Adriana A. Davies

From Sojourners to Citizens

Alberta's Italian History

GUERNICA
EDITIONS

TORONTO • CHICAGO • BUFFALO • LANCASTER (U.K.)
2021

Michael Mirolla, editor
Cover design: Allen Jomoc Jr.
Interior layout: Rafael Chimicatti
Guernica Editions Inc.
287 Templemead Drive, Hamilton (ON), Canada L8W 2W4
2250 Military Road, Tonawanda, N.Y. 14150-6000 U.S.A.
www.guernicaeditions.com

Distributors:
Independent Publishers Group (IPG)
600 North Pulaski Road, Chicago IL 60624
University of Toronto Press Distribution,
5201 Dufferin Street, Toronto (ON), Canada M3H 5T8
Gazelle Book Services, White Cross Mills
High Town, Lancaster LA1 4XS U.K.

First edition.
Printed in Canada.

Legal Deposit—First Quarter
Library of Congress Catalog Card Number: 2020947922
Library and Archives Canada Cataloguing in Publication
Title: From sojourners to citizens : Alberta's Italian history / Adriana A. Davies.
Names: Davies, Adriana A., 1943- author.
Series: Essential Essays ; 78.
Description: First edition. | Series statement: Essential Essays ; 78 | Includes bibliographical references.
Identifiers: Canadiana (print) 20200375717 | Canadiana (ebook) 20200375725 | ISBN 9781771836548 (softcover)
ISBN 9781771836555 (EPUB) | ISBN 9781771836562 (Kindle)
Subjects: LCSH: Italians—Alberta—History. | LCSH: Immigrants—Alberta—History.
CSH: Italian Canadians—Alberta—History.
Classification: LCC FC3700.I8 D38 2021 | DDC 971.23/00451—dc23

To my sons Alexander and William Davies
My daughters-in-law Catherine and Sabrina
And my grandsons Ciaran, Oliver, Dawson and Miles

Contents

Acknowledgements

IT WAS MY GRANDFATHERS AND PARENTS who chose to come to Canada and defined me as an immigrant, and as an Italian-Canadian. They left their homes in the small town of Grimaldi, Provincia di Cosenza, Calabria to seek adventure. I would like to acknowledge them: Vincenzo Potestio and Francesco Albi, who were sojourners; and my parents Raffaele and Estera Albi, who came to stay. They span several eras of immigration to North America. Nonno Vincenzo went to the US with his family as a small boy in the 1880s and returned to Italy where he married. In 1913, he travelled to New York with my paternal grandfather Francesco Albi, and both ended up working in Canada. Both worked on the railways. Nonno Vincenzo did not have my grandmother, Assunta, join him. Nonno Francesco died of pneumonia, alone, in Revelstoke, BC, in 1916. He left a widow, Nonna Alessandra, and two young sons, Giuseppe and Raffaele. My father came to Edmonton in 1949 and my mother, siblings Rosa and Giuseppe and I joined him in 1951.

It was my parents who instilled in me a love of learning and supported me through all levels of schooling and university. I would not be who I am without their efforts and sacrifices. Studies at the University of Alberta and the University of London, England shaped my intellect as well as honing my research and writing skills. This enabled me to work in publishing and the museum and heritage sectors. It was a volunteer activity, however, that inspired my interest in Italian immigration history. In 1983, Father Augusto Feccia, pastor at Santa Maria Goretti Parish in Edmonton, invited me to take part in a twenty-fifth anniversary project for the parish. He knew that I was a senior editor on Mel Hurtig's *Canadian Encyclopedia* and felt that he could make use of my research skills. He established the Italians Settle in Edmonton Society, obtained a grant, and recruited volunteers to undertake the project. We undertook oral histories, prepared a photographic exhibit and produced a commemorative booklet. The following served as mentors: Italian-American historian Dr. Rudolph Vecoli, Director of the Immigration History Research Center, University of Minnesota; Jim Parker, University of Alberta Archivist; and David Goa, Curator of Folk and Religious Life, Provincial Museum of Alberta.

Sab Roncucci brought me to the next level of involvement in the community: he recruited me in 1986 to become President of the National Congress of Italian Canadians, Edmonton

District. I served for six years and learned an enormous amount about the workings of Italian communities across the country. I participated in the Second Rome Conference on Immigration in 1988 and, beginning in 1989, through the NCIC took part in the preparation and submission of a brief to the Government of Canada regarding enemy alien designation and internment. I was, thus, able to live the later history of the community as it was being made.

My life as Executive Director of the Alberta Museums Association exposed me to the work of curators and historians researching settlement history. In 1999, I became Executive Director of the Heritage Community Foundation and Editor-in-Chief and founder of the *Alberta Online Encyclopedia* (www.albertasource.ca). With the support of the Board and staff we created the first "born digital" encyclopedia in Canada. A proud moment was the launch of the *Celebrating Alberta's Italian Community* website, developed with the support of the NCIC, Edmonton District. I thank President Carlo Amodio and his board as well as volunteer Lina Amodio, who undertook much translation work. Finally, participation in the Villa Charities-Columbus Centre Memories of World War II Project allowed me to research the Italian communities of the prairies in this painful period of our history.

Other projects built on my knowledge of Alberta's Italian history and I thank the people who made them possible: Michale Lang at Glenbow and later at the Whyte Museum of the Canadian Rockies; Ron Ulrich at the Galt Museum in Lethbridge and later the Fernie Museum; and Maria Mauro at the Ital-Canadian Seniors Centre. A research grant from the Alberta Historical Resources Foundation enabled me to do the in-depth research and writing that has resulted in this book. The NCIC, Edmonton District and the Santa Maria Goretti Community Centre also provided me with seed grants. I thank their boards for their confidence in me. The publication of this book has been made possible by the inaugural Edmonton Heritage Council Heritage Writers' Reserve Award and my publisher, Guernica Editions. I would like to thank David Ridley, Executive Director of the Council, and Michael Mirolla and Connie McParland of Guernica.

I would also like to thank Allen Jomoc Jr. for the cover design and Rafael Chimicatti for the book layout.

No type of historical research could be done without the holdings of our public archives. I want to thank the Glenbow Archives (now the Glenbow Western Research Centre at the Taylor Family Digital Library, University of Calgary), Provincial Archives of Alberta, Crowsnest Archives, Galt Archives, Red Deer Archives, Whyte Museum and Archives of the Canadian Rockies, Jasper Yellowhead Archives, Medicine Hat Archives, Lac La Biche Archives and the Fernie Archives. I also want to acknowledge all of the organizations that undertook oral histories in Alberta including the Dante Alighieri Society, Italians Settle in Edmonton Society, Calgary Italian Club, the People of Southern Alberta Oral History Project, and the Ital-Canadian Seniors.

Alberta is blessed with a range of community histories made possible by Government of Alberta funding; these enabled historical committees and societies to solicit family histories, and explore the settlement history of their town and region. Some of the family stories have found their way into the book. Individuals and families have also given me information and I thank them.

While I provide demographic information as well as a range of historical information, above all, I wanted to make the people who lived "Alberta's Italian history" come alive. In the process, I hope that I have challenged stereotypes and ill-founded assumptions. Above all, the book is a celebration of past lives. Any errors of commission or omission are my own.

Adriana A. Davies, CM, PhD, Cavaliere d'Italia
Edmonton, Alberta
January 2020

Scrivano family and others aboard ship on their way to Canada, ca 1929, donated by Sam Scrivano. Photo courtesy of Provincial Archives of Alberta A10881.

CHAPTER I

Introduction

AS WITH OTHER ECONOMIC MIGRANTS of the last half of the nineteenth century, Italians were motivated to leave their homeland by the desire to find work and make money. Italian unification in 1861, while ending the oppression of the Austrians in the north and the Bourbons in the south, did not magically improve the economy, nor end age-old rivalries, in particular those between the North and South. For labourers, whether agricultural or industrial, well-paying work remained a dream, as did advancement through education. Industrial development was largely confined to regions north of Naples, and with it came economic and political power. Thus, there were "have" and "have not" regions and, at the bottom of the pecking order was the South including largely agrarian provinces such as Calabria and Sicily.

Immigration from Italy has been described as an immigration of poverty and desperation, and exceeded that from other countries in Eastern and Western Europe: in the period from 1861 to 1914 various sources place the number of emigrants at between nine and 16 million.[1] Gianfausto Rosoli in *Un Secolo di emigrazione Italiana 1876-1976* (One Hundred Years of Italian Immigration from 1876-1976) provides the following statistics: from 1860 to 1900, 3,723,672 left northern Italy, while 1,534,239 left central and southern Italy; from 1901 to 1915, 4,621,057 left northern Italy, while 4,148,728 left central and southern Italy. In the period 1876 to 1900, immigration from the north exceeded that from central/southern Italy in a ratio of about 3:1 (about 69.5 percent); in 1901 to 1915, the figures are very close though slightly more northerners immigrated. The total immigration in these two periods totaled 14,027,696. The majority was from the countryside rather than cities. (Naples was the exception.) About two-thirds of immigrants had trades training of some kind while the others were unskilled labourers.[2]

---

[1] For data specific to immigration from Italy, a key source is George E. Pozzetta and Bruno Ramirez, eds. *The Italian Diaspora: Migration across the Globe* (Toronto: Multicultural History Society of Ontario, 1992). The book is a *festschrift* for Robert F. Harney.

[2] Gianfausto Rosoli, *Un secolo di emigrazione italiana 1876-1976* (Roma, IT: Cser, 1978). See also Francesco Saverio Alessio's table that lists immigration numbers by Italian provinces, Associazione Internet degli Emigrati Italiani, URL: http://www.emigrati.it/Emigrazione/Esodo.asp, retrieved July 26, 2017.

With respect to immigration to Alberta, based on local and oral history sources, it would appear that northerners were the earliest to come, and their numbers were greater in the last decade of the nineteenth century and first decade of the twentieth century; after that, the split appears to be 50:50 as per Rosoli's calculations. Among these immigrants were adventure seekers and dreamers. Giorgio Pocaterra, a minor aristocrat, was fascinated by the "Wild West" and arrived in Calgary in 1903 and found work at the Bar D Ranch near High River. Civil engineer Felice De Angelis arrived in Edmonton in 1914 as an agent of the Italian government sent to help set up an agricultural colony in northern Alberta. Lorenzo Grassi obtained work with the CPR in Ontario but asked to be transferred to the Rockies so that he could climb mountains.

The vast majority of immigrants, however, were ordinary men who wanted to improve the lot of their families by seeking work abroad, making money and returning to create a better life in Italy. They were known as "sojourners" or "birds of passage." While some labourers (the designation for unskilled day labourer in Italian passports was *bracciante*) went to France, Germany, Switzerland, the Austro-Hungarian Empire and North Africa, the lure of North America was strong. While many Italians immigrated to South America, by the latter half of the nineteenth century the United States and, later Canada, became preferred destinations. The building of transcontinental railways and urban infrastructure as well as opening of mines promised work and prosperity for all.

Immigration Restrictions

While Canada and the US required labourers to realize expansion westward to the Pacific coast, this did not mean that immigration was open to everyone. Selective immigration was the rule and anthropological studies in the latter half of the nineteenth century were used to prove "scientifically" the superiority of Anglo-Europeans. Just as Darwin had demonstrated the evolution of species from single-celled organisms to complex *Homo sapiens*, in the emerging field of anthropology, some nineteenth century scientists applied similar techniques to cultural studies, and demonstrated that European cultures were at the peak of human development. Taken to the extreme, these theories would be used by Germany to justify the concept of a "superior" Aryan race that needed to fulfill its manifest destiny by dominating other, inferior races.

While some dismissed theories of racial superiority, many accepted them including government representatives and, like a genie that is let out of the bottle, they wreaked havoc not only in the past but also in the present allowing countries and individuals to separate "desirable" from "undesirable" immigrants, based on pseudo-science. There were liberal, more "modern," views about race at the time, but these views did not come to dominate the thinking of government leaders and the intelligentsia until the mid-twentieth century after the horrors of the Holocaust.

From the late nineteenth century to the 1950s, British colonies such as Canada, Australia and New Zealand, and the US government, viewed British and Northern Europeans as the most desirable settlers; Southern and Eastern Europeans, Asians, Southeast Asians, Africans and other races were considered less desirable. The reasons for selective immigration and the need for assimilation and "Canadianization" of settlers were made clear by J. S. (James Shaver) Woodsworth, Superintendent of the All Peoples Mission in Winnipeg, in his book *Strangers Within Our Gates: Or, Coming Canadians*.[3] The book was published in 1909 by the Missionary Society of the Methodist Church, Canada and had a number of editions. Methodists were adherents of the Social Gospel movement, which focused attention on the alleviation of social ills including poverty and drunkenness. A number of Methodist missions were located in urban areas including Toronto, Winnipeg, Edmonton and Vancouver. Woodsworth, the son of a Methodist minister, graduated from Methodist College in Winnipeg, in 1896, and studied theology at Victoria College in Toronto where he witnessed first-hand the condition of immigrants. The Fred Victor Mission, established by wealthy philanthropist Hart Massey in 1894 and named after his youngest son, tended to unemployed and homeless men.[4] The mission building was situated on the corner of Queen and Jarvis Streets and Italians were among the clients they served.

Woodsworth also spent a year in Oxford, England and visited London to observe missions in slum neighbourhoods. He brought these learnings to bear on his ministry in Winnipeg. The city at the time was the last outpost of eastern Canada and a bridge to the new West. It was a railhead and trains from eastern Canada stopped there, and settlers travelling westward embarked on new trains once the railway was built. Winnipeg was thus a crucible for immigrant interaction with mainstream society, and a testing ground for integration.

In Winnipeg, Woodsworth was exposed to immigrants and their first experiences in the new Canadian society that was emerging in the first decade of the twentieth century. While Methodism and other religions were responsive to the plight of the poor, there were those who distinguished between the "deserving" and "undeserving" poor. This same type of judgment, some

---

[3] See James S. Woodsworth, *Strangers Within Our Gates: Or, Coming Canadians* (Toronto, ON: University of Toronto Press, reprint of the 1909 original edition, 1972). Marilyn Barber provides biographical information about Woodsworth in her introduction to the book and makes the case that the Methodists, including Woodsworth, were genuinely sensitive to the needs of poor immigrants while espousing the racist attitudes of the British and Canadian establishment (xx-xxi).
[4] Fred Victor website, "Our History," URL: http://www.fredvictor.org/fred_victor_beginnings, retrieved March 22, 2017.

would say, equivocation, is at play in Woodsworth's classification of ethnocultural groups as to their suitability for citizenship. In this he was no different from other Methodist brethren, or those of other faiths such as Anglicans, Presbyterians and Roman Catholics. The chapter sequence in *Strangers Within Our Gates* can be viewed as a ranking of races from most to least desirable. It is as follows: Great Britain, United States (including the Mormons), Scandinavians (including Icelanders), Germans (including the Mennonite), French, Southeastern Europe (including Russians, Doukhobors, Lithuanians), Austria-Hungary (including Bohemians, Slovaks, Ruthenians, Poles, Hungarians), Balkans States, Hebrews, Italians (North and South), Levantine Races (including Greeks, Turks, Armenians, Syrians, Persians), Orientals (including Chinese, Japanese, Hindus) and Negro and Indian.

The tone of the book is fear-mongering – the prefatory section titled "Immigration – A World Problem" describes "A vast and endless army" marching from northern, eastern and southern Europe at the rate of 1.5 million per year towards "the civilized world."[5] It is an "invading" army. Woodsworth also provided tables of immigration to Canada based on country of origin to support the notion of invasion by foreigners (Chapter I: Who Are We?). Ironically, this language is not much different from that being used by politicians and the popular media in the UK, some Western European countries, the US and Canada just over 100 years later to describe the migrants and refugees from the Middle East, Africa, Southeast Asia and Latin America, who are leaving their impoverished, and sometimes war-torn homelands, for a better life. It is not surprising that most are visible minorities and Muslims. This bears out notions that history tends to repeat itself and that we do not learn the supposed lessons of the past.

When historian Howard Palmer wrote about "the rise of nativism" in Canada in the first decades of the twentieth century, he likely could not imagine a resurgence of such sentiments in the twenty-first century. He was writing in the 1970s as government policies on multiculturalism gained acceptance and were ultimately entrenched, in 1982, in Canada's Charter of Rights and Freedoms. As Palmer noted, by 1914, "Anglo-Saxon Protestants, mostly from Ontario and Britain, had established almost exclusive control of the political, legal, cultural, and educational institutions in Alberta as well as in the other prairie provinces.[6] They were the "native" majority and wanted to entrench their own belief systems.

---

[5] J. S. Woodsworth, *Strangers Within Our Gates, Coming Canadians* (Toronto, ON: Frederick Clarke Stephenson, Missionary Society of the Methodist Church, Canada, 1909), 11.

[6] Howard Palmer, "Strangers and Stereotypes: The Rise of Nativism, 1880-1920," in the *Prairie West: Historical Readings*, edited by R. Douglas Francis and Howard Palmer (Edmonton, AB: University of Alberta Press, 1992), 310.

In this period, Canadian immigration policy, while restrictive, did not impede immigration of "less desirable" people so long as they could serve the economic development of the country. In the period 1900 to 1981, an estimated 666,178 Italians arrived in Canada. The two boom periods were 1896 to 1914 and 1950 to 1980. Between 1901 and 1911, Alberta's population grew more than fivefold, from 73,022 to 374,295; by 1916, it was 496,000. The censuses reveal the following number of Italians in the province: 1901, 109; 1911, 2,150; 1921, 4,028.[7] The numbers were low in contrast to other groups (British, Americans and Germans exceeded them by far) but they were growing. In 1924, John Blue, Provincial Librarian and the province's first historian wrote:

> Fears have been expressed at various times by men of affairs and publicists that there is a danger of foreign immigration swamping the native born and destroying the distinctive character of Canadian laws and institutions. Up to the present time such fears are groundless. There is enough Anglo-Saxon blood in Alberta to dilute the foreign blood and complete the process of assimilation to the mutual advantage of both elements. The census of 1916 and the census of 1921 show in a general way the ethnological groups that are fusing to produce a rich and virile nationality in Alberta, as is true throughout the entire West.[8]

There is an inherent irony in that "native born" does not mean Indigenous people but rather, the colonists.

In Chapter 13: "The Italian," Woodsworth acknowledged the growing Italian presence and provided a historical account, though biased, of how these immigrants were faring. His book perpetuated the stereotype of the difference between "northern" and "southern" Italians, and also legitimized it. In every Italian community in North America the rivalries between the regions have been documented. These have, in some cases, led to antagonism and conflict within such communities across the country, and also hampered the development of Italian cultural organizations and institutions created to reflect Italian ancestry and memorialize it.

Woodsworth wrote: "AN ITALIAN! The figure that flashes before the mind's eye is probably that of an organ-grinder with his monkey. That was the impression we first received, and it is difficult to substitute another. Italian immigrants! The figure of the organ man fades away, and

---

[7] Howard and Tamara Palmer undertook demographic analysis and accomplished benchmark work in determining the populations of various ethnocultural groups. Tables of demographics based on census records appear in the book they co-edited, *Peoples of Alberta: Portraits of Cultural Diversity* (Saskatoon, SK: Western Producer Prairie Books, 1985).
[8] John Blue, *Alberta Past and Present: Historical and Biographical* (Chicago, IL: Pioneer Historical Publishing Co., 1924), 218.

we see dark, uncertain figures, and someone whispers, 'The Mafia – the Black Hand'."[9] While Woodsworth's profiling of Italians is offensive, it is important to acknowledge that not just Italian immigrants but others who were subjected to this type of racism had to come to terms with it, and overcome it in order to make a living and a home in Canada.

While acknowledging that this is a stereotype and asking what "dirty Dagos" have to do with the much-admired Italian freedom fighters Garibaldi and Mazzini and the classical Roman past, Woodsworth pointed out that Italians were the second most numerous of "non-English immigrants" in Canada and suggested "we cannot afford to remain ignorant concerning them." He continued, "In 1901 there were only about 10,000 Italians in Canada. Now there are 50,000 [1909], and the stream is only starting to flow in our direction. Two hundred thousand a year leave Italy, yet so prolific is the race that the population continues to increase rapidly. With the tightening of immigration restrictions by the United States, there will be a tendency for the Italians to crowd more and more into Canada."[10]

Woodsworth differentiated between the taller, lighter-complexioned and more intelligent "Northerner" and the swarthy, less intelligent "Southerner." The former could usually read and write and had a trade or skill, while the latter did not. In addition, the Northerner's immigration was purposeful and aided by family and friends. Woodsworth compared the Northerner favourably with Scandinavians. On the other hand, the Southerner was the "descendant of peasantry illiterate for centuries," could seldom read or write, was a farm labourer and dependant on the *padrone* (master), who frequently took financial advantage of him. Woodsworth also repeated the claim that criminality was systemic in the "Neapolitan zone." Finally, he affirmed that American statistics about Italian immigration likely applied to Canada, and noted that "over 80 per cent are from the south; over 80 per cent are between the ages of 14 and 45; almost 80 per cent are males, and 80 per cent are unskilled labourers."[11] This view on the prevalence of immigration from the south was perpetuated by Italian-Canadian scholars in the 1970s and 1980s, which was the heyday of academic focus on Italian immigration.[12] As has been noted, none of these assertions are borne out by the actual immigration statistics. In the late nineteenth and early twentieth centuries, immigration from the North was higher than from the South.

---

[9] *Ibid.*, 160.

[10] *Ibid.*, 160-161.

[11] *Ibid.*, 163.

[12] As late as 1999, Antonella Fanella asserts this in *With Heart and Soul: Calgary's Italian Community* (Calgary, AB: University of Calgary Press, 1999).

Woodsworth completed his Italian profile by noting that there were 12,000 Italians in Montreal, 6,000 in Toronto and, likely 2,000 in Winnipeg. Many worked in railway construction (he noted that Canadians should be grateful to them for this) and that they were hard-working and saved their money to send back to their families in Italy. The desire to save meant that they could only afford to live in tenements: "Many Italians, unaccustomed to city life, do not know how to make the most of the poor accommodations they have; so there come filth, disease and crime."[13] Positive features that he noted include the fact that they are "temperate" (it is important to remember that Methodists espoused Temperance and supported Prohibition); "rarely tell deliberate lies"; "family morality is high"; "sixty per cent are illiterate, but the children are quick and ambitious," and that they would move from labouring work to "factories and business establishments." A final observation was that Canada's Italian immigrants came through the US. At the end of the nineteenth century and beginning of the twentieth century, Italian immigrants as well as others in the "less desirable" groups faced discrimination in all aspects of their lives. For example, in spring 1897, the *Alien Labour Act: An Act to Restrict the Importation and Employment of Alien Labour* was passed to limit contract labourers entering the country.[14] This applied particularly to Italian and Chinese railway workers from the US.[15]

Movement of Labour

Based on immigration records and oral history accounts, very few immigrants came directly from Italy to a Canadian destination in the period 1896 to 1914. This confirms Woodsworth's observation that most Italian immigrants to Canada came via the US. In fact, few Italians made distinctions between the US and Canada: it was the US that was the destination of choice. Since much of the work available was seasonal in nature, or dependent on cycles of boom and bust, it became common to follow work on railways and in mines from the Eastern US, through the midwest (or even south and southwest to Colorado, Nevada and California) to the Pacific Northwest and, then, to BC and Alberta. It became customary to travel great distances to obtain work.

---

[13] *Ibid.* 164.

[14] Collections Canada, *Alien Labour Act: An Act to Restrict the Importation and Employment of Aliens*, in "Moving Here Staying Here. The Canadian Immigrant Experience," retrieved March 1, 2017, URL: https://www.collectionscanada.gc.ca/immigrants/021017-119.01-e.php?&document_code=021017-71&page=1&referer=021017-2350.02-e.html&section_code=pl-labour.

[15] See Donald Avery, "European Immigrant Workers and Labour Protest in Peace and War, 1896-1919," in *The History of Immigration and Racism in Canada: Essential Readings,* edited by Barrington Walker (Toronto: Canadian Scholars' Press Inc., 2008) 125, 126.

Fathers and sons, brothers, cousins and townsmen came together and sponsored others. In some instances, labour agents or *padroni* acted as middle men promising jobs and advancing monies for fares, food and accommodation. They recruited in their home town or region. This type of immigration pattern has been described as "chain migration" and the term applies not only to the country from which the groups emigrated but also to the settlement pattern in the host country. Relationships in immigration were familial involving blood, marriage or kinship ties such as *compare* (best man), *padrino/padrina* (godfather/godmother as a result of a baptism or confirmation) or *paesani* (townsmen).

On July 20, 1871 British Columbia became Canada's sixth province. In order to link the Eastern provinces of the Dominion of Canada and the new province, Parliament determined that a transcontinental railway needed to be built by 1881. While railways already existed in central and eastern Canada, the move west required railway building on a much grander scale. Since this had already occurred in the US in the first half of the nineteenth century, there were both positive and negative models as well as individuals who could be recruited to assist. These included figures such as Cornelius Van Horne and Andrew Onderdonk, seasoned American railway builders. Such an enterprise required both public and private capital, and fortunes were made and lost, and the Government of Sir John A. Macdonald fell, in 1873, as a result of corruption associated with railway dealings. The CPR would finally be incorporated in 1881 after Macdonald returned to power (1878).

The building of the CPR and branch railways brought Italian migrant workers to BC and Alberta. Once the bulk of the railways had been constructed, the coal mines provided ample employment. By 1911, the region from the Elk Valley in BC through the Crowsnest Pass to Lethbridge and Drumheller, in Alberta, produced most of Canada's coal. By 1919, Italians comprised 14.5 percent of the work force in the Crowsnest Pass. Mines were also found along the eastern side of the Rocky Mountains in Bankhead (near Banff), Canmore, Nordegg, the Coal Branch and at Pocahontas in Jasper National Park. Edmonton and region also had extensive mines. Italian immigrants worked in all of them.

While initially some Italians were used as strikebreakers and were unaffiliated, eventually, the majority supported unionization and were members of the United Mine Workers of America. Labour organizations, based on the nature of activity performed, were in keeping with the European guilds and trades organizations dating back to the Middle Ages. Many Italian miners in Alberta supported the One Big Union – an effort to strengthen the union movement by getting rid of the restrictions based on "craft" or type of labour (for example, mine workers and carpenters). The 1919 General Strike, which spread across the country, found strong support in mining communities in Alberta. In fact, the strike lasted longer in Drumheller than in any other area in the country, and mounted Alberta Provincial Policemen were used to charge strikers. Italian immigrants were in the picket lines. At the 1919 Royal Commission hearings held by the Government of Alberta, S. Centazzo testified on behalf of local miners.

Italian miners also set up their own fraternal or benevolent societies – the Società di Mutuo Soccorso (Mutual Aid Society) – modeled on Italian predecessors dating back to the early 1860s. These were developed to provide sickness and death benefits for members who paid monthly dues. Beginning in 1899, the next 20 years saw societies established in Rossland, Fernie, Michel and Trail, in BC and, in Lille, Coleman, Nordegg, Lethbridge, Drumheller and Edmonton, in Alberta. The Fernie lodge charter, dated 1913, indicates that the organization was incorporated under the Federazione Colombiana della Societa Italo-Americane (Colombian Federation of the Italo-American Society), established in 1893. These lodges existed in mining communities throughout the US and, since many Italian immigrants had worked first in the US, it was logical for them to affiliate with American counterparts.

The Lure of the Land

In 1895, Minister of the Interior Clifford Sifton launched a campaign that saw over a million pamphlets advertising the West in more than a dozen languages distributed abroad. Slogans included: "Prosperity Follows Settlement," "The Wondrous West," "The Last Best West" and "Canada: Land of Opportunity." Alberta was presented as an agrarian paradise.[16] The program was hugely successful – more than one million settlers arrived in the period 1896-1914. Incentives included bonuses to agents and steamship lines. It was not just the CPR that promoted settlement: the Canadian Northern Railway produced a brochure in 1912 with the title "Western Canada Has a Home for You" to entice settlers to northern Alberta.

In spite of the promised returns of agricultural settlement, relatively few Italians homesteaded in Alberta although small agricultural colonies were set up in Naples, in 1906, and Venice-Hylo, in 1914-1915. While a significant number of Italian immigrants had been agricultural labourers in their homeland, prairie agriculture was significantly different from the small mixed farming operations that they were used to. Perhaps the more significant reason for their lack of interest

---

[16] See Kenneth H. Norrie, "The National Policy and the Rate of Prairie Settlement," in *The Prairie West: Historical Readings*, edited by R. Douglas Francis and Howard Palmer (Edmonton, AB: The University of Alberta Press, 1992), 243-263. See also Jeffrey S. Murray, Library and Archives Canada, "Printed Advertisements," in *Moving Here. Staying Here. The Canadian Immigrant Experience* for an overview of Government of Canada agricultural promotional campaigns for Prairie West. URL: https://www.collectionscanada.gc.ca/immigrants/021017-1100-e.html, retrieved March 1, 2017.

in agriculture was the fact that work in the railways and mines was so readily available and the opportunities for making money on the land were less secure. A number of families also homesteaded around the communities of Lethbridge, Delia and Edson.

Far different from the experience of the "sodbusters" was the life of Giorgio (George) Pocaterra, the son of Italian minor aristocrats. His story resembles that of the so-called "Remittance Men," the younger sons of British aristocratic families who went to the colonies because they had nothing better to do since they were not heirs, so they ranched in southern Alberta and played polo. In 1905, Pocaterra set up the Buffalo Head Ranch. Everything about him is extraordinary including the fact that he converted his ranch to a guest ranch and married Norma Piper, a Canadian opera singer.

Cities and Towns

Edmonton and Calgary, as well as Lethbridge, Medicine Hat and Red Deer, drew Italians who did not want to work in mines and railways. All were experiencing a surge in growth and required tradesmen. Italian stonemasons helped to construct major buildings such as the Alberta Legislature as well as assisting in building civic infrastructure such as roads, bridges and tramways. In 1907, Nick Gallelli began a construction business in partnership with brother-in-law Harry Cicconi, in Calgary. He was joined in the business by sons Nado, Harry, Bill and Aldo, and it became one of the largest construction companies in western Canada. Brothers-in-law Felix Nigro and James Anselmo, in the mid-1920s, began work in road building and, later created New West Construction. Their company helped to build Imperial Oil's Strathcona Refinery adjacent to Edmonton. Such firms provided employment to Italian immigrants.

While railway and mine work served as an entry point into the work force, those who had trades wanted to pursue these once they made the transition from sojourners to citizens. In cities and towns, Italian immigrants operated grocery stores, shoe shine shops, hotels, restaurants, garages and other types of small businesses, and thrived. Some became major entrepreneurs.

Hard Times

During the First World War, while Italy was an ally of the UK, Italian workers in mining communities were lumped in with "the foreign element" with whom Canada was at war. The "enemy" was a fairly elastic term that included not only Austro-Hungarians and Germans but also Poles, Slovakians, Ukrainians and other eastern Europeans. At this point, parts of north-eastern Italy were under the dominion of the Austro-Hungarian Empire and census records of immigrants from these regions described them as "Austrian." Mines and railways were essential to the war effort and suspicion fell on their foreign work force. The Russian Revolution and international labour movements were also seen as a threat not only to industry but also Canadian values. With the ending of the war, the Government of Canada amended the 1910 *Immigration Act*.[17] A further amendment in 1919 was prompted by growing anti-foreign sentiment targeted at war-time enemy countries and enemy aliens residing in Canada; labour unrest; and the post-war economic downturn. Immigration was barred from enemy countries and restrictions were expanded on so-called "dissidents." Cabinet had extraordinary powers and could restrict immigration based on nationality, race, occupation and class system, and also exclude people who had "peculiar customs, habits, modes of life and methods of holding property." The last clearly referred to Communism and its challenge to traditional land ownership. While Italians were not enemy aliens, these restrictions were applied to them and the Italian population of Alberta remained stagnant as revealed by census data: 1921, 4,028; 1931, 4,766; and 1941, 4,872. In a period of 20 years, the number of people of Italian ethnicity in Alberta increased by only 844.

The rise of Fascism in Italy under Benito Mussolini would further damage the standing of Italian immigrants, whether naturalized or not. In 1922, Mussolini became Prime Minister and with him came a resurgence of patriotism and a vision of a heroic national identity based on the ancient Roman past. The governments of Canada and the US demonstrated admiration for Mussolini and his program for the revitalization of Italy as well as his defeat of Communism. Mussolini's desire to propagate Fascist beliefs to Italians abroad coincided with the Government of Canada's desire to attract agricultural settlement. In 1923, Italia Garibaldi, the granddaughter of Giuseppe Garibaldi, visited Canada to promote the formation of Italian agricultural colonies. She went to Edmonton, the Venice Colony and Calgary. Garibaldi linked Italian communities in Canada with Fascism. In 1924, following on the high of her visit, *fasci* (Fascist locals) were set up in Edmonton, Calgary, Lethbridge and Venice. These were among the earliest organizations of this kind in Canada. On December 8, 1926 a provincial Fascist organization was established at a meeting in Calgary led by Felice De Angelis, a founder of the Venice colony, who had returned to Alberta on a number of occasions and styled himself as "the royal Italian consul at Edmonton."

By the mid-1930s, Italian consuls had created strong Fascist organizations in a number of Canadian cities including Toronto, Montreal and Vancouver, and raised funds locally to support the Italian government. At this time, the RCMP stepped up surveillance of community members

---

[17] The 1910 *Immigration Act* increased the list of prohibited immigrants and expanded Cabinet's power on admissibility and deportation. Immigrants "unsuited to the climate or requirements of Canada" were barred and charities could no longer sponsor immigrants.

involved in these organizations. When Mussolini signed a pact with Hitler and, following in his footsteps, sought to build an Italian empire by attacking Abyssinia (Ethiopia) in 1935, and occupying Albania in 1939, Italian-Canadians were regarded with suspicion. Italy's declaration of war on Britain on June 10, 1940 brought Canada into the war. Prime Minister W. L. Mackenzie King invoked the *War Measures Act* and, under the Security of Canada Regulations, the RCMP identified about 600 Canadians of Italian descent with ties to Fascist organizations. They were arrested and interned in camps in Kananaskis, Alberta; Petawawa, Ontario; and Gagetown, New Brunswick.

Those who had not become naturalized Canadians before Mussolini came to power were declared enemy aliens and were fingerprinted and had to report to the RCMP. In Alberta, six men were interned, the most prominent being Antonio Rebaudengo, who had arrived in Calgary in 1921 and had been employed by the CPR in the Ogden Yards. He served in Calgary as the consular agent and was a strong supporter of the Mussolini regime. Other Albertan internees were O.J. Biollo and Rudolph Michetti from Venice-Hylo; Emilio Sereni, a farmer from Balzac, who had obtained Canadian citizenship in 1904; Giovanni (Johnny) Galdi, who arrived in Alberta in 1914 and worked in the mines in Nordegg; and Santo Romeo from Calgary. Most were released within a year; however, Michetti served almost two years and Rebaudengo until September 1943 when Italy was defeated by the Allies.

Whether any of the internees would or could have done anything to damage the Canadian war effort is a moot point. The distrust levelled at members of the Italian community resulted in a moving away from Italian organizations created for mutual support and social purposes. When the new wave of immigration began in 1949, there were virtually no societies to assist.

Building Community

While many Italian immigrants arriving in Alberta in the period 1896 to 1914 came to make money and return, those arriving after 1949 came to stay. At the end of the Second World War in 1945, the economies of European countries were in disarray and there was massive unemployment. In Canada, the economy was beginning to boom and primary and secondary industries, and the service sector, were hiring. In January 1947, war-time measures to restrict movement and rights of enemy aliens ceased and the doors to immigration re-opened. In 1967, new immigration regulations created a point system based on education, occupational skills, employment prospects, age, proficiency in English and French, and personal character. Those receiving at least 50 points out of 100 were granted entry, regardless of race, ethnicity or national origin.[18] This did not

---

[18] Immigration Regulations, Order-in Council PC 1967-1616, 1967.

mean that racist attitudes ceased to exist; in fact, Italians were still viewed by some as "Dagos," "DPs" and "WOPs." All were pejorative terms and of diverse origins: Dago may have referred to an Italian or Portuguese speaker but, by the nineteenth century, was used in the British navy to refer to Spanish sailors and, later, in North America, referred to Italians; DPs were "displaced persons" forced to leave their homeland because of war or persecution; and WOP referred to an illegal immigrant or criminal.[19]

While urban centres such as Toronto and Montreal were the primary draws for Italian immigrants, they also spread across the country. This was due, in part, to the growing economy of the West but also because of kinship ties. Labour agents, as in the early part of the century, played a role in initial recruitment. Canada's total Italian population increased from 150,000, in 1951, to 450,000, in 1961. Comparable figures in Alberta were: 5,996, in 1951; 15,025, in 1961; 24,805, in 1971; and 26,605, in 1981. Thus, Alberta's Italian community more than quadrupled in 30 years. By 1996, the number was 58,140 and, by 2011, 88,710 individuals indicated Italian ancestry in the census (2.5 percent of the province's population). Criteria for self-identification of ethnicity in various censuses changed over the years. In both Edmonton and Calgary, the most prominent sources of immigration were the Italian provinces of Calabria and Abruzzo-Molise, with smaller percentages from Campania, Puglia and the northern regions of Veneto, Friuli and Piemonte. With respect to Edmonton, the 1961 census listed 3,465 individuals with Italian as their mother tongue; in 1986, 9,865 individuals listing Italy as their single country of origin. In Calgary, the Italian community grew from 4,720 in 1961 to 9,810 in 1971.

The strength in numbers gave the new immigrants much more confidence than their predecessors. In addition, some of those who came in the 1960s were better educated. Together they forged a new Italian-Canadian identity and "Little Italies" emerged in Edmonton and Calgary. The majority still worked as labourers for the railways and in the construction industry, in petroleum refineries, steel-making and fabrication, meat-packing, and civic, provincial and federal governments and other institutions. Most insisted that their children better themselves through higher education. A few immigrants with qualifications moved directly into the professions. Many women joined the work force as seamstresses in garment factories, in the retail sector, in cafeterias

---

[19] According to the Merriam-Webster dictionary, the term "wop" was first used in the US in 1908 and is attributed to the southern Italian dialect term "guappo" meaning thug or pimp. Its origin was the Spanish term "guapo," which meant "bold" and "beautiful." Since parts of Italy were under the control of Spain since 1559 to 1714, the passage from Spanish into colloquial Italian was definitely possible. In Neapolitan dialect the term referred to a "flashy" criminal using extortion and prostitution to obtain money. Clearly, it came into use in immigrant communities at the same time as various criminal organizations – the Black Hand Society, Neapolitan Camorra and Sicilian Mafia – established themselves in the eastern US, in particular the city of New York.

and as cleaning staff. While some children (male and female) were sent to work as soon as they turned 16, a significant number went on to higher education. The push to professionalization, which had occurred in earlier eras of immigration, from the 1950s onwards was accelerated.

The desire to purchase homes and establish institutions that supported community life and values became driving forces. Since real estate in inner-city areas was cheapest, Italians bought properties and established businesses in what became Edmonton's Little Italy comprising the McCauley and Boyle Street neighbourhoods. A parallel phenomenon was at play in Calgary and the Italian presence in the established heartland of the Italian community – the neighbourhoods of Bridgeland/Riverside – grew.

In academe, as immigration studies came to the fore in the 1970s as a result of an emerging emphasis on social history, attention was focused on the concepts of assimilation and pluralism. It was viewed as a truism that in the US, assimilation was the preferred option and the country was, thus, a vast "melting pot." This was differentiated from the Canadian pluralist model, which embraced respect for people of different ethnicities, cultures and religions.

As government policies began to change traditional views that nurtured the distinction between "them" (the immigrant, the outsider) and "us," Italian community leaders were at the forefront in Edmonton and Calgary. The Canadian Multiculturalism Policy implemented by Prime Minister Pierre Elliot Trudeau, on October 8, 1971, recognized Canada's diversity and committed to assisting communities to preserve and share cultural traditions and remove discriminatory barriers. The *Immigration Act* 1976 included new provisions on refugees as a class of immigrants, and acknowledged provincial and municipal government role in successful integration. These liberalizing measures culminated in 1988 with the *Canadian Multiculturalism Act*, the first in the world.[20]

The Province of Alberta, under Culture, Youth and Recreation Minister Horst Schmid, proclaimed the *Alberta Heritage Day Act*, in 1974, establishing the first Monday in August as a cultural heritage holiday.[21] Two organizations – the Cultural Heritage Council and the Cultural Heritage Foundation – were established to consult with qualifying groups and provide grants. Alberta's support for multiculturalism was entrenched in the 1984 *Alberta Cultural Heritage Act*. Individuals such as Sabatino Roncucci, a founder of the Dante Alighieri Society and its Italian language school in Edmonton, collaborated with Minister Schmid from the outset. The mandate

---

[20] Museum at Pier 21, see summaries of various pieces of immigration and multiculturalism legislation. URL: https://www.pier21.ca/research/immigration-history/canadian-immigration-acts-and-legislation, retrieved May 25, 2016.

[21] Horst A. Schmid is an important figure in Alberta politics and a model of the post-war immigrant making good. In 1971, he was elected a member of the Legislative Assembly of Alberta for the Progressive Conservative Party under Peter Lougheed. It was under his stewardship that support programs for the arts, culture and multiculturalism were implemented.

of the National Congress of Italian Canadians (NCIC), Edmonton District included not only preservation and sharing of Italian culture and traditions but also contributing to the greater good.

The impact of the federal and provincial legislation on the building of ethnic pride and a sense of belonging in Alberta's Italian communities cannot be understated. At the most basic level, it affirmed that while of different ethnicity, Italians and other immigrants belonged. They were no longer "strangers at the gates." The proliferation of Italian community organizations, in particular in Edmonton, was evidence of this.

Funding programs leveled the playing field between mainstream organizations and those created by immigrants. In 1969, amendments to the Criminal Code of Canada gave provinces authority to licence and operate lotteries and casinos. Funds derived from these sources were dedicated by the Government of Alberta to cultural and community-building purposes. The Alberta Lottery Fund allowed the Government to make funding available for festivals and events as well as for building community facilities. Cynics might say that it was the creation of major new sources of funding by the Government of Alberta, in the 1980s that was the cause of the building programs of various ethnocultural organizations. But the same thing happened with community leagues, churches, seniors' centres, and sports and recreation entities. In a sense, this enabled ethnocultural organizations to become part of the mainstream.

With respect to the development of post-war Italian societies, Calgary was the first at bat. The Italo-Canadian Society was started in May 1952 and among its objectives was to "acquire land" and "erect or otherwise provide a building for social and community purposes." The society merged, in 1955, with the earlier entity, the Loggia Giovanni Caboto, and reflected a unified front by adopting the name the Calgary Italian Club. The club's first home was a barn, purchased in 1959, and eventually they had a purpose-built building. By the 1980s, the club was threatened by attempts to create other societies based on regional lines. This occurred to some extent in Calgary. In Edmonton, there were many societies before a unitary one was created. The National Congress of Italian-Canadians, Edmonton District was established in 1979. The 1980s saw the building of the Italian Cultural Centre, new Santa Maria Goretti Community Centre, Piazza Italia Seniors' Residence and the Ital-Canadian Seniors Centre in Edmonton. The number of societies continued to grow and, by the early 1990s, there were more than 40, many based on the region of origin of the group. The age-old division between North and South was thus re-created in the New World.

A desire to document Italian community history emerged and oral history projects, the most current vehicles for creating social history, were initiated. In Edmonton, the Dante Alighieri Society, in 1973-1974, undertook a project with pioneers mostly from Edmonton and a few from Calgary and other areas of the province. In 1983, to celebrate the 25th anniversary of Santa Maria Goretti, Father Augusto Feccia established the Italians Settle in Edmonton Historical Society.

Rudy Vecoli, Director of the Immigration History Research Center at the University of Minnesota and Italian-American historian, was brought to help initiate an oral history project. The project was led by teacher Frank Sdao and then *Canadian Encyclopedia* Editor Adriana (Albi) Davies. In 1985, the Calgary Italian Club undertook the Calgary Italian Club Historical Project. In 1987, Glenbow in partnership with the University of Calgary began the *Peoples of Southern Alberta Oral History Project*. This included a number of Italian oral histories. In 2001, the National Congress of Italian Canadians, Edmonton District partnered with the Heritage Community Foundation, led by Davies, resulting in creation of the multimedia website *Celebrating Alberta's Italian Community*.[22] Launched in 2002, the website contains excerpts from oral histories including some undertaken for the website. In 2007, the Ital-Canadian Seniors' Association, in partnership with the Heritage Community Foundation, undertook oral histories largely with post-war immigrants.

Community identity was also nurtured through a number of communications initiatives including a series of radio programs beginning in the mid-1950s that ran on CHFA, CKUA and CKER; the last was the first fully multicultural radio station. Edmonton took the lead in this. *Il Congresso* newspaper was established in Edmonton by Carlo Amodio, Rudy Cavaliere and Alessandro Urso. Milena Alzetta, followed by Carlo Amodio and Frank Cappellano, ran the *Panorama Italiano* program in Edmonton on Shaw Cable TV until 2012.

As Canada's Italian communities gained in strength and confidence, the issue of Italian internment in the Second World War was finally addressed. The National Congress of Italian-Canadians and regional congresses spearheaded documentation of this painful history. A brief was submitted to PM Brian Mulroney addressing the need for an apology and reparations. This followed Japanese community efforts that, in 1988, resulted in an apology and $330 million compensation. At the NCIC national conference in Toronto, on November 2-4, 1990, Mulroney apologized to the Italian community.

Some Observations

Alberta's Italian community today is at a crossroads. Italian immigrants have been enormously successful and are integrated into all aspects of Canadian life. This success has meant that there is no longer the same need to maintain the vehicles for preserving and affirming identity. In addition, the volunteers maintaining the Italian societies are seniors in their seventies and eighties struggling

---

[22] The *Celebrating Alberta's Italian Community* website was one of the 84 multimedia websites comprising the *Alberta Online Encyclopedia*. Adriana (Albi) Davies created the encyclopedia and wrote about Italian settlement in Alberta as well as the entries on cultural life, sports and recreation and religion.

to engage Italian-Canadian youth in the running of these venerable organizations. The *Il Congresso* newspaper and the Shaw Cable *Panorama Italiano* program ceased operations. While there might still be potential readers and viewers, death and old age have diminished the capacity to produce newspapers and television programs.

The 2017 broadcast list for Monday at CKER suggests why: 12 to 5 am: World Beat Music; 5 to 6 am: Nitnem Path (South Asian Religious); 6 to 7 am: Hukamnanma and Viakhia From Golden Temple (South Asian Religious); 7 am to 12 pm: Morning with Raj (South Asian); 12 to 1 pm: Corazon Latino (Spanish); 1 to 3 pm: Mandarin Radio; 3 to 5 pm: Cantonese Radio; 5 to 6 pm: Himig Pinoy (Filipino/Tagalog); 6 to 7 pm (Ukrainian Edition); 7 to 10 pm: Basota (South Asian); 10 pm to 11 am: Rahul's Playlist (South Asian); 11 to 12 am: Naz at Night (South Asian). Italian programming is now confined to Sundays: 8:30 to 8:45 am: Mezz'Ora Con Voi (Italian Religious); 8:45 to 9 am: 15 Minuti Con La Terza Eta' (Italian) and 9 am to 12 pm: Ciao Italia (Italian).

New immigrant groups dominate the CKER play list and they need telecommunications media, community centres and program funding to establish and affirm their presence in Canada. There is a similar occurrence in university studies. The once thriving program of Italian studies at the University of Alberta has been cut back because of lack of demand. Italian language schools run through the Calgary Italian Club and the Dante Alighieri Society in Edmonton are still successful but not simply because they teach the grandchildren of Italian immigrants; they are catering to parents who want their children to acquire a world language that links them to an ancient civilization or a hot tourist destination.

Successful assimilation may ultimately result in turning the lights off at Italian cultural institutions just as surplus churches are being torn down or finding new uses. The Italian Canadian Cultural Centre in Lethbridge has provided a vision of the future: it still exists but is now a community centre open to anyone.

I have discussed this issue with friends of the same generation who were also part of the third-wave of immigration from Italy. Most of us agree that we are not left with a sense of regret about the potential closure of Italian centres; we view it as a measure of success. It means that our children and grandchildren need not go through this rite of passage from one society to another, from Old World to New World. It is much more comfortable to be within the gates than outside waiting to be let in.

It is important, however, to remember the challenges faced by Italian immigrants today when Canada's Charter of Rights and Freedoms guarantees fundamental rights and privileges to economic migrants and refugees alike. In addition, there are a range of economic and social safety nets. Canada's willingness to admit refugees is noteworthy as other western democracies attempt to close their gates to "less desirable" immigrants. Prime Minister Justin Trudeau gained worldwide positive attention by the ready acceptance of 35,000 Syrian refugees after coming to power in 2016. Donald Trump espoused selective immigration policies while on the campaign trail in 2016 and, as president in 2017, through a presidential directive barred Muslims from selected countries from admittance to the US. In his first address to Congress, he praised Canada's points system for ranking potential immigrants.

As a nation of immigrants, Canadians must be ever conscious of the rights and privileges that we enjoy and the trials and tribulations it has taken to arrive at this point in time. Democratic policies are not set in stone and must evolve to address changing societal needs not just within our own country but also in response to international crises. It was particularly important to remember this in 2017, the 150th anniversary of Confederation. History has its winners and losers, and Canada has yet to address the needs of its Indigenous peoples who unwillingly made our way of life possible. The quest to maintain a just society is a never-ending one.

ENGLISH. This card should be kept carefully for three years. It should be shown to government officials whenever required.

BOHEMIAN. Tato Karta musi být drřená přes tři lete. Na po...ni lidi ůrednich jim oddaná.

RUSSIAN. Этую бумажку нужно сохранять через три года. На запросъ чиновниковъ державнихъ, слѣдуетъ ею отдать.

RUTHENIAN. Сю картку треба держати через три роки. На жадане держав-них урядниківъ, треба еі віддати.

GERMAN. Diese Karte muss drei Jahre sorgfältig aufbewahrt werden. Wenn immer Regierungs beamte dieselbe verlangen, muss selbe vorgezeigt werden.

FRENCH. Cette carte doit être conservée soigneusement durant trois ans. Elle doit être montrée aux officiers du Gouvernement lorsque requis.

DUTCH. Deze kaart moest drie jaare goed bewaart worden. Deze kaart moest gewezen worden wanneer een ambtenaar door regering hetzelve begeert.

HUNGARIAN. Ezen jegy 3 eves at jol megörizendö. Mindig megmutatandó allami hivatalnoknak akar mikor az követeli.

SWEDISH. Detta kort bor väl förvaras i 3 år. Det bör uppvisas till Regeringens tjenstemän vid anfordran.

POLISH. Ta kartka musi byc trzymana przez trzy lata. Takowa ma byc oddana urzendowym ludziom zazondana przez nich.

ITALIAN. Questa carta dove stare conservata per tre anni. Dove mostrarli agli uffiziali del governo quando demandato.

האלט דיעזע קארטע אונד פאסט עס אויף פיר 3 יאהר צייט
צייט עס צום נאוונערנמענט בעאמטע, ווען.נור ער עם פֿאָדערמ

Immigration identification card, Canada, 1914. The card is printed in English, Bohemian, Russian, Ruthenian (Ukrainian), German, French, Dutch, Hungarian, Swedish, Polish, Italian and Yiddish. It states: "This card should be kept carefully for three years. It should be shown to government officials whenever required. Photo courtesy of Glenbow Archives, Archives and Special Collections, University of Calgary NA-2181-2.

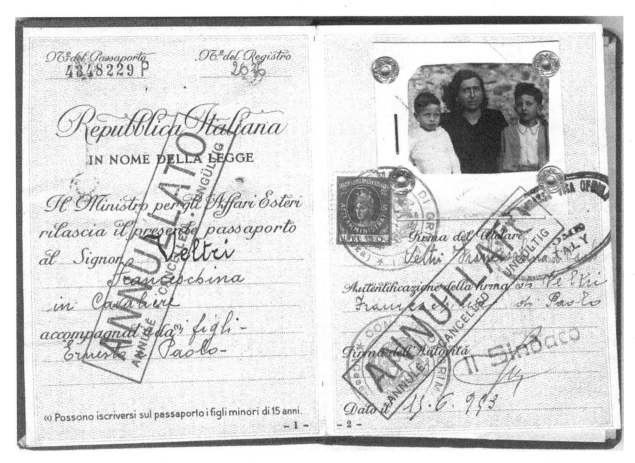

Passport belonging to Franca (Veltri) Cavaliere including sons Paul (left) and Ernesto Rodolfo (Rudy) (right). Photo courtesy of Rudy and Rita Cavaliere.

View of the Canadian Pacific Railway's Crowsnest Branch framing gang in the Lethbridge Millyards, April 16, 1898. Many Italian sojourners worked on railway gangs. Photographer: Steele & Co. Photo courtesy of Provincial Archives of Alberta A3948.

CHAPTER II

Working on the Railways

IN 1871, THE GOVERNMENT of Sir John A. Macdonald made a binding commitment to link British Columbia to Eastern Canada when the province joined Confederation. A transcontinental railway would create a united Canada, enable economic development, and provide the means for transporting settlers. On February 16, 1881, a syndicate of Scottish-Canadian businessmen incorporated the Canadian Pacific Railway (CPR). The company was given a monopoly in railway construction and operation. Other powers allowed it to run transportation and communications industries, coal mines and other industrial operations, as well as promote settlement. The CPR also obtained a subsidy of $25,000,000, and 25,000,000 acres of land. The federal government tried to remove any barriers to the success of the CPR, seeing its work as synonymous with the public interest. Building it required laying tracks westward across 1,600 km of challenging terrain, from the granite base of the Canadian Shield and muskeg of Northern Ontario through the three prairie steppes, the Canadian Rockies and mountain ranges of the interior of BC to Vancouver. The line began at Bonfield, Ontario, where the first spike was driven.

In 1879, the federal government hired Andrew Onderdonk, who built the San Francisco seawall, to lay the rails from Vancouver to Savona, near Kamloops, but he continued building until he ran out of rail at Eagle Pass in 1885.[23] Cornelius Van Horne from the Chicago, Milwaukee and St. Paul Railway was hired by the CPR as general manager and his primary responsibility became the laying of track westward as well as gaps in Ontario.[24] In 1882, work on the prairie portion began and Van Horne quickly realized that earnings could only be achieved through speed in finishing tracks and opening them to traffic. His aim was to make savings on the prairies to offset extra expenses anticipated for construction in the mountains. He needed a tight money manager

---

[23] Onderdonk's first major project was the San Francisco seawall including the harbour. See Robert D. Turner, "ONDERDONK, ANDREW," in *Dictionary of Canadian Biography*, vol. 13, University of Toronto/Université Laval, 2003.

[24] Theodore D. Regehr, "VAN HORNE, Sir WILLIAM CORNELIUS," in *Dictionary of Canadian Biography*, vol. 14, University of Toronto/Université Laval, 2003.

and brought in former colleague Thomas George Shaughnessy, who became chief purchasing agent. Fundraising by syndicate members had fallen short while construction costs mounted.

While the railway route through the prairies was easily established, the route through the Rockies was a political issue. In 1872, Sandford Fleming, a Scottish-Canadian engineer, had recommended a northerly route that would follow the North Saskatchewan River through the fertile prairies and cross the Rockies through the Yellowhead Pass. Instead the CPR chose a more southerly route closer to the American border. This was done to prevent American interests from encroaching on their market. Albert Bowman Rogers, who had worked for the Chicago, Milwaukee and St. Paul Railway, was hired to find a pass. The promised reward was $5,000 as well as the naming rights.

The mountainous terrain presented enormous challenges; for example the steep gradient of the Kicking Horse Pass. From the west of the summit (1,625 metres), the Kicking Horse River drops 350 metres. In 1884, this required the CPR to build a 7-kilometre length of track with a steep 4.5 percent gradient (the normal grade was considered to be 2 percent). The "Big Hill" also required a number of safety switches and a speed limit of 10-km per hour. In spite of these precautions, several runaways happened, including the first locomotive to test the line. The summit was reached on August 17, 1885. The tracks ascended the eastern flank of the Mountains towards Rogers Pass. There, a 50-metre-high trestle was built spanning 331 metres across the valley walls. The bridge built at Stoney Creek was 64-metres high, believed by the engineers to be the highest in the world. The line continued from Rogers Pass to the Columbia River and on to Eagle Pass through the Monashee Mountains, where on November 7, 1885, Ross's crew met the crew coming from the Pacific. The last spike was driven at Craigellachie, 48 km from Revelstoke. While the railway was completed four years after the original 1881 deadline, this was more than five years ahead of the new date of 1891 that Macdonald had given Parliament in 1881.

Van Horne's final challenge in the Rockies occurred in spring 1885 when a strike occurred because of the CPR's inability to pay its contractors. The North-West Mounted Police was used to keep men working while Van Horne struggled with the directors to ensure that a pay car was dispatched. Ironically, it was the CPR's assistance in putting down the North-West Rebellion that resulted in further funding from the Government of Canada. In the end, Van Horne's services were recognized with election to the Board of the CPR and the office of vice-president as well as general manager.

The story of the CPR is well-documented as it is part of the Canadian narrative of nation-building. Lesser known is the history of the labourers who laid tracks and built the other necessary infrastructure including stations, shops and railyards. Gordon Lightfoot's "The Canadian Railroad Trilogy," a CBC commission to commemorate the Canadian centenary in 1967, gave the "navvies, who worked upon the railway," a heroic stature that was denied them in their lifetimes.[25] The achievements of the "railway barons" must therefore be balanced with the stories of the ordinary men who accomplished the great feat at great personal cost including death and dismemberment. The Italians and many other ethnocultural groups are part of this chapter of our history, and their achievements must be drawn from memoirs, oral and community histories, and newspaper accounts of the day.

Father Nicolas Coccola: Saving Money and Souls

A first-hand account of railway building is provided by an unlikely source: Oblate missionary Father Nicolas Coccola. A Sardinian who spoke Italian, he arrived at St. Mary's Mission near Kamloops in 1880. As with many Oblates, he was an adventurer who relished travel on the frontier and embraced his duties in evangelizing Indigenous people, and supporting the settlements developing in the region. It was another Oblate of Mary Immaculate, Father Albert Lacombe, who would assign him to minister to railway workers. After helping to set up the Lac Ste. Anne Mission in northern Alberta and the Metis settlement at St. Albert, near Edmonton, Lacombe settled in Calgary where he continued his work. In 1883, the CPR reached Calgary and the company was readying for a push into the Rockies and BC interior. Lacombe had an established relationship with the CPR leadership, and began to minister to Catholic railway workers.[26] He quickly realized that he needed help and requested that his order assign an Italian-speaking priest to tend to their spiritual needs. Coccola was appointed and his area of responsibility became Kamloops to Calgary.

Coccola's 1934-memoir, while primarily dealing with his mission work, also provides some information on railway construction and early Italian immigrants. Writing about a visit to Eagle Pass, west of Rogers Pass and Revelstoke, he captures the rough-and-tumble of the railway camp as follows:

> Father LeJacq told me: "Here is your field of labor go to it." I went on, my first stop was Eagle Pass. No construction work there yet except surveyors and engineers' camps locating the best pass for the R.R.R. [*sic*] but there was much activity on the part of the forerunners of the men

---

[25] The term "navvy," short for navigator, came into use in the era of canal building in Britain and later was applied to manual labours working on constructions projects.

[26] See Raymond Huel's biography of Father Albert Lacombe for the *Dictionary of Canadian Biography*, URL: http://www.biographi.ca/en/bio/lacombe_albert_14E.html, retrieved March 14, 2017.

to be employed on construction consisting in gamblers, whisky sellers and toughs of every description. Saloons and dens of all sorts were going up waiting for the railway builders to come with their wages and spend the last dollar they would earn at the cost of so many hardships. Those saloons keepers lived by preying upon the navvies who might appear amongst them on pay day and get trunk.[27]

He continues, distinguishing between the opportunists and more serious immigrants as follows: "Things were better when I came to the construction camps. If there were men who would dissipate and throw their money away, the majority of the men in those camps were coming from good Catholic families anxious to earn enough to send their cheques to their parents. I would write their letters and enclose the cheques before they were cashed, that was a part of my work. Saving money and souls."[28] So as not to interfere with the working day, Coccola said Mass and gave Communion at 5 am and finished well before 6 am to allow the men to have breakfast and start work at 7. For cooks, he did this at 3 am. On Sundays, he said High Mass at 9 am and men came from surrounding camps to attend and, on one occasion, built an altar at the foot of a high tree. Coccola noted that numbers rose to 200. He ministered not only to Italian workers but also to other Roman Catholics including Irish, Polish, Austrians and Germans. He stayed in camp only three days so as not to be seen to be interfering with the men's work.

Coccola's account provides insight into the hardships experienced by the men and he observes:

> At Rogers Pass, where I was calling often on account of the many men employed in rock work, the buildings were carried off in the following spring by avalanches of tremendous force and power bringing along trees and immense rocks. The continual blasting was the cause of it. Glaciers which had never moved from their rocky beds above the clouds, came down with a tremendous roaring; by the pressure of the air one of those avalanches not touching the ground below of the valley rose up many hundred feet on the other side burying a construction train with 19 men ....[29]

---

[27] Margaret Whitehead, ed. *They Call Me Father: Memoirs of Father Nicolas Coccola* (Vancouver, BC: University of British Columbia Press, 1988), 99-100. Whitehead provides an introduction to the memoirs and a context for the evangelization of Indigenous people in the area, and also for the coming of the railway and economic development.

[28] *Ibid.*, 100.

[29] *Ibid.*, 100. On March 4, 1910, the largest avalanche accident in Canada occurred at the Rogers Pass killing 58 men most Japanese labourers. Snow sheds were then built to protect the tracks.

He expressed surprise that there were relatively few accidents and attributed this to the fact that experienced men handled the explosives. Coccola referred to "mountain fever or rather typhoid" as being prevalent and noted that the young doctors visited the work camps frequently to try to keep the diseases under control. Their efforts were hampered by bad sanitation and damp. Coccola also provides information about labour troubles. In 1883, on a visit to Donald, a divisional point for the CPR, he noted:

> One afternoon there was some excitement; the track men declared a strike. A train loaded with gravel was on the main track and a freight with passengers was due in the evening. I was asked to speak to the men, which I did, but they complained of not being paid for the past month and would not work unless settled at once. I assured them that settlement would be made soon, but by wasting time their cheque would be only smaller on the next pay day, that the company had no desire to defraud them of their dues. The Mounted Police came also to speak to the men having heard of threats to set fire to the station under construction, but what could five or six police do in a crowd of desperatos [sic]? I showed the harm they were doing to themselves: striking would deprive them of return tickets to go East and going in their own account how costly it would be. After a moment of silence one said: "I am willing to go to work if the others consent."[30]

The very close relationship between southeastern BC and southern Alberta is made clear by Coccola who writes: "Calgary was nearer to me than Kamloops, where I could renew my supplies for Mass. Father Lacombe received me very cordially." He noted: "Calgary built on the bank of the Elbow River was promising to be a big town. The Catholics had there already a little chapel and a priest house, a large school under the direction of the Faithful Companions of Jesus, and a splendid hospital under the management of the Grey Nuns."[31] The community had benefitted from the CPR's decision to take a southern route, which in Alberta, went, from east to west, through Medicine Hat to Calgary and, eventually, Banff. In the first decades of the twentieth century, Calgary was a growing urban centre and a desirable base for Italian immigrants doing railway work and, later, settling.

---

[30] *Ibid*, 101.
[31] *Ibid*, 102. The Faithful Companions of Jesus and Grey Nuns were women's religious orders that followed the Oblates West.

A letter dated February 10, 1886 from Coccola to a friend in France provides specific information about Italian workers as follows:

> I arrived at one of the camps where the foreman told me there were many Catholics. He gave me every opportunity to speak to them. The men did not seem friendly. Some questioned, "are you a priest?" When I said "yes," they said "impossible a priest would not venture alone on such a mission in such a country." Others shouted, "he is here to beg for our money." They did not intimidate me. I waited until they settled down, I spoke first in English, then in Italian wishing success to all in return for the curses that had been hurled at me. When the Italians heard me speak their language they were ashamed. They probably thought I had not understood. The news of the arrival of an Italian priest spread quickly along the line. The following day I had a very small congregation. I was not discouraged.[32]

While initially suspicious, the Italian railway workers came to depend on him to draft correspondence, resolve queries about wages and provide spiritual support. Coccola's engagement with Italian immigrants was solidified when, in 1904, he became resident priest for a year at Holy Family Church in Fernie.[33] Italians comprised about a third of the congregation and most had moved from railway construction to work in the area's plentiful coal mines.

Chain Immigration and Labour Agents

In order to understand how Italian labourers came to be involved in construction of the CPR, it is important to examine the relationship between railway building in the US and Canada. By the 1860s, Chicago had become a hub for immigration to the western US and was served by 11 railway companies. While the port of New York was still the primary entry point for immigrants into the North American continent, in the 1880s and 1890s, Chicago was a hub for recruitment of railway workers who were then sent westward to Wisconsin, North Dakota, Montana, Idaho and Washington State, and, then, north to BC.[34] This was the second wave of railway building in the US, the first wave had occurred prior to 1860.

---

[32] Quoted by Whitehead in her introductory essay, 64-65.

[33] In 2016, I developed the content for the Fernie Museum's virtual exhibit titled "Fernie's Italian Pioneer Heritage," which received funding support through the Department of Canadian Heritage Community Memories Program.

[34] See Marie-Christine Michaud, *From Steel Tracks to Gold-Paved Streets: Italian Immigrants and the Railroads in the North Central States* (New York, NY: Center for Migration Studies, 2005). She explores the movement of Italian immigrants on various railway projects.

The CPR drew not only on American railway builders but also the railway workers, thus, becoming a part of the larger, American labour chain. The first part of the railway west involved the portion between Flat Creek in what became Kananaskis Country and Fort Calgary. The CPR awarded the contract, in February 1882, to General R. B. Langdon of Minneapolis and his partner D. C. Shepard of St. Paul. Both were experienced in railway construction – Langdon as a stonemason and Shepard as an engineer. Historian Pierre Berton describes the scale of hirings as follows:

> On the day after the contract was signed, Langdon and Shepard advertised for three thousand men and four thousand horses. The job they faced was staggering: it would require no fewer than three hundred subcontractors. Between Flat Creek and Fort Calgary the partners would have to move ten million cubic yards of earth. They would have to haul every stick of timber, every rail, fishplate, and spike, all the pilings used for bridge-work, and all the food and provisions for 7,600 men and 1,700 teams of horses across the naked prairie for hundreds of miles. To feed the horses alone it would be necessary to distribute four thousand bushels of oats every day along one hundred and fifty miles of track. It was no wonder that Van Horne's boast about building five hundred miles in a single season was openly derided.[35]

At peak of construction through the Rockies and the interior of BC, the CPR employed more than 10,000 men. Some Chinese workers were brought in from San Francisco by Andrew Onderdonk but it is estimated that an additional 6,500 were brought in from China making them the primary group by ethnicity. At least 4,000 men were of other ethnicities including American, English, Canadian, Irish, German, Polish, Swedish, Russian and Italian. With respect to construction in the Rockies and the Selkirks, some accounts indicate that most workers were Swedes or Italians from the eastern US, and that Oriental and "Native Indians" were not employed.[36]

CPR President Thomas Shaughnessy defined ideal railway workers as follows: "Men who seek employment on railway construction are, as a rule, a class accustomed to roughing. They know when they go to work that they must put up with the most primitive kind of camp accommodation … I feel very strongly that it would be a huge mistake to send out any more of these men from Wales, Scotland or England … It is prejudicial to the cause of immigration to

---

[35] Berton, 101-102.

[36] Robert D. Turner, *West of the Great Divide: An Illustrated History of the Canadian Pacific Railway in British Columbia 1880-1986* (Victoria, BC: Sono Nis Press, 1987), 17-18.

import men who come here expecting to get high wages, a feather bed and a bath tub."[37] From 1901, the CPR increased its recruitment of Italian workers. The Grand Truck Pacific and Canadian Northern were also laying track. In the period 1907 to 1914, it is estimated that 60,000 to 70,000 workers were hired. Historian Donald Avery throws light on these hirings as follows:

> A survey of the labour demands of railroad contractors in 1909 revealed that the most popular immigrant workers were "non-preferred" Southern European immigrants; these, it was claimed, "were peculiarly suited for the work." Wheaton Bros. of Grand Falls, New Brunswick, reported that it "would not employ Englishmen;" the Toronto Construction Company announced that it was entirely dependent "upon Italians, Bulgarians, and that class of labour"; while the Munro Company of La Tuque, Quebec, expressed a preference for "foreigners" – "Polaks, Bulgarians, Italians."[38]

Members of the Montalbetti family of the Crowsnest Pass were among the first Italian workers hired by the CPR. They are unique in having had railway building experience before coming to North America. They were among a group of immigrants from the Lombardy region of northwestern Italy, who came to Canada specifically to work on construction of railways, and some of whom later worked in the mines of the Elk Valley, BC and the Crowsnest Pass, Alberta. Italian historian Ernesto R. Milani in an essay titled *"Appunti per una storia dei lombardi in Canada"* (Notes for a History of the Lombards in Canada) provides some information on Carlo (Charles) Montalbetti, who in 1888 was working on railway construction at Rat Portage, near a local reserve in northwestern Ontario with other workers from the municipalities of Sumirago, Mornago and Cadezzate in Lombardy.[39] Census records reveal that the following Montalbettis worked in the Crowsnest Pass: Felix, who was born in 1852 and immigrated to Canada in 1886; Giuseppe (Joe), born in 1865 and immigrated in 1888; Enrico (Henry), born in 1871 and immigrated in 1893; and another Carlo, born in 1876 and who immigrated in 1900.

---

[37] Cited by Donald Avery in *"Dangerous Foreigners": European Immigrant Workers and Labour Radicalism in Canada 1896-1932* (Toronto, ON: McClelland and Stewart, 1979), 25-26.

[38] *Ibid.*, 27.

[39] Ernesto R. Milani, "Appunti per una storia dei lombardi in Canada" ("Notes for a History of the Lombards in Canada"), in Lombards in the World portal, URL: http://portale.lombardinelmondo.org/nazioni/nordamerica/Articoli/storiaemi/canada, retrieved April 26, 2017. Milani is attached to the Ecoistituto della Valle del Ticino, Cuggiono, Italy and has written about Lombards in the US. The translation is by Adriana Davies.

R. Aldo Montalbetti, the son of the last Carlo (Charles), in a family history in *Crowsnest and Its People*, notes that his grandfather and two siblings had worked in railway construction in Italy prior to coming to Canada.[40] There was a division of labour: one brother obtained government contracts; another supervised the work; and the third managed the family farm where they raised heavy horses. Their last project was helping to build a railway in central Sardinia linking Oristano, Ozieri and Olbia with the capital Cagliari. This opened in July 1879. According to Aldo, the Montalbettis then went out of business because of poor management. Aldo observed that a cousin involved in the family enterprise immigrated to Canada and began work for the CPR in Fort William, Ontario (this work was done in 1882), and then followed the railway west. He was soon joined by other family members.

Aldo provides information about his uncle Felix Montalbetti, who served as construction foreman for the building of the railway between Fort Macleod and Cranbrook, having earlier worked in Medicine Hat. The line linking Fort Macleod to Kootenay Landing, BC was opened in October 1898. Aldo writes: "After completion of the steel, Uncle Felex [*sic*.] built section houses for the crews. These houses consisted of six rooms, one room being the operator's quarters. This same type of C.P.R. building is still in existence in Coleman. Uncle Felex built two dry stone culverts six feet by six feet east of Burmis, which for the past 50 years took care of Rockcreek run off."[41] In 1899, Felix was appointed as the first station foreman at Blairmore. In the spring of that year, he and H. E. Lyon, the CPR station agent, erected log houses at what was known as the 10th siding or "The Springs." As noted in *Crowsnest and Its People*, "The time as to when these houses were constructed was the basis for the long litigation over the ownership of the townsite. With the town booming due to the start of the mine at Frank, land became valuable and Lyon and Montalbetti both claimed squatter's rights to the townsite."[42] Local historian Ian McKenzie expands the story as follows:

> The dispute arose when station master and future mayor Henry Lyon attempted to claim homestead rights on the entire quarter section on which the fledgeling settlement was located, then section hand Felix Montalbetti submitted a counter-claim based on coincident but more substantial residency. The case considered who had built buildings and of what nature, who had planted a

[40] R. Aldo Montalbetti, "Charles Montalbetti" in *Crowsnest and Its People*, 721-722.
[41] *Ibid.*, 722.
[42] *Anon.*, "Blairmore," in *Crowsnest and Its People*, 75.

garden, etc. Montalbetti sold his claim to lawyer Malcolm McKenzie who ultimately obtained title to the quarter section, with Lyon receiving some small concessions. The matter then went to court, and Lyon later charged Montalbetti with perjury, but the decision in favor of McKenzie stood. The federal Conservatives then attempted to make a national scandal of the matter (McKenzie was a Liberal). Malcolm McKenzie became Alberta's provincial treasurer in 1912.[43]

McKenzie died in 1913. The fact that Felix would take on Lyon, a retired colonel who had fought in the First World War, is remarkable and shows a tough-mindedness and desire to succeed. McKenzie subdivided the lots and put them up for sale and the townsite developed and became a village. Felix continued to be employed by the CPR and, in the 1901 census of the Northwest Territories, is listed as residing in Blairmore with wife Rose and daughters, Tesline and Iedda (the non-Italian spellings were likely due to census errors). By 1910, Felix had opened the Mercantile Store in Bellevue and went on to develop other commercial enterprises. The 1916 census lists another Montalbetti, George, who was born in Italy in 1879, and immigrated in 1893; he is residing in Frank with Irish-born wife, Dazzie, and brother Isadore, who was born in Ontario in 1889.

Aldo's father, Charles, arrived in the Pass around 1900 and the following year became the section foreman in Sparwood, BC. He later worked in Frank and Michel laying tracks for the mines. He decided to remain in Canada and, in 1902, Maria came from Italy to marry him. Their home in Frank was destroyed by the 1903 Frank Slide. At 4:10 am on April 29, over 82 million tonnes of rock slid down Turtle Mountain engulfing the eastern side of the town, the CPR line and the coal mine. Between 70 and 90 people were buried in the rubble. It is thought that mining activity as well as weather conditions caused the side of the mountain to sheer away. The family returned to Italy in 1907 likely because Maria was traumatized by the slide, and the deaths of friends and neighbours. Charles returned to Canada and worked for the CPR building a section house in Frank where he became foreman. In 1912, he arranged for his wife to return. Immigration records reveal that Maria and three children – Adriano (Andy), Aldo and Ernestina – arrived at the port of Quebec on the *SS Polonia* on September 12, 1913. Andy and Aldo joined their father in work on the railways. Aldo subsequently trained as an electrician and ended his career in 1944 as chief electrician at the McGillivray Mine.

While the Montalbettis emigrated from Italy as a large extended family, others needed the services of labour agents, who served as "middle men" between potential workers and employers. Some of these agents amassed other powers becoming unofficial bankers and also forming alliances

---

[43] Ian McKenzie, "Why Blairmore and Coleman Are Different," in *Heritage News: Discover Crowsnest Pass,*" issue #35, June 2014, footnote 4, np.

with shipping agencies and other elements of the infrastructure required to move seasonal labour between Italy and North America. The Italian term "*padrone*" (patron/owner) has been assigned to this system.[44] Local labour agents emerged in every city that required temporary workers and they prospered. These included New York, Buffalo, Providence, Fall River, Boston, Chicago, San Francisco, Seattle, Portland and Spokane in the US, and Montreal, Toronto and, later, Winnipeg and Port Arthur, in Canada.

Ultimately, the Italian government was forced to examine and regulate foreign recruitment of labour as accounts of abuses reached home and were taken up by local newspapers. In 1901, for example, newspapers in Milan published a series of articles exposing unscrupulous labour practices centred around the town of Chiasso. Labourers travelled either on British steamship lines via Liverpool or French ships from several ports and found themselves stranded in northern Ontario working camps, or unemployed in Montreal and Toronto. This embarrassed the Italian government and, in 1902, the Commissariato Generale dell'Emigrazione (General Commissariat for Emigration) in Rome sent Egisto Rossi to investigate. He visited New York and Montreal and discovered that labour agents in those cities were in collusion with steamship companies (for example, Beaver Lines and the Compagnie Générale Transatlantique) to bring Italian labour to North America.

The town of Chiasso, strategically located on the Swiss-Italian border, was significant in the flow of migrant workers because agents representing various steamship lines were based there, and received payment for each labourer recruited and transported. It was an established market centre and had silk mills and tobacco factories that attracted labour. It was also well connected by railways to northern Italian cities such as Como. The prominence of Chiasso in the movement of labour from Italy explains why so many immigrants went from Northern Italy to North America in the late nineteenth and first part of the twentieth centuries. They came from the northern states of Piedmont, Lombardy, South Tyrol, Trentino, Liguria, Emilia Romagna, Veneto and Friuli Venezia Giulia. This is confirmed in accounts in Alberta community and oral histories.

Antonio Cordasco was the most prominent *padrone* in Montreal rivalled only by Alberto Dini. Cordasco emigrated likely from Calabria and arrived in Canada in 1886 where he learned English, and was among the first generation of Italian workers in railway construction. He was based in Montreal and was employed as a labourer by CPR eventually becoming a foreman. Based on his own experiences, he chose to become an exploiter rather than a victim of the immigrant labour system.

---

[44] See Robert F. Harney, "Montreal's King of Italian Labour: A Case Study of Padronism" in *Labour/Travail*, Volume 4 /Volume 4e (1979); Bruno Ramirez, "Brief Encounters: Italian Immigrant Workers and the CPR 1900-30," *Labour/Travail*, Volume 17, Spring 1986; and "CORDASCO, ANTONIO," in *Dictionary of Canadian Biography*, vol 15, University of Toronto/Université Laval, 2003.

At the time, Montreal was the hub of three railways – the CPR, the Great Northern and the Grand Trunk – as well as being a port. The opportunities for labour agents were boundless, and the clever Cordasco prospered. Historian Gunther Peck describes the Montreal labour scene as follows:

> If Canada's railroads transformed Montreal's economy by opening up a vast hinterland of goods and markets for its own manufactured goods, they also transformed the shape and structure of the labour market in both Montreal and western Canada. As thousands of workers moved west either to settle land or work on the CPR each spring, labour in Montreal became much scarcer and had to be replaced by workers from outside the city – first from the countryside of Quebec and Ontario, then the cities of New York and Boston, and eventually villages of northern Italy. In so doing, Canada's railroads greatly expanded the regions that reciprocally influenced each other within Montreal's labor market.[45]

By 1901, Cordasco was the primary supplier of Italian labour to the CPR. In that year, he helped the CPR break a strike in Vancouver. The company had tried to replace striking workers, which included Italians, with Italian workers from Montreal. This angered Italian strikers because they were either related to some of the strike-breakers, or were from the same region.[46] Cordasco saved the day for the CPR by bringing 2,000 Italian workers from the northeastern US. He later brought in labour directly from Italy, in particular, Northern Italy via Switzerland.

While labour agents or *padroni* can be criticized for their exploitation of labourers, the relationship ultimately was symbiotic. Those who were desperate to leave Italy but could not do so because they had no kin to sponsor them, and were also too poor to make immigration arrangements, needed the help of the *padrone*. That is why it is not surprising that on January 23, 1904 Italian labourers paid tribute to Cordasco presenting him with a ceremonial crown and parading in Montreal chanting: "Viva Edouardo VII, Viva le Canada, Viva Antonio Cordasco, Viva le Canadian Pacific Railway!"[47] For them, he was the "King of the Workers," as was reported in the *Corriere del Canada* newspaper.[48]

---

[45] Gunther Peck, "Mobilizing Community: Migrant Workers and the Politics of Labour Mobility in the North American West," in *Labor Histories: Class, Politics, and the Working Class Experience 1900-1910* (Urbana and Chicago, IL: University of Illinois Press, 1998), edited by Eric Arnesen, Julie Greene and Bruce Laurie, 26-27.

[46] Avery, *Dangerous Foreigners*, 50.

[47] Peck, 185.

[48] Harney, in "Montreal's King of Italian Labour," presents a trenchant attack: "Antonio Cordasco, the protagonist of our story, appears in the end as a nearly perfect Italian parody of the 'negro king,' that peculiarly ugly phenomenon of an ethnic or colonial puppet who serves those who really control the society and the economy" (59).

Cordasco did not hold the crown for long. In May 1904, unrest caused by 6,000 unemployed Italian labourers in Montreal, the result of over-recruitment and a delay in the start of the working season caused by bad weather, led to protests by officials including Mayor Hormidas Laporte and charitable organizations involved in the relief of poverty. On May 31, the mayor wrote to PM Laurier complaining about the unrest and its threat to the city's inhabitants. He noted that the Italian society had tried to assist the unemployed but did not have sufficient resources.[49]

The *Royal Commission Inquiry into the Immigration of Italian Labourers in Montreal and the Alleged Fraudulent Practices of Employment Agencies* was established to investigate the causes of the unrest.[50] In the introduction to the report, Commissioner Mr. Justice John Winchester noted that he had interviewed two Italian labour agents – Antonio Cordasco and Alberto Dini – as well George E. Burns of the CPR in the first five days of hearings. A total of 64 witnesses were examined. Winchester describes "The Circumstances Inducing Italian Immigration" as follows:

> The evidence shows that for some years past a considerable number of Italians have been employed in connection with the construction of railways and other public works in Canada; that during the year 1903 the Canadian Pacific Railway alone employed 3,144. Of these, 1,200 were in Montreal and the remainder came from the United States.
>
> Mr. Burns in his examination stated that since the summer of 1901 he engaged Italian labourers for the Canadian Pacific Railway, almost exclusively through Mr. Cordasco. Previous to that year he had employed other agents, namely, Mr. Dini, the two Schenkers, and possibly one or two others, in obtaining Italian labourers for the company, but that in the year 1901 there was a strike on the Canadian Pacific Railway, and he made special arrangements with Mr. Cordasco to obtain Italian labourers for the railway. Cordasco in turn employed agents in the United States to assist him in getting the required number.[51]

Witnesses stated that Cordasco charged them for arranging work and, in addition, money to cover supplies and food was deducted from wages and paid directly to Cordasco. Other allegations were that Cordasco charged from 60 to 150 percent above cost and continued to bring in labour in 1904 in excess of need simply to make more money.

---

[49] Letter from H. Laporte to Sir Wilfrid Laurier, May 31, 1904, URL: https://www.collectionscanada.gc.ca/immigrants/021017-119.01-e.php?&document_code=021017-76&page=1&referer=021017-2352.03-e.html&section_code=pl-labour, retrieved March 19, 2017.
[50] See *Report of commissioner and evidence* (Ottawa, 1905), in Can., Parl., *Sessional papers*, 1905, no.36b.
[51] *Ibid.*, xi.

Dini, who supplied labour to the Great Trunk Railway as well as other companies, was no less unscrupulous. His labour recruitment was more diverse than Cordasco's – he recruited for other industries and also developed his own enterprises offering services to the local Italian community. In his commission testimony, he mentioned that he was an agent for a number of steamship lines including North German Lloyd's Line, Hamburg-American Anchor Line and the Italian La Veloce, and represented about 10 or 20 contractors. Dini was in an expansionist mode and, in 1903, had set up a branch of his Montreal labour agency in Toronto.[52] He was also vice president of Montreal's Italian Immigrant Aid Society, which was established in 1902. Peck describes the Society's intent as follows:

> Founded in 1902, the Italian Immigration Aid Society proposed to eliminate sojourning among Italian immigrants by settling them on vast tracts of public land in the Canadian Northwest. Stabilizing this vast migratory population on landed plots would solve the "problem" of how to represent sojourning Italians in two ways. First, as agriculturalists they would be members of persistent and therefore respectable Italian communities in North America and, second, they would no longer need Cordasco's "protection."[53]

The Society later became directly affiliated to the Italian government through the Italian consulate in Montreal. This signaled that the government wanted to control the labour recruitment process. In a very real sense, Dini was a wolf in sheep's clothing being both a labour agent and Immigrant Aid Society supporter. In his testimony to the Commission, the Society's Secretary, R. Candori, noted that they were recruiting from the region of Venice a better class of Italian worker who would be a good citizen once work on the railway ceased.[54]

The title of the Commission already suggested the outcome – at fault were the "fraudulent practices" of the agents. While the agents certainly were at fault and exploited the system, employers who wanted to pay the lowest possible wages must share the blame. The findings ended Cordasco's relationship with the CPR and, while the recommendations called on licensing and regulation, they did not end the practice of bringing in numbers of labourers without means of support until they began work. It was not in the interest of railway companies to do this since a large labour pool helped to keep wages low, and also made workers think twice about striking

---

[52] John E Zucchi, *Italians in Toronto: Development of a National Identity, 1875-1935* (Montreal, PQ and Kingston, ON: McGill Queen's University Press, 1988), 212.
[53] Peck, "Mobilizing Community," 185-186.
[54] *Ibid.*, 80.

since they could be easily replaced. The *Alien Labour Act of 1897* had been sponsored by the trade union movement and made it illegal for any "person, company, partnership or corporation" to assist or encourage importation of labour or immigration of "aliens" or "foreigners" through the prepayment of transportation or any other means.[55] In practice, it had no impact. The need of industry was so great that there was no way of stopping the flood of migrant workers.

An examination of the Italian family histories in *Crowsnest and Its People* reveals that at least a quarter of the men got their start in railway work and were part of labour chains in Europe and North America. Some were part of the earliest immigration wave to the US in the 1880s. Francesco D'Ercole was born in L'Aquila, Abruzzo in 1874 and at the age of 13 went to work in Marseille, France as a labourer, one assumes with older relatives.[56] In 1888, he travelled to Boston where he worked as a brick layer, in quarries and helped to install part of the city's sewer system. In 1891, working for the Great Northern Railroad he helped to build lines from the US into BC. The family history notes that he worked with Chinese labourers. He shifted to work in mines in Morrissey before settling in the Crowsnest Pass. Paul Baratelli was born in northwest Italy near the Swiss border, and trained as a blacksmith. He immigrated to Canada in 1900 and worked for the CPR at Michel and then as a blacksmith in mines in southern BC and the Pacific Northwest before settling in Blairmore where he worked in the West Canadian Collieries Ltd.

Domenico Campo left the Basilicata region of southern Italy with his uncle and arrived in North America at the age of 13 (around 1897) and first worked in Chicago as a shoeshine boy. He took on a variety of jobs in the US and Mexico and eventually helped lay tracks for the Great Northern Railway and the CPR. Work with the CPR as a section hand brought him to Blairmore, in 1917, where he settled. Campo also helped to lay streetcar tracks in Calgary. Virginio Marcolin immigrated from Loria in northern Italy, the oldest of a family of 11, and worked for the CPR around Lake Superior. He arrived in Frank shortly after the 1903 slide and he and wife Maria (nee Bassani) settled in Bellevue in 1909 where he worked in the mines. Frank Amatto emigrated from San Giovanni-in-Fiore, Calabria in 1904 with his two brothers and worked for the CPR in Corbin, Blairmore, Vancouver, Creston, Nordegg and Grouard before turning to work in the mines. Paul Caletti left Mornago in the region of Lombardy arriving in Frank in 1904 where he worked on the railways.

Giovanni (John) Marconi (originally Mucciarone) came to Canada from Campobasso in southern Italy around 1903 and initially worked in construction in Montreal and on CPR work

---

[55] *"Alien Labour Act,"* in About Moving Here, Staying Here, URL: https://www.collectionscanada.gc.ca/immigrants/021017-119.01-e.php?&document_code=021017-71&page=1&referer=021017-2350.02-e.html&section_code=pl-labour, retrieved March 19, 2017.

[56] Ronald E. D'Ercole, "D'Ercole, Francesco," in *Crowsnest and Its People*, 492-493.

gangs. Andrea (Andrew) Mascherin left Pordenone in the Friuli-Venezia Giulia region of northern Italy in 1905 with a brother and arrived in Fort William around 1905. He laid track across the west and ended up working at the Hillcrest Mine and, later, in Coleman. Giuseppi Nastasi left Reggio, Calabria with his brother in 1901 and worked on a CPR gang in Morrisey, BC before settling in Coleman and working in the mines. Angelo Pozzi left Milan and arrived in the Crowsnest Pass in 1903 where he worked for the CPR before turning to the mines. Pietro (Peter) Rizzo left Italy, in 1913, at the age of 16 to join his brother-in-law who was working in the US. He travelled with a number of acquaintances to New York and, then, to Montreal. He worked for the Grand Trunk Pacific Railway in BC and later in the mines in Coleman. Filippo (Philip) Sacco arrived in the Crowsnest Pass as a CPR car man and worked for the company for 46 years. As can be seen, a significant number of railway workers in the Pass came from northern Italy and those who came in the period 1901-1904 were likely sponsored by Cordasco and were linked to the labour agents in Chiasso on the Swiss-Italian border.

As their numbers grew, and value to their railway employers, Italian workers in the first decade of the twentieth century occasionally used strikes to defend their own interests. By this time, they were involved in other areas of railway work including handling freight in both eastern and western Canada. In 1907, Italian railway workers at Nanton struck to protest bad conditions in CPR camps. While concessions were made to them, officials decided to transfer some of the discontented men to avoid further trouble.[57] In 1903, the CPR was involved in irrigation workings to promote settlement. The Department of Land and Natural Resources had created the Irrigation Block comprising Eastern, Western and Lethbridge sections in order to facilitate farming.

The Welch Family – Bridging Waves of Immigration

The Veltri family is important in the West because it comprises several generations of labour agents involved in railway work. Vincenzo and Giovanni Veltri from Grimaldi, Cosenza, Calabria began as railway workers and then established their own small construction company and recruited labour from their home town. Giovanni's memoir, written in the early 1950s, provides insight into their experiences, as well as labour practices.[58] The brothers were orphans who entered the work force early. Elder brother Vincenzo immigrated to the US and worked in railway construction in

---

[57] Avery, *Dangerous Foreigners*, 50.
[58] See John Potestio, ed, *The Memoirs of Giovanni Veltri* (Toronto, ON: The Multicultural History Society, 1987). Potestio, also from Grimaldi, translated the memoirs.

the Pacific Northwest. Giovanni went to North Africa in 1882 with cousins Pietro and Francesco Veltri, and friends Giovanni Albo and Francesco Potestio. They found employment building a railway line around Batna, Algeria. In 1885, Giovanni was injured and, in response to prompting from his brother, he and brother-in-law Antonio Nigro and friend, Antonio Iachetta, went to the US. They arrived in New York in October and headed for Montana where Vincenzo was working for Keefer and Larson, who were building the Montana Central Railway. It became part of the Great Northern Railway in 1889 and was a branch of James J. Hill's St. Paul, Minneapolis & Manitoba Railway. They went on to another contract in Butte City, Montana with fellow Calabresi and Abruzzesi including Fortunato Albo and Fortunato Veltri.[59] Historian John Potestio, editor of the memoir, notes: "Vincenzo's propensity to rely on his home-town connections (a typical time-sheet shows that out of twenty men in his employ seventeen were Grimaldesi, a type of 'Paesanism' adapted to North American conditions) was also evident, in the partnership he formed with another Grimaldese, Gaetano Iachetta."[60]

The memoir provides detailed information about Italian labour in railway construction including pay and conditions of work as follows:

> We were paid two-and-a-half dollars per day and charged a dollar for room and board. This project lasted eleven months. Later, the company sent us to build other branch lines and clearings for the construction of the huge mills and kilns at Anaconda, Montana. We worked in Anaconda until May 1887. The same month we left for Spokane, Washington. We went to work for Milone and Castelli, 100 miles from Spokane. A short while later, we left for Rocky Creek to work on the building of a railway from California to Oregon which joined Albany to Corvallis. Having arrived there, my brother was made work superintendent with his own work-yard and provisions store.[61]

In 1889, Giovanni returned to Italy and, in December, married Rosa Anselmo. Their son Raffaele was born in 1894 and would eventually join his father in Canada. In this period, the brothers changed their surname to Welch perhaps because it made them seem more English.

---

[59] The Albo brothers emigrated from Grimaldi to Spokane and like the Veltri brothers set up construction companies. They changed their name to "Albi." My grandfather, Francesco Albi, was the youngest brother in the family left behind in Italy to look after their mother, Rosa.

[60] John Potestio, *In Search of a Better Life: Emigration to Thunder Bay from a Small Town in Calabria* (Thunder Bay, ON: Thunder Bay Historical Society, 2000), 51.

[61] Potestio, *Veltri Memoirs*, 23-24.

In March 1895, Giovanni joined brother Vincenzo on building a branch line from Kaslo to Three Forks, BC for the Great Northern. Giovanni became foreman for the laying of 12 km of track, which was completed in three-and-a-half months. They next worked for the CPR on a branch line from Revelstoke to Arrowhead Lake. The contractor was Don McGillivray and the sub-contractors were Welch and Iachetta. The pattern of railway work continued and, in October 1897, Welch and Iachetta were given a contract to construct 22-km of track from Kootenay Landing to Goat River, BC for the CPR. The Welch brothers and Giovanni Albo (Albi) were in charge. The company paid $1.75 a day in wages and $5 a week for board.

Tragedy struck 20 days into the project: Luigi Alpini, the foreman, made an error in loading the mine and an explosion occurred, which resulted in his leaving work. The next mine was loaded by Giovanni Albo and, during the explosion that followed, a rock struck and killed Raffaele Greco, the uncle of the Welch's partner Gaetano Iachetta. John noted: "He died in my arms and was later buried in Nelson." It was likely the tragic death of his uncle that prompted Iachetta to return to Italy, in 1898, and Vincenzo bought him out.[62] It was in this period that the brothers sponsored their nephew, Fidele (Felix) Nigro, and he became involved in their work. Aware of how dangerous the work could be, John kept him constantly on his team. Felix would later set up a construction company in Alberta with his brother-in-law James Anselmo. New West Construction based in Edmonton, in its turn, provided work for many Italian immigrants.

The Welch brothers benefited from a number of CPR contracts and Giovanni observes:

> In the autumn of 1898, we moved the work-yard to the vicinity of Grand Forks [BC] on the CPR line. We worked there for nearly two months preparing the clearings for the construction of the new smelter. We also built a line to transport the raw material from the mines to the smelter. We spent the rest of the winter in Grand Forks.
>
> In March 1899 we were notified to load everything in order to move to Nelson. We worked around Nelson until the middle of December. This thirty-mile line went from Five-mile-Point to Balfour. The J. V. Welch Company obtained five miles of it, adjacent to the stretch of work assigned to Big Red Jack McMartin. The other sub-contractors were Pat Welch [no relation], McLean and others. Head contractor was Foley, Larson & Company; the general superintendent was J. W. Stewart; and the engineers were McLeod and Proctor.[63]

62 *Ibid.*, 31.
63 Potestio, *Veltri Memoirs*, 32-33.

In 1899, Vincenzo decided to move their operations to Ontario where he obtained work from the CPR. In 1901, he became involved in a mining operation that did not work out and lost a great deal of money, which resulted in a nervous breakdown requiring him to be hospitalized in Selkirk, Manitoba. In December 1904, Giovanni returned to Italy and, while he was away, Vincenzo sold their company to another contractor, for $3,000. Whether this was due to his breakdown is not known. Giovanni returned from Italy in October 1905 and found that his brother was ill again and had to be hospitalized.

The brothers then made Winnipeg their base of operations. In 1906, they obtained a contract for 93 km of track for the National Transcontinental Railway east of Winnipeg River. Giovanni wrote of their next project, in 1910-1911, which was plagued by bad weather: "The work was west of Balcarres [southern Saskatchewan], on a branch of the Grand Trunk Pacific which ran from Regina to Melville. The work consisted of heavy clay removal, too hard for the horses. Furthermore, the work was ill-begun and poorly planned, and the poor horses died daily. During that season, we lost forty, all recently bought. Of the 100 horses sent in 1909 there were only a few left and those in poor condition."[64] These were prized work horses the purchase of which had required bank loans of $19,000.[65] Giovanni noted that they made minimal profits on the job. In 1913, Vincenzo died of peritonitis while in Port Arthur, Ontario leaving Giovanni as sole owner. Vincenzo's death signalled a new era for the company and it became John Welch (J. V.) Company. John's son, Raffaele (Ralph), had joined him in Canada in 1905 at the age of 11, and, in the years ahead, would play a leading role. Nephew Felix continued to be involved on various projects, which included some in Alberta. (He settled on a farm in central Alberta and raised heavy horses as well as taking on railway work in his own right.)

After the First World War, the great era of railway building slowed down dramatically as a result of an economic downturn and the fact that virtually all economically-viable lines had been built. The Welch company moved to Port Arthur (now Thunder Bay), Ontario, and, in 1931, Giovanni returned to Italy. Ralph took over the business and it became the R. F. Welch Company Ltd. Having survived 20 lean years by doing maintenance work for the Canadian National Railway (CNR), the company was poised for the post-war wave of immigration beginning in 1949. Their solid work was rewarded and they obtained a lucrative contract for hiring work gangs for the CNR that included catering. Ralph continued to bring men from his home town to work in Canada, in particular, BC and Alberta. At the Italian end, his father Giovanni and younger brother Vincenzo saw to the recruitment. The end of the immigration boom in the 1970s also signaled the end of the company.

---

[64] *Ibid.*, 31-32.
[65] *Ibid.*, 51.

The Railway and Urban Development

Railway development spelled economic prosperity in the development of the West. Communities courted railway companies and the outcome of being bypassed spelled a death knell for would-be towns. The arrival in Calgary of the CPR, in 1883, gave the community a distinct advantage: the following year it incorporated as a town, the first in Alberta, city status followed in 1894. Edmonton incorporated as a town in 1892 and as a city in 1904. In 1911, based on the federal census, Calgary's population was 43,704 while Edmonton's was 24,900. Municipal census figures were higher: by 1914, Calgary was about 76,000 and Edmonton about 72,000. Alberta's population reached 375,000 by 1911and 57 percent were immigrants.[66] In 1916, it had grown to 496,000. There were 119,510 families, 277,256 males and 219,269 females.[67] The economic downturn and enlistment impacted the population of both cities with Edmonton dropping to about 50,000 and Calgary to about 55,000 by the end of the war in 1918.

Calgary was thus a natural destination for Italian immigrants leaving railway jobs; they went there to find work and settle, or used it as a stepping-off point to other destinations. This was the case for a number of individuals from the Abruzzo region. Giovanni Masciangelo left Fossacesia, Chieti, in 1901, and worked in Montreal for three years before returning to Italy and doing military service. He returned to Canada in 1906 and worked laying tracks for the Niagara, St. Catharines and Toronto Railway (it became part of the Canadian Northern Railway in 1908) between St. Catharines and Welland, Ontario. A sign promoting homesteading in Alberta prompted him to head west. His brothers Daniele (Dan) and Nicola (Nick) joined him in 1904 in St. Catharines to work for the railways. After four years, they went to work in the mines of the Crowsnest Pass before heading for Calgary. The family quickly changed its name to Marshall, in order to fit in.

Fellow countrymen from Abruzzo, cousins Giovanni and Carlo Angelozzi, arrived in St. Catharines in 1903 and worked on the railroad before heading west to Alberta, where they initially worked in the mines in the Crowsnest Pass. The family changed their name to "Battle." Giovanni's brother Felice (Felix) arrived in Canada in 1911 and also began his immigration journey in St. Catharines. As had his brother and cousin, he headed west where he worked for the CPR in Hillcrest before moving to Calgary. Antonio DiGiano emigrated from Lanciano, Chieti, Abruzzo in 1908 and arrived in Montreal. He worked his way across the country mostly

---

[66] Howard and Tamara Palmer, eds. *Peoples of Alberta: Portraits of Cultural Diversity* (Saskatoon, Saskatchewan: Western Producer Prairie Book), 1985, 6-7.
[67] *Ibid*, 217.

on railways and ended up mining in the Crowsnest Pass. In 1909, he settled in Calgary for a time. City living did not suit the Marshalls, the Battles or DiGianos and they ended up homesteading near Delia.

Calgary was also an important divisional point for the CPR and, in 1911 the decision was made to build a major repair shop and yards. A crew of up to 5,000 men worked for a year on the Ogden Yards project, named for Vice-President I. G. Ogden. At its peak during the First World War, 1,400 men were employed in repairing rolling stock. In 1920, the Railway Association of Canada petitioned the federal government to allow 20,000 Italian railway workers to come. The petition stated: "Canadian Railways are rapidly approaching a very serious situation ... of obtaining an adequate supply of track labour to carry out the heavy maintenance and improvement work ... The difficulty arises out of the steady exodus to Europe of those classes of foreign-born persons upon whom the railways have long been dependent for track work ... and the aversion of native-born and other Canadians toward this class of work."[68] Of course, this was opposed by war veterans and others who viewed foreigners with distrust. Antonio Rebaudengo was one of the lucky ones. He was sponsored by his brother Cesare and arrived in Calgary with wife Angelina and infant son Mario in spring 1922 from Piozzo, Cuneo, Piedmont. The Rebaudengos settled in the Bridgeland/Riverside neighbourhood where other Italians had already established themselves and Antonio, who was a machinist, was hired by the CPR to work in the Ogden shop.[69] In the 1920s, when Antonio began work, there were about 600 employees and there were likely other Italians among them[70] It would take nearly 50 years for an Italian to become the works manager at Ogden: Angelo G. Vulcano served in that position from 1969 to 1975, and 1978 to 1984.

Italian immigrants working for the CPR in its push westward contributed to the development of Medicine Hat though they have left few traces. The railway went through the southern portion of the North-West Territories and linked Maple Creek, Saskatchewan, to what would become the community of Medicine Hat. The first train arrived on June 10, 1883 and spurred the development of a village; it was incorporated as a town in 1899 and, as a city, in 1906. The growth was directly related to the CPR and the community boasted nearly 1,100 km of tracks within the city limits making it the largest divisional point in Canada for the railway. There was an abundance of gas and it was cheaper to produce than coal. The gas strike had been made

[68] This is cited by Donald H. Avery, *Reluctant Host: Canada's Response to Immigrant Workers, 1896 to 1994* (Toronto, ON: McClelland & Stewart Inc., 1995), 86.

[69] Angelina and Antonio Rebaudengo Fonds, 1892-1982, Glenbow GLEN glen-1923.

[70] CPR, History of Ogden Shops, Calgary, Alberta, Canada, URL: http://www3.telus.net/hildavid/Ogden/history.htm, retrieved March 19, 2017.

fortuitously, in 1883, when the CPR was drilling for water. Local businessmen quickly envisioned the range of industries that could be attracted. It was the geology and geography of the region that made possible what became the area's largest industry: clay that could be used for the manufacture of industrial materials such as pipes for the transmission of water and other materials as well as bricks and ceramics for domestic and industrial use.[71] Early potteries included Medalta, Hycroft/ Medicine Hat Potteries, Alberta Clay Products, National Porcelain, Plainsman Clays and Medicine Hat Brick and Tile. Medalta was the most successful and, in the period 1920 to 1940, it was the largest manufacturer of pottery west of Toronto.

According to the 1911 census, there were 292 Italians in Medicine Hat indicating that the city was a large draw for immigrants; in contrast, Calgary had 369, the Crowsnest region had 813 and Edmonton had 231. By 1921, Medicine Hat's Italian population had decreased to 71, and, by 1941, it had increased slightly to 109. The decrease in the population suggests that the Italian community largely comprised railway workers who either moved on or settled and with the worsening economy of the city, beginning in 1914, moved on to other areas to find work.

The Bellagente family is closely associated with Medicine Hat. Pacifico (Enrico) and Teresa (Buffoni) Bellagente arrived in 1914 from Sarmato, Piacenza, Emilia-Romagna and he initially got work with the city as a labourer.[72] He had arrived in New York in 1906 and was employed as a bricklayer by the company that recruited him. His future brother-in-law, Antonio (Toni) Buffoni, also worked there. Enrico moved on to Quebec City where he was based from 1906 to 1912. Enrico returned to Italy on three occasions; the most important visit was in 1912. At the request of Toni, he went to visit the Buffoni family and met his sister, Teresa, and they were married in February 1913. In March 1913, Enrico returned to Quebec with his brother Camillo and they were joined by Teresa and a third brother, Ernesto, in April. The family has no knowledge of why Enrico and Teresa headed for Medicine Hat but it was likely they heard of job prospects through other countrymen from their region.

In 1919, Enrico was employed by the Ogilvie Flour Mill Company Inc. Since the city's largest employers were clay-related, Enrico next worked for the Birnie Brick Company. From January 1921 until his death in 1951, he worked for Alberta Clay Products. The Bellagente children – Victor, Zerma and Clara – worked there in the 1930s and early 1940s. Enrico suffered from lung disease due to the dust in the work place and died in 1951. Victor Bellagente worked as a potter's

---

[71] Anne Hayward, *Alberta Pottery Industry, 1912-1990*, Mercury Series History Division Paper 50 (Ottawa, ON: Canadian Museum of Civilization, 2001).

[72] The family history of the Bellagente Family was given to me by descendant Aimée Benoit, Curator, Galt Museum & Archives, October, 2017.

helper and then got work with the CPR as a trainman. When the Second World War broke out, he enlisted and trained at Brandon, Manitoba in spring 1941 and, in July, was transferred to the No. 8 Bombing & Gunnery School, based in Lethbridge. Due to sickness, he could not complete the course and had to repeat it at Pearce, Alberta, where the British Commonwealth Air Training Plan No. 3 Air Observer School was based. From 1944 to 1945, he was based overseas and served as a rear gunner on a Lancaster plane. He spent the remainder of his career working for the CPR.

While Edmonton, as a fur trade fort, is one of Alberta's oldest communities, its development was hampered by the CPR's decision to take a southern route. This decision can be seen as one of the causes of what became the Calgary/Edmonton rivalry. Though advantaged politically as the province's capital, economically, Edmonton was hampered by its lack of railway connections. The unknown author of *Edmonton Alberta's Capital* enthused about "Edmonton – Gateway of the Peace River Country":

> Vast stretches of farm lands are there; millions of acres of grazing; hills and valleys, open country and wooded slopes give feed and shelter for countless cattle; river sands yield gold; lakes hold millions of food for fish; coal, oil, and gas are known to be there; iron, tin, lead, gypsum, marl, asphalt, limestone – all of these other minerals besides – have been found in Edmonton's hinterland. The quality and kinds of riches contained in the Peace River country have been determined, but it remains for more careful exploration to fix the extent of these riches. Railroads are building into the Peace River country rapidly, towns are springing up, trade, commerce and general business are advancing with strong and sturdy strides.[73]

The Calgary and Edmonton Railway (C & E) was built from Calgary, in 1891, to the settlement of Strathcona and became part of the CPR. In 1902, the Edmonton, Yukon and Pacific Railway (EY & P) created a link between the C & E station via a line down the Mill Creek Ravine crossing the river via the new Low Level Bridge. This branch line became part of the Canadian Northern Railway (CNoR). In 1905, the CNoR's main transcontinental line from Winnipeg finally reached Edmonton and its station and railyards were located at what is today 104 Avenue and 101 Street, with adjacent yards to the west. The Grand Trunk Pacific (GTP), in 1909, reached Edmonton from the east connecting to Jasper in 1911. The railway also built the Macdonald Hotel in Edmonton's downtown in the same year. The CNoR and GTP, in 1916 and 1919, respectively, became part of the new Canadian National Railway (CNR) and their lines were consolidated. The completion of Edmonton's railway hub occurred in 1929 when the Northern Alberta Railways

---

[73] *Edmonton Alberta's Capital 1914*, 14.

(NAR) was established merging the Edmonton, Dunvegan and British Columbia Railway (ED &
BC), the Alberta and great Waterways Railway (A & GW), the Canada Central Railway (CCR)
and the Pembina Valley Railway (PVR). The NAR eventually merged with the CNR in 1981.

As the era of railway building ended, many jobs became available in operations and maintenance and Italians were hired as part of this new work force. Sam Scrivano, who was born in
Spezzano della Sila, Cosenza, in 1901, was sponsored by his sister Assunta Gaudio, who with
her husband Joe operated the Venice Grocery in Edmonton.[74] Sam arrived in January 1923 and
got a job with the CNR as a labourer; he went on to become an inspector of trains, assistant
mechanic and, finally, a mechanic. His starting salary was 39 cents an hour. He worked for the
company for 42 years. Joe Medori arrived in Jasper in 1940 and operated a snow plough to keep
the tracks clear.[75]

Venice-Hylo and the Railway

The men of the Venice-Hylo Italian colony had a very special relationship with the local railway:
for many, it offered seasonal employment, while for others it became full-time, life-long work.
Otto Michetti notes: "My first encounter with the Alberta and Great Waterways Railway occurred
on April 4, 1917, when my mother and an older brother boarded the train in the vicinity of 121
Street and 104 Avenue, together with my father, who had come to meet us in Edmonton following our arrival from Italy, and proceeded to Hylo."[76] The A&GW's history had been fraught with
financial difficulties that caused Premier Rutherford to resign. Eventually, rails were laid and the
railway reached Lac La Biche in 1915 and, then, Waterways. An article in the *Edmonton Bulletin*
on May 17, 1917 noted: "The grading outfit of Felix Negro [*sic.*], with about twenty-five teams,
is expected to join the outfit working. Messers. Foley Brothers are subcontracting for ten miles
of construction and Mr. W. Grant, seven miles. Mr. P. A. James is the walking boss, looking after
the McArthur interests in general on this construction."[77] This was likely Felix's first job as an
independent contractor separate from his Welch relations after settling in central Alberta.

Otto began work for the railway as a 14-year-old and notes: "We worked sixty hours per
week with the occasional overtime those days, and needless to say, I was the baby of the family

---

[74] Sam Scrivano, oral history interview, Italians Settle in Edmonton Society, 1983, Provincial Archives of Alberta,
305.851.Lt1.

[75] *Ibid.,* "Medori, Joe and Jessie," 285-286.

[76] Otto Michetti, "The A&GW – First Impressions," *Hylo-Venice: Harvest of Memories* (Hylo, AB: Hylo-Venice History
Book Committee, 2000), 31.

[77] Cited by W. M. Tichonuk, "The Arrival of the Railroad," *Hylo-Venice: Harvest of Memories*, 30.

in a gang of men." The foreman, Frank Dunnigan, Otto believes, was very fair and praised him on his work: "Otto, from where I stand, I can see each of the four ties trimmed by you around this curve. You keep this up and you will surely become a Roadmaster some day."[78] Many of the men worked in tie camps since it was the practice to put in spur lines to timber stands where trees could be cut to make railway ties. Otto also provides insight into the working conditions as follows: "Boxcars no longer fit to haul tonnage were converted to bunk cars, with sixteen bunks for sixteen men in each car with a floor area of 334 square feet. There were no sanitary facilities other than two pails full of water and two wash basins in each car for use by sixteen men in the short time between reveille and breakfast or before supper. There was no time to wash at noontime."[79]

In 1930, Otto began working for the Northern Alberta Railway as a section man and continued to work for them through the Great Depression that saw the decline in volume of traffic. This translated into smaller work crews and harder work for the men who did not lose their jobs. Things changed dramatically with the start of the Second World War, and the Alaska Highway and Canol projects. Both were related to the Allied war effort: the former enabled transport of men and materials and the latter was intended to increase petroleum supplies necessary for land and air transportation. A pipeline was built from Norman Wells, Northwest Territories, along the Alaska Highway to Whitehorse, Yukon, where a refinery was built. The American Corps of Engineers oversaw both projects, which produced dramatic changes in northern Alberta. Otto observes: "Traffic requirements amplified from three way freights and two passenger trains per week, to as many as twenty-eight trains dispatched out of McLennan in one day."[80] The men who were not of fighting age quickly found work on the railways. Otto asserts that no greater demands were made on railway crews in the period 1942 to 1945 anywhere in North America than were made on the NAR.

Some Observations

There is no doubt that the building of the CPR, as well as the web of local railway lines in the Province of Alberta, provided work for migrant labourers. The railways were also instrumental in settlement: town sites followed the lines and fanned out into agricultural areas. Railway building also led to the development of urban centres that, in turn, increased job opportunities. The first Italian communities developed in railway and coal mining centres and the cities and towns that

---

[78] Michetti, 31.
[79] *Ibid.*, 31.
[80] *Ibid.*, 31.

sprang up along railway lines. In the south, this included Medicine Hat, Calgary and Lethbridge. Towns quickly grew in the Rocky Mountain corridor including Crowsnest, Frank, Lille, Coleman, Bellevue, Blairmore, Hillcrest, Passburg and Burmis; and at Banff and Jasper where national parks were developed. The building of railways in central and northern Alberta gave an impetus to the development of the cities of Edmonton, Red Deer, Grande Prairie, Peace River, Lac La Biche and other northern communities. Railway work would result in Italians settling in all of these communities as well as on the land. Italian railway workers were undaunted by lengthy maritime and land journeys required to find work. Some joined the work force as early as aged eight or nine travelling with their fathers to France and Germany as sojourners, In North America, they followed well-established chain migration routes. Many fell prey to unscrupulous labour agents such as Cordasco and Dini but others from Calabria benefited from the more enlightened practices of the Welch brothers. Railway jobs were also significant for immigrants arriving in Alberta in the post-1950s era, some of whom were sponsored by labour agent Ralph Welch, who took over the family business.

View of the tracks and work crew in front of the Fort Macleod Canadian Pacific Railway station, July 25, 1898. Italian sojourners were involved in laying tracks from Winnipeg into the interior of southeastern BC. Provincial Archives of Alberta A3957.

The laying of the Alberta and Great Waterways railway track, Bon Accord area, Alberta, 1914. Some of the clearance work was done by Felix Nigro and his construction crew. The railway would allow settlers to reach the Italian agricultural colony at Venice-Hylo. Otto Michetti started work for the A&GW at the age of 14. Photo courtesy of Glenbow, Archives and Special Collections, University of Calgary NA-1646-19.

Employees of the Blue Diamond Coal Company, Brule Mines, Alberta, carrying lunch pails and miners' lamps, ca 1917-1918; Valentino Dotto is pictured in the front row, third from the right. Photo courtesy of Glenbow, Archives and Special Collections, University of Calgary NA-5124-28.

CHAPTER III

When Coal Was King

THE DEVELOPMENT OF THE CANADIAN WEST was spurred by the knowledge shared by federal and provincial politicians that its mineral wealth could benefit the nation. Historian John Blue presented a resource-rich and dynamic province in his 1924 history *Alberta Past and Present*. He noted: "Alberta contains 85 per cent of the coal deposits of Canada and 18 per cent of the coal deposits of the world." This potential wealth was regionally based: "The coal is found in three horizons distributed from the summit of the Rocky Mountains eastward over the entire prairie region to Manitoba and from the International Boundary Line to the Mackenzie River. Each Horizon produces coal of different qualities depending upon its age and distance from the mountains."[81] Blue noted that the Geological Survey of Canada estimated the quantities of coal as follows: anthracite, 697,625,065 metric tonnes; bituminous, 40,530,292,628 metric tonnes; and sub-bituminous and lignite, 920,002,353,191 metric tonnes. Anthracite, the purest form, was the most desirable because it burns hottest making it ideal for smelting operations; bituminous was ideal for heating purposes and powering steam engines such as locomotives; and sub-bituminous, because it contained more moisture, was valuable for electricity generation. Lignite, found on the prairies, was soft and brittle and the least desirable though it was nonetheless useful for heating and electricity generation.

For eastern and foreign entrepreneurs (including the railway builders) the coal resource became an irresistible lure. In 1905, there were 600 mines operating in Alberta. By 1906, the work force totaled 2,800; by 1914, over 8,000; and by 1924, 12,500. In the period 1900 to 1920, production increased from 282,542 metric tonnes to 6,267,669 metric tonnes. Blue placed the value of the annual output at $30 million with over $14 million paid out in wages.[82] Thus, mining was a huge economic driver for the province and companies sprang up wherever there were deposits. Development of the industry is crucial to an understanding of Italian settlement in Alberta.

---

[81] John Blue, *Alberta Past and Present: Historical and Biographical* (Chicago, ILL: Pioneer Historical Publishing Co., 1924.), 363.
[82] Blue, 368.

The coal industry created a new labour force that reflected the class structure of the developing West, and the hierarchy of desirable immigrants described by Woodsworth in 1909. Management was of British origin whether Canadian, American or British, and workers were largely drawn from Southern and Eastern Europe. Very few had worked in mines though some men from northern Italy had worked in construction of roads and railways in France and Belgium, and rock tunnels in the Alps. Since labour agents were actively recruiting for workers in the Piedmont region of northern Italy this accounts for the large presence of northerners in Alberta's coal mining work force. In the early decades of the twentieth century, Italian men made up from 14 to 19 percent of the work force in mines located in communities from the Elk Valley in southeastern BC, through the Crowsnest Pass, along the eastern slopes of the Rocky Mountains, Lethbridge and Drumheller valleys, and on both sides of the North Saskatchewan River in Edmonton.

The Crowsnest Pass

At the beginning of the twentieth century, the Crowsnest Pass was the place to go to obtain work. Having found themselves there to build the railways, Italians saw the opportunities to improve their lives by staying. For those from northern Italy, the mountain environment was also reminiscent of home. While it is difficult to obtain information on Italian immigrants in Alberta working in railway construction because of the transient nature of the work, information about their work in mines is plentiful. Many Italian miners remained in their communities throughout their working lives, as did their children and grandchildren.[83] Ample information is found in the community histories *Crowsnest and Its People* (1979) and *Crowsnest and Its People: Millenium Edition* (2000). Mining continued the longest in Crowsnest communities than in any other part of the province and is reflected in the multi-generations of Italian families comprising part of the work force. In addition, the records of the Italian miners' society are located in the Crowsnest Museum in Coleman.

Census records make very clear the significant numbers of Italian workers in Pass communities. In 1911, of a total population of 1,137 in Blairmore, the breakdown based on ethnic origin was as follows: English, 293; Irish, 98; Scots, 202; French, 105, German, 34, Austro-Hungarian, 44; Belgian, 65; Chinese, 38; Dutch, 1; Italian, 224; Japanese, 2; Jewish, 1; Polish, 9; Swiss, 17;

---

[83] There is a great deal of documentary evidence in local history books funded by Alberta Culture from the 1970s. Besides descriptive essays, these volumes include histories provided by family members.

and other, 4.[84] Italians comprised over 19 percent of the population. In 1921, the breakdown of the total population of 1,552 was: English, 40, Irish, 108, Scots, 245; Other British, 36; French, 112; German, 9; Austro-Hungarian, 2; Belgian, 101; Chinese, 32; Dutch, 6; Finnish, 23; Italian, 308, Jewish, 10; Polish, 35; Russian, 7; Scandinavian, 32; Ukrainian, 5; and other, 131. Again, Italians comprised over 19 percent. The numbers for 1931 were roughly the same and suggest that there was little or no outward migration of Italians. It is interesting to note that the Italian population of the community grew from 224 in 1911 to 308, in 1921, and declined slightly to 297 in 1931. The total population increased from 1,137, in 1921 to 1,629 in 1939. The decline can be attributed to the fact that, after the First World War, immigration became more restrictive and focused on family reunification and agricultural settlement.

In Coleman, the Italian population was 119, in 1911; 216, in 1921; and 185, in 1931. The percentage of the total population in Coleman was 7 percent for 1911; 17 percent for 1921; and just under 11 percent for 1931. The Italian population for Frank was 60 percent in 1911, 22 percent in 1921; and 7 percent in 1931. The total community population for the same years was 806, 401 and 268. With the mine disaster of 1903, the community was no longer a viable economic enterprise. The Italian population of Hillcrest was 481 in 1911, 0 in 1921 and 0 in 1931. The total population of the community in the same years was 481, 1,362 and 1,200. The mine disaster clearly had an impact on the Italian community and miners moved away.

In summary, the Italian population of Crowsnest communities was 503 in 1911, 546 in 1921 and 489 in 1931. In the same time period, the Italian population of the province was as follows: 1901, 109; 1911, 2,150; 1921, 4,028; and 1931, 4,766. Crowsnest communities were, thus, the earliest recipients of Italian immigrants and, in 1921, comprised over 13 percent of the Italian population of the province. The 1920s saw a shift from resource-based communities to the cities and this can be seen in the 1931 statistics when the Italian population of The Pass decreased to just over 10 percent. The beneficiaries were, in particular, Edmonton and Calgary.

Blairmore had a "little Italy," which is still discernible with its typical small houses surrounded by large gardens and outbuildings to house animals. Most Italians raised chickens and some had other livestock in the back yard. St. Anne's Roman Catholic Church was built in 1910 and, according to the family the first recorded baptism was that of Charles Montalbetti. What is surprising is that a northern Italian, Enrico Pozzi, who arrived in 1905 and worked in the mines for half a year, became the largest builder in The Pass responsible for most of the commercial and residential buildings in Blairmore.

---

[84] The census date is drawn from the Ethnic Research Project, Glenbow Alberta Institute, 1960, M3553 undertaken by Dan de Vlieger, a Glenbow staff member.

Frank Village was established in 1900 by Samuel W. Gebo (Gibeau) whose family originated in Quebec and who had begun mining enterprises in Montana and Wyoming.[85] According to the family history, Charles and Maria Montalbetti's house was destroyed in the Frank Slide of April 29, 1903.[86] The village of Crowsnest developed as a divisional point for the CPR but soon grew to include a post office, hotel, general store, school and church. Theresa Sacco gave birth to the first baby to survive in the community. When the Lille mines became uneconomic in 1912, and the town ceased to exist, even railway tracks were removed (some were used to connect to mines in Blairmore and Bellevue). In 1937, Valentine Rinaldi, who owned land across from the tracks, laid claim to the remaining rails and sold them. While this was challenged by the West Canadian Collieries, the Court sided with Rinaldi.

With closure of the Lille mine, the fortunes of Bellevue increased dramatically and the town continued to grow and even possessed an Italian pool room and a grocery store owned by Luigi (Louis) Fidenato, who was born in the Treviso region. He arrived in Bellevue in 1903 and worked in mines there and in Hillcrest where he lost a leg in an accident. He was then employed in the poolroom owned by Tony Cantellina (Cantalini). In 1924, he started a grocery store and operated it until his death in 1958.

Adjacent to Bellevue and below the Mohawk Mine tipple was the unincorporated community of Maple Leaf, also known as "Bushtown" or "Il Bosc" (The Wood). Its population was largely Italian and it existed from the first part of the century to 1955. Brothers J. and T. Alzetta worked in the mines in 1909-1910 and then set up the Allazetta (*sic.*) Brothers' Grocery Store. The Cantalinis also operated a beer store. In the late 1940s, Aristide Brazoni and son Enzo operated Quality Meats. Other residents included Giovanni and Silvio Gatto and family; Sesto Fidenato; John Petrini; Giovanni Scodellaro; the Louis and John Vandresco families; Fred, Epanio and Angelo Bosetti family; Giovanni Artico; Angelo Filipuzzi family; Benedetto Maniago family; Tony De Zarzi; Batiste Lenardon; Marco Facin; Joseph Scodellaro family; Pio Vigna; and Giovanni Bosa. The community had an outdoor bocce court and space for dances and gatherings.[87] In the period 1904 to 1978, the following Italians served on Coleman Town Council: A. Toppano, A. Gentile, A. De Luca, F. De Cecco and R. C. Montalbetti. The town also had a dedicated Italian Hall built by members of the Società di Mutuo Soccorso (Society for Mutual Support), that is the Italian miners' fraternal society.

---

[85] Karen Davidson Seward, "Gebo/Gibeau: Cousins reunited in the Crowsnest Pass," in *Heritage News: Discover Crowsnest Heritage*, Issue 5, September 15, 2010, unpaginated.

[86] R. Aldo Montalbetti, "Charles Montalbetti," in *Crowsnest and Its People*, 722.

[87] Adic Rinaldi, "Maple Leaf," in *Crowsnest and Its People*, 155-157.

By 1979, the publication date for *Crowsnest and Its People*, mine closures had impacted on the Italian population of the region; however, there were a significant number of pioneer families still living there. The book provides a record of multi-generational mining families and also reveals a pattern of intermarriage within the Italian community. The impact of education can also be seen as members of the second generation moved into other types of employment as well as a shift from working to middle class. A number of families have been chosen who depict these characteristics.

Giuseppe (Joseph/Joe) Alampi arrived at Ellis Island in 1896 from Pellaro, Reggio Calabria.[88] He was in his fifties and brought his son Francesco (Frank) with him. They arrived in The Pass in 1900 to work on the railways. Because of ill health, Joe returned to Italy shortly after but Frank persevered and worked in mines in Lille and Coleman, and was a founding member of the Italian fraternal society. He became a Canadian citizen in 1905 and, in 1907, returned to Italy to marry Angela Oliva but did not bring her to Canada with him. He fought for the Italian Armed Forces in the First World War and, after demobilization in 1919, returned to Canada and worked at the International Coal and Coke mine. According to the family history, "Francesco had a myriad of sea-faring experiences as he traversed the Atlantic Ocean between Italy and Canada numerous times from the time he was 14 years old in 1896."[89] The Alampi children were conceived during periodic trips to Italy and were raised by their mother. In the 1920s, Frank built a house in west Coleman assisted by members of the Italian community.

On January 10, 1930, Frank was joined by daughter Giovanna (Joanne), aged 21, and son Giuseppe (Joe), 14. In 1931, his wife Angela and other children arrived: Genoeffa (Effa/Jenny), 21; Francesco (Frankie), 13; Anna, 12: and Giuseppina (Josie), 3. They left Italy on December 28, 1930 on the liner *SS Caronia* sailing from Genoa and had a grim winter journey to Halifax. Family historian Josephine Aristone observes that her grandmother had heard "terrible stories" from relatives: "Stories of severe winters, primitive conditions in the Crowsnest Pass, mine disasters and especially when she heard the story of Turtle Mountain cascading onto the town of Frank in 1903 dissuaded her from taking that momentous step. It was a great relief to the family in Coleman when she was finally persuaded to leave Italy."[90] It was customary to marry into other mining families. Joanne Alampi married Giorgio (George) Aristone in 1929; he had come to Coleman from Reggio Calabria at the age of 17 in 1921 and worked for International Coal and Coke. Jenny married Peter Rizzo in 1931; Anna married Jack Marconi in 1939; and Joe married Catarina (Catharine) Mascherin in 1940.

---

[88] Josephine Alampi provided the family history in Crowsnest Historical Society, *Crowsnest and Its People Millenium Edition* (Lethbridge, AB: Crowsnest Historical Society, 2000), 480-486.

[89] *Ibid.*, 481.

[90] *Ibid.*, 481.

Francesco Oliva and son Leandro (Andy) arrived in Coleman around 1906 from the US and the elder Oliva went to work in the mines. Alberta's coal mining history inspired author Peter Oliva's novel *Drowning in Darkness* (1993). It is a poetic but bleak account of immigration from southern Italy to the Crowsnest Pass and draws on the experiences of three generations of his family.[91] Methane gas, coal seams and rock are presented as aspects of a "dark ocean" whose depths miners sailed. The dark tides threaten them and Oliva writes of death resulting from the filling of the mine with methane gas in a way that mutes the horror: "The gas softens the cobbles, eggs, nuts, peas and fines of coal into sponge, cushioning the miner's fall. It penetrates and turns coal soft, making the rock just as boneless as his legs but more often than not the methane pulls him further away than the coal floor, further into darkness. Carried along by sleep, with the current tugging, swirling around him, he drifts deeper into the mountain. Hours later, his safety light fades in the distance."[92] The loneliness and alienation of the wives who came from Italy to join their men is also presented as a wave that threatens to drown them.

In the novel, an illiterate miner named Celi, whose wife was unhappy in Canada, reminisces about his youth in Italy when he caught birds to sell for food. He dreams of nights in the scented bergamot orchard where he watched for birds to trap. The physical and metaphorical darkness of the mining community is contrasted with the sunny, pastoral life in Italy. Oliva describes the mining town as follows:

> Dagotown. A group of houses built tight, squeezed into twenty-five-foot lots, all of them one to four feet apart and slightly angled, spilling foundation corners and room splinters into their neighbours' properties like frustrated elbows fighting for an armrest. Rainwater fell on one house, slid down the walls of another and was bailed into a third. Coal dust from each stove chimney mushroomed and joined the collective black billows hovering over the street and the nearby mine tipple. And a sneeze from one home brought a muttered salute, or more often an unconscious wipe of the nose, from its neighbour, the casa del vicino [the neighbour's house].[93]

Many of the immigrants came from rural areas in Italy and never became accustomed to underground work in the mines and the proliferation of coal tips and dust that blighted mine sites. They breathed the dust and took it home in their clothing and hair.

---

91 Peter Oliva, *Drowning in Darkness* (Dunvegan, ON: Cormorant Books, 1993); the book won the Writers Guild of Alberta Best First Book Award and was shortlisted for a Bressani Prize.
92 *Ibid.*, 7.
93 *Ibid.*, 19.

While Oliva's account is bleak, for most immigrants who found steady work in the mines, life was an enormous improvement from conditions in Italy. As has been noted, the Crowsnest Pass experienced significant immigration from northern Italian communities. An important example was the Aschacher family of German/Dutch/Swiss descent from the village of Macugnaga and city of Domodossola in the Piedmont region (today the province of Verbano-Cusio-Ossola).[94] Joe arrived in Lille in 1905 and worked in various mines for 45 years until his retirement in 1950. He returned to Italy, in 1910, and married Brigida and the couple had a daughter, Olga, and then returned to Canada and settled in Bellevue where sons Martin and Henry were born. Mine work took Joe to Blairmore and, in 1916 he sponsored brothers Battista, Peter and John. All worked in the Greenhill Mine for West Canadian Collieries and built many of the entries into the mine. Joe was a founding member of the Italian miners' society in Lille and eventually served on Blairmore's Town Council. Peter married Mary Emelia Brunetto in 1920. Her family had emigrated from another northern town, Brosso, Province of Turin, and arrived in Bellevue in 1906.

The Avoledos of Valvasone, Udine (now Pordennone) are interesting because they had a history of being migrant workers before coming to Canada. Father Giaccomo went to work in Germany where skilled bricklayers were in demand and was joined by his four sons.[95] He had a small land holding and could not support his family of eight. During the winter, they went to Germany, which was in need of skilled cement workers and bricklayers. David, the youngest, decided to immigrate to Canada with two brothers and arrived in Hosmer, BC, at the age of 17 in 1905. He was another founder of the Lille Italian society. He returned to Italy to complete military service with the famed Alpini regiment, a trained ski patrol unit. While in Italy, he married Elisabetta Nocente but returned to Lille alone; she joined him in Blairmore, in 1913, where he worked in the West Canadian Collieries. The couple had three children – Guerino (Jerry), Alberto and Berta (Bertha). David worked in mines at Lille, Blairmore, Bellevue and Frank. Daughter Bertha Yagos *in Crownest and Its People* notes: "Our lives revolved around the mine, of course, since that was our livelihood, and every night we would listen for the whistle which would signify whether or not there would be work the following day. When the work was really scarce, the men would gather in silent clusters to wait, probably gaining a little courage from each other's presence, for times were getting worse."[96] She refers specifically to 1931 and 1932 when there were strikes in Bellevue and Blairmore. She writes of the eight-month strike in 1932 as follows:

———

[94] Bill Aschacher, "Joe and Brigida Aschacher," in *Crowsnest and Its People*, 388-390.
[95] Bertha (Avoledo) Yagos, "David Avoledo – The Way it Was!," in *Crowsnest and Its People*, 392-394.
[96] *Ibid.*, 393.

It was a time that caused neighbour to resent and hate his neighbour, and children learned two new and terrible words: "Red" and "Scab." It was the time of the huge meetings where Harvey Murphy spoke and Tim Buck was elected to the labour party in Ottawa; it was the time when men went to work in stock-racked trucks and the R.C.M.P. were brought in to protect them as they moved through the picket lines. How they used their clubs to keep the picketing men and women back! It was the time when our parents were pushed to their limit to keep things going.[97]

Bertha's mother had a breakdown and returned to Italy for nine months to regain her health; friends provided financial assistance to make this possible. Like other families, the Avoledos took in boarders to make ends meet.

Giovanni (John) Bovio left Brosso, Turin, and arrived in Bellevue in 1909.[98] Son John observes in the family history, "His arrival coincided with the movement of many other families from the alpine regions of Northwest Italy to the coal mining areas of Alberta and British Columbia in the early 1900s."[99] John worked in the mines for 25 years and played the mandolin in the Bellevue Band. It is significant the frequency with which Italian men recreated the home-town band in their new homes in Canada. Wife Irene Bolettino arrived in 1912; her brother Stefano had been killed in a mining accident in Canmore in 1901. The couple had three children, a son, Johnny, and two daughters, Eva and Vera. Tragedy continued to stalk the family: in 1927, at the age of 17, Johnny drowned in Lee Lake. According to the *Blairmore Enterprise*, he had completed high school and won a gold medal in a sports competition. Daughter Eva married John Raymaker of Bellevue and their son, Darryl, was born there in 1939. In 1959, the family moved to Calgary where Darryl attended the University of Calgary and qualified as a lawyer.[100] Daughter Vera married Joe Krkosky Jr., a member of a Slovakian family. Joe Senior worked in the mines in Fernie and then settled in Blairmore. Joe Jr. followed him into the mines and became a respected union leader and town councillor; he was one of the union activists elected to Council after the bitter 1932 strike. Joe worked in the West Canadian Colliery with two brothers and an

---

[97] *Ibid.*, 393. Murphy was a Polish-born immigrant living in Ontario who became a Communist in the 1940s and was a militant leader within the Mine Workers Union of Canada in the 1940s. Buck was the long-time general secretary of the Communist Party of Canada.

[98] John Bovio, "Bovio, John," in *Crowsnest and Its People*, 399-400. There is a second account in *Crowsnest and Its People: Millenium Edition* (512-513).

[99] Bovio, *Crowsnest and Its People: Millenium Edition*, 512.

[100] Darryl Raymaker in his blog posting, "Italian Sentimental Journey: Back to Brosso," October 22, 2007, provides information about his paternal grandfather, John Bovio, as well as his grandmother Irene's family, the Spolettinos. See, URL: http://darrylraymaker.blogspot.ca/2007/10/italian-sentimental-journey-back-to.html, retrieved October 1, 2017.

uncle. He was killed by "a fall of top coal" at the Greenhill Mine on October 11, 1944 at the age of 35.[101] Joe and Vera had one son, Garry, who studied at the University of Alberta and was a Rhodes Scholar (1958). He was employed by the Department of Fisheries and Oceans in Ottawa and, after leaving the government service, worked as a consultant.

The Angelo Cervo family provides a snapshot of the itinerant life of some miners resulting from mine production highs and lows.[102] Angelo was born in Posina, Vicenza, Veneto, and arrived in Coleman around 1900; he was joined by wife Roselina and daughter Maria (Mary). Their remaining children (Angelo Junior, Adriano, Augusto, Vera and Marcel) were born in different mining towns as he followed work. These included Coleman, Lille, Blairmore, Frank and Sentinel. In 1910, he filed for a homestead in Burmis. This also became a pattern in areas where mines were located close to arable land. Roselina and the children looked after the four cows, milked them and carried a five-gallon can to Blairmore where they measured out the desired amount to customers, who paid one dollar for 12 quarts. Angelo had a narrow escape as described in the family history: "In 1914 Mr. Cervo was employed at the Hillcrest mine. On June 19 he started from home to walk to work but at the gate decided to turn back. Mrs. Cervo scolded that he could not afford to miss a shift. He turned back from the gate a second time but received the same greeting from his wife. The third trip he went through the gate but joined friends in Frank for a poker game. Mr. Cervo's partner was at work and lost his life in the Hillcrest explosion."[103] Many Italians were and are superstitious and believe in the importance of fate in their lives; in this case, Angelo's Guardian Angel was looking after him. The family was not able to avoid tragedy around 1928. The farming enterprise had grown and, in addition to milk production, they made and sold cheese. After completing milking in the barn, the family went outside to find that their house was on fire. Fortunately, no-one was hurt and they were able to rebuild.

Andrea (Andrew) Mascherin was born in 1883 in Cordenons, Udine and worked in Germany before immigrating to Canada in 1905 with his brother.[104] He headed west laying track for the CPR until he reached Hillcrest around 1914. He worked in the MacGillivray Creek Mine in Coleman until 1922 when he returned to Italy. There he met his wife Maria and they returned and settled in East Coleman. The family history notes: "Their grandiose shack in Bushtown consisted of two rooms, relatively well air-conditioned to the elements. On many occasions in winter,

---

[101] Gerald Friesen, *The Canadian Prairies: A History* (Toronto, Buffalo, London: University of Toronto Press, 1987), 298-299.

[102] *Anon.,* "Cervo, Angelo Sr. and Jr.," in *Crowsnest and Its People,* 458-459.

[103] *Ibid.,* 459.

[104] *Anon.,* "Mascherin, Andrew," in *Crowsnest and Its People,* 689-690.

Maria would awake to find her hair frozen to the bedpost because of the icy wind and snow which filtered through the cracks in the walls."[105]

The 1924 strike provided the opportunity for the Mascherins to return to Italy where, in 1926, son Elidio was born. Andrew returned to Coleman alone leaving his wife to work in a local cotton mill. Andrew's family did not return to Canada until 1937. Whether Maria chose to remain in Italy is not known but the family history notes that Andrew was content after their arrival and describes his life as follows:

> His wants were simple. Steady work at his mine, the Sunday cards or "boche," [bocce or Italian lawn bowling] and his wine maturing in his basement barrels. The men on second street (Italian Town) would gather on Sunday to play cards or boches. There were two boche lanes, one directly west of D'Appolonia's lumber yard, paralleling the tipple and the other on the side of the hill at the west end of second street. Here, on a Sunday afternoon, one could hear the shouts of "Curta! Curta!" The names of the players ring in memory like long remembered poetry – "Pete C.P.R.," "Fulfone," "Nan DeCecco," "Zonnini," "Chavon Rinaldi," "Zaun Rinaldi," "Secondo," "Pete Fontana," "Burcit Toppano," "Futin DeCecco," "Sardinia," and many others, each with his own affectionate nick-name, each unique and beloved. Over cards, the adventures and misadventures of each would be retold and laughed at in warm camaraderie.[106]

While the men were "playing," wives waited not knowing when the game would finish, and whether or not the men would be drunk on their return. According to this story, Maria arrived at one of the matches with a mine bucket with supper in it and gave it to her husband. The unnamed family historian notes: "Andrew calmly took it, opened it, ate its contents, while concentrating on the game, after its contents were eaten, closed the bucket and gave it back to Maria. During his procedure, Maria stood in silent rage. Someone finally laughed, and broke the taut silence, where-upon Andrew remarked: 'Did you expect me to throw it out like Pete Fontana would'?"[107]

The anecdote while, on the surface humorous, demonstrates that it was very much a man's society. Some men chose not to have their families join them preferring the single life. While some remained celibate, others either played the field or had a common-law wife. The wives in Italy sometimes also took up with other men. While some families accepted illegitimate children as par for the course, for others it was a shameful secret and, even 100 years later, there is discomfort in

---

[105] *Ibid.*
[106] *Ibid.*, 690.
[107] *Ibid.*, 690.

discussing the subject. Nonetheless, it was a reality of immigrant life. Alcohol was also a problem and many women had to take in laundry or other revenue-generating activity since their husbands drank away their pay cheques. That is why leaders in the suffrage movement targeted the mining communities of the Crowsnest Pass.

Andrew retired in 1945 because he contracted silicosis or "miners' lung" and died in 1950. This disease was also a reality of life underground and the necessity of making a living forced acceptance of the risk. Accidents too were viewed with a kind of stoicism. Self-sacrifice to advance the family's fortunes became a truism. Only education could break the unending cycle of mine labour. While in some families, the focus was on sons, in other families, daughters were also included in the desire for betterment. It depended on the culture of the individual family. Italians were not unique in this and education for women was an issue not only in immigrant communities but also establishment families. In the Mascherin family, daughter Catherine followed the norm: she married miner Joe Alampi. Son Elidio attended the Faculty of Education at the University of Calgary and returned to Coleman to teach before moving on to Innisfail. He eventually became principal of George McDougall High School in Airdrie. Elidio's teaching career spanned 35 years and, in the latter part of his life, he was active in Calgary's Italian community.

While northern Italians made up a significant portion of the mine work force in The Pass, southerners also came. Domenico Campo was born in Potenza in the southern region of Basilicata (bordering on Calabria), and went to the US with an uncle at the age of 13.[108] His uncle died shortly after leaving him to fend for himself. According to daughter Rose Anderson, he had no formal schooling but could read and speak English fluently. He worked in Chicago as a shoeshine boy but eventually got work on the railway and laid tracks for the Great Northern Railway, the CPR line through Fort Steele, and some of the last streetcar tracks in Calgary. In 1917, he arrived in Blairmore as a CPR section hand and settled there. He met Juliana Schilling, a Hungarian, in Calgary and they were married. The couple had six children – five daughters (Victoria, Mary, Dorothy, Rose and Constance) and a son, Ivan. Domenico worked in the Greenhill mines and became a prominent member of the community called upon to act as an interpreter as well as helping others with immigration issues. He was the Mine Workers Union president during the 1932 strike, and was temporarily blacklisted for his dedicated fight for mine safety, better compensation and pensions. Domenico also played guitar in the Mountaineers Orchestra and served on the Blairmore School Board. During the Second World War, he sold war bonds and was proud

---

[108] There are two family histories: Rose Anderson and Dorothy Kennerd, "The Campo Family," in *Crowsnest and Its People*, 451-453; and Rose Anderson, "Campo, Dominic and Juliana," in *Crowsnest and Its People: Millenium Edition*, 539-543.

that his son and sons-in-law were in the Canadian military. In 1943, the National Film Board of Canada produced a film titled "Coal-Face, Canada" in which some real miners were featured, including Campo.[109] It explored the importance of the industry in war time and also the possibility of improving the lot of miners.

At a time when Italian-Canadians were designated as enemy aliens and some were interned, the Campo family was contributing to the war effort. Son Ivan was shot down in 1943 and was imprisoned in Stalag Luft III, the camp featured in the film *The Great Escape*. After the war, Ivan joined the federal civil service in the area of customs and excise. Victoria married miner Floyd Smaniotto and continued to live in Blairmore. Mary went to Calgary and worked as a waitress in the oilfields. She married Jack DieBold at Camp Shilo, Manitoba. He was killed in Sicily while fighting with the Allied forces in the liberation of Italy. With her sister, Dorothy, Mary was employed as a war worker in a sheet metal shop in Calgary. Dorothy married James Kennerd, a soldier serving with the Calgary Highlanders, in 1940. Their son, Jimmy, was born in 1942 on the same day his father left for the Front. Rose married Ivan Anderson, in 1941, before he went overseas. She joined the Canadian Women's Army Corps (CWAC) and received medical and clerical training, and served in an Army hospital.

Guglielmo Carlo(s) D'Amico, who was born in Campobasso, Molise in southern Italy, began his immigration journey by going to Brazil but this did not go well and he returned to Italy.[110] Around 1909, he decided to try Canada and immigrated to Corbin, BC, to work in the mines before moving on to Bankhead where he obtained his stationary steam ticket, and worked for the CPR Coal Mining Company. After the mine closure, he moved to Blairmore and sponsored his second wife, Anna Maria Tortorelli. On May 9, 1925, he was killed by a fall of coal in the Hillcrest Mine and left his 32-year-old widow with nine children to care for (the youngest was only 48 hours' old). The children refused to speak Italian to force their mother to learn English; the family survived on a small Widow's Pension and the casual work done by her sons. Only Gabriel went into mine work becoming maintenance foreman at the International Mine in Coleman until the 1950s when demand for coal plummeted as railways turned to diesel fuel. Rinaldo made a career in the construction industry. Ric served in the Canadian Air Force as a pilot in the Second World War and pursued a career as a plumber in Edmonton and Victoria. Sam joined the Canadian Navy and saw active service with the British Navy and, after the war, made a career

---

[109] The NFB 1943-film "Coal-Face, Canada" was produced by Graham McInnes and has as its central character a young soldier who returns to his coal mining home town and returns to work in the mines to further the war effort. See information on the film at URL: https://www.library.yorku.ca/find/Record/2941341, retrieved May 23, 2017.
[110] *Anon.*, "Carlos D'Amico Family – Hillcrest," in *Crowsnest and Its People*, 486-487.

in the military. Mike joined the Air Force as ground crew and, after the war, worked as a civilian fire fighter with the Department of National Defence. Fel served with the Canadian Army in Germany and remained as part of the Army of Occupation into the early 1950s. Eleanor became a school teacher and taught at Blairmore and Calgary. Rose, who was a baby when her father died, became an RN.

Giovanni (John) Marconi (Mucciarone) was born in Santa Angela, Campobasso and arrived in St. John, New Brunswick around 1903 and travelled to Montreal.[111] He worked in construction in Montreal and spent the summers on CPR gangs in western Canada as a water boy. In 1906-1907, he ended up in Lille working in the mine as a chute loader. According to son Jack, "One day, at work, a dead man came down the chute and into the mine car he was loading. It upset him so much he quit the mine and got a job as a porter at the Lille Hotel."[112] John followed Grand Union Hotel owner George Clair to Coleman in 1909-1910 where he met his future wife, Margaret Mary Davidson, a hotel employee, and they married in 1911. Because of better pay, John returned to mine work as a teamster at the International Mine, in 1914, a position he held until 1930. At that point, he became a blacksmith's helper and worked in this area until retirement in 1954. Jack noted that his father was illiterate and lost his passport and could not prove the correct spelling of his name and, therefore, there were many variants. He eventually had it legally changed to Marconi. The couple had four children: Jack, Gordon, Francis and Catherine.

Jack Marconi, who was born in 1915, did not go to high school; he does not say why though it is clear in his brother Toby's history that the family was desperately poor and the children had to go to work as soon as they were of age. He was lucky to get a job at the International Mine as a trapper, an individual who opened the mine doors to allow coal cars to get in and out and observed: "My wage was $3.50 a day. Work at the mines was very slack and unsettled during this period, and in 1932 we had a bitter strike which saw a lot of tension between the miners of which there was a wide variety of different nationalities. I witnessed the picket line at Bellevue and the violence that erupted between the R.C.M.P. and the miners and their wives. When the strike was finally settled and work resumed ill feelings still persisted because of the discrimination against a number of men who were not rehired."[113]

In 1934, Jack experienced a potentially dangerous situation in the mine when a fire broke out on the mine's 103 slope. He and Andy Buckna were instructed by fireboss Tom Flynn, to rush around to all the rooms and inform the men to exit via the York Creek workings. Buckna tripped

---

[111] John Marconi, "John Marconi (Mucciarone)," in *Crowsnest and Its People*, 686-687.

[112] John T. (Jack) Marconi, "John Thomas Marconi," in *Crowsnest and Its People*, 687-688.

[113] *Ibid.*, 688.

and sprained his ankle and Jack had to help him as they did this. Fortunately, an orderly withdrawal occurred and no-one was injured. The fire could not be extinguished so the mine was flooded with water from York Creek. It remained sealed until 1944 when it was reopened.

Jack realized that, in order to improve his prospects, he needed to continue his studies and attended night classes. In 1939, he obtained a fireboss certificate and, in 1946, the overman's certificate. The last position is second only to the mine manager in authority and is responsible for ensuring safety of operations. These positions were traditionally held by miners of British ancestry so his achievement is not only a personal success story but also demonstrates that some Italian miners were able to move up the ranks. In 1950, Jack became head pitboss and served in that capacity until mine closure in 1954. He then moved on to the McGillivray Mine in the same role and, finally to Vicary to open up a new mine to supply coking coal to Japan. Jack was thus a part of the mining "elite" work force in the latter part of his career. In 1939, Jack married Anna Alampi, the member of another mining dynasty.

Toby Marconi was born in 1917 in Coleman and notes in his history that money was scarce in their household and that he went to work at the age of 16 in the local theatre as a janitor.[114] Toby followed his brother in work at the International Mine in 1935. He joined the Canadian Army and was stationed in Nanaimo for a time until he was sent back to work in the mines since it was an industry important to the war effort. He continued to work for International until mine closure in 1954. He then worked at Vicary until his retirement; he spent over 40 years as an underground miner. In 1958, he was part of a crew that prospected for coal in the Smoky River region of Alberta for US Steel.

Bankhead, Exshaw and Kananaskis

It is difficult to determine the Italian work force of the Bankhead Mine: after over a decade of strikes (1909-1922) and increasing competition, the mine was shut down and the miners moved on to other jobs. Historian Ben Gadd in *Bankhead: The Twenty Year Town* mentions two Italian families, the D'Amicos and the Tronos, and Narcissus Morello. The last is remembered as one of two men who died jammed inside a coal chute deep inside Cascade Mountain. On November 25, 1914, Narcissus and Walentey Packney were swept down the chute when the coal face collapsed.[115] Gadd observes: "Only the deaths appear in the Bankhead records. Broken bones and lacerations

---

[114] Gordon Marconi, "Gordon Marconi," in *Crowsnest and Its People*, 689.
[115] Ben Gadd, *Bankhead: The Twenty Year Town* (Banff, AB: Minister of Supplies and Services, 1989), 49.

do not. Mining companies of the day didn't offer compensation to permanently injured miners who would never be able to work again, nor did the government."[116] In 1922, the Dominion Parks Commissioner instructed the CPR to move the entire town and the miners not only lost their jobs because of mine closure but also their homes. In 1926, 38 houses were moved to Banff. Housing and other structures were important commodities and were recycled when possible. The Trono family settled in Banff and the D'Amico family in Blairmore.

At least some Bankhead miners found work in the cement plant at Exshaw. In 1904, Sir Sandford Fleming was serving as the president of the International Portland Cement Company in Hull, Quebec. When son Hugh Fleming and Dan Diver discovered high-grade limestone and also shale deposits near Seebe (these contained silica, alumina and iron required for cement production), he staked a mineral claim on a 2.8 hectare parcel of land. Western Canadian Cement and Coal Company (WCCCC) was established and plant construction began in August 1905. The location was ideal because it also had coal to fire the kilns. The town site that developed at the base of the quarry was named for another shareholder, Fleming's son-in-law William Exshaw.[117]

Orlando Martini, who contributed the family history in *Exshaw: Heart of the Valley*, noted that many of the Italians who settled there came from the Veneto including not only his own family, the Orlandos and Martinis, but also the Lazzarottos, Sassos, Smaniottos, Nardinos and Manzardos.[118] His maternal grandfather, Leonardo Orlando, arrived from Valstagna in 1906; he was joined in 1907 by his wife Angela Scremin. The couple had two children: Caterina, born in Exshaw in 1908: and Alberta, born in 1910 (her name shows the family's commitment to their host province). Caterina was Orlando Martini's mother. Leonardo helped to build the cement plant and worked there until 1920 when the family returned to Italy where he bought a small farm and grew tobacco. Daughters Caterina and Alberta continued their education and became fluent not only in English but also Italian. Around 1930, Orlando returned to Exshaw with daughter Caterina, who married Angelo Martini in 1932. According to Orlando, his grandfather's intention was for him and Caterina to work hard and generate a "nest egg" that would allow them to return permanently to Italy. This was not to be because Martini had recently arrived from Italy. Grandfather Leonardo had a tragic death; he drowned in the Bow River as he crossed to get firewood.[119]

[116] *Ibid.* 51.
[117] Rob Alexander and Dene Cooper, eds., *Exshaw: Heart of the Valley* (Exshaw, AB: Exshaw Historical Society, 2005), 120-21.
[118] Orlando Martini, "Orlando/Martini – 1906," in *Exshaw*, 188-191.
[119] *Ibid.*, 189.

Giovanni (John) Martini was born in Merlengo, Treviso and married Virginia Borsato in 1907.[120] The couple had four children. John immigrated in 1913 and initially worked in BC; in 1918, he moved to Lethbridge where he tried to homestead without much success. The family history notes that this was due to the dry conditions. After trying to find work in Calgary, he moved to Exshaw where he began work in the cement plant. Six months' work at the plant and six months' work in the coal mines at Drumheller became the pattern of his life for the next few years. He did not have his family join him and grandson Orlando Martini, observes: "His older son, Angelo (my father), speculated that John Martini wanted to return to Italy eventually, but was thwarted first by World War I (1914-18) and later by his wife's premature death in 1922."[121] Virginia had not seen her husband since his immigration to Canada (a total of nine years) and raised their children alone.

While today, parents strive to protect their children from the uncertainties of life, this was not possible in the late nineteenth and early twentieth centuries. Not only did boys enter the work force in their early teens, they also travelled alone from Italy to North America. This was the case with the Martini family. In 1929, John sent money for Irma, Angelo and Bert to join him (daughter Eugenia was already married). All were under the age of 20. The trip across France by train and ship was a nightmare but they eventually arrived in Quebec City on October 20, 1929. Their father had wired $50 so that they would have money for the last part of their journey but, because they landed on a Sunday, they couldn't access it. Thankfully, the Salvation Army, which met trains in Calgary, involved the Italian consular agent, Antonio Rebaundengo and wife Angelina and they put the young people on the train to Exshaw. They had not seen their father for 16 years and the transition was a difficult one – the boys immediately joined their father, in cement plant and mine work in Exshaw and Drumheller. Irma took care of the house. In the height of the Depression, they were grateful for whatever work they could get.[122]

The Martini children married other Italians: Angelo married Caterina Orlando (1932); Irma married Pietro (Pete) Martini (1933), the owner of the ABC Coal Mine in Drumheller; and Bert married Olga (Rita) Violini (1940). In the family history, Orlando notes that the family lived "in a humble two-room frame house situated 'across the tracks'."[123] This was definitely the wrong side of the tracks: houses had no indoor plumbing and coal-fired stoves. Family historian Aldo also remembers difficulties experienced during the Second World War:

---

[120] *Anon.*, "Martini: John and Virginia – 1922," in *Exshaw*, 257-259.
[121] Orlando Martini, 189.
[122] *Ibid.*, 258.
[123] Orlando Martini, 189.

Soon after the outbreak of the war, a small group of Exshaw residents circulated a petition which asked the Canada Cement Plant superintendent to arrange for the deportation of all Italians in Town to detention camps (at that time, Exshaw was a Canada Cement Company Town without a Mayor or Town Council). The response of the Superintendent, Mr. Vic Hamilton, was quick and decisive. He tore up the document and told the instigators to mind their own business; the Italians in the Town were in no way responsible for the actions of Mussolini. This hostility towards Italians was largely responsible for my parents leaving Exshaw in 1941 and moving to the Town of Weston, Ontario (now part of Toronto).[124]

Orlando attended Western Collegiate and, after graduation in 1952, obtained a BA in Civil Engineering (1956) and Masters' in Environmental Engineering (1968) from the University of Toronto. He worked throughout Canada and abroad.

Bernardo Sasso was born in Bassano del Grappa, Vicenza, and arrived in Exshaw in 1907. He returned in 1908 and married Pierina, who joined him in 1909. According to son Angelo (born 1910), his father worked on the construction of the plant. The Sasso family had a long history as migrant labourers. Angelo notes in the family history:

> When my dad was nine years old, the family moved to France and he worked in the mines from age nine. He learned to speak French fluently and then the family moved to Germany and he learned to speak German fluently, but he could never learn English fluently. This was due, in part, to the fact that living in the Italian section of Exshaw he spoke Italian and when at work at the plant, he spoke French as the manager was French; although when an English manager took over he had difficulties.[125]

Angelo and brother Valentino completed high school though Angelo notes that they were bullied because of being Italian: "We had to put up with it. Sometime I try to forget it, but some of the boys treated us roughly; they would gang up on us and beat the devil out of us … My brother went to grade 12 and we both did good in school, but there was envy again."[126] Bernardo's immigrant story did not end well – on May 19, 1934, he was buried under 22 tonnes of cement. Angelo makes a stoic observation: "If you leave cement for too long in bins it kind of hardens. He just

---

[124] *Ibid.*, 189.
[125] Angelo Sasso, "Sasso: Bernardo and Pierina – 1907," in *Exshaw*, 198.
[126] *Ibid.*, 198.

happened to be in the wrong place when that came down. He was 51 years old."[127] The fatalism about danger on the job was a common attitude among those who stayed in labouring work.

Angelo worked as a temporary railroad station agent in Exshaw, Calgary, Disbury and Olds but was laid off in 1932 and it was impossible to find work at that point. The manager at the cement plant invited him to work for them. Angelo was an avid learner and progressed to senior supervisor; this caused jealousy and he notes that when he joined the company, there were only four people with a high school education (the manager, him, the chemist and the office clerk). He enlisted in the Army and went overseas and ended up in England where he did administrative work and benefited from University of Alberta President Henry Marshall Tory's Khaki University program. Angelo attended university for a year and, in 1946, returned to Canada and to work at the plant. He was a life-long learner and, after retirement, studied to become a chef at SAIT but didn't think there was a future in it and then turned to studies to become a police magistrate. When these were completed, he worked for the next eight years at the Morley Reserve in an administrative capacity. He moved to Calgary and joined the Italian Club and served as president for two years.[128]

Giovanni (John) Lazzarotto was born in Valstagna, Vicenza, Veneto and arrived in Exshaw in 1914 joining his brother. He worked in the plant but like others, he also filled in with mine work. John worked in the cement plant for 30 years as a repairman (millwright). Son Jino was born in 1924 and went to work in the plant in 1941 at the age of 16 and worked for the company for 45 years. He describes his work history as follows: "I started as a labourer and worked myself up into the quarry as a driller and from there I went down to the shale pit at Seebe where I ran a shovel. I worked there for 23 years and then came back here to the plant as a bulldozer operator in the quarry. I liked my job. I like the people I worked for. First, it was Canada Cement, a good company to work for. Canada Cement merged with Lafarge and later Lafarge dropped the Canada Cement name."[129]

Jino describes the neighbourhood in which they lived and provides insight into the conditions of the working class in the community: "There were a lot of houses here on the south side of the train tracks. There were a lot of shacks because people didn't intend to stay here, they would just make a little money and go again. They called it Little Italy but there were a lot of nationalities, all kinds of people: Polish, Ukrainian, Germans, French, Belgian. A lot of the old shacks were torn down and new houses built. There must have been 40 families on the south side of the track."[130]

[127] *Ibid.*, 198.
[128] *Ibid.*, 200.
[129] Jino Lazzarotto, "Lazzarotto: Jino and Millie – 1912," in *Exshaw*, 235-236.
[130] *Ibid.*, 236.

Jino and brothers Silvio and Tony served in the Canadian military: his brothers overseas and he on the east coast with the engineers. On their return, they all went back to work in the plant. Jino's sons worked in the plant during the summer breaks from school and he notes:

> They could have stayed on permanent, but they said they didn't like the dust. I said, "You know what it means. Back to school." Ronnie is an electrician at the plant. Rickie has his own company as a pipeline inspector in the oil business, and Lionel worked for Cummings Diesel for several years as a heavy duty mechanic. Now he's working on his own. They all turned out good. Ronnie's the only one who stayed in Exshaw. He was lucky because they apprenticed him here.[131]

In his own family history, written around 2004, son Ron observes that he started work as a labourer at the plant when he finished high school in 1970. That was a crucial year – in May 1970 Canada Cement and Lafarge merged. A $30-million plant expansion occurred and this involved tearing down the old town.[132] While father Jino was of the older generation and mourned the old company and town, son Ron was able to benefit. Because of seniority, the company allowed him to choose a trade – he chose electrician – and attended SAIT in Calgary for four years for two-months' of instruction; the rest of the time he worked in the plant. He also studied instrument mechanics. Ron became a union man and served as president of the National Brotherhood of Boilermakers union at Lafarge and Baymag.[133] The Lazzarotto family's experience of powerlessness in the first generation, to the mastery of the third generation is representative for many Italian immigrant families.

Nordegg

Martin Nordegg's Brazeau Collieries began mining in 1911 but a town site was not developed until 1914 when the railway arrived from Red Deer.[134] The Royal Commission on Coal of 1925 noted that the mine work force at Nordegg had a disproportionately-high percentage of Italian workers, the largest in Alberta, exceeding that of people of Slavonic origin. When Johnny Shanks, the Mine

---

[131] *Ibid.*, 239.

[132] Alexander and Cooper, *Exshaw*, 532.

[133] *Ibid.*, 421.

[134] Anne McMullen Belliveau, *Small Moments in Time: The Story of Alberta's Big West Country Upper North Saskatchewan River Corridor, Shunda Basin, Brazeau Collieries and Nordegg* (Calgary, AB: Detselig Enterprises Ltd., 1999), 110-111 and footnotes 11 and 2 in "Nordegg: A Town is Born" chapter.

Manager at Fernie, took on this position at Nordegg, a number of Italian miners followed him. Local historian Anne McMullen Belliveau observes:

> The Nordegg Italian population was drawn from specific locations within certain Italian provinces [i.e., regions], but the provinces from which they came were widely scattered. Approximately 30% came from Sicily and Calabria, the most southern provinces. The original homeland of these Italians was one of the poorest in Italy. About 30% of Nordegg's Italian population had come from the province of Abruzzi in the mid-regions of Italy, along the Adriatic Coast southeast of Rome, while the remaining 40% came from the northern areas of Veneto, Friuli, and Liguria.[135]

In 1922, Stuart Kidd, Manager of the Brazeau Trading Company, went so far as to recommend to immigration authorities that the travel costs of bringing the family of an Italian miner should be guaranteed because he was a good worker and had a secure job.[136] This is unheard of in other mining areas in the province. But this action does not mean that the miners were treated equally and Belliveau observes that "British miners seemed to be getting all the good jobs" and continues: "There was a definite ethnic distinction which resulted in a certain amount of friction. After the Officials' Club had been done away with in 1918, all Brazeau employees, whether management or labour became members of the Miners' Club, and each man had membership fees deducted from his pay. Class distinction, which had been based upon the hierarchy created by divisions between labour and management, had begun to give way to stratification following ethnic lines. Ethnic societies and mutual aid organizations began appearing."[137]

Belliveau believes that community solidarity developed in spite of ethnic divisions because of the mine's remoteness. Families had at least five children and supported the miners' fraternal society – the Ordine Indipendente Fior d'Italia. By the 1940s, Italian entrepreneurs represented a significant percentage of the business district operating the bakery/coffee shop, a service station, two boarding houses, the only hotel, the beer parlor, shoe repair shop and Bighorn Transport.[138] Second-generation Italian miners also occupied some junior-level management positions.

One of Nordegg's first Italian workers, Paul Bifano, had a tragic end. He was born in Grimaldi, Cosenza, Calabria and found work in the mines in Fernie. In 1914, he enlisted in

---

[135] *Ibid.*, 127-128.
[136] *Ibid.*, 128.
[137] *Ibid.*, 128.
[138] *Ibid.*, 184.

the 1st Depot Battalion, 13C Regiment (an Alberta regiment) but was discharged as an "Italian Subject." Italians were not enemy aliens in the First World War though for some employers, all foreigners were viewed with distrust. Paul moved to Nordegg with Shanks and was killed on October 31, 1941 in the Nordegg Mine Disaster. The *Lethbridge Herald* reported on November 1: "Nordegg, Alta., Nov. 1 – (CP) – Thirty-one coal miners were killed by an explosion yesterday in the Brazeau Collieries according to the first official detailed report made available early today. John Shanks, general manager of the mine, said 'there are 19 of the men who were killed now removed and it is believed there are 12 more to come.' Earlier Mr. Shanks and other officials said there was no hope any would be found alive."

Zupito (Zupi), the son of George and Maria D'Amico, was born in Nordegg, and experienced the disaster first-hand.[139] At the age of 25, Zupi was working as a timberman responsible for mine beam repairs in the tunnels of the No. 3 Mine. It was Halloween and he was looking forward to going to a dance after his shift ended and with brother, Guido and three other workers was involved in repairing the beams in a mine room that had collapsed the previous day. They were about 853 metres down the mine slope at about 91 metres below ground. This was the fourth level of the mine and below them was the bottom of the mine, which was covered by water. Another crew was adjacent to them in room 13, led by fire boss Jock Armstrong, who was preparing to set off dynamite charges to loosen coal. An electrical charge from a battery was used to ignite the dynamite. The first two shots released methane gas, which then caught fire. Zupi described feeling a "bump" and a sudden change of air pressure in his ears.[140]

The article in the *Lethbridge Herald* concludes: "The tragedy stunned this little town in the foothills of the Rockies, whose population is about 800, and sent a wave of sadness throughout as the citizens mourned their dead and launched plans for a mass burial." The bodies of 29 miners were taken to the washhouse to be cleaned and then to the Show Hall in the Empress Hotel where family and friends could view them. In addition to Bifano, Rudolph D'Amico, the son of Charlie and Celine D'Amico, was killed. He was Zupi's cousin. Two other members of the D'Amico family had been killed in a 1925 accident at the Hillcrest Mine. The mine was closed for six weeks and a trial found the company criminally responsible and fined it $5,000. As a result of the accident, Brazeau Collieries introduced the pneumatic pick system for breaking up coal, the first company to do so in Alberta. Zupi served in the Second World War and, on demobilization in 1945, attended the University of Alberta and, in 1948, graduated with a degree in mining

---

[139] Johnnie Bachusky, "*Ghost Town Stories of Alberta: Abandoned Dreams in the Shadows of the Canadian Rockies*" (Victoria, BC: Heritage House Publishing, 2009), 20-21.

[140] *Ibid.*, 23.

engineering. He returned to work at Brazeau Collieries and was the engineer in charge when Brazeau closed its Kananaskis Mine at Mount Allen in 1952, and the mines at Nordegg in June 1955. He entered the oil business and, in 1996, founded Edmonton-based Larsen & D'Amico Manufacturing, a firm specializing in oilfield machinery and equipment.[141]

The Blasettis from the Antrodoco, Lazio region of central Italy were another prominent Nordegg family. The first of the brothers to immigrate was Andrea (Andrew) who arrived at Ellis Island in February 1910. He obtained work in the under-sea mines in Nova Scotia and likely worked at the Princess Colliery of Old Sydney Collieries, Nova Scotia Steel & Coal Company. Perhaps the work did not appeal to him for he headed for Calgary where he joined Italians in road construction work and also in the Burns packing plant. In 1912, he sent for wife Bernardina (nee Serani) and then moved to work in Nordegg. Because the town site had not yet been built, he left Bernardina in Calgary and, in June 1914, she joined him with their nine-month-old son Guido. They rode on the floor of a box car among men going to work in the mines. Bernardina was the first woman to live in the community surviving in a tent until their house was completed in the fall.

The family history provides a level of detail that demonstrates the resourcefulness and resilience that was typical of most immigrant families. Andrea not only worked in the mines but also supplied wood to neighbours; he hunted and fished to supplement the family's food supply. Bernardina kept an extensive vegetable garden but also foraged for wild berries, dandelion greens and wild mushrooms. She was famous for her cooking, in particular, recipes using wild game. She also took in laundry and sold home-made bread to the community's bachelors. The couple was married for 61 years of which 41 were spent in Nordegg. They experienced both joys and sorrows: sons Ernest and Frank were killed in mining accidents. Son Guido was an accomplished entrepreneur who established a number of local businesses, his most successful being Big Horn Transport, a major hauling company.

Four Sartor brothers – Giacomo, Giovanni Battista (Tita), Antonio and Domenico – from San Giorgio della Richinvelda, Pordenone, immigrated to Canada early in the twentieth century. Their father was a miller, who eked out a living for the family of 16 (eight sons and eight daughters). Giacomo arrived in Quebec in June 1907 with a group of Friulani and worked until 1912 in the mines at Lille and, then at Hosmer.[142] Domenico joined him in 1909; Tita, in 1911; and Tony, in 1913. The enormous mobility of Italian workers is evidenced through Giacomo's

[141] Zupito D'Amico Obituary, *Calgary Herald*, September 13, 2009.
[142] This information is derived from a typescript account titled "Itinerario di Sartor Giacomo" given to me for the Italians settle in Edmonton Oral History Project, in 1983; it was likely created by Tony Sartor.

moves in the next years. In 1912, he returned to Italy to complete his military service. By 1913, he was back in Hosmer and then Fernie with his brother Tony. Although Giacomo had taken out citizenship papers, according to Tony, he still experienced problems at work. In 1914, he moved to Blackfalds, Alberta, and worked for a time on a farm. By the end of 1915, he was homesteading in Venice near Lac La Biche but returned to work in the mines in Hosmer until they closed in 1916. Giacomo then moved to the Pocahontas Mine in Jasper National Park until the end of 1917 when he went to Butte, Montana, for three-month's work. This was followed by three months in Spokane before returning to work for short periods in Rossland, Trail and Sault Ste. Marie. In 1916, brother Domenico returned to Italy to fight with the Italian forces, was taken prisoner and died in 1919.

The itinerant work in the mines continued for Giacomo in 1918 and 1919 in Nordegg and Cadomin. He then went to Banff for treatment for sciatica. He returned to Italy in 1919 and married Olimpia D'Andrea and two children were born – Tullio and Longino. In October 1922, Giacomo left for Sydney, Australia to work in the mines. In spring 1923, he embarked for Honolulu and subsequently arrived in Vancouver. From 1923 to 1929, he worked at Cadomin and had his wife and children join him in 1925. Sadly, his wife died in July 1928 and he was forced to send his sons to the Grey Nuns' convent in St. Albert for a year. He returned to Italy with his sons during the summer of 1929 and remained there for a year. He then married Giuseppina Marascutti and the family returned to Cadomin in January 1930. In 1933, he returned to Italy and acquired a farm in Pordenone. His working history is very much that of the "bird of passage." What is amazing is that this continued for a period of 26 years.

Tony Sartor, in an oral history account, described his epic 1913 immigration journey that took 22 days. He travelled from Italy by land through Switzerland and France to embark at Liverpool to cross the Atlantic.[143] He then travelled from Maine to Spokane by train and eventually reached the Crowsnest Pass. He immediately began work transporting coal but, after two months, the mine closed and he went to work in Nordegg. The 1916 census shows Tony living with a number of Italian workers (Peter Mazotto, Anthony Martinella, John China, Joseph Foschia, Louis Bortulussi and Silvio Rovado) in a boarding house; he was the youngest at age 18. Tony later worked for a time in the mines at Brule before returning to Nordegg and, eventually moving on to Pocahontas in Jasper National Park. By 1920, he was tired of the mines and went to Edmonton where he found work as an assistant baker at the MacDonald Hotel.

---

143 Tony Sartor interview, Italians Settle in Edmonton Oral History Project, 1983, , PAA PR0915.

The Coal Branch

Local historian Toni Ross describes the Coal Branch town of Mountain Park as follows: "More than 80 dwellings in all, painted white with green facings to harmonize with the snowcapped mountains and green spruce and jack pine trees. The workmen's houses were 28 feet by 28 feet, some with cottage roofs and the other with gable roofs. Gable roofed houses had large second floor rooms with access gained by an outside staircase. These were designed in such a way that families could take in boarders and still attain complete privacy. The chief officials were provided with handsomely designed six-room bungalows."[144] Like Nordegg, Mountain Park was envisioned as a model town and was a far cry from the dingy, dirty communities that developed in BC's Elk Valley and the Drumheller Valley. Historian Andy A. den Otter, drawing on surveys done in 1918 and 1925, notes: "Both surveys agree that those of British origin formed the largest group (41.5 percent in 1925) and that the Italians, Serbians and Ukrainians were also substantial groups while smaller clusters consisted of Poles, Americans, Rumanians and Swedes."[145]

Prominent Italian miners included John Baruzzini, Primo Piccoli, Frank Livero, Jim Bello, Louis Dominic, and Pete and Joe Chiesa.[146] Baruzzini came from Italy to work in the Crowsnest Pass and moved to Mountain Park in 1921.[147] He returned to Italy to marry in 1922 and his wife gave birth to a daughter, Mary, before joining him in Canada. The couple had seven children at Mountain Park (Zita, Silvino, Dora, Isidor, Loretta, Caroline and Secondo). John worked in the mines until he lost his eyesight in 1944. In 1950, the family moved to Luscar where sons Isidor and Secondo worked in the strip mines. When the mines closed, the family moved to Edmonton. Secondo died tragically at the age of 26, in 1957, in an accident when he was working in Canmore for Mannix Construction. At the age of 17, Silvino went to work underground in the mines and did this until mine closure in 1955. He then worked in construction and, finally, for the Alberta Liquor Control Board in Edmonton. Isidor worked for CP Transport.

Pietro (Peter) Chiesa came to Canada in 1908 and initially worked in the mine at Copper Cliff, Ontario; he then moved westward to the mines at Michel.[148] In 1912, he walked to

---

[144] Ross, *Oh The Coal Branch: A Chronicle of the Alberta Coal Branch*, 33-34.

[145] Andy A. den Otter, "Social Life of a Mining Community: the Coal Branch," in *Alberta Historical Review 17*, Historical Society of Alberta, 1969, 17-4 Autumn, 1-11.

[146] *Ibid.*, 31-32.

[147] Silvino Baruzzini's account of his father Giovanni's life at Mountain Park is described in an essay titled "A Ranger Rode 30 Miles," in Toni Ross, *Oh! The Coal Branch*, 259-262.

[148] This account draws on a short essay titled "You Don't Dream About Girls when You're Hungry," the story of Pietro Chicsa in Ross, *Oh! The Coal Branch*, 206-209.

Mountain Park to find work. At the age of 37, he returned to Italy to marry and left his new bride, Julia, pregnant to return to work in Canada. Son, Nino was born in 1922 in Udine and, in 1923 mother and son arrived in Mountain Park. The couple had three other children – Regina, Alvio and Pete – and Julia died shortly after Pete's birth in 1929 as a result of complications in the delivery. Pietro could not take care of the children and they were sent to the convent in St. Albert. In 1932, through an arranged marriage, his second wife Maria arrived from Italy and the family was reunited. The couple had another child, a boy called Lucino.

Peter had the distinction of being the oldest miner in Mountain Park on June 20, 1950 when the mine closed and in July performed his final duties as mine watchman. Marjorie Jones in a July 24 article titled "Miners at Mountain Park Mourn Over Town's Death" writes:

> Mountain Park's oldest miner is making his last rounds at his last job as watchman in this dying town. At the end of July his work will be finished. So will the town. The Mountain Park Coal Mine whistle which first blew 39 years ago, blasted its last on June 20, when the mine was shut because of lack of orders, but its echoes still ring in the mountains. Reluctant ears of 110 miners whom it threw out of work, and their worried wives, hear it yet. As they pack to leave they hear it. As they say quick goodbyes to neighbours who in 30 years are more like family than friends they hear it.[149]

On mine closure, Peter bought the old hospital and two houses and moved them to Edson where he used them to construct a home. Son Nino served in the Canadian military in the Second World War seeing service in North Africa and Italy where he was captured and sent to a German prisoner-of-war camp. After the war, he returned to Mountain Park where he worked as a clerk in the Mercantile Store and, in 1949, purchased it with friend Jack Roome. When mining operations ceased, Nino and family moved to Edson where he owned the By-Rite Food Store.

Joseph Ciciarelli left Blairmore around 1917 to work at Mountain Park as a foreman responsible for building the round table required for the railroad engines to turn around and return to Edson. Daughter Teresa Girardi tells the story of when the family (her mother, three sisters and a baby brother) joined him:

> The train trip was really something to remember. From Blairmore to Edmonton where dad met us was not too bad, but from Edson to Mountain Park was terrible. It took one day and one night to go from Edson to Mountain Park. The train, it must be a museum coach now

149 Cited by Ross, 160-161.

– old wooden coach, wooden slat seats, coal oil lamps nailed to brackets on coach walls, and an old wood and coal stove for heat. If you wanted air in the coach, the brakeman would come along with a long handled stick with a hook on the end to open the vent in top of the coach. I won't forget that as I still have the scar from one of the vent windows which was jerked too hard, fell out and crashed down and the glass cut my arm.[150]

She was eight years old at the time. Joseph participated in a political rally in Mountain Park in April 1917 when the Hon. O. C. W. Cross spoke. He undertook the translation into Italian. His wife became a member of the Ladies Cross Club. Their time in Mountain Park was short-lived; according to Teresa, "the climate was too high for mother," and, after two years, they moved to Edson where he worked for CN as a boilermaker's helper.

Albano Paron was born in Valvasone in northern Italy and arrived in Canada in 1907 and for over 20 years led the life of a sojourner. He worked in mines in the Crowsnest Pass, Michel and Fernie. In 1914, he returned to Italy to marry Elisa Valentinuzzi. The couple had three daughters: Maria (1914), Evelina (1916) and Amelia (1917).[151] With the ending of the war in 1918, he returned to work in the mines in Cadomin and Nordegg. After a year, he went back to Italy and the couple had two more daughters: Jennoveffa (1920) and Assunta (1922). Because of fears of an upcoming war, in 1939, Albano sponsored Elisa and daughters Jennoveffa, Assunta and Amelia. Grandson Renso Castellarin notes in the family history that they crossed the border into France mere hours before it was closed and caught a ship leaving Cherbourg for North America. Albano built a home for them with the assistance of fellow miner Luigi Raffin. In Cadomin, Amelia went to work in a local hotel and Assunta started cleaning houses. In an oral history interview, Amelia noted that she made more money in a week in Canada than she could in a similar position in Italy.[152] She married Luigi Raffin in 1941. He had immigrated in 1928 and worked in the mines in Michel, Nordegg and Cadomin. Raffin tried to get out of mine work and got a job in Windsor in one of the automobile plants but, when the authorities discovered he was a miner, he was forced to return to Cadomin to help with the war effort.[153] Since mines there were working only a couple of days a week, he went to work in Hillcrest. By 1956, he was seriously ill with silicosis resulting from years of mine work and the Compensation Board found him a job in Edmonton.

---

[150] Teresa Girardi's account is titled "Train Backed Up All the Way to Mountain Park," 263.
[151] Renso Castellarin, "Paron, Albano Family," in *Crowsnest and Its People: Millenium Edition*, 547.
[152] Gus and Assunta Dotto (Emilia Raffin), oral history interview, Italians Settle in Edmonton Oral History Project, 1983, PAA PR0915.
[153] Renso Castellarin, "Raffin, Luigi Family," in *Crowsnest and Its People: Millenium Edition*, 547-548.

Valentino Dotto and wife Albina Favaro arrived in Edmonton in 1914.[154] The year following, she gave birth to twin boys – Agostino (Gus) and Giuseppe (Joe). When the twins were six months old the family moved to the mining community of Pocahontas in Jasper National Park, and, later, to Brule, where Valentino worked until 1928 when he went to work in Cadomin. The couple would have six more children.

Gus Dotto met Assunta Paron shortly after her arrival in Cadomin in 1939. They fell in love but she decided to move to Edmonton and found work at the Great West Garment Company (GWG), which was busy making uniforms for Allied troops. They continued to see each other and became engaged in 1942 when Gus was serving in the military with the Mountain Rangers. Because of a knee injury and trouble with his hearing, he was put on reserve in 1944. After the war, he returned to Cadomin to work in the mines. The couple married in 1945. With mine closure, the family moved to Edmonton where Gus found a job with the Molson Brewery and worked there until his retirement. Assunta continued to work and spent many years running a cafeteria in a health facility. She was an avid family historian and wrote a memoir and was interviewed a number of times by oral historians.[155] Daughter Lydia Dotto became a distinguished science journalist and photographer. Joe's brother Albino Dotto moved to Edmonton after the mines closed and found work at the Imperial Oil Refinery.

Family reunification brought Evelina Paron and husband Pio Castellarin and their four children to Canada in 1949; Elisa Paron, Evelina's mother, provided the travel money.[156] The Castellarins were *contadini* who farmed and grew grapes. According to son Renso, six Castellarin families lived in their courtyard home. Brother-in-law Louis Raffin got Pio a job at the Mohawk Mine in Maple Leaf. After a year, he was laid off but a friend, Johnny Podgornick, helped him get a job in Blairmore where he worked for five years until the work week was reduced to a couple of days and he went to Michel for full-time work. A mine accident resulted in a broken leg and he retired after 22 years in the mines. Son Renso became a teacher and served as a principal for 37 years working in three schools in the Crowsnest Pass and one in Pincher Creek.

[154] Gus and Assunta Dotto and Emilia Raffin oral history tapes and family photos are in the Gus Dotto Fonds PAA-7626. There is a short account titled "Dotto, Augusto Family," in *Crowsnest and Its People: Millenium Edition*, 548.
[155] See Catherine C. Cole, *GWG: Piece by Piece* (Goose Lane Editions: Fredericton, NB, 2012) and the accompanying website *Piece by Piece: The GWG Story*, URL: *https://www.royalalbertamuseum.ca/exhibits/online/gwg/en/images/3-1-4.html*, retrieved October 10, 2017. The author interviewed her in 2013 for the Columbus Centre Project on Italian Canadians as Enemy Aliens: Memories of World War II, URL: http://www.italiancanadianww2.ca/collection/details/icea2011_0009_0001, retrieved October 12, 2017.
[156] Renso Castellarin, "Castellarin Family," in *Crowsnest and Its People: Millenium Edition*, 548.

Some Italian miners who worked in the Coal Branch are only remembered because of accidents. Enrico Carretti was suffocated at the Cadomin mine on June 11, 1931. Dan Spinazzi (aged 48), John Burnside (41) and James Maddams Jr. (29) were killed in a methane gas explosion on the last working day in 1939. Toni Ross, writes:

> The fatality took place in No. five panel, a panel in which the 'pillars' were being drawn. Normally a warning sound indicates the presence of gas when it frees itself. But there was no warning. Fireboss Nicholson had made his rounds of inspection only a few minutes before and almost within seconds of his return, the tasteless, odorless terror crept down, leaving in its wake the stricken men caught in a merciless gas trap…. Whistles did not blow at midnight signaling the New Year, and all social, public and private gatherings were cancelled as Cadomin paid tribute to its dead. [157]

The pallbearers for Spinazzi were Louis Raffin, John Luccini, John Vadrasco, John Passamero, Max Ongaro and Attilio Esquenni, who came from the same town as Spinazzi in northern Italy. The bodies were taken to Leyland and put on a train for interment in Edmonton.

A cave-in in February 1940 killed Paul Ciputa (50) and Anthony Resek (44) at the Mountain Park Collieries.[158] The men were recovered 548 metres underground. At 7:30 pm on August 5, 1942, Victor Alleggretto (41), John Vallance (52), Joseph Dombrowski (55), Carl Stocks (52) and pitboss John Logan (63) were killed when a torrent of water broke through panel pillars from an old mine working in Cadomin.[159] Rescuers had to dig through tonnes of rock and mud to bring the bodies to the surface. Peter Laghi and A. Bennedetti were two of the three miners who escaped death and testified at an inquiry. In 1942, Alex Marconi was killed when he was buried by a fall of coal at the Foothills Mine; he was 41 and a bachelor.[160] J. Dominchelli was a pipefitter in the Luscar Collieries when an explosion occurred on May 12, 1945 that killed five men: W. Belik, M. Zozuk, D. Astley, P. Zokuk and Steve Zayezierski. He was one of the witnesses at the hearing in Edson in spring 1947.[161]

---

[157] Ross, 122-123.
[158] Ross, 124.
[159] Ross, 140.
[160] Ross, 141.
[161] Ross, 145.

Canmore

Ludovico (Italo) Massole immigrated from Lessole in 1905 and went to Canmore where he worked as a blacksmith at the mine.[162] He was joined by a hometown girl, Adelina Caffaro, in 1911 and they were married. Sons Ricardo and Italo were born in 1913 and 1914, respectively. They are said to have been the first Italian family in Canmore. In 1919, Ludovico sponsored his 14-year-old brother-in-law Attilio Giovanni Caffaro. Attilio was an orphan and the only one who could immigrate to earn money to send back to his family. Attilio's son, Peter, noted in an oral history interview that the majority of the miners in Canmore were Piemontese who had been contracted by the CPR in Europe to work in Canada.[163] Attilio lied about his age and immediately went to work in the mine but was passionate about education and made an arrangement with local principal Munroe Macleod to attend night school. Attilio completed grade 12 and went on to get steam engineer and welding credentials. He worked at Canmore Mines ending his career as mechanical superintendent responsible for all surface workings. He was a strong supporter of the UMWA and, according to Peter, "John L. Lewis was synonymous with God," for his father. Lewis was President of the UMWA from 1920 until 1960. In the 1920s, strikes occurred almost every two years with the longest, in 1924-25, seeing a reduction in wages of 33 per cent.[164]

In 1927, Attilio returned to Italy and fell in love with his cousin, Caterina (Rina) Adelaide Giono. In spite of opposition from her father, Mario Battista Giono, a wealthy contractor, they married in 1932. Used to having servants, Rina had to learn how to cook and clean house. Peter believes that his father had a "leg up" because he completed his education in Canada and also spoke excellent English. He observes: "The pattern is the first generation gets an economic foothold and the second generation gets educated." This was certainly the case in the Caffaro family and their close friends the Rivas. Attilio strictly enforced the importance of higher education with his children. Peter stated that in the summers he worked in the mines to earn money and the pay was seductive; however, his father always gave him the worst jobs in order to force him to leave the valley to study. The strategy worked: Peter received his Bachelor of Law degree in 1957 from the University of Alberta and was admitted to the Law Society of Alberta in 1958 and practised in Edmonton. On November 20, 1989, he was sworn in as a Judge of the Provincial Court of Alberta, Criminal Division. In 1970, he became the Italian Consular Agent and, later, Honorary Vice Consul, a

[162] Edna (Hill) Appleby, *Canmore: The Story of An Era* (Calgary: D.W. Friesen & Sons Ltd., 1975).

[163] Peter Caffaro interview, Memory Lane Oral History Project, Ital-Canadian Seniors Association, 2007.

[164] Water Riva, *Survival in Paradise: A Century of Coal Mining in the Bow Valley* (Canmore, AB: The Canmore Museum, 2008), 59-60.

position he held until 1982. In 1988, he became a Queen's Counsel. Peter was active not only in Edmonton's Italian community but also provincially and nationally in a range of professional and community organizations. He was made a Cavaliere della Repubblica Italiana in 1980. Brothers George and Paul Caffaro also completed university and the former became a teacher and taught at St. Francis Xavier High School in Edmonton and the latter, a doctor, practised in Slave Lake.

The Riva family is another mining dynasty. John Riva arrived in 1900 and was working in Canmore in the mine and boarding with his brother Joseph, and three other Italians (Mike Perota, Dominic Miglia, and Dominic Ammonitto). His great-grandson, Walter Joseph Riva, would be instrumental in bringing coal mining in Alberta into the modern age after it was dealt a death blow by the coming in of the Leduc and Redwater fields. Walter was born in Canmore in 1922, a third-generation coal miner who used enlistment in the Second World War to leave mining. He served as a navigator in the RAF and was able to attend the University of Alberta through the Veterans' Program. He specialized in mining engineering and graduated with honours in 1949. He returned to the Canmore Mines in management ending over 20 years of service as executive vice president. Riva later became president of Kaiser Resources and served as president, CEO and chairman of the board of a number of companies including Westar Resources and the British Columbia Resources Investment Corporation. He served as President of the Canadian Institute of Mining and Metallurgy and was inducted into the Canadian Mining Hall of Fame in 2004. An amateur historian, he completed a history of mining in the Bow Valley at the age of 86. Walter took great pride in his family's history – each of the family men worked in the Canmore Mines for about 40 years.

Walter provides an interesting explanation for the founding of the McNeill Co. Colliery Band. The Canadian Anthracite Coal Mine was experiencing a labour shortage and, as part of a recruiting campaign, built the Memorial Hall in 1921 for $150,000 (a staggering amount at the time). It had a gym, pool hall, barber shop, library, dance hall and tennis courts. Riva writes:

> The manager, Stan Young, a YMCA trained gymnast took advantage of the new building to improve recruiting programs and add significantly to activities available for family entertainment in the town…. hockey players and band musicians were sought from all corners of the west, even Bankhead. These programs not only added to community activities, but also developed a sense of community and pride as the hockey team won provincial championships and the band achieved wide recognition under the leadership of Peter Balla, an international celebrity for having been a guest artist at a John Philip Sousa concert (Sousa was a famous conductor and composer in the late-1880s and early 1900s).[165]

---

[165] Riva, 59.

Thus, Italian immigrants not only contributed their labour but also enriched the life of the community. Italian names are also found on the Roll of Honour of men who fought in the First World War as follows: O. Carsana, J. and T. Giovanozzo (Giovinazzo), B. Manolini, O. Massolini and P. Moini.[166] Immigrants and sons of immigrants also played on local sports teams. Louis Sandrelli and Vic Riva played in the Canmore Hockey Team, which in 1920-1921 was the Intermediate Champions of Alberta. Riva Heights in Canmore was named in his honour. Walter Riva played on the team in the 1930s. Cardo and Fred Marro and Angelo Sasso played in the National Park Baseball League in the 1920s.

Canmore's best-known miner is Andrea Lorenzo (Lawrence) Grassi though not for his prowess in the mines but rather his love of mountaineering. He was born in the village of Falmenta in the Cannobino Valley, Piemonte, a mountain community with proximity to Switzerland and France. Lawrence's father, Giuseppe Grassi, annually worked as a woodsman in forests surrounding the French city of Grenoble in southeastern France at the foot of the French Alps. From the age of 12, after completing elementary schooling, Lawrence accompanied him. In 1912, he decided to go to Canada. Grassi's passport lists his occupation as "*boscaiolo*" (woodsman). He travelled from the port of Le Havre on the steamship *La Provence* belonging to the Compagnie Générale Transatlantique to New York.[167] He was employed by the CPR on a section gang near Lakehead in winter 1912-1913.[168] Grassi brought two significant items to Canada – a 1912-edition of an *Accelerated Grammar Italian-English* as well as the Whymper's Guide to *Chamonix and the Range of Mont Blanc* (1908 edition).[169]

The camp was at Jackfish Lake, a fishing village, coal port and CPR railway section stop east of Fort William.[170] According to his biographers Elio Costa and Gabriele Scardellato, by 1911, there were 56 adults and children from the village of Falmenta in Fort William. Grassi, thus, found a welcoming community of compatriots and, like other single men, boarded with an Italian family. Grassi chose to go west, in 1913, continuing to work for the CPR at Hector situated in the high

---

[166] Appleby, 87.

[167] The Lawrence Grassi Fonds are located in the Whyte Museum of the Canadian Rockies Archives. In 2011, I researched Grassi for the museum's new permanent gallery titled Gateway to the Rockies. Elio Costa and Gabriele Pietro Scardellato had begun their research and co-authored *Lawrence Grassi: From Piedmont to the Rocky Mountains* (Toronto, ON: University of Toronto Press, 2015).

[168] Jon Whyte, *Tommy and Lawrence: The Ways and the Trails of Lake O'Hara* (Banff, AB: Lake O'Hara Trails Club, 1983), 52.

[169] These are part of the extensive Grassi Fonds in the Whyte Archives.

[170] Antonio Pucci examined immigration to these communities in his Master's thesis titled "The Italian Community in Fort William's East End in the Early Twentieth Century," Lakehead University, May 1977.

Rockies, so that he could climb mountains. Grassi worked there for about two years and, from 1916 to 1945, for the Canmore Mines.

Grassi worked to live but lived to climb mountains and make them accessible to others; he distinguished himself as a solo mountaineer and as an unofficial guide. Costa and Scardellato note that Grassi's reputation as a great mountaineer solidified in the late 1920s, as he guided members of the Canadian Alpine Club in various climbs. They cite an article by Ferris Neave "Climbing at Banff Park," which appeared on August 15, 1926 in the *Canadian Alpine Journal* as "the moment when the Grassi myth was born...."[171] A chapter of *Lawrence Grassi: From Piedmont to the Rocky Mountains* is dedicated to his climbing exploits. His reputation as a mountaineer prompted members of the Alpine Club to seek him out for assistance in ascending a number of mountains on the Alberta and BC side of the Rockies. Grassi also undertook rescue work; in 1926, he was climbing Bastion Peak of the Rampart Range with Dr. R. G. Williams of Calgary and the doctor fell and fractured his ankle. Grassi carried him out on his back. In 1939, he found the body of the son of H. E. Bulyea, Dean of the School of Dentistry at the University of Alberta.

His lasting legacy was as a trail builder and he developed masonry skills in order to do this. In 1921-1922, Grassi built his first trail. Banff historian Jon Whyte notes: "The Youth Hostel Association was then constructing a series of hostels from Bragg Creek to Banff National Park. Only one stretch was without a trail, a distance of about six or eight miles east of Canmore on the south side of the river. Lawrence, hearing of the gap, without anyone's asking him, set out to make the trail."[172] During a miner's strike in 1924, he constructed a trail from the twin lakes in the region connecting Mount Rundle and Chinaman's Peak (now called Ha Ling Peak).[173] He also developed a trail at the Alpine Clubhouse on Sulphur Mountain in Banff.

Grassi's intense mountaineering and trail building activities in the 1920s resulted in an unexpected honour. Aphrodite Karamitsanis, in *Place Names of* Alberta writes: "The name Grassi Lakes, after the well-known mountaineer and guide, was submitted to the Canadian Board on Geographical Names for approval in a letter dated 9 March 1927 from Mr. E. Mallabone, President, and Mr. W.M Ramsay, of the Canmore Advisory Council. The Board officially adopted the name 3 May 1927."[174] The lakes are located above Canmore, beyond the Rundle Reservoir.

---

[171] Costa and Scardellato, 130.

[172] Whyte, 52.

[173] Whyte, 53.

[174] Aphrodite Karamitsanis, *Place Names of Alberta: Mountains, Mountain Parks and Foothills*, vol 1 (Edmonton, AB: Alberta Culture and Multiculturalism and Friends of Geographical Names of Alberta Society and University of Calgary Press, 1991), 102. This date is confirmed by the Canadian Geographical Names database. Costa and Scardellato note that a letter dated March 17, 1960 from the Canadian Youth Hostel Association, Mountain Region to the Canadian

Both nominators were involved in the coal industry. Ramsay was a director of the H. W. McNeill Coal Company and the English-born Ernest William Mallabone worked in the No. 2 mine in Canmore. He died on September 24, 1929 as a result of an injury while working underground: a runaway coal car crushed him.

N. A. Wait, a mining engineer who arrived in Canmore in 1922, became Grassi's friend and in 1969 wrote a moving tribute titled "Grassi of Canmore."[175] The sub-title – "A Miner Who 'Did His Thing' and Gave Alberta, a heritage of Beauty" – suggests the high esteem in which he held his friend. Wait provides some biographical details as well as examples of Grassi's exploits including the account of the memorable climb of Mount Bastion in the Tonquin Valley of Jasper National Park. Dr. R. G. Williams of Calgary broke his leg during the descent and Wait writes: "Grassi carried him down the ice and rock slopes to the timberline where they were met by another party. 'Lawrence Grassi is a superman,' Dr. Williams stated."[176]

In the recounting of great deeds, myth sometimes eclipses fact and there is some controversy about the date of the renaming of the lakes. Wait states:

> In 1938 Dr. J. S. Woodsworth, MP for Winnipeg, that gentle soul who was the leader of the CCF Party, now the NDP, speaking in support of legislation which would change the name of Twin Lakes in Whiteman Pass to Grassi Lakes, paid the following tribute to Lawrence. The quotation from Hansard, sincere, eloquent, and with a fullness of content, sums up the spirit of the deeds of Grassi. A quiet man, who lived alone, who labored as a master miner at the face of coal tunnels, because of his daring mountain deeds and his outstanding community activities – this man was sought out and honored by both distinguished and common Canadian men and women.[177]

The Woodsworth tribute Wait provides is, in part, as follows:

> Last summer I spent a month in a little mining town in the Rockies. For me, the most interesting individual in the community was Lawrence Grassi, an Italian miner ... In the course of a prolonged strike, instead of loafing about the village, he set off into the hills, axe on shoulder,

Board on Geographic Names made a request for the official re-naming of Grassi Lakes (161). A letter of response dated April 6, 1960 noted that the name change was official in 1927.

[175] N. A. Wait, "Grassi of Canmore," in *The Canadian Golden West*, 1969, 24-25.

[176] Wait, 25.

[177] Wait, 24.

to make trails to points of interest. It was a labor of love. He loved the mountains, but enjoyed having others share their beauty…. The world needs Grassis. In the realm of the spirit, in the search after truth, in the field of social relationships, in politics, in economics, in international affairs, we need trail makers ….[178]

Edna Appleby in her 1975 Canmore history, and Jon Whyte in *Tommy and Lawrence* (1984) repeat Wait's dating and Woodsworth's role in the renaming.[179] This was accepted until Costa and Scardellato pointed out that the naming of Grassi Lakes occurred in 1927 and there was no record in Hansard. They note that Woodsworth and his family met Grassi in 1927 when he guided them during a vacation in the Rockies. They cite two articles by Woodsworth in which he praises Grassi: the first appeared in the July 1927 issue of *Weekly News*, the newspaper of the Manitoba Independent Labour Party; and the second, titled "The Trail Maker" in the September 23, 1927 issue of the *Jewish Post*. He writes in the latter:

> This summer I spent a month in a little mining town in the mountains. For me, the most interesting individual in the community was an Italian miner, Lawrence Grassi. He came into public notice two years ago when at great personal risk he performed a feat of strength and skill in carrying an injured Alpine climber to safety. But years before he was recognized in the community as being different from those about him. In the course of a prolonged strike instead of loafing about the village he set off into the hills, axe on shoulder, to make trails to points of interest. It was a labour of love.[180]

According to Appleby, the Woodsworth family spent two summers in Banff as guests of the "Y" (Canadian Youth Hostel Association, Mountain Region).[181]

It is ironic that the Methodist minister who offered a less-than-flattering view of Italians in his book *Strangers Within Our Gates*, should praise one individual who was both an immigrant and a member of the working class. This about face was due to the fact that Woodsworth had undergone a crisis of conscience after the Winnipeg General Strike of 1919 and had taken up the labour cause as well as championing socialist beliefs. This prompted him to run for Parliament

---

[178] Wait, 24.
[179] See Appleby, 103-104 and Whyte, 53-54.
[180] Costa and Scardellato, 163.
[181] Appleby, 100.

in 1921 in Winnipeg Centre.[182] In 1926-27, Woodsworth introduced a bill supporting the first minimal old age pension. In his working life, while Grassi was a miner and member of the working class, his achievements in trail building and mountaineering elevated him to another level, and challenged negative stereotypes of Italians. Final honours for Grassi include the naming of Mount Lawrence Grassi, located south of Canmore and east of the Spray Lakes Road, a Province of Alberta Achievement Award, which he received in 1977, and the naming of the Lawrence Grassi Middle School in Canmore.

Lethbridge Valley

Census records reveal that Italian immigration to Lethbridge in the early decades of the twentieth century was limited: the Italian population numbered 19 in 1911 but increased to 204 by 1921.[183] The majority worked in the mines. Other mining communities developed in the region, among them Diamond City, in 1905; Coalhurst (originally Bridgend), in 1911; and Commerce (originally Coalgate), in 1912. A significant number of Italian workers resided in these communities; for example, by 1921, Coalhurst had 99 Italians and Commerce had 92. The Chinook Company Limited mines in Commerce and Coalhurst, in 1918, had 43 and 29 Italian workers, respectively, of a total of 166 and 366.[184] While Lethbridge grew as the regional urban centre providing a range of services, the development of the other communities strictly depended on the health of the mines. Coalgate was a boom and bust community with a peak population of 360 in 1921 but, with closure of the Chinook Mine in 1924, the population dwindled to about 100; it finally dissolved in 1926. The mine in Coalhurst located northwest of Lethbridge continued to prosper and the town had a population of about 1,200 in 1935 when disaster struck the Imperial Mine. Afterwards, most immigrant miners moved to Lethbridge for work but the community survived because agriculture was well established. Historian Howard Palmer noted that the 204 Italians in Lethbridge in 1921 were likely mostly single miners who lived on the north side.[185] In fact, many were married and had families. These included the Ermacoras, Simeones, Bacedas, Lizzis, Locatellis, Bridarollas, Valerios, Cattois, Chistes and others. While there are conventional histories of

[182] Woodsworth's interest in labour resulted in his becoming a founder of the Co-operative Commonwealth Federation, the CCF political party, a precursor of the NDP.

[183] See Howard Palmer, *Land of the Second Chance: A History of Ethnic Groups in Southern Alberta* (Lethbridge, AB: The Lethbridge Herald, 1972), 175-177.

[184] Alex Johnston, Keith G. Gladwyn and L. Gregory Ellis, *Lethbridge: Its Coal Industry* (Lethbridge, AB: The Lethbridge Historical Society, Occasional Paper No. 20, 1989), 51.

[185] *Ibid.*, 176.

Lethbridge, there is no community history to provide immigrant stories; however some Lethbridge mining families are found in *Our Treasured Heritage: A History of Coalhurst and District* and *The History of Diamond City and Commerce*, since the men moved from mine-to-mine in the region.[186] As with other mining communities, many of the Italian families came from northern Italy.

The most significant and tragic event in Coalhurst's history is the the mining disaster of December 9, 1935. Between 4 and 4:30 pm, while shifts were changing, a methane explosion deep in the mine killed 16 miners. Three, badly-burned men struggled to the surface and rescue teams immediately set to work and recovered 16 bodies in three trips underground. The casualties included three Italians dead – Angelo Ermacora, a father of 10, Albino Simeone, single, and E. Rota, a father of two – and one injured, John Saccardo. Had the disaster occurred during a full shift, the casualties would have been much higher. A Royal Commission was called and the rumour circulated that a mine worker may have dropped his electric safety lamp resulting in a shattered bulb, creating a spark that ignited the gas.

Funerals took place on Friday, December 13; Mayor D. H. Elton of Lethbridge arranged for a special train to bring up to 400 mourners from mining communities from the Crowsnest Pass to Drumheller. Reflecting the different religious denominations of those killed, there were three church services: a 9 am Catholic Mass at the Greek Catholic Church in North Lethbridge; a 10 am Mass at St. Patrick's Roman Catholic Church; and a Protestant service at 3 pm. A funeral cortege comprising numerous cars brought families and mourners to the Catholic and Protestant cemeteries in the city. Residents lined up to pay their respects and some walked the route to the cemeteries. The Canadian Legion participated and various bands paraded with covered drums. The local paper estimated that about 5,000 mourners gathered at the cemetery where a bugler played the "Last Post."[187] Lethbridge stores and other businesses closed for an hour to honour the dead and all flags in the city were flown at half-mast.

Angelo Ermacora came to Canada in the early 1900s from Arzene, Pordenone. He homesteaded in the Lac La Biche area and, after a year of struggling, moved to southern Alberta and obtained work in the Royal View Mine in Lethbridge. He later worked at the mine at Commerce and, in 1912, was able to bring his wife and children Louis, Teresa and Bertha over (daughter Yolanda was left behind with her grandparents). Their next move was to Coalhurst in 1914 where

---

[186] Italian family profiles in the Lethbridge region can be found in *Our Treasured Heritage: A History of Coalhurst and District* (Lethbridge, AB: Coalhurst Historical Society, 1984) and *The History of Diamond City and Commerce* (Diamond City, AB: Diamond City Historical Society, [1996]).

[187] Details of the funeral are presented in an article titled "No Christmas this Year" by Janine Coombes, in *Our Treasured Heritage*, 154-161.

they lived in a company house and the family continued to grow. Besides working in the mine, Angelo delivered coal and water in the community. He saved his money and purchased a 60-acre parcel of land from the Coalhurst Collieries and built a house. Like other miners who had the opportunity and skills, he farmed for six months in spring and summer and worked in the mines during the winter months. Son Louis joined him in the mines at the age of 14. The family had to sell the farm on his death and their only support came from l'Ordine Indipendente Fior d'Italia.

Camillo Bridarolla left Trento and came to Canada in 1924 and, according to an oral history interview, he decided to join his uncle in Lethbridge to escape the conflict between the Fascists and Socialists.[188] Because of a strike, he was unable to find work initially; he succeeded eventually obtaining work at Coalhurst and was employed in the mine until 1931. He felt that he made good money – $7 to $8 a day – not in salary but contracted based on tonnage extracted. He noted that this was more money than he could earn by farming and he worked shorter hours. During the Depression, he worked for two years in what he described as a "gopher hole mine" near Lethbridge. The mine was a simple hole in the ground with no workings. With an Italian partner, he then operated a similar coal mine and noted that many Italians worked for them. All of the work was done manually. Farmers came to the mine to buy coal for $2.50/ton. In 1944, he sold out to his partner and moved to Lethbridge. He did this for the sake of his family – he had three daughters and one son – and wanted them to get a good education and it was too far for them to travel to Lethbridge for schooling. He did not return to mine work but operated a bakery for four years.

Antonio Valerio immigrated in 1904 and worked as a farm labourer in Lethbridge region initially before going to work in the mines.[189] The 1911 census shows his occupation as miner and he is a boarder in the household of an Italian couple, Darla and Elmira Basarich and their two children, who also immigrated in 1904. Antonio left behind his wife and two sons and a daughter. In 1913, he sponsored son Louis, who was 17, and who joined him in the mines.[190] Louis met wife Maria in Lethbridge and son Tony, named in honour of his grandfather, was born in 1923. In an oral history interview, Tony notes that the Italian community was not large, and the majority of men worked in the mines. Most came from the Friuli region (north-east Italy). He believes that it was not a tight-knit community – except for the miners who worked in the No. 3 mine. They had an Italian Club, which was the only Italian organization. His father worked in the mines for over 40 years and was committed to his sons' education so that they need not work

---

[188] Camillo Bridarolla, oral history interview, Dante Alighieri Society, 1973, PAA AN 74.106/4.

[189] Tony and Nina (Carloni) Valerio oral history interview, August 18, 1988, People of Southern Alberta Oral History Project, Glenbow Archives RCT-854.

[190] Louis Valeria, misspelled as "Vallairs" appears in the 1916 Census of Canada.

in the mines. Tony observed that at least 50 percent of Italian young people left the community and his mother advised him to do so. He completed high school and, in 1942, was drafted into the Canadian Army (he had been a cadet in Lethbridge) but preferred to join the Air Force. From 1942 to 1945, he served as an armourer in Calgary, Ireland and Wales. After the war, with funding support from Veterans' Affairs, he took sheet metal courses and then worked for 28 years at the Southern Alberta Institute of Technology (SAIT).

Drumheller Valley

The mines in the Drumheller Valley attracted many Italian immigrants and their stories are told in *The Hills of Home: Drumheller Valley*.[191] More than 130 mines operated in the period 1911 to 1979 and, in the early part of the twentieth century, the *Calgary Albertan* reported that Drumheller was "the fastest growing town in Canada, if not all of North America."[192] With the coming of the railway, the town became a commercial and coal-mining centre. Frank Moodie established the Rosedale Mine in 1912 and actively recruited European miners because he could pay them less than miners from the UK, or other parts of Canada. Moodie rejected unionization but, by 1919, many of the miners threw their support behind the One Big Union (OBU). Returning First World War veterans resented the fact that individuals who they viewed as "enemy aliens" had jobs and they did not. Moodie hired returning vets and not only the Rosedale Mine but also others in the valley saw violent confrontations as the 1919 General Strike took hold in coal mining communities in western Canada. The UMWA sided with government and the Royal North West Mounted Police to stop strikers from destroying mine equipment. With the failure of the OBU, Moodie re-hired immigrant miners and let the returning vets he had hired to break the strike go (some have suggested that they were let go because they were ineffective and lazy).

The population of the Drumheller Valley reached about 10,000 by 1920, about one quarter of that in the town. In that period, the 29 mines employed 200 men, which increased to 700 by the end of the decade. In comparison to the work force in mines in the Crowsnest, Nordegg and Coal Branch regions, this is a smaller number and, therefore, the Italian population of these communities was small and most left with mine closures in the 1950s. Italians worked at most mines in the Valley and there was a significant presence at East Coulee, Rosedale, Wayne

---

[191] Drumheller Historical Association, *The Hills of Home: Drumheller Valley* (Drumheller: Drumheller Valley Historical Association 1973).

[192] *Ibid.*, 37.

and the Sunshine Camp. Early families included the Cattinis, Castellis, Clozzas, De Bernardos, Miglierinas, Pedrinis and Stoccos.

There is a significant phenomenon in the Drumheller Valley that does not occur in the larger mining communities – ownership of some of the mines by Italian immigrants. The most significant Italian mine owners in the area were the Stocco family. Santo and Luigia (nee Mozzocco) Stocco arrived in Canada in 1913 as honeymooners but decided to stay. They initially lived in Calgary but, in 1916, moved to Drumheller and started the Roma Grocery Store and boarding house on Railway Avenue. The couple had three children – Reno, Rinaldo (Jim) and Tegla. In 1920, they sold the store to the De Bernardo family. With a group of shareholders (mostly family and friends), they took over the Sunshine Mine, two miles from Wayne. When the deposit was mined out, they started a second mine, the Superior Grade Mine, also in the Drumheller Valley; this too was known as the Sunshine Mine. In 1929, Santo died and Luigia continued the mine operation with the other shareholders. This was an incredible act of courage and defies the stereotype of the submissive Italian wife whose domain was the kitchen and garden. When the second Sunshine Mine closed in 1932, Luigia and her associates – Joe Sandino, Pete Martini, Giovanni Guidolin, Joseph Florian and Emil Eggenberger – bought the Scranton Mine at Midlandvale.[193] When the coal ran out, they bought the remaining leases held by the Western Gem Mine and created the Brilliant Mine. The mine operated from 1935 to 1957, among the last mines in the area to close. It was managed by Joe Sandino and Angelo Clozza, who had married Tegla Stocco in 1943; he served as fire boss and, from 1949, was the top boss.[194] Matriarch Giulia Clozza was there at the end and saw her son-in-law Angelo sell off the assets.

Angelo Clozza was born in Varmo, Udine and was sponsored, in 1927, by his sister Rosalia whose husband Verginio had immigrated and worked at the Newcastle/Drumheller mine. The 17-year-old became the family's breadwinner since Verginio was ill and helped raise his two nephews, Orfeo and Nello, and niece Leanna. He worked initially in the building of the East Coulee railway and then at the North American Collieries and the Western Gem mines. He also studied for pit boss qualifications. After the Brilliant Mine shut down, Angelo worked for a short time at the Hy-Grade Mine. He ended his working life as a store clerk in his brother-in-law Jim Stocco's grocery store in Drumheller – Jimmie's Super Market. Angelo and Tegla had two children

[193] Ancestry.ca searches reveal that a Giovanni Guidolin and Joseph Florian resided in Carbon, Alberta, and were miners; Emil William Eggenberger resided in the Red Deer area.

[194] Tegla (Stocco) Clozza, "Recollections of Life in the 'Sunshine Camp'," in *The Hills of Home: Drumheller Valley*, 572-576. See also "Stocco, Clozza family helps build an industry," in the *Drumheller Mail*, 30 April, 2011.

– Gordon and Louise. Gordon became a lawyer and subsequently an Alberta Provincial Court Judge in Drumheller; Louise had two careers, first as a teacher and later as a librarian.

Tegla (Stocco) Clozza was born in Drumheller in 1917, thus, she was among the first Canadian-born children of Italian miners in the community. In *The Hills of Home: Drumheller Valley*, she provides a loving account of the early days at the Sunshine Mine. While she recounts her own experiences, they are representative of life in coal mining communities and pioneering life in Alberta. She writes:

> Having no electricity, coal oil lamps were used, pails were hung by ropes into a well serving as refrigeration; in the winter the weather took care of this. We had coal stoves and out-door privies. The homes inside were roughly finished. There were wide boards nailed throughout. Winter time, we judged the cold by the higher frozen nail, whereas with summer rains, containers were placed here and there to catch the dribbles of water seeping in. Mouse traps were in most corners of the homes. The summers were great for continual swimming in the creek. Apart from this, there were only sponge baths or our yearly trip to Calgary, and the glory of getting into a real bath tub. All laundry was done by hand, in tubs, using wash-boards. [195]

She also provided details about how families avoided purchasing store-bought food and raised their own. Many not only had extensive vegetable gardens but also kept chickens, geese, pigs and cows as well as hunting and fishing.

Her mother served as a midwife as well as providing home remedies to the community: "Many were our remedies – for stomach pains the castor oil was always ready. Pure olive oil for sun-burn, also for the hair in that once in a while attack of lice, common among children in those days. Goose grease as an ointment for itch or rash, bed bug marks. Our daily vitamin Cod liver, the picture on the bottle of 'the man struggling with that Cod fish,' as big as himself.... More serious cases, the invalids were placed on a railroad hand-car and taken to the hospital in Wayne or Drumheller."[196] With respect to the social and cultural life of the community, she describes ball games, Saturday night dances with the "self-made orchestra," the weekly picture show in Wayne, group singing, outdoor bowling and card games. She also notes that the families made their own wine and "moon-shine" even though it was illegal.[197]

---

[195] Tegla Clozza, "Recollections of life in the 'Sunshine Camp,'" 573.
[196] *Ibid.*, 574-575.
[197] *Ibid.*, 576.

Some families were dogged by tragedies. In 1907, Antonio Violini married Maria Livieri and, in 1909, left his home in Pesaro, central Italy, to come to Canada. He was sponsored by brother Giovanni, who had immigrated in 1906 and worked in the Bankhead Mine. Antonio also worked in the mine but returned to Italy to marry finally returning to Canada in 1912 with his wife and four-year-old daughter. Around 1914, the family moved to Drumheller so that he could work in the mines. The move did not bring them luck – in the 1920s, the couple lost three young children. They were so poor that one of the children, who died in 1922, was buried in a "Free Lot" (the equivalent of a pauper's grave). This was to be the fate of an additional baby, born in 1927. Maria supplemented the family's meagre earnings by doing laundry for the local doctor and the funeral parlour. A strong religious faith allowed them to bear their misfortunes and one child, born in 1915, entered the Grey Nuns and became Sister Violini. The family eventually moved to Calgary living in the Italian community at Sunnyside.[198]

The Martinis were relatives of the Violinis and had a parallel immigration history. John Martini was born in Treviso and came to Canada around 1907 to work in the Bankhead Mine and later in Exshaw. Brother Umberto joined him in 1912 at the age of 34 and worked winters in the mines in Drumheller and summers in the cement plant at Exshaw from 1912 to 1929. The younger Umberto (Bert) tried his hand at farming but then worked with his father in the mines and cement plant. He married Olga Violini in 1939 and the couple settled in Vegreville where son Gerald was born and twin sons Larry and Barry. Bert's sister Irma married Pete Martini (no relation), a co-owner of the Brilliant Mine, and their grandson is figure skater Paul Martini.[199] He partnered with Barbara Underhill and, from 1979 to 1983, the pair was Canadian national champion; and, in 1984, World champion. The couple represented Canada in the 1980 Winter Olympics placing ninth; in 1984, they placed seventh.

Giovanni Battista (John) Castelli came to Canada in 1912 and worked in the mines at Corbin, BC. He returned to Italy in 1922 and married Santina Miglierina. The couple returned to Canada and joined her brother Ercole Miglierina and sister-in-law in Drumheller. Unable to find work, John and Santina returned to Corbin where their son, Louis, was born in 1923.

---

[198] There are two accounts of some miraculous activities associated with Father Gene, specifically with respect to St. Joseph Mission church in Cowley, Alberta. Paul Fournier wrote an article titled "Father Gino (Eugene) Violini: Eucharistic miracle in Alberta, Canada," posted on Sunday, August 1, 2004 in the website titled *Michael for the Triumph of the Immaculate*, URL: http://www.michaeljournal.org/articles/roman-catholic-church/item/eucharistic-miracle-in-alberta-canada, retrieved July 6, 2017. See also Kathy Roe, *Memories of Father Gino Violini* (Calgary: Self-published, 2014. URL: http://www.blurb.ca/b/5894952-memories-of-fr-violini), retrieved July 6, 2017.

[199] This information is drawn from an interview conducted by the author with Larry Martini and on an article titled "Dragon finds family roots in Drumheller," by Patrick Kolata, which appeared in the *Drumheller Mail*, February 25th, 2004.

Their daughter Maria was born in 1926, the same year in which he was able to find work in Drumheller for the Elgin Coal Company and, later, Hy-Grade Coal. The Castellis were strong believers in education and both children completed their schooling in Drumheller and went on to the University of Alberta. Louis completed a B Sc in Electrical Engineering (1946) and M Sc in Mathematics and Physics (1948). He went on to postgraduate studies at the Sloane School of Business at the Massachusetts Institute of Technology in 1967. He had a stellar career in the petroleum industry beginning work as district geophysicist for Mobil Oil Canada Ltd. in 1950 and moving up the ranks to district exploration manager (1960) and chief geophysicist (1964). He then became region exploration manager for Mobil in Denver (1966); general manager Corpus Christi division in Texas (1969); and a number of other positions culminating in his appointment as vice president exploration and producing services in 1975. In 1981, he became president and CEO of Moore McCormack Energy, Inc. In 1982, he was appointed Director of the Institute of Petroleum Computation at Colorado State University. Maria completed a degree in Home Economics and worked for the Calgary General Hospital.

Giovanni (John) Michielin was born in 1885 and arrived in the Drumheller Valley in June 1914. He worked in various mines until development of the Moonlight Mine. Son, Ido, in the family history provides a devastating picture of the life of local miners as follows: "During these years 1923-1926 I watched many of the miners' pitiful shacks being built. Many were made of the grain and coal doors which were used to seal the box cars when they were loaded. These were taken at night from the mine spur tracks. The night watchmen closed their eyes to this pilfering, because they knew what little money was earned was needed for food."[200] The appalling nature of miners' housing was noted in the 1919 Alberta Coal Mining Commission report. This was not a "model" mining community like Nordegg, Mountain Park and Cadomin. The family's story is one of initial tragedy, which Ido describes as follows:

> My Mother died of Typhoid Fever three months after I was born. She washed her clothes in the Red Deer River as she did in Italy as a girl. She became ill because of drinking the water on a hot summer day. She was extremely shy and timid and could not be persuaded to enter the new Hospital which had been built in 1919 at Drumheller. She preferred to stay in the floorless shack until she died early in 1921….When Mother died I was raised by the same lady, as Dad never remarried. He moved from mine to mine and helped to keep me and her family because her husband was invalided for many years.[201]

[200] Ido Michielin, "Ramblings and Reminiscences of 50 Years in the Drumheller Valley," in *The Hills of Home*, 467.
[201] *Ibid.* 467.

Virginia was just 29. Ido went to school in Drumheller and remembers the 1926 strike when supporters of the OBU and the UMWA clashed with each other and mounted police: "Quite a few heads were thumped with pick-handles and the like. I remember too a column of Mounted Provincial Police and police cars with Lewis guns mounted on the fenders. They paraded up the length of Ploeg St. in a show of strength."[202] As a boy, he spent week nights with other children on the slag heaps finding lumps of coal missed by slate pickers to be used for heating and cooking in their homes. He continues: "Later during the early thirties many families mined their own coal. The coal seam was a bare twelve feet under the houses. I knew of at least ten families who mined their own coal and it was not unusual to hear a miner's pick digging away under your feet while we played in the back yards."[203] The Great Depression struck mining communities hard and miner's son Roy Berlando took part and documented hunger marches in Drumheller, Calgary and Edmonton in 1932.[204] The glory days of the second decade of the twentieth century when Drumheller was viewed as Canada's "Miracle City" and its population had leapt from 50 in 1911 to 3,000 in 1916, were long gone.

While recounting stories of hardships, Ido also reminisces about happy moments observing:

> At the Newcastle across from the present Dinosaur Hotel the mine Union picnics were held. There was quite a mixture of sports indulged in. I can recall the coal loading contests, climbing the greasy pole for the big ham that was tied to the top; releasing a greased pig amongst the huge throng of miners and their families; the games of quoits and horseshoes; playing cricket, and the bagpipes of the Army and Navy Veterans club playing for the Highland dances. I can remember the Hungarian Fruit Dances in the old Demett's hall and the many Ukrainian dances at the Labor Temple, not to forget the old Army and Navy hall which stands today as an old warehouse. Many a square dance I enjoyed there.[205]

Ido also provides insight into prostitution: "Long after I was married, my dad told me of the girls who plied their ancient trade there [in the old Newcastle Hotel] on a circuit which took in many of the mining towns through the Crowsnest Pass and Lethbridge."[206] There were four whorehouses and, during Prohibition, bootlegging and gambling flourished.

---

[202] *Ibid.*, 468.

[203] *Ibid.*, 468.

[204] See Roy Berlando Fonds, Provincial Archives of Alberta PR1882.

[205] Michielin, 468.

[206] *Ibid.*, 469. The buildings in Drumheller with prostitution linkages are mentioned by Michael Gaschnitz in the *Drumheller Main Street Programme Historical Building Report*, August 28, 1989.

Ido joined his father in the Midland Mines and "batched" with him until 1939 when he enlisted in the Royal Canadian Air Force. Because of the scarcity of men, miners at this time stayed at their jobs and did not drift from one mine to another. Army service had an unexpected benefit – it resulted in improved living conditions for families. Ido writes: "Their wives settled down and improved the little Company houses and waited for their men to come home. After the war these homes were bought from the mine owners and further improved to make some of the nice homes we see in Midland today."[207] In 1945, Ido married Anne, an Edmonton girl who had been orphaned at five years of age, in 1928, and had been raised by nuns and thought she was going to be a nun until she decided to join the Canadian Women's Army Corps. In 1944, she had an adverse reaction to a vaccination and was blinded. She joked about visiting Drumheller in 1943 during Christmas leave and later marrying the first man she met. Son, Rick studied music at the University of Alberta and made his career in teaching music in Edmonton at the Louis St. Laurent High School and as a saxophone player.

Edmonton

Over 100 mining companies operated from 1880 to 1970 in Edmonton. Italian immigrants worked in many, in particular, at the Humberstone Mine located in Beverly (later annexed by Edmonton), which was situated on the north bank of the North Saskatchewan River, and the Black Diamond Mine, on the south bank of the River. Miners included Giuseppe Pecori; Joe Marta; Giovanni Rosso; Giacomo and Giovanni Sartor; Silvio Tona; the Del Bosco brothers – Luigi, Celeste, Giovanni and Federico; cousins Antonio and Giuseppe Biamonte; and Francesco (Frank) De Filippo.

A number of members of the Biamonte family, brothers and cousins, from Gimigliano, Calabria came to Edmonton at various times. Antonio (Tony) Biamonte was the first and ended up working in labouring jobs in Buffalo, Pickering, New York, Niagara Falls and Winnipeg. In 1905, with members of the Zagordi family, he travelled to Edmonton and was hired by Alex Dunne, owner of the Black Diamond Mine. In 1912, he sponsored his younger brother Domenico and cousin Giuseppe (Joe) Biamonte. Tony found them jobs in the Black Diamond Mine and eventually they also obtained company housing onsite; these were very modest cottages. Niece Loretta (Biamonte) Villeneuve wrote in a family history: "Tony eventually took a correspondence course in Stationary Engineering and became the Chief Engineer of the Black Diamond mine – a position he was to hold for forty years. Tony's older brother Giuseppe (Pep) arrived at some

---

[207] *Ibid.*, 471.

point and worked with Tony at the mine until his death from a flu-type illness in 1916 at 34 years of age (nine years before Dad came to Canada)."

With the death of older brother Giuseppe in 1916 and, then, younger brother Domenico in the mid-1920s, Tony became the family member with the greatest financial responsibilities. He was financially shrewd and invested in real estate. He purchased a two-shop building at 10271- 97 Street and this became an income property. Tony's wife Angelina Marazzo joined him and they had four children, Maria, Aida, Aurora and Domenic. His relative wealth allowed him to build a home on Valleyview Crescent in the 1950s; this was one of Edmonton's new wealthy neighbourhoods in the west end. Tony was a fervent believer in the importance of education and was a visionary in ensuring that his three daughters received a full education becoming teachers. Aida taught at St. Mary's High School (now J. H. Picard) and Maria at St. Joseph's High School in Edmonton. Aurora received a doctorate in education from Columbia University in the US and taught psychology and statistics there. Maria and Aurora created the Antonio & Angelina Biamonte Clinical Research Memorial Fund at the University of Alberta Hospital Foundation as a tribute to their parents.

Joe Biamonte, Tony's cousin (the two families had a number of names in common), became the principal breadwinner for his branch of the family in Italy and could not shed this responsibility until he recruited the next-youngest brother to immigrate. He married Annina Marazzo, the sister of Tony's wife, in 1923, and the couple had two sons, Tony Biamonte, who became a popular broadcaster in Edmonton and Robert Donald (Don) Biamonte, a teacher and amateur actor who taught at Archbishop Macdonald High School. On his death in 2012, Don endowed a literature prize at the University of Alberta. Joe sponsored his other siblings, Napoleone, Luigi (Loretta's father), Garibaldi (Gary) and Salvatore (Sam), who came to Edmonton later.

S. Centazzo is an enigmatic figure the only traces of which are his testimony in Edmonton at the Coal Mining Industry Commission in 1919; memories of a few of Edmonton's Italian pioneers; and a few entries in genealogical materials. Pioneers remembered his Communist ideology that brought him out to Market Square downtown each May Day for labour marches and his expressed desire to have the "Red flag of the Revolution" draped over his casket. According to online records, Silvano Centazzo arrived in New York in 1905 on the *SS Touraine* from Le Havre and his birth date is noted as about 1887 and place of origin as Udine. Another travel listing is for "Sylvane" Centazzo, who arrived in August 1913 in Quebec on the *SS Ascania* from the port of Southampton.

David Bercuson included his testimony in *Alberta's Coal Industry 1919*, a summary of key testimony at the coal mining commission hearings after the 1919 General Strike. The Edmonton hearing took place on Monday, October 6, 1919. Centazzo's observations are intelligent and reveal that he worked in mines throughout Alberta in the previous 15 years, and that he was a strong union man. When asked by W. H. McNeill where he worked last, he responded, "Bush mine." When asked if he was working at present, he answered that he was not and, when asked why, continued: "Because it's impossible to get a job. I was one of the leaders, and I am under discrimination and you know very well all the leaders from the United Mine Workers they're up against it today. One is working on the section, and other one working on the section south and one way and another."[208] He notes that he had to get a job "in town" for three or four days a week. McNeill was the industry representative on the commission and managed the McNeill Brothers Coal Mines in Canmore. In 1912, he was appointed commissioner (executive secretary) of the Western Coal Operators Association.

Centazzo's testimony expresses the union's position with respect to pay, right to be a union member, the 8-hour day, mine safety and conditions of work. By the time he gave his testimony, he had heard company positions that were anti-union including that of G. S. Montgomery, General Manager, Alberta Coal Mining Co., Edmonton who states:

> Strikes are called without any reason, without any sense. The strike that was called on May 24th at our mine was the most senseless and silly strike that was ever pulled off in Alberta. There was not a single demand made on us for higher wages, the conditions were satisfactory, and the men were all satisfied. Why should they strike? Along came one of these fellows – a parasite that lives off these people. He cracked his fingers and all these fellows came out and stayed out all summer. These labour leaders are very solicitous for the welfare of the miners. They lost those fellows $85,000 in wages; lost us $414,000 in business and damages in our mine. For what?[209]

The strike certainly was intended to demonstrate labour solidarity across the country but the issue for miners were very real. Montgomery notes that contracts should have penalty clauses and that the 8-hour day should be abolished. (He mentions that their employees who have homesteads want to work as many hours as possible.) He goes so far as to observe: "That compulsory 8-hour law is tyrannical, autocratic, it's un-British."[210] He continues on this tack noting that only British subjects should be eligible to become union members because the "troublemakers" in the union

---

[208] David J. Bercuson, *Alberta's Coal Industry 1919* (Edmonton, AB: Alberta Records Publication Board, Historical Society of Alberta, 1978), 42. The volume comprises edited transcripts of the hearings. The Centazzo testimony appears on pages 42-52.
[209] *Ibid.*, 37.
[210] *Ibid.*, 38.

movement were "aliens" and had too much power. When challenged by Commissioner W. Smitten on denying rights to certain miners, Montgomery observes – "Because it is a British country."

As chairman of the Edmonton Miners' Local, Centazzo was at loggerheads with Montgomery and the tension in both their testimonies suggests personal animosity. Centazzo picks up on Montgomery's observation that only English miners should be allowed to speak and questions whether he has permission to speak since he is not English. This demonstrates wit on his part but also a subliminal desire to make fun of his adversary. He is told to go ahead by Chairman J. T. Stirling, provincial Chief Inspector of Mines, and focuses on grievances including the poor condition of the washhouses in mines throughout Alberta. Centazzo notes that the Mining Act prescribed that water should be available but, in his experience, it frequently was not. As well, the wooden box used to dry clothes was not a screen box but rather a solid box so that clothes cannot dry. He also focuses on safety lamps observing: "We have cold weather in this country, some time 45 below zero, and the miners go to stand outside there waiting for the fire boss to put the lamp – examine the lamp. The miners have to stay there 15 to 20 minutes in some mines where there's a big crew. It seems to me, speaking humanity, there should be a big room there so the miners can go in and warm themselves instead of stay in the cold weather outside."[211]

Centazzo proceeds to make a series of recommendations including: each miner be allowed to carry a small electric lamp in his pocket in case of emergency because this could save lives; several blankets and first-aid materials including a stretcher should be placed in every section of the mine; and enforcement of the 8-hour day. He is questioned about his nationality, which he states as Italian, and admits that he is not "nationalized" and observes that he arrived in Alberta in September 1913 from London, England. He also admits that he is an OBU supporter, which is doubly damning since the UMWA had sided with the federal and provincial governments in opposing them.

Francesco Chiarello left Savelli, Crotone, Calabria in 1905 and first worked on the railroads in Minnesota and then followed other immigrants to Edmonton where he worked in the mines.[212] He returned to Italy in 1907 and married Costanza Anselmo and the couple had a son, Domenico. In 1912, he returned to Edmonton to work in the mines and three years later filed for a homestead near Legal (SW-2-64-23-4). In 1924, Costanza and Domenico joined him in Edmonton and father and son worked at the mine on Big Island near Edmonton and at Cardiff. In an oral

---

[211] *Ibid.*, 47.

[212] Histoire de Legal History Association, "Chiarello, Francesco & Constanza and Domenico & Nella (Anselmo)," in *Vision, Courage, Heritage: Legal 1894-1994, Vimy – Waugh – Fedorah*," vol. 2, Altona, MB: Histoire de Legal History Association, 1995), 300-302.

history interview, Domenico reminisced about the 16 days spent on the boat before arriving in Halifax.[213] He and his mother next took a train to Edmonton and passed another five days and six nights before reuniting with his father, who he had not seen in 12 years. Aged 17, he was the youngest worker in the mine. The community history notes: "He often spoke of the hardships endured during those years when he spent many 12-hour shifts, working in mine shafts so shallow that you could not stand upright. Often, he dreamed of getting enough money saved so that he could return to Italy. However, once he learned the language and became accustomed to life in Canada, he settled in and got his mining certificate while working at the Cardiff mine in 1927."[214]

Desiring to better their lot, Francesco and Domenico began to prospect for coal near their homestead and found a good seam. In 1927, they began operating the Legal Coal Mine #351 (SW-25-57-25-W4), which was large enough to require horses to work it. The community was grateful to have a ready coal supply. The Chiarellos also farmed and sold barley and wheat. In 1942, Domenico married Nella Anselmo of Edmonton and she joined him in Legal. Francesco died in 1947, and Domenico gave up his interest in the mine and decided to move his mother, wife and new-born daughter, Francesca (Frances) to Edmonton. There he started the Venice Confectionery, located at 97 Street and 106 Avenue. The couple assisted many of the Italian immigrants who arrived in the 1950s.

Some Observations

Coal mining was the Province of Alberta's first resource industry and it is clear that Italian workers played a vital role as can be seen in the geographically-based accounts. While the industry and the economic benefits that resulted have been studied by historians, the contributions of specific ethnocultural communities are still largely unexplored. The accounts of individuals and families have been catalogued for several reasons: first, they demonstrate the large presence of northern Italians in mining communities in Alberta; second, the motivations of immigrants to escape poverty and for economic betterment become clear at the level of the extended family. Oral and family histories have also allowed some of the specifics of the immigration and settlement experiences to be expressed in the words of the people who lived this part of our history.

Focusing on a single industry enabled discussion of the evolution of the Italian work force in a period of over 100 years. Boom and bust cycles, changes in technology and labour legislation have

---

[213] See Domenico Chiarello oral history, Dante Alighieri Oral History Project, 1973, interviewer Charles Grelli, Provincial Archives of Alberta AN 74.106/7; and Domenico Chiarello Fonds, PAA PR 1401.
[214] "Chiarello," *Legal History*, 301.

also been explored through their impacts on individual lives. In addition, as mining modernized and changed to meet the challenges of oil discoveries in Leduc and other areas of north-central Alberta in the late 1940s, the children of Italian immigrants, who had worked in the industry for over 50 years, were able to play significant roles as change agents in the rebirth of the mining industry.

From the earliest days, education was a driving force in social mobility. What is surprising is that, in some instances, movement out of the working class into the professions and other occupations occurred in the first generation. This was due to the exceptional commitment to education by individual families; what is surprising is that, frequently, this was not focused solely on male offspring. While racism did restrict options, it did not inhibit individuals from realizing their dreams of a better future not only for themselves but also their families.

Widow and child mourning at the grave of Luigi Ponti, Coleman, Alberta, January 6, 1924. He was born on May 20, 1900 in Italy and, according to the Blairmore Enterprise, worked for local livery and contracting firm Ponti & Bielli. He was loading railway cars with mine props near Crowsnest when some logs broke loose and he was crushed. He died in hospital in Lethbridge. His wife Josephine is 17. Photographer: Thomas Gushul. Glenbow Archives NC-54-2772.

The Canmore Elks Band, Canmore, Alberta, pictured in 1923. It had a number of Italian members: front row left to right: John Bertino, Harry Rhodda, Ben Rock; Heine Hubman, O. Verdesia, Leslie Hill, Harry Musgrove, John Balla, Lawrence Faletti, conductor; 2nd row left to right: Nellio Torino, Fred Verhuslt, John Verdesia, J. Giovanetti, A. Marro, Fred Marro, Tom Rappel, Ken Balla, Edward Dunbar; 3rd row left to right: William Lytkowski, Paul Hubman, Pete Balla, Sylvester Latvala, Charles Cochrane, Carl Kendall, William Musgrove, Edward Lewis, Cliff Dewis; 4th row L-R: Attilio Caffaro, C. Johnson, Charles Cochrane, Stewart Lynch, George Freethy, (first name unknown) Meili, Joe Bestwick, Albert Grainger; 5th row left to right: Ludwig (Ludovico) Massole, R. Smales, Harry Hunter, Dub Mackie and Bill Bobyk. Photo courtesy of Glenbow, Archives and Special Collections, University of Calgary NA-4073-1.

Francesco and Carolina Rusconi and daughters Angela and Florence at their Edmonton home in 1915. The Rusconis helped to set up the Naples Italian settlement in 1906. Photo courtesy of Provincial Archives of Alberta A10913.

CHAPTER IV

Settling the Land

WHEN CLIFFORD SIFTON, Liberal Minister of the Interior from 1896 to 1905, envisioned agricultural settlement, it was people of British, American and Northern European ancestry that he saw homesteading. The federal government initiated a major advertising campaign to entice "suitable" settlers to come to the Canadian west. Promotional literature included: *Twentieth Century Canada: Agriculture, Minerals Forestry*, published in 1906; and *The last best West: Canada West: Homes for millions: Grain raising, ranching, fruit raising, mixed farming, dairying*, 1908. Local municipalities followed suit; for example, the booklet *Edson, Alberta*, was published in 1915 by the board of trade and included testimonials from recent settlers. Homestead numbers in the Canadian Northwest increased from 2,384 in 1897 to 33,699 in 1912.[215] There was, however, a downside according to the Commission of Conservation Canada 1917 Report: the productivity in Alberta and Saskatchewan in wheat and cattle depressed the prices of these commodities thereby reducing earnings for farmers in eastern Canada. Western settlement exceeded the wildest dreams of Sifton and his successor Frank Oliver, and the pitting of east against west became the standard for interprovincial relations.

In this grand scheme, Italians did not even rate as potential settlers though some saw the promotional literature and responded to it. As well, a policy shift had occurred: the Montreal-based Italian Immigration Society from its founding in 1902 established the goal of eliminating sojourning and promoting settlement in the "Canadian Northwest." Subsequently, this became a function of the Italian consulate.[216] Of the men who came to work on the railways, few turned to agriculture. The conditions were radically different from those in Italy where farming occurred almost everywhere due to the temperate climate. Crops included grains, olives, grapes and a range of fruits, nuts, vegetables and livestock including beef and dairy cattle, water buffalo, sheep and goats,

---

[215] Commission of Conservation Canada, *Report of The Eighth Annual Meeting Held at Ottawa January 16-17, 1917* (Montreal, PQ: The Federated Press, 1917), 134. According to the report, eastern farmers "had to compete with wheat at 50 cents a bushel and cattle at 3 cents per lb., live weight," 134.
[216] Peck, "Mobilizing Community," 185-186.

swine and poultry. The majority of the land was held by landowners who made use of *contadini*, labourers or sharecroppers, who lived in conditions similar to medieval serfs, and who could never aspire to ownership. Where land was held by ordinary families, inheritance reduced plots to such a diminutive size that families could not be supported on the crops and animals they raised.

While their numbers may have been small (it would appear that not many more than about 150 Italian immigrants homesteaded), they nonetheless contributed to Alberta's agricultural development. Chain migration patterns also applied to agricultural settlement. The settlement experience prompted marriage and, if the individual was already married, then, family reunification. Thus, in the first two decades of the twentieth century, immigration numbers increased as women and children joined the men in the new land. Clusters of families farmed around communities such as Delia, Mayerthorpe, Lethbridge, Barrhead, Edson and Stettler. An unplanned agricultural colony developed at Naples in central Alberta and a planned colony in the Venice-Hylo area of northern Alberta. Whenever possible, men worked in mines or logging operations in the winter to earn money, and on their homesteads in the summer. This placed enormous strains on wives and children. Many of these early farmers were from northern Italy. The family histories provide an interweaving narrative of the joys and sufferings of settling the land.

Mines and Homesteads

Among the earliest who transitioned from sojourning to agriculture were friends from Fossacesia, Abruzzo in east-central Italy. The families are unique in also having Anglicized their names. Perhaps their experiences as sojourners led them to believe that they would have greater success with English surnames. They homesteaded around Delia and Craigmyle in southern Alberta. The former was 45 km northeast of Drumheller making mine work accessible. Among the most prominent families were the Marshalls, who changed their name from Masciangelo (Marsciangelo).[217] They were typical of Italy's agricultural poor. Michele and wife Anna Domenica by 1900 had ten children, six sons and four daughters. They lived on a small farm and the pressure for some sons to emigrate was enormous. Four sons made their way to Canada. The family serves as a case study for Italian agricultural settlement in Alberta and, since there are a number of family histories in *The Delia Craigmyle Saga*, their story can be fully fleshed out.[218]

---

[217] Jean Marshall, "The Giovannio Masciangelo Story – Better Known as Mr. and Mrs. John Marshall," in *The Delia Craigmyle Saga* (Lethbridge, AB: Southern Printing Company Limited, 1970), 360.

[218] The 1911 Census reveals that a number of Masciangelos settled around Medicine Hat including Donato Masciangelo, 26 years old, immigrated in1902; and Nicolo (22) and Lela (18), likely Daniele, who are described as brothers.

Giovanni (John) Masciangelo was born in 1883; left Italy in 1901; found work in Montreal with the assistance of a labour agent; and then moved to St. Catharines, Ontario to lay tracks for the Great Western Railway. The year 1904 was important: John went back to Italy to do two years of military service and brothers Daniele (Dan) and Nicola decided to immigrate and went to St. Catharines to work. John returned to Montreal in 1906 where he became friends with John Battle (formerly Angelozzi). There are several stories as to who made the decision to go west. John's wife Jean states that it was her husband and Battle who, at the St. Catharines train station, around 1908, saw a poster stating "Go West and Homestead." The fare to Winnipeg was $10. The friends left and worked for some farmers at Christmas City for two months, and then continued to Vancouver for a fare of $35. Having no luck in finding work there, they returned to Calgary where their job seeking also failed. They succeeded in obtaining 12-weeks' work in a logging camp in the Crowsnest Pass for $35 a month. They then spent a year working in the mines at Blairmore where they were paid two dollars a day. Jean notes:

> They decided in 1909 to go homesteading, so they came out to the north side of the Hand Hills and picked out the homesteads side by side. John Marshall took SW 1/4 27-30-17-W4 and John Battle took the NW ¼ 27-30-17-W4. The friendship of these two men continued through life. They were like brothers. The cost of the homestead was $10.00 for 160 acres. They had to break 30 acres and build a $300.00 house, which they did. Then after six years they were allowed a pre-emption quarter section at $3.00 an acre. John Marshall took the SE ¼ 27-30-17-W4 and John Battle took the NE ¼ 27-30-17-W4. This gave them each a half section. The next few years, when they were not farming, they worked out.[219]

According to Dan's daughter, Gladys Lewis, it was her father and his brother Nick who filed for homesteads (Section 25, Township 30, Range 17) in 1908 and were joined by brother John in 1909. She observes: "Dan and John operated a mine on the north side of the Hand Hills and got coal from there for years after. The three of them lived in a so-called shack, on Dan's farm. Then in 1912, Dad went back to Italy to get married. On March 19 of that year, he married Grace Luciano, who was only 16 years old. From the way they spoke about it afterwards, I think they eloped."[220]

Grace was totally unfitted to roughing it: not only was she homesick, she couldn't cook and had to be shown how to make simple things by her husband. The loneliness that Grace felt on the land

---

[219] Delia Craigmyle Historical Society, 360-361.
[220] Gladys (Marshall) Lewis, "Mr. and Mrs. Dan Marshall," in *The Delia Craigmyle Saga* (Lethbridge, AB: Southern Printing Company Limited, 1970), 349.

was the same as that experienced by many pioneer women. The family's tragedies were also those of other pioneers. These began when Nick died in 1911 or 1912 (accounts vary) as a result of an abscessed tooth; he was 23. The brothers were working on construction of irrigation ditches in the Bassano and Brooks area. They took Nick to a dentist in Brooks but the tooth was so badly infected that it could not be removed. Lockjaw developed and he died a very painful death shortly after.

The close relationship between the brothers is noted in all the family histories. Dan was the first to marry (Grace). John returned to Italy in 1913 and married Giancinta (Jean) Antonnelli.[221] Unlike her husband, who was barely literate, Jean had attended school and notes in the family history: "I had learned to crochet, knit, spin and weave linen. At one time I was able to weave twelve different patterns in linen. Thus I had a very nice dowery [sic.] of homemade linens to bring to Canada with me. Seven pairs of sheets, twelve towels, twenty serviettes and many pairs of pillow cases."[222] She recounts that, as a city girl, she felt alien but decided to learn English and adapt to her new circumstances. Their housing was primitive: they started in a one-room shack; water had to be brought in from the well; and a small coal stove was used for cooking and heating. Jean continues: "We had four horses with which we did the farming and also were used for driving teams. Groceries and shopping were got from Stettler or Munson and the Hand Hills store, where we also got our mail. Then the C.N. Railway came through Highland (now Delia) and businesses opened in town. From then on we could do most of our business and shopping in Delia."[223] The two siblings and their families lived parallel lives and helped each other: in order that John could work in the mines, Dan farmed his land.

The accounts include many details about the lives of women, in particular, childbirth. The sisters-in-law gave birth in 1913 – home births assisted by midwives. Jean notes: "On December 21, 1913, our first son was born prematurely. He was very small, with no fingernails or eyebrows or eye lashes. Mrs. James Scott came to assist me as midwife. We just had to do the best we could. Baby Michael was three weeks old before the doctor could come to see him." Other children quickly followed: Carl in 1915; Arthur, 1916; Anna, 1917; Mary, 1918; Patricia, 1920; Irene, 1922; Catherine, 1924; Violet, 1925; Jeanne, 1927; Lorraine, 1928; Josephine, 1931; and Elsie, 1932. A large family meant many hands to do farm work. While John and Jean's family was large, its ratio of three sons to 10 daughters would have been viewed as a disadvantage; typically, Italian families wanted male children rather than female. At the most basic level, their earning power was greater.

---

[221] *Ibid.*, 362.
[222] Jean Marshall, 362.
[223] *Ibid.*, 362.

The female perspective draws attention to the nature of medical assistance in pioneer communities. Jean notes: "Lorraine, our eleventh child, was born November 10, 1928, at the home of Mrs. Chas. Lees in Delia. Confinement was 10 days and we paid $3.50 a day, but the care was wonderful. Lorraine grew up and became a Registered Nurse and later a stewardess with Air Canada." In contrast, daughters Josephine and Elsie Jean Louise were born in the Craigmyle Hospital, under the care of Drs Kidd and Hicks, on August 19, 1931 and November 28, 1932, respectively.[224] A hospital birth attended by a doctor was likely the greatest wish of most pioneer women because of high rates of infant mortality in childbirth. Jean's pride in her daughter becoming a nurse demonstrates the high regard in which the medical profession was held. All branches of the Marshall family valued education and this included their daughters, which was a rarity in immigrant households.

In 1927, John's 20-year-old sister Margaret came from Italy to help look after the children. This type of family reunification was common since there were advantages on both sides: help in the household for the sponsoring family and possible marriage for the young immigrant woman. Sadly, this did not occur – she died two years later of spinal meningitis. Jean noted that Margaret was not only attended by Dr. Kidd but also two other doctors who made the diagnosis. This was important so that family in Italy would not infer that her illness had been neglected. Tragedy struck again in 1944 when daughter Violet died of "anaesthetic poisoning" while undergoing an emergency appendectomy.

Dan's wife Grace had a much more difficult time not only in childbirth but also in the health of her children. Her first child, Ernest, was born in 1913; Nick, in 1914; the couple's third child, Alfred, born in 1915 died of convulsions the same year while his mother was nursing him. Anna, the fourth child, was born in 1917 and died from an infection from improperly sterilized equipment in the midwife-assisted delivery. The next child, Fred, was sickly and almost died from scarlet fever. Happily, the next three children, Gladys (born 1921), Lily (1923) and Albert (1925) were all healthy. The families had a strong Catholic faith and the children were baptized at Holy Family Church in Delia.

The sisters-in-law were friends and Jean recounts that she and the children frequently walked three miles, to visit Grace. The women went to town once a month; the men went more frequently. The acquisition of a Model T Ford changed this and trips to Drumheller to Bernardo's General Store where they traded for groceries became frequent. Eventually the families went to Delia on Saturday to do the shopping and visit friends. Jean's account documents not only her own family's history but also that of the community and region. What is remarkable is that, unlike in mining

---

[224] *Ibid.* 364.

communities where social mobility was limited for Italians since many viewed them with distrust as enemy aliens, unionists or socialists, in this area of rural Alberta the Marshalls were accepted and prospered. Bearing an Anglo-Saxon name likely helped but all of the older generation spoke broken English so their "Italianness" was obvious.

Changes in housing marked the rise in the fortunes of the Marshall clan: both John and Dan built new homes in 1918. Jean notes that her house had four bedrooms upstairs, and a large farm kitchen, living room and dining room on the ground floor. The basement housed a furnace, which was the height of luxury. Jean notes that the builder was Mr. Scotty Murdock and that the men worked for $1.25 an hour. In 1928, four rooms were added to the east side of the house and the builders were Roger Rose and Bill Barss. The fact that others could be paid to do the work was an enormous step up from the homesteading experience. A large cistern in the basement provided hot water for the kitchen and bathroom, which had a large cast-iron tub. It did not, however, have a toilet so chamber pots and the outhouse remained part of daily life.

Gladys notes: "We had a happy and enjoyable home, lots of company and happiness but even so, times were hard. Dad always provided for us as he was a hard working man. He would take the two oldest children to the field and they would ride the horses all day while ploughing or discing or whatever had to be done. He was always a good father."[225] In 1927, Dan and Grace and four of the children visited Italy for six months. The fact that they had prospered sufficiently to return reinforced the belief that the streets of North America were paved with gold. According to Gladys, they all learned Italian but they were glad to return to Canada. This suggests that the Marshalls had established their lives in Canada on a solid foundation and did not experience nostalgia for the homeland. The family histories also document farming success and diversification into activities beyond simply tilling the soil. Jean notes that they built a big barn in 1922 and that they had 18 head of horses plus a stallion and that her husband always entered a team in the annual Delia Fair. The family entered all of the competitions and, for two years in a row, Jean won first prize for her apple pie.

In his portion of the family history, John and Jean's first-born, Michael notes that he did not begin school until he was eight because there was no school in the district.[226] Eventually, he and his brother Carl attended Georgetown school and then high school at Delia. He quit school when he turned 15 to help his father. He also helped John Battle in road-building in the Delburne area. Michael drove a four-horse team and in eight weeks earned $200. He thus contributed not

---

225 Gladys Lewis, 350.
226 Michael P. Marshall, "The Michael P. Marshall Story," in *The Delia Craigmyle Saga* (Lethbridge, AB: Southern Printing Company Limited, 1970), 367.

only his labour to the family farm but also cash. From the age of 14, he also helped his father and Battle run the steam engine and threshing machine and, from 1929 to 1941, was the bookkeeper for the business.

Michael's lack of extensive formal education did not limit his prospects: he was a self-starter and, in 1929-1930, he took an electricity course at the Southern Alberta Institute of Technology in Calgary. He stayed with the Nick Gallelli family, pioneers involved in construction. Michael understood the importance of mechanization and, in 1937 went to Calgary to buy a tractor. When he returned to the farm, he couldn't make it work so he traded it in for a new John Deere Model D. He paid $1,700 for it and negotiated a $550 trade-in for the old tractor that he had bought for $450. He knew instinctively how to use debt to improve the family's economic circumstances. He and brother Arthur borrowed $100 from a friend, Pete Caravaggio, and bought a 10-foot tiller and did custom work power binding. In 1938, with Harry Gallelli, he bought a 2-ton Ford truck and did commercial trucking for two years. He also built up the family's herd by using the government bull. In order to do this, six farmers had to sign up to use the bull and pay $10 a year each and jointly care for the animal.[227] When brothers Carl and Arthur joined the army, Michael continued to work on the farm. It appears that he did the day-to-day running of the farm because his father, from 1937, took over the management of the Blossom Coal Mine. Michael also worked in the mine in the winter. In 1943, he married Maude Margrette Morton of Hand Hills and the couple moved to the John Battle farm that was run by John Jr., who at the time was serving in the military. On his return, Michael and Maude moved to town. In 1948, they bought their own section of land. Their sons Stanley and Paul studied agricultural mechanics and worked the land with their father.

The outbreak of the Second World War brought changes to Dan and Grace's family: Ernest, Nick and Fred enlisted but returned unwounded. In 1940, daughters Gladys and Lily went to Calgary and found employment at the Palace Bakery earning $7.50 a week and, after a few months, got higher-paying jobs at McGavin's Bakery ($13.50 a week). In 1943, the federal government offered jobs for women in the Boeing Aircraft Plant in Vancouver and the two sisters decided to go. Lily worked there until the end of the war but Gladys returned to the farm as a result of surgery. On recovery, she returned to Calgary to work, initially, as an elevator operator at the Prince of Wales Hotel, then at the Jenkins Groceteria and, finally, at the Hudson's Bay store. She married Arthur Lewis, a CPR employee, in 1948.

Nick served overseas with the Royal Canadian Army Service Corps and Fred served with the Royal Canadian Electrical-Mechanical Engineers. The brothers brought back English war brides.

---

227 Jean Lewis, 369.

Ernest had married a local girl, Darlene Foye, in 1942. The brothers did not return to the land: Ernest worked in the mines at Drumheller; Fred at the Longmates Garage in Drumheller as a mechanic and bodyman; and Nick as a mechanic at Greyhound in Calgary. Albert, the youngest, continued to farm and, in 1950, as part of the second wave of Italian immigration, Dan's youngest sister, arrived at the farm. In 1948, Dan and Grace retired to Vancouver because "it reminded them of Italy with the fruit and mild winters," and Fred took over their farm.

Ernest had worked at the Willow Creek coal mine during the winters of 1936 to 1938 for his future wife's father, Ed Foye. In summer 1942, he returned to work at the North American Mine because they were short of labour and the coal industry was deemed critical to the war effort. He next worked at the Italian-owned Brilliant Coal Mine until 1949, when coal orders declined. He got a job at Drumheller Motors for a time and then returned to run the family farm. But all did not go smoothly and he observes: "In 1951, winter came in September and our crop laid out under the snow all winter.... In August, 1954, we were hailed out 100% and I was lucky enough to get a job as flagman when they were paving the No. 9 Highway between Delia and Drumheller."[228]

John Battle Sr., in his family history, recounts that he left Italy in 1903 at the age of 15 and met John Marshall on the boat to Canada. He writes:

> On a warm spring day in 1909 we arrived at our respective homesteads. My land, consisting of a half section, lay north of John's and a mile from the Hand Hills. The first night was spent in the log cabin of Mr. Skippen. We appreciated his hospitality as the cold wind was howling and blowing hard outside. To our dismay the next morning we found six inches of snow on the ground. Early that morning we drove over to our homesteads. We pitched our tent and unloaded all our belongings before travelling to the Hand Hills Store for supplies.[229]

They erected a barn for their horses; since it took four to pull the plough, they rented two from a neighbour and John proudly concludes: "We liked farming; it was great to be our own bosses and work in the fresh air."[230] As if to reinforce his decision to homestead, John notes that the man who replaced him at the Hillcrest Mine was killed.

---

[228] Ernest Marshall, "Ernest Marshall," in *The Delia Craigmyle Saga* (Lethbridge, AB: Southern Printing Company Limited, 1970), 356.

[229] John Marshall, "Story of John Battle Sr.," in *The Delia Craigmyle Saga* (Lethbridge, AB: Southern Printing Company Limited, 1970, 320.

[230] *Ibid.*, 320

But all did not go smoothly on the farm: after returning from doing some railroad work in Coronation, his horses escaped and headed for home. He had to walk home and comments that homesteaders along the way, though poor, were generous and housed and fed him. It would appear that Battle, like the Marshalls, did not experience discrimination. It took him two days to walk home and find the horses. He then went south to work at the irrigation project at Brooks for two months. A second, more-serious setback occurred in 1912 when a prairie fire burned his tent and destroyed the barn. In addition, he had to replace a horse at a cost of $250. This meant that he had to return to work in Brooks. In 1913, he married Faye Friedley, and she joined him in Brooks and cooked for the men while he worked on the irrigation ditches. While a capable wife was a huge asset, marriage outside the Italian community provided additional legitimacy. John and Faye, members of the Marshall family and other Italian immigrants worked on a historic irrigation project.[231] In 1908, the CPR created the Eastern Irrigation system, located in the Palliser Triangle, to transform range land with insufficient rainfall for cultivation into land for settlement (60 farms were created). Construction of the Bassano Dam began in 1909 and, in addition to the dam 4,800 km of ditches were created at a total cost of $10 million. Both the dam and the community were named for Napoleon Maret, the 3rd Duc de Bassano (1844-1906), a CPR shareholder from Quebec.[232]

In 1914, Faye gave birth to a son, Johnny, and Robert was born in 1916. The homestead yielded bumper crops in 1915 and 1916 though in the latter year, the crop froze. The next year, John built a home and purchased his first car, a Ford. In 1919, he was elected to the Michichi Municipal Board and served for three years; he also served as a Delia school trustee for eight years. A third son, Thomas, was born in 1920 but died at six months of whooping cough, which according to John, caused many deaths that year. Daughters Irene and Louise were born in 1922 and 1924, respectively. The family's run of good luck ended in January 1926 when Faye caught a cold resulting in a general infection and she died of septicemia in a Calgary hospital. John was left to care for four young children ranging in age from two to 12. He had a series of housekeepers to

---

[231] See A. A. den Otter, *Irrigation in Southern Alberta: 1882 – 1901*, Occasional Paper No. 5, Whoop-up Country Chapter, Historical Society of Alberta, Lethbridge, Alberta, 1975.

[232] The peerage was bestowed on Hugues-Bernard Maret, a journalist, diplomat and statesman by the Emperor Napoleon in 1809. It was linked to Bassano, a community in northern Italy, which was part of the Kingdom of Italy, established by Napoleon in 1805. The 3rd Duc, Napoleon Maret, appears to have been in Canada by the 1880s and was an investor in the Ontario and Quebec Railway and the CPR. According to the Place names of Alberta, the town was named in 1884. In records, he is referred to as Marquis or Duc. He married an Englishwoman, Marie Anne Claire Symes, and in records she is referred to as Marquise, Lady, Dame and Duchesse. The town of Duchess near Bassano was named for her.

help him; the last, Mrs. Welles, returned to Drumheller and took the two girls with her and looked after them until 1931 when they came home. Irene was then nine years old and Louise seven.

In 1933, John married Catherine Saraceni, who had arrived from Italy six years before to help her aunt, Jean Marshall. The couple had two children – James (1942) and Roger (1944). After the war, he sold the farm to son Johnny and purchased another in 1955. All of the children did well: Johnny and Jim farmed; Bob made a career in the federal civil service and served as Assistant Deputy Minister of Indian Affairs in Ottawa; Irene married Allan Parry, who worked for the Meteorological Bureau of Canada in Ottawa; Louise married Vic Kathrens, who worked for Canadian Industries Ltd. in Calgary; Louise was a supervisor with the Bank of Montreal; Margaret Rose taught at an elementary school in Calgary; and Fred worked as a surveyor for Bird Construction.

John's younger brother, Felice (Felix), joined him in Canada in 1910 at the age of 18. It was an escape from the grim life he had experienced from the age of eight assisting his father in field work.[233] At Ellis Island he got separated from his guardian and was sent back to Italy. His parents saved the money for his second trip and, in spring 1911, his guardian handed him off to an uncle in Philadelphia where he stayed for a couple of months. Felix joined cousins Charles and Sam Angelozzi in St. Catharines. Around 1912, he travelled westward with the CPR and found work at Hillcrest, and his account states that he was there, in 1914, for the Hillcrest mine disaster that killed 189 men. He appears to have moved back and forth between brother John's homestead and Hillcrest but also, for a time, worked laying street car tracks in Calgary for the Calgary Municipal Railway's Route No. 5.

In February 1913, Felix filed for homestead NE¼ 18-30-17-W4. He provided a graphic account of his trip to the unnamed individual who compiled his family history: "Early on the morning following his filing at the Land Registration Office, he set out on foot to return to Delia. He was without funds for the train fare and had neither overcoat, overshoes or gloves – ill prepared for a one hundred and ten-mile walk! What had started out as a beautiful day turned into one of leaden skies with a strong wind. By noon, a heavy fall of snow was coming down."[234] He stumbled through the blizzard and arrived safely in Carbon.

Felix initially farmed with his brother and was also involved in the threshing operation with the Marshalls. He worked in the Joberg coal mine at Miller Coulee for B. Norton-Taylor and, later, for Norton-Taylor and Sam Pocklington at the Pioneer Livery Stable. He married Maud Crossley in Calgary at St. Andrew's Presbyterian Church in May 1918 and the couple built their first home on Felix's homestead. It is noteworthy that he appears to have converted to

---

[233] This account is found in a typescript in the Glenbow Archives.
[234] *Ibid.*, 414-415.

Protestantism in keeping with the change of name and new identity. This was rare among Italian families. His prized team of matched Clydesdales won many prizes at agricultural fairs and he was involved in various community activities including curling. He served as a council member for the Municipal District of Michichi (four years from 1922); Enterprise Valley School Board (four years); member of the Michichi Rural Electrification Association; and charter member of the Alberta Wheat Pool. Perhaps to acknowledge his achievements in his new homeland, in 1928, he officially changed his name from Felice Angelozzi to Felix Angelozzi Battle. The couple had six children who attended school in Enterprise and Delia. The original homestead was sold in 1945 and another farm was purchased in the same area.

The Lethbridge area had a number of Italians who worked in mines but also farmed including Achille (Archie) Briosi, who was born in Tenno, Trento. In 1910, he arrived in Lethbridge with wife Maria Pellegrini and daughter Vittoria, and filed for a homestead in the Taber area.[235] They had four additional children: Ina, Andrew, Elda and George. It was son Andrew who would bring distinction not only to the family but also Alberta's Italian community. He assisted his parents in farming from an early age and, by 18, had his own farm. After marrying Jessie Learmont of Grassy Lake, he purchased 12 hectares east of Picture Butte and began to raise sugar beets on contract. Not desiring to spend money on expensive equipment (he came of age in the Depression), his inventive spirit led him to creative solutions. The family history notes: "One winter he produced single handedly 16 self-propelled, hand-controlled, sugar beet weeder-thinners. When early snow and mud made it virtually impossible to pick and top the beets Andy developed a straight disc topper which was far more successful than more expensive and complicated machines. It was capable of topping two rows at a time and elevating the beet tops into a tractor-drawn cart equipped with an automatic dump which emptied at the end of the field."[236] These machines were made from salvaged parts. Andrew went on to invent over 50 pieces of agricultural equipment including a pick-up loader, a vacuum grass seed harvester, a potato top annihilater, a semi-trailer for hauling wet pulp, a long-handled asparagus cutter and fertilizer spreaders. He succeeded in obtaining patents for only four: the front-end loader, two sugar beet toppers and lifter wheels. The companies that he contacted about his inventions generally modified the plans and patented them themselves. In 1975, Andrew was invested in the Order of Canada at the same time as Max Ward, founder of Wardair, and Hugh Dempsey, prominent curator and archivist at the Glenbow Museum. He was the first Albertan of Italian ancestry to receive this honour. In the same year,

---

[235] Achille's older brother, David, born in 1866, also immigrated around the same time.
[236] Taber History Committee, *From Tank 27 to Taber Valley: A History of Taber, Its District and People* (Taber, AB: Taber History Committee, 1977), 55.

Premier Lougheed presented him with the Province of Alberta Achievement Award. In 1982, Andrew was inducted into the Alberta Agriculture Hall of Fame.[237]

A number of families developed dairy herds including the Pavans and Fabbis. They began by making deliveries to local homes and then moved on to establish dairies. Giuseppe (Joe) Pavan, a farm boy, left Breda di Piave, Treviso and arrived in Lethbridge in March 1911; according to daughter Ginger Erickson, he brought with him an English-Italian dictionary.[238] For five months, he worked for the city laying mains and wooden sewer pipes and, in 1912, went to work as a fireman in the No. 3 Mine. He was joined by fiancée Maria Morandin in August 1914 and they were married. While focusing on establishing himself on a solid footing in the new land, he did not forget his family in Italy. In 1912, he sponsored brother Giovanni; in 1914, his brother Antonio; and, in 1921, brother Pietro.[239] Joe had a dream of having a farm of his own; the couple saved and, in 1917, they were able to put a down payment of $1,500 on the Cave Estate (comprising 32 hectares) located northeast of Hardieville. Ginger notes: "Times were hard and money was scarce. The money from the job at the mine was needed, so Dad continued to work at the mine on eight-hour shifts. It was either 7 am to 3 pm, or 3 pm to 11 pm, or 11 pm to 7 am. He also carried on with his farm work between shifts during the day. Dad and Mother moved out to the farm on March 19, 1918 with their three children: Louis, Marguerite and Elide."[240]

The Pavans raised dairy cattle and, by the early 1920s, used a horse and buggy to deliver milk to miners' homes. In 1923, Joe finally quit work at the mine and began to deliver milk door-to-door in Lethbridge with a horse-drawn milk wagon. The business continued to grow and, in the early 1930s, he purchased a delivery truck and had "Pavan Dairy" painted on the doors. Ginger describes the dairy operation as follows:

> The cows were milked in the mornings before we went to school and again in late afternoon. That day's milk was bottled and some was separated for cream, then put into a cooler for the next morning's early delivery. The milk was cooled and kept cool by the tons of ice that had

[237] Alberta Agriculture and Forestry, "Briosi, Andrew Arthur – 1982 Hall of Fame Inductee," Alberta Agriculture Hall of Fame, URL: http://www1.agric.gov.ab.ca/$Department/deptdocs.nsf/all/info1982?opendocument, retrieved October 18, 2017.

[238] Ginger (Pavan) Erickson, "Joseph and Maria Pavan," in *Sunnyside Area: A History of the Royal View/Eight Mile Lake and Crystal Lake School Districts* (Lethbridge, AB: Sunnyside Area Historical Society, 1988), 524-526. Pavan family documents comprise the Ginger Erickson Fonds at the Galt Archives 2012 1067.

[239] In 1947, Joe also sponsored three nephews.

[240] *Ibid.*, 525.

been harvested in the winter months when the ice was thickest on the lake. It was stored in an icehouse with coal slack or sawdust for insulation between blocks of ice to keep it from thawing. Milk was sold for as low as 5 cents per pint and 7 cents per quart. Cream was also delivered and any that was not sold went into making butter or delicious ice cream.[241]

The Pavans continued to buy land and their holdings increased to 323 hectares of which one-quarter was under irrigation. Joe also rented 64 hectares on which he grew feed for his herd. All work was done by hand until 1935 when he bought a tractor. In 1942, with enlistment (including son Carl's), it became impossible to get help, and home delivery was stopped. The Pavans sold the retail and wholesale portion of their business to Purity Dairy, owned by the Fabbi family, although they continued to supply bulk milk to them.

Joe was not only skilled in animal husbandry and milk production but he was also a talented inventor developing a range of equipment to enhance operations. He constructed all of the farm buildings and built the farm's water system. Ginger writes:

> He used the boiler from an old steam engine which was set up so that it could be fired to build up a good head of steam. This was in a shop near the barn. Pipes from the boiler were connected to steam radiators in the house, thus the house was comfortable on cold or chilly days. The boiler was fired all year round. The steam also provided hot water for the taps in the house, hot water and steam in the milkhouse for washing and sterilizing the milk bottles and cans, etc. The cows always had warm drinking water in the wintertime.[242]

The farm also had the first electricity in the area – Joe built his own power plant – and used a stationary steam engine with a 12-volt generator to power the milking machines. The Pavan sons continued the dairy operation and also setup their own farms.

In his family history, son Benny writes of the transition to the second generation: "The partnership at the dairy continued unchanged until 1965 when Carl left to farm on his own, and in 1973 my mom passed away. Louis and I, the eldest and youngest of the children, carried on with the dairy, expanding until we were the largest privately owned dairy in Alberta. When the cows and quotas were sold in 1978, Berniece [his wife] and I had already started building a house in Lethbridge. We moved into our new dream home on December 20, 1978. The dairy, both land

---

[241] *Ibid.*, 525.
[242] *Ibid.*, 525.

and equipment was sold by auction in March 1979."[243] The sale took two days, March 16 and 17. The Pavan Dairy Farm, comprising 181 hectares and located two miles north of the Lethbridge city limits, was acquired by the city. In 1986, the city designated the land as Pavan Park: It is an ecological preserve and is a fitting testament to an important pioneer family.

Simeon Fabbi and wife Laura left Rome and came to Alberta in 1911 settling on a farm near the CPR line north of Lethbridge. In 1923, they made the decision to leave farming and move to Lethbridge and start a dairy. Purity Dairy was a very basic operation run by the couple helped by sons Stanley, Eugene and Romeo. Romeo describes it as follows: "Our parents cared for the cows. The milk was just strained through a flannel cloth, measured into five pound Red lard pails, a very generous quart, and then delivered morning and night to neighbourhood customers."[244]

Deliveries were done by the boys. After two years, deliveries were done by horse-drawn wagon. The opportunity presented itself to acquire a herd of cows and an established milk route owned by Whitney James and this resulted in expansion and a move to a new site near St. Basil's School, which included a large house and barn. The basement of the house became the milk room and functioned well for two years until the business required further expansion. This prompted another move to a location near present-day 10 Avenue South and Scenic Drive South. Because of an increase in customers, a better wagon was acquired and Simeon did the deliveries. The labour was still provided by the family with the boys helping with milking, cleaning bottles and equipment, and also the cow barn and yard. Again, the basement of the house was converted into the dairy plant and, in 1933, new pasteurization technology was introduced. A typical work day was 4 am to 6 pm or later. Stanley and Romeo took over operation from their father in 1935. In March 1939, Stanley obtained the Engineer's Special Certificate enabling him "to have charge of and operate a Creamery" with a boiler capacity of 100 horsepower.

In 1940, the brothers purchased the Majestic Theatre and refitted it as a state-of-the-art dairy. They sold the dairy herd and bought milk from surrounding farmers. The product line expanded to include other products such as butter. This site also became too small and a large addition was built. Stanley notes with pride that their "equipment and facilities [are] second to none for the production and processing of quality Dairy products for which Purity Dairy have become noted and jealously guarded with modern day Lab facilities and staff."

[243] Benny Pavan, "Benny and Berniece Pavan," in *Sunnyside Area: A History of the Royal View/Eight Mile Lake and Crystal Lake School* Districts, 521. Carl Pavan was killed, tragically, in a two-vehicle crash in 1966.
[244] The Purity Dairy history is drawn from an account written by Stanley Fabbi at the request of Iain C. S. Macnab, the Editor of the *Canadian Dairy and Ice Cream Journal* outlined in a letter dated January 11, 1966. Galt Archives 2009.1033007.

Branches were established in Medicine Hat and Calgary and delivery expanded to Taber, Fort Macleod, Drumheller, Red Deer and southwestern BC. They acquired large, refrigerated trucks to be able to do this. In 1962, they acquired the old brewery in Cranbrook and converted it to a modern dairy. In 1963, new premises were purchased in Edmonton. Romeo justified the move to Edmonton as follows: "It became evident Edmonton and district is where the future growth of Purity Dairy lies. Here is where the largest portion of the population of the province of Alberta is. Here is where the Bread Basket of the milk supply is – Edmonton and District." The company invested in an Impco-Plastic Blow Mold machine that enabled them to introduce plastic milk bottles, the first dairy in Canada to do so. The firm also expanded deliveries into southwest Saskatchewan and southeastern BC. In 1970, the Fabbi brothers sold their dairy, the last independently-owned one in Alberta, to Purity Co-op Limited. The firm changed ownership several times and, in what is perhaps an ironic but fitting historical coincidence, in 1997, the Italian company Parmalat purchased it.

Naples Colony

The town of Barrhead, about 96 km northwest of Edmonton, was established in 1906 on the old overland trail to the Klondike. Among the earliest settlers were brothers Francesco and Carlo Rusconi, who came from Lecco, Lombardy.[245] They arrived in Canada in 1906 and cleared the land and built a log cabin in the community that became Naples located between Barrhead and Westlock. Formal homestead records – 295381 NW 16-60-2 W5 – were filed on May 4, 1908. In 1912, Carlo returned home and married Sofia Farinati; the couple journeyed to Naples, in 1913, with her sister Carolina who married Frank. By this time, there were enough people in the area to support the building of a school but a post office was not built until 1923 and received the formal name "Naples." Frank and wife soon moved to Edmonton so that he could get work with the Grand Trunk Pacific Railway since the homestead was not making money. The couple had one son and five daughters. Carlo and Sofia continued to farm and had six children.

The Rusconis were staunchly Catholic and, in 1923, Frank provided the land to build a Roman Catholic Church – Our Lady of Mount Carmel – at the prompting of Father Eugene Rooney of Westlock. Prior to this travelling priests said Mass in homes or the local school. The church building became a community project with George Lazzer, Joe Maykut and Stanley Cherwonka comprising the building committee. The first marriage celebrated was that of Angela

---

[245] Loretta Biamonte Villeneuve completed a family genealogy and also an essay on her family's history in Canada; this was shared with me by her brother, Richard Biamonte, in 2016.

Rusconi, Frank's daughter, and Charles Tonsi of Edmonton. The first babies baptized were Mary Balen and Robert Cherwonka.

The community history, *The Trails Northwest: A History of the District of Barrhead, Alberta*, states that some homesteaders did not come directly from Italy but rather from the US. Jim Andreis, who is described as an Italian (like the Marshalls and Battles, he must have changed his surname) told the history book compilers that Frank Oliver, the publisher of the *Edmonton Bulletin* (and also Minister of the Interior in charge of immigration) "was responsible for him and several Italian neighbours leaving Springfield, Illinois where they were choking to death from the coal dust in the big mines."[246] Andreis had seen one of Frank Oliver's fairs in St. Louis, Missouri with its displays of produce and livestock. In 1907, he filed for a homestead on his own behalf and, by proxy, for friends Paul Bassani, Giuseppe (Joe) Crippa, and brothers Gaspare and Giovanni Ciochetti. Andreis was 25 when he arrived and was led to a "good quarter" by Land Guide Andy Tuttle. He lived in a tent all winter and the following summer until his wife Effa and children Ross and Pinky arrived in 1907. He continued to work in mines in Alberta during the winter until 1914 – the money was required for essentials and also the purchase of equipment. The homestead did not produce crops until 1909 and it wasn't until 1916 that he hauled his first grain crop to Westlock. He purchased one of the first threshing machines in the area and spent winters doing custom threshing from Belvedere to Fort Assiniboine and east to Rossington. The farm was sold in 1944 though Andreis continued to live in the area. The NW section 33 where his farm was located north of Belvedere was known as "Andreis Corner." He also helped to establish the Co-op Store in Barrhead.

Basile (Paul) Bassani, his wife and three children arrived in 1908 and, according to the family history, he had a twenty-dollar gold piece that he vowed not to spend so that it could be passed on to the youngest child. The couple had an additional 11 children of whom two died of diphtheria in 1914. The bleakness of prairie life is epitomized in the observation: "There were no funeral homes. Joe Maykut made caskets, women lined them with cloth and prepared bodies for burial."

Gaspare Ciochetti was born in Torino and went to the US in 1903 and initially worked in the Boston area. According to the 1916 census, Gaspare arrived in Canada in 1908. His first name is listed as "Jasper" and his wife's name as Chia, a misunderstanding by the enumerator of her maiden name, Chiarodo; her first name was Domenica. Their daughter Rebecca was born in Edmonton before they could move to the homestead. Their son, Peppino, who was born in 1918, became a prominent member of Edmonton's Italian community with many immigrants going to his barbershop for haircuts and gossip. The Ciochettis were close friends of the Properzi brothers

[246] Barrhead and District Historical Society, *The Trails Northwest: A History of the District of Barrhead, Alberta* (Barrhead, AB: Barrhead and District Historical Society, 1967), 176.

and, in 1914, the two families set up a syndicate and purchased a threshing machine. They then did all the community's threshing until a second machine was purchased by the Messmer brothers. In addition, a number of the homesteaders partnered to obtain a registered bull in order to improve their stock.

Four Properzi brothers – Tony, Carmen, Salvadore and Luigi – emigrated from Aquila, Abruzzo. Tony arrived in the US in 1901 and worked in Chicago. Tony returned to Italy to marry and, in 1908, moved to Edmonton and filed a homestead at NE ¼ 4-61-2-5. According to the Naples history, he returned to the US and brought his wife and brothers, Carmen and Salvadore, to the homestead. The 1916 census lists his age as 36 and that of his wife Mary as 37; the older children, Americ, Mossa and Dominick were born in the US and the youngest, India and Mary, on the homestead. In 1910, Tony gave up the first homestead and filed for another at SE ¼ 33-60-2-5; this was closer to his brothers' homesteads. Tony and wife and children continued operating the home farm and other land. Tony served on the local school board as well as on church committees.

Brothers Carmen and Salvadore homesteaded together and, in 1916, Carmen bought another quarter, one of the first settlers in the area to do so. In 1922, he decided to return to Italy to find a wife and sold his livestock so that he did not have to worry about its care while he was gone. He and wife Angela had two children, sons Abraham and John, who continued to farm in the district. Salvadore had to wait to file for a homestead until he came of age. To make ends meet, he worked on road construction crews in the summer. An accident with a rifle resulted in the loss of vision in one eye but a doctor in Westlock managed to save the eye. A young woman, Victoria Grosso, and her cousin arrived in Naples and Salvadore convinced her to marry him. There is a touching account of Victoria putting in a garden the first spring after their marriage only to see the plants wilt and die. The family history notes: "A neighbour came to see what was the trouble, discovered it was cutworms and showed her how to look for them just below the surface of the ground. She took a small stick, dug for the worms, got them on the end of the stick, and threw them over the garden fence. The neighbour laughed at her and said, 'Be sure you tell them not to come back'!"[247] Another anecdote also points out her inexperience:

> A few years later, Salvadore was walking through the bush with his gun, saw a coyote, shot it and carried it home. He was so proud of it, he took it into the kitchen to show it off, and leave it so it would not freeze until he could skin it. Victoria was preparing a meal, turned from the stove, and there the coyote was on its feet weaving about. She was so frightened, grabbed the children

247 Barrhead and District Historical Society, *The Trails Northwest*, 251.

to her and ran part way up the stairs to the landing, where she stood clutching the children. When Salvadore came in a few minutes later, he laughed at her and asked if she thought the coyote couldn't get up those few steps.[248]

The couple had four children, three girls and a boy. Son Meric continued the family farm and purchased other land.

A fourth brother, Luigi Properzi, came to Canada in 1925 and lived with Salvadore and family until he filed for his own homestead. In 1933, Luigi married Teresa Dompe, the oldest of five children born to Peter and Lucia Dompe of Edmonton. The couple had four children. From 1940 to 1945, Luigi rented the farm and moved to Edmonton with the family and worked as a painter at the Burns Packing Plant. A family online post notes that he hunted and fished as well as making his own sausage, ham, bacon and wine. The traditions from the homeland were thus continued in Canada not only by Luigi but many others.

The Naples homesteaders did not achieve the success of those in the Delia, Lethbridge and Drumheller areas; this was likely due to a combination of factors. In the latter, the families undertook mechanization and also specializations such as sugar beet and dairy farming. Continued work in the mines also added to family incomes. It would appear that the families were also more entrepreneurial. Our Lady of Mount Carmel Cemetery was the resting place of many members of Naples' Italian community. The tombstones provide a lasting memorial to the Italian pioneers and family members ensured that their names and dates of birth were accurate in contrast to the census records.[249]

Venice-Hylo Colony

The settlement in Venice-Hylo in the Lac La Biche area of northern Alberta was unique in having been promoted by the Italian government. Whether it was the government that led the initiative or the local Italian fraternal society – La Società Vittorio Emanuele Terzo – is not known. Felice De Angelis, a civil engineer born in 1886, was the consular agent assigned to the project.[250] He obtained the maps, survey blueprints and other documents required to establish homesteads.

---

[248] *Ibid.,* 251.
[249] Naples Catholic/Our Lady of Mount Carmel RC Cemetery, Canada Gen Web Cemetery Project, URL: http://geneofun.on.ca/cems/AB/ABBAR0159, retrieved July 25, 2017.
[250] The diary comprises the Felice de Angelis Fonds, donated by Tony Bonifacio, 1995, Provincial Archives of Alberta PR1995.0022.

According to an article in *The Edmonton Bulletin*, on July 27, 1914, De Angelis, Guiseppe Billos (O. J. Biollo), Beniamino Maragno, Pio Bonifacio, and Antonio Piemonte and son Teofilo set out to view the land. The article noted that Edmonton's Italian population numbered about 600; the figure was likely provided by De Angelis and was clearly an exaggeration as revealed by census records. The settlers were assisted by Industrial Commissioner George M. Hall's Department and the Society provided tools, a tent for camping and food sufficient for three weeks.[251] Hall was an American journalist who had headed the Winnipeg Industrial Bureau before coming to Edmonton, in 1912, to become Industrial Commissioner. In 1913, the title was changed to Industrial and Publicity Commissioner. When the Italian colonists set off, Hall told the media:

> Italians are not known and understood in Western Canada as they should be … I believe this colony of Italians in the Edmonton district will be the means of demonstrating the value of the Italian as a colonizer and agriculturist. They are an adaptable people and send their children to the public schools with the result that the second and third generations are teachers, lawyers, doctors, bankers – in short, they take their place side by side with the native people and hold their own with signal success.

Hall's observation is remarkably free of prejudice. From July 27 to August 3, De Angelis and the colonists looked over the area they intended to settle, and decided it was suitable for farming. Later, they walked to the Lac La Biche Mission where they registered their homesteads. On August 28, 1914, the second group of 22 men, led by De Angelis, left Edmonton by train for Colinton. A picture at the railway station including families and hunting dogs accompanied an article titled "Leaving For A Different Kind Of 'Front'," in *The Edmonton Capital*, August 28, 1914. The headline was referencing the start of the First World War.

Members of the second group included Giuseppe Michetti, Augusto Marini, Paolo and Domenico Morelli, Antonio Lavigni, Antonio and Pietro Riva, Atillio Perini and Giuseppe Baldoni. An article in *The Edmonton Journal* on August 29 described the Italians as "natural farmers." The settlement was named Venice on establishment of the post office on September 8, 1916 and Biollo became the postmaster. He was instrumental in naming the community for the capital of his region, which pleased the majority of the settlers who were from northern Italy. Among their numbers were some who came directly from Italy while others came from other parts of Canada or the US.

---

[251] Gisella Biollo, in *Hylo-Venice: Harvest of Memories*, notes that the Italian Society was established in 1913 in order to help organize the immigrants from Italy. The first president was Mr. Cantera and the Italian consular agent replaced him with her father.

De Angelis kept a diary and excerpts, translated from the original Italian by Gabriele Erasmi, were included in the *Hylo-Venice: Harvest of Memories* book, published in 2000.[252] Tony Bonifacio describes the settlement in an unpublished manuscript titled *Venice Alberta 1914: The Pioneers and Others That Lived There*. In a handwritten note on the copy of the diary in his memoir, Bonifacio notes that, prior to coming to Edmonton, De Angelis had been in London, England for one or two years and had studied English.[253] The diary provides an account of the exploratory party's adventures and the first days of the settlement. At the outset of the second trip north on Friday, August 28, De Angelis writes:

> It seems the Italian Colony will materialize, after all. This morning a group of nineteen strong and willing Italians left Edmonton. I am proud to be their leader and guide: it's a lively advance patrol of civilization. We leave Edmonton at eight, as usual. First, a group photo in front of the railway station: Mr Hall wants to get some publicity out of it. My good Italians are all pleased with the picture taking.
>
> From Edmonton to Colinton nothing remarkable happens. I get acquainted with the first Italian woman who will join the Colony. She is attractive, intelligent, truly and typically Italian. When we reach Colinton, there is a bit of frenetic activity to unload the tools and flour from the train: part of it is to be brought along and part of it is to be stored here. Baldoni even brought some potted basil. What a practical man! Two dogs of the female variety are also part of the company. They are quite unaware of the honour of being the first bitches of the Italian Colony. One of them is blind, poor thing! Dinner with the big chiefs and the fellow from Piedmont at the home of Mr. Mocafi, also a Piedmontese and a resident of Colinton.

Frank Mocafi of Novara filed for a homestead at Athabasca Landing in September 1912; his previous residence was in Washington State. De Angelis is struck by the beauty of the countryside and writes in the same entry:

---

[252] The diary ended up in the hands of De Angelis' niece Matilde (Crespi) Bigiaretti (1915-2012), a journalist and the wife of Italian author Libero Bigiaretti (1905-1993). To promote her husband's work, she attended writers' conferences and, in a quirk of fate, met Gabriele Erasmi, a professor at McMaster University, and gave him a copy. According to Tony Bonifacio, Erasmi met an Edmonton academic of Italian descent who enabled him to contact Venice descendants in Edmonton, and share the manuscript and translation with them.
[253] In June 1994, Bonifacio drove Erasmi to Venice-Hylo and Lac La Biche where he gathered information from local residents. He spent four days in Edmonton with Bonifacio and visited the Provincial Archives to search for information about the pioneers. In 1995, Bonifacio donated a copy of the English translation of the diary to the Archives.

It's ten o'clock: I've gone outside to look at the night and I feel deeply moved: the most beautiful aurora borealis marks the sky from west to east. It's the first one I've seen in my life; it makes quite an impression on me. A white light with irregular bands makes a path among the stars on a clear, starry night. It is mysterious, divine. It's like a word from God written with fire. It's a day worth being alive, a new experience in my life, and I thank God for it.[254]

De Angelis enjoyed playing the role of heroic adventurer and leader of a motley group of common men. In his diary, he explores the notion of their creating a utopia, but is grounded by the squabbles between Michetti and Piemonte, the difficulties of building roads and bridges over sloughs, poor quality of the food, inclement weather and hordes of mosquitoes. The language of the narrative is that of a witty, educated young man and is at times condescending as would be expected of someone of his education and social class towards labouring men.

The larger world intrudes and he records on September 8, 1914: "I go and spend some time with the railroad people, camped nearby. They too, are absolutely fed up [with the rain]. The conversation turns on the war. Only a distant echo of death, slaughter, and destruction reaches us here, but it is frightening. It must be a nightmare, it cannot be true. I give Marini an English lesson and it's the only well spent time of the day. Alas, it's not enough. I turn nostalgic and think of my wonderful, exalted, distant Italy. It keeps raining." On November 9, he records a discussion on capitalism and labour and notes: "Poor people, they are so ignorant. How much hatred has been fostered upon them against the ruling class!" De Angelis expresses admiration for Giuseppe Michetti, noting: "His company is very pleasant: a strong and generous man from the Abruzzi, he fought as a *bersagliere* in the Chinese Campaign. He's got a lot of interesting stories to tell."[255]

During the first winter, settlers built cabins, beginning with that of Giuseppe Baldoni in Hylo (Section 33 SE), Antonio Piemonte in Venice (Section 1 NW) and Joe Michetti (this last was shared with his brother Paul and friend Ascenzio Varze). They survived on hunting rabbits and other small game but also had to ask the Italian Society for money to buy food. Entrepreneur O. J. Biollo set up the community's first general store. Spring brought fish to creeks and streams as well as other animals. A lifeline to civilization was established when, in February 1915, the first train from Edmonton arrived in Lac La Biche and the siding near Baldoni's section was called

---

[254] Felice De Angelis Fonds PAA-8663.

[255] The *bersaglieri* made up the Army of the Kingdom of Sardinia established by General Alessandro La Marmora in 1836 and which, later became the Royal Italian Army. They fought in China to give Italy a foothold as the country was opened to western trade.

Hylo. According to local lore, railway workers named the station after a popular card game.[256] New arrivals to Hylo included Felice Rizzoli and Carlo Meardi and to Venice, brothers Pietro, Attilio, Francesco and Ferro Macor, father-and-son Andrea and Aurelio Tuia, and Andrea Simioni. Since Venice did not have its own station, Biollo with the support of De Angelis appealed to the Premier and the siding that had been named Delgany and, which was some way away, was moved and the hamlet of Venice was born in 1916. Jealous of this success, Marini tried to get Hylo renamed Trieste for his home city but failed.

The small colony's fortunes continued to improve and many settlers qualified for a $500 loan from the government of Alberta to purchase cattle.[257] In 1917, a government official came to encourage enlistment but because the men were working the land, they were exempted from service. The end of the First World War saw some of the single men leave the homesteads to work in coal mines and the railway but they were replaced by newcomers including Angelo Guerra, Angelo D'Angela, Frank Rycroft and Luigi Catalani who came to Venice, and Paul and Joe Michetti who came to Hylo. Luigi Fabbri took over the homestead abandoned by Angelo D'Angela. Tragedy struck in 1919 when fire fueled by debris from logging operations destroyed part of Hylo. Thankfully, no homes were destroyed and an unforeseen benefit resulted: the fire burned stumps helping to clear the land. The burn ended logging in the region.

By 1920, there were enough children in the two communities to require a school. Several sites were suggested (Julius Rossi offered to donate the land) but an agreement could not be reached and, eventually, each community built its own. The Venice school was built on the Gambacorta homestead and opened in 1926. Until this time, children had gone to the Lac La Biche Mission School and had to learn French. With the growth in population, desire for a church was expressed and eight acres were donated by Olivo Biollo.[258] The cornerstone for the Holy Redeemer Church was laid in 1924 and work on the basement was begun. It was a community effort: the Biollo and De Angelis/Marini sawmills donated lumber; and Pio Bonifacio, Salvatore Giacobbo, Joe Michetti, Augusto Marini, Frank and Attilio Macor, Angelo and Leonardo Guerra, Eric Parent and Joseph Benoit donated their labour. It was completed in 1925 and Father Carlo Fabris came from Rome

---

[256] A letter from Alberta Community Development dated September 1996 notes: "It [Hylo] was originally established in 1914 as a station on the Alberta and Great Waterways Railway line. According to available sources it was named out of the following: During construction of the A&GWR the workers played a game known as faro, which used counters, shuffling boxes, and the like. One of the oldest of all gambling games played with cards, faro was one of the favorite pastimes of upper class Europeans in the eighteenth and nineteenth centuries. Faro was introduced to North America with the flood of European immigrants" (*Hylo-Venice Harvest of Memories*, 19).

[257] See Tony Bonifacio, *Venice Alberta 1914*.

[258] This was officially registered in 1936.

to be the first pastor. The infrastructure continued to grow and, by 1922, the community had a grain elevator. Fire continued to be an enemy and, in fall 1923, the elevator burned down and was replaced with the addition of a flour mill.

The cycle of destruction by fire continued: 1926 saw the elevator burn down again and the Michetti sawmill in 1926; both were rebuilt. To celebrate, a picnic was held in June, the first of many that continued even after many Italians had left the region. In 1927, the community leaders erected a community hall, again with donated labour and materials contributed by Biollo. The Great Depression of the 1930s hit the community hard but the founders collaborated in the range of farming, construction and logging activities and survived. Medical services continued to be unavailable: local women acted as midwives and a visit to Lac La Biche or Edmonton was required to see a doctor. But it was the rise to power of Benito Mussolini in Italy that would have the strongest impact not only on Venice-Hylo but also Italian communities throughout the province. De Angelis and Father Fabris established the Fascio de Venice to support Mussolini; it received extensive community support and, on Italy's declaration of war in 1940, resulted in enemy alien designation and internment of two community members, Olivo Biollo and Rudolph Michetti. A separate chapter has been devoted to the rise of Fascism and enemy alien designaton and internment in Alberta's Italian communities.

Many family histories were submitted to *Hylo-Venice Harvest of Memories* and, based on this record, there were about 30 founding households most of whom stayed in the region. Breakdown, based on point of birth, is as follows: Abruzzo: Vincenzo Donofrio, Giuseppe Michetti, Paul Michetti, and Ascenzio Varze; Calabria: Salvatore Grandinetti; Campania: Guiseppe (Joe) Tisi; Lombardy: Carlo Meardi, Enrico Marchesi, Luigi Rizzoli; Marche: Augusto Marini; Parma: Julio Rossi and John Rossi; Rieti: Pio Bonifacio; Sardinia: Efisio Manca; Friuli-Venezia Giulia: Aurilio Ferro and son Francesco, Luigi Fabbro, Macor brothers (Pietro, Francesco, Attilio and Gildo) and Antonio Piemonte; Veneto Region: O. J. Biollo, Secondo Edwardo Fornari, Salvatore Giacobbo, Celeste Giacobbo, Romano Tedesco and Anthony Torresan; and Campania: Antonio Zevola. This analysis provides further evidence that in the first two decades of the twentieth century, the majority of immigration to Alberta was from Northern Italy.

The most prominent family was that of Olivo Biollo.[259] There are variant spellings of the surname including Billos and given names including Olivo, Oliver, Giovanni and John. He was born in 1883, the son of Giuseppe and Valentina (Carraro) Biollo, and was the youngest of seven children. According to Mary Doyle (Biollo's daughter), the family supplied milk to the Roman Catholic Patriarch of Venice (later Pope Pius X) and Olivo was the delivery boy. As a consequence,

---

[259] Mary Doyle, "Biollo, Olivo John and Anne," in *Hylo-Venice*, 258-262.

he wanted to become a priest but was rejected because he had asthma. He then attended an agricultural college in Padua. Biollo immigrated to Canada in 1902 as a prospective employee of the CPR but instead worked off his commitment with the National Transcontinental Railway.

Biollo sponsored brothers Angelo and Santo and the three settled in Winnipeg, in 1904, where Olivo went into partnership to acquire the Savoy Hotel at 686 Portage and Main Street. The three brothers operated the hotel and, in September of that year, Olivo was part of a group that formed an Italian benevolent society, the Società di Mutuo Soccorso.[260] In 1905, he became a Canadian citizen and joined with other Italian immigrants to set up the Western Co-operative Construction Company.[261] The three brothers also worked in several Italian restaurants including the Venice Restaurant.[262] By 1907, they were ready to build their own hotel, initially known as the Mount Royal Hotel and, later, the Wellington Hotel, on Garry Street south of Portage Avenue. The five-storey brick and stone building in the Classical Revival Style was built for a total cost of $50,000.[263] This was a staggering amount that the three brothers could not possibly have got together and would therefore have had to have partners and a mortgage. According to an article in the *Manitoba Free Press* of November 21, 1907, the hotel boasted an electric elevator and had 12 suites with their own bathrooms, in addition to 31 single apartments, main-floor rotunda and dining room, second floor parlour, large banqueting hall and "grotto." Construction was done by Western Cooperative Construction, which also built the impressive 3-storey red brick house at 294 College Avenue in which the Biollo brothers and their families resided. [264] Olivo had married a Polish woman, Annie D'Mitruzinski in 1907.

All did not go smoothly with the family business: Biollo had been given permission to build a temperance hotel, a fact that he neglected to note. The Province of Manitoba had passed a Prohibition Act in 1900 and, though this was deemed unconstitutional, the Temperance Movement was so strong that, in a 1906 amendment to the Liquor License Act, an area of downtown Winnipeg was designated a "non-licence" area and this impacted on hotels built there. Olivo sought to

---

[260] M. Peterson, *287 Garry Street Garrick (Wellington) Hotel*, a report prepared for the City of Winnipeg Historical Buildings & Resources Committee, April 2016. The report presents the historic significance of the building and provides some details of O. J. Biollo's businesses in Winnipeg. Notice of the setting up of the Italian fraternal society appeared in the *Manitoba Free Press*, September 30, 1904, 3.

[261] Cited by Peterson, 2; the article appeared in the *Manitoba Free Press*, April 17, 1905, 9.

[262] *Ibid.*, 2; the article appeared in the *Manitoba Free Press*, January 14, 1909, 7.

[263] Peterson's report was intended to support historic preservation of the hotel, 3. According to an inflation calculator, $100 in 1914 would be worth $2,165 in 2017; thus, in today's dollars, the hotel would take about $108 million to build.

[264] Peterson notes that Western Cooperative Construction operated only in 1905 and 1906 and built small, single family homes valued at $75,000 (5).

obtain a liquor licence after-the-fact but was unsuccessful. In addition, Biollo had obtained credit from John Arbuthnot, a local lumber company owner and former mayor of Winnipeg, to build the hotel. Arbuthnot also held the mortgage. The family lost the hotel and it was the belief of the Biollo children that their father's partners had cheated him. While there might have been an element of truth in this, it may simply have been inexperience and getting in over his head.

In 1910, Olivo moved his family to Rivers, Manitoba, and the following year to Edmonton. In spite of the failures in Winnipeg, it is clear that Olivo had been able to save some money since he purchased a store on the corner of 96 Street and 99 Avenue, and also operated the Family Theatre (a movie theatre) in the neighbourhood. Daughter Mary noted that he took courses from McTavish Business College to better equip himself for success. He became involved with the local Società Vittorio Emanuele Terzo and became its second president, in 1913. According to Mary, it had a membership of about 200.

Olivo filed for land at Section 12, Township 66, Range 15, West of the 4th Meridian 12-66-15-W4, part of the Venice Colony. Surrounded by Lake Missawawi, it was an ideal location that provided fish for food as well as water for agricultural and domestic purposes. The extent of his business network is revealed by documents in the Provincial Archives.[265] With respect to the settlement, he served as a sub-agent/contractor for a range of companies including the Cunard, White Star and Anchor-Donaldson shipping lines; the Northern Alberta Railways; Treasury Branch; Alberta Government Telephones (AGT); and the Department of Lands and Mines. He was a crop correspondent for the Dominion Bureau of Statistics and also served as postmaster for Venice from 1916 to 1940. Biollo also dealt with the Italian consulate on behalf of settlers, in effect, acting as the regional consular agent.

Olivo began his empire by purchasing a small general store, known as the Mercantile Company Limited, owned by a Mr. Kish (or Kiss). It supplied logging and lumbering camps in the area. The family lived in a lean-to attached to the store until 1917 when Olivo built a large, eight-room house on the lake shore. He availed himself of the Government of Alberta's offer of pure-bred animals for the breeding of cattle and pigs. Beginning with horses for farm work, he then moved on to tractors and other machines to improve efficiency. He purchased a threshing machine that he used to service all the farms in the area. In 1921, he bought a sawmill and hired Jacob Schaub from Plamondon to operate it. In 1922, he became the first agent for Alex Fraser's grain elevator. A red barn was erected to accommodate the horses from Plamondon, Egg Lake,

---

[265] See Biollo Family Fonds at the Provincial Archives PR1370 (1923-1955), Mercantile Company Limited Fonds PR 1382 and Venice Post Office Fonds PR 1391. In addition, there are the Mary N. B. Doyle Fonds, 1912-[1973] PR 1392 and PR 1992-0258.

Beaver Lake and Brierville, which had to be sheltered overnight. The United Farmers of Alberta (UFA) Co-operative Local was run out of his Mercantile Company. Starting as a farmer's interest group, it eventually became a political party and formed the Government of Alberta from 1921 to 1935; after this period it became primarily an agricultural supply co-operative.

Biollo was aided in his endeavours by wife Anne, who gardened, made butter and cheese, preserved meat, mended and made clothes, served as a midwife, and, at times, as the postmistress. The couple had 10 children (Valentina, Florence, Mike, Mary, Arthur, Fidelia, David, Valentino, Gloria and Gilbert). In 1925, Olivo saw to the formation of Venice School District #4102 and a school was built. He served as the secretary-treasurer from 1928 to 1939. The first four children received their education at the Lac La Biche Mission and, for reasons unknown to the family, their surname was registered as "Bellis." When daughter Mary finished her education, she became the teacher at the Venice School. Olivo with other community members saw to the purchase of the McArthur Inn in Lac La Biche and its conversion into St. Catherine's Hospital.

The family also experienced setbacks. In 1925, Biollo served as the District returning Officer in the provincial election and there appears to have been some fraud and he was sentenced to serve a term in the St. Albert penitentiary. In 1927, Mrs. Biollo moved to Edmonton to run the store; she took with her six of the children. The business did not prosper and they returned to Venice in July 1928, and the family businesses in Edmonton were wound down. During the Depression, the Venice Store also was hard-hit; people were buying less and taking advantage of credit and, then, defaulting on the debt. Some had to avail themselves of a government program that provided financial aid ranging from $5 to $14.

To help the family's finances, Olivo became foreman on a road building crew; a bridge across the narrows of Lake Missawawi was begun and completed in 1931. His financial situation improved enough so that, in 1930, he was able to trade in his Model T Ford for a Chrysler Coach, and, in 1934, he had a new store. The rebuilding of the family's fortunes continued when, in 1936, Olivo obtained the position of road supervisor with the provincial government for a new improvement district comprising Venice, Lac La Biche and Plamondon. The job paid $4 per day with an additional $3 per day expense allowance. The work lasted for two years and meant that he was constantly on the road. With his three sons, he continued to work two quarter sections of land that he had homesteaded as well as another quarter section not as yet registered; this totaled 101 hectares under cultivation.

Olivo's luck ran out on September 19, 1940, when he was arrested and interned. Marital problems peaked and he moved to Edmonton in 1943 where he worked as night clerk at the Ritz Hotel. He built a house in Edmonton and was joined by some of the children; his wife continued to operate the store in Venice. He returned briefly to Venice in 1953 to revive the store but this failed. He died in May 1963 at the age of 80 in St. Joseph's Hospital in Edmonton after a bout of pneumonia.

The lives of other original families are also of interest. Pio Bonifacio was born in Toffia, Rieti, southeast of Rome and married Lucia Macor, in spring, 1911, and left for the US in the fall with a friend, Pangrazio (Pete) Rauco.[266] They landed in Boston and then worked in the coal mines of Pennsylvania and Kansas. They ended up in Winnipeg and, then, moved to Edmonton to work on railroad construction. Pio was a friend of the Biollos and, when Lucia joined him in 1915, she stayed for a time with the family while Pio worked out-of-town. He established a homestead on NE1/4 1-66-15-W4 and to earn money to support farming, he worked as a logger. The couple had five children (Tony, Joe, John, Quinto and Bernice). Pio operated the farm with the help of his sons. In 1942, Pio, Quinto, Peter Rossi and Frank Ferro cut cord wood for the Northern Transportation Company Limited along the Mackenzie River in the Northwest Territories. The company was one of the first haulers on the Mackenzie River and had started at the time of the Yukon Gold Rush. In 1947, Pio and Lucia retired to Edmonton where, for a time, he worked in the kitchen of the Misericordia Hospital. Preferring a more adventurous life, he then worked for a tree-cutting crew in the Redwater-Egremont area preparing for the construction of Highway 28.

Anthony P. (Tony) Bonifacio was the first child to be born in Venice in June 1917.[267] He attended school at the Lac La Biche Mission and learned French; he did not learn English until 1926 when the school in Venice opened. After grade eight, he quit school to work on the farm and, in 1935, went to work for the Northern Alberta Railways as a section man at Mile 199, north of Lac La Biche. When brothers Joe and John enlisted in 1940, he returned to work on the farm. In 1948, Tony moved to Edmonton and, in spring 1949, worked with New West Construction, which was doing finishing work on the Imperial Oil (Strathcona) Refinery. He continued to work for the company (one of the first Italians to do so) for 31 years until his retirement. In 1949, he married Rina Macor, the daughter of Frank and Anna Macor, another founding family, and the couple had three sons. As has been noted, he was a passionate community historian.

Joe Bonifacio worked on the farm in the winter and in railway tie camps in summer, which involved cutting and removing the limbs from trees for railroad ties. In 1942, he was conscripted into the Army and received his discharge papers in 1946. He returned to Lac La Biche to work on the farm but also took on other paid work including building of the Lac La Biche airport. Joe married Antoinette (Nini) Maccagno, youngest daughter of Tomaso and Giovanna Maccagno, in 1947, and they had three children. As with other Italian families, when the elders could no

---

[266] Anthony P. (Tony) Bonifacio, "Bonifacio, Pio and Lucia Bonifacio, Anthony and Rina (nee Macor)," in *Hylo-Venice*, 273-280.
[267] *Ibid.*, 279-280.

longer farm, the next generation took over. In fall 1947, Joe and Nini bought the family farm. Brother John served in the Army and after the war worked with Edmonton Transit driving streetcars. Quinto Bonifacio worked in construction of gas plants and refineries in Alberta including Suncor's oil sands plant in Fort McMurray.

Antonio Piemonte was born in Buia, Udine not far from Venice, and with son Teofilo immigrated and arrived in Boston in 1909.[268] Antonio and Teofilo found work as sextons at Sacred Heart Church in Boston. They moved to Scranton, Pennsylvania, to work in the mines and then to Mountain Park in the Coal Branch. They arrived in Edmonton in time to join the colonists. De Angelis documents the squabbles between the senior Piemonte and Giuseppe Michetti, which may have had regional differences as their source. The Piemonte homestead was section T66 R15 NW1. According to their family history, it was Antonio who proposed naming the colony (as has been seen, Biollo also claimed this honour). In March 1920, Angela D'Angela arrived from Codroipo, Udine, to marry Teofilo. The young couple continued to live with Antonio for about a year-and-a-half helping him on the farm. The Piemonte story is interesting because it is untypical of the experiences of the other settlers. In 1923, the family chose to leave Venice: Antonio returned to Italy, and Angela and Teofilo moved to Salem, Massachusetts.

Vincenzo (Jim) Donofrio was born in Villemagna, Chieti, Abruzzo.[269] An orphan, he came to Canada in 1903 with an aunt and cousin. She died on the voyage and was buried at sea. The two boys were met by Vincenzo's uncle, who found out from them that his wife had died. In 1914, Jim filed for land at T65 R15 SW36 and homesteaded. He married Elizabeth Tremblay, the daughter of a pioneer Francophone family from Egg Lake, Alberta, in 1917 and the couple had seven children. He worked for the NAR and became a foreman. His family lived with him in the section house for many years until he bought a house in 1928. While he worked on the railway, his wife and children looked after the farm. Elizabeth served as one of the community's midwives and assisted in the birth of 52 babies.

Eldest son Nick Donofrio, who was born in Venice, worked for the NAR and enlisted in the Canadian Army.[270] He achieved the rank of Lance Sergeant with the Royal 22nd Regiment, RCIC, and was based in Aldershot, England. In 1942, he married in Edinburgh and he and wife Barbara had a son, Bill, in 1943. Nick was killed in action on December 29, 1943. The regiment,

---

[268] Angela Piemonte, "Piemonte, Antonio/Piemonte, Teofilo/ D'Angela, Luigi/D'angela, Angelo)," in *Hylo-Venice*, 457-458.

[269] Margaret and Virginia (no surname), "Donofrio, Vincenzo and Elizabeth (nee Tremblay)," in *Hylo-Venice*, 313-314.

[270] *Ibid.*, 314.

known as the Van Doos (an Anglicization of the French "22"), was a predominantly Francophone regiment headquartered at Valcartier, Quebec. The fact that Nick chose to enlist in this regiment was probably a tribute to his mother and the result of his early education at the Lac La Biche Mission School. He lost his life at the Battle of Ortona (December 20-28, 1943) as the Allies moved up the boot of Italy.

The Macor brothers – Pietro, Francesco, Attilio and Gildo (Guido) – were born in Grions, in the province of Udine.[271] Theirs was a family of migrant workers and, at the age of 10, Frank was already working in Germany in a brick fabricating plant. The brothers left Italy in 1911 when Pietro was 25, Frank, 23, Attilio, 21 and Guido 16; the brothers worked in Nordegg, Luscar and Cadomin. In 1914, two of the brothers registered homesteads in Venice: T65 R14 NW30 (Peter) and SW30 (Attilio). Land was cleared and a house built on Peter's homestead in the first year; the other brothers continued to work in the mines. Guido did not like farming and left to work for the CPR in the Crowsnest Pass; he worked for the company for over 49 years. Frank and Attilio then built a house at SW¼ 30-65-14-W4. Since Attilio was already married to Erminia (Vinti), Frank's thoughts turned to marriage and, he remembered a girl – Anna Bizzaro – from the village of Flaibano, Udine, and began to write to her. After a lengthy correspondence, she agreed to be his wife and, in May 1922, joined him and they were married at St. Joachim's Church in Edmonton. The couple shared a house for seven years with Attilio and Erminia. In 1929, Frank with the help of Attilio built a three-room, log house on the northeast corner of section 24, and the family moved there and operated their own farm. In 1932, they built a larger house to accommodate their growing family which included three daughters and a son. In 1961, Frank, Anna and daughter Lydia moved to an apartment in Edmonton because of health issues. Their daughter Rina married Tony Bonifacio, in 1949, and they moved to Edmonton as well. Louis Macor and wife Elizabeth took over operation of the family farm, in 1958.[272] The couple had seven children, six daughters and a son. Louis not only raised cattle but also did veterinary work until a trained vet was enticed to the area.

Carlo Meardi, who was born in Voghera per Bastida dei Dossi, Pavia, filed for a homestead on section SE¼ 33-65-15-W4.[273] Due to some discrepancy, the government took back the title and he lived with his uncle's family on the next quarter until he married Dominica (Maimie) Marini,

[271] Lydia Macor and Rina Bonifacio, "Macor, Frank and Anna," in *Hylo-Venice*, 403-406.
[272] Elizabeth Macor, "Macor, Louis and Elizabeth," in *Hylo-Venice*, 406-407.
[273] Cecile Kirkbride as told by Maimie Meardi, "Meardi, Carlo and Dominica (Maimie) (nee Martini)," in *Hylo-Venice*, 425-428.

daughter of Augusto Marini, another settler, in October 1923. In spring 1924, the young couple moved to their own homestead at SE¼ 5-66-15-W4; Maimie, in her own right, filed on a quarter across the railroad (NE¼ 32-65-15-W4). They decided that Maimie would look after the farm while Carlo worked as a section man for the NAR. She looked after the chickens, milked cows and did the other chores and this continued until 1943 when their economic circumstances were such that Carlo could afford to leave the railway and farm full time. In 1952, he chose to return to full-time work for the Department of Highways, when major road construction occurred in the area.

In an oral history interview in 1973, Maimie reminisced about the family's early history in Alberta.[274] She noted that she arrived in Canada at the age of 14 in 1920 with her mother and brother and they joined her father, Augusto Marini, who was working in the mines at Cadomin to make money. In 1922, the family settled on the homestead and she was shocked to see that their home was a log shack with a sod roof. She noted that the land that was available was hard to clear and that you could only make a go of it if the men worked on the railways or other jobs. But this was a catch-22 situation because, if you couldn't clear the land yourself, you had to hire someone else to do it. Her father was the postmaster for Hylo and she helped him until she married. She felt that her family was lucky because her husband worked on the railways during the Depression and earned $100 a month as foreman. She noted that some families lost their farms. Having survived the Depression, the family was unprepared for the coming of the Second World War and designation of Italians as enemy aliens. In 1940, her father had to give up his job as Hylo postmaster because of suspicions about the loyalty of Italians.

Their son Bruno was born in Hylo in 1925 and quit school at the age of 15 to improve his family's finances; he earned money by helping farmers throughout the region and also worked in logging camps. In 1940, he purchased a truck and began a trucking business. In 1942 Bruno found full-time work for the NAR at McLennan. This was a period of enormous growth for the NAR: it was the only railway that could service Alaska Highway Mile 0 at Dawson Creek, BC, and was used to transport men and supplies. In addition, the British Commonwealth Air Training Plan built training bases in both the Peace River and Fort McMurray regions, which also saw increased traffic for the NAR. In 1947, Bruno began work for the Department of Highways as a grader operator. He also trucked livestock to Edmonton for area farmers for over 40 years. In 1944, Bruno married local school teacher Olga Shalapay. Their daughter Cecile married J. Michael Kirkbride and was instrumenal in development of *Hylo-Venice: Harvest of Memories*, published in 2000.

---

[274] Maimie Meardi (nee Marini) oral history, Dante Alighieri Oral History Project in 1973, PAA 74.106/11.

The Maccagnos of Lac La Biche

While Tomaso Maccagno was not part of the Venice colony, the Maccagno family is important to the region and Alberta's political life. Tomaso immigrated in 1921 going directly to Lac La Biche with wife Joanne Calligio and son Michele (Mike), who was born in 1914. Tomaso and Mike for many years operated a mink farm but Tomaso believed in higher education and Mike attended the University of Alberta. It is likely that Mike was the first immigrant to attend university. In 1935, he married local girl Valentine Lebas and they had eight children. Mike joined the Liberal party and ran successfully in the provincial election on June 29, 1955. He defeated Social Credit MLA Harry Lobay by less than 100 votes and was re-elected in 1959 becoming the only Liberal with a seat in the Legislature. In 1964, he became interim Liberal leader (the leader, Dave Hunter, failed to win a seat in the Legislature), as well as the official leader of the Opposition. In 1966, when Adrian Berry who had been elected Liberal leader, failed to obtain a seat, Mike was chosen as leader of the Alberta Liberal Party. This was a huge achievement for an Italian immigrant; in fact, Mike was the first to become the leader of a major political party in Canada. In the 1967 provincial election, Mike served on various standing committees including agriculture, colonization, immigration and education, all of which resonated with his immigrant roots.

The interest in government and the law, no doubt, can be traced back to the designation of Italians as enemy aliens and the negative impact this had on the entire community. This may also have triggered his desire to run for political office in the first place. Mike resigned his seat in the Alberta Legislature on May 27, 1968 to run in the federal election in the Athabasca Riding but lost by about 1,200 votes to Progressive Conservative candidate Paul Yewchuk. He was bitterly disappointed because he was a strong supporter of Pierre Elliott Trudeau. He was appointed to the National Parole Board serving in Saskatoon but eventually returned to Lac La Biche and focused on local affairs.

Passionate about the history of the region, Mike fought for the designation of the Lac La Biche Mission.[275] In 1989, Notre Dame des Victoires (Our Lady of Victories) became a national historic site of Canada in recognition of its importance as an Oblate mission (established in 1853) and its historic role in the fur trade and settlement of the early west. In 1988, Mike authored *Rendez Vous: Notre Dame des Victoires* and, in 1991, with co-author Edward J. McCullough, *Lac La Biche and the Early Fur Traders*.

---

[275] Thomas Maccagno, in 2006 and 2008 donated materials relating to his father's work to the Provincial Archives of Alberta – the Michael Maccagno Fonds PR2311.

Tom Maccagno, who was born in 1939, obtained a law degree from the University of Alberta, the first person from Lac La Biche to do so. In 1965, he was engaged by the Metis Association of Alberta and, in 1969, under President Stan Daniels, litigation began to assert Metis rights. In 1961, Tom married Annette Favennec and the couple had four children. He served as Mayor of Lac La Biche from 1990 to 1995. Tom was an active community volunteer and served on the Lakeland Park Advisory Committee, Airmen's Memorial Cairns Committee, Lac La Biche Mission Historical Society (president), Lac La Biche Bicentennial Committee, and Lac La Biche Birding Society (president). He was active in historic designation work including that of Portage La Biche as a Province of Alberta Historic Resource and the expansion of Sir Winston Churchill Park to include all of the islands on Lac La Biche. Tom was awarded the Alberta Achievement Award for Preservation and Conservation (1983), Emerald Award for services to the environment (1998), Canada's Recreational Fisheries Award (2002), Queen Elizabeth II Golden Jubilee Medal (2002) and Canadian Environmental Conservation Gold Award (2003). The Beaver Lake Cree Nation made him an Honourary Elder in 2008.

Edson Region

A number of Italians homesteaded in the Edson region and remained there growing crops and also doing some ranching. John Camarta immigrated to the US from Genga, Ancona in the Marche region of east-central Italy in 1909 when he was 18 years old and ended up working in an iron ore mine in Minnesota. Whether his wife Estera joined him then or later is not known; their first child, Nello, was born in 1913 in Eveleth, Minnesota. In 1914, the family moved to Alberta. In an oral history interview, he noted that his first impressions were very favourable because there was work.[276] He homesteaded on 64 hectares near the Grand Trunk Railway at Shining Bank near Edson. In 1915, he left his wife and son on the homestead and went to southern Alberta where he worked on a farm for two years. In 1917, he went to work in the mines in Castor and Drumheller until the spring of 1918 when he returned to the homestead. The couple had an additional six children. During the Depression, he attempted to work in the mines in Drumheller but was put on a waiting list since the mines had been unionized during his absence. After a month's wait, he was given a job. He was highly-motivated and began to study to improve his knowledge of mining and started a mine in the Morinville area at Cardiff. He prospered until petroleum replaced coal as the primary energy source and he closed the mine in 1957. In an oral history interview,

[276] See John Carmata oral history, Dante Alighieri Oral History Project, 1973, PAA 1974.0166.

John referred to the changes brought about by the coming in of oil in 1947, specifically family allowance and medicare.

Nello Camarta spent his entire life farming and logging in the Shining Bank area. He worked in his sawmill into his nineties and died in 2017 at the age of 104 in a nursing home in Edson.[277] Nello married Elizabeth Neale in 1952 and they had three children, a son and two daughters. Grandson Neil, born in 1953, made his career in the industry that gave traditional coal mining its death blow. In an interview, Neil observed that his parents knew nothing about university and that he was tempted to go to work with his uncles who were welders at Suncor since many of his contemporaries were leaving school to work there. Instead, he decided to attend the University of Alberta and study chemical engineering.[278] In 1975, Neil began work with Shell Canada Ltd. and, later, was put in charge of the $6-billion Athabasca Project. After 30 years with Shell, he joined Petro-Canada in 2005, and became senior vice president in charge of oil sands operations. His working life culminated with overseeing what has been described as a "mega-merger" – the integration of the natural gas operations of Petro-Canada and Suncor in 2009.

Italian Cowboys

The romance of the iconic cowboy riding his horse across the plains has survived to the present day, perpetuated by the Calgary stampede and rodeos in communities throughout Alberta. This vision of the west and the exoticism of Indigenous people attracted Giorgio (George) Pocaterra and Roberto Basilici to Alberta. They were adventurers and dreamers rather than poor immigrants wanting to better their economic circumstances. In contrast to the numbers of individuals of British and American descent who ranched in Alberta, the number of Italian immigrants who did this is minute. Perhaps it was the fact that the outlay on buildings and animals was high and ranching did not lend itself to doing seasonal work in the mines. The stories of Pocaterra, the son of a northern Italian industrialist and minor aristocrat, and Basilici, an artist who married a wealthy, titled German woman, are therefore unique in the history of Italian immigration to Alberta. Their stories resemble those of the "Remittance Men," younger sons of British aristocratic families who went to the colonies and received generous allowances to stay away. Pocaterra arrived in Canada in 1903 and the Basilicis in 1911.

---

[277] Nello Salvador Camarta obituary, *Edmonton Journal*, September 21, 2017, URL: http://www.legacy.com/obituaries/edmontonjournal/obituary.aspx?page=lifestory&pid=186722533, retrieved October 12, 2017.

[278] Neil Camarta interview, Oil Sands Oral History Project, Canadian Petroleum Society, Glenbow Archives M-9491.

Giorgio Guglielmo Cesare Pocaterra was born in September 1882 in the town of Piovene Rochette, Vicenza, Veneto. He was the middle child of Giuseppe Pocaterra and Ubaldina Talin; the couple also had two daughters, Emilia and Marta. The parents were from established families, Giuseppe of Roman and Ubaldina of Venetian descent. The memoir "Son of the Mountains," jointly written by George and wife Norma Piper, notes that his great-grandfather, Giuseppe Pocaterra, was a friend of Napoleon and fought in the Russian campaign.[279] Grandfather Cesare fought with Garibaldi, was imprisoned by the Austrians and released on a family appeal to Emperor Franz Joseph. He died as a result of a prison fever, leaving George's father, Giuseppe, an orphan at the age of seven. Giuseppe made a career with textile manufacturer Lanificio Rossi and was financially comfortable and well-known in the region.

As a child, George revealed a remarkable aptitude for languages (the number ranged from four to six). He also prided himself on his physical fitness – his father was a director of the Club Alpino Italiano and took his son with him on climbing expeditions.[280] Giuseppe wanted his son to follow him in the textile business and, following attendance at a boarding school in Padua, he was sent to the Academy of Commerce in Berne, Switzerland for six years. This was capped by a year in Bradford, England. George returned to Rochette in 1902 and began work at Lanificio Rossi but life in the business world did not keep his attention for long. He was a dreamer who painted in water colours and read books by American James Fennimore Cooper (the *Leatherstocking Tales*). The catalyst that launched George into the greater world was a clergyman, the Reverend Robert E. Spence, from Glenboro, Manitoba. The two met on a train in Switzerland in 1900 and Pocaterra translated for Spence. The two became friends and began corresponding on the latter's return to Manitoba. Spence's accounts of the development of the west seduced George and he decided to accept an invitation to visit. Giuseppe let him go but gave him limited funds.

George set out in February 1903 and stopped in London before going on to Liverpool to board the *SS The Parisian*. The ship carried many less fortunate Italians including future railway workers sponsored by Italian labour agents. George arrived in Calgary in fall 1903. His friend Reverend Spence's housemate, journalist W. T. Shipley, had given him a reference to Ernest Daggett, who lived in the High River area, and who gave him work at his ranch, the Bar D.[281] Unlike young men of his class in Italy, George was undaunted by the care of animals and upkeep

[279] George and Norma Piper Pocaterra, "Son of the Mountains," unpublished manuscript, ca. 1970, Glenbow Archives, 74-75.
[280] See Jennifer Hamblin and David Finch, *The Diva & the Rancher: The Story of Norma Piper and George Pocaterra* (Surrey, BC: Rocky Mountain Books, 2006).
[281] *Ibid.*, 11.

of buildings and fences. But, of course, this type of work did not define him because he chose to do it rather than being born to it. Over 100 years ago, there was a large and unbridgeable divide between white and blue collar work and his father would have viewed this as a betrayal of his class.

George determined that he wanted to own his own ranch and was joined by his older cousin, Arturo (Arthur) Talin, who had spent time in Brazil and Venezuela (both countries had extensive cattle ranches). The two found an ideal place near Pekisko, 35 km south of Longview, and north of the Highwood River. The area had excellent rangeland and the community was located in traditional Blackfoot territory (the name Pekisko was taken from the Blackfoot Cree word "*i ta pisko*," or "rolling hills"). The Prince of Wales would also be seduced by the landscape and, after his 1919 western tour, purchased a ranch. Today, the community and the ranches surrounding it are part of the historic "Cowboy Trail."

Like young men in an adventure novel, George and Arthur lived in a tent to stake their claim. But, if living rough was not bad enough, the former, according to his own account, did not have the money for his portion of the $10 registration fee. In a 1965 talk to the Kiwanis Club, and the unpublished memoir, he recounted that, in order to address this need, he resorted to playing poker. The epic game lasted two days (Saturday and Sunday) and George emerged triumphant.[282] On February 22, 1905, George filed for NW 36-17-4-W5 at the Dominion Land Office in High River; and, on March 27, 1905, Arthur filed for NW 6-18-3-W5. With the help of an experienced Norwegian builder, they erected a log cabin that was nearly five square metres. Next, they acquired brood mares, a stallion, cows, calves and a bull. They named the property the Buffalo Head Ranch (ostensibly because of bones George found on the property) and the co-owners registered the "XN" brand for cattle and a buffalo-head-shaped brand for horses. They had modest success and George described this period as follows:

> For about thirty years of my early life I averaged seven hours a day riding over my lands, through the herd of cattle and horses, and looking over 30 miles of fences, most of the time alone in hilly country, within less than an hour's easy ride to the higher peaks of the Rockies. Thus I had plenty of time and opportunity for thinking about Life in general and in detail, gradually acquiring a better understanding of the forces which condition human life, and learning to adapt myself so as to collaborate with them.[283]

---

[282] *Ibid.*, 16-17.
[283] Letter from George Pocaterra to Dr. Halford J. Morlan, May 28, 1963, Glenbow Archives M6340/17.

This is the observation of a philosopher rather than a hard-headed rancher and evidence of the fact that George was more interested in the idea of ranching than its practicalities.

What George really wanted to do was to experience the wilderness and the life of the Indigenous people who populated it, and he had ample time to do this. His first encounter became a story that he loved to tell. In an article in the *Alberta Historical Review*, he writes:

> As I struck a match and lit my cigarette I suddenly saw five Indians standing behind me in a half circle, every man with a rifle in the crook of his arm. They looked like the Indians of "Deerslayer" by Fenimore Cooper. They were dressed in leggings, breechclouts and blanket coats with the capote at the back, and all had their hair done in tresses, and some had either feathers or ermine skins woven into their tresses. Somehow I managed not to be startled. One living in those early conditions was usually set and ready to meet sudden crises. One had to train oneself for that. I smiled and handing my tobacco pouch to the nearest Indian, said: "Have a smoke with me." All five broke suddenly into a smile, and one of them said to the others: "Ne washshidjoo tah-ah-ko gheenee-ashin." I started learning foreign languages when still very young, and so I was always keen to grasp the sound of any strange words. I found out that what the Indian had said meant: "This white man is not afraid of anything."[284]

George developed a number of strong friendships including with Spotted Wolf (Paul Amos), who later became a blood brother; his father Three Buffalo Bulls; his brother-in-law Dog Nose (Elijah Hunter); King Bearspaw; and others. These individuals not only gave him an entrée into their traditional life but also were a source of stories that he shared with others and also wrote down.[285] In the harsh winter of 1906-1907 that negatively impacted ranchers in the foothills, George joined Spotted Wolf and Dog Nose in a trapping expedition in Kananaskis country that also included prospecting. The depth of the snow caused difficulties for the men and pack horses alike but they succeeded in setting up traplines in the area of the headwaters of the Kananaskis and Palliser rivers. George was nearly caught in an avalanche. Adding insult to (almost) injury, the trapping was poor. An unexpected outcome was that Three Buffalo Bulls declared that George was

---

[284] George W. Pocaterra, "Among the Nomadic Stoneys" in the *Alberta Historical Review*, vol 11, No 3, Summer 1963, 12-13; see also "Son of the Mountains," 18-19. The publication was edited by his friend Hugh Dempsey, curator/director of the Glenbow.

[285] The *Calgary Herald* published two of his articles: "The Last Buffalo Hunt, as told by a Stony [sic.] Chief," (January 23, 1932) and "Lone Warrior Defies Tribe for Revenge" (October 22, 1932).

his son and, therefore, a Stoney, and gave him the name "Nya-he-taush-kan" (Mountain Child). In addition, he told him of deposits of black rocks and suggested that he stake a claim.[286]

Throughout his period on the Buffalo Head ranch, George would go on to several failed coal mining ventures as well as attempts to strike oil. Worry about money became a constant companion but, in later years, George would bear this alone. On June 4, 1908 his cousin and best friend, Arthur, committed suicide in Calgary. The *Herald* of June 5 in a short notice on page 1 reported that an Italian, the business partner of "George Pocatero of Pekisko," had shot himself behind the CPR station and that the body was being held by Graham and Buscombe Undertakers until his friends were notified.[287] I have been unable to find any information on Talin's suicide. Perhaps the harsh winter and financial difficulties resulted in depression; or perhaps it was more personal reasons. The outcome for George was that he became sole owner of the ranch and that he relied on his Indigenous friends for companionship and escape. In 1909, he became a naturalized British subject and embarked from New York for a trip to Italy. While on his own behalf, he could report to family that his ventures in Canada had succeeded; the death of Arthur was clearly a sign of failure and brought great pain to the family. Perhaps that was the motivation for his trip – to provide a first-hand account of what happened.

Having accomplished his duty visit to family, George returned to the country where he could truly be himself. His looks and European charm would bring about an era of relative prosperity. Allen Seymour of the Canadian Pacific Railway had a vision of bringing wealthy tourists to Alberta and housing them at ranches so that they could experience life on the land. In 1924, Pocaterra and neighbour Guy Weadick at the Stampede Ranch were approached and agreed to participate. Historian David Finch observes: "By the late 1920s, European dudes were paying up to $50 per week to stay with the multilingual Pocaterra, who spoke five languages fluently: Italian, French, Spanish, Portuguese and his heavily accented English. American dudes stayed upstream at the Stampede Ranch."[288] A lavishly-illustrated brochure – *Buffalo Head Ranch in the Foothills of the Canadian Rockies* – was produced targeted mostly at American guests. It described "A Playground for people who wish an outing amongst the most beautiful of scenery, in a ranching country, with its picturesque, care-free life and customs, and where besides riding, one can go hunting and

---

286 Pocaterra, "Son of the Mountains," 25.

287 This is found in death records, URL: http://search.ancestry.ca/cgi-bin/sse.dll?gl=allgs&gss=sfs63_home&new=1&rank=1&msT=1&gsfn=Arturo&gsfn_x=0&gsln=Talin&gsln_x=0&msypn__ftp=Highwood%2C%20Alberta%2C%20Canada&msypn=5001&msypn_PInfo=5-%7C0%7C1652393%7C0%7C3243%7C0%7C5001%7C0%7C0%7C0%7C0%7C0%7C&cp=0&catbucket=rstp&MSAV=0, retrieved August 10, 2017.

288 David Finch, "Romancing the Dudes," in *Research Links: A Forum for Natural, Cultural and Social Studies*, vol 5, no 3, Winter 1997, 5.

fishing during the open season." Guests were housed in cabins and teepees, supplied with horses and offered guided trips. Those not wishing to ride were offered a reduced rate of $35 a week. The brochure observes: "There are abundant short trips one can take on horseback from the ranch; for instance, the E.P. Ranch of H.R.H. the Prince of Wales, and the well-known Bar U Ranch are only a few miles away...."[289] A willingness to customize trips is touted including forays into the mountains and foothills to experience unspoiled nature.

While Pocaterra was good at the socializing and organization of trips, he was not great at actually running the ranch and had to borrow money to keep the operation afloat. His run of good luck ultimately ran out. In spring 1932, he was struck low by appendicitis and, while in hospital, heard that the mortgage holder on the ranch was calling in the loan. He was bailed out by his friend Raymond M. Patterson, also a lover of the west and an adventurer, who on October 14, 1933, assumed his mortgage, covered his outstanding debts, paid him $700 in cash and gave him title to his own Ghost River property. George was then able to return to Italy to deal with his father's affairs (he had died in 1933).

An inheritance improved George's finances and the stars also aligned romantically. In February 1934, George received a letter from a Calgary friend, William S. Park, informing him that a friend's daughter was studying singing in Milan.[290] He provided George with a letter of introduction to the young woman, Norma Piper, who was a talented soprano. She was born in October 1898 in Leamington, Ontario and had joined her father in Calgary in 1918 where he had a dental practice, and dabbled in oil and other stocks. She studied music with local teachers and had made her Canadian debut in 1931. Her father had used his connections to arrange for the Men's and Women's Canadian Clubs to sponsor the concerts, on February 19, in Calgary at the Central United Church and in Edmonton, on February 25, at the Macdonald Hotel. The Calgary *Albertan* gave it a positive review as did the *Herald*.

Establishing an operatic career in Italy for Norma became the focus of George's life for the next few years. He used his own funds and Norma obtained further monies from her father. In the end, international events put paid to her prospects. On October 3, 1934, Benito Mussolini launched an attack on Abyssinia (Ethiopia) and skirmishes occurred in November and early December. The next few years were not a good time for a foreigner to make her way in the operatic world as the Italian government prepared for war. George blamed this on anti-English sentiment in Italy, which reflected negatively on Norma. To give her some legitimacy, they were finally married

---

[289] Buffalo Head Ranch brochure, 4, Pocaterra Fonds, Glenbow Archives M6340/198.
[290] Pocaterra, "Son of the Mountain," 29.

on June 18, 1936 in a civil ceremony conducted by the Mayor of Milan.[291] For whatever reason, the couple did not notify her family in Canada and created tensions there. Money became an issue when Norma's brothers refused to further support her career though she pointed out that George had spent $10,000 in the past three years in furthering her interests.

In May 1939, when Mussolini signed a military alliance with Hitler, the Pocaterras knew that they had to leave Italy. Greater urgency was added by the fact that George's passport was expiring in October and, according to the couple, his naturalization papers had to be renewed. They left for Switzerland without letting anyone know and embarked for New York on the *Vulcania* from Trieste in September 1939. George had to borrow money from friends in Italy and Canada for the travel costs. They arrived in New York on October 2 and, on October 7, flew to Calgary. The couple faced the prospect of starting again with little money. George had to resort to writing begging letters to better-off friends. The country was gearing up for a declaration of war with Germany and Italy and, in addition, by this point, Norma was too old to begin an operatic career. However, the couple continued to pursue this elusive goal and made trips to Montreal and New York and had discussions with the CBC which led to auditions and some broadcasts.[292] Norma also took small musical engagements, for example, musical clubs.

In spring 1943, they chose to build on the Ghost River property with the expectation that they might operate a small guest ranch. The log home totaled 148 square metres and was named "Valnorma" (Norma's Valley). Their finances were so tight that George had to do most of the construction work. The couple lived there for 13 years. George pursued elusive coal mining and other ventures while she taught at the Mount Royal Conservatory (she did this until the 1970s), as well as through her own studio. She was thus able to pass on her extensive knowledge of operatic music to the next generation of aspiring singers. In 1955, the couple moved to Calgary since it had become inconvenient for them to make the trek for Norma's work. (They had to be in Calgary from Wednesday through Saturday.)

By the 1960s, Pocaterra was a high-profile individual in Calgary. The post-war wave of immigration had increased the city's Italian population enormously and resulted in the establishment of the Calgary Italian Club in 1955. In 1961, the Club presented him with a ceremonial pen in recognition of his status as a pioneer. George also enjoyed the attention of Antonio Rebaudengo, the honorary consul of Italy, who brought visiting dignitaries to the Pocaterra home. Pocaterra Creek, Pocaterra Ridge, Pocaterra Tarn and Pocaterra Mount in Kananaskis were named in his honour and are a testament to his knowledge and love of the land. Norma stated in an oral history

---

[291] Hamblin and Finch, 159.
[292] *Ibid.*, 199.

interview in 1973 that a surveyor, without George's knowledge, had named these features for him.[293] The naming of the Pocaterra Dam in his honour, in 1955, did not please him since he was not happy with Calgary Power developments that diminished the natural beauty of the area.

While George spent the majority of his life in Canada, Roberto (Robert) Basilici's experience was different.[294] He was born in 1882, the second son of Giuseppe Basilici and Adele Mannucci (brother Carlo was two years older). Giuseppe was a successful engineer, who in 1890 with two partners helped develop the Prati district of Rome. The parents supported their sons' artistic leanings (Carlo in poetry and Roberto in art). They received a classical education and Roberto attended the Academy of Fine Arts in Rome and also also studied at the Atelier Sabatté, a private art studio.[295] At the age of 20, Roberto helped to illustrate the first issue of *Fantasio* magazine, published on March 22, 1902 in Rome by Casa Editrice Tipografia Carlo Colombo. The venture was short-lived (it only published 16 issues) but drew positive attention to him. His early works were in the Art Nouveau style that dominated Europe in the last decades of the nineteenth and early decades of the twentieth century.[296] Roberto and Carlo belonged to a number of artistic and political circles including the Circolo Giovanile Socialista (Young Socialists' Circle). In addition, Roberto became enamored with the "idea of America" espoused by German painters who were fascinated by not only the sweeping vistas but also the Indigenous people.

In fall 1905, Roberto, impressed by the new publication *Jugendstil*, decided to study in Munich. Georg Hirth, an eminent writer and publisher had founded *Jugend: Münchner illustrierte Wochenschrift für Kunst und Leben* (Youth: the illustrated weekly magazine of art and lifestyle of Munich), in 1896, and helped popularize Art Nouveau. In fact, the German word for the movement, *Jugendstil*, came from the magazine's name. Roberto quickly made himself at home in Munich joining a large group of young Italian artists studying there, who were part of an Italian expatriate community of about 20,000. Roberto met Hirth and the older man was impressed with his talent and included six of his works in the magazine.[297]

---

[293] Norma Pocaterra, Dante Alighieri Oral History Project, 1973, PAA AN 74.106/14.

[294] There are only three sources of information about Roberto and Elisabet Basilici: Jane (Rummel) Fisher, "Basilici, Elisabet 'Mater' Elsa, 1879-1966," in *Our Foothills* (Calgary, AB: Millarville, Kew, Priddis and Bragg Creek Historical Society, 1975); Ruth Oltmann, *Baroness of the Canadian Rockies* (Exshaw, AB: Ribbon Creek Publishing, 1983); and Paolo Basilici, "Il Pittore Roberto Basilici" (Edizione aggiornata a marzo 2016), URL: http://www.basilici.info/personaggi/roberto.pdf, retrieved August 17, 2017.

[295] *Ibid.*, 4.

[296] *Ibid.*, 6. In Italy, the movement is known as "Lo stile Liberty" named for the British store that specialized in fine arts and handicrafts of the period.

[297] These were: "*Die Oberin*" (Mother Superior), 1906, No. 44; "*Frieden*" (Peace), 1907, No. 45; "*Mademoiselle B.*" (Miss B.), 1906, No. 46; "*Im Bade*," (The Bather), 1906, No. 47; "*Windstille*" (Calm Wind), 1907, No. 48; and "*Am*

The professional relationship led to socializing and resulted in Roberto's meeting Hirth's daughter Elisabet (Elsa) in November 1907. The family was part of the cultivated and artistic elite of Munich and Elsa was charming, sophisticated and a lover of the arts. She was three years older than Roberto (born in 1879 in Munich) and was a twice-married "woman of the world," who spoke four languages and enjoyed travel. Her first husband, Baron Gustav von Rummel, was an adjutant in the army and also an aspiring actor who used Gustave Waldau as his stage name. The couple had three daughters: Elizabet (Lizzie), born in 1897; Johanna (Jane), 1898: and Eugenie (Nina), 1901. The marriage did not last because of his womanizing and they divorced in 1902; she, did, however keep the title baroness, as did her three daughters. In 1903, she married Fritz Weinmann, a classical pianist and composer of Jewish descent. Tragically, he died in October 1905 of peritonitis but left Elsa and the girls well-provided for.

The handsome and talented Roberto captured Elsa's attention and they were married on December 21, 1907 and he appears to have formed a strong bond with her daughters. Elsa loved the "good life" and Roberto quickly came to value the carefree living that wealth allowed. The family travelled within Germany but also abroad. It was on a trip to England in 1909 that the girls took riding lessons from George Welsh, who was Scottish, at his riding school in Shepperton, England. Jane (Rummel) Fisher describes this encounter as follows:

> In 1910 we lived for a summer in Shepperton, near London, England. Mother rented an estate and nearby was a school where western riding and roping was taught. We enrolled and it was here that our love for horses and riding began. Some time later, at a dinner party at our Grand-father's home in Munich, one of the guests told Mother that he had a friend who had a ranch in Alberta, Canada and he might sell it, if Mother was interested. The friend was contacted and agreed to sell and we bought it sight unseen. This was the Gate ranch at Kew.[298]

In April 1911, the family left Germany and sailed for Halifax and then travelled by train to Calgary and eventually arrived at Priddis. They were met by Louis Taylor, who took them to the Gate Ranch (32 km southwest of Priddis). The family fell in love with it and Jane writes: "The buildings were situated on the North Fork of Sheep Creek and the view of the foothills and the mountains beyond was a sight we would always love."[299] They spent a glorious summer but, by fall, Elsa was fed up with life in the Wild West and the family returned to Germany. They were in

---

Tiber" (On the Tiber), 1902, No. 49.

[298] Fisher, 86.

[299] *Ibid.*, 86.

Canada long enough to appear in the 1911 census which enumerated the household as follows: Roberto Basilic (29), Elsa Basilici (32), Lizzie Basilice (14), Jane Basilice (12), Nena Basilici (10) and Guido Mannucci (28). Mannuci, Roberto's cousin, joined them in their western Canadian adventure and travelled with them for several years.

At the girls' insistence, the family returned the summer of 1912 in time to see the first rodeo in Calgary (which became the Stampede), and Jane writes:

> What excitement for us to see all the cowboys and cowgirls in their western clothes; that year the Mexicans were there to compete in the Stampede events and with them [*sic.*] and the Indians in their colorful costumes; it was thrilling to girls so recently over from Europe. Mother bought a silver mounted Mexican saddle for Nina. George Welch [*sic.*], whom we had met when he was an instructor in the Western school at Shepperton, competed in the trick roping and placed third. Returning to Okotoks at the end of the show we got our horses and returned to the hills, Nina on her pony trying out some of the trickriding she had seen in Calgary.[300]

Neither Elsa nor Roberto knew anything about ranching but, luckily, she had hired Welsh to run the property. They returned again in 1913 and 1914 when the outbreak of the First World War trapped them in Canada and placed Elsa in the position of being an enemy alien. Since the family used the surname Basilici, Elsa and her daughters did not encounter the difficulties that other German immigrants experienced.

Money became a major worry since it could not be obtained from Germany and Roberto and Elsa had no option but to make the ranch pay. Jane mentions that they had two milk cows and bought a Clydesdale stallion and some mares from neighbour George Bell. They also acquired stock; Elsa acknowledges the assistance of the Burns ranch manager Jack Dempsey. In 1913, Roberto executed an oil painting titled "Gate Ranch," which remained in the possession of Lizzie until her death. Whether this was done in Canada or Germany is not known. Another painting, which was sold in 2017 by a German auction house, is a wonderful oil depicting a man ploughing a field with two heavy horses. There is an Impressionist quality to the work and the colours are extremely vivid suggesting that Roberto had a strong link to the land.

With the capable Welsh running the ranch, they muddled through but tensions developed between the couple. Ruth Oltmann in *Baroness of the Canadian Rockies*, a biography of Lizzie, notes that Roberto became violent and threatened to take the ranch from Elsa perhaps to sell it to obtain funds. Elsa had registered it in his name, which is borne out in the homestead records,

[300] Fisher, 86.

which show that Roberto filed on March 4, 1915 for SE 20-20-4-5. While the threat of violence was decidedly unpleasant, its motivation is explainable. Visiting the prairies in summer for an extended holiday and returning to civilization in winter was, no doubt, idyllic; when it was replaced by what would have seemed to both Roberto and Elsa an eternity of roughing it in the bush, it resulted in depression and despair. While Oltmann blames Roberto for the tensions, daughter Jane mentioned, after their first summer on the ranch, that her mother was anxious to return to Europe. Even George Pocaterra who had adjusted admirably, on his return to southern Alberta after a seven-year stay in Italy complained about the cold and snow, and joked about heading to a warmer climate.

The tension between their mother and stepfather does not appear to have affected the girls, who loved the life and happily took on chores. They were home schooled by their mother and lessons were blended with chores, riding, reading, listening to music as well as the round of social activities. The family also acquired the old John Ware homestead. He was a renowned Black cowboy whose life came to a tragic end when his horse stumbled in a badger hole causing him to fall; the horse landed on him crushing him. While necessity forced the family to make their ranches going concerns, Jane observes: "We soon became fair ranchers and learned to put up our own hay. We were members of the North Fork Stock Reserve and ran our cattle in the Bow River Forest Reserve and now our sons are doing it."

Roberto must have felt some kinship with Canada, in spite of his discontent, since he enlisted in the Lord Strathcona's Horse (Royal Canadians) on October 28, 1918 (regimental number 2294031). He served until April 7, 1919 and held the rank of captain. His attraction to this regiment is understandable since many of its officers and men were former members of the North-West Mounted Police as well as cowboys and ranchers. His attestation papers list his occupation as a rancher living at Kew. The marital and money problems continued and, in 1919, Elsa sold the oil rights on the ranch for the family to be able to visit Germany to see her ailing mother.[301] She and Roberto lived in separate houses in Munich and she returned to Canada with her daughters in 1920 and Roberto remained behind. It is at this time that he began to act in films.

Roberto returned to Canada in 1921 and the couple separated in 1922 when he returned to Europe to live. They divorced in 1925. It is clear that Roberto, while enjoying the Canadian West as a holiday destination, was unsuited for life there in the long term. He needed the stimulation of the German artistic scene in order to be able to create and the post-war scene was particularly exciting in the area of film production. In the period 1918 to 1933, more than 3,500 feature films

---

[301] Oltmann, 16.

were produced. Roberto continued to act and, by the time of his death in Berlin of throat cancer in October 1929, had completed another seven films.

The family remained on the ranch since the girls loved the life and Elsa travelled back and forth to Germany. Jane married Joe Fisher, the son of an area rancher. Nina married Pat (Paddy) Rodgers, whose family farmed in the Okotoks region. Lizzie became a passionate environmentalist and supporter of the Alpine Club of Canada. She managed a number of mountain lodges including Skoki, Temple, Lake Louise and Sunburst. She was awarded the Order of Canada in 1979 for her passionate championing of the natural environment. Lizzie also became great friends with Lawrence Grassi, a Canmore miner who became renowned for his mountaineering and trail building activities, and for whom Grassi Lakes were named.[302]

Some Observations

Alberta's Italian farmers were incredibly resourceful. Not only did they have to learn a new type of agriculture, but they also had to contend with weather conditions unlike any they had ever known. Regional differences are evident: while settlers in Naples, Edson and Venice-Hylo, succeeded, it was not to the same extent as experienced in the Delia/Lethbridge/Drumheller areas. While the backgrounds of all the immigrants were similar, it appears that conditions in southern Alberta enabled a greater degree of innovation and entrepreneurship than in more northernly regions The dairy operations in the southern communities prospered and, in addition, the adoption of mechanization aided in farm production and brought additional revenues as the equipment was used to thresh grain for others. The harsher climate of northern Alberta also imposed limits on types of crops and yields. The shift into business and professions in the southern agricultural communities was also greater.

The practice of working at other occupations including on the railways, in mines, construction and lumber camps enabled them to bring in the cash required for necessities, and they were able to survive bad crop seasons and even the Great Depression. Wives also had to adapt and resign themselves to the fact that their men would be away for half the year, and that they and their children would need to look after the farm. It was accepted that sons, after completing grade 8, would find paying work. But the next generations benefitted from schooling and moved into the professions. Sons (and some daughters) served in the military in the Second World War in spite of the fact that their parents were under the shadow of enemy alien designation. It would appear

---

[302] Elio Costa and Gabriele Scardellato in their book *Lawrence Grassi: From Piedmont to the Rocky Mountains* (Toronto, ON: University of Toronto Press, 2015) provide a monograph on Lizzie (179-181).

that, in rural areas, Italian immigrants gained greater acceptance and integrated more quickly into the community at large. Marriage with individuals of other ethnicities also helped. This situation was unlike that in mining communities in which class and ethnicity, as well as the conflict between bosses and labour, resulted in polarization that served as a stumbling block to acceptance.

With respect to the Italian cowboys – Pocaterra and Basilici – their experiences were atypical but their stories are of interest because they are outside the norm. They shared a love of the "romance" of the West and, because of their education and class, did not encounter the discrimination experienced by their compatriots. Their photographic collections in the Glenbow Archives captured not only early ranching but also the close relationship that both enjoyed with Indigenous people.

Venice and Hylo Italian settlers: standing (left to right): Luigi Rizzoli, Paul Michetti, Efisio Manca, Otto Michetti, Rosaria Varze, Santina Michetti; sitting: Gisella Michetti, Lydia Michetti, Paolo or Domenico Morelli, Pio Bonifacio. The agricultural colonies were set up in 1914-15 by consular agent Felice de Angelis. Photo courtesy of Lac la Biche Museum & Archives.

George W. Pocaterra, from an aristocratic Italian family, was enamored of the life of the cowboy and set up a ranch at Longview in southern Alberta. He is pictured on his horse Don, ca. 1911. Photo courtesy of Glenbow, Archives and Special Collections, University of Calgary NA-695-1.

The People's Bakery van with Curly Miglierina in front with an unknown child, Drumheller, Alberta, August 15, 1918. Photo courtesy of Glenbow, Archives and Special Collections, University of Calgary NA-2389-31.

CHAPTER V

Shopkeepers, Tradesmen and Entrepreneurs

WHILE THE EARLIEST WAVE of Italian immigration (1896-1914) largely comprised labourers, there were skilled individuals among them. Italy had an established trade apprenticeship system, and skilled craftsmen such as carpenters, masons, metalsmiths, tailors, shoemakers, jewellers, watchmakers and others had standing in the community denied to unskilled labourers. In fact, *mastro* (master) was an honorary address. In all eras of immigration, individuals used their trade as a tool for economic improvement but it was not just tradesmen who started businesses; there were entrepreneurial individuals who despite limited education and skills prospered. These businesses did not necessarily continue into future generations; in some instances, this gave credence to the old adage that the first generation made the money, and the second or third generations spent it. A more significant reason for businesses not surviving was the value placed on higher education that resulted in children and grandchildren entering the professions. Others did not survive because of economic forces, for example, the Great Depression of the 1930s.

Initially, small businesses provided services within the Italian community, but success built on success, and many ended up serving the larger community. The family-run grocery store (described by Italians as *generi alimentari*) became a staple in many communities, as did the bakery and shoe, tailor and barber shops. Other immigrants set up construction companies, manufacturing establishments and other services. Such ventures expedited movement into the mainstream. The following account focuses on prominent individuals in the first half of the twentieth century.

Hoteliers

The first example of the rise to prominence of an Italian entrepreneur ended in tragedy. The so-called "race" card had everything to do with the downfall of Emilio Picariello, a prominent shopkeeper and hotelier in the Elk Valley and Crowsnest Pass regions. Emilio is not remembered for his hard work and enterprising nature but rather as the convicted murderer of Alberta Provincial Police Constable Stephen Lawson, as a result of a Prohibition "sting" operation gone wrong.[303] Emilio's crime reinforced the belief that Italians were not to be trusted because of their innate "criminal" instincts noted by Rev. Woodsworth in *Strangers Within Our Gates*. Although Picariello was born on November 27, 1879 in Capriglia, Avellino, Campania, in the bootlegging literature, he is said to be Sicilian because of that region's association with the Mafia. While the location of his birthplace could be found, no-one bothered to check. Campania is located in central Italy and its capital is Naples.

Picariello's father, Modestino, was a tenant farmer who believed in education. His sons were taught to read and write at the local convent. Members of the extended Picariello family were established in the US and were encouraging the oldest son, Pellegrino, to immigrate. Because he had a sweetheart, he was not interested, so Emilio went in his place around 1899-1900.[304] He arrived at Ellis Island and settled in Allentown, a community in Buffalo, New York. Unable to find his uncles, he found work as a labourer and also attended English classes. A poster advertising the position of electrician's helper with the Guelph Radial Railway brought him to Canada in September 1902. He lived in a boarding house and saved money during the fall so he could afford to buy a run-down store in Toronto. He fixed it up and opened for business Christmas 1903, and subsequently opened another confectionery in Montreal. Maria Marucci (born 1883), whose family had emigrated from San Marco, D'Cavotti, Calabria, to Pennsylvania, was visiting her brother Antonio and wife Anna in Toronto, and went to the store. Picariello asked for permission to court her and the couple married in April 1904 in Arlington, New Jersey at the home of her brother, Joseph. Mariannina ("little Mary") assisted him in the Toronto store, which flourished. Son Stefano (Steve) was born in 1905 and Angelina Rose (Julie), in 1907.

Picariello made friends with Frank Celli, an agent for Italian food suppliers, who encouraged him to go to Fernie to take over management of the Columbian Macaroni Factory. An article titled "Off to a Good Start" in the *Fernie Free Press* of May 26, 1910, provides a glowing overview of the block-long, two-storey brick structure with a fire-proof roof to be built by the Marinaro Bros. as well as a two-storey duplex residence. In 1911, Picariello sold his stores and the family moved to Fernie. When the Marinaros left to set up another factory in Lethbridge, Picariello purchased the business and duplex. Picariello went on to open a cigar factory, ice cream plant and other food retail outlets as well as purchasing a small farm in the Spokane Valley from which

[303] I first encountered the Picariello story when I developed the *Celebrating Alberta's Italian Community* website for the Alberta Online Encyclopedia in 2002. I chose him as one of the six "maverick" characters I was contracted to prepare for the new Western Canadian Gallery at Glenbow (2004-2005). In 2015-2016, I developed a travelling exhibit for the Fernie Museum and wrote the book *The Rise and Fall of Emilio Picariello* (Fernie, BC: Oolichan Press, 2015).
[304] I have been unable to locate travel documents in online searches.

he trucked produce. The success of the businesses placed him above the miners, and he became known for his generosity particularly during strikes. Around 1914, Picariello became the Fernie representative of the Pollock Wine Company and collected and bought used bottles for re-sale to brewers and distillers. This led to a monopoly and, in 1916, he advertised in the *Free Press* as "E. Pick, the Bottle King." He hired Carlo (Charlie) Sanfidele, and a mechanic, Jack McAlpine, to help him. Stephen and Julie helped to roll cigars and Steve operated the horse-drawn ice cream cart that Emilio built to sell cones around the city. In advertisements, Picariello invited the public to come to the Macaroni Factory to watch ice cream being made and also offered free cones to children in exchange for bottles. It took Prohibition becoming law in Alberta on July 1, 1916 and, in BC, on October 1, 1917, that presented a business opportunity that he could not pass up and that would set the course of the remainder of his life.

In spring 1918, Picariello purchased the Alberta Hotel in Blairmore from Frits Sick, a founder of the Fernie-Fort Steele Brewery who had moved to Lethbridge to set up the Lethbridge Brewing and Malting Company. Picariello became the brewery's sole agent in the Crowsnest Pass selling their Temperance beer with 2.5 percent alcohol content. The family moved into the second floor of the hotel. During the Spanish Influenza outbreak of 1918, it is said that Emilio allowed the hotel to be used for the care of victims. He also bought war bonds. Around 1920, Picariello set up the Crowsnest Pass Clothing Company on the ground floor of the hotel in partnership with John Bannatyne Risk, a former APP officer. He invested $11,000 in the business, which was run by Risk, and they shared profits 50/50. Charlie Sanfidele, who had married Filumena (Florence) Costanzo, the daughter of a Fernie miner in 1915, continued to work for him, as did McAlpine. Charlie and Florence went on a honeymoon trip to the US and, on returning to Fernie, Charlie assumed a new name – Lassandro (Losandro) – ostensibly because he had entered the US illegally.[305] Both men assisted Picariello in bootlegging as did Italian friends in the Crowsnest Pass, Fernie and the Elk Valley. The Lassandros, for a time, also resided in the hotel and Florence helped Mariannina with care of the children.

In 1921, the *Prohibition Act* was repealed in British Columbia and led to a proliferation of liquor warehouses in Fernie. Liquor could be bought legally in BC but could not be transported across provincial lines to Alberta, or state lines to the Pacific Northwest. In addition, a range of import/export liquor companies straddling the two provinces were set up to facilitate the trade. The Brown Export Co., Blairmore, which represented the Pollock Wine Co., Ltd., Fernie,

---

[305] Jock Carpenter, in her fictionalized account of Florence Lassandro's life *Bootlegger's Bride* (Hanna, AB: Gorman & Gorman, 1993), ascribes another motive stating that Charlie was involved in crime in the US and also used Florence for purposes of prostitution. There is no proof of this.

Carosella Liquor Co., Fernie, and the Michel Liquor Co., Natal, BC was one example; the Fernie Liquor Exporters, which partnered with the King's Exporting Agency, Limited, Lethbridge was another. The individual behind the latter was Mark Rogers, an American from Massachusetts who settled near Lethbridge.

Since both the Elk Valley and the Crowsnest Pass had voted against Prohibition, there was no stigma attached to making money in this way. The majority of warehouses were run by men of British or American ancestry. The owners of the dozen or so hotels in Fernie were also involved in the liquor trade not only selling Prohibition beer in their bars but also operating liquor warehouses. Italians were, thus, in the minority among the ranks of professional bootleggers in The Pass and Picariello became an object of jealousy.

Cases of liquor were hidden in coal cars and many railroad workers made money aiding professional bootleggers. The extensive railway network linking BC with Alberta and the two provinces with the Pacific Northwest, and beyond to Eastern Canada and the US was just too large to police. Bootleggers also hid cases of liquor in the trunks of speedy vehicles, in particular, the McLaughlin-Buick. A typical run involved three vehicles, two to serve as lookouts and the third to carry the liquor. The convoy would pick up liquor in Fernie and transport it through the Crowsnest communities of Coleman and Blairmore to Lethbridge, and then south via the "Whiskey Gap" to Montana. The pass was used to bring liquor into Alberta from the US but, after 1919, the flow was reversed to satisfy liquor-starved Americans.

Picariello's bootlegging business prospered and he bribed local politicians and provincial MLAs. Some local mayors even ran liquor themselves. The coming to power of the United Farmers of Alberta on August 13, 1921, was to have an enormous impact on the enforcement of Prohibition. Premier Herbert Greenfield came under fire from the media and the party's grass roots, the majority of who supported passage of Prohibition. In response, the Alberta Provincial Police, in April 1922, appointed a new superintendent, W. C. (Teddy) Bryan, a former North-West Mounted Police officer. Bryan added an additional 50 men to the force and many were deployed in the Crowsnest Pass and Lethbridge regions. Picariello became the target of the new team of officers in The Pass, which included sergeants James O. Scott and John James Nicholson, and Constable Stephen Lawson, hired in spring 1922. Lawson was the former police chief of Fernie and had first-hand knowledge of Picariello. A "sting" operation was set up with the support of two of Picariello's rivals: Mark Rogers, an established Lethbridge businessman, and Jack Wilson, a recent immigrant from Ireland to whom Picariello had lent a thousand dollars to set up in the liquor trade in Fernie. The former was known as "Mr. R." and the latter as "Mr. Big."

In a book titled *The Rise and Fall of Emilio Picariello*, I make the case that a liquor order placed by Rogers with Picariello as the delivery agent initiated the sting that occurred on September

21, 1922.[306] The APP and local police tracked Picariello, McAlpine and Steve as they drove from Blairmore to Fernie to pick up liquor and then returned to the Blairmore Hotel. Steve's taking part in the run was unusual – his mother refused to have him involved in the liquor trade. When challenged by police, Picariello motioned to Steve, who was carrying the load, to make a run for Fernie. Steve drove through Coleman where Constable Lawson was on the lookout and, when told to stop, continued driving; Lawson fired and wounded him in the hand. Steve arrived in Natal where he met a BC Provincial Police officer and asked for medical help, and later telephoned his father to let him know he was alright.

Later that evening, Sergeant Scott told Picariello to bring his son in otherwise there would be trouble. Picariello, accompanied by Florence Lassandro, went to the APP barracks in Coleman where he confronted Lawson. The only witness was Lawson's nine-year-old daughter Pearlie, who was playing behind Picariello's vehicle. She testified that she saw her father standing on the running board of the car hugging "Mr. Pick" and then heard a shot and saw her father fall. After the shooting, Picariello drove back to Blairmore where he dropped Lassandro off at a friend's place and then returned to the Alberta Hotel. There he heard that Lawson had died and went into hiding at a friends' home in "Italian town."

A police manhunt resulted in his arrest at 4:30 pm the afternoon of September 22; Florence turned herself in. The APP then continued their catalogue of errors led by Sergeant Scott who did not take any notes of the interviews with the two accused. Picariello and Lassandro were charged with murder. A preliminary hearing was held in the Coleman Opera House on October 2-3, 1922, and the couple was bound over for trial. After a sensational trial in Calgary, lasting from November 27 to December 2, 1922, in which the accused were tried jointly and defended by John McKinley Cameron, a bastion of Calgary's legal establishment, they were found guilty of murder. The entire trial was attended by Alberta's Attorney General John E. Brownlee (another violation of accepted trial practice). The press reportage pitted the Anglo-establishment against the immigrant community.

Cameron's defence was lacklustre and focused on trying to discredit police with respect to what today would be described as violating the rights of the accused, and procedural matters including the fact that Scott had intimidated Lassandro into confessing that she had murdered Lawson. She had been carrying a firearm and had fired it in self-defence when she heard gunshots while Lawson was grappling with Picariello seated behind the steering wheel of the car. A bullet hole was found in the dash and the windshield of the Picariello vehicle was shattered. The fact

---

[306] I found this among the papers of his lawyer, J. McKinley Cameron (Picariello/Lassandro Trial) Fonds, Glenbow Archives M 6840, NA 4691.

that the majority of glass debris was found inside the vehicle supported Picariello's claim that there was a shooter in the alley. Lassandro could not have shot Lawson from inside the vehicle because Picariello blocked her view of him and, in addition, he was shot in the back, again corroborating Picariello's claim of innocence. It is unlikely that Lawson, in the middle of a tussle with Picariello, would have turned his back to run away thereby providing an excellent target. Cameron did not call any witnesses including a Red Deer lawyer who claimed that he had evidence of police corruption with respect to other Prohibition cases. It was likely that Cameron believed that it was a trial that he could not win. He did, however, bring up what he described as the "race card" suggesting that Picariello was being pilloried for being Italian.

Extensive correspondence in Cameron's files reveals that he believed in his clients' innocence. Picariello told his lawyers that his rivals – Wilson and Rogers – were in the Pass at the time. The collusion between the APP and rival bootleggers was supported by the discovery made by his supporting counsel, prominent Fernie lawyer Sherwood Herchmer, that Rogers drove Sergeant Nicholson and other members of the APP and the RCMP from Lethbridge to Blairmore for the manhunt. Rogers also drove the police team and Picariello to jail in Lethbridge. An appeal to the Appellate Division of the Supreme Court of Alberta succeeded; however, there was one dissenting opinion that allowed an additional appeal to the Supreme Court of Canada. This failed and Picariello and Lassandro were hung on May 2, 1923 at the Fort Saskatchewan Gaol. Picariello's fall, while tragic for the protagonists and their families, served as an abject lesson to other immigrants about the importance of keeping a low profile, learning English and assimilating as quickly as possible.

Picariello and Lassandro's story has featured in bootlegging literature as well as artistic productions. John Estacio and John Murrell's opera *Filumena* is based on the premise of Picariello's guilt and Lassandro's innocence. The opera enjoyed public success when it was premiered in Calgary by the Calgary Opera Company in 2003 and, again, in 2005, as part of Alberta Scene, the arts tribute to Alberta's centenary at the National Arts Centre in Ottawa. In February 2017, the opera was COC's tribute to Canada's 150th anniversary and Canada Post issued a commemorative stamp. The company brought in the "Rise and Fall of Emilio Picariello" exhibit from the Fernie Museum, which I curated, and it was set up in the lobby of the Southern Alberta Jubilee Auditorium. Visual artist Gisele Amantea created 14, black and white panels including cartoons dealing with the Picariello/Lassandro story in the communities of Fernie and Coleman. The exhibit, titled "Reading History Backwards," was featured in 2002 at the Dunlop Art Gallery, Regina Public Library. In 2007, these were published in book form as *The King v. Picariello and Lassandro*.[307]

---

[307] Gisele Amantea, *The King v. Picariello and Lassandro* (Toronto, ON: Frank Iacobucci Centre for Italian Canadian Studies at the University of Toronto and Dunlop Art Gallery, Regina Public Library, 2007).

A counterpoint to the Picariello story is provided by Giorgio (George) Giuseppe Cantalini; he dabbled in bootlegging but prospered. He was born in 1885 in Navelli, L'Aquila, Abruzzo, and immigrated to Canada in 1904, settling in Lille where he worked in the mines. An article in the *Medicine Hat News* in 1953 notes that George's family had operated grocery stores and worked as wine merchants in Italy. It continues: "George was well acquainted with the wine and liquor business and, as soon as he reached the age of 21, in 1906, he took a job in the Cross liquor store in Blairmore. He later worked in the Mike Rossi liquor store in Blairmore and in the Fernie Brewery Store in Frank."[308] A. E. Cross was a prominent Alberta rancher who, in 1892, set up the Calgary Brewing and Malting Co. as well as a number of liquor stores. The article continues: "During the Prohibition era, besides handling Sicks' products, Mr. Cantalini purchased and operated three poolrooms in Bellevue."[309] In fact, he was an employee, a fact confirmed by the 1916 census, which lists his occupation as worker in a liquor store.

The reference to Mike Rossi's liquor store is extremely important. Rossi, who also spelled his name "Rosse," immigrated to the US in 1886 and lived in New York for a time before moving to the Crowsnest Pass, in 1903. He started working in the mine at Lille and, in 1905, purchased a liquor wholesale business in Blairmore. Rossi prospered and local historian Ian McKenzie writes: "With the coming of Prohibition in 1916, Mike's liquor outlet was converted to a pool hall. With his connections within the liquor distribution trade, Mike became one of the better-known sources of illegally imported alcohol. He was also Blairmore's police commissioner! The *Blairmore Enterprise* and other papers often joked about the presence of 'blind pigs' in the Rosse mansion."[310] A blind pig was a speakeasy, an establishment that stocked liquor for the consumption of patrons during Prohibition. Rossi was fined for liquor infractions but this did not affect his standing in the community.

While Cantalini may have been as pure as the un-driven snow, it is highly unlikely based on who he worked for, and the fact that he had money to invest when he moved to Medicine Hat in 1927 and purchased the Corona Hotel. There is no doubt that George was clever and entrepreneurial. According to the *Medicine Hat News*, hotel bankruptcies were common in the city but George's enterprises not only survived the Great Depression but went from strength to strength. In 1931, he acquired the historic Assiniboia Hotel and, in 1934, the Royal Hotel. In 1944, the old Assiniboia Hotel burned down and George vowed to rebuild when circumstances permitted. After the fire, he purchased the Cosmopolitan Hotel, which became the firm's headquarters. There would be delays in rebuilding the Assiniboia due to war-time shortages but the acquisition

308 *Anon.*, "Assiniboia is New Success for George Cantalini," *Medicine Hat News*, Tuesday, January 6, 1953.
309 Cantalini Family Fonds, Medicine Hat Archives/Esplanade Archives, MED-753.
310 Ian McKenzie, "The 'Colorful' Mike Rosse," *Heritage News: Discover Crowsnest Pass*, issue #27, May 2013.

of a site occurred in 1946. This was the Huckvale Block at the corner of Third Street and South Railway Street. A number of the Cantalini children became involved in the business beginning with oldest son Alfred, who started as a clerk at the Corona.

There was much media interest in the future hotel. In the *Medicine Hat News* of May 18, 1951, there are four articles on page 16. The lead one is titled "New Assiniboia Hotel Replaces Old Landmark Hostelry." It observes that rising costs of materials was a concern for the owners and also notes that the projected cost was $750,000, a significant investment for the time. The old Huckvale Block was being incorporated into the structure, which was four storeys and had a square, modernist look. A second article titled "Largest and Most Modern Structure for Gas City" provides details of building finishes, the banquet-ballroom and coffee shop. In another article Cantalini is praised for giving business to local firms. The *Medicine Hat News* of January 6, 1953 reported that the opening of the Assiniboia Hotel occurred on the twenty-fifth anniversary of "Mr. Cantalini's entrance on the Medicine Hat business scene."[311] The business venture is described as an act of great civic-mindedness providing employment to 65-70 people with a payroll of $100,000. Mayor Henry Veiner participated at the ribbon-cutting ceremony, which was attended by Senator Dr. F. W. Gershaw, MP W. D. Wylie and R. H. A. Lacey of the Chamber of Commerce. Cantalini's rags to riches story took him from the ranks of miner to saloon keeper/bootlegger to hotelier. All the children were educated and contributed to the business. In 1953, Alfred managed the Assiniboia and Royal hotels; daughter Elsa was the bookkeeper for the Cosmopolitan Hotel; Joseph managed the Corona Hotel; and Maurice, the Cosmopolitan Hotel. Elsa's obituary describes her as "a highly respected business woman" and notes that she worked as the accountant in the family business for over 40 years.

Angelo (Monte) Montemurro parlayed a thriving hotel business in Mayerthorpe into political office. The Montemurro brothers – Frank, Jack and Angelo (Monte) – left Cosenza, Calabria, in 1905, to join their father who was working on the railways. Monte was only 12 years old.[312] The family settled in Vancouver where Monte learned to speak English and attended school until grade ten. He also studied music and performed with a local orchestra. By 1918, the three brothers were working in the mines in Wayne near Drumheller. Monte next went to work for the railway and ended up with responsibility for booking lodgings for railway workers. This gave him an informal business education and, in 1926, he purchased a general store, butcher shop and boarding house at Saunders Creek, a coal mining community west of Rocky Mountain House.

[311] *Anon.*, "Assiniboia is New Success for George Cantalini," *Medicine Hat News*, Tuesday, January 6, 1953.
[312] Mayerthorpe and District History Book Society, "Angelo Mario Montemurro," *Three Trails Home: A history of Mayerthorpe and Districts*, 396-397.

In 1930, Monte and wife Adelina Graham moved to Mayerthorpe where they purchased the Hub Hotel. The building of the Canadian Northern Railway, in 1919, gave the community strategic importance and it was incorporated as a village in 1927. At the time, it had a population of 149 but was ripe for development. In 1933, Monte ran for town council and was elected and served for eight years. In 1934, he built the first theatre in the community and on Saturdays provided free shows for children. It burned down in 1935 but Monte quickly rebuilt it. He also started a brass band that played Saturday evenings and attracted area farmers to the town. In 1938, he went directly to Nathan Tanner, Minister of Lands and Mines, and was instrumental in obtaining land that was divided into 62 lots for a new subdivision.

Monte continued to serve on town council and was the town's mayor from 1949 to 1952 and was instrumental in establishing a Treasury Branch in the town. In 1952, he ran as a Social Credit candidate for the riding of Lac Ste. Anne and won. The community history notes: "During the four years with the Alberta government, through his suggestions to the ministers and the Premier, acts such as assistance to the mentally affected children, the homestead act, the divided highways and hotel restrictions from five hundred to one thousand population for the first license were amended or changed or annexed."[313] He was narrowly defeated and returned to running his business further expanding the hotel. In 1963, Monte was re-elected mayor and served a number of terms.

Grocers and Tradesmen

The presence of Italians in Alberta created a demand for Italian goods and, as a result, grocery stores proliferated. Some may have had experience in Italy as shopkeepers but the large majority risked all to try a new venture that avoided work in the mines. It was the mining communities that provided the largest opportunities since in the early decades of the twentieth century they had larger Italian populations and provided an alternative to the company store that gouged miners of their hard-won wages. The earliest-recorded Italian immigrant grocer was likely Giuseppe (Joseph) Defeo (also Defee or Dafoe), who operated a confectionery in Canmore. He had an untimely end: the store was robbed on November 24, 1899 and he was beaten to death. The inquest found that about $400 had been stolen.[314] No-one was ever charged with the offense.

Italo Rader and Andy Oliva started grocery stores in the Crowsnest Pass; both prospered but Rader went on to gain political profile and power. The self-styled "Macaroni King," when interviewed in old age, claimed to have brought pasta to Albertans. He was born in Pesaro, Urbino,

---

313 *Ibid.*, 396.
314 Rob Alexander, *The History of Canmore* (Banff, AB: Summerthought Publishing, 2010), 91.

and, in 1900, at the age of 17, saw a CPR display at the Paris World's Fair advertising Canada as a "Land of Opportunity" and was inspired to immigrate. His story is told in a 1953-article in *The Vancouver Sun* titled "Local 'King' Back from Italy: $37 Stretched into Macaroni Fortune."[315] Italo was 71 years old and reminiscing about his life in Canada, which began in 1906 when he arrived in Blairmore. He had learned barbering during military service and this is how he initially made a living. In 1906 he opened a grocery store and operated it until 1915 when he sold it and started a macaroni factory in Lethbridge. He noted: "When I started, Canadians were eating a half a pound of macaroni per person; now it is four pounds per person per year."

The linkage between the various macaroni plants in the Elk Valley and southern Alberta is interesting. A macaroni factory was begun in Calgary around 1905 but it failed; no information is known about who did this. The Marinaro Bros. built the Columbian Macaroni Factory in Fernie in 1910 and moved to Lethbridge where they built the Columbia Macaroni Factory in 1913 at Second Avenue and 12th Street. It is likely that Italo took over this factory. In 1922, because of his stature as a business owner, the Government of Italy appointed Rader as the consular agent for Calgary and Lethbridge. An article in the *Lethbridge Daily Herald* of March 21, 1925 titled "Lethbridge Has Two Consuls: Consular Agent for Italy Heads Macaroni Factory," explores the roles of consuls in Alberta. Journalist Charlotte Gordon presents Rader as a far-sighted individual:

> Mr. Rader has large business interests in Lethbridge and Calgary as president and manager of the Columbia Macaroni Company. He has always taken a keen interest in educational matters and kept in close touch with the schools, considering that the younger generation of Italians are trained and moulded, through the medium of education, into fine Canadian citizens. He encourages his people to grasp the opportunities afforded in a new country…. Mr. Rader gives particular attention to opportunities on the land, for his countrymen…. There are quite a number of Italians engaged in farming, in mining and in business of various kinds.[316]

Italo mentions that he had held the consular agent office for three years and served about 3,500 Italians in southern Alberta. He told the reporter that prior to the war, he had imported macaroni from Italy but rising labour costs in the country had resulted in price increases and helped his locally-made product, made from western Canadian hard wheat, which he describes as

---

[315] *Anon.*, "Local 'King' Back from Italy: $37 Stretched into Macaroni Fortune," *Vancouver Sun*, October 26, 1953. I would like to thank historian Ray Culos for providing me with a copy of this article.

[316] Charlotte Gordon, "Lethbridge Has Two Consuls of Foreign Nations," in the *Lethbridge Daily Herald*, March 21, 1925. The other consular agent is for the US.

"second to none in the world." He noted that, during the war, the British government purchased "a million pounds weight" of macaroni in Alberta and that "they were willing to pay extra freight charges instead of purchasing in Montreal because of the fine quality of macaroni made from Western hard wheat." Italo took his "trade commissioner" responsibilities very seriously and noted that facilities in Alberta could not handle export trade to Italy but that this was an opportunity to be developed. He mentioned that current trade from Vancouver to Italy went via the Panama Canal and included grain, salmon, lumber and condensed milk.

A letter to the editor of the *Lethbridge Herald*, which appeared in April 16, 1925, further demonstrates his expertise in matters of trade and also how assiduously he courted the media. Under the heading "The Tariff," Rader observed that the US had imposed higher tariffs on Canadian-made steel from Ontario and Quebec entering the US because the exports had benefited from lower freight rates. The US accused Canada of "dumping" this merchandise. This is a surprisingly current issue as is Italo's observation:

> This shows how the United States government, through its treasury department, protects its own industries and maintains employment for its people. This is only an indication of the well-known policy.
>
> Our Canadian cattle and other farm products are shut out by prohibitive tariffs. The market that our fishermen had created in the United States was swept away when the United States raised the duty on fish. A special duty shut coal mined in the maritime provinces out of the Eastern States.

In 1928, Italo sold the business to the Catelli Company for a reputed $80,000 (over $1.2 million in 2020) but was required to continue working for them to prevent competition. In 1930, he moved to Vancouver to start another plant for Catelli.

Because of his Fascist sympathies, Rader would be interned but, after the war, his fortunes rose again and he was appointed honorary consul of Italy in Vancouver. He was a great believer in education and his children prospered: Theresa became a teacher; Louis obtained a Ph D in Electrical Engineering at Cal Tech and joined General Electric in the US; Albert was a dentist; and Tiny studied Electrical Engineering at UBC receiving his degree in 1935. He served in the Canadian army and, after demobilization, started his own company, Rader Pneumatics, and, in 1956, sold it to his staff and joined Allen-Bradley Canada, a manufacturer of automation equipment, as a sales manager in Galt, Ontario.

Leandro (Andy) Oliva was another early entrepreneur. He was born in 1890 in Pellaro, Reggio Calabria, but his story is atypical because he was brought to the US, in 1892, by his father

Frank and received his entire education in North America.[317] In 1906, when he was 16, his father returned to Italy and Andy decided to stay. He joined relatives in Coleman and obtained a job as foreman in the mine. In 1910, he built a grocery store and operated it for three years and then sold it to go the US. Within two years, he was back in Coleman running the Italian Co-operative store. The two-storey structure was built by the Italian miners' fraternal society, the Società di Mutuo Soccorso, and had a large hall on the second floor used for social gatherings. Andy's success brought him a job offer to work at a co-op in Drumheller and he moved there in 1917. His earnings totaled $225 a month and this enabled him to save and build four houses, which he rented. By 1921, he was back in The Pass residing in Blairmore with wife Anita. In 1937, he founded The Pass Furniture Company, which he operated until 1945. The two-storey frame building initially housed the offices and presses of the *Blairmore Enterprise* newspaper on the second floor; Oliva converted this space into a hall similar to the Italian Hall in Coleman and made it available for rentals. Over the years, it was used to host dances, concerts, card tournaments and meetings by groups such as the Elks, Order of the Eastern Star, the Lions Club and Loyal Order of the Moose. Eventually, he also started a confectionery store that he operated until 1974.

Not all enterprises were single proprietorships: friendships sometimes resulted in commercial ventures. Primo De Cecco was born in northern Italy and began work as a boy of nine or 10 in Hungary helping carry bricks on building projects; in the process, he learned the mason's trade. After service in the Italian army, in 1908, he left Trieste with his best friend Louis Fidenato and embarked on the *SS La Touraine* and arrived at Ellis Island. The two made their way westward and found work in mines at Lille and Coleman.[318] In 1913, Primo sponsored a young woman of 16, Angela, so that he could marry her. She was accompanied by John D'Appolonia and his mother and sister as well as a 15-year-old boy, Angelo Toppano, who was joining his father in Coleman.

In an oral history interview, in 1973, Toppano recounted that he joined his father in May 1913 from Udine where the family had lived for generations.[319] His father had come to Coleman in 1906 as a sojourner but decided to stay and sponsored his son. On his arrival, Angelo was placed in grade 3 with 8 year olds and felt totally out of place but, as a concession to his father, whose dream it was to see him educated, he attended night school. But he wanted to work and make money, so he got a job picking rocks on the mine tipple. He next got work at the International

---

[317] "Oliva, Andy," in *Crowsnest and Its People*, 745-746.

[318] Ferucio De Cecco, "De Cecco, Primo," in *Crowsnest and Its People*, 489.

[319] See "Toppano, Angelo (1898-1976)," in *Crowsnest and Its People*, 867-868. Toppano was interviewed in 1973 for the Dante Alighieri Oral History Project, Provincial Archives of Alberta PR0915.

Mine in Coleman as a "dinky driver." This is where his friend Primo worked firing boilers – the plant generated electricity not only for the mine but also for the town.

In 1928, Toppano and De Cecco decided to open a grocery story on Second Street (this was the store built in 1910 by Andy Oliva) and it was run by their wives, Ines and Angela. The men continued to work in the mines. In 1943, Angela died and Primo decided he no longer wanted to be involved and the Toppanos became sole owners. In the interview, Angelo noted with pride that he became known as the "Maccaroni King" of Coleman. He also expressed concern about the effect that big corporations who "grab everything" were having on small businesses and which might be forced to "give up." He noted that, if that happened, "they'll be sorry because independent business is the backbone of the nation." He was active in community affairs and served on town council, the Coleman Board of Trade, the Elks, and the Italian Society, the Ordine Indipendenti Fior d'Italia.

Hard work did not guarantee business success; this was certainly the case with the Carmelos. Nicola (Nick) Ciarmelo (Carmelo) left Italy in 1899 when he was 16 and travelled to Argentina, New York and Chicago before moving to Canada in 1906 to work in the mines at Hosmer. In 1909, mining work took him to Coleman and, in 1911 he was joined by wife Carmela. Nick built a large house in West Coleman with a bakery and barber shop on the ground floor. Carmela did the baking. The next move was to Beaver Mines where Nick again built a house and bake-shop. Carmela was both the brains and brawn in the bakery as the family history makes clear: "As Mrs. Carmelo had no equipment, she mixed a batch of dough from fifty pounds of flour by hand. When Nick was able to help, they would use one hundred pounds of flour. The bread was baked in specially-constructed brick ovens. Mrs. Carmelo sold large loaves of bread at three for 25 cents. In this way she made a profit of $5.00 on a hundred pound sack of flour that cost her $3.00. For three years they operated the bakery."[320]

In 1917, tragedy struck when their infant daughter Lily died as a result of an allergic reaction to a bee sting. Carmela gave birth to another daughter, Agnes, 18 days later. The family's troubles were compounded when a fire of unknown origin destroyed their home and business. The family went on to homestead without great success and then Nick set up a lumber business and supplied timber to the newly-opened McGillivray Mine. Bad luck struck again: he contracted mumps and this resulted in the quarantining of his lumber camp for six weeks with no money coming in and 60 men to feed. In addition, the timber on the land that he leased turned out to be rotten and could not be harvested. He sold his equipment and, in 1924, filed for a homestead in the Cowley area and invested $6,000 in farming. While Nick with a hired man did the farm work, Carmela did the milking, and raised pigs, turkeys, geese and chickens as well as keeping a large

---

[320] Anon., "Nick Carmelo," in *Crowsnest and Its People*, 455.

garden. She also made butter and cheese for sale. Eventually they returned to Coleman. While the Carmelos did not achieve great material success, their honest labour earned them a good living.

What was probably one of Calgary's earliest Italian grocery stores was set up by an unlikely individual: Giovanni Mamini, who had served in the Royal Italian Navy and achieved the rank of Commander. He was referred to as "Cavaliere," the Italian for knight and whether the title was a military or civilian honour is not known. He was born in 1864 and arrived at Ellis Island on January 29, 1901 from northern Italy. By 1908, he was operating a store on Fourth Street East. His education and rank conferred distinct advantages and he also appears to have had money.[321] Giovanni became involved in real estate with Leopold Jacques, who was operating a Real Estate Trust Money Club. In Calgary's over-heated property market prior to the First World War, there were many investors who were looking to make money through purchase and resale of property. Giovanni bought shares in a venture involving six lots in Block 29, Regal Terrace, which Jacques had purchased for $4,500, and was selling shares worth $10 each. Significant properties were built in this subdivision, which was located on the Edmonton Trail hill and offered stunning views of southeast Calgary and the lower Bow River Valley. Mamini also undertook property purchases in his own right and had dealings with the CPR. In 1907, he was joined by wife Laura. Giovanni died young, in May 1913, during a mountaineering expedition in the Swiss Alps, leaving his widow and three children: Robert, Daisy (Brawn), and Joan Lilyan (Stuckey).

Giovanni was also an agent of the Western Canada Insurance Company and his association with Switzerland suggests that he may have been involved with Canadian Pacific and other steamship lines bringing contract labour from Italy to North America. His widow and children appear in the 1916 Census in which Laura is listed as an alien and her birthplace as Austria. Son Bob became sports editor at the *Calgary Herald*. (Gerald Brawn, Daisy's husband, was also an editor.)[322] Daisy and Gerald's son, Robert, graduated from the University of Alberta with a degree in Chemical Engineering and worked for Mobil Oil Canada and other companies in Calgary. He sat on the Board of the Calgary 1988 Winter Olympics and was inducted into the Calgary Business Hall of Fame.

Domenico Gasbari's grocery store is associated with the early history of Calgary's Italian community. He was born in Abruzzo and, according to daughter Flavia Santucci, completed his education in Italy and trained as a shoemaker before immigrating to the US in 1899.[323] He first

[321] The Giovanni Mamini Fonds, Glenbow Archives M-807, consist of legal, land and business records of Mamini's enterprises in Calgary in the period 1908-1911. They were gifted in 1965 by Gerald Brawn, the husband of daughter Daisy.
[322] In 1958, the Scott-Mamini Award, was created by the Calgary Press-Radio-TV Sports Club, to recognize the city's Athlete of the Year. It was named for hockey player Harry Scott, sports editor of the *Calgary Albertan*, and Bob Mamini.
[323] Flavia Santucci oral history, Calgary Italian Club Historical Project, May 22, 1986, Glenbow Archives RCT-869-23.

worked in stone quarries in Vermont for 35 cents an hour. His wife joined him in 1902 but Flavia was left behind in the care of her grandmother. She was expected to help on the family farm and was therefore not sent to school. On her grandmother's death in 1907, her mother returned to Italy and brought her to the US. In 1908, before a planned move to California, Domenico decided to visit an old friend in Calgary. On the train, the family made friends with Harry Cicconi who was going to Calgary to visit his sister Giulia Gallelli; the Gallellis were one of Calgary's founding Italian families. Harry convinced him to stay and Domenico started the Roma Grocery.

Flavia noted in an oral history that her father imported food from Italy and eastern Canada as well as repairing shoes in a shed behind the store. In 1911, on her mother's death, Flavia had to leave school and care for the family home until her father remarried shortly after. She also worked in the family store and it was there that she met Flavia Coradetti when she arrived in Calgary in 1918 and the two became friends. Mary Cioni, the latter's granddaughter, described the store as follows: "The Roma Grocery catered to the tastes of the small Italian community, selling food in bulk so that minimal amounts could be purchased when money was tight. There were salami and prosciutto hanging over barrels of olives, a large container of olive oil with a spigot to fill vessels with liquid gold, and mouth-watering cheeses – mild, blue, and hard – challenging the aroma of dark-roasted coffee."[324] Domenico was a shrewd businessman and saved money and used it to buy houses to rent to Italian immigrants. Flavia mentioned that there was a competition for boarders and that members of the Italian community undercut each other regularly: if someone was offered a $5 rate, someone else might offer $4.

The Lethbridge region had a number of early grocers. Domenic Tedesco initially came to Canada in 1905 going to Guelph to work on the railways.[325] In 1910, he married Isabella Ross and the following year they headed west and settled in Lethbridge where they built a brick store on 9th Avenue North. The couple followed the mines moving first to Wigan and, then, Coalhurst. In the last, they opened the Coalhurst Meat Market and Grocery Store, which also sold hardware and furniture. Seeing the increasing number of vehicles on the road, Domenic opened the Coalhurst Garage and hired Mike Bublik as the mechanic. He also bought a farm next to the mine property and, when the mine closed, bought additional land and continued to farm until the mid-1940s. Domenic served as Mayor of Coalhurst for two terms and also as a school board trustee. On his retirement, he moved to Lethbridge and set up a construction company and built homes.

---

[324] Mary Cioni, *Spaghetti Western: How My Father Brought Italian Food to the West* (Calgary, AB: Fifth House, 2006), 16.
[325] Coalhurst History Society, "Domenic Tedesco," in *Our Treasured Heritage: A History of Coalhurst and District* (Lethbridge, AB: Coalhurst History Society, 1984), 533.

Antonio (Tony) Pavan was a successful grocer in southern Alberta. He was born in Breda di Piave, Treviso and came to Canada in 1914 settling in Lethbridge where he worked as a boiler washer at the No. 3 mine, and part-time waiter at the Silver Grill.[326] In 1919, he married Isabella Tokar who was born in Romania and who had come to Canada in 1912 on her own. In 1919, they moved to Wigan where they operated a small store and, then, to Coalhurst where they built a general store on Main Street. It included not only groceries and dry goods but also a meat market. Tony had his own slaughter house located just outside town and, in addition to doing his own butchering, hired and trained Inez Cattoi. Tony prided himself on customer service – orders were delivered twice daily and once on Wednesdays. He also gave credit to miners and farmers. The couple operated the store until 1938 when ill health forced them to sell. Tony served as councilor for the Village of Coalhurst, as a trustee of the Lethbridge School Division and as Chairman of the West Lethbridge Committee in the Community and War Services Drive. He was also a founding member of the Lethbridge Italian-Canadian Club.

Ercole (Curly) Miglierina was born in Varese, Lombardy, and came to Canada in 1911 and initially worked on the railway at Frank.[327] He next worked in mines at Hillcrest, Bankhead and in the Drumheller Valley. In 1917, he erected a building on Third Avenue East in Drumheller and operated the People's Bakery with wife Teresa Rosetti until 1949. The basement served as a temporary isolation unit during the Spanish Influenza epidemic.[328] The bakery became a community gathering place popularly known as "the Peeps." Curly and Teresa were expert marketers and not only had the bakery name on the side of the delivery van but also created coin tokens that could be exchanged for a loaf of bread. The couple's daughter, Gina, helped but they also hired local Italian girls to work in the bakery. Curly's brother Enrico joined him in Drumheller in 1923, and assisted in the bakery. After Ercole's death in 1958, Teresa continued to run the bakery for a number of years. A Drumheller landmark, it was sold after her retirement and burned down in 1972.

Nicola (Nicolino) Alvau had perhaps the strangest occupation of any Italian immigrant – he was a herbalist and arrived in southern Alberta in the late 1920s from Sardegna.[329] He advertised in the *Lethbridge Herald*, beginning in 1928. He practised in several Alberta communities including Lethbridge, Blairmore, Macleod and Carmangay; however, the majority of his working life was spent in Lethbridge. Nicolino's story can be traced through his encounters with the law

[326] Geraldine Pavan VandenHeuvel, "Tony Pavan," in *Our Treasured Heritage*, 462.
[327] *Anon.*, "Ercole Miglierina," in *The Hills of Home: Drumheller Valley*, 285.
[328] *Anon.*, "Spanish Influenza Paralyzes Early Drumheller," in the *Drumheller Mail*, March 21, 2011.
[329] The information is drawn from the accession records of a photograph of Nicolino and Florence Alvau, January 5, 1937 in the Galt Archives 199110004298.

documented in the pages of the *Herald*. He used the title "doctor" but was not, in fact, a qualified practitioner and all charges were based on practicing medicine without a license. He was pursued by the Alberta College of Physicians and Surgeons, in 1932, and a hearing was held on April 1, when he was practising in Carmangay but charges were dismissed on a legal technicality. The short article refers to him as Dr. Alvau.

In 1934, he was at the centre of two cases involving inquests on patients who died: Jack Carr, a schoolboy, and Elisha Karren, a farmer from Magrath. The *Herald* reported on the former case in an article titled "Chronic Nephritis Cause Boy's Death, Verdict of Jury" (December 20, 1934). Both cases were instigated by local doctor D. B. Fowler, who treated both patients. Carr's father testified that Alvau had said the boy did not have kidney trouble, Fowler's diagnosis, and had given him Epsom salts and gentian to treat his stomach upset and charged him $3.50. Dr. W. S. Galbraith conducted the autopsy and is quoted as follows: "Dr. Galbraith thought neither would have any effect on the patient so far as causing his death was concerned. Gentian is a stomach tonic with no curative effect, and Epsom salts a cathartic. The latter would be helpful he said, in kidney disease." The jury, after an hour's deliberation, ruled on December 20: "We the undersigned jury find from the evidence submitted that Jack Carr came to his death at the Galt Hospital, Lethbridge, Alberta on December 4, 1935; cause of death, chronic nephritis. We the jury, observe that one Alvau, herbalist, of Lethbridge, Alberta, did not make a proper diagnosis of his patient, Jack Carr, before prescribing medicine and giving advice." The boy died of kidney failure.

A *Herald* article titled "Activities of Lethbridge Herbalist Told at Inquest" reported on the second inquest.[330] While the headline deems Alvau guilty this would not be the jury's finding. Dr. Fowler had been treating Karren since 1931 for heart trouble resulting from a childhood bout of inflammatory rheumatism. Fowler advised him not to do any hard work, difficult for a busy farmer, and prescribed some medicine that might help his condition indicating that he would need to take it until the end of his life. Legal action was begun when Fowler refused to issue a death certificate and Coroner J. E. Lovering, MD, of Lethbridge called for an inquest. The first witness, Thos. Dudley, a friend, recounted that he had gone to the Karren farm to help the deceased take hogs to the stockyard. Afterwards, they did some Christmas shopping and also had several beers. Karren was complaining about pains and shortness of breath. The deceased's wife testified as follows: "About two months ago he consulted the herbalist, N. Alvau, who told him the same thing, that he could not cure him nor help him, but he gave him a tonic to build him up." Nicolino was next on the stand and the article noted:

---

[330] *Anon.*, "Activities of Lethbridge Herbalist Told at Inquest: Declines to Name Herbs Used in Medicine Sold to Late Elisha Karren," *Lethbridge Herald*, December 27, 1934.

He had been in Canada for 24 years, was a naturalized Canadian citizen. His profession was that of an herbalist. He had practiced 20 years; had practiced in Alberta alone five years, two years away and two years in Lethbridge. He received his general education in Milan and Rome. He has never attended any college nor university nor any medical school whatsoever. He has no degree giving him authority to practice only a licence from the City of Lethbridge, for which he pays $25 per year, which allows him to practice as a herbalist in Lethbridge.

Nicolino testified that he had no X-ray or other equipment to help him diagnose patients and that he "allow[ed] the patient to tell what ails him and then he prescribes." In the case of Karren, he gave him herbal remedies to help him with "stomach trouble." On December 27, 1934, the jury deliberated from 12 noon to 12:55 pm and found that the death of Karren on December 22, 1934 was from heart failure resulting from over-exertion rather than any treatment he had received from Alvau. Two other charges would be laid in 1935 and he was found guilty and fined $50 in both instances. A final charge against Alvau was made on January 14, 1950 and he offered no defense and pleaded guilty and was fined $50. The case related to a young Indigenous girl, 20-year-old Mable Black Plume, who had tuberculosis. Alvau treated her with herbal remedies beginning three months before her death.

Alvau's personal life is also of interest because it provides an example of a marriage failure resulting from immigration. His wife, Rosaria Mazzuca, and son Paolo were left behind in Piane Crate, Calabria, and she subsequently refused to join him. Nicolino established a relationship with an Albertan, Florence Gilmar Willoughby, and they passed as man and wife. A formal portrait, dated 1937, by the De Jourdan's Studio Ltd. in the Galt Archives shows a prosperous, middle class couple. They are pictured in their substantial living room with an impressive chandelier and decorated Christmas tree. It would appear that the irregularity of their relationship was not known in the community and that Nicolino continued to use the title "doctor." The couple was finally able to marry in 1954 after Rosaria's death in Italy.

The Red Deer Bottling Company, established in 1911 by A. J. Pingrey and F. L. Brown from Kansas, had several Italian owners. The plant, located on Gaetz Avenue south of Alexander Street (now 48th Street), had fallen on hard times during the First World War when sugar was rationed and lack of discretionary money made luxury purchases difficult. According to historian Michael Dawe, the company manufactured soft drinks and aerated waters as well as a unique beverage named "Jersey Crème."[331] It was acquired, in 1927, by the Maggiora brothers, Constantino (Con)

---

[331] See Michael Dawe, "Red Deer Bottling celebrates 100th anniversary," in *Red Deer Express*, October 12, 2011 and *Anon.*, "City pioneer dies at 78," in the *Red Deer Advocate*, December, 1977.

and Natale, who had run soft drink manufacturing plants in BC. Dawe points out that timing was in the brothers' favour – the summer of 1927 saw celebrations of the Diamond Jubilee of Confederation and large quantities of soft drinks were sold at community events. In 1928, the brothers moved the plant to the north-east corner of Gaetz Avenue and 2nd Street SW.

In 1933, a new partner came onboard – Romano Valentino Truant. He arrived in BC in 1921 from San Martino Al Taglimento, Udine, and worked in highway construction and in a lumber camp. In 1923, he moved to Nordegg and worked as a timberman's helper in a coal mine. Tragedy struck when he was blinded in one eye and had to spend nearly a year in hospital in Edmonton. He was joined in Canada by his wife Roma in 1925 and the couple opened a tavern in the Lakeview Hotel in Nordegg in 1927. In 1933, Romano moved the family to Red Deer to expand their opportunities for economic betterment and was offered shares in the Red Deer Bottling Company Ltd. by Con Maggiora.[332] The following year, Romano purchased the company and continued to grow it. Products initially included Cal-aid, Delaware Punch, Kings Court, and Canuck Dry Ginger Ale. In a brilliant stroke, Romano purchased the franchise rights to new soft drinks named Coca-Cola and Orange Soda. Deliveries were made by Romano in a Model T Ford to stores from Three Hills to Hobbema, and Nordegg to Compeer near the Saskatchewan border. In 1942, the plant was moved to a building at Gaetz and 46th Street.

On Romano's retirement, sons Alfio and Dino took over the business and, on his death in 1977, became sole owners. In 1995, when Dino left the business, Alfio's son Mike became general manager. The company moved several times to larger premises and, in 2001, to a new facility in the Edgar Industrial Park. The company still retains its Coca-Cola franchise and their inventory includes more than 50 different soft drinks. A separate company, M.A.C. Munchies, was established to stock vending machines throughout Central Alberta.[333] Romano served on the board of Parkland Industries, as President and Director for the Alberta Lung Association and was a member of the Rotary Club, the Knights of Columbus, Elks Club and the Fish and Game Association. Truant Crescent in Red Deer was named in his honour.

While the Italian population of Medicine Hat dwindled as railway work finished, a few immigrants were successful in establishing long-lasting businesses. Baptiste Carnelli left Turate, Como, Lombardy, in 1923, and arrived in Medicine Hat in November.[334] Without a word of

---

[332] Anon., "Red Deer Bottling Company History," URL: http://www.reddeerbottling.com/briefhistory.htm, retrieved September 19, 2017.

[333] Dawe, op. cit.

[334] See Baptiste Carnelli obituary, Medicine Hat News, May 2, 1998; and Ron Carnelli obituary, Medicine Hat News, June 17, 2014.

English, he was able to get a job at the Ogilvie Flour Mills and stayed there long enough to save money to start his own business. He had been trained as a master shoemaker and, in 1926, opened the Carnelli Shoe Clinic. Baptiste married Mary Agnes Bolger in 1932 and the couple had one child, Ronald Francis. Ron attended Montana State University in Bozeman but, after two years, decided to return to Medicine Hat to help his father. Because both father and son were keen fishermen and hunters (Ron was also a self-taught gunsmith), they established Carnelli and Son Sporting Goods and continued to operate the shoe store. By the 1950s, Baptiste was a director of the Medicine Hat Fish and Game Association. In 1953, at a meeting of the association, he made a novel proposal reported in the *Medicine Hat News*: "The suggestion of more promotion of wildlife attractions in the city and district was raised by Baptiste Carnelli, with the proposal that the Club consider establishing its own office, which would feature wildlife exhibits, and a shooting gallery. There should be more public picture showings, and the showing of wildlife films in the schools, said Mr. Carnelli."[335] It would appear their store had cornered the sporting goods market. An advertisement in the *Medicine Hat News* of August 20, 1955 noted: "Hunters! Carnelli is Ready! Are You? THE ELK, DEER, MOOSE, BUFFALO, DUCKS, GEESE AND PHEASANTS ARE READY Do you want to be caught without a CARNELLI gun, without a CARNELLI scope, without a CARNELLI adjustment of your weapon? Spare yourself that horrible embarrassment by seeing CARNELLI at once, today, tomorrow or yesterday at the latest." Ron's son Danny eventually joined the family business. When gun control legislation was introduced in the House of Commons in 1976, the *News* spoke to Baptiste to get his opinion: "Carnelli said he does not sell guns to strangers and believes only qualified gunsmiths should be permitted to sell them. Many guns are bought and sold by people who know nothing about them, Carnelli said. He feels someone attempting to obtain a gun for criminal use will do so regardless of any laws."[336]

Guido Blasetti and wife Julia Poscente of Nordegg used a series of small businesses as stepping stones to major success. Guido was born in Calgary in 1913, the first child of Andrea and Bernardina Blasetti. His father obtained work at the Brazeau Collieries. Guido received his initial education in Nordegg but, from 1927 to 1931, he and his brother Ernesto were sent to the convent in Lac La Biche to study. Their parents believed that they would receive a better education there. Having studied in a Francophone institution, in 1932, Guido continued his studies at the College St. Jean in Edmonton. He then taught briefly in Lac La Biche before finally returning to

[335] *Anon.*, "Fish-Game Group is Considering City Permanent Headquarters; Bill Clark, Re-elected President," *Medicine Hat News*, January 13, 1953.
[336] *Anon.*, "Controls trigger protest from Alberta sportsmen," *Medicine Hat News*, February 26, 1976.

Nordegg where he met Julia and they were married. They operated a range of businesses including a service station, Bighorn Motors, a bake shop and restaurant, butcher shop and a boarding house. They anticipated community needs and provided services such as delivering milk and groceries; selling policies for Crown Life Insurance; men's suits for Edmonton-based LaFleche Brothers; and cars, fridges, stoves, washing machines and dryers.

Guido was a visionary who saw the importance of road transportation and, in 1946 he purchased a 3-ton truck for $3,000 intending to haul coal for the mines. When this opportunity did not materialize, he started hauling mail, groceries and other commodities from Rocky Mountain House and Red Deer to Nordegg. By 1947, this venture was so successful that the couple was forced to rationalize their business activities; they focused on the garage, bake shop and restaurant, and bus and truck service. The last gave birth to Big Horn Transport Ltd, which was run by Guido while Julia dedicated herself to the bake shop and restaurant, and looked after the family.

By the early 1950s, when mines were closing, Guido sold the Nordegg businesses and moved to Red Deer. There he expanded Big Horn Transport buying more trucks and taking on bigger transportation contracts. By 1957, the strategic decision was made to move the business to Calgary where more and larger contracts for freight and mail could be obtained. Sons Andrew and Philip joined the family business in 1965; Guy, Raymond and Ernie became involved by 1976. The family business was poised for further expansion and also to create a number of branches which began with acquisition of equipment (stock rose to over 90 trucks and over 300 trailers). Calgary remained the head office but Ernest was sent to manage an Edmonton branch while Andrew managed the Lethbridge branch and US accounts. Youngest son Mark then joined the business. In 1990, they expanded into Saskatchewan and set up an office and yard in Regina. Their operations covered western Canada and the US from Alaska to Texas. Guido ran the family business for 50 years until his death in 1993 leaving the second and third generation in charge.

While there are references in oral histories to Italian grocers in Edmonton, there is virtually no information about them. O. J. Biollo, one of the founders of the Venice-Hylo agricultural colony when he arrived in Edmonton in 1911, purchased a store on the corner of 96 Street and 99 Avenue and ran it for a number of years. By 1923, Joe and Assunta Gaudio had established the Venice Grocery. Domenico Chiarello, in 1948, established the Venice Confectionery. It would be the post-Second World War wave of immigration that would bring the population numbers to support the development of a whole new generation of grocers and wholesalers.

The Builders

The first decade of the twentieth century saw a building boom throughout Alberta that lasted until the worldwide recession at the beginning of the First World War. Italian craftsmen and labourers played a significant role. For example, in 1907, building of the Alberta Legislature was begun; it was a steel-frame, sandstone and granite structure and was completed in 1913. Many terrazzo workers immigrated to the US from the 1880s onwards from the northern Italian regions of Friuli-Venezia-Giulia to work in the US and Canada.[337] A "Mr. Zuchett," an Italian mason and mosaic artist, worked on the terrazzo floors of the Legislature. Antonio and Maria Zuchett lived in the Rossdale flats and Maria found employment at the Great West Garment Company as a seamstress. Giacinto Arnano, a mason, immigrated to New York and worked on six-month contracts at the Legislature (workers were brought to Edmonton in the summer returning to the US in the winter). Francesco De Filippo also worked on the Legislature and the original Royal Alexandra Hospital. Construction of the Canadian Pacific Railways' High Level Bridge, which included a road and pedestrian walkway as well as a railway line, began in 1910 with the three levels of government contributing funding. More than 500 workers including Italian immigrants such as Luigi Cantera worked on the project that was completed in May 1913.

It was inevitable that some would succeed in setting up their own construction businesses. Among the earliest were Domenico Ciccone and sons, Enrico (Harry) and Frederico (Fred), who arrived in Calgary in 1902 from Antrodoco, Rieti, Lazio.[338] In Italy, Domenico raised horses; in Calgary, he initially worked for the CPR. As soon as he could, he purchased a small farm in the Bridgeland/Riverside neighbourhood where he raised heavy horses – from 12 to 15 – and became a teamster working on various construction projects. In an oral history interview, daughter Giulia mentions that she, her mother Rita and sisters, Anna and Pasquina, joined the men in Calgary, in 1908.[339]

The Ciccone family fortunes are intertwined with those of Nicola (Nick) Gallelli, who with brother, Giuseppe (Joe), left the family home in Albi, Catanzaro arriving in New York in May 1900. The brothers headed for Pittsburgh and found work in the mines. Shortly after, Joe went to Philadelphia for work. In the meantime, Nick travelled west to Blairmore to work in

---

[337] Javier Grossuti, "Immigration from Friuli Venezia Giulia to Canada," University of Trieste, undated, URL: http://www.ammer-fvg.org/_data/contenuti/allegati/eng/en_grossutti_canada.pdf, retrieved February 14, 2018.

[338] The 1921 census says the Ciccones arrived in 1906.

[339] Giulia (Ciccone) Gallelli oral history, Calgary Italian Club Historical Project, May 28, 1985, Glenbow Archives RCT 869.

the mines; Joe joined him in 1903. It was not long before the brothers moved to Calgary where they worked on various construction projects until 1905 when they established a homestead near Crossfield (SE1/4 16-28-2-W5). In 1906, Nick returned to Calgary and purchased two horses from Domenico Ciccone and he and Harry began to work together. Delores Gallelli (the wife of Bill Gallelli) notes in the family history: "So Nick and Harry bought a cart, a wheelbarrow, a shovel, a slick and a pick, hitched up the horses and gravel onto the cart and began delivering it to various construction sites around the city. From this small beginning grew a thriving business. These men contributed to the construction of some of Calgary's landmark buildings, including the Hudson's Bay Store, the main Calgary Post Office and the Centre Street Bridge."[340]

Nick met Harry's sister Giulia and the two fell in love and were married in St. Mary's Cathedral in January 1912. They settled in Bridgeland and built a large barn so that he could continue to develop the business. Sadly, Harry died aged 24 in 1912 and Nick had to continue the business on his own, digging basements, and supplying sand and gravel to construction sites. He also started to supply cement to contractors and this enabled him to get a city contract for curbing and sidewalks. Giulia took on the administration work including ordering supplies. In addition, she cared for the couple's five children: Nado (1912), Harry (1914), Mary (1916), Bill (1917) and Aldo (1920). As their sons got older, they joined their parents in the business. Daughter Mary was not allowed to work, a sign of the family's wealth and standing in the community. The Gallelli business became the first place of work for many Italian men arriving in Calgary.

In 1926, the Gallellis expanded from their Bridgeland home at 218 – 6A Street NE into a lot next door at 222 – 6A Street NE. Horsepower was replaced by mechanized equipment including a gas-powered cement mixer and, in 1928, they purchased their first truck and another property on 1st Avenue NE. In 1929, they built a large two-storey home on that lot, which also housed the business office. The land also served as the yard for the heavy equipment and included a garage for mechanical work. The mechanization continued and a crawler tractor was purchased in 1941 and Bill designed an overhead loader for it. Harry left the business for 10 years beginning in 1935 (he returned 10 years later) and Nick changed the business name from "Nick Gallelli, Contractor" to "N. Gallelli and Sons, Contractors" to acknowledge his sons' involvement.

Nick's retirement in 1949 resulted in restructuring – the business became Gallelli and Sons Company Limited – with parents and sons as joint owners but Giulia as the majority shareholder. Daughter Mary assisted her mother in her administrative duties, particularly after her father's

---

[340] Delores Gallelli, "The Story of Nick and Julia Gallelli and Family: Founders of the Gallelli Company: A Pioneer Calgary Firm," unpublished manuscript, 2009, 1. Gallelli and Sons Ltd. Fonds, Glenbow Archives M-9113, M-9222, PA-3675. Delores married Bill Gallelli in 1951.

death in 1952. Giulia lived to the ripe old age of 96 and died in 1990. The *Calgary Herald*, in a June 13, 1966 article titled "Mother's Character, Dedication Key to City Family's Success" noted: "She fostered the growth of the business from the days when the total equipment consisted of pick and shovel, horse and wheelbarrow, to the $1,500,000 enterprise it is today. Julia Gallelli might be called a matriarch. She admitted in an interview that she 'rules with an iron hand.' Her daughter, Mrs. P. J. Prokopy, verifies it. 'There is no doubt she is a self-made woman, that she is resourceful and driving'." Her sons built homes on the hill above their parents' home and the family was a tight-knit one mixing business and pleasure.

The family was positioned to benefit from Alberta's second building boom resulting from the 1947 discovery of oil in Leduc. In 1950, they purchased land at 630 Riverside Boulevard NE and erected a building to serve as offices and shops. In 1954, the City of Calgary purchased the land for the widening of Memorial Drive and the business relocated to 703 – 48 Avenue NE on a 94-hectare lot that included a gravel pit, asphalt plant, cement plant, offices and repair shops. In the same year, the company was split into separate divisions: Bill ran Gallelli Sand and Gravel Company Limited; Nado, Transcrete Company Limited; and Aldo and Harry, Gallelli and Sons Company Limited. The restructuring resulted in greater efficiencies and Gallelli and Sons took on major road-building contracts with the governments of Alberta and BC as well as municipalities. As Calgary continued to grow, the plant site was once again sold in 1966 and new land at 103rd Avenue and 15th Street in southeast Calgary was acquired. The 190-hectare parcel was close to Fish Creek. The gravel, asphalt and concrete operations were located there and, according to Delores, "the capacity of the asphalt plant was sufficient to handle all the paving needs of the City of Calgary."[341]

The Gallelli boys had started work in the family business before they reached their teens and were instrumental in its growth. Ultimately, their interests diverged and the companies were acquired by Canada Cement Lafarge Limited. The achievements and community involvements of the brothers are noteworthy. Delores writes about the eldest son Nado: "At eight years of age he began to work Saturdays and holidays with his father in the excavation of building sites and at nine years of age accompanied his father and his team of horses hauling sand from the cemetery to the new technical school site, begun in 1921 and now known as SAIT Polytechnic."[342] He married Margaret Kerstiuk and the couple had a son, Daniel. By 1968, Nado felt burned out and sold his interest in the company to brothers Harry and Aldo, and bred thoroughbreds at his farm south of Calgary. Retiring from the family didn't mean that Nado was idle: he invested

---

341 Delores Gallelli, 5.
342 *Ibid.*, 7.

in hotels; served as a director of Carma, a Calgary-based land development company, and for North West Financial Ltd; and as manager of the Odan Construction Co. Limited and Dan Mar Holdings Ltd. (named for his son). He also supported neighbourhood softball and hockey clubs including the Stampeder Hockey Club.

Harry Gallelli, who was named for his uncle Harry Ciccone, started work in the family business at the age of 16. In 1936, he moved with his wife Florence Zimmer to Portland, Oregon, where he studied diesel mechanics and played hockey. In 1945, he returned to the family business and specialized in excavations and, then, in the crushing operation that supplied gravel to the provincial and municipal governments. Delores noted: "The Gallelli firm was spectacularly successful with these accounts as there were few construction companies at that time who could market their services in such a sincere and personal manner. Selling was a necessity in growing the business and the considerable talents of Harry, who devoted so much of his energy and enthusiasm toward these ends, contributed greatly to the success of Gallelli and Sons. Harry was a 'hands-on' manager who could handle any piece of machinery when he was needed, but was second to none at operating the crusher."[343] Harry's son, Garry, obtained an MBA from Harvard and became the company's general manager. In 1980, in celebration of Alberta's 75th anniversary, Premier Lougheed recognized Harry with an Alberta Heritage of Pride award.

Bill Gallelli attended St. Mary's High School but left to join the family business when he was 17. He focused on the sand and gravel side, and also did the estimates. He eventually ran the Gallelli Sand and Gravel Company and managed Gallelli Construction Materials Limited. He helped to set up the Calgary Italian Sportsmen's Dinner and volunteered at the Calgary Zoo. In 1969, Bill and Nado sold their shares in the business and Bill, wife Delores Stothers, who he married in 1951, and son Nick formed a new company, Bill Gallelli Investments, and built warehouses and townhouses for rental purposes.

Aldo Gallelli, the youngest child, attended St. Mary's High School and Henderson's Business College before joining the family business. He focused on the finances and was instrumental in the change to a corporate structure in 1949. His responsibilities increased until he was put in charge of highway construction and general operations. According to the family history, he was sounded out by the University of Calgary with respect to an honorary engineering degree but refused it. This was likely for the company's participation in the continuous pour of cement required to build the Calgary Tower. In 1972, he left the Gallelli companies and set up Stoneway Crushing, which was taken over by his oldest son Greg.

---

[343] *Ibid.*, 10-11.

Enrico Giuseppe Pozzi was to Blairmore what the Gallellis were to Calgary; he was born in Udine and was trained in coke oven construction. Coal mining was an important industry in the town of Nimis near Udine and in neighbouring Slovenia, a part of the former Yugoslavia. Enrico arrived in Frank in 1905 and was joined in 1906 by Stella Vanoni and they were married. After six months of work shoveling coal into rail cars, his skills came to the attention of management at the Canadian Metals Company and he was hired to supervise the building of a zinc smelter near Frank. Designed to be North America's largest, it was situated to make use of zinc deposits and coal from BC, as well as good railroad transport to markets. The company experienced financial and technical difficulties and the smelter never went into commercial production. But with one door closing, another opened: West Canadian Collieries opened the Greenhill Mine in 1913 and, as a result, Blairmore underwent a major period of development.

In 1914, Enrico purchased the lumberyard and construction business of Thomas Frayer and Daniel Sinclair, early Blairmore builders. He moved buildings from both Lille and Frank to Blairmore, when mining ceased, and also got the contract to remove mine workings from Lille as scrap metal after the First World War. In 1923, he purchased the failed zinc smelter buildings in Frank and this provided him with salvaged brick and other materials for use in construction projects. The final piece of his empire was the building of a sash and door factory. In the 1920s, the "Greenhill Addition" at the west end of Blairmore's main street was planned.[344] West Canadian tendered the work and Enrico's bid was successful and he was responsible for construction of more than 70 residential, commercial and institutional buildings. At its peak, he employed up to 200 men, many of whom were Italian.

West Canadian was conscious that in order to get good staff it needed excellent accommodation. In 1915, Pozzi constructed a one-and-a-half storey duplex designed to house two mining engineers. In 1920, he built the Greenhill Apartments with all the modern conveniences required by company personnel. The two-storey brick structure had four large apartments. Also in 1920, he designed and built the West Canadian Collieries General Office. Besides offices, the two-storey structure also had employee apartments on the second floor. A companion building, the Greenhill Grill was built in 1922 housing two businesses on the main floor and apartments above. The ground floor also had an elegant dining room that served the Greenhill Hotel located across the street. In 1920, Enrico built a department store for F. M. Thompson; it is a two-storey brick building with large display windows. He also designed the first motion-picture theatre, the Orpheum, for fellow Italian immigrant Peter Ubertino in 1921. In 1923, he completed the

---

[344] Donald Grant Whetherell and Irene Kmet, *Town Life: Main Street and the Evolution of Small Town Alberta 1880-1947* (Edmonton, AB: University of Alberta Press), 182.

Union Bank and a building for the Blairmore Garage Company. Joe Fumagalli bought this in 1929 and renamed it Red Trail Motors. This was subsequently taken over by Charles Sartoris who renamed it Blairmore Motors. Enrico also designed more modest buildings such as the G. B. Catonio Grocery Store.

With respect to the J. E. Upton Block, the heritage significance for designation as a provincial historic resource notes: "The building reflects the history of Blairmore's main street and commercial development in the Crowsnest Pass area. Unlike many commercial buildings built in the early 20th century, however, it includes more than just a 'boomtown' front. The decorative parapet and oriel window are unusual features and suggest an Italianate design. The building is also a main street landmark and one of the oldest commercial buildings still remaining in Blairmore."[345] Grocer Angelo Toppano observed that craftsmen from northern Italy including masons, stucco-workers and plasterers decorated their rough wooden shacks in a manner reminiscent of their homeland.

Enrico's son Louis studied architecture and engineering and began work in the family business in 1924. After his father's early death in 1930, he continued the business alone. The Thirties in Blairmore were extremely difficult: the mining companies imposed wage cuts and this resulted in demonstrations. On May 1, 1932, International Workers' Day (now Labour Day celebrated in September) saw protests; four days later over 1,200 miners and their families battled with 75 members of the RCMP. The economic hard times resulted in the end of the Pozzi building empire in 1936.

Louis went to work as supervisor in charge of the Youth, Vocational and War Emergency Training Programmes, a federal/provincial initiative, and this involved a move to Medicine Hat where the training facility was built. During the Second World War, he joined the Air Force and was made Commanding Officer of the No. 3 Construction and Maintenance Unit responsible for airfields in Alberta associated with the British Commonwealth Air Training Plan. After the war, he returned to his former position and then moved on to work in the engineering division of CPR. In 1949, he was hired by the Mannix Company in Calgary and moved up the ranks from assistant chief engineer, to chief engineer, manager of the railroad division, chief estimator and, finally, assistant to the construction manager and president of Techman Ltd., the engineering branch of Mannix. Louis worked on many iconic structures in Calgary including the Hudson's Bay Parkade, Skywalk and store addition; AGT Toll Building and Micro-wave tower; a number of hotels including the Stampeder, Forest Lawn and Bow Valley; Faculty of Education, Engineering, Gymnasium and Library buildings at the University of Calgary; and McMahon Stadium.

[345] J. E. Upton Block, Alberta Heritage Survey Program, Canada's Historic Places website, designation date August 16, 1995, URL: https://hermis.alberta.ca/ARHP/Details.aspx?DeptID=2&ObjectID=HS%2030055, retrieved September 2, 20017.

He also managed construction of Red Deer's City Hall; railroad work throughout Canada, the US and Australia; and dam construction in South America. He retired in 1974 but was hired by the federal government to oversee construction of the new terminal at the Calgary International Airport but illness forced his final retirement two years later. He was interested in local history and contributed the Emilio Picariello story to *Crowsnest and Its People*.

Edmonton's equivalent of Gallelli Construction was New West Construction, established by brothers-in-law Felix Nigro and James (Jimmy) Anselmo. As has been noted, Felix's father, Antonio, immigrated from Grimaldi to the US in 1885 and began work with his brother-in-law John Welch on railways in the Pacific Northwest and the Crowsnest Pass. Felix joined his father in 1897 when he was 15 and, worked on various construction projects with the Welch Company.[346] In 1913, he returned to Italy and married Amelia Anselmo and the couple made their home in Winnipeg where he continued to work for his uncle. There appears to have been some tension between Felix and his uncle subsequently with respect to debt repayment and this may have motivated the former to decide to homestead at Clive, near Red Deer.[347] Felix raised heavy horses and set up as an independent contractor doing railway work. (He appears as such in the 1916 census.) He did land clearance for a branch railway line in the Venice-Hylo area near Lac La Biche. In 1925, the family moved to Edmonton with their children.

Jimmy Anselmo was born in Grimaldi, Calabria in 1900 and arrived in Winnipeg at the age of 14 likely joining his father Domenico, who also worked with the Welches. For the next six years, he did a range of work including a stint as camp cook. He also learned English. In 1920, he went west to Edmonton where he obtained work in a lumber camp north of the city. For the next five years, he saved his money and, then, partnered with Felix Nigro on roadwork contracts. In 1925, they created Nigro & Anselmo Limited in which he invested his savings of $2,500. In an article in *Construction World* in 1958, Jimmy described this period in construction history as "horse-and-scraper" and noted, "Just to keep the company going both Nigro and I held many jobs – we were foremen, timekeepers, barn bosses, teamsters, and when necessary cooks. But we were both impressed as we visualized the great possibilities the construction field had to offer in the West."[348]

---

[346] Elizabeth (Betty-Anne) Nigro Pearson and Susan (Nigro) Grant provided information on the family's immigration history for the *Celebrating Alberta's Italian Community* website. This included a video interview with her father Bill Nigro.
[347] John Welch's memoir expresses discontent with family members, for example, the quality of Felix's work; this should be taken with a grain of salt. According to the family, Felix's father, Antonio, the husband of John and Vincent Welch's sister Anna, left her in Italy and took up with another woman (Rosaria Cassana) in the US and she bore him two sons. To make up for his father's betrayal, Felix supported his mother and a sister, Caterina, in Italy.
[348] *Anon.*, "James Anselmo Points to Guideposts for Success," in *Construction World*, May 1958, 40.

Their first sub-contract was not profitable and they learned that they needed to be precise in costing for bids. The business continued to grow and considered a 16 km contract for a season "good going" and, over two seasons, they built one third of a 56 km rail line from Busby to Barrhead for the Northern Alberta Railway Co. (1925-1926). In 1927, they did grading work for the Canadian National Railways from Glendon to Bonnyville; this was followed, in 1928, by a 29 km contract for the NAR from Whiterock to Fairview in Peace Country. In 1929, they got a contract with the CPR for work from Lake Alma to Minden, Saskatchewan; this continued in 1930 with a contract from Debden to Middle Lake. At the time, they had 50 horses to draw equipment including an elevating grader, 10 dump wagons and two Fresno scrapers, horse-drawn machines used in constructing canals and ditches in sandy soil.

Then, the Depression hit and Jimmy observed: "It was difficult to obtain contract work from 1931 to 1936." The partners worked for others but kept their own business going. Jimmy served as a foreman for a Saskatchewan firm and also spent two years in Italy, beginning in 1932. He returned so that the firm could take on a sub-contract on the highway between Edmonton and Jasper (now the Yellowhead Highway). While in Italy, he married Teresina Belmonte and their first child, John, was born there in 1934. They subsequently joined him in Edmonton. Things continued to improve and Jimmy noted that the new Social Credit government, in the period 1936 to 1939, did not issue any contracts but, rather, "The government hired our horses, tents, equipment and paid my partner and me foremen's wages."[349]

The coming of the Second World War changed everything. In 1939, Nigro & Anselmo obtained a sub-contract from the Department of Transport in Fort St. John, BC, to build the first grass-landing strip in Canada; the contract was worth $17,000 and they bought their first Caterpillar excavator. In 1940, they constructed a similar airport at High River, Alberta. In 1942-1943, they partnered with the Western Construction and Lumber Co. Ltd. and built the airport at Grande Prairie. In 1943, they changed the company name to New West Construction Co. Ltd. and Nigro became president and Anselmo, vice president. J. W. Millar of Western Construction and Lumber took a financial interest in the company. The influx of capital was used to buy better equipment as well as increasing the office staff. (Prior to this the two partners did everything.) The gross volume of business rose from $250,000 a year to $2.5 million.

In a 1958 interview, Jimmy pointed out the importance of the bidding process and outlined a number of rules for success: understanding, location, availability, sources of credit, regulations and profit. Bill Nigro, in an oral history interview, noted that his father could walk 10 miles (16 km)

---

[349] Allan Fenton, "New West Construction – From horse to computers," in *Engineering and Contract Record*, December 1967, 61.

of a road, and then turn around and tell you how much dirt had to be moved, how much rock had to be removed, and estimate the cost of building the road. Anselmo took aim at the bidding process as follows: "It is disturbing to notice the unrealistic bidding which has taken place during the last few years. I have always felt that, unless a contractor obtains a fair price for his work, he will not produce a good job, no matter how hard he tries. A factor which has often contributed to unrealistic bidding is the lack of information and preliminary data available to the contractor before he bids, especially as concerns profiles and soil testing."[350] He echoed this sentiment in a 1967 interview with Allan Fenton, Managing Editor of *Engineering and Contract on Record*, when pointing out that business growth was not without its difficulties: "Anselmo recalls that the company was successful tenderer to construct a canal and dam near McGrath, Alberta. There was about 1,000,000 cu yd [over 760,000 cubic metres] of material to move. 'Our price was so low that the more we moved the more we lost … We bid it at 15 cents a yard and it cost us 19 cents. It nearly broke us but we survived'."[351]

The war-time boom resulted in increased revenues and, around 1946, they acquired a significant interest in Hett & Sibbald Limited, a lumber company that produced railway ties. It was at this point that Felix's son, Bill, got involved in the family business. He was educated in Edmonton but after a less-than-stellar first-year at the University of Alberta, in 1935, his father sent him and brother, Monty, to St. Michael's College, University of Toronto. Bill completed a Science degree and then two years towards a medical degree. In 1940, he went to work for CIL in Nobel, Ontario, as part of the war effort. In 1942, he married Norvel Mary Faught and the couple moved to Montreal. In 1946, the family moved to Edson so that Bill could take over the lumber business.

In the early 1950s, New West bought Hett & Sibbald and the company produced 500,000 ties per year equivalent to over 320 kms of track. They later acquired S. N. A. (Sibbald, Nigro and Anselmo) Lumber Co. Ltd. with a mill in Edson. It produced about 14,160 cubic metres of lumber as well as constructing about 90,000 doors for railway grain cars. In 1954, Felix died and the company's assets were divided between the Nigros and Anselmos. The Nigros took on the two lumber companies and Jimmy kept the construction company. Bill moved to Edmonton, in 1956, to become president of Hett & Sibbald and brother, Monty, became vice president. In 1968, Bill served as president of the Alberta Forest Products Association. The company's offices were in the Royal Bank Building in Edmonton.

[350] *Anon.*, "James Anselmo points to Guideposts for Success," 40.
[351] Fenton, 62.

With the division of New West assets, Jimmy's sons, Albert and Felix, joined him in the business, the former as his assistant and the latter as head of accounting and payroll in the BC office. In 1958, the company did about $6 million in general contracting and earthmoving work and had 150 pieces of major equipment including a Cessna 310 aircraft. In 1964, they discontinued bidding for industrial buildings because they found it difficult to get qualified staff and focused on road and railway work, dams and scarification projects for pulp mill operations; the last involves scraping the forest floor to promote germination of tree seeds. Projects in 1967 included paving work from Hobbema (Maskwacis) to Calgary ($500,000); road construction and paving of the Big Bend to Mica Dam road ($3.7 million); a scarification project for Northwest Pulp and Paper; and grading work for the Alberta Resources Railway. This was a 1965 Government of Alberta initiative to establish railway lines to service the resource area along the eastern slopes of the Rocky Mountains from Hinton to Grande Prairie. The company invested $1.5 million in equipment including 25 Cats, five draglines and two shovels and trucks.

The 1967 Fenton article was titled "Anselmo of New West Construction – pioneer from horses to computers," suggesting the company's new thrust. The magazine was examining the boom in construction to celebrate Canada's centenary. New West had made the transition to using computer systems. While Jimmy's attitude to mechanization was visionary, he revealed an anti-union bias, which perhaps was typical of company management at the time. Fenton notes: "He finds the work today is far more technical than in the past and he deplores the strength of the unions when it means, for example, the inability for a company to move men from a job in British Columbia to Alberta or vice versa. He thinks it's a weakness in the industry that some contractors bid without the equipment. If they get the job, he says they rent it but often they can't get enough and the job suffers."[352] While 1967 was a peak year for the company, its fortunes would be affected by Jimmy's death in 1976; it ceased operations in March 1981. Son John Edward Anselmo graduated in Medicine from the University of Alberta in 1958 and specialized in surgery at Georgetown University, Washington, DC. On his return to Edmonton, he became Chief of Surgery at the General Hospital and set up the first intensive care unit. He next moved to the Grey Nuns Hospital and finally to the University of Alberta Hospital where he practised until his retirement in 1999. He served for two terms on the Alberta Cancer Board and was an innovator in early detection and treatment. He was also an advocate for persons with developmental disabilities.

Red Deer was the base of another family construction business. Giovanni (John) Paolo Comis was born in Belluno, Veneto, in the Dolomite Mountains, and was trained as a mosaic and terrazzo artisan. He arrived in Red Deer in November 1912 with his brother-in-law Fred

---

[352] *Ibid.* 62.

Nachtmann.[353] They partnered in construction work and set up Parkvale Cement Industries, which derived its name from the new Parkvale neighbourhood established in 1905 by the Town of Red Deer. An ad in the *Red Deer News*, May 21, 1913 noted that they made cement blocks of every type as well as tombstones and edging stones, and mosaic and terrazzo flooring. The business venture did not succeed because an economic downturn and the declaration of war in 1914 shifted government priorities to other areas, in particular, mobilization.

John established his own concrete business and, in 1919, purchased land on the Burnt Lake road from the original homesteader, a Mr. Darlo, and built his own home. In 1919, the partners also built a home for Fred and wife Anna. The house demonstrated their building techniques and is described in the *Red Deer Historical Walking Tours* booklet as follows: "The concrete block used in its construction indicates the acceptance by the middle class of an imitation stone as a less expensive substitute for sandstone, the 'aristocrat' of building materials. Called architectural or 'artistic' concrete block, its use spanned a fifty-year period from the 1870s to about 1920. The 'rock-face' block used here was the easiest and, therefore, the cheapest form of imitation stone which could be made." In 1922, John was injured in a work accident and was not able to resume work until 1924. He was an excellent craftsman and was involved in the construction of many Red Deer buildings but few have survived as a result of later building booms. It is said that he laid the terrazzo floor of the old Bank of Montreal building, and built the Roger's House, a sandstone building in the Crossroads District.

John passed on his trade to his sons and grandsons. Otto served in the Medical Corps; Bruno with the Military Engineers; and Yvo with the Provost Corps (the military police corps of the Canadian Army) in the Second World War. After the war, the brothers returned to the construction business. Beyond his work, Bruno was a renowned sportsman who loved hunting and fishing. He became involved in speed skating in 1956 and, until 1968, coached the Red Deer Lions Speed Skating Club leading them to regional, provincial and national championships where his skaters won many medals. Two of them represented Canada at the Olympics. Bruno also was one of the organizers of the Northwest International Meet, one of Canada's largest competitions at the time. He was named Sportsman of the Year in 1960 and Coach of the Year in 1964. In 1968, he moved and became active in the Calgary Speed Skating Club. Bruno was inducted into the Alberta Sports Hall of Fame in 1978 for his coaching contributions.[354] In 1987, he was inducted into the Canadian Speed Skating Hall of Fame.

---

[353] Poplar Ridge Historical Committee, *The District's Diary: 95 Years of History of the Crossroads, Poplar Ridge, Norma and Durham Districts* (Red Deer, AB: Poplar Ridge Historical Committee, 1981), 30-31.
[354] Bruno Comis entry, Alberta Sports Hall of Fame & Museum website, URL: http://ashfm.ca/hall-of-fame-honoured-members/browse/speed-skating/comis-bruno, retrieved January 11, 2018.

Arthur Joseph Dorigatti was an important builder in Lethbridge. He appears in the Canada Voters List for 1945 described as a "carpenter." A number of articles in the *Lethbridge Herald* describe his career as a builder. He set up Dorigatti Construction and his first project appears to have been the Bigelow-Fowler Clinic, the city's first medical-dental building built in 1948.[355] It was a two-storey, steel-and-brick building designed by Lethbridge architects Meech Mitchell and Meech and cost just over $128,000. Dorigatti next build two churches – St. Basil and St. Patrick. In 2000, the former celebrated its fiftieth anniversary and the *Herald* showcased this event in three articles by Garry Allison under the banner headline – "The Way We Were." The article titled "Building St. Basil's was a community effort," noted that a building committee was struck in 1950 headed by Dorigatti, who was a parishioner. This suggests that there was no formal bid process. Allison continues: "The church was built by the parishioners, in all kinds of weather, pounding every nail … The bricks were laid by the men of the church too, and it was all done under the direction of Art Dorigatti."[356] Christmas Mass in 1950 took place in the unfinished church and it was completed on March 10, 1951. Many parishioners were Italian and the fiftieth anniversary dinner was held at the Italian Canadian Club.

The first St. Patrick's Church was established in Lethbridge in 1887 by Bishop Vital Grandin, head of the Missionary Order of Oblates of Mary Immaculate in Alberta. In 1951, it was decided that a new church was needed and parishioners were involved not only in fundraising but also the fabrication of the church.[357] Dorigatti Construction was given the contract in April 1951. The Oblates supervised all aspects of construction of the steel, concrete and brick building. The basement of the old church served as the parish hall. No expense was spared on the fixtures. The stained glass windows including a circular "rose" window over the altar contain 22,000 pieces of coloured class, and were created by the Rault Studio of Rennes, France.[358] The church's organ was built by Casavant Frères of Quebec, Canada's most renowned builders. St. Patrick's opened on September 24, 1952.

Dorigatti's next work would be secular in nature. The *Herald* of April 26, 1952 reported that the city had issued $10 million in construction permits: "Emphasis Moves to Business and Public Spending." The post-war building boom had arrived in Lethbridge. Dorigatti was initially

---

[355] Dave Mabell, "City's first clinic has new lease on life," *Lethbridge Herald*, April 29, 1998.

[356] Garry Allison, "Building St. Basil's was a community effort," *Lethbridge Herald*, October 1, 2000.

[357] Oblates of Mary Immaculate, *St. Patrick's Church – At Last Completed* (Oblates of Mary Immaculate: commemorative booklet, 1952).

[358] Patrick Burns, "Vitraux d'Art E. Rault: Rault Frères: Maîtres Verriers Rennais, 1898 – present, Rennes, France," Institute for Stained Glass in Canada, URL: http://www.glassincanada.org/news/vitraux-dart-e-rault/, retrieved January 13, 2018.

assisted by his brother Alfred (Fred), who worked for the CPR until his retirement in the 1970s. The company grew quickly and on July 9, 1955 the *Herald* reported that Dorigatti Construction had merged with Phaff Construction and Four Square Alberta Lumber.[359] The new company had assets in excess of $800,000. The article continues: "The Company, Mr. Cundy said, will provide plans, lots, utility services, a consulting service and the final home in a package deal. In this manner the financing becomes a simpler operation he said." Work on two subdivisions is mentioned: 8th and 9th Avenues S and 21st Street and Mayor Magrath Drive, and Lakeview.

City Council and the school board, in 1955, approved the building of two new schools. Dorigatti-Phaff Construction's bid in the amount $293,240 to build General Stewart Elementary was successful. The eight-room masonry and brick building was located on Corvette Crescent in the Veterans Subdivision. The name was suggested by the local Army, Navy and Air Force Veterans Association to honour the local dentist who fought in the Boer, First and Second World Wars as well as serving as an MLA and MP.

Dorigatti was also involved in the building of two ethnocultural centres. He donated the material to build the Italian-Canadian Cultural Centre, which opened on May 24, 1977. The Lethbridge Hungarian Oldtimers Club was founded in 1927.[360] With the influx of new arrivals after the 1956 Hungarian Revolution, community members pushed to have their own building. The contract was given to Dorigatti's company; he was a member of the society and his wife, Annie Zasadny, was Hungarian. The society had collected $120,000 but actual building costs were $198,000. Members of the community shouldered the shortfall and were repaid by 1984. The celebration dinner and dance on November 25, 1979, saw 580 in attendance. In 1982, the building was damaged by fire and Dorigatti did the repair work at no cost. The Dorigatti Estate made a gift to the University of Lethbridge.

Dorigatti's buildings served their users well and some still exist and others have been repurposed (for example the clinic has seen major renovations and now accommodates professional offices). The churches are less fortunate. In 2011, Bishop Fred Henry of Calgary decreed that three Lethbridge churches (St. Patrick's, St. Basil's and Our Lady of Assumption) would be sold to build a 1,200-seat "mega-church" to meet the needs of contemporary worshippers. St. Patrick's was closed the same year and the other two churches subsequently. The Save Our Churches Association was established to attempt to block this but it is unlikely to succeed because of the decline in church membership.

---

[359] *Anon.*, "Three Building Companies Become One," *Lethbridge Herald*, July 9, 1955.
[360] Judy Robins, "Hungarian Cultural Society of Southern Alberta" profile (unpublished), Galt Archives, 2011, Hungarian Cultural Society of Southern Alberta Fonds 20101011000.

Restaurateurs and Chefs

At the beginning of the twentieth century, Italian food was considered alien in Alberta. While local pasta manufacturers and grocers helped to introduce Italian products to the general public, it would be pioneer restaurateurs who would build the popularity of Italian cuisine. While individuals worked as cooks in commercial kitchens likely from the earliest days of immigration, Italian restaurants would not emerge as a culinary force until the post-Second World War wave of immigration.[361] Soldiers who fought in Italy acquired a taste for Italian food and looked for it in Italian neighbourhoods back home. Historian John Gilchrist observed in a 2011 article that new immigrants settle near each other and, "Quickly, entrepreneurs open shops that sell foods and materials from the homeland. And soon, a restaurant or two opens to serve the needs of the community." He continues:

> Adventurous diners from across the city venture into the cultural enclave to sample the wares. They report back to their friends and more 'outsiders' arrive, bumping up business. In time, entrepreneurs may move or open a second location in the city's business centre or 'outsider' community, expanding the clientele, and helping connect their community to the broader population.... In Calgary, this pattern applies to the two cultural enclaves – Chinatown and Bridgeland – that date to the early 1900s and to the development of many local Chinese and Italian restaurants.[362]

Gilchrist refers specifically to Gene Gioni whose daughter Mary authored *Spaghetti Western: How My Father Brought Italian Food to the West*.[363] Her claim that her father brought Italian food to the west might seem extravagant but he certainly appears to have created Calgary's first Italian restaurant at 111 - 4th Street NE on the edges of the Italian district of Riverside/Bridgeland.

Genesio Ciono was born in Antrodocco, Rieti, Lazio, the son of Sabato Cioni, a shoemaker, and his second wife, Flavia Cardellini. Sabato died in 1908 leaving his widow to care for five children. The connection to Canada occurred when 15-year-old daughter Gisa, from the first marriage, went to Calgary to marry a man she did not know – Ricardo Santopinto. Gisa's letters painted a glowing picture of Calgary and inspired in the 37-year-old Flavia, who felt trapped in

---

[361] My maternal grandfather Vincenzo Potestio worked as a cook on Welch gangs and also for the CPR in the Kapuskasing to Winnipeg run.

[362] John Gilchrist, "Project Calgary," in *Calgary Herald*, November 28, 2011,

[363] The book *Spaghetti Western: How My Father Brought Italian Food to the West* developed from two essays Mary Cioni contributed to the anthology *Mamma Mia! Good Italian Girls Talk Back* (Toronto, ON: ECW Press, 2004), edited by Maria Coletta McLean ("Answering Rafaela," 13-24, and "What's in a Name?" 175-186).

poverty, a desire to immigrate. Relatives arranged a marriage with Annibale Corradetti, a 49-year-old widower who worked for the city as a labourer. According to Mary, he was mean-spirited and stingy, and did not honour his promise to Flavia to give her money to bring her sons (Genesio and Sabatino) to Canada. A resourceful woman, she saved money from her household expenses and sent it to Italy. It was enough for only one fare and, Gene, the elder, came to Calgary in 1923. He turned 16 on shipboard. Flavia wanted Gene to become a barber and he worked at the Calgary Shoe Hospital to save money. Two years later he enrolled at the Hemphill Barber School and graduated in 1925. Tragically, his mother died of a ruptured gall bladder in 1926, and Gene blamed his stepfather for lack of attention to her health. This freed him from a trade that he had not embraced and, through his cousin and best friend Mario Grassi, he obtained a job at the Palliser Hotel as a busboy (Mario was a waiter). Soon after, he became sous-chef and learned the CPR repertoire of largely English and French specialties.

In 1931, Gene worked on trains preparing food for gangs repairing lines in Alberta and BC and began to add Italian dishes to the work-a-day fare. His culinary apprenticeship continued in Vancouver where he worked for the Pini family, seven brothers who operated several Italian restaurants.[364] It was there that Gene learned how to cook Italian specialties and the skills needed to open his own restaurant. In 1938, he returned to Calgary and, according to Mary, worked in a gambling club and then ran the Perfection Store and Ice Cream Parlour. In 1939, he married Martha Arndt, who assisted him in his various ventures. The couple purchased the Pacific Lunch that they renamed Martha Lunch and served soups, sandwiches, meat loaf and other Canadian staples. In 1940, their son Gary was born and, according to Mary, just as Genesio had changed his name to the English "Gene" (for boxer Gene Tunney) to fit in, his son was named for film star Gary Cooper. The desire to Anglicize did not prevent the young couple from falling within the provisions of the federal Enemy Alien Act (Martha was German) and both had to register and report to the police on a monthly basis during the Second World War.[365] After two years, the 16-hour days took their toll and they sold the restaurant. Gene went to work as manager of the dining room at the Shamrock Hotel and Martha at Olivier Chocolates. In 1943, he was hired to run the cafeteria at the Burns plant. In 1947, the couple started another cafe venture opposite the Stampede grounds but found that business was good only when the festival was on so they sold it.

By 1951, Calgary had a population of 129,000 but things were happening that would turn the small prairie town into a metropolis. Cioni opened Gene's Spaghetti Parlour in March 1949 and it was an instant success. According to Mary, this was due not only to hard work but also to the following:

---

[364] Keith McKellar, *Neon Eulogy: Vancouver Cafe and Street* (Vancouver, BC: Exstasis Editions, 2001), 114.
[365] Cioni, 45.

He had come of age as a cook and manager in Calgary; he understood the mood of the city and seized the opportunity. Gene envisioned American executives, business people, soldiers, the Stampeders and their fans, the established Italian community and newcomers all dining on his Calgary cooking – Italian style. He consulted relatives and trusted friends and was overwhelmed by their enthusiasm. A *paesano*, Vittorio Cioni, loaned Gene a few thousand dollars, and another *paesano*, Louis Carloni, said that he could rent the basement of an apartment house he owned in Riverside.[366]

Carloni suggested that he renovate the building next door to create a ground-floor restaurant space that Gene could rent. According to Mary, the deal was done on a handshake and Gene's Spaghetti Dine & Dance was born on December 31, 1949. Carloni opened a banqueting hall on the second floor, the L. C. Ballroom, which also prospered. Gene catered major events booked there. After two years, problems developed between the partners that led to threats of litigation. Mary blames the Carlonis for this. Gene felt that it was his reputation as a chef and his name that brought in the customers. Carloni had problems with this and was less than generous with his offer of compensation; in fact, he succeeded in preventing Cioni from using his trademark name in his next restaurant venture.[367]

This setback prompted Gene to create the La Villa Supper Club, located in a large, two-storey historic home on the edge of the city near the Shaganappi Golf Course and Calgary Gun Club. This would appear to have been a risky move but Mary describes her father's reasoning as follows: "I need the space. The distance is good. In America, people are going crazy for nightclubs. My villa will be a nightclub, serving the best Italian food. People will drive the distance for the food. The spot is perfect. Adds to the mystique. It'll be harder for the police to patrol illegal drinking."[368] He envisioned the facility as not only a supper club for adults but also as a destination for families on Sunday drives to the country. His insticts proved right and the restaurant became a destination for Calgary's elite. The family lived above the restaurant until 1956, when they moved into a new home.

Gene was a generous, kind-hearted person and embodied the "perfect host." In fact, these early Italian restaurateurs were the prototypes of today's "star" chefs, renowned not only for their cooking expertise but also their charisma. Mary provides various examples of her father's savvy in dealing with influentials. Anecdotes include the names of the wealthy elites of Calgary such as

---

366 *Ibid.*, 55.
367 *Ibid.*, 92. According to Mary, Carloni and his nephew Leo Fabi, on October 12, 1951 signed legal agreements to carry on the business using the name "Gene's."
368 *Ibid.*, 82.

Ras Mikkelson, who was in the oil business; Hal Gooding, chief pilot for Imperial Oil; Hy and Jenny Belzberg, owners of Christy's Furniture Store; Shirley and Jack Singer, a real estate mogul; members of the Calgary Stampeders football team including Paul Rowe, who was part of the 1948 Grey Cup winning team; sports announcers Ed Whalen and Ted Soskin; the Holdsworths, Hunts and Quigleys, who were part of the booming real estate and insurance business; city councilor Don McIntosh; and Stu Hart, wrester and promoter, with stars Gene Kiniski, Killer Kowalski and Mighty Ursus. Italian businessmen also came including the Amantea brothers – Jack, Ralph, Mike and Frank – who had established Amantea shoes. Mary sums up the restaurant's appeal as follows:

> This cheerful group of Stampeders, and all the other La Villa customers there that night, knew that my parents provided the essentials of enjoyment, Italian style; the best food in town, music, and dancing. The Wurlitzer pumped out Guy Lombardo and his Royal Canadians and Perry Como, and the jazz beat of Ella Fitzgerald, Louis Armstrong and Count Basie. A powdered wax, sprinkled across the hardwood floor every afternoon, removed friction to free the soles. A customer with one leg shorter than the other had found a warped rise in the oak boards. Planting himself on the secret spot, he danced the night away.[369]

Sadly, Gene was unable to fulfill his potential as an entrepreneur because he died in 1958, aged 51, of a heart attack after surgery to remove gallstones. He therefore did not witness his children's success: Gary graduated with a law degree from the University of Alberta in 1960 and retired in 2015 after serving nearly 44 years as an Alberta provincial court judge with the distinction of being the longest-serving judge in the province's history. Mary is a specialist in international education and an author; she did not pursue a career in the opera, which was her father's dream when he arranged for her to have private lessons with Norma Pocaterra.

Luca (Louis) Carloni's story is told by wife Adelina (Adelaide) Cardellini and daughter Nina Valerio in oral history interviews.[370] Poverty had prompted Adelaide's father to immigrate from Antrodocco, Rieti, Lazio; the family owned a small parcel of farmland and raised sheep, but this was inadequate to their needs since there were 11 children. Adelaide was born in 1905 and was brought to Canada in 1923 by her father, who had arranged a marriage for her with a man she did not know. Her intended was Luca, who had immigrated in 1913 and worked in the mines

---

[369] *Ibid.*, 8.

[370] See Adelina (Adelaide) Carloni interview, Calgary Italian Club Oral History Project, June 10, 1985, 1985, Glenbow Archives RCT-869-5; and Nina and Tony Valerio interview, Peoples of Southern Alberta Oral History Project, August 18, 1988, Glenbow Archives RCT-854.

at Nordegg. While some of these marriages between strangers failed, that of the Carlonis was an enormous success; they were married at St. Mary's Cathedral 10 days after her arrival. The couple became an "instant" family since Luca had taken on responsibility for his sister's children Ringo, Leo and Benny Fabbi when they were orphaned by the Spanish Influenza in 1918.

The Carlonis initially settled in Nordegg. On moving to Calgary's Bridgeland/Riverside neighbourhood, in 1927, Luca partnered with Rocco DiLeandro, who arrived in Calgary in 1913, and they opened the Canadian Shoe Shine store.[371] The partners subsequently parted ways and Luca opened two other shoe shine businesses. It would be the partnership with Gene Cioni that launched Luca in the restaurant business. After the breakup, Luca set up the Isle of Capri on 34th Street and 1st Avenue NW near the Edmonton Trail; this combined a restaurant with a dance club. According to daughter Nina, her father couldn't find a decent hall for her wedding to Tony Valerio, in 1949, and this was the inspiration for the restaurant. She states that it was Calgary's first Italian restaurant and was a supper club with no liquor service. It became popular with the Italian community and, in 1955, when Luca and other community leaders promoted the merger of the Giovanni Caboto Loggia and the Associazione Italo-Canadese, the new organization met at the restaurant until 1959 when the Calgary Italian Club acquired its own premises. Clearly, La Villa and the Isle of Capri were competitors but the market was large enough to accommodate both.

Valentino (Tino) DeValter was born in Medicine Hat in 1933. His parents, Sante and Amelia, were part of an earlier generation of immigration to the city.[372] Tino completed grade 11 and then had several casual jobs working in the oil patch and at Dominion Glass. He next worked at Val Marshall Printing and trained as a printer. For a change, he began to work in restaurants and managed several including one at the local Elks Club and the Dog n Suds fast-food outlet. In 1958, he married Margaret Ormston and, in 1967, they opened Tino's Drive-In, which quickly became a popular hangout for young people. Tino was well-known in the community as a talented curler who had played in many championships. In advertisements in the *Medicine Hat News*, he offered special rates for curlers. Son Terry followed in his father's footsteps and became a champion curler. Tino was a member of a range of local clubs including the Elks, Moose, Legion and Shriners and was also a shareholder with the Lethbridge Hurricanes, Medicine Hat Curling Club, the three Medicine Hat Golf Clubs and Medicine Hat Rattlers Football Team. He was also a Director of the Medicine Hat Exhibition and Stampede organization. The motto for the diner remains "where the hamburger is king" and it is still run by the family. In 2017, the restaurant celebrated its fiftieth anniversary and, to keep current, introduced vegetarian burgers and gluten-free buns.

---

[371] The Glenbow Archives holds the Canadian Shoe Shine Fonds, 1931-1971, M-6166.
[372] Collin Gallant, "Hat's favourite burger man passes," *Medicine Hat News*, April 15, 2014.

Barbers and Retailers

Community histories provide the names of a number of Italian barbers, for example, Florindo Comin who set up the Venice Barber Shop on 97 Street in central Edmonton in the 1930s, but there is little or no information about them. This is not the case with barber extraordinaire Luigi (Louis) Biamonte, who was born in Gimigliano, Calabria. Louis completed five years of education and also tried a number of trades including tailoring, shoemaking and carpentry but didn't take to any of them. His abiding love was music and this was the subject that he took seriously at school.[373] Unable to find a job in music, in 1925, he was forced to join his brother Joe and cousins who worked at the Black Diamond Coal Mine in Clover Bar (Edmonton). He was then 16 and accompanied by a family friend, Giacomo (Jack) Iuliano. Daughter Loretta Villeneuve notes that he did not adapt quickly and was extremely homesick for three years. Joe got him a job as a water boy on the railway in the Coal Branch but this did not work out because it was winter and Louis was inadequately dressed. To encourage him, Joe told him that he would arrange for him to play with the Edmonton News Boys' Band and he did but, because Louis was doing casual work at the Black Diamond Mine, after a couple of months he had to quit. The pattern of short stints in railway work and the mines continued for a number of years until Italian grocer and friend, Frank Romeo, suggested that he go to barbering school. In 1930-1931, Louis took an eight-month course at the Dominion Trade School on 101 Street and 102 Avenue. A year later he became a naturalized British subject.

Louis initially worked for Comin at the Venice Barber Shop with another young immigrant barber, Pep Ciochetti. Pep's wife Julie remembers that the barber shop was where the Italian men hung out to get community news and find out about work.[374] According to Louis, the Italian population of Edmonton in the 1930s was about 1,500 of which most were men. Louis took on partners and set up a number of shops, the first being Don McElroy with whom he operated a shop in the back of Frank Pitingolo's Majestic Pool Hall (where the MacDonald Hotel Annex now stands on Jasper Avenue). Loretta notes: "It took Dad 3 years of losing money to finally build a small clientele of steady customers and earned $15.00 - $20.00 a week clear. At that point Frank, as the shop owner, suggested that Dad share half his profits with him, so Dad started looking for

[373] Daughter Loretta Villeneuve tells his story in an unpublished family history, "Luigi Biamonte Family History," unpublished manuscript, undated.

[374] Julie Ciochetti oral history, Ital-Canadian Seniors Memory Lane Oral History Project, April 29, 2007, Ital-Canadian Seniors Centre.

another shop site."[375] Cousin Tony Biamonte offered him one of the shops in the building he had purchased at 10271- 97th Street and Louis and brother Napoleone lived in one room behind the shop. It continued to be hard for him to make a living and Loretta observes:

> Being an independent businessman in the depression was not easy. Until Dad built up a regular clientele, there were some days when not a single customer would walk in, and others when his take-home pay was 25 cents, the price of a haircut, shave, or shampoo. On the occasional really quiet day he would close the shop in the afternoon and go to a movie at either the nearby Dreamland or Gem Theatres. Gradually he built up a clientele of steady customers, and eventually had to hire a second barber to assist him.[376]

In 1948, he opened Louis' Barbershop near the current Citadel Theatre with old friend Bruno Lavorato and also hired brother-in-law Frank Rusconi. (In 1936, Louis had married Florence Rusconi, whose parents helped to found the Naples agricultural colony.) Others who worked for him in the 4-chair shop included Amilcare Durante, his nephews Louis and Paul Biamonte (Napoleone's sons) and his youngest brother, Salvatore (Sam). The brothers-in-law set up a second shop on 114 Street and Jasper Avenue, which Frank operated alone. There were several other moves but the one that occurred in the 1960s into the new Batoni-Bowlen Avord Arms building housed not only a barbershop but also a travel agency, a new venture. Louis had begun selling Italian Line steamship tickets in the barbershop and saw that it was a potential money-maker; he then partnered with Angelo Biasutto and worked for Bing Mah's Columbus Travel Agency. In 1962, the partners purchased shares in William Bressmer's Europa Travel on 96th Street in Little Italy. By 1965, when men chose to keep their hair long, business declined and Louis closed the shops (except the one on 99th Street operated by Sam) and with Angelo purchased Europa Travel outright. Wife Florence and son Richard helped in the agency and owned shares. In 1981, the agency was sold.

The 1950s and 1960s was a period when a new confidence emerged among entrepreneurs in the Italian community and many forged connections with civic and provincial politicians, in particular, Edmonton Mayor William Hawrelak, himself from an immigrant family and who liked to thumb his nose at establishment, largely Anglo, figures. Many of Louis's clients were politicians and Loretta notes:

---

[375] Villeneuve, 16.
[376] *Ibid.*, 16.

As a child I remember newly-arrived immigrant families, complete with small children, coming to our house, to ask Dad, whom they had never met, for employment assistance. He never turned anyone away and he was always profoundly embarrassed when they would bring him a bottle of wine to thank him. His two best contacts were his clients Mayor W. Hawrelak and Mr. Peter Hyndman, who was in charge of the Alta. Government Personnel office. As a student, Richard [her brother] was hired by the city parks department during the summer, and I got on as a file clerk in the offices of the provincial legislature, because of Dad's contacts.[377]

Louis used his political contacts to help Italian immigrants obtain jobs, mostly labouring or maintenance positions with the city or province. In 1972, he became a Notary Public to assist immigrants with oath-taking, affidavits and certificates.

Musical activity paralleled Louis' busy work life and he was a professional musician for more than 50 years. He played the saxophone, clarinet and mandolin, and worked with various bands travelling around the province before setting up his own. In 1933, he played banjo in a 13-piece string band directed by a Mr. Patucci; in 1936, he played with the 17-piece Ukrainian Band; and in 1939 with the Social Credit Band. During the war, Louis played with the volunteer band of the Loyal Edmonton Regiment. He also had his own eight-piece group from 1941 to 1946 called the Edmonton Serenaders. They played at the Palace Gardens Dance Hall on Jasper Avenue and 96th Street as well as for Catholic Youth Organization dances held in the basements of Sacred Heart Parish and St. Joseph's Cathedral. In 1949, his band helped to inaugurate Edmonton's French radio station CHFA. In the 1950s and 1960s, the era of "dine and dance," his next orchestra, the Louis Biamonte Band, played at Friday night dances at the Moose Temple. His other bands played at the MacDonald Hotel, the Blue Hole, the Palace Gardens and Rainbow Ballroom, and he continued to perform into his eighties.

According to Loretta, her mother Florence made her father into a church-goer and both contributed to the building of Santa Maria Goretti Church. The church was the gathering place of the community and, in the 1960s and 1970s, events were well-attended and the Biamonte band played at many Italian weddings. While outwardly confident and even arrogant, Loretta observes that her father was very conscious of his poor education and his less-than-perfect English. His great fears were poverty and criticism. The Biamontes were committed to higher education and son Richard became a lawyer and daughter Loretta, a school teacher, who later accompanied her diplomat husband, Lucien Villeneuve, in postings abroad.

---

[377] *Ibid.*, 27.

The Forzani family has deep working class roots in Calgary: Giuseppe Forzani was born in Borgomanero, Novara, and arrived in the city in the first decade of the twentieth century. In 1921, he sponsored wife Maria and four children. Oldest son John ended up working in a service station and, according to wife, Audrey Denegri, got up as early as 2 am to ensure that repairs were done for customers. Audrey (Andreana) was born in Calgary in 1914. Her father, Giacomo (Jack), a bricklayer and plasterer, arrived in 1911 from Genoa and worked in construction including the building of the Louise Bridge over the Bow River. In 1913, Jack sponsored wife Caterina and older daughter Giulietta. It is a tribute to Audrey's parents that they encouraged her to complete her education and she graduated from St. Mary's High School in 1933 as class president. She took secretarial courses and found work with the Hudson's Bay Company eventually becoming a store manager; she helped Italian immigrant women to obtain jobs in the store. She chose to marry rather than accepting a promotion involving a move to Nelson, BC and, then, dedicated herself to husband John and sons Joe (1945), John (1947) and Tom (1951).

The Forzani brothers are unique in their passion for sports. All were talented high school football players – they played for the Saint Francis Browns – and attended Utah State University where they played for the Utah State Aggies. All made their mark on the Calgary Stampeders of the Canadian Football League: Joe and John were part of the 1971 Grey Cup winning team. Tom was still at university but became an all-star selection at wide receiver in 1973, 1974 and 1977. His No. 22 was retired by the Stampeders in 1984. The brothers made a bit of sports history in Canada playing together for the Stampeders from 1972 to 1976, unique in CFL history.

In 1974, the brothers and friend Bas Bark, also a Stampeder, started a sporting goods store in Calgary, Forzani's Locker Room, at 17th Avenue. Their only assets were $9,000 in seed capital and their profile as sports personalities. John, with degrees in business and physical education, became chairman and CEO; Joe with a Masters in Psychology provided insight into customer motivation; and Tom was the general all-round sportsman. This enterprise became the foundation of an empire, the publicly-traded Forzani Group Ltd. (FGL), which grew into a billion dollar business, the largest and only national sporting goods retailer in Canada. Product lines catered to mid- and high-end customers and included their own brand goods, Sport Chek, Sport Mart and Coast Mountain Sports. The business was so successful that they franchised and this resulted in 160 stores; at its peak, the empire totaled 550 stores across Canada. The partners were able to anticipate growth in the leisure and fitness markets and led the trend. Product lines included athletic footwear, athletic/leisure apparel and sports equipment. When asked by Claudia Cattaneo, at the *Financial Post* newspaper, in 2011, why he started the business, John observed: "We were very lucky. This whole issue of physical fitness and health and wellbeing was just starting. In 1973, the average guy went for two martinis and a pack of smokes for lunch. Nobody was jogging. Nobody was going to health clubs. When my brothers and I were playing for the Calgary Stampeders, they were buying their football shoes out of the country. And we said: 'If we had this little store, with products that real athletes wanted to have,' and who knew it would grow so much?" [378] He acknowledged his mother's contributions in the early days as a part-time, unpaid cashier.

They also pioneered in web sales through the Sportchek.ca website. In 2011, the company, which was valued at $771 million, was sold to Canadian Tire. There were 600 stores and 40,000 employees at the time. John stepped down as Chairman and CEO, in 2006. In 2005, John became part of an investors' group that bought the Stampeders and, in 2012, when the Calgary Flames became majority owners, he retained a minority interest. In 2016, the brothers and friend Basil Bark were inducted into the Alberta Sports Hall of Fame.

The brothers learned from their mother's life-long volunteerism (she was involved in organizations such as the Calgary Boys and Girls Club, Calgary Meals on Wheels and the Catholic Women's League) and supported a range of charitable enterprises through events such as the annual Mother's Day Run and Walk (started in 1977). These efforts culminated in 2000 with establishment of the Forzani Group Foundation to fund health, wellness and sports projects. The brothers started the Forzani McPhail Colon Cancer Screening Center, the only publicly funded facility dedicated to colon cancer screening in Canada, at the Foothills Medical Centre in Calgary. John was named Alberta Venture Business Person of the Year in 2002. In 2015, the Forzani Group Foundation gifted $1.5 million to the University of Calgary Dinos, the largest single gift in their history.[379]

Some Observations

The move into business happened very early in the history of immigration from Italy to Alberta. Italian shopkeepers, retailers and builders also appear to have moved into the middle class more quickly than their counterparts in labouring work or on their own farms. They also ensured that their children went to school and, when they did not follow them into the family business, entered the professions. While a few were aided by their trades, others were born entrepreneurs with the instinct to excel in whatever enterprise they took on. Wives and daughters worked in the family business but very few continued the family business or set out on their own. While oral histories of the 1970s and 1980s asked the obligatory question about discrimination, it is clear that in

---

[378] Claudia Cataneo, "John Forzani on the right time to sell," in *Financial Post*, May 16, 2011.
[379] Ben Matchett, "$1.5 million Gift Honours Memory of John Forzani," Dinos website, April 23, 2015, retrieved September 18, 2017.

the earlier eras of immigration those seeking to make a living through their own wits simply did it, irrespective of obstacles in their paths. They were prepared to risk their savings on the chance that they would succeed in business. While some made only a modest living, others such as the Gallellis, Blasettis, Nigros, Anselmos and Forzanis achieved great wealth. A number chose to give back to the community at large establishing a tradition of philanthropy. This was frequently directed not at organizations within the Italian community but rather to the community at large since this is the arena in which they operated.

The Fumagelli brothers, Luigi and Alfonso Rinaldo (Joe) owned Red Trail Motors in Blairmore, Alberta and were not averse to bizarre advertising stunts. The 1929-photograph shows them with two circus elephants and the sign plays on the Barnum & Bailey Circus slogan, "The Greatest Show on Earth." Photographer: Thomas Gushul. Glenbow Archives NC-54-2223.

Harry Gallelli operating equipment likely at Trochu, Alberta, ca1947. The company was started by his father, Nick Gallelli in Calgary. Photo courtesy of Glenbow, Archives and Special Collections, University of Calgary PA-3675-17.

The executive of the Alberta Fascio in a photo taken at the formation conference on December 6, 1926 in Calgary. Front row, left, Antonio Rebaudengo from Calgary; Italo Rader, Italian consular agent for southern Alberta; Felice de Angelis, Italian Royal Consul for Alberta (a founder of the Venice and Hylo Italian agricultural colonies near Lac la Biche in 1914-15); Louis Trono, young musician from Banff; probably Emilio Sereni, who had homestead near Balzac (he returned to Italy to fight in the First World War). Second row, probably Victor Losa from Edmonton; Pietro Butti, electrician, from Edmonton; Giuseppe Michetti, farmer, from Venice (he had served in the Italian military in China); and Pietro Colbertaldo, consular agent for central Alberta. Back row, unknown; Rodolfo Michetti, son of Giuseppe Michetti. Rebaudengo Fonds, Glenbow. Photo courtesy of Glenbow, Archives and Special Collections, University of Calgary NA-5124-7.

CHAPTER VI

Enemy Alien Designation and Internment

AFTER THE FIRST WORLD WAR, Communist and Fascist supporters fought for the hearts and minds of Italian citizens. In 1922, Benito Mussolini became Italy's fortieth Prime Minister and with him came a resurgence of patriotism, and a vision of a heroic national identity based on the ancient Roman past. Mussolini quickly realized that it would be very beneficial to instill Fascist beliefs in Italians living abroad. The Government of Canada's interest in agricultural settlement provided an entry point and he chose a dynamic woman with an international reputation to investigate the possibilities. Italia Garibaldi, the granddaughter of freedom-fighter Giuseppe Garibaldi, was sent to Canada in late 1922. A memorandum from F. C. Blair, Department of Immigration and Colonization dated Ottawa, February 6, 1923, noted: "Miss Garibaldi arrived in Canada on the 4th December and expects to sail from St. John on the 10th instant. During this period Miss Garibaldi has visited the Federal Government in Ottawa and the Provincial Governments at Winnipeg, Regina and districts, Montreal, the mining districts of Northern Ontario, Toronto, and various points in the Western Provinces, not including British Columbia."[380]

A short "teaser" article, accompanied by a picture, appeared on the front page of the *Edmonton Journal* on January 9, 1923 titled "Signorina Italia Garibaldi, who is visiting Canada in the interests of the fascisti movement in Italy." The longer article headline trumpets: "Men Who Overthrew Communists in Italy Would Bring Wives and Families to Alberta Farms." The author continues:

> The black-shirted Fascisti are coming to Alberta.
>
> Not for conquest and bloodshed – not for new principles and new ideals – not to overthrow governments and establish something more modern in this most modern of countries – but coming simply to till the land.
>
> With their wives and families, these men who fought a war in the clouds from 1915 onward, waist-deep in the snow of their native Alps, they are coming, fresh from stirring contact with pioneers from the four corners of the earth, to adopt as their future home this land where the skilled and trained agriculturist may be always sure of a living.

---

[380] Stan Carbone, *Italians in Winnipeg: An Illustrated History* (Winnipeg, MB: University of Manitoba Press, 1998), 100.

The men who fought in the Italian or Alpine Front are presented not only as war-time Allies but also as "a good type of settler." More than 1.5 million were killed, injured or taken prisoner in fighting with the Austro-Hungarian and German armies. The author knew that the audiences who heard Italia were fascinated by her heroic actions and those of her brother, General Ezio Garibaldi. During the First World War, Italia served as an army nurse in the Balkans and helped set up Red Cross committees. The author catalogues her honours as follows: "One French War Cross and two Italian war crosses (given for three years' service in the zone of army operations), a Balkan medal, and one given for Red Cross service of the highest grade, prove Signorina Garibaldi the worthy descendant of the great name she bears."

The press lionized her and there is no doubt that members of the Italian community were delighted to claim her as their own. Besides promoting immigration, Italia was also selling Mussolini's regime to Canadians. Knowing that the western democracies were extremely anti-Communist, she talked about the Fascist struggle with Communism as follows:

> Dealing with the Fascisti movement, Miss Garibaldi related the conditions which existed at the end of the war, when her country was in the throes of socialism, when war decorations were torn from the tunics of the soldiers of Italy in the streets of her cities; when factories and estates were taken possession of by the Communists, and when chaos reigned until the everyday people, rising as did the same people of old under the first Garibaldi, swept the forces of Communism before them, and established in the new Italy, a new and democratic government, under Mussolini.

Italia emphasized that Mussolini had the support of the people: "With the labourers giving one hour's work free each day to the new government, and the school children contributing their mites the success of the new government was assured claimed Miss Garibaldi, and it was these same people, who were now coming to western Canada to take up land." Italia presented Northern Italians as ideal colonists: "They were adaptable, quiet living people, who loved the land, and who would ask nothing better than to live on the land. Just such settlers as the west needs…." Finally, being part of a military family, her reference to the Communists' attacking veterans had her audience eating out of her hand: "A hearty vote of thanks was given to Miss Garibaldi at the conclusion of the meeting, several of the ladies present staying after the meeting, to make the personal acquaintance of this distinguished lady, who is the first Italian woman to address the people of Western Canada."

On January 10, 1923, she travelled to Calgary and the *Herald* headline was: "Granddaughter Noted Garibaldi Visiting Calgary Is Investigating Possibilities of Immigration Into Canada Italians

Anxious to Improve Circumstances Outlet for Surplus Population Of That Country Must Be Found." Again, the emphasis is placed on immigration from the North:

> From the narrow mountain ledges of Lombardy where toil wrung peasants painfully carry baskets of earth to get another foot of land whereby the fruits of the soil may be coaxed for their sustenance; from the plains of Venice where every yard of ground is regarded as treasure, and where intensive cultivation has reached the heights of an art, known only in densely populated countries; from these places are looking toward Canada thousands of farmers who hope, if plans in their behalf materialize, to seek their fortunes in Canada, and apply their agricultural art, not to a narrow strip of ground, but to at least a quarter section, a wealth of land, which to them would be far beyond the dreams of avarice.

Italy's suffering in the war and the fact that immigration to the US was closing to Italians (this would be formalized in the *Immigration Act of 1924*, which established quotas for ethnic immigrants) are emphasized. When asked whether new immigrants from Italy would "mingle with the people already here," her response was:

> "Of course," she said, "the older folk would never want to forget their native land, but regarding the British and the Canadians as their friends, they are eager to bring their children up with the people of the country. The Fascisti believe in the gospel of hard work and are strongly opposed to Communism. Those who will be sent are people who are educated and many have traveled. All the men have had military training and many went through the war. We believe there is a place in Canada for the Italian, and we believe he brings the best ideals of citizenship."

She described the potential immigrants as "a thrifty people, a people of a nation with the best ideals, they will come here endowed with gifts which, in the great melting pot of the west will aid in building the new nation of the world." One wonders whether she was the first to use "the great melting pot of the west" phrase, which in the latter half of the twentieth century came to dominate dialogue around the diversity of the US and Canadian populations.

Italia met with the Hon. George Hoadley, Alberta Minister of Agriculture, and heard first-hand about a new irrigation district in southern Alberta. This initiative was described in the December 31, 1922 issue of the *Journal*, in an article titled "More Settlers, Mixed Farming Alberta Slogan: Southern Farmers Who Have Cut Out Wheat Game Are Making Success." It reported on a conference in Lethbridge on December 21 that brought together representatives from the Dominon Experimental Farm, Lethbridge; the Brooks CPR farm; and representatives of financial institutions. While there is no evidence of any attempts after her visit to establish any other agricultural colonies in Alberta, an agricultural colony was founded, in 1925, in Lorette, Manitoba. This was the North Italy Farmers Colony Limited established by Joseph Ghezzi of Winnipeg and which shut down in 1928 because it was not financially viable.

Italia was much more successful in exciting interest in Mussolini and Fascism. For Italian immigrants who heard her speak, she communicated that Italy's star in international politics was rising and that they too could be a part of this. As a result of her trip, Fascist locals were set up in Toronto, Winnipeg, Montreal, Edmonton and Calgary as well as a provincial body in Alberta. This was not just a Canadian phenomenon: in the period 1923 to 1925 more than 150 fasci were established worldwide.

The Beginnings of Fascism in Alberta

While oral histories mention enemy alien designation, there is very little information about the local fasci. This is understandable since being on the wrong side of the epic struggle between Nazi Germany and the western democracies had left the generation involved traumatized. Evidence that Italia's visit bore fruit is found in three articles in the *Calgary Herald*.[381] The first, dated December 8, 1926, is titled "Alberta Fascisti Forge Firm Ties Through Province." The author notes: "The Black Shirts of Italy, Mussolini's Famous Fascisti, are represented in Alberta by an organization that has sections in four communities and aims within the next year to represent the seven thousand Italians who make their home in Alberta. Pledged to the principles of the Fascisti, delegates representing more than two hundred of their comrades have just concluded the first annual provincial convention of the Alberta Branch of the order."

The Italian population figure is inflated (the 1921 records place the number of Italians in the province at just over 4,000) and was likely supplied to the journalist by organizers to add importance to the event. Other than gatherings organized by branches of the Ordine Indipendente Fior d'Italia, this was the largest gathering of Italian immigrants that had ever occurred in the province. The "Provincial Body" is described as a "federation in which sections in Calgary, Edmonton, Lethbridge, and Venice, Alberta are represented." The meetings took place in the Oddfellows Hall and

SOJOURNERS
TO CITIZENS

216

[381] The author advised Villa Charities/Columbus Centre in development of a grant proposal to Canadian Heritage for the Italian Canadians as Enemy Aliens: Memories of World War II Project and served on the Advisory Committee. She was field researcher for the prairies. undertook three oral histories, authored reports and the paper titled "The Black-Shirted Fascisti Are Coming to Alberta," in *Beyond Barbed Wire: Essays on the Internment of Italian Canadians*, edited by Licia Canton, *et al.* (Toronto, ON: Guernica Press, 2012).

elections were held with the following results: "F. de Angelis, royal Italian consul at Edmonton, was elected provincial president; I. Rader, consul for Calgary and Lethbridge, vice president; and A. Rebaudengo, Calgary, secretary." The regional delegates were A. Michette, Venice; P. Colbertaldo, P. Butti, M. Sestini and A. Gottarolo, Edmonton; O. Anofri, P. Credico, and I. Rader, Lethbridge; and A. Rebaudengo and E. Sgreni, Calgary. Several of the names are misspelled.

The author reported that a flag for the Calgary Fascio was dedicated, the first in the province, and that the organization's intention was one of service to "their own countrymen who come to this province as immigrants." The messages communicated echo those of Italia Garibaldi. The article outlined the organization's objects as support for religion, nation and family; respect for law; support for the Dominion of Canada; opposition to theories and ideas that undermine the nation, religion or the family (a veiled reference to Communism); support for Italian immigrants becoming good Canadian citizens; support for Italian immigrants' lawful rights in Canada; promotion of a better understanding of Italo-Canadian politics, economy and culture; and promotion of athletics. In essence, the founders did not want to antagonize anti-immigration Nativists. These values were also in keeping with those professed by the American fraternal organization Ordine Indipendente Figli d'Italia (Independent Order Sons of Italy), established in the first decade of the twentieth century in the US. What is different is that the fasci rather than being independent organizations would be controlled by the Italian government.

The convention concluded with a banquet organized by the Calgary Fascisti at the Hudson's Bay restaurant, hosted by De Angelis. A head and shoulders photograph in military uniform accompanied the article. This historic event was memorialized in a photograph, a copy of which is part of the Antonio Rebaudengo papers gifted to the Glenbow. Of the 11 men pictured (the executive and regional delegates), five are in some type of uniform including the Fascist black shirt. De Angelis is wearing a Fascist uniform.[382]

The following day, Thursday, December 9, another article appeared titled "Many Italians Against Fascisti, Says Alex. Picco: Lodge Official Declares no Need for Movement in Canada: Urges Italians to Retain Citizenship: Alleges Intimidation in Attempt to Secure Memberships." It is clear that Picco approached the *Herald* and presented a strong, dissenting argument. Picco's stance demonstrates that Fascism had already caused dissent in Calgary's Italian community. Picco is described as the "grand deputy" of the Giovanni Caboto Lodge, the eighth branch of the Ordine Indipendente Fior d'Italia headquartered in Fernie. It was Calgary's oldest Italian organization, established in 1918. The article continues: "In the course of an interview with The

---

[382] Antonella Fanella, a Glenbow archivist at the time, drew my attention to the photograph of the Alberta Fascio founders in August, 2011.

Herald, Mr. Picco declared that at the meeting on Sunday, Mr. Rader who occupied the chair, stated that the Fascisti were going to fight to the last drop of blood in their veins to gain control over the non-Fascisti and that they would mark the name of the Fascisti movement on the big prairies of Canada."

Picco's objections included the fact that Mussolini abolished "all societies and lodges," the "election of mayors, aldermen and members of parliament," and "set up a dictatorship." He also presented the fasci as a challenge to Canada's sovereignty and attacked a member of the executive as follows: "At the Sunday meeting, also, according to Mr. Picco, Antonio Rabandengo, secretary of the Fascisti party, declared that all those who do not belong to the Fascisti Party are idiots and stupid." Picco goes on to make a damning allegation about the "bully boy" tactics of local Fascist supporters: "According to Mr. Picco, the Fascisti movement has between 12 and 18 members in Calgary but the leaders are now trying to increase their enrolment by methods of intimidation, by stating that unless they join the movement their property in Italy will be confiscated." Picco also mentioned that Rev. Father Buchini had refused to dedicate the flag noting that, if he were in Italy, he might "support the Mussolini form of government, but while in Canada he was a Canadian and therefore has no desire to bring in any controversy among the Italians residing in this country."

Picco also made a startling revelation: "The Fascisti press of Montreal has been very insulting to Italians who do not care to support the movement here.... Libelous statements were issued and we tried to take legal action against the publication. Although our lawyer advised us that we might get damages we have not sufficient funds to prosecute. At any rate, in view of the fact that the articles appear only in Italian, they have very little effect."[383] The notion that there were individuals within Calgary's Giovanni Caboto Lodge who considered legal action against the Fascist press in Montreal is not only surprising but also suggests a high degree of awareness of national and international affairs.

In a 1984 article in *Alberta History*, John G. Fainella notes that Picco had personal reasons for opposing Fascism – he had served a one-year prison sentence in Italy for his opposition to Fascism.[384] On December 11, 1926 a third article appeared titled "Fascisti Backing Present Form of Canadian Gov't: Respect for Laws of Canada Being Taught, Declares Italo Rader." In his role as a consular agent, Rader attempted to do damage control and is presented as rejecting

[383] Oral history interviews note that Italian-Canadian newspapers were readily accessible in Alberta. Angelina Rebaudengo mentions that a local store in Calgary sold the Toronto paper. The dominant newspapers were *L'Italia* of Montreal, *Il Bollettino italo-canadese* (*Italian-Canadian Bulletin*), published in Toronto, and the *L'Eco italo-canadese* (*The Italian-Canadian Echo*) in Vancouver.

[384] John G. Fainella's "The Development of Italian Organizations in Calgary," *Alberta History*, vol. 32 (Winter 1984) is the only article that provides information about Fascism in Alberta. His source was Ovindolo Onofri (24).

Picco's assertions "in toto." Noting that he did not want to prolong a newspaper debate, Rader challenged Picco's assertion that the Italian government wanted immigrants to retain their citizenship. He observes: "In conclusion we would point out that 75 per cent of our members in the city of Calgary are Canadian citizens. Of those who are not yet naturalized, most of them are unable to take out papers as they have not been here for the full period of five years."

Role of Italian Consular Agents and Consuls

The history of Fascism in Alberta is tied up with a few charismatic figures: Felice De Angelis, Italo Rader, Pietro Colbertaldo and Antonio Rebaudengo. While De Angelis did not settle in Venice-Hylo, after starting the colonies in 1914, he made regular visits and, on April 20, 1920, filed for a homestead, which was granted on July 31, 1923. Rader had a successful business in Lethbridge; Pietro Colbertaldo set up a jewellery store in Edmonton in 1923; and Antonio Rebaudengo arrived in Calgary in spring 1922. All were Northerners and, in the 1920s, all but Rebaudengo were *agente consolare* (consular agents), the term used to refer to Italian government representatives. A second term also became current – *regente consolare* (royal consul). While the latter sounds more professional, in fact, in the early days both were honourary positions. The point at which the transition from *agente consolare* to *regente consolare* occurred is not clear; nor is that from *regente consolare*, as an honorary position, to a member of Italy's professional consular corps. From 1914 to the early 1930s, in Alberta and the rest of Canada, the terms *agente consolare* and *regente consolare* appear to have been interchangeable and those who held the positions acted as notary publics (assisting with documents such as passports, pensions, etc.). The positions were unpaid but could bill for services.

De Angelis is the most mysterious of Alberta's consular agents: there is very little information other than that contained in the colonization diary, travel documents and incidental references in community and oral histories. At the time of the formation of the Alberta Fascio, he was in his mid-thirties. The diary is important not only for the settlement history of Alberta but also for what it reveals about him. References to Italy and the larger world are few but noteworthy. On Sunday, August 2, 1914, he writes: "And it is at this point that we get the dreadful news of the Russian-German war. Is it really true? If it is true, it's awful. This notion hovers upon us like a nightmare through the rest of the day. Shreds of news are relayed to us by farmers coming from the city, but they are mostly confusing. Only one thing is clear and that is an immense tragedy is about to happen, and that thousands of mothers will weep tears of endless sorrow." On Wednesday, September 2, he observes: "Piemonte has fallen in love with this land. And rightly so. This interminable extension of yellow wild-corn gives a very vivid idea of what the Italian Colony will become one day, a fertile spot of Latin blood in the midst of these vast solitudes." The notion of "Latin blood" was part of the language associated with Benito Mussolini, who in 1914 established the Fasci d'Azione Rivoluzionaria in the hope that Italy's participation in the war would enable it to claim lands held by Austria-Hungary. In 1915, Mussolini founded the Fascist Revolutionary Party, which in 1921, became the National Fascist Party.

De Angelis also expresses admiration for Giuseppe Michetti, noting: "His company is very pleasant: a strong and generous man from the Abruzzi, he fought as a bersagliere in the Chinese Campaign. He's got a lot of interesting stories to tell." The China reference is intriguing and reinforces De Angelis' ties to the government of Italy. Like other western countries, Italy had an interest in opening China to trade. It also had what has been described as a "mythic" relationship to China dating back to Marco Polo in the fourteenth century and Jesuit missionary Father Matteo Rossi in the seventeenth century. The latter was described as "the apostle and geographer of China." But Italy also had contemporary interests in China and was part of the Eight-Nation Alliance that succeeded in breaking the Siege of the International Legations during the Boxer Rebellion of 1900. As a result of winning the Battle of Peking, the participating foreign powers obtained the right to station troops in China to protect their legations.

While there is no documentary evidence to support this assumption, on his return to Italy, De Angelis went into the military. He returned to Alberta in November 1919 and was in Venice-Hylo in 1921 to set up a sawmill.[385] Whether De Angelis remained in Canada, moving between Edmonton and Venice, from 1921 to 1926 in its entirety, or spent part of that time in Italy, is unknown. In this period, like so many young men of his generation, he espoused Fascist principles and his travels between Italy and Canada kept him current. According to Gisella Biollo, O. J. Biollo's daughter, on November 25, 1925, Pietro Colbertaldo, Antonio Rebaudengo and Gafolla (Iafolla) came up from Calgary to help set up the fascio. Tony Bonifacio noted that all the Italians in Venice and Hylo became members, about 40 in all, and got membership cards.

De Angelis was also involved in the establishment of the church at Venice, in 1924, and arranged for the assignment of a priest. This suggests that the ties between the colony and the Italian government were strong. In Italy, the church was one of the pillars of the Fascist regime, solidified by Mussolini and Pope Pius XI through the Lateran Treaty in 1929. Father Carlo Fabbris came from Italy to become the pastor of Il Redentore Church (Holy Redeemer) and, according to the local history, helped to establish the fascio and blessed the party flag. Bonifacio also mentions that Father Fabbris hoped that establishment of the fascio would help them to obtain a subsidy

---

[385] According to Ellis Island records, De Angelis embarked from the port of Genoa and arrived in New York on November 2, 1919.

to set up a convent school. Fabbris returned to Italy in 1927 but was unsuccessful in obtaining monies for the school; however, in the 1930s Italian language classes were held with materials from Italy. Mary Biollo Doyle was the teacher.

Pietro Colbertaldo is another elusive figure; he was born in San Zenone, Treviso and attended a watchmaker's school in Turin. [386] In 1921, he married and with wife Paulina lived for two years in Venice. The couple arrived in Edmonton around 1923 and he set up a jewellery store, which prospered. Son Joseph Colbertaldo was born in Edmonton. Henry Butti in an oral history interview in 1983 noted that Colbertaldo set up a consular agency in Edmonton and that, after a few years, he wanted to become the consul and went to receive training in Italy. This detail is of enormous significance. In the 1930s, Mussolini required individuals holding consular positions abroad to become part of the professional consular corps. According to historian John Zucchi, "Mussolini's program of 'exporting fascism' to Italian immigrants abroad began with the institution of Fasci all'Estero (Fascists Abroad) in 1923. This propaganda agency of the Italian Fascist party, and, beginning in 1927, of the Italian Foreign Office, was to organize and oversee the activities of hundreds of *fasci* (Fascist Clubs) in Little Italies around the world."[387] He also points out that, in 1928-1929, the Italian government established 70 new consulates and appointed 120 career consuls. In Canada, this resulted in elevation of the Toronto consular agency to a vice-consulate headed by war veteran and Cavaliere Giovanni Ambrosi.[388]

Colbertaldo went to Italy around 1932 and was among the first generation of Fascist-trained consuls. In 1934, he became vice consul in Vancouver where he set up a number of Fascist organizations. An article dated January 9, 1937, in *L'Eco Italo-Canadese* titled "Carriera Diplomatica Del Vice-Console" mentions that he set up the Regia Scuola Italiana, the Lega Femminile (Women's League) and the Giovani Italiane (Italian Youth). Historian Ray Culos confirms that Colbertaldo was instrumental in advancing the Circolo Giulio Giordano in Vancouver, which became known as the Lodge of the Fascio. It was established in 1927 under consular agent Nicola Masi. The Vancouver Fascio, thus, was established later than its Alberta counterparts.

Colbertaldo's professional zeal as a Fascist organizer is evident in his final remarks to Vancouver Italians before departing for his next post in Winnipeg. The *L'Eco Italo-Canadase* on May 26, 1937 quoted him as follows: "And finally, guided by the genius of the *Duce*, with the cooperation of fascism and with all its good and courageous people, Italy has conquered those lands before denied

---

[386] See Victor Losa oral history, Dante Alighieri Oral History Project, 1973-1974, PAA PR0915.
[387] John E. Zucchi, *Italians in Toronto: Development of a National Identity, 1875-1935* (Montreal, PQ and Kingston, ON: McGill Queen's University Press, 1988), 168.
[388] *Ibid.*, 168-169.

but which by destiny were to be part of the new Italian Empire of which we celebrated the first glorious anniversary on the 9th of May. In the conquest of the Empire, you, together with other Italian people of the Province, have done your part too, by donating money, gold, and even by volunteering."[389] The gold referred to the donation of wedding bands requested by Mussolini as a show of support for the African campaign. Collections were also held by Alberta fasci.

Another article titled "Vancouver Girls Guest at Banquet of Winn. Consul," reported that five school girls had been selected to go to Italy by Consul Colbertaldo in Winnipeg: "The girls, whose ages range from 15 to 18 years, are on their way to Rome for a two months' holiday tour as guests of the Italian government. The trip is given to 50 Canadian girls each year in recognition of their work in learning the Italian language, in addition to their Canadian studies." Colbertaldo told the newspaper that Il Duce originated this idea "in an effort to familiarize the children of former citizens with the homeland of their parents." Zucchi noted that, in July 1934, 19 Italian girls from Toronto and six from other Ontario cities attended a meeting of world-wide fascist youth in Italy.[390] I have been unable to discover whether anyone from Alberta attended.

A *Winnipeg Tribune* article by Lillian Gibbons titled "An Album of Winnipeg Women" provides further background on the Italian vice consul's family.[391] She interviewed Paulina Colbertaldo and quotes her as describing her husband's formal title as "Regent of the Royal Italian Vice Consulate for the prairie provinces." It would appear that he was given oversight of not only Manitoba but also Saskatchewan and Alberta. Paulina also mentioned that he had recently received an honour, "corresponding to English knighthood which entitles him to prefix Cavaliere, or in abbreviation, Cav." Paulina describes their role as follows: "We are here to further the amity and the commercial relations of Canada and Italy." Colbertaldo's knighthood is significant since these were awarded to only those who, according to historian Angelo Principe, had provided significant service abroad in promoting Fascism.[392] Colbertaldo used his base in Edmonton as a stepping-stone to move up the ranks of Italian Fascist consuls in Canada until he was expelled from the country along with other consuls in June, 1940.

Italo Rader's rise to prominence as a businessman was charted in Chapter VI: Shopkeepers, Tradesmen and Entrepreneurs. His alter ego, "I. Rader, consul for Calgary and Lethbridge," vice

---

[389] Cited by Raymond Culos, *Vancouver's Society of Italians*, vol 1, 73. Culos notes that Italians from Vancouver had volunteered for active military service in the Ethiopian campaign.

[390] Zucchi, 191.

[391] I would like to thank Stan Carbone for this article. He is the author of *The Streets Were Not Paved with Gold: A Social History of Italians in Winnipeg* (Winnipeg, MB: Manitoba Italian Heritage Committee, 1993) and *Italians in Winnipeg: An Illustrated History* (Winnipeg, MB: University of Manitoba Press, 1998).

[392] Principe, *The Darkest Side of the Fascist Years*, 21.

president of the Alberta Fascio, is more elusive. Fainella in his 1984 essay writes: "In 1925, in Leth-bridge, a pasta factory owner and Ovindolo Onofri, an employee who reports that he was coerced into co-operating, did promote the organization of a fascio, but were unable to obtain more than 15 members out of all the Italian miners, whom Onofri described as 'all Bolsheviks'."[393] Fainella continues: "Edmonton was the provincial centre of Alberta's Fascist organizations which reported and sent dues to the national headquarters in Montreal. As late as 1926 a convention of all *Fasci* in Alberta was held in Calgary under the direction of a special envoy of the Italian party, a *Sotto-tenente della Milizia* by the name of Gottad. In 1927, the Lethbridge Fascio was broken up due to internal sabotage."[394] The failure of the Lethbridge fascio can be directly attributed to opposition from the local branch of the Independent Order Flower of Italy, a miners' fraternal society. Both organizations ceased to exist. After selling his Lethbridge factory, Rader moved to Vancouver and became involved with the local fascio and was arrested on June 10, 1940 and was interned at Camp Kananaskis in Alberta and, later, at Camp Petawawa, Ontario. He was released on November 19, 1941 and, after the war, the Government of Italy appointed him consul in Vancouver.[395]

Antonio Rebaudengo was born in Piozzo, Cuneo, Italy and married Angelina Ceresero in 1920. In spring 1922, they arrived in Calgary with their infant son Mario, sponsored by Antonio's brother Cesare. Antonio undertook various unskilled jobs before finding work with the CPR at the Ogden yards. In an interview, Angelina stated that her husband wanted to leave Italy because he was an anti-Communist and the Communists controlled work in Torino.[396] She affirmed that he had to choose either to support the Communist Party or the fascio. Tony Bonifacio writes: "The Mussolini rise to power in Italy had a strong effect on some Italians in Alberta, and it began in Calgary. Antonio Rebaudengo organized and founded the Fascist party in Calgary, and having known about the Italians in Venice through Rudolph Michetti, he came to Venice. With Rudolph Michetti, Efisio Manca, and Benedetto Colli the Fascist Party was organized, and formed in Venice."[397] Bonifacio also provides information about the relationship between Rudolph and Rebaudengo as follows: "Rudolph Michetti was sent to a technical school in Calgary for a six month term to learn the trade of machinist and mechanic. In Calgary he boarded with an Italian family and there he met and got acquainted with a young man, Antonio Rebaudengo, and he had

---

[393] Fainella, 23.

[394] *Ibid.*, 23.

[395] Lucy Di Pietro in the entry for Rader in *Italians Canadians as Enemy Aliens: Memories of World War II* website, notes that his defence lawyer made the case that he was interned because he appeared on a list in the office of the Italian Consul.

[396] Angelina Rebaudengo oral history, People of Southern Alberta Oral History Project, February 23, 1987, Glenbow Archives RCT-856, 1-2.

[397] Bonifacio, 40.

formed the Fascist Party in Calgary, so he played an important role in the forming of the Fascist party in Venice later on."[398]

Picco's claim that Rebaudengo was a hothead and bully is supported by Ovindolo Onofri, who told Fainella, that "the Fascist promoter … active in Calgary in 1922," preached "beatings for dissenters." Onofri also spoke of "a heated encounter in the Riverside consular office between himself and the fascist promoter that eventually resulted in an attempted appeal by the former against the latter for police protection." Fainella further notes: "The *Fascio* in Calgary seemed to have existed as a separate organization outside of the *Giovanni Caboto Loggia No. 8*. The sources did not reveal the extent of the Fascist membership among Calgary's Italian community; yet it seems probable that it was considerable though not as pervasive as in other parts of the country."[399] Whether or not Antonio used intimidation tactics, he actively preached his Fascist beliefs. Audrey (Denegri) Forzani recounted that he was avoided by those who had got fed up with hearing him repeat the same things over and over. Angelina ascribed negative attitudes to "jealousy" of Antonio's education and believed that it was this that had kept him out of the Loggia. In fact, with Picco as the secretary, it was clearly opposition to his Fascist beliefs. In the early 1930s, Antonio would be instrumental in setting up the Piemontese Club with others who shared his beliefs. This was the de facto Calgary fascio. Rebaudengo succeeded Rader as the consular agent for Calgary and southern Alberta in 1930. The Rebaudengos took on the range of consular functions with Angelina doing the bulk of the work.

Victor Losa completes the line of Fascist consular agents in Alberta. He was born in Turin and trained as a watchmaker. Colbertaldo sponsored him as an assistant in his jewellery business and, when Colbertaldo went to Italy for training, Losa ran the store. In an interview with Sab Roncucci, Losa explained that he became the consular agent first and then consul later: "Yes, regent, because they don't appoint you right away. But then in 1936 I was appointed, nominated, with a patent 'patente' of 'agente consulare.'" The date was, in fact, earlier since Colbertaldo left for Vancouver in 1934. Losa showed Roncucci the appointment paper signed by the Italian Ambassador. He also provided some insight into the work of the consular agent noting that his duties involved the entire province and also Saskatchewan. The only source of revenue for the position was notary-type fees that did not recompense him for his time. Losa also mentioned that the local authorities treated him well as they did other Italians. Roncucci tried to get him to talk about internment and enemy alien designation but he refused.[400]

---

[398] *Ibid.*, 15.

[399] Fainella, 22.

[400] In his unpublished memoir, Henry Butti mentions that, at his marriage to Mira Cantera in 1929, Father Nelligan who married them at St. Joseph's Cathedral got two witnesses: Francis Shaplowski and his sister Salome, who later married Losa.

Alberta Fascio Delegates

The Alberta Fascio delegates named in the *Herald* article were a very diverse group united by love of their homeland. They were also under the sway of the consular officials. As Angelo Biasutto, a post-war honorary consul in Edmonton told me, the consuls were "like their fathers" and Italian immigrants believed implicitly everything they told them. I have been unable to find any information on M. Sestini, A. Gottarolo and P. Credico. According to the Ellis Island records, Ovindolo Onofri arrived in New York on April 21, 1911 and was 21 years old. He was born in Outro D'Oro in southern Italy and left from the port of Naples. According to the 1921 Canadian census, he was a boarder residing in the Calgary home of Giulio Cicconi (mispelled as Ciacaoi); his occupation is listed as "shoemaker." At some point, he moved to Lethbridge where he worked in Rader's pasta factory. Fainella interviewed him in 1974 just two years before his death. Onofri was one of the few people who wanted to talk about Alberta's Fascist past.

"E. Sgreni" is Emilio Sereni and, according to the Ellis Island records, arrived in New York on November 10, 1903 on the ship *Sardegna* from the port of Genoa. The place of birth listed is Borgomanero, Novara, Piedmont; he was 23 and single. Emilio filed for a homestead in 1905 near the Morley Reserve.[401]. He must have returned to Italy because, according to travel records, three Sereni brothers left Novara, in 1904. Mario (born January 1876) and Emilio (February 1880) homesteaded near Balzac, and Pietro (October 1880), a master baker, worked for the Johnson family at the Palmetto Bakery in Calgary from 1908. Emilio purchased a tract of land on the southwest corner of the Renfrew neighbourhood, which became the Sereni Estate and, in 1907, attempted to sell lots.[402] Because of delays in the City of Calgary's installation of water and sewer pipes, Emilio sold the land by 1911 though the area still retained his surname for a time. The Sereni Cottage School was built in 1911 at 826 4th St NE and was later renamed Mount Pleasant School.

According to Fainella, Emilio was one of 67 Italian Calgarians who volunteered with the Canadian forces in the First World War.[403] Italy's May 23, 1915 declaration of war on the Austro-Hungarian Empire prompted Italian reservists who wanted to return to fight to board the immigrant train travelling from Vancouver to Montreal for embarkment. Sereni's military service is confirmed in the 1916 census, which shows him as serving abroad and his wife Enrichetta

---

[401] Sereni also appears on the register of Western Land Grants 1870-1930 on the Archives Canada website.

[402] Information on the Sereni family can be found in the brochure of a historic Calgary walking tour, "2017 Historic Calgary Week Sidewalk Stamp Tour- stopping points," URL: https://www.calgaryheritageauthority.com/pdf/sidewalks-stamp-walking-tour-crescent-heights.pdf, retrieved December 6, 2017.

[403] Fainella gives his source as James Barbaro, "Fifty Years of Italian Community – Place and Needs," in *Rivista della Communita Italiana*, 2:1, January 1976.

maintaining the family farm. Emilio achieved the rank of captain in the Italian army. In the *Calgary Daily Herald*, Tuesday, October 29, 1935, there is a "Card of Thanks" advertisement in which Captain Sereni thanks everyone who extended condolences on the death of his wife; the placement of the card suggests some standing in the community. Sereni was arrested on January 9, 1941 and interned on January 28.

"A. Michette" is Giuseppe Michetti, who was born in the small town of Corropoli, Abruzzo and who left Italy in March 1910 to find work in the US. In 1912, he moved to BC and worked on construction of the Canadian National and Grand Trunk railways. In 1914, he was one of the founders of the Venice colony and appears frequently in De Angelis' diary. Giuseppe was joined by wife Filomena and sons Rodolfo (Rudolph) and Ottone (Otto). Rudolph, who was born in 1908, by the age of 12, was working on a construction gang and, by 15, on a railroad gang. As has been noted, in 1924, his father sent him to study steam engineering at the Alberta Institute of Technology in Calgary and he met Antonio Rebaudengo. A very young man in a black uniform appears in the Fascist photo and this is undoubtedly Rudolph.

"P. Butti" is Pietro Butti, who was born in Ospitaletto Mantova, Lombardy. His father, Cesare Butti, was one of the "Garibaldi 1000," who fought to establish an independent Italy.[404] Pride in his lineage was central to his personality and he was an Italian patriot. Pietro studied steam engineering and found work operating steam engines in silk mills in northern Italy. He left Italy on March, 1912 to work in the coal mines in BC. For the next 20 years, he led the itinerant life of a miner. He worked in the Crowsnest Pass at the Bellevue Mine and next moved to the mines in Canmore where he was joined in January, 1917 by wife Ida, son Enrico (Henry) and daughter Rosa. Work also took him to Trail, BC, Wayne, near Drumheller and, finally, Nordegg where he worked at the Brazeau Collieries. There, the father and son became members of the miners' fraternal society and subsequently Pietro became president and Henry, secretary. In May, 1926, the family moved to Edmonton after Pietro injured his eye in an accident.

In oral history interviews in 1973 and 1983, Henry mentions that his father had been one of the "hotheads" who had started a fascio in Edmonton, and noted that the men got together to talk politics and drink beer.[405] Henry indicated that he did not join the club because he did not believe that it should exist in Canada: "Personally, I was dead set against it because I never was a Fascist, never. My Dad was, and Losa, and all the bunch here. They had the Fascista Gagliardetto [pennant] and they had their little meetings. They did everything to get me in there … they used to tell me how good Fascism was. I said fine, it may be OK in Italy; it made the trains run on

---

[404] Peter J. Butti provided me with information on the family including a memoir written by his father, Henry Butti.
[405] *Ibid.*

time. Fine, but here the trains run on time. We don't need Fascism here." Henry's son Peter, in a 2013 oral history interview noted that, according to family history, his grandfather Pietro had been involved with Fascism even in the Nordegg days and also referred to photographs of the Loggia as a gathering of Fascists.[406]

It is important to emphasize that belonging to the local fascio was largely an expression of Italian patriotism and not an elaborate cover for nefarious activities. In this period, many world leaders admired Mussolini. Even PM Mackenzie King was an admirer and, in a diary entry of September 27, 1928 noted: "All morning and afternoon on the train I continued reading Mussolini's life – a fascinating story. He has won his way deservedly to his present position, a truly remarkable man of force of genius, fine purpose, a great patriot. It seems to me the people are truly governing themselves under his direction."[407]

The Lead-Up to War

In the period 1926 to 1940, it was not just Italian immigrants who tracked events in Italy: the pages of the *Calgary Herald* and *Edmonton Journal* provide ample evidence of the public's fascination with Mussolini's activities. At the same time, a debate was in progress that questioned immigration to Canada from certain countries. Two days after the *Herald* reported the formation of the Alberta Fascio, a lead article by C. W. Peterson appeared (December 10, 1926) titled "Eastern European Peasant Class is Colonization Need." Peterson notes:

> It has become a habit with us to regard our foreign population as a problem if not an actual menace. Sensational journalism, class interests, unscrupulous political argument and mental indolence, to the extent that we cannot be bothered with ascertaining the facts, are responsible for this. I do not wish to pose as the apologist for the foreign inhabitant of our industrial centres, largely from Southern Europe, who represents whatever menace there may be to Canada in foreign immigration. But I desire strongly to emphasize the point that even in the face of the admitted handicap of the shortcomings of the city slums, the foreign population of Canada as a whole compares favorably with the British stock in point of literacy and general morality.

---

[406] The author interviewed Peter Butti in 2011 for the Villa Charities/Columbus Centre *Italian Canadians as Enemy Aliens: Memories of World War II Project.*
[407] Cited by Principe, "A Tangled Knot: Prelude to 10 June 1940," in *Enemies Within*, 41.

This is an incredibly enlightened perspective for the time. . In the December 11 paper, Herbert Bailey, British United Press Staff correspondent, in an article titled "All Europe Keeps Eye on Sig. Mussolini," reports on Mussolini's takeover of Albania and interest in North Africa as follows:

> The recent rumours of a secret clause in the new treaty between Italy and Germany, indicating that Italy has offered to support Germany in freeing the Rhineland and that unless the League of Nations will give Italy room for expansion Germany will support Italy in a movement against Turkey, has increased the anxiety although there is absolutely no official confirmation of any such clauses in the treaty, and the British foreign office laughs at the idea that any secret agreements are included.

While the British foreign office did not take these actions seriously, they hint at things to come. On a more light-hearted note, in the December 13, 1926 issue, there is a charming profile of Princess Maria of Savoie, youngest daughter of the King and Queen of Italy under the headline "Italy's War Baby Grown Up."

The *Journal*, as the paper of Alberta's capital city, had greater coverage of international affairs. In the November 3, 1926 issue, there is a lengthy article titled "Frenzied Mob Slays Youth Who Fires Shot At Benito Mussolini: Italian Dictator Escapes Sixth Attempt on Life." Anteo Zamboni made the attempt at the opening of a sports stadium in Bologna. In the Wednesday, November 3 issue another article titled "Fascist Italy Venting Fury on Opposition" reports on suppression of all opposition as a result of the attack on Mussolini. A third article in the November 3 issue is titled "Italy Seethes in Rage of Fascists." On November 6 another headline trumpets "Mussolini to protect Life in New Post: Becomes Minister of Interior Making His Seventh Portfolio." On November 10, another article titled "France Warns Italy Against More Intrigue: Repetition of Garibaldi Affair May Threaten Peaceful Relations." The article begins: "France has issued a warning that repetitions of intrigue within her borders similar to that of Colonel Ricietti [Riciotti] Garibaldi, alleged agent of the Italian secret police, may seriously threaten her peaceful relations with Italy." Riciotti is Italia's father and a staunch supporter of Mussolini. Clearly, there was enormous press interest in what Mussolini was doing.

While Mussolini's expansionist agenda continued to unfold, so did his control of the consular agents in foreign countries. In the period 1934 to 1936, trained Fascists were in place across Canada and the RCMP began to take notice of participants in Fascist meetings. Historian Luigi Bruti Liberati notes that the RCMP began monitoring the Communist party through the 1920s as a potential threat to national security and makes a case that surveillance of Italian-Canadians began as early as 1926. He draws attention to a 1931 document, which highlighted the spread of

Fascism in Canada and there is an Alberta reference as follows: "Concrete proof of the existence of Italian fasci in Canada had been collected in 1931, when the RCMP had been informed that a certain L.T., manager of the Cascade Hotel in Banff, Alta, had received from Rome a quantity of membership cards for the Italian Fascist party."[408] It is likely that an informant from the Italian community, perhaps Alex Picco, gave the RCMP this information.

The mysterious "L.T." was Louis Trono, who was born in Bankhead where his father Mario worked in the mine. Mario came from Baio Dora, Piemonte, with wife Laura in 1898 to join family members. When the mine closed in 1922, the family moved to Banff. Louis is remembered as an excellent musician who had a successful career in Alberta and the fact that he is named in an RCMP document is totally out of keeping with his career and life in Banff. Louis was taught to sing and play the guitar and mandolin by his father and taught himself to read music. He began work as a bus boy at the Banff Springs Hotel in 1923, when he was 14.[409] He saved his tips and bought his first trombone and became the youngest player in the Banff Citizens Band, conducted by Major F. A. Bagley.

The men of the Trono family had all done service in the Italian military and their connections with Calgary's Italian community exposed Louis to Fascism. It is not surprising therefore that he joined the party (in 1931, he was 22 years old) and even served in an administrative capacity. He was certainly not the manager of the Cascade Hotel in 1931. In the 1930s, Trono played in regional bands such as the Gerry Fuller Orchestra. From 1938-1942, he played at the Banff Springs Hotel, Chateau Lake Louise and the Palliser Hotel. The flirtation with Fascism did not last: in 1942, Louis joined the Royal Canadian Navy and was posted, first, to Victoria and, then, to Greenock, near Glasgow, Scotland. He played in the Navy band in Britain. On his return to Canada after the war, he became a professional musician and later worked for Parks Canada.

The Trono story casts doubt on the RCMP's intelligence gathering and reliability of community informants who, it would appear, were encouraged to inflate information that they provided. Intensive monitoring of Italian consuls and fasci by the RCMP began in 1936, after the invasion of Abyssinia (Ethiopia) and Bruti Liberati notes: "Local Italian-Canadian informers were hired in ever greater numbers and charged with reporting to RCMP offices any subversive fascist activities; and investigations of suspected agents of the Opera Vigilanza Repressione Antifascismo (OVRA) [Organization for Vigilance and Repression of Anti-Fascism, which served as Mussolini's secret

[408] Bruti Liberati, "Internment of Italian Canadians," in *Enemies Within*, 77. Liberati consulted the Norman A. Robertson Papers at Library and Archives Canada.

[409] See Bill Pasnak, "It's Been a Long, Long Time: A sentimental Journey with Louis Trono, musician," for *Calgary* magazine (November, 1983) and Genevieve Svatek, "Banff loses a legend: Louis Trono remembered for his stories, humour, talent, love and music," in *The Banff Crag & Canyon*, May 25, 2004.

police] were carried out, as well as of propagandists who arrived from the United States. A special effort was devoted to the surveillance of schools for teaching Italian."[410] By 1938, paid RCMP informants existed across the country.

The June 6, 1939 Edmonton Journal not only reports on German advances but also on events in Italy noting: "Hint Mussolini Will Call Mass Meet to Declare Italian Nation Is at War." On June 7, a headline states: "Italian Ships Ordered To Enter Neutral Ports; War Thought Imminent." In the same paper, a short article observes: "Aliens' West Farms Called 'Arsenals.'" The statement was made by A.W. Hanks at an annual meeting of the Manitoba division of the Canadian Weekly Newspapers Association. The article presents the spectre of immigrants on the land armed to the teeth. The issue of June 8 has a very interesting short article titled "Alberta Italians Plead With Duce": "LETHBRIDGE June 8 – Grand Order of Sons of Italy, which has a membership of about 800 in eastern British Columbia and south Alberta, has sent a cable from headquarters at Fernie, B.C., to Mussolini asking him not to go to war against the Allies. 'The 800 membership of the Ordine Independente Fior d'Italia wishes to beg your excellency not to go in this war against the Allies, namely Great Britain and France,' the message said." This surveillance was not discussed in the pages of the *Journal* or *Herald*. An article of June 4, 1940, in the *Journal* titled "Italians Set Good Example," notes:

> An example that could be followed with profit by Canadians of German descent has been set by the 400 members of the Italian community of Trail, B.C. Noting the threat of Italy to enter the war on the side of Germany, they have affirmed their loyalty to Canada and have given up, voluntarily, all firearms in their possession…. Beyond question most aliens and citizens of foreign descent are loyal to Canada and to the things for which Canada stands. Canadians of German extraction know they are under a general cloud of suspicion because of the extensive organization of Nazi fifth columns in all countries. They would go a long way to reassure their neighbours of their loyalty if they would turn in their firearms.

The tone changed soon after in an article titled "Convict Pitingolo Subversive Talk" in the June 5, 1940 paper, which states: "Frank Pitingolo, city poolroom owner, was convicted by Magistrate Millar in police court Wednesday on a charge of uttering subversive statements and was remanded to Thursday for sentence." In his sentencing, the magistrate noted: "I am satisfied that the statements made by you were subversive and do come under this section of the defence of Canada regulations." The article observes that Pitingolo was the second city man to be arrested on the same charge (the other was David Pick) and the complainant was a soldier in an Edmonton

---

410 Bruti Liberati, "The Internment of Italian Canadians," 79.

regiment who had had arguments with Pitingolo about the war. A former pool-room employee also testified that he argued daily with Pitingolo: "This used to make me plenty mad because I was a boy in France in the last war and had to run to the cellars plenty of times to get out of air raids," the former employ[ee] declared. He added that Pitingolo once told him France and England 'are all capitalism.' Defence witnesses said that they had known Pitingolo for many years and during that time he had never said anything to them that was against the Allies or against Britain's part in the war." Pitingolo, a Calabrese, who had worked in the mines in Nordegg, was well-known in Edmonton's Italian community. The Majestic Pool Hall, located near the Macdonald Hotel, was a gathering place for the men of the community and was also the location of Louis Biamonte's barbershop. Pitingolo, who was Henry Butti's brother-in-law, was a member of the local *fascio*.[411]

In the same issue, an article titled "The Enemies in Our Midst" reports on a talk given by Watson Kirkconnell, professor of history at the University of Manitoba. The tone of the talk was fear-mongering as can be seen from the following excerpt:

> Prof. Kirkconnell recognized as our greatest authority on immigration and assimilation of the foreigner in Canada, informed members of the Canadian Historical Association that for the past six years a Nazi press has been pouring "virulent propaganda into German-Canadian homes in the West." It is true that of Canada's 600,000 German-Canadians only four per cent are estimated to be Nazi, but the westerner reminds us this four per cent is composed of men who take a personal oath of loyalty to Hitler. The Deutsche Bund has been assiduously building up a fifth column movement.

Attention is also turned on Italians and Kirkconnell is quoted as follows: "Finally the historian dealt with the group of Italo-Canadians. Their political and racial sentiments are served by newspapers in Montreal, Toronto and Vancouver. In these sheets they find a strong and heady brew 'rhapsodically pro-Fascist.' The influence of these papers is believed to reach into more than half of the Italian homes in Canada." While giving currency to these views, the journalist is surprisingly balanced in his conclusion:

> While these statements from a man in a position to know are timely, and while Canadian authorities must be scrupulously vigilant to guard against every sort of traitorous movement, we must not allow our natural resentment to develop into an unfair discrimination against the 96 per cent of absolutely loyal German-Canadians, nor against those Italo-Canadians who see eye to eye with us in our faith in democracy and the Canadian way of living.

---

[411] Frank Pitingolo was married to Josephine Cantera, the oldest sister of Mira (Myra) Cantera, Henry's wife.

On Monday, June 10, the feature article in the *Journal*, "Canada Parliament Approves Declaration of War on Italy," reported on the Order-in-Council that defined enemy aliens as "all persons of German or Italian racial origin who have become naturalized British subjects since September 1, 1922." At the time, citizens were "naturalized" by becoming British subjects since Canada could not grant passports and citizenship on its own. A second Order-in-Council outlawed the Communist Party. Twenty-six internment camps were set up across the country. A second article titled "Police Watching Alien Activities" noted that city police were co-operating with the RCMP in this work at the request of city aldermen. The author continues: "Resolution urging compulsory registration of all persons in Canada more than 16 years of age will come before Monday's meeting of council. The resolution recently passed by Ottawa city council was sent here by the city clerk of the capital." The resolution was approved on June 11, 1940. That issue also reported that of the 120,000 people in Canada of Italian origin, only about 15,000 were not naturalized.

Paul Raeding from the *Journal*'s Ottawa Bureau noted: "In what may be its last statement to the press, the Italian consulate-general estimated Monday that there are approximately 120,000 persons of Italian origin in Canada. The last Canadian census is nine years old, and probably out of date in this matter." A report prepared by Gérald Fauteux of the joint Department of External Affairs/RCMP committee tracking Fascists puts the number of individuals of Italian origin in Canada at 115,000 with a possible 3,500 of them supporting Mussolini." The article also provides an overview of activities by a number of Italian communities as follows:

> TRAIL, B.C., June 11 – Leaders of Trail Italian groups again pledged their loyalty to the British Empire Monday, in the face of Italy's entry into the war, and dissociated themselves from Mussolini's action.
> TORONTO, June 11 – A number of Toronto's establishments owned by Italians were stoned Monday night while reinforced police squads stood guard in Italian centres of population.
> VANCOUVER, June 11 – More than 300 Italo-Canadians, representing a score of Vancouver and district Italian groups, met here Monday night and pledged "unswerving loyalty to Canada and the Empire in the face of Italy's declaration of war."

A separate article, reported on the expulsion of Italian diplomats from the country.

On June 12, 1940, the *Journal* reported: "Canada Nabs Italian Aliens: 'Several Hundreds Held in Eastern Canada; No Alberta Action'." In contrast to the several hundred arrests in Ontario and Quebec as well as seizure of guns and ammunition, literature and black-shirt uniforms, the paper notes: "Much work remains for Alberta police, however, in the registration and fingerprinting of all unnaturalized Italians, as in the case of unnaturalized Germans. Number of Italians in Alberta was said to be 4,802." The article concludes: "Lifting Tuesday of the censors' ban against announcement of the intensive police drive was taken to indicate that most Italian nationals regarded to be too dangerous to be at large, have been detained." About 600 individuals, the majority from Ontario and Quebec, were arrested.

The article noted that most of the Italian nationals in Alberta were miners living in the Crowsnest Pass, Edson, the Coal Branch and near Lac Ste. Anne. It also announced that a third internment camp would be established in addition to those at "Petawawa, Ont., and Kananaskis, Alta." Great attention was focused on the raids conducted in Montreal by "nearly 1,000 R.C.M.P. officers of half dozen forces." The article further observes that Italian clubs and restaurants in Toronto, Windsor, Hamilton and North Bay were targeted and several arrests were made in Vancouver. This level of RCMP activity generated mass hysteria among the Canadian populace and also inspired fear among members of Italian communities across the county. While the Alberta authorities were not ready to name names, it is clear that the RCMP were prepared with a list of potential internees. However, based on my reading of issues of the Edmonton *Journal*, at this time, there appears to have been no overt "fear mongering." The Calgary *Herald* did not have the broad range of coverage of these issues though it did report on the war in Europe.

Sensitive industries that had large numbers of Italians in their work forces such as mining, smelting and railways came under RCMP scrutiny. In the June 11, 1940 *Journal*, a one-paragraph article titled "Miners Won't Work With Italian-Born," notes that miners in Glace Bay, NB, refused to work with "Italian-born men" after the declaration of war. This also happened in Alberta mines. Local historian Toni Ross notes in *Oh! The Coal Branch* that the mines were militant about enforcing enemy alien provisions. She writes:

> A meeting of residents in this district met at Sterco on Sunday afternoon, June 2nd, 1940 when 55 British subjects were in attendance to discuss the employment of enemy aliens to fill the positions left open by men joining the C.A.S.F., and it was moved that a petition be sent to the management as follows:
>   1. No enemy aliens or any naturalized since 1939 be employed for the duration of the war;
>   2. Preference be given to British subjects as foremen;
>   3. Positions vacated by men enlisting in the C.A.S.F. be filled by British subjects.[412]

---

412 Ross, 127.

The motion was carried unanimously. Methods of "combating fifth column activities" were also discussed and it was decided to report all "anti-allied activities." For Italian miners who had worked for years in these communities, the witchhunts that ensued inspired not only insecurity about employment but also fear.

In the June 14, 1940 issue of the *Journal*, a headline trumpets: "Start Registering Alberta Italians: Some have Turned Firearms over to the R.C.M.P. Officers: No Arrests Made." The article notes: "Registration of all unnaturalized persons over 16 years of age and of Italian nationality or who were born in territories under the sovereignty or control of Italy as of April 1, 1940, was being carried out in Alberta on Friday, R.C.M.P. in Edmonton announced. Those who are required to do so must register immediately with the nearest R.C.M.P. detachment. They must be accompanied, if necessary, by an interpreter." The author notes that some firearms had been turned in but, as yet, there were no arrests or internments and concludes: "Like German nationals, Italians who fail to register with R.C.M.P. will be liable to prosecution. They are required to answer a number of questions and submit to finger-printing."

Some measures reflected paranoia, for example, on June 19, under the headline "Foreign Tongues Banned by City," the *Journal* reports: "English and French have been announced as the 'official languages' to be used by all civic employees while on their jobs. An order sent to all city department heads by commissioners Tuesday said by banning foreign languages on the job 'unpleasantness' might be avoided." In Calgary, the *Herald* reported on June 11 that over 200 members of the City's Italian community met at St. Francis Church to condemn the declaration of war and affirm their loyalty to Canada. The City went so far as to fire its 24 Italian employees, mostly in the water and sewer department, only to rehire them shortly after. The Calgary *Albertan* reported on June 24, 1940 that the Associazione Italo-Canadase had raised $1,000 with the help of the Italian Ladies' Lodge; activities included a concert. The monies were used to purchase war bonds. Fainella notes: "Considering that in 1940, as nearly as can be estimated from newspaper reports, about 10 percent of the 108 Italian families in Calgary were on relief, the amount donated to the war effort may have been more than the associations could bear."[413]

National directives continued to be implemented and, on June 27, even more stringent motions were passed in the Coal Branch including: "That any enemy sympathizers in the employ of the Coal Valley Mining Co. Ltd., at the present time be discharged"; "That this meeting expresses itself as being against immigration of nationals of any country with which we are at war during the present conflict, for a period of 25 years after the cessation of the hostilities"; and

---

[413] Fainella, 24.

"That the Coal Valley Mining Co. Ltd. be requested to have their employees refrain from speaking anything but English or French."[414]

While Italians were being interned throughout the country on the hypothesis that they might be dangerous to Canada and Canadians, the Calgary *Herald* on August 2, 1940 published a well-executed cartoon titled "Axis Duet," which depicts an arrogant cigar-smoking Hitler and a rotund Mussolini playing a harp. "Groucho Hitler" and "Harpo Musso" are singing: Hitler sings "All we want is Peace" and Mussolini answers: "– a piece of this and a piece of that." The suggestion is that the dictators are comparable to the Marx Brothers comedy team. The cartoon is by Taylor Boothe of the *Vancouver Province*.

The Alberta Internees

In a 1973 interview, Romano Tedesco observes: "Some people from Venice went to concentration camp. Italians spied on other Italians and reported them to the authorities. You had to keep your thoughts and beliefs to yourself. But many talked badly about Mussolini. You had to watch who you talked to. If Italians had not spied on each other, the authorities would not have known anything."[415] Tedesco had been assisted in immigration from Bersano, Veneto, in 1923, by Pietro Colbertaldo, and homesteaded in Venice. He was designated an enemy alien.

There were six Alberta internees: O. J. Biollo, Rudolph Michetti, Antonio Rebaudengo, Giovanni Galdi, Emilio Sereni and Santo Romeo.[416] Antonio Rebaudengo is the most interesting and important. His story can be fully fleshed out because his wife Angelina kept the letters he wrote to her and their son Mario from the internment camps where he spent nearly three years.[417] Angelina is a potent force in the correspondence. She was a strong woman who fought to assert his and, by extension, her innocence. The letters reveal how she waged a personal war to ensure that the authorities knew the hardships that internment caused the family. Oral history interviews with Angelina and son Mario also document their internment experience. Antonio was the first

[414] Ross, citing the *Edson-Jasper Signal*, 128.

[415] Romano Tedesco and Irma (Tedesco) Giacobbo oral history, Dante Alighieri Oral History Project, 1973, PAA 74.106/16.

[416] Galdi, Sereni and Romeo were discovered by Travis Tomchuk, a researcher on the Villa Charities/Columbus Centre project.

[417] In 1997, Mario Rebaudengo gifted a number of family papers and photographs to the Glenbow Archives, among them a hand-written "diary." Actually a collection of letters that Antonio wrote to his wife and son from the camps, it is incomplete: most of the Kananaskis letters were kept by Canadian authorities as evidence against him. The letters from Angelina and Mario do not appear to have survived.

person of Italian heritage to be interned in Alberta – he was arrested on June 10, 1940 and was held until August 10 in the Calgary Mounted Police Barracks. From August 10, 1940 to July, 1941, he was at Kananaskis (Seebe) Internment Camp, Alberta (P.W. 525); from August 1941 to July, 1942 (P.W.1107), in Camp Petawawa, Ontario; and from August 1942 to September, 1943 in the Gagetown Camp ("Ripples"), near Fredericton, New Brunswick (P.W.1107). Antonio's prisoner of war number "525" indicates the sweep West after initial arrests in Ontario and Quebec (the total of internees was about 600).

As a first-hand account of life in an internment camp, Rebaudengo's letters, which he described as a diary, are of national significance.[418] Though he masks the identity of his fellow prisoners, there is enough information allowing for identification by a social historian well-versed in Alberta Italian history. The letters reveal the psychological changes that Rebaudengo undergoes as his imprisonment lengthened and he lost hope. His view of himself as a Christ-like figure, though stylized, is typical of someone who seeks the consolation of religion. The letters fall into a number of thematic groupings including worry about his wife and son; the daily round of camp life; the happenings in the Italian community in Calgary focused on his betrayers; and the battle with officialdom for his release.

The first surviving piece of correspondence is a Christmas postcard dated December 20, 1940. There are two compelling images: a drawing of the camp with barbed wire and observation towers in the foreground against a backdrop of mountains; and a cottage surrounded by birds and flowers. Antonio notes that these are the landscapes of "hell" and "heaven." The heading for the camp is "1941: Cool days at Kananaskis" and his home, "1940: Home Sweet Home." The card is personal and sad. The incongruity of an iconic mountain beauty spot as the location of a prisoner-of-war camp was not lost on internees. But it was the very remoteness that had prompted its use as a camp in the First World War housing mostly Ukrainians interned as Austro-Hungarians. Camp Kananaskis was located in the foothills of the Rockies 65 km southwest of Calgary and 11 km south of Seebe. The message is simple: in a time of trial and tribulations, he wishes his family Merry Christmas.

The letters are hand-written in Italian; the English translation was done by University of Calgary professor Valeria Lee, for the Glenbow Archives with some editing by archivist and historian Antonella Fanella. The first is dated 10 March, 1941, nearly 10-months after his arrest and imprisonment; Rebaudengo writes:

---

[418] The only comparable account is that of Mario Duliani, a Montreal author who was interned and wrote about his experience in Italian; published in French, in 1945, as *La ville sans femmes* and, then, in 1946, in Italian as *Città senza donne*. The English version, *The City Without Women*, translated and with an introduction by Antonino Mazza, was published in 1994.

I mentioned in a previous letter it is problematic to write and I outlined some of the reasons, for the moment I have found a subject; I'll jump from one topic to another, not making sense, believing what is not true, since the pen is free to write what it likes even if my thoughts are different. After nine months in prison one cannot expect to be in the right frame of mind but I remember one of the Ten Commandments: "Do unto others as you would have them do unto you." And I feel ashamed in being unproductive, clothed, maintained and cared for by the government, which needs lots of money to wage the war … victoriously.

He presents himself as a solitary figure surrounded by other Italians, who are playing cards and arguing. He advises his wife to send her letters to Ottawa because at Kananaskis there was no censor for the Italian language and provides the following address: 525 Department of Secretary of State, Ottawa.

In trying to arrive at a chronological view of Rebaudengo's internment, it is important to take into account some material that appears at the end of the collection of letters with the final entry being: "Fui rilasciato dal campo il 25 Settembre 1943. Era di sabato." (I was released from the camp on the 25 of September, 1943. It was a Saturday.) Immediately following, there are two pages of typescript that appear to be diary entries or perhaps excerpts of letters written in April 1941 when he was at Camp Kananaskis. There is also another possibility that these are remnants of censored letters. In the diary, there is only one letter for April, dated the 3rd. In it, he describes life as a vale of tears and also refers to the Cross that he and Angelina and others bear. He refers to Angelina's visit to his brother and writes: "I am glad you went to see Cesare even if he does not feel his brother is a victim of the situation." His brother's indifference to his plight was particularly galling for Antonio since the reason he immigrated to Calgary was to join him. The letter further notes that he writes her three letters and four postcards every month so that she would know if any were kept back (in fact, a number were held). He also observes that her letters do not reach him regularly and in chronological order

The type-written excerpts provide information about camp life and mention other prisoners. The typescript page begins with "Quaderno No. 7" (Notebook 7) implying that there may have been others and the page is numbered 356. The short entries, which begin on April 8, 1941, mention other Italian internees. I have selected a few passages of interest as follows:

8 Aprile. Yesterday and today were two days since I came to the camp in which I truly worked with a few comrades and we cleared and leveled a new place to play bocce, among the hardest working was Rodolfo [Michetti].

10 Apr. My wife continues to complain that only one in three of my letters arrive. Since the content is not inflammatory and even if the censor doesn't like it, why not cancel or cut but, by God, send her at least a piece of the letter.

11 Apr. A food package arrived from home, and I will have enough to supplement the weak food from the kitchen. In the package there was also a fountain pen but it was taken away from me so the interior could be "censored." What a joke. What secret could my wife give me that could possibly damage national security.

13 Apr. Easter. A spring day, at 8 am, the majority of ours made their holy communion. At 9 a boxing match, which was won by a blonde Swede, who is able in all sports but who is seen always alone. Many of his comrades believe he is a spy for the commandant. From 10 to 11 a concert performed by the German prisoners. Billo [Biollo] yesterday received a game of bocce. Now we have two sets in camp and now more can play more easily, who before had to wait their turn. The Rev. Bortignon from Vancouver sent all of us Italians two packs of cigarettes each; others contributed some crossword puzzles from the US.

14 Apr. I will now talk about a change in accommodation. Two new barracks were today occupied by Germans; in one all of the married men were housed, in another, the single men. Rita [Angelo, from Vancouver] would play 24 hours a day, he leaves the bocce and picks up cards. Because there are prisoners who are working reduced hours and played in their free time, the Colonel suspended these games while others were still working.

25 Apr. The head of barrack and Father Fabri [Alimando, the father of Victor, who was also interned] changed lodgings; my friend Tenisci [Fioravante or Fred from Trail] was nominated in Enio's place. A German comrade, who authored an anti-English letter, earned himself 28 days in prison. It took great courage.

29 Apr. One of the bocce games was broken but thanks to my old work mate Gino Rosso we have a new one. Many thanks. A beautiful day, many who work in the camp are bare-chested; others have short pants; others who are more fearless are lying on a blanket in the sun nude. After lunch seated in a group we are joking, the usual chatter, War, camp, the future, Italy, fascism, among Rader [Italo], Cillis [Felice or Felix from Vancouver], Baesso [Rino from Vancouver], Biollo and the Communist from Winnipeg who is clearly anti-Fascist and launches attacks on Italy, the military and Italians in general.[419]

---

[419] Translation is that of the author.

These entries confirm that the other internees from Alberta – Michetti and Biollo – were there as was Rader. A Gino Rosso appears in the 1916 Census as a railway worker residing in Prince Albert, Saskatchewan; Rebaudengo mentions him as a work mate, so he clearly moved to Calgary. The "Communist from Winnipeg," Carlo Roggiani, is actually from Saskatchewan. There were no internees from Manitoba. The excerpts also show that the internees were tracking what was happening on the Front and, on April 14, Rebaudengo mentions that the gossip is that Czechoslovakia has capitulated and in a few days it is expected that Greece will follow. On April 3, he advised her: "Do not send sweets or ravioli, instead send things that will keep like anchovies, salami or preserves." He also expresses envy that she has attended a concert and enjoyed beautiful music.

While there are elements of humour and irony in the April 1941 excerpts, the tone changes as Rebaudengo's imprisonment lengthened. The letters document his increasing anger at being interned; his sense of betrayal and obsession about who may have denounced him; his relationships with others in the camp (including other Italian internees); and his longing for his wife and son. The letters also offer a reflection on Canadian democracy and the treatment of internees. Rebaudengo was certainly aware of his legal rights and the lack of due process in the government's implementation of internment.

The length of Rebaudengo's internment (over three years), suggests that the RCMP believed they had overwhelming evidence of his guilt. His dossier has not survived because, according to Library and Archives Canada, it was destroyed in keeping with Government of Canada policy.[420] A number of appeals were denied and these are mentioned in the letters with increasing frustration. On June 9, 1941, on the anniversary of his arrest, Antonio writes about the men with whom he shares a shack:

> A touchy, uncouth character who does not want to hear ill words against that particular company [left blank by author], in which he worked for many years, always speaks in confidence, he is a coward. Two united by a fictitious family relationship *(compari)*, idiotic chatterboxes, one with a hoarse unpleasant voice, the other with a Stalin-like physiognomy, not in his political inclinations, his ideas change every hour, from pessimistic to optimistic, money in the forefront of his thoughts, they make a very stolid, but rather reasonable pair. Two dark men, one prays morning and night, both of them are rather taciturn and serious, differences: one gambles, the other does not, both protected by Saint Crispino. The tenth suffers the heat, he is blonde and

---

[420] I visited Library and Archives Canada to look at the records in 2011 and found those of Rudolph Michetti and Emilio Sereni. These should not have survived but the fact that they did, provides useful information. I made an access to information request with respect to Rebaudengo and the others but nothing was found.

has odd ideas, with his beard looks like a false Christ. The last two, one has a beard like Balbo's, the other has one like Grandi, they are in agreement, rarely do they intervene and when they do, they are abrasive, which hurts the weaker opportunists. As you do not know my bunkmates you certainly will not find my description of them ridiculous, but in the meantime I managed to fill the page.

At times the religious imagery is difficult to fathom, for example, the reference to the protection of Saint Crispino. Saints Crispin and Crispinian were the patron saints of shoemakers and leather workers. One account notes that they were twins and that their good works in aiding the poor resulted in their being beheaded on October 25, 285 or 286 AD. If this was Antonio's judgement of those around him it is difficult to follow his reasoning, or it may be that he is simply amusing himself as he indicates. According to Angelina, her husband studied for the priesthood so religious imagery came naturally to him.

Peter Krawchuk, a Communist who was also interned, provides another perspective:

> A second group in the camp was comprised of Italians who had been interned in June, 1940, after Benito Mussolini dragged Italy into the war on the side of Nazi Germany. The Italian group was made up of some 40 men, almost as many as us. Among them there were only a few ardent fascists (particularly from Vancouver) who belonged to an organization, subscribed to fascist newspapers and magazines, supported Mussolini and travelled to Italy in official delegations. The majority of them was made up of small-time upstarts, charlatans, gamblers, ruffians and the owners of cheap hotels. True, this was a receptive element for fascist propaganda. As far as I know, in the entire group there were only two workers — a miner from Coleman, Alberta, and a railway worker from Saskatchewan, Carlo Roggiani. It should be noted the Carlo Roggiani was a fervent antifascist and the entire time supported our group. [421]

His conclusion was that "generally speaking, the Italians were not interested in politics" and did not get into arguments or fights; rather, they were passionate card players. He does, however, note an exception: "Just a few Italian fascists ensconced themselves in the canteen and raised toasts of lemonade to Il Duce Mussolini and the "great Italian empire." The "miner from Coleman, Alberta" that Krawchuk refers to was Giovanni Galdi, the fourth Italian internee, who worked in Nordegg.

---

[421] Krawchuk, *Interned Without Cause*, Socialist History Project, URL: http://www.socialisthistory.ca/Docs/CPC/WW2/IWC12.htm, retrieved February 13, 2018.

On June 23, 1941, Rebaudengo asks Angelina not to "write verses since they would not let them go through" and also observes that he did not write on June 10, the anniversary of his internment, because he was not in a good mood and "I would have probably uttered some raw truths, which would have been censored, therefore I postponed writing until today." On July 7, he writes the following enigmatic statement: "Is it necessary? My days are all alike after all and I believe Mrs. Anastasia will find nothing to complain about, I will not name names." This becomes a recurrent theme in which he emphasizes his honour in not denouncing others. Nonetheless, it must have been a real fear within Calgary's Italian community. On July 14, Antonio mentions that he has moved shacks (the third time) and notes: "There are ten Italians, I am the only one from Alberta, two are from Trail, B.C., all from the worker class. We are divided according by region: four Venetians, three Abbruzzesi, one Neapolitan, one Calabrian, none really old, all around fifty." The Trail internees were Vito Di Pompilio, Ennio Fabri, Francesco Federici, Silvio Romano and Fiorvante Tenisci and they were likely all miners. The Calabrian is Galdi.

In order to make way for the first wave of German prisoners-of-war, the internees were moved to Camp Petawawa in Ontario in July 1941. According to Krawchuk: "The Kananaskis internment camp was divided into two groups: one group (antifascists, Italians and German Canadians) was sent to Petawawa, Ontario. The other group (German aliens and German sailors) was sent to Fredericton, New Brunswick." They were taken to the station at Seebe by truck and then put on a train (each car held 50 internees) where their movements were limited and they had to be accompanied to the washroom. Even there, they had no privacy since the door had been removed to ensure that the prisoner did not break the window and attempt to escape.

On July 31, Rebaudengo writes from Camp Petawawa and notes that the weather is better and the food was "cooked Italian style." (There were cooks and bakers among the internees.) He observes that Angelina's letters arrived more regularly. There were many more Italians and the letters reveal an awareness of this. On August 28, Rebaudengo writes: "Tell Mrs. Moretti that her cousin is not here and never was; he may be in some other camps." This suggests that some relatives do not know where family members were interned. There is no Moretti on the list of internees though he may have had a different surname. Antonio requests some letters to support an appeal: "Do you think it would be possible to obtain three letters stating my good civil conduct; from the mayor, the bishop and Mr. McCafery; if you could have them addressed to the Minister of Justice and I will send you the exact address. Do not regard these requests as humiliations. Some persons found my August 28 letter harsh, but the truth should be told to everybody." He informs her that he has not been interrogated and doesn't know whether he will be and that some of his "shack mates" had been freed in the last few months.

Increasing pressure was being put on him to divulge names, the suggestion being that if he implicated others, his own internment would be terminated. He writes on September 16:

> Today I have received your much appreciated letter, dated September 12. I will get immediately to the point; first of all I must tell you that the judge was perfectly aware of my political behaviour, who informed him I don't know, certainly I confirmed I was a fascist when Fascism in Canada was legal, namely before June 12, 1940, the day in which all so-called subversive associations were dissolved and therefore I was not against the law of this country; the judge knew I had cooperated in the collection of gold for the homeland in 1936 and knew other facts regarding my activity which continued until June 12, 1940, as I have always stated, that is to say while it was permissible. Then there is my letter, dated 28 September 1939, to my sister Giuseppina. It was a private letter as much as my opinion was private when Italy was not yet at war; furthermore I wrote convinced I had the right of freedom of thought and of speech that is so often preached by newspapers and personalities who label this a free country.

The reference to a letter to his sister Giuseppina falling into the hands of the RCMP raises the question of how the RCMP obtained it. It would appear that there were also a couple of his bosses at the CPR who spoke against him. In 1935, after the League of Nations imposed sanctions on Italy for its attack on Abyssinia (Ethiopia), to show support for the homeland, Italians at home and abroad were asked to donate their wedding bands or other gold.

In a letter dated September 26, he mentions two individuals, Iafolla and Sereni, who shared his beliefs but were not arrested and wonders "what is the meaning of justice?" In fact, Emilio Sereni was arrested and was released in January, 1941. On October 17, Rebaudengo writes: "I am not surprised by the unjust reply, it seems they want to give me a hero's aureole. I am gratified by your positive mood. Even before your letter, I already said what I think of the carrot: am I interned for my personal security? Utterly ridiculous! Why was I not told to change city for the duration of this mess? Yes, I have become somewhat philosophic, between Saint Francis and Saint Job; better times ahead." The reference to his being given a halo (aureole) suggests that some friends in Calgary, who were relieved by his silence, viewed his behaviour as that of a saint. The reference to "personal security" is more difficult to understand. The suggestion that he was imprisoned to keep him safe is absurd as he states.

Antonio and Angelina also have cryptic discussions about who betrayed him. In a November 6 letter, he writes: "Iafolla's behaviour is proper of his foul conduct, forget about it. Talking about the future elections I invite you not to vote for anybody, because it does not matter who conducts the orchestra the music will still be the same, as long as Canada does not belong to Canadians." Since Iafolla was mentioned as one of the founders of the fascio in Venice by Gisella Biollo, it would appear that he gave evidence against his former Fascist colleague. The Iafollas were a family of 13 from Villalago and the older brothers, Ascanio and Diomede, immigrated in the late 1920s; the former was born in 1910 and the latter in 1912. Diomede married Irene Pompilio in 1934 in Calgary. Either brother could be the informer but Diomede is the more likely candidate. The brothers were masons who worked in New York and Diomede went there to live in 1953. Younger siblings came as part of the post-war wave of immigration in 1949.

Rebaudengo continued to track the release of other Italians and was upset that Rader was released before him. On November 26, he writes:

> Picco's Circle is allowed to meet again, the police know these turncoats of cheap patriotism, one of them Sciorli's mother. This unjust internment of mine is harsh, however it has opened my eyes, and you can be certain that if I'll remain in Canada after the war I'll keep away from every group and our group in particular. The Canadians have only now realized that the Jews have taken advantage of the situation, because they who know the former to be blind and gullible, but I hope that this deception will end. The matter of Uncle Sam is not clear as yet, but I believe that he too will join the dance, though there will be little difference in the music.

"Picco's Circle" was the Giovanni Caboto Lodge; "our group" was the Piemontese Society. The Picco he refers to is his nemesis Alex Picco, who opposed the formation of the Alberta *fascio* in 1926 and had acted as an informant to the RCMP.

Anti-Semitic statements appear in a number of letters; while Rebaudengo may have been anti-Semitic in the conventional definition, his use of the term "Jews" in the context of the diary is as betrayers of Christ. By extension, he is Christ and the Jews are his Calgary betrayers. On December 6, he writes an enigmatic letter full of religious symbolism:

> Yes Lapunte has pulled his socks, good, he was an unjust person. In recent days we received news across the ether, or as you wish, from a well informed person or on good authority that Saint Peter did not admit him into Paradise. Saint Peter sent him to Purgatory with a letter which will keep him there for an undetermined amount of time waiting for the eternal father's signature on the sentence which will rush him to Hell. The day we received the news we all had tears in our eyes, many started to praise the Lord, others cursed the dead man so, that he would have hastened his departure had he heard them.

The "Lapunte" referenced is Ernest Lapointe, Canadian Minister of Justice from 1921 who signed the order-in-council that labelled more than 31,000 Italian Canadians as enemy aliens. He died in office on November 26, 1941, and was succeeded by Louis St. Laurent. Rebaudengo, who sees him as the instrument of his torture, imagines him first being sent to purgatory and, then, to hell.

In a letter dated January 5, 1942, he comments: "It is strange that Cesare will not greet you one day and extend hypocritical wishes the next. Carmine belongs to that jittery gang." It would appear that Angelina is being shunned by some members of the Italian community including her brother-in-law fearing that associating with her will somehow "taint" them. The letter also refers to a potential appeal:

> The *cincio's* trip is for an advertisement like that of the scare-crow. Iafolla and Picco are vile, they cannot know about my arrival unless they work for the Mounties. I cannot appeal again because I must have new evidence, "proof", to present to the commission, only some high ranking person working through the local Canadian Legion could move the Calgary Police in my favour and point out that in February 1940 I presided over the Italian committee of the "Pro Canadian Red Cross."

Rebaudengo continues to harp on his betrayal by Iafolla and Picco in a letter dated January 15:

> I am waiting for an answer to my letter to Ottawa hoping for another trial even if I don't expect positive results; the letters I wrote from the other camp [Kananaskis], which you did not receive, are also against me. My advice to Mario is not to take steps towards citizenship until my case will be cleared. The man who confiscated that newspaper and his fat friend are responsible for my arrest; I think there should be another copy of that newspaper at home because we had two copies of it…. Even if Toresan returns, I urge you to not be friendly, he is of the wooden leg type.

The observation about the letters Angelina did not receive explains the nine-month gap between his internment on June 10, 1940 and commencement of the letters in the diary in 1941. Something in their correspondence prompted the RCMP to hold on to the letters. The reference to Mario's citizenship is important because, as a citizen, he would be eligible for the draft. Though not stated, Rebaudengo was wondering whether his son, who was a minor when he himself became a citizen in 1931, was included in the naturalization. The papers are in the Glenbow Archives and confirm that Mario was naturalized at the same time as his father.

On February 4, Antonio writes:

> The radio news concerning Article 21 and those from Alberta, is nothing more than a sick fantasy of
> some politician. I am glad you did not bind yourselves to the lawyer because it is certain he would
> not have done anything. There is no hope for us: we know the ministry functions and the principles
> and tactics it adopts. As you know Fabbri [Alimando/Armando] from Vancouver was set free. He was
> not only the secretary, but also the inspector of the Fascio; Rader then had a set of responsibilities,
> but you see, they whined and made promises in front of the judge, they bent over backwards.....

It would appear that a lawyer was promoting some kind of joint appeal and he warns Angelina
not to get involved. He is appalled by the fact that Rader, who was more senior than himself in
the Alberta and Vancouver fasci, had been released while he had not. He cannot be blamed for
a sense of paranoia. At one point, Angelina appealed for help to George H. Ross, Member of
Parliament for Calgary East.

The internees avidly followed the release of fellow prisoners and, in a letter dated February 24,
1942 Rebaudengo writes: "Of the three Ghislieri one son was released, Paolo D. has received order
to stay. In my last letter I mentioned my teeth which are not broken, but poorly fixed. Gregorio F.
too, who had been approved by the Committee, must stay." The three Ghislieri brothers – Erminio,
Federico and Mario – were all internees from Vancouver. A letter of February 26 has only this
statement: "Your letter of February 21 has reached me and I enjoyed it a lot. Did you read in the
papers the declarations of the new justice minister, small j, to a Toronto Committee, it seems they
are starting to confess their mistakes, let us hope they will quickly find a remedy. If, as stated by the
authorities, only those accused of spying and sabotaging should be detained, I should regain my
lost freedom." It would appear that some members of the Canadian government had indicated that
the sweep of arrests of Italians may have been too broad and innocent men were caught in the net.

Antonio continued to worry that his son would be drafted and a letter dated March 16
reveals his anger at the possibility:

> I ask myself why is it that in dictatorial countries the only son of a mother without a husband is not
> called to arms, while here they cover their lewd democracy under a chaste veil, calling those born in an
> enemy country, those whose father has been kept, like a wild beast, behind bars for more than twenty
> months. I was accused of being a disloyal citizen, although in my statement to the police I declared
> and swore to be ready to fight for Canada, and I was interned. It is good that you wrote to Edmon-
> ton, if it will not suffice, write to Ottawa and also the Argentinean Consul, which is closer to you.
> Mario is twenty one and no longer naturalized, as long as I am interned he cannot be a good soldier.

At this point, Rebaudengo had been interned for about 22 months and his despair is palpable. Internment tested and changed him and, in the end, broke his spirit. It becomes difficult for him to write but he forces himself to do so. Others continue to be released because of influence mongering and he writes on April 5:

> Do not delude yourselves, treachery and lack of humanity have fertile soil here. If you only knew how many injustices take place, nothing could surprise you anymore. Leaders of political parties go free since they can pay a lawyer; those with a proven criminal record; those without family, a job, money, fixed residence, they too go free. Here gentlemen, family men, hard working citizens are imprisoned without a way out; look at my case: I am fifty years old, I can strongly claim never to have been involved in a fight, I have no criminal record, in twenty years in Canada nobody ever saw me drunk, I never lost, without a reason, a day of work, I was never involved in Canadian political parties, and yet I am labeled dangerous, in the wrong because according to them I think differently from the ruling classes; twenty years is not enough to demonstrate that I respect the law and I am mild-mannered.

He concludes: "But can they explain why in Canada there are eighty thousand Italians and in the last two years no subversive or violent event has occurred? They would like us to believe that the dangerous ones are interned and yet half of the internees have been released and nothing has happened; how do they explain it?"

Rebaudengo had become a citizen on July 31, 1931 and, therefore, fit within the legal requirements for naturalized citizens to be interned. Mario is listed on the Naturalization Certificate as a minor child. (He was 10 years old.) As time passes, Mario's letters become less frequent and he comments on this and, on May 12, he writes addressing his son:

> Do not think about yourself: you tell me how can it done; your experience is as young as your enviable years; but I better tell you that a father has the sacrosanct duty to watch over his children, especially in our case; it was in a free country, as a Canadian citizen, that I was arrested in this country of freedom like a common criminal and for the last two years I have lived behind barbed wire only because I wrote and said what was allowed. Others who have done the same, are now free. Those of us born in Italy are not guilty as charged by the Government.

It is clear that Mario felt oppressed about his father's situation and withdrew – the oral history interview in July 1985 reveals that he was embittered by the whole experience. In essence the period of his young manhood was destroyed by his father's internment.

In a letter dated May 17, 1942, the first sign of optimism appears. Antonio hoped that Mario's going into service might result in clemency towards him and release. There was a rumour that Mario enlisted in order to assist his father; in fact, he was drafted. Rebaudengo's hopes were dashed and he was among the last group of internees to be released. He continued to worry about Mario and writes on June 16:

> The society of G. Buccini tries to appear what it is not, the patriotism of these hypocrites and opportunists is weak, will these persons have the courage to keep talking about national brotherhood when the storm is over? I don't doubt Mario's right sentiments, but he is lucky because he is young, nevertheless he lacks experience; he should be careful in signing documents, he should be tough, not fearful, the fact that he is not a citizen weighs in his favour.

According to the 1916 census, Giuseppe Buccini arrived in Calgary in 1912 aged 25 from Villalago; he worked as a labourer.[422] He was joined the following year by his wife Maria Michela Iafolla and daughter Dora. Rebaudengo indicates that he was part of Calgary's Giovanni Caboto Lodge; the fact that he is married to a Iafolla also made him suspect. Antonio notes that only the love of his wife and his faith keeps him going but also reveals, in a letter dated June 21, that he has undergone a crisis and has been unable to eat or sleep. He writes: "With love all is good, all is beautiful, without it, everything is mediocre. I am bored, life bores me, I fear the empty hours, the multitude of hours which are in store for me, so slow in passing, one after the other, all veiled and gray. I feel like shouting 'have Mercy' but they do not hear my voice." He was suffering from extreme depression but, somehow, his fervent faith enabled him to accept the misery and injustice and transcend them. He did, however, experience relapses.

In July 1942, Rebaudengo was transferred to Camp Gagetown near Fredericton, N.B. The Camp's capacity was 900 in contrast to Kananaskis, which had 650, and Petawawa, which had 800. He writes On July 24: "Since Friday the 17th I have received no news from you, the reason being that in this camp there is no censor for our language; the correspondence goes to Ottawa and as we know from previous experience, the severe and hysterical madam Anastasia is there." On August 15, he notes: "The government as yet has not given you the subsidy, it is a disgrace. We internees know the RCMP and we value them for what they are worth...."[423] The Rebaudengo fonds in

---

[422] Joe Boccine (Buccini), 1916 Canadian census, URL: https://search.ancestry.ca/cgi-bin/sse.dll?indiv=1&dbid=1556&h=759340073&tid=&pid=&usePUB=true&_phsrc=ReY1817&_phstart=successSource, retrieved December 3, 2018.
[423] The Glenbow Archives has various documents pertaining to her struggle to obtain the Dependents' Allowance. Her situation was exacerbated by a bout of Scarlet Fever. To cope she had taken a tenant, Barbara, into her home.

the Glenbow Archives contain a letter signed by Major Sydney Wood, Department of Defence, Army headquarters, M.D. 13, Calgary, dated September 11, 1942. The rejection contained in the letter can be described as a "Catch-22" situation: "The Dependents' Allowance Board advise that unless it is considered that Mr. Rebaudengo would be totally incapacitated from earning a living were he living at home, that you are not eligible to receive an allowance. If you have any reason to consider that Mr. Rebaudengo is incapacitated please let us know and further representations will be made to the Authorities at Ottawa." The implication is that her son Mario would support her.

A letter from George H. Ross, Member for Calgary East, to the Hon. N. A. McLarty, Secretary of State, on behalf of Angelina, provides additional information as to her circumstances:

> Antonio Rebaudengo who is an Italian by birth has been interned since June 1940. He has a wife and one son. Antonio and his wife own a home at 324-5th Avenue East in Calgary. They are anxious to sell the home in order that Mrs. Rebaudengo may have the realization from the sale to live on. What I would like to know is this; suppose she should sell the home will the realizations from the sale be frozen for the duration so that she will not be able to get her hands on it [or] will it be turned over to her so that she can use it to live on for the duration of the war? Would there be any difficulty in giving a conveyance in view of the fact that the home stands in the name of both husband and wife and he is in the internment camp. I presume we could send a transfer to the internment camp and have it executed by him and she could sign here.

He further observes that their son Mario was conscripted and has assigned his $20 monthly pay to his mother since he has been unable to get a Dependents allowance for her. He concludes: "She has relatives in Eastern Canada and she would like to go there and rent a couple of rooms for herself and live in that way on the money that she would receive from the sale of the property."[424] Fortunately, Angelina did not pursue the harebrained scheme of selling their property. It would appear that there were some who wanted to profit from Antonio's imprisonment by exploiting his wife: "I already told you about the kind and willing custodian; he would always have either the house or money in his hands so I don't think that it would be convenient to sell it, because you would be without the house and without money." It is appalling that there were members of the Italian community who wished to profit from the misfortune of others by masquerading as friends.

---

[424] Travis Tomchuk, a researcher on the Villa Charities/Columbus Centre Project, found this letter in the Rebaudengo's Custodian of Enemy Property file and photographed it and shared it with me on August 23, 2011 (RG117, Vol 690, File 7680).

On October 1942 a hearing was held in Calgary and Angelina succeeded in obtaining a Dependents' Allowance in the amount of $20 a month for the duration of her husband's internment retroactive to June 12, 1942. The first payment totalled $92.67. On November 9, he writes in anticipation of his release: "My working tools, which are in the basement, especially those for wood working, should be oiled and kept clean since it will not be easy for me to buy new ones; and my clothes should also be aired now and then." His hope is dashed when the Commission confirms his internment and he writes on November 12: "Yesterday I received the long awaited response from the Minister of Justice, my internment is confirmed; the thin thread of hope broke when I had heard that you would have received a subsidy for our son; they have bought him for twenty dollars per month." This is a twisted reference to the 20 pieces of silver that Judas received for betraying Christ.

Angelina continued to protest to her local MP and even went so far as to write to Prime Minister Mackenzie King. On February 7, 1943 he comments on another hearing:

> Last month you wrote to me that my case would have been probably reviewed in January, but it was not so; as I already said to you the Commission, made up of the same people, came to town on 25th of last month and questioned many of our fellow countrymen, half of them have been released by now; on the 5th of this month the same Commission left Fredericton until the new orders, and I was not summoned; my three comrades from the West were called and one has already gone home. As you see I am unlucky, I hope, however, that the Investigative Commission will soon return and will act with more discretion this time.

He was photographed and fingerprinted, which added insult to injury and writes: "It is the third time and, by now, they have my face in three styles; without beard, with beard and now with the moustache only."

On February 23, Angelina received a letter from the Deputy Minister of Justice as follows: "With reference to your letter of the 19th instant, I may say that an Advisory Committee recently reviewed your husband's file and in view of the information disclosed thereon, including letters from yourself and your son to him, is not prepared to alter the recommendation previously made, namely, that his detention be continued." Rebaudengo continued to plan for his release and writes on February 26: "I am sure that the nursery rhyme of questions in my last letter made you laugh, in any case I was not trying to worry you, only to stay within the realm of reality. To those to whom I advised you to turn, you can add Mr. Rossetti, pasta factory in Lethbridge, and Mr. J. Kelly too, director at Ogden, who could find me a job in some shop in the province, in a branch of his department: in Medicine Hat, Edmonton, Lethbridge, Revelstok[e]."

Rebaudengo provides a brief reference to some violence at the camp. Bruti Liberati describes an incident involving Salvatore Mancuso, a doctor and director of the Montreal fascio. He was attacked by another internee, Gentile Dieni, also of Montreal. Bruti Liberati notes: "In this instance, Dieni, an ardent Fascist, appears to have vented his anger for the internments against a fascist leader, Mancuso, whom he accused of having betrayed the cause. Mancuso was released shortly after the attack."[425] Dieni was sent to a psychiatric hospital. After the lengthy imprisonment, it is not surprising that some internees suffered from psychotic episodes.

In a letter dated March 10, Rebaudengo observes that the censors had cut out a significant portion of Angelina's last letter because she had allowed herself to vent about the most recent rejection from the Justice Minister. The Investigative Committee was visiting the Camp frequently and the number of releases was increasing. The maintenance of a loving relationship with a spouse across the barriers of time and physical distance was enormously challenging for the Rebaudengos as it was for other internees. That they succeeded is a testament to their love for each other and moral fortitude. However, her tenacity may have acted against his release. Rebaudengo in a letter dated April 8, 1943, states categorically that her letters and actions may be hurting his cause.

It would appear that Angelina and Mario were kept under surveillance until the very end. A letter dated August 29 contains the cryptic statement: "The blank promissory note on Mr. Corradetti's life is about to expire, patience." Could the Italian expression be equivalent to the English expression that Corradetti will "get his just desserts?" The Corradetti to whom Rebaudengo refers is likely Annibale Corradetti, who worked for the city as a labourer and also owned properties and was a member of the Loggia. The last entry in the diary is: "I was released from camp on September 25, 1943. It was a Saturday."

Rebaudengo, while longing to see his wife and son, was also likely dreading meeting those who had spoken against him. The fears, doubts and insecurities were not left in the camps. They were a legacy that continued to haunt internees and their families to the end of their lives. Is it any wonder that a "collective amnesia" fell over Italian communities about this painful episode in their history? Rebaudengo returned to Calgary and work with the CPR and, according to Angelina, he refused help from the Italian community though their friends organized a twenty-fifth wedding anniversary party for them. In 1949, he was appointed honorary consul and served until 1967. Antonio's doubts about Canadian democracy were laid to rest and he supported the mayoral campaigns of Grant MacEwan, Don MacKay, Harry Hays and Rod Sykes and, according to Angelina, delivered "the Italian vote." He refused to assist local Italians seeking public office because he felt

---

[425] Liberati, 91.

that they lacked education and experience. Angelina continued to view Antonio, son Mario and herself as victims.[426]

Tony Bonifacio recounts the story of the two Venice internees in his unpublished memoir as follows:

> Someone reported to the R.C.M.P. in Lac La Biche that the party had existed in Venice, and that led to an investigation by the police. Although the party had ceased to exist for many years, the police located records that Mr. Coli in Hylo still had and some of the names led to the arrest of O. J. Biollo first. He was taken to Calgary and sent to a concentration camp in Kananaskis. A short time later Rudolph Michetti, Augusto Marini, Efisio Manca, and Joe Michetti were arrested and taken to Edmonton, and after a hearing the three were sent home only Rudolph was sent to Kananaskis to keep O.J. Biollo company.[427]

These observations were confirmed by Mary Biollo Doyle.[428] After her marriage in 1936, she moved to Edmonton to teach but was visiting the farm when an RCMP officer arrived to arrest her father. He was not allowed to change his work clothes or say goodbye to the family. In a 2011 interview, she indicated that one of the people who denounced her father was a business rival, Jean/John Piquette, the agent of the grain elevator company. After Biollo's internment, Piquette took over the post office. Another individual who spoke against Biollo was a young member of the colony, Lydia Michetti, the daughter of Giuseppe Michetti. In an unpublished family history, Mary writes:

> Mr. James S. Johnston, a returned British soldier of World War I, gave testimony in a letter: "I know there is no reason to intern Mr. Biollo and that complaints turned against him were made to satisfy personal spite and grudges and not patriotic reasons …I have lived beside the Italians here twenty-one years and find them good neighbours."… [pause is Mrs. Doyle's] This letter was submitted by Mr. R. D. Tighe K.C. to Chief Justice Mitchell. Mr. Alex Fraser and Mr. Adrian Crowe, both of Edmonton testified as to Mr. Biollo's character. From the two hearings

---

[426] The Glenbow created a digital educational resource titled "Letters from the Trunk" about the Rebaudengo internment story. Besides working on this resource, Antonella Fanella contributed the essay "The Rebaudengo Family," to *Beyond Barbed Wire: Essays on the Internment of Italian Canadians*, 274-280.

[427] Tony Bonifacio, unpublished manuscript.

[428] Mary Biollo Doyle oral history *Celebrating Edmonton's Italian Community Oral History Project*, 2001, University of Alberta Archives. The second interview in 2011 was conducted by the author for the Villa Charities/Columbus Centre project.

before Chief Justice Mitchell, a report was sent to Ottawa. With this information, and with the help supplemented by Constable Hanna of Lac La Biche, Mr. Biollo was released from Camp Petawawa and returned home in September of 1941.

Rudolph Michetti's RCMP dossier can be found at Library and Archives Canada.[429] The fact that it survived is remarkable since the records of internees were to be destroyed. The document in its entirety is as follows:

SECRET

Memorandum To:

The Inter-Departmental Committee

Re: Rudolph MICHETTI, Hylo, Alta.

This subject was born in Italy in 1907, came to Canada in 1910 and acquired naturalization by Virtue of his father's naturalization in 1918. He is married, has five children and resides at Hylo, Alberta.

2. Our inquiries reveal that this man was one of the main organizers of the Italian Fascist movement at Venice and Hylo, Alberta, in 1926 and was elected President. It was learned that MICHETTI on several occasions approached different citizens in Hylo and Venice with a view of obtaining membership in the Fascio. In one instance he approached one Salvatore Giacobbo, a farmer of the Venice district, and he stated that anyone who refused to join the party would be dealt with as they did in Italy with those who refused, namely the castor oil treatment. This threat against Giacobbo caused him to leave the district until such time as the Fascist party in that area was organized. It was reported that on several occasions he used force and intimidation in obtaining members for the Fascio and did not hesitate to express the opinion that "some time they would wish they had joined".

3. MICHETTI, as well as other executives of the local organization, kept a constant fear amongst the members, in this way endeavouring to hold the group together.

---

[429] The Villa Charities/Columbus Centre team obtained Rudolph Michetti's RCMP dossier, Reference: RG18 F-3 Vol 3563 Part 2, Library and Archives Canada.

4. On one occasion he placed an Italian flag in a church during his sister's wedding and said, "This is the only flag" and that "some day the people of this country will have to respect it".

5. It is understood that, until the war starts, he wore a black shirt at all Italian functions as a symbol of Fascism. In 1927 he was Provincial Regent of the Italian Fascist Movement.

6. He is known as one of the staunchest supporters of the Fascist organization in his area. MICHETTI has been known to express anti-British sentiments on several occasions but since the war he has been more cautious in his remarks. It is reported that the subject is a potential saboteur and, should the occasion arise, he would undoubtedly cause trouble.

7. In view of the above, it is recommended by the Officer Commanding, "K" Division, that he be interned, which recommendation is concurred in at these Headquarters.

OTTAWA, 22-11-40

40 D 269-1-H-1171

GAK/LIJ

Rudolph's birth date and date of arrival in Canada are wrong: the former is given as 1907 and the latter as 1910. Rudolph was born in 1908 and came to Canada in 1917. The informant, Salvatore Giacobbo, settled in Venice in 1924 and, in 1929, married Florence Biollo. There is an element of tit-for-tat here: Lydia Michetti informed against O. J. Biollo and Giacobbo, married to a Biollo, informed against a Michetti. The details in Michetti's dossier including threats, use of the castor oil treatment, wearing of the black shirt were typical charges but the most damaging was the suggestion that he was a "potential saboteur."

On May 11, 2011, I interviewed Alberto Michetti (born August 8, 1921 in Hylo), Rudolph's cousin. He confirmed the details of the arrest and noted that, when Rudolph went from Edmonton to Camp Petawawa, he was shackled to a German, Hans Brauer, from Stony Plain. He stated that, initially, his Uncle Joe wasn't arrested because he was ill. He confirmed that Rudolph's family suffered during his internment and noted that, when he was arrested, his wife was pregnant. He mentioned that his Uncle Joe helped them with food and clothing, and the Sunshine Society from Edmonton also sent them used clothing. Michetti was released in September or October, 1941. Alberto observed that, on his release, Rudolph set up a blacksmith shop. He appears not to have been considered a security risk because, in 1942, he went to Fort McMurray to work at the Abasands Plant, the province's project to extract oil from the tar sands.

Emilio Sereni's RCMP dossier has also survived.[430] It is included below in its entirety.

---

[430] Researchers from the Villa Charities/Columbus Centre Project obtained a copy of the RCMP record pertaining to Sereni, Reference: RG18 F-3 Vol 3563 Part 2, Library and Archives Canada.

Memorandum To:

The Inter-Departmental Committee

Re: Captain Emilio SERENI, Balzac, Alberta.

The person was born in Italy February 4th, 1880 at Novara, Italy; arrived in Canada via Niagara Falls, Ontario, 1903, and is reported as having acquired Canadian citizenship in 1904.

2. He is a widower and resides with a brother on a farm at Balzac, Alta.

3. He was secretary of the Fascist Party in the Calgary District from 1923 to 1928. During this period of time he endeavoured to establish a branch of the Ballila Section of the Italian Youth Organization Abroad in Southern Alberta, but this fell through owing to the opposition of some Italian members of the Communist Party, in Calgary, Alta.

4. He is a member of the Italian Veteran Officer's Association, having held rank of Captain during the last Great War. He is reported as being well educated and a good speaker in English, French, German and Italian and an ardent admirer of Mussolini.

5. During a conversation this subject had with a member of this Force he remarked, "that he was surprised that he had not been one of the first Italians to be picked up when Italy declared War", and added, "that he did not care if he were picked up."

6. He is a confirmed Fascist and certainly a bad influence amongst local Italians. He is distinctly anti-British on his own admission and appears to be very disloyal to this country.

7. Due to his previous activities and his present attitude, the Officer Commanding "K" Division recommended that he be place[sic.] under Appendix III, or that an order be issued to restrict his movements in having him report to this Force at least once a month.

OTTAWA, 11-12-40
40 D 269-1-H 1182

The belligerent attitude with which Sereni confronted the RCMP, in my opinion, not only reveals a fervent Fascism but also a deep-seated depression triggered by the death of his wife. The statement that he is surprised that he was not arrested immediately suggests that he had given up on life.

Giovanni (Johnny) Galdi was born in Aprigliano, near Cosenza, Calabria, in 1897 and arrived at Ellis Island in 1914 when he was 17. He came with his older brother Francesco, who had immigrated earlier and worked in the mines in Alberta along with other family members. According to niece Maria Muto, Galdi got in trouble when he drank in the local social club and talked about Mussolini. A younger friend, Tony Mele, confirmed this.[431] When asked whether Giovanni was an alcoholic, he noted that nobody could afford to drink too much because they were working only 2-3 days per week. Mele observed that Galdi was a good and gentle person and stated that there was no fascio in Nordegg though people did know about Antonio Rebaudengo in Calgary. Galdi was arrested in June, 1940 and sent to Camp Kananaskis. When he was released on September 17, 1941, he was ill with gall bladder problems. Galdi returned to work until he got too ill and the doctor sent him to hospital in Calgary. Mele drove him and Galdi died in the operating room at Holy Cross Hospital. According to Muto, Giovanni was illiterate and could not have done anything to threaten Canada.

Santo Romeo from Calgary was added to the list of Alberta internees through the Villa-Charities/Columbus Centre projet. An individual of that name appears in the 1911 census living in Macleod; he is unmarried and was born in 1888 and immigrated to Canada in 1906. In 1914, he married Carmela Quintera in Hosmer, BC. It is likely that he was a miner who moved to Calgary to find other work. He appears again in the 1916 census and is described as a labourer working in the cement works, likely, at Exshaw.

Alberta Enemy Aliens

Based on a federal report, there were about 115,000 Italians in Canada in 1940 of which about 3,500 supported Mussolini (about three percent of the Italian population). Using this percentage, based on Alberta's total Italian population of 4,802, 144 would have been Fascist supporters. This is in keeping with the 200 figure mentioned in the Calgary *Herald* article of 1926. Suspicion, however, fell on all of the Italian community, in particular, those designated as enemy aliens. They had to carry a Certificate of Exemption, which was renewed annually, report to the RCMP monthly, and notify the RCMP if they needed to travel outside their community. Many Italians distrusted government and its police and must have felt that the new lives they had established in Canada were built on a foundation of sand. In many communities, enemy alien designation served to unleash the latent racism inherent in Canada's immigration policy. No wonder that community members could be intimidated into revealing the names of community members whom they did not like when asked to do so by the RCMP.

---

[431] The information was provided to me in telephone conversations with Maria Muto and Tony Mele in 2012.

Victor Losa, surprisingly, was not interned though he was involved in the Fascist cause in Alberta for 14 or 15 years. The question arises: "Why?" His oral history interview in 1973 is understated about enemy alien designation and internment. While Sab Roncucci tried to draw him out about Fascism, Losa stated that he ceased to be the consul in 1936. The interview, as a whole, reveals Losa's rather patronizing attitude towards other Italian immigrants (specifically that they were labourers and uneducated) as well as his pride in his association with Canadian government officials.

Henry Butti, in an interview with Roncucci, noted that a local Italian businessman quickly shut his mouth about Fascism otherwise his store windows would likely have been broken by local residents. This was likely Losa's jewellery store. If Losa was acting as a spokesperson for the Italian government on the invasion of Ethiopia, how could he not have been caught up in the internment net? Resignation of his consular responsibilities should not have saved him (he fit enemy alien criteria) unless he collaborated with the RCMP with a guarantee of immunity, and named names. This is simply a theory and cannot be proven since anyone who would have known is deceased. After the war, Losa was reappointed honorary consul and was succeeded by Angelo Biasutto in 1954. Losa was a generous benefactor of St. Joseph's Cathedral and also of the Italian Cultural Centre. In 1982, Terra Losa, a subdivision in Edmonton's westend, was named in his honour at the suggestion of Carlo Amodio, president of the National Congress of Italian Canadians, Edmonton District.

Henry Butti provides a first-hand account of how the RCMP treated enemy aliens as follows:

> The Mounties came over to the house right away because I was the president of this society [Cristoforo Colombo Club, also referred to as the Italo-Canadese Society] and right away they wanted a copy of things, the constitution, etc. Anyway, they came to the house and Myra [his wife] says, "Well, he's out of town." They say, "As soon as he comes in, tell him to come over and see me." So, I went there and boy, oh boy, they put me through the grills. And they asked me if I was a British subject. I say, "Yes." They say, "You're lying." I say, "What do you mean I'm lying?" He says, "Yes, you are." I say, "When my Dad took his papers out, I wasn't 21 yet and they told me at the time that automatically I was a British."

In fact, Henry had turned 21 the year his father was naturalized and had not automatically obtained citizenship. He was photographed and fingerprinted and was warned that he could not leave town. Henry told them that his occupation as an electrician required him to work out of town and a more sympathetic sergeant winked at him indicating that he understood. The other Mountie, who according to Henry had been sent from Ottawa, was enforcing the government line.

Assunta Dotto came to Canada as a young woman with her mother and sisters Melia and Genoveffa in April, 1939 to join their Father Albano Paron in Cadomin. She writes in an unpublished personal history:

> As the war progressed in Europe, we were not able to get any news from my sister Evelina and her family in Italy. This worried all of us. Then, all of a sudden, Italians and Germans in Canada became enemy aliens, which meant we had to report to the RCMP and be fingerprinted. Most people realized it was not our fault; still, some in Cadomin gave us a hard time. The procedure to process us went very slowly and we had to wait outside the police barracks. Some passersby made snide remarks about the "aliens."
>
> The RCMP took this registration to extremes. One woman who was born in Canada was married to an Italian-born man who immigrated to Canada when he was two years old; since he was considered an enemy alien, his wife also had to be fingerprinted. My father was fingerprinted, even though he had spent most of his life in Canada and had been a Canadian citizen for many years.
>
> One English woman took it upon herself to advise the mine manager he had better intern all German and Italians because we could be dangerous. His response was: "If I do that, I would have to close the mine," adding that "your English husbands will not go underground."

She remembered having to report to the RCMP when she went to Edmonton to visit and eventually moved there to work at the Great West Garment Company.

In Calgary, Tony Valeri's application to become a pilot and navigator in the Royal Canadian Air Force was rejected because of his status as the son of an immigrant. Antonella Fanella quotes Audrey Forzani (nee De Negri), a Hudson's Bay Company employee, as follows:

> War breaks out, Jean Santopinto, Mary Bussi, Dora Buccini and me were pulled into the office of Mr. Trimble, he was the superintendent of The Bay. No he says, 'War's been declared and Mussolini's gone with Hitler.' We were all wondering what he's talking about because we were all born in Calgary, and he says, 'You know, girls, if you keep your mouths shut and don't give your opinion about anything, we will keep you on. But the minute you cause a little bit of trouble, or if there's a ripple around that you say something derogatory against the war, we will have to let you go.' [We wondered] What's he talking about? For Pete's sake! We were warned not to say anything or give our opinion. I don't remember having an opinion. War was over there, we felt sorry for the people, but we never discussed the war.[432]

---

[432] Cited by Antonella Fanella, 45-46.

For many Italians who had immigrated near the turn of the century and were rooted in their communities, the questioning of their loyalty was hurtful and the fact that their livelihood could be at stake was patently unfair. Orlando Martini, whose paternal and maternal grandfathers worked in the Canada Cement Plant in Exshaw observed in the family history: "This hostility towards Italians was largely responsible for my parents leaving Exshaw in 1941 and moving to the Town of Weston, Ontario (now part of Toronto)."[433]

Some Observations

It is clear from primary sources that Fascism was a significant force in Alberta's immigrant communities. The catalyst for the formation of the Alberta fascios was a pivotal visit by Italia Garibaldi in January, 1923. Sent to promote Fascism and find opportunities for the establishment of Italian agricultural colonies, she met immigrants in Venice-Hylo, Edmonton and Calgary. She used the language of patriotism to engage their hearts and minds. The consular agents played a key role in the establishment of fasci and the dissemination of Fascist values. While these organizations were largely social in nature, there were among their membership individuals who were fervent Fascists and resorted to fear and intimidation in their dealings with opponents. The fasci in Venice, Edmonton, Calgary and Lethbridge organized social events at which uniforms were worn and Fascist symbols displayed.

To have avowed Fascist sympathies at a time when Italy's star was in ascendance and Mussolini was hailed as its saviour was almost inevitable. The pact that Mussolini signed with Hitler raised some concerns but it was only when he followed in Hitler's footsteps and sought to build an Italian empire, beginning with Ethiopia, that the Western democracies began to experience doubts. At a time of war and within the legislative framework of the *War Measures Act*, the Government of Canada had "just cause" for the internment of a few individuals in Alberta.

While, at the time, suspicion of guilt was enough justification for Draconian measures that limited the civil liberties of citizens, whether born or naturalized, and immigrants, the passage of time allows for further reflection and perhaps clarity on painful episodes in our collective history. The claim that all internees were innocent is not true, in law or in fact. There were ardent Fascists in Canada who placed the welfare of their homeland above that of Canada. Whether or not Italians who were interned or were designated enemy aliens qualified as "enemies within" is a more difficult question. The idea of "third columnists" within the Italian community with the benefit of hindsight seems far-fetched. This would presuppose that such individuals would have the desire

---

[433] *Ibid.*, 189.

and capacity to harm Canadians and have an impact on the war effort. In this instance, "intent" or "suspicion of intent" is enough for preventive measures, which is, in fact, what internment and enemy alien designation were about.

While the number of internees in Alberta was small, the experience of internment and enemy alien designation would affect the Italian community for years to come.[434] Rebaudengo, in his last letter from Camp Gagetown to his wife, indicated that he would cease to be Italian. In his case, this venting did not prevent him from resuming his consular duties in peace time. One wonders whether this was a reward on the part of the Italian government which could do nothing for those interned. For others, all aspects of their "Italianness" including language and associations would disappear.

[434] Luigi Bruti Liberati includes a table with information about the province of residence of 362 internees. Alberta's six internees roughly reflect the percentage of the Alberta population (4.85%) in the 1931 census.

Guards on a five-man patrol at Camp Kananaskis, Alberta, ca 1940. Italians from Alberta and British Columbia were interned at this camp including Antonio Rebaudengo from Calgary, and O. J. Biollo and Rudolph Michetti from the communities of Venice and Hylo in Northern Alberta. Photo courtesy of Glenbow, Archives and Special Collections, University of Calgary NA-5474-3.

While the Glenbow Archives indicates that this photo of internees was taken at the camp at Kananaskis, Alberta, comparisons to other photos of the time indicates that it was taken at the Internment Camp near Fredericton, New Brunswick, ca 1942-43. Antonio Rebaudengo is in the front row, second from the left and immediately behind him with his hand on his shoulder is Osvaldo Giacomelli from Hamilton. Photo courtesy of Glenbow, Archives and Special Collections, University of Calgary NA-5124-22.

Frank Spinelli and partner Remiro Zalunardo set up the first Italian Centre Shop in 1959 in what became Edmonton's Little Italy. Frank is seen (fourth from right in his customary white uniform jacket) with a number of male customers. The shop was a popular hangout where gossip could be shared and also opportunities for work, ca 1960. Photo courtesy of the Spinelli Family.

CHAPTER VII

Strength in Numbers

THE END OF THE SECOND WORLD WAR left Italians defeated on several levels: the war had been lost with attendant physical and psychological damage, and the bright dreams of becoming a world power that Mussolini had offered were in ruins. On February 10, 1947, the Treaty of Peace with Italy was signed in Paris and came into effect on September 15. Italy was punished monetarily when war reparations of $360 million in American dollars (set at the 1938 value of the dollar) were imposed. The payouts went to Yugoslavia ($125 million), Greece ($105 million), Soviet Union ($100 million), Ethiopia ($25 million) and Albania ($5 million). Italy was spared war crimes tribunals.

From 1945 to the early 1950s, the general feeling in the population was one of unrelieved economic gloom. It was as if Italy had returned to the turmoil of the post-unification period in the 1870s that had resulted in massive immigration. The political situation was also unstable with the Communist Party growing in strength. In the end, the Marshall Plan began Italy's economic recovery so that it could be part of the Allied bulwark in Western Europe being established to combat Soviet Communism. In the period from 1948 to 1952, Italy would be awarded $1.5 billion for post-war recovery through the Plan. The impact of this investment, intended to bolster a democratic regime in Italy, would be felt over time; so also economic changes resulting from formation of the European Common Market in 1957.

Italy's economy began to recover: in the 1950s and 1960s, the growth rate represented in the GDP was in the 5 to 6 percent range. However, there was a distinct division between the "haves" and the "have nots." Industrial development occurred in the north leaving an "underclass" of uneducated poor, particularly in south-central and southern Italy. As in the previous century, many Italians took the well-established route of immigration for economic betterment. This was particularly true for unskilled and semi-skilled labour, whether agricultural or urban. The emerging society with its emphasis on science and technology had no place for them; the better educated stayed thinking that the new world order might provide opportunities but this too would change and with it the nature of immigration. The "brain drain" from Italy in the late 1960s and 1970s, as a result of strikes and the oil crisis in 1973 that depressed the economy, would impact the nature of Italian communities wherever these immigrants settled.

In January 1947, war-time measures to restrict movement and rights of enemy aliens ceased and Canada opened the doors to immigration to initiate a new era of economic development. PM Mackenzie King stated in the House of Commons on May 1, 1947: "The policy of the government is to foster the growth of the population of Canada by the encouragement of immigration. The government will seek by legislation, regulation, and vigorous administration, to ensure the careful selection and permanent settlement of such numbers of immigrants as can advantageously be absorbed in our national economy."[435] He justified Canada's position noting: "With regard to the selection of immigrants, much has been said about discrimination. I wish to make it quite clear that Canada is perfectly within her rights in selecting the persons who we regard as desirable future citizens. It is not a 'fundamental human right' of any alien to enter Canada. It is a privilege. It is a matter of domestic policy."[436] Selection of immigrants was an important issue and Australia, like Canada a former British colony, became the prototype of a democracy with extremely restrictive immigration legislation. Canada, on the other hand was viewed as more liberal.

In the period 1948 to 1975, about 375,000 Italians immigrated to Canada; many in response to government labour programs. The first surge occurred in 1951 when 24,351 came and this became the average until 1967.[437] The peak year was 1968 when 31,625 came. After that, a steady decline occurred indicative of the growing strength of the Italian economy. About 100,000 men came to help address farm labour shortages but, after fulfilling their time commitment of six months to a year, most left for other employment.[438] In 1957, the federal government made family sponsorship a requirement. In 1967, new immigration regulations created a point system based on education, occupational skills, employment prospects, age, proficiency in English and French, and personal character. Those receiving 50 points or more out of 100 were granted entry, regardless of race, ethnicity or national origin.[439] This served as an inducement for educated young people who were unemployed or under-employed. But this regulation did not help doctors and lawyers who desired to immigrate. They had to learn English as well as retrain and write qualifying exams. Journalist A. V. Spada decried the waste as follows: "It would be interesting to know how many technicians are washing dishes and cleaning rest rooms in public institutions to make the few dollars necessary to subsist while waiting to get a more suitable position, or earn enough money

———————

[435] Cited by A. V. Spada, *Canada Ethnica VI: The Italians in Canada* (Ottawa, ON and Montreal, PQ: Riviera Printers and publishers Inc., 1969), 128.
[436] *Ibid.*, 128.
[437] See Canadian Museum of Immigration at Pier 21, Italian Immigration, National Statistics, Pier 21 website, URL: https://www.pier21.ca/culture-trunks/hungary/statistics, retrieved January 10, 2018.
[438] Spada sets the figure at 100,000, 129.
[439] Immigration Regulations, Order-in Council PC 1967-1616, 1967.

to return home. Why solicit the immigration of a professional, who has spent years acquiring an education, and not immediately supply him with proper work?" Professional associations still regulate and maintain barriers to practice.

According to census records, Canada's total Italian population increased from just over 150,000, in 1951, to 450,000, in 1961. In Alberta, there were 5,996 individuals of Italian ethnic origin in 1951; 15,025, in 1961; 24,805, in 1971; and 26,605, in 1981. Thus, Alberta's Italian community more than quadrupled in 30 years. By 1996, the number was 58,140 and, by 2011, 88,710 individuals indicated Italian ancestry in the census (about 2.5 percent of the province's population).[440]

Toronto and Montreal with their established Italian communities were the most popular destinations but cities across the country benefitted. While Vancouver was the most popular western destination, Edmonton and Calgary also received large numbers of immigrants. With respect to Edmonton, the 1961 census listed 3,465 individuals with Italian as their mother tongue; and the 1996 census reported 9,865 individuals listing Italy as their single country of origin. Calgary's Italian community grew from 4,720 in 1961 to 9,810 in 1971, and 11,420 in 1991. In contrast, the 2016 census lists Edmonton's Italian population as 3,050 based on place of birth and Calgary's as 3,945 reflecting the death of immigrants of the post-war generation. In both Edmonton and Calgary, the most prominent sources of immigration were the Italian regions of Calabria and Abruzzo-Molise, with smaller percentages from Campania, Puglia and the northern regions of Veneto, Friuli and Piemonte.

Economist Eric J. Hanson in *Dynamic Decade: The Evolution and Effects of the Oil Industry in Alberta* answered the question "Why come to Alberta?" He pointed to increasing world demand for oil and observed: "More than twice as many wells were drilled in the world in 1956 as in 1946. The capital expenditure of the petroleum industry in the United States and the rest of the free world rose from $2.7 billion to $8.2 billion from 1946 to 1955, a threefold increase. During this decade, total capital expenditures exceeded $56 billion of which $18 billion was spent outside the United States."[441] The Leduc and Redwater fields put Alberta at the centre of oil-fueled growth and, between 1946 and 1956 the population grew from 803,000 to 1,123,000, an increase of 320,000."[442] Hanson notes:

---

[440] Criteria for self-identification of ethnicity and language grouping in various censuses changed over the years and this had implications for the figures reported. For example, according to the 1986 census, Edmontonians who listed Italy as their single country of origin totaled 9,865; Edmontonians who list Italian as one of their ethnic origins totaled 8,110.
[441] Eric J. Hanson, *Dynamic Decade: The Evolution and Effects of the Oil Industry in Alberta* (Don Mills, ON: T. H. Best Printing Company, Ltd., 1958), 1.
[442] *Ibid.*, 282.

Edmonton and Calgary became the fastest-growing metropolitan areas in Canada. Edmonton, which was the ninth largest city in Canada before the oil development, became the sixth largest by 1956, surpassing, Windsor, Quebec City and Ottawa. If its present rate of growth is maintained through 1956-61, it will become Canada's fourth city by 1961, exceeding Hamilton and Winnipeg, assuming that the current rates of growth for these cities are maintained, Calgary which ranked tenth before the great oil development surpassed Windsor and Quebec City to rank eighth in 1956.[443]

By 1956, 54 percent of the population of Alberta was in urban centres.

There are many immigration stories to tell. The following account groups them in geographical terms to demonstrate the regional character of Italian settlement. Within these parameters, there are thematic groupings including individuals whose immigration was facilitated by labour agents, federal government work programs or family sponsorship. Also included are the stories of "strong women" who achieved things in Canada that they could not have dreamed of in Italy. Finally, some examples are provided of individuals who were not happy with their immigration experience.

Edmonton's Italian Community

Italian immigrants arriving in Edmonton worked in railways and construction, refineries and petrochemical plants, meat-packing, dairies and flour mills, retail and government service. They also worked in the mines of the Northwest Territories. Family and friendship ties were of primary importance not only in the decision to immigrate but also in the settlement experience. The Albi, Veltri and Mantello families demonstrate this interconnection. Ottavio Iachetta and Francesco (Frank) Albi, Winnipeg labour agents, were involved in their immigration and directed them to Edmonton. Since Iachetta and Albi were from Grimaldi, Calabria, they assisted many of their relatives and *paesani*. Iachetta sponsored Raffaele (Ralph) Albi and Paolo (Paul) Veltri, who were brothers-in-law. Their stories are both unique and representative.

Ralph's story bridges several generations of immigration history. In a 1983 interview, he noted that his uncles went to Spokane and established themselves as contractors. His father, Francesco, was the last to immigrate in spring 1913 and left behind his pregnant wife, Alessandra, and two-year-old son, Giuseppe (Joe). Francesco died of pneumonia in Revelstoke in 1916 never having returned to Italy and seen his second son, who was born in September 1913. Two of the

---

[443] *Ibid.* 284.

uncles in the US sent money to support Alessandra and the children and she ensured that they received trades training: Joe became a mason and Ralph, a carpenter. Like their contemporaries, they served in the Italian army in the Second World War and were stationed in Ethiopia. The fact that Ralph contracted malaria, and was sent back to Italy to a desk job, saved him from being taken prisoner with the defeat of the Italian Forces. Joe was interned at Kew Gardens near London. In May 1939, Ralph married local girl, Estera Potestio. Her father Vincenzo had been a close friend of his father's and had been a sojourner in Canada until his death in 1950 in Port Arthur, Ontario.

Immigration was, thus, in Ralph's blood and his favourite book was an Italian translation of *Gulliver's Travels*, which he brought to Canada in 1949. He landed in Quebec, and then took the train to Winnipeg. After working on a farm for a few months to fulfill the terms of his immigration, he heard that work was available with the Italian-owned New West Construction in Edmonton. He attended language classes and could both read and write English. This fluency enabled him to sit in as translator for recent arrivals on many trade exams including carpentry. He was well-known in the Italian community and fondly referred to as "Mastro Raffaele (master for his carpentry trade)." In turn, I was "la figlia di [the daughter of] Mastro Raffaele."

Ralph became a permanent employee of Imperial Oil (New West was a subcontractor for work at their Strathcona Refinery), which in today's terms would be considered a "paternalistic" employer. For immigrants, this was a "dream" job that came with a good pension and health benefits. The company demonstrated interest in the well-being of its employees through an annual picnic and Christmas party where children were given gifts. The only blight on his working life was the fact that his British foreman did not treat him or any of the other Italian employees well. He did, however, have the support of Joe Gray, an American engineer who was part of the company's management, and this made Albi's working life tolerable. Gray and wife Helen, the company nurse, were life-long friends of the Albis.

In 1951, Ralph was joined by wife Estera and children – Rosa (10), Adriana (7) and Giuseppe (4). Estera immediately found employment at the GWG plant where brother-in-law Paul Veltri worked in the cutting room. Paul helped a number of Italian women obtain work at the plant.[444] Estera was likely the first Italian woman to enter the work force in Edmonton in the post-war immigration era. She learned English on the job and with the assistance of her children. Her work life was hard: she found sewing the heavy jean fabric for men's workwear extremely difficult and, the blue dye stained her hands and her fingers cracked and bled. The bright artificial light in the large sewing room gave her headaches. GWG historian Catherine C. Cole observes:

---

[444] Paul Veltri interview, Italians Settle in Edmonton Oral History Project, 1983, PAA PR0915.

While some workers stayed for many years, many left within days or a few months after the training period, when their pay shifted from hourly wages to piecework. Some who were well-educated and had been professionals in their home countries found the work demeaning. Some did not enjoy the work – it was stressful trying to work as quickly as possible without making any mistakes – but they felt they were lucky to have a job. Some were afraid of losing their jobs if they complained or, in the pre-maternity leave era, if the company found out that they were pregnant. Some were afraid to leave their machines and resented that their time in the bathroom, for example, was monitored.[445]

Estera's working life improved when she found employment at Toni Lynn and White Stag, which produced women's clothing. She helped many friends obtain work with these companies.

Paul Veltri arrived in Winnipeg in 1949 and got a job in snow removal. Unlike other immigrants of the time, he had already worked in the US and Canada having been given the money to immigrate in 1929 by his father-in-law, Vincenzo Potestio, who worked on train gangs in Ontario. This earlier immigration journey ended in 1933, when he was arrested when caught illegally working in the US, and was deported. In 1950, he moved to Edmonton to join brother-in-law Ralph Albi. Lacking a trade, he held various jobs including working for the GWG, running a restaurant, working as a caretaker at Immigration Hall and, after retirement, part-time work as a relief caretaker for businessman Charles Allard, who owned several buildings in Edmonton's downtown. Through his work for the federal government, he was able to help new arrivals from Italy. His wife, Teresa, joined him in 1952 and they lived for a short time in a boarding house on 97 Street and 103 Avenue. The inner-city Boyle-McCauley neighbourhoods were the "stopping off" place for immigrants: rents were cheap and property was available for purchase.

Teresa decided that she wanted to run her own boarding house and they purchased a large house in the nearby Oliver neighbourhood. Her clients were working class men most of whom were not Italian. She was known fondly as "Mamma Teresa," and was renowned for her cooking. She learned to make "Canadian" food and dinners in the Veltri home featured roast beef and Yorkshire pudding, and popular desserts such as lemon meringue and Boston cream pies. Tired of the strain of operating a boarding house, the couple purchased a historic fourplex and rented out rooms and suites until Paul's retirement. Over the years, Paul sponsored a number of his Veltri relatives. Grandson Rudy Cavaliere remembers that when Paul went to Holy Cross Cemetery to

[445] Catherine C. Cole, "Accommodating an Increasingly Diverse Work Force," *Piece by Piece: The GWG Story* website, Royal Alberta Museum/Virtual Museum of Canada, URL: https://www.royalalbertamuseum.ca/exhibits/online/GWG/en/labourforce/middleeast.html, retrieved January 21, 2018.

choose burial sites, he noted two empty plots near Allard's crypt and chose those because of his connection with the high-profile businessman.

The couple had one daughter, Franca, who was born in 1926; she was married to Ugo Cavaliere and the mother of two sons, Ernesto Rodolfo (Rudy) and Paolo (Paul), when her father left for Canada. Ugo also immigrated and was living in Kapuskasing, Ontario, and Franca was waiting to join him. When he failed to sponsor her, her parents stepped in and she arrived in Ontario in 1954. She discovered that her husband had formed a relationship with another woman and decided to join her parents in Edmonton. Her husband later sent their sons by train to Edmonton; they travelled alone. Franca was a woman of courage and lived with her parents and raised her sons. She worked in the garment industry and drapery business until her retirement. Her story is representative of family breakdowns resulting from immigration. These betrayals were considered "shameful" and not talked about in the community. The offending husband stayed away from the community in which his wife resided since he would have been ostracized. Extra-marital affairs were also taboo though, of course, they did occur.

Winnipeg labour agent Frank Albi also sponsored Francesco (Emilio) Mantello and Raffaele Anselmo. Mantello and Anselmo were related by marriage not only with each other but also with their sponsor. They left Italy in 1949 and worked in farms south of Winnipeg near Ste. Agathe. Neither were farmers but, in order to get into the country, they were prepared to start there. Mantello was born in 1910 and, in 1932, married Giulia Amantea. According to son Silvio, Frank went to Ethiopia in 1937 and, when the Second World War broke out, was conscripted into the Italian army. He was captured by the British and spent the rest of the war as a prisoner of war in Kenya and Haverfordwest, Wales. He returned to Italy in 1945.

After completing the farm work commitment, in 1950, Mantello went to Edmonton and found work at New West Construction. Others who got their start with the company included Angelo Santarosa, Attilio Gatto, Teodoro Cimino, Eugenio Falcone, Vittorio Facchin and Frank Bossio. There are many stories about established Italian employers welcoming immigrants and providing them with their first jobs; there are also many stories about these same employers taking advantage of their workers. This presented enormous difficulties because the men needed the work and were afraid to say anything in case they were fired. This happened with Albi, Mantello and others with New West which paid its Italian workers less than the going rate at Imperial Oil, which they received as subcontractors. In their defence, they would state that they gave their workers a "step up" on the work ladder in Canada. Eventually, some Italian employees informed friends in Imperial Oil management that they were being paid less, and they were offered full-time work.

The outcome was not so fortunate for Mantello. Son Silvio observes:

> My father was a rather impulsive individual and was not very happy working with the Nigros and Anselmos. He figured that since he was loosely related to them he should have been given better work rather than just being sent from one job site to another. Therefore, when he heard news that the Crow's Nest Pass Coal Company was hiring, he immediately left Edmonton for the coal mines of Michel, BC. As was the custom, he got the invitation to move to Michel from Alessandro Iacino, another relative of my mother's.[446]

His earnings increased from $6 to $11 a day and the work made use of his blacksmith's trade. With changes in technology, he moved into the machine shop as a heavy duty repairman. While son Joe joined him earlier and worked alongside him, the rest of the family – wife Giulia, daughter Teresina and son Silvio – did not arrive until 1957. Giulia was born in 1912, the third daughter of seven children born to Francesco and Caterina (Nigro) Amantea. Her family had a very early immigration history in North America: her father Francesco and various relatives worked in Colorado, Utah, the Crowsnest Pass and Winnipeg on various railway construction projects with the Welch brothers. Giulia was also related to the Vecchio and Gatto families of Grimaldi.

Mantello suffered from severe rheumatoid arthritis and had to quit work with Kaiser Resources (which had taken over the mine) and, because he had not accumulated the required pensionable years, he lost his pension allocation. In 1968, he moved to Lethbridge where his oldest children had settled, and son Silvio was attending the university. He was able to sell his home in Sparwood and purchase one for roughly the same amount in Lethbridge. Needing to work, he joined son-in-law Aldo Vercillo in the welding business that he had set up, as did son Joe. Eventually both left the business: Joe got a job with the City of Lethbridge as a welder and the elderly Mantello retired. The last years of his life were comfortable since he was able to collect his Canada Pension.

Attilio Gatto was born in Grimaldi, in 1911, the youngest of four brothers and three sisters.[447] His father was a contractor for roadways. After completing elementary school, he was apprenticed to a carpenter and moved to Cosenza for further carpentry training. He then signed up for military service and was sent back to Grimaldi and became part of the civil guard. Wife Stella was also born in Grimaldi, in 1921, the youngest of three girls (her older sisters were Maria

---

[446] This information is drawn from a short biography that I asked Silvio to provide me for the book, which he did on November 12, 2017.

[447] Attilio and Stella Gatto interviews, Italians Settle in Edmonton Oral History Project, 1983, PAA PR0915.

Teresa and Luisa); the family was completed by brother Gennarino. Her father, Fiore Amantea, had immigrated to Canada and worked as a blacksmith and was later joined by son Gennarino.

Attilio and Stella were married in 1943 and, soon after, he began to experience hip pain after an accident and could no longer do carpentry work. He tried travelling around the region selling wood but was not making much money and began to consider immigration. There were two possibilities open to him: Stella's brother Gennarino in Vancouver could sponsor them, or Attilio's two brothers in New York could. Vincenzo was a tailor and Gabriele, a tile setter, and both were well established. According to younger son Pasquale, Attilio's decision was motivated by the fact that he had lost many friends in the war. Since he knew that the US had the draft he decided to go to Canada to avoid this outcome for his son.

In 1949, the couple embarked on the SS *Vulcania* with five-year-old Emilio; Stella was pregnant and son Pasquale was born in Vancouver. Things did not go well there either on the personal or work front. The sister-in-law did not make them feel welcome and Attilio found work in a local sawmill physically challenging. The pay was only 95 cents an hour and, without the money they had brought with them from Italy, they could not make ends meet. It was at this point that he decided to leave for Edmonton where his best man, Ralph Albi, got him a job at New West Construction and they worked as carpenter assistants at the Imperial Oil Refinery; they were paid $1.25 an hour. Stella and the boys joined him 10 months later. When he became an Imperial employee, his pay jumped to $6 an hour. Things had begun to change for the better; however, Stella wanted desperately to return to Italy but Attilio was dead set against it – he had lost all his contacts and was uncertain whether he would be able to find work. Attilio, in the end, allowed her to return with the children. After six years, she decided to rejoin him in Edmonton to reunite the family. Her quality of life improved enormously since there were many young Italian families to socialize with (including that of her sister Maria Teresa Vecchio) as well as a church and Italian grocery stores.

In 1949, labour agent Frank Albi also sponsored several members of the Vecchio family including father Giambattista, and son Serafino (Sam). Their stay in Winnipeg, however, was short since his wife Maria Teresa's cousin, Ralph Welch, offered them work in Kamloops doing maintenance for the CNR. Younger son Fiore joined them in 1950 and, after a short stint in Vancouver, settled in Edmonton in 1952 where with the assistance of family friend Ralph Albi he obtained work as a carpenter. Giambattista and Sam worked for Welch for six years and, then, joined Fiore in Edmonton. While Giambattista continued to work as a labourer, Sam obtained welding qualifications and eventually obtained work at C. W. Carry Ltd. The company was established in the 1960s and specialized in the fabrication and erection of structural and other steel for refineries, chemical plants and pulp and paper mills. Fiore, a talented musician and composer, qualified as a real estate agent.

Vittorio Facchin was born in 1929 in Treviso and arrived in Edmonton in 1951 where he obtained work with New West Construction and was then hired by Imperial Oil. He worked there until 1965 when he returned to Italy unsure whether he would go back. Since his father owned a flour mill, he decided to try his hand at pasta-making. With the growth in the number of Italians in Alberta, he felt there would be a strong market. Facchin apprenticed with the Pavan Pasta Company in Padua and, on his return to Edmonton, used his savings to set up Roma Pasta and hired four people to help him. Business went well and, a few years later, he enlarged the plant, invested in new equipment and hired more staff. He produced more than 340 types of pasta which were sold mostly between Vancouver and Winnipeg and, on occasion, in several US cities.[448] In 1987, Facchin sold the plant to Primo Foods, a division of Nabisco Ltd. Canada.

While Vittorio Facchin had seen an opportunity to create an Italian product in Alberta, Franco (Frank) Spinelli saw the need for Italian imported foodstuffs and decided to capitalize on this emerging market. Frank emigrated from San Pietro al Tanagro near Naples in 1951 where his father Pietro was an established farmer and also served as the town's mayor. This life held no appeal for Frank, who sought adventure, and he ended up working in the silver mines in Mayo, Yukon Territory, which was part of the Silver Trail. A significant number of Italians worked in Mayo and Elsa, and used Edmonton as their base. Two years later, Frank broke his back in a workplace accident and was flown to hospital in Edmonton where he spent a year-and-a-half in traction. After that, he could only do casual work and kept busy with a number of occupations including bartender at the Ritz Hotel.

In 1958, Santa Maria Goretti Church was built in the inner-city neighbourhoods of Boyle-McCauley. Since many new immigrants were settling there, in 1959, Frank decided to invest his savings in a business. With partner Remiro Zalunardo, he bought a small store on the corner of 109 Avenue and 95 Street, and began importing Italian products. The business prospered. He was assisted by wife Rina Quagliarello, a hometown girl chosen by his mother, whom he married in 1960. In 1964, Spinelli became sole proprietor and built the Italian Centre Shop at 108 Avenue and 95 Street as well as starting a wholesale operation. Frank missed the village square in Italy where people shopped, ate and met to pass the time and wanted this to happen in Edmonton. He saw Princess Patricia Park across from his store as the perfect venue. Going to Mass on Sunday and then to Little Italy to buy foodstuffs, newspapers and magazines, and gossip became a community tradition. The Italian Centre Shop remains the largest business in Little Italy. The appeal of "Spinelli's," as it is commonly known, expanded beyond the Italian community to include all

---

[448] Sab Roncucci, "Vittorio Facchin: Un Pioniere Dell'Industria Leggera" ("Vittorio Facchin: A Pioneer of Light Industry," *Il Congresso*, anno 2, no 8, August 1985; translated by the author.

of Edmonton region and a range of ethnicities. Frank was a community builder who sponsored a range of recreational and cultural activities as well as providing financial support to community organizations and Italian immigrants. Spinelli's bronze statue, commissioned by daughter Teresa, sits in the park playing a game of cards, a symbol of the many games he played with friends including local and provincial politicians. Spinelli was inducted into the Junior Achievement Alberta Business Hall of Fame in 2013.

Welch railway gang work enabled brothers Franco (Frank) and Maurizio Saccomanno and Vincenzo Annichiarico to come to Canada. While the former moved from labouring work, the latter continued to do this to the end of his life. The difference in their circumstances is likely that with a young family Annichiarico was risk averse while the newly-married Saccomannos had less to lose and were therefore more adventurous. The Saccomannos worked for two years in Port Arthur, Ontario on railway track repairs before coming to Edmonton in 1951 and working in construction. In 1965, the brothers set up Saccomanno Brothers grocery store on 95 Street in Little Italy. They added a small restaurant, which they ran with the help of their wives. In 1959, Frank had married Maria Magliocco, a home town girl, at the Santa Maria Goretti Church, one of the first marriages celebrated in the new building.[449] Her father, Emilio Magliocco, had also come to Canada in 1951 to work for the Welch Company as a railway repair man in BC and she, her mother and younger brother Sergio had followed him to Canada. Maurizio married Maria Arnieri, whose father had also immigrated to Edmonton. After working together for a time, the brothers went their separate ways, and Frank established Saccomanno Importing Ltd., a wholesale food company. Frank has supported a range of community causes not only within the Italian community but also outside the community; the latter included the Salvation Army and Habitat for Humanity. Maurizio went into business with son Stella's husband, Carmelo Rago, and they established the Sorrentino Chain of restaurants.

Vincenzo Annichiarico arrived in 1952 from Zungoli, Avellino, Campania, and initially worked in railway camps in northern Alberta, and, then, settled in Edmonton. In 1955, he sponsored his wife Concetta and children. Daughter Lina Urso noted in an interview: "Mother was very brave to come with four children, seven days on a boat. People were very helpful. Then, after four or five days on the train, we arrived in Edmonton. My only memory was of arriving at the train station and being picked up and kissed by a man who I didn't know and who was my Father."[450] Annichiarico had a furnished house ready for them near Clarke Stadium in the

---

[449] Frank and Maria Saccomanno interview, Memory Lane Oral History Project, April 29, 2007, Ital-Canadian Seniors Association.

[450] Alessandro and Lina Urso interview, Celebrating Edmonton's Italian Community Oral History Project, June 27, 2002, University of Alberta Archives.

inner city. Lina remembers walking to Sacred Heart Parish to hear Mass in Italian before Santa Maria Goretti Church was built in 1958. Vincenzo sponsored his brothers and sisters and the Annichiarico home was open not only to kin but also other immigrants.

Antonio Innocente Frattin immigrated to Edmonton from Castelfranco, Veneto, after his marriage to Aurora Assunta Tedesco in 1956. He arrived in July and she, in November. He worked as a baker for Honeyboy Bakery and eventually became superintendent. Aurora also worked at the bakery. The couple sponsored seven of his siblings as well as his widowed mother. In 1960, the couple set up the Italian Bakery at 90 Street and 121 Avenue. In 1962, they moved to the current location at 106 Avenue and 97 Street. In 1968, they opened Capital City Recreation on 95 Street and 108 Avenue; the facility had 10 pool tables, a pizza oven and also served espresso and Italian ice cream. In 1986, they bought a building in Beverly and it became the Italian Bakery #2. Their most recent endeavour is the Italian Bakery's Mercato in St. Albert which includes a café and deli. The family business expanded to involve their children and the couple assisted new immigrants to become integrated in the community. They have supported various Italian societies and donate baked goods to a range of causes. When the City of Edmonton promoted the beautification of Edmonton's inner city, the couple had a mural painted on the side of their 97th Street bakery.

Two women arrived in Edmonton in 1957 and would go on to have rich working lives and become important Italian community volunteers. Luciana De Santis was a young mother who left L'Aquila, Abruzzo, to join husband Mario while Maria Caria was 18 and travelled with her mother Elvira to join brothers Joe and Tony. Luciana received a degree in Home Economics from the Institute of San Bernardino L'Aquila and taught at a private school for two years. [451] In Edmonton, she worked at a tailor's shop for two years and, then, for the Hudson's Bay Company, first as a tailor and then as supervisor of the tailor shop. In 1982, she became head of men's wear where she worked until her retirement. Luciana has been active in the Italian community for many years and was one of the founders of the Giovanni Caboto Society and Festival; co-founder of the Abruzzese Club; fundraising volunteer for the building of Santa Maria Goretti Parish and president of the Donne Del Santo Rosario; and volunteer for the Ital-Canadian Seniors Association. In 1990, Luciana was a co-founder and member of the Comitato Italiano all'Estero (Committee of Italians Abroad), established by the Italian government. In 2006, she was honoured by the Government of Italy with a knighthood: Cavaliere Dell'Ordine della Stella della Solidarità Italiana (Knight of the Order of the Star of Italian Solidarity).

Maria Caria left her hometown Grimaldi and, in a 2007 interview, remembered the arrival in Halifax on December 28, 1957 as follows: "We were welcomed by Canadian Immigration and

---

[451] Luciana de Santis interview, Memory Lane Oral History Project, April 29, 2007, Ital-Canadian Seniors Association.

brought into a warehouse; our entire luggage went through inspection. From Halifax we took a train with wood benches which were very uncomfortable to sit on for four days. We stopped in Winnipeg for a couple of days and visited my cousins Ercolino and Franco Albo. We spent our first Canadian New Year's Eve in Winnipeg. We finally arrived in Edmonton January 3, 1958 at 6:30 in the morning at the railroad station. My brother Giuseppe and some of his friends were waiting for us. What a journey!"[452] Maria attended a nine-month course in tailor technology at NAIT and, on obtaining a diploma, went to work as a sewing machine operator at White Stag. She rose through the ranks to assistant to the vice president of production. She moved to the tailor shop at the Hudson's Bay Company and then to Tip Top Tailors. In 1986, she decided on a career change and became the General Manager of the new Santa Maria Goretti Community Centre, a position she held for two years. Over the years, she continued to update her education completing English 10, 20 and 30 at Grant MacEwan College and qualifying as a teaching assistant. In 1963, Maria married Giuseppe Salvatore (Joe) Mauro, also from Grimaldi. Maria has been an active volunteer in many Italian community organizations and, as president of the Ital-Canadian Seniors' Association was instrumental in setting up the Alberta Italian Museum in their centre near Commonwealth Stadium.

Tony Falcone, Alessandro Urso and Carlo Amodio were under-employed and were part of the brain drain from Italy. Falcone was born in Celico, Calabria and was sponsored, in 1959, by his father, who had arrived in Edmonton in 1951.[453] Tony was a trained teacher, who had graduated in 1953 but had only been able to find work as a substitute teacher and that for only a year-and-a-half. To improve his prospects, he decided to sit the civil service exams to become a courtroom clerk in the Justice Department. He ranked 550th of a total of 11,000 individuals; after an oral exam, he ranked 2,500th. Since this would mean a three-to-five-year wait for a job, he felt that his only option was to join his father in Canada. An older brother had already done so. Tony had also completed military service and had been attached to NATO doing security checks.

On his arrival, Tony had to learn English and retrain. This began with completing high school credits, which put him in the ludicrous position of being 25 at St. Mary's High School. To support his studies, he worked as a carpenter. He believes that he was well-treated at the University of Alberta: Dean of Education Ronald Coutts advised him about classes to take. In the second year of the B Ed program, he signed a contract with the Northlands School Division for

452 Maria (Caria) Mauro interview, Memory Lane Oral History Project, April 29, 2007, Ital-Canadian Seniors Association.

453 Tony Falcone interview, Celebrating Edmonton's Italian Community Oral History Project, July 3, 2002, University of Alberta Archives.

1963-1964 to teach on the Janvier Reserve in return for their subsidizing his fees. In 1964-1965, he taught what were described as "trainable retarded children" aged 13 to 17 at the Father Lacombe School. The next year he did this work at Sacred Heart School. Tony spent the majority of his career at O'Leary High School until his retirement in 1999. He became the first teacher of the Italian language at the Dante Alighieri School and was instrumental, with Tony Caria, in initiating teaching of Italian in the Catholic School System in Edmonton and, eventually, provincially.

Alessandro Urso was born in Avola, Siracusa, Sicily and was a graduate of the Instituto di Pharmacologia (Institute of Pharmacology) at the University of Genoa. In a 2002 interview, he mentioned that, although post-war reconstruction had been successful, the Italian economy was stagnant and there were few job opportunities for young graduates.[454] He saw a newspaper advertisement for work in Canada and, within three months, arrived at Pier 21 in Halifax. The group of young men with whom he immigrated partied for the entire seven days of the journey. The federal government had determined that he would work in Armstrong, a small town near the Maine border, and he took a train there. He had no English and only school French. There was no work there and he was told to go to Sherbrooke where Immigration Services sent him to the Maison St. Georges, which was a shelter operated by the Beni Fratelli. He found room and board but couldn't find a job. Immigration suggested that he next try Quebec City, which he did, without success. He was then directed to Montreal, again with the same results. Urso realized that he had to take control of his own future and found a job in the lab at Domo Chemicals in Montreal. The city reminded him of his home city of 800,000 people; he was definitely an urban Italian.

At the Montreal lab, Alessandro met a young Spanish chemist who had worked in Edmonton and Fort McMurray and recommended it. A year later, he moved to Edmonton where he found work with the Government of Alberta in environmental protection (in particular, water pollution); he continued to work for the provincial government in various positions until his retirement. He remembers hanging out at the Italian Centre Shop, which was the destination for young men since it stayed open until 9 pm every day. That's where he met friends Carlo and Lina Amodio as well as his future wife, Lina Annichiarico. Another popular hangout was the Italian Gardens Restaurant started by Salvatore Prete, who cooked for single men for a monthly fee. Alessandro attended the Santa Maria Goretti Youth Club meetings and dances – this was a parent-approved place where young courting couples could go. He was a co-founder of the *Il Congresso* newspaper with friends Amodio and Rudy Cavaliere.

---

[454] Alessandro and Lina Urso interview, Celebrating Edmonton's Italian Community Oral History Project, June 18, 2002, University of Alberta Archives.

Carlo Amodio was born in Naples and graduated in 1965 with a diploma in land surveying. His first job was as a site supervisor at Italsider Bagnoli, a national smelting company. He got the job through his yoga teacher, who owned a small construction company. In his memoir, Carlo observes:

> In 1966, when I was 23 and she only 19 [Lina d'Aquino his fiancée], we made one of the most important decisions of our life, to emigrate. Although I always had a job, I never felt I was secure. To be realistic, given the economic conditions of Naples at the time, we felt that we would never be able to get married as so many couples that don't have real jobs ... So when both Canada and Australia placed ads in the local newspaper looking for people with technical training and offering to advance a loan for a one way flight to their country, I jumped at the idea. Lina was also happy at the opportunity ... So one sunny day we took our little Fiat 500 and went to Rome.[455]

Carlo arrived in Edmonton in 1967 and remembers the kindness of Sab and Elena Roncucci, who made him feel welcome and helped him to become oriented to the city. Not able to speak English, he could not find work based on his education, so he took a number of labouring jobs including working for the CNR. For the first time in his life, he picked up a pick and shovel and quickly developed calluses. Carlo, eventually, found employment as a blueprint operator with the Government of Alberta but lost it when, in March 1968, he returned to Italy to marry Lina and return with her to Edmonton. While his boss liked him, Carlo had no holiday time and was ineligible for unpaid leave since he had not worked long enough.

On his return, Carlo took on a number of casual jobs including work for Peter Batoni's construction company building warehouses in Saskatchewan. He sank into depression for a time. Things began to change for the better when he got a job working in the drafting section of the Water and Sewer Department of the City of Edmonton. He continued his studies and became a real estate appraiser. In the following years, he moved up the ranks of the city Planning Department and retired early, after 30 years of service. He then set up as an independent contractor working for developers until he had the opportunity, in 1999, to work for the Government of Alberta disposing of surplus land and buildings. Carlo is one of those individuals who not only works hard at his day job but is also a full-time volunteer. In 2007, the Government of Italy awarded him the Knighthood of the Order of the Star of Italian Solidarity. In 2012, he was awarded the Queen's Diamond Jubilee Medal for volunteer service. Lina, who received a Diploma in Foreign Languages (French and English) from the Institute Salvatore Rosa in Naples, taught at the Dante

---

455 Carlo Amodio, *Downloading Memories* (Edmonton, AB: Carlo Amodio, self-published, 2010), 58.

Alighieri School for many years as well as teaching non-profit extension classes. She has volunteered for the Edmonton Food Bank and other organizations

Other well-educated immigrants would play important roles in the construction industry. Pasquale A. (Pat) Giannone studied art before coming to Edmonton where he partnered with Don Johnson and built four hotels. In 1954, with J. B. Starkey, he built Edmonton's most modern hotel – the Cromdale – on 118 Avenue. Costing $450,000, it had 44 fully-equipped rooms with bath, telephone and television. A newspaper article noted that Pat commissioned two art students from the University of Alberta (Eunice Walter and Mary Hallett) to complete murals for the men's and women's lounges. The hotel housed Frank Cappello's Coffee Shop (Frank had worked as a cook in Edmonton for over 40 years), which featured Italian spaghetti. The proximity to the Edmonton Gardens, the city's largest arena and performance space, ensured its success. Pat was also a business partner of Edmonton Mayor William Hawrelak and undertook a number of projects with him including hotels and shopping centres. In 1974, Hawrelak appointed him to the Edmonton Exhibition Association Board, an incredibly powerful board comprising members of Edmonton's business elite. Pat supported the building of Santa Maria Goretti Church and Santa Maria Goretti Community Centre.

Peter Batoni studied architecture in Florence and Lausanne, Switzerland, and came to Edmonton via London, England, and Montreal. He established his own construction company – Batoni Properties Ltd. – and, in partnership with Pat Bowlen, grew the small company into Batoni Bowlen Enterprises. Initially a major player in western Canada, it later expanded into other regions of the country and the US. The partners moved from traditional poured concrete to precast concrete construction. Over a period of about 30 years, Batoni-Bowlen built 60 percent of the bridges in Alberta, and prominent Edmonton landmarks such as the Coliseum, College Plaza and Renaissance Place. The building of the Coliseum was a hotly-debated issue from 1963 to 1970. City councilors and citizens fought about whether or not to build the complex and, if so, where it should be located. The design was innovative – circular like Vancouver's Pacific Coliseum – with excellent sightlines for fans. A range of difficulties were encountered including the fact that the land was swampy and had to be stabilized with crushed gravel; costs rose from $10 million to $12.5 million to $15 million. The pressure to complete the project spurred innovation and journalist David Staples observed: "To speed things up, contractor Peter Batoni put a giant crane on a circular railway track. It could chug around to wherever it was needed on the site."[456] Most of the construction crew comprised Italian immigrants including Erminio Floreani, project superintendent, and Luigi Zorzetto, project manager. Batoni-Bowlen faced delays in arrival of building materials and strikes. To signal the building's completion, they observed an Italian tradition and

456 David Staples, "The Rise and Fall of the Edmonton Coliseum," *Edmonton Journal* (April 6, 2016).

placed a spruce tree on the roof signifying that the building had reached its full height. Without the Coliseum, Edmonton would not have been able to get an NHL team in 1979. The new Katz Ice District arena – Rogers Place – has replaced the Coliseum and it is likely to be demolished.

Luigi Zorzetto was born in Venice and studied Industrial Chemical Engineering at the University of Padua and Marghera. On completing his studies, he worked for Giuseppe Baraldi Construction in Venice and, in 1954, married Mara Enrica Baraldi.[457] In spite of being well-established, a sense of adventure motivated him, in 1956, to come to Edmonton; his family joined him in 1958. He found work with Batoni-Bowlen, and moved from the position of manager to senior vice president. Besides Batoni-Bowlen, he worked for Clark Lumber, Alberta Oxygen & CG Oxygen, Kanuka Construction, Parkins Construction and, since 1986, for the Triple 5 Corporation that built and operates West Edmonton Mall and Mall of the Americas in Minneapolis-St. Paul. Zorzetto has been an active volunteer in the Italian community and served as project manager for the renovation of the Santa Maria Goretti Community Centre and Church. He has served as chair of the SMGCC board.

Massimiliano (Max) R. Berretti was born in Pisa and obtained a degree in civil engineering from the local university.[458] He met Annabel Keith, an English girl, in Florence in 1953 and desiring to marry, he began to look for work abroad. The couple arrived in Edmonton in 1955 and he obtained work in the engineering department of the City of Edmonton. After two years, he partnered with several engineers to create the firm Richards, Berretti and Jelineck. The firm designed the Edmonton Public School Board Building and the University of Alberta Student's Union Building both in the Modern Style with extensive use of steel, concrete and glass. The former, built in 1960, is a concrete cube structure with windows found only on the west side. It was made redundant by the board and has been used for various purposes since. The latter was built in 1967 and includes the 720-seat Horowitz Theatre. Berretti's next firm, Morrison Berretti Engineering (later MB Engineering) specialized in work in the north. The Citadel Theatre in downtown Edmonton, which opened in 1976, is considered Berretti's landmark building. It was built at a cost of $6.5 million and its heated atrium filled with plants keeps theatre-goers and downtown workers in a constant "spring-like" environment. His largest project was the design and build of the Confederation Bridge between PEI and NB. Max was a member of a number of professional associations and served on the Board of Governors of the University of Alberta. He was a great lover of wilderness and, with his partners, gifted land in the Edmonton area to the Nature Conservancy of Canada.

457 Luigi and Mara Zorzetto interview, Memory Lane Oral History Project, Ital-Canadian Seniors Association, April 29, 2007.
458 Anon., "Berretti, Massimiliano (Max) Romualdo," in *Edmonton Journal*, December 7-10, 2016.

Calgary's Italian Community

Historian Antonella Fanella summarizes the achievements of Calgary's immigrants as follows: "Owning a business was the dream of many Italian immigrants, and what they lacked in education they made up for with good business sense, hard work and fierce determination. While Italians tended to concentrate in the ownership of restaurants, grocery stores that specialized in goods imported from Italy, clothing stores, bakeries, construction and contracting firms, they also owned a variety of other businesses."[459] While setting up a business was the favoured vehicle for moving from the working to middle class, not all immigrants became successful businessmen. Many were content working for others and led modest lives. Giovanni Ambrogiano and Luigi Bontorin offer examples of the two poles of modest achievement and business success.

Giovanni's immigration history reinforces the stereotype of the Italian immigrant as a poor, illiterate labourer. He was born in Fossacesia, Chieti, Abruzzo, to agricultural labourers. In a 1985 interview, he recounted that his father could not afford to buy him shoes so he attended school barefoot. The teacher refused to allow him to do this so he completed only two years of education; his father then sent him out to look after the family's sheep. In 1930, he married Francesca Marsciangelo (Masciangelo) and they struggled to raise a family. In 1940, he was drafted into the Italian Army; on discharge, in 1945, he returned to work as a farm labourer. Life was grim: the house had been bombed in 1943 and the family slept outside and cooked on an open fire. He noted that they ate bread and polenta (cooked cornmeal) and vegetables they grew in their garden; they only had meat on Sundays. He was one of nine children and all of the family was in dire straits. He was sponsored by his brother-in-law John Marshall, who was part of an earlier wave of immigration.

Giovanni recounted that he left his hometown, and boarded a ship in Naples, which arrived in Halifax in June 1949.[460] He spoke no English and had his destination written on a piece of paper. He took the train to Montreal and, then, changed trains in Winnipeg arriving in Calgary during the Stampede. He then mistakenly took a train to Edmonton. Eventually, he connected with the family in Delia – his wife had three brothers all of whom farmed in the region – and worked for them to fulfill his farm labour obligations. He noted that his wife's family in Italy was much better off than his because they received money from Canada. Money sent home to support family became as significant in the 1950s and 1960s as it had been in earlier eras of immigration.

---

[459] Fanella, *With Heart and Soul*, 53.

[460] Giovanni and Francesca Ambrogiano interview, Calgary Italian Club Historical Project, May 23, 1985, Glenbow Archives RCT-869-1 & 2. There are some variations in dating indicative of memory lapses.

In Calgary, Giovanni found work with Gallelli Construction and earned 80 cents an hour. He paid $75 a month in rent. He was fortunate to find employment with the City of Calgary and remained there until retirement in 1973. Wife Francesca and their children joined him in 1950. He took pride in the fact that he came with nothing and was able to save to buy his first house, in 1956, for $3,300; his brother-in-law co-signed the bank loan. He bought a second house five years later. In 1963, Giovanni returned to Italy for his son's wedding in Pescara and noted that conditions had improved. The visit confirmed his belief that he was right to immigrate and his economic circumstances continued to improve and he purchased a car in 1967. He shared his good fortune and, in turn, sponsored three brothers and two sisters. Giovanni was a staunch supporter of the Calgary Italian Club.

Luigi Bontorin was born in Romano d'Ezzelino, Veneto and completed military service with the Alpini regiment after the Second World War.[461] The oldest of 10 siblings, he immigrated arriving in Calgary in 1954. He found work clearing logs in Kananaskis for 25 cents an hour. He next drove a delivery truck for Canadian Oil Companies Ltd. but lost the job in 1962 when the company was taken over by Shell. In 1958, he was boarding with an Irish family in Calgary and met the second-youngest child, a daughter, Myrl. They married in 1959. The couple decided to take a risk and start a bakery. In Italy, Luigi had worked for his uncle at his bakery near Bassano del Grappa, Vicenza. The Bontorins' Calgary Italian Bakery, near the St. Louis and King Eddy hotels, cost them $7,000 and opened in October 1962; it produced 200 loaves a day. Business was cutthroat – there were seven independent bakeries vying for the same business. According to the famiy, competitors resorted to "dirty tricks" such as squeezing apple turnovers and poking fingers in pies to make them unsaleable. Luigi decided to be proactive and targeted a number of Chinese grocers offering free loaves to sample. They responded favorably and his sales soared. This gave him the courage, in 1965, to purchase a larger facility, a former Italian supermarket, but business was slow and he was on the hook for $36,000 to various creditors. At this time, the couple had two sons, Louis and David, and Myrl was expecting another child (daughter Teresina). Though Luigi was advised to declare bankruptcy, he chose to reduce staff and work day and night. Two years later the business turned the corner and, according to a short history, "what began as a tiny downtown bakery with a couple of Italians working up front and a couple more in the back evolved over the

[461] Alberta Agriculture website, "Calgary Italian Bakery," nd, URL: http://www1.agric.gov.ab.ca/$department/deptdocs. nsf/ba3468a2a8681f69872569d60073fde1/bfa872a0a60df8ad8725784e007dfe1a/$FILE/CalgaryItalianBakery.pdf, retrieved January 28, 2018.

past 50 years into a huge plant in the city's southeast industrial area. Calgary Italian Bakery now employs more than 75 staff who can turn out 3,000 loaves or 1,500 dozen buns every hour."[462]

Alberto Romano was born in Altilia, Cosenza, Calabria where his parents farmed and operated a grocery store.[463] He followed his older brother Carlo to Edmonton; he had been sponsored by labour agent Ralph Welch in 1951 and worked on one of his CNR gangs. Carlo moved on to work for New West Construction in Edmonton and Alberto joined him in labouring work. This did not suit him, nor did work scrubbing medical instruments at the Misericordia Hospital where he was employed next. A low in Alberto's working life was at Canada Packers where a number of Italians worked in butchering meat. When he was offered some supervisory responsibilities, he decided that he did not care to work in the cold and bloody environment and, again, quit. The fact that his brother had found work with Honeyboy Bakery and been transferred to Calgary, opened up new opportunities. In December 1954, Alberto joined him in Calgary and worked briefly for Honeyboy Bakery and then for the CPR. He next worked at Dominion Bridge for about 18 months (1956-1957) until he was laid off.

By this point, he was 26 and ready to commit. When someone suggested that he set up as a realtor, he convinced a local firm to give him a chance. He observed: "I didn't really know Calgary or even how to drive a car very well but knew where Italians went to church and showed them a property there, and they bought it for about $8,000. My new bosses were thrilled and I had found my calling."[464] The many immigrants who came needed someone who spoke Italian and knew how to find houses, make a deal and obtain a mortgage. When obtaining credit became difficult for clients, Romano helped to found the Columbus Credit Union. Eventually, with partner Pat Roland, he established Tempo Real Estate Ltd., and became an agent for New York Life.

Alberto became a mainstay of the Calgary Italian Club and one of his favourite causes involved taking on the Government of Alberta when the RCMP raided Italian homes in 1964 and seized wine-making equipment and wine. He attended a planning meeting and hit it off with young lawyer Darryl Raymaker, who was prepared to work for free, and with community leaders in both Calgary and Edmonton, strategized about how to get the law changed. The strategy worked. Sara Lacentra, in a 1985-article in *Il Congresso*, provided an indication of Romano's commitment:

---

[462] *Ibid.*

[463] Information was drawn from three interviews: Alberto Romano, Calgary Italian Club Oral History Project, 1985, Glenbow Archives RCT-869-22; Peoples of Southern Alberta Oral History Project, 1987, Glenbow Archives RCT-788; and telephone interview with the author on February 12, 2018.

[464] The information was provided to the author by Romano in a telephone interview on February 12, 2018.

There is not one cultural or social initiative in Calgary to which Alberto has not linked his name; he played a role in the setting up of a soccer club, Juventus, helped found the Columbus Credit Union … helped to organize the Italian School of which he has been the president for many years, was part of the Committee that established the Sportsman's dinner of the Italian Club and the Ferrari raffle, which was so lucrative for the club. The list is extremely lengthy, and particularly illustrious. It includes the Folk Art Council, the Alberta Cultural Heritage Council, the Italian Professional Person's Club …and for 16 years, the presidency of the National Congress of Italian Canadians [Prairie Region].[465]

In November 1984, he received an Alberta Achievement Award and, in 2006, he was made a Cavaliere d'Italia.

The immigration history of Pasquale (Pete) Fornaro sees him move from poverty on the land in Italy to life as a business owner in Canada. In a 1985 interview, he remembered having to leave his home at Città Sant'Angelo, Pescara, Abruzzo, as the Allied bombings occurred.[466] The family returned on June 13 to find their home had been destroyed. Food was scarce and they had difficulty bringing in the harvest because of land mines. Pete was then conscripted into the Army but deserted after three months because soldiers were not being paid. He fled his hometown but was arrested by the *carabinieri* (federal police) and returned to service. He deserted two more times and eventually bribed a local official to be released from military duty. He observed that post-war life in Italy was harsh for those working the land. Twelve-hour days in the fields were common and everything was done by hand. The final catalyst for immigration was a hailstorm in June 1956 that destroyed the crops, followed by poor crop yields in the next two years.

Pete and wife Ida arrived in Calgary in March 1959 and he found work in construction and she at Benito's Restaurant. In addition, they both cleaned buildings on evenings and weekends. They had a burning desire to succeed but they also had a debt of honour – Ida's brother lent them $1,000 for the trip to Canada as well as housing them on their arrival. By each working three jobs, they were able to pay the debt as well as buy their first house and car. Pasquale noted that he earned $1.45 an hour on construction jobs and $1.65 on Union jobs. Ida earned $25 a month.

The couple was eventually able to buy the Hatchwear Uniform Company in 1971, which produced products for men, women and children. (They renamed it the New Hatchwear Uniform

---

[465] Sara Lacentra, "Una Vita per La Comunità," in *Il Congresso*, year 2, no 11, November 1985. The translation is by Adriana Davies.
[466] Ida and Pasquale Fornaro interview, Calgary Italian Club Historical Project, June 3, 1985, Glenbow Archives RCT-869-10.

Company.) The entire family worked in the business and, on Pasquale's retirement in 1977, son Vittorio (Victor) took over. In 1976, they began a tradition of creating the costume for the Stampede Queen.[467] Victor was involved in the establishment of the Italian Dancers and the company made the first costumes. Pete and Ida returned to Italy in 1970 and in 1979 and found that the country had undergone enormous changes. They observed that few people were involved in agriculture and generally people were more affluent. They no longer felt at home there. In 1988, Adrian Bussoli became Hatchwear's co-owner and eventually took the company over, and further developed it.

The post-war wave of immigration spurred the opening of a number of grocery stores. Alberto and Christina Iamartino, in 1956, opened a small store in the Italian neighbourhood of Bridgeland.[468] In 1958, they set up Great West Italian Importers, which repackaged and distributed imported Italian goods under their own label, Scarpone Foods. They competed with established companies and their territory eventually extended from Victoria to Thunder Bay. The fact that the city wanted their land for the Crowchild Trail enabled them to relocate to a larger warehouse in Inglewood. Daughters Sera and Sue, born in Calgary, became involved in the business. In a 2014 interview, Sera noted: "After school, I would take the bus and go help them do the shelves. They didn't speak English very well so I even did most of their paperwork. Then, they started selling to Safeway. I remember I would go and fill up the shelves for Safeway because you had to make the stuff look good or they wouldn't buy it from you. It was a lot of hard work." Sera's husband, Mike Duros, and Sue's husband, Giovanni (Gio) Oliverio, with the elder Iamartinos operate two divisions: The Italian Store, which opened in 2001, is the retail end, and Scarpone's Quality Italian Foods, the wholesale portion. The younger generation has shouldered the burden of day-to-day operations.

The heads of several Calgary families began their immigration journeys by working in mines. Vincenzo Scarpino was born in Bianchi, Palinudo, Cosenza, Calabria, to a farming family.[469] He served in the Italian Army and fought at the Battle of Tobruk during the Western Desert Campaign. Italian reinforcements were fighting with the German Army and were defeated by the Allies in 1942. About 20,000 prisoners were taken. Vincenzo spent the remainder of the war in England working on a farm as a prisoner-of-war. In 1957, he was sponsored by his brother, Antonio Scarpino, who had immigrated in 1951 and went to work in the mines in Fernie.

---

[467] Jennifer Hamblin, *Calgary's Stampede Queens* (Banff, AB: Rocky Mountain Books, 2014).

[468] Scarpone's Great West Italian Importers Ltd. website provides some information; see also Jeff Collins, "All in the family at the Italian Store and Scarpone's," *Culinaire Alberta*, June 17, 2014, URL: http://culinairemagazine.ca/all-in-the-family-at-the-italian-store-and-scarpone-s/, retrieved February 14, 2017.

[469] Serafino Scarpino kindly provided me with information about his family's immigration history in a telephone interview, January 22, 2018.

Vincenzo left wife Ermelinda and children behind. He did not last long in mining work and then found employment at a local sawmill. To improve the prospect of bringing his family to Canada, he decided to move to a large urban centre.

In 1959, with a group of young Italian immigrant friends, Vincenzo moved to Calgary where they lived in an Italian-owned boarding house. He obtained work with Burns and Dutton Construction (later the CANA Group) and saved money to sponsor his family and buy a house in Inglewood. They arrived on September 7, 1962 in a snowstorm – the children were in shorts and sandals. The weather improved enormously and they had a beautiful fall, which boded well for their new life in Canada. In the mid-1970s, Vincenzo got a job with the City of Calgary Parks and Recreation Department and noted: "We were paid a little less than in construction but you had security which was best for *la famiglia*." Ermelinda never worked – she had five young children to look after and no-one to help. Vincenzo was proud that Ermelinda didn't have to work. Son Serafino says she was a superb seamstress, housewife and mother. She made clothes to order for community members and could look at a garment and create a pattern and replicate it perfectly. Happy childhood memories include the morning routine of egg-yolks whipped with sugar and milky coffee poured over them and stirred in the belief that the concoction would bolster the immune system; beautifully-prepared lunches; and the clothing she made for them.

Vincenzo Girimonte was born in Castelsilano, Catanzaro, Calabria, the youngest of 11 children, and trained as a cabinet-maker. His father had a woodworking shop but, with limited means, he could not finance further education for the children. Vincenzo worked in his father's shop until his sister, who lived in Fernie, was able to sponsor him. He arrived in 1962 and went to work in the mines. After three months, he moved to Calgary where he got a job as a cabinetmaker with the Alberta Trailer Company, based in Airdrie. The company employed many Italian men so lack of English was not a problem and he learned to speak on the job. Vincenzo was lured away by a specialist wood-working company, which offered him more money, and, when it went out of business, in the early 1980s, he started Castello Woodcraft. In a 1987 interview, he emphasized that Italian craftsmen were extremely skilled in comparison to their Canadian counterparts since in Canada mass production was the norm.[470] He married Rosa Alfieri, a Neapolitan girl, and their courtship was traditional. Her parents, Antonio and Lucia, had arrived in Calgary in 1963 with their three daughters. Vincenzo was not allowed to be alone with Rosa and could only visit her at her place of work, the Co-op. He observed that there were 35 families from his hometown in Calgary and that they socialized with each other and also frequented the Calgary Italian Club.

[470] Vincenzo Girimonte interview, Peoples of Southern Alberta Oral History Project, July 13, 1987, Glenbow Archives RCT-855.

Vincenzo expressed no regrets about coming to Canada noting that Italy was class-ridden and that there was little social mobility.

Michele (Mike) Ciccaglione was born in Sessano del Molise, Isernia, Molise and, at the age of 16, went to Lucerne, Switzerland, to study restaurant management and business administration at the Union Elvetia School. He completed six years of studies and, at the prompting of his sister, Maria Petrollini, joined her in Calgary in 1962. Like so many others, he found that his credentials gave him no advantages. He started work as a waiter, first at the popular Hy's Steak House and then at the Calgary Inn and a restaurant in Banff. In a 2003 interview, Mike noted that the tips were good and he remembered serving European specialties including beef Chateaubriand and set alight the cherries jubilee, which was a crowd pleaser.[471] In 1967, with the help of family members, Mike bought the Prairie Dog Inn on 17th Avenue SW, one of the few restaurants that served Mexican food. He described his success as follows: "You have to surround yourself with good managers, good waiters and good chefs. You surround yourself with good people and you give the people hospitality and good food. It's not magic. Good food and hospitality has been around since the days of the Romans, I guess."[472]

Ciccaglione saw the growing popularity of Latino food and, in 1972, established El Molino Foods of Canada, which distributed foods and sauces. The company grew from a small operation with a staff of five to a large plant, built in 2009, that produces its own line of products including tortilla chips and salsa, and supplies individual restaurants as well as Mexican food chains. The current plant is located in Claresholm and houses three lines: El Molino Foods, Bear Creek Foods and Del Comal Foods. Bear Creek supplies frozen burritos, cabbage rolls, taquitos and quesadillas to retailers; and Del Comal manufactures tortilla chips from its own cooked white or yellow corn. Ciccaglione has also introduced production of some Italian specialty foods such as antipasto and bruschetta.

While succeeding as a food manufacturer and distributor, Ciccaglione did not abandon restaurant operations. In 2003, he noted: "When I came here, Calgary was a meat-and-potatoes town. Now, I don't think there's one cuisine you won't find here. And the fastest growth is in Italian restaurants."[473] He noted that Canadian students, who had been travelling to Italy with their backpacks, returned with a taste for trattoria-style food, and this appetite had only continued to grow. Ciccaglione established the Buon Giorno restaurant in 1987 in the former premises of the Prairie Dog Inn and it became extremely popular. It was subsequently sold and continues to

---

[471] Gyle Konotopetz, "Life's El Grande for Calgary's Nacho King," *Business Edge News Magazine*, January 15, 2003.
[472] *Ibid.*
[473] *Ibid.*

thrive. Ciccaglione also opened a series of food outlets including the Mexican Village chain, the Pied Pickle chain, Il Giardino restaurants, Zips Pizza and the Royal Duke English Pub. The Pied Pickle and Royal Duke involved partnerships. Mike Junior followed his father in the business and opened the Black Cat Lounge & Grill. Italian options were added to the menu and, according to David Parker in a 2013 article, "Ciccaglione's elder sister Maria [Petrollini] makes the gnocchi at home from her own recipe – very tasty."[474]

Calgary also benefitted from the "brain drain" from Italy. Dr. Luciano Mazzolani was born in Rimini and studied medicine at the University of Milan graduating in 1954.[475] He immigrated to Saskatchewan and worked there until 1968, first at the Regina General Hospital and, then, at St. Paul's Hospital in Saskatoon. In Calgary, he set up as a general practitioner. Bruno Scrobogna attended the Nautical Institute of Fiume and, in 1929, obtained a captain's licence.[476] He served in the Italian Navy and then worked for the city of Fiume from 1933 to 1939. He immigrated to Calgary with his wife Lucilla and their two children and obtained employment with the city of Calgary as a waterworks technician and retired in 1974.

Sandro Silenzi received a doctorate in geological sciences from the University of Rome in 1963 and was drawn to Alberta by the oil boom. He arrived in Calgary in 1964 and worked for TransCanada Pipeline Ltd. and other companies. Sandro's consulting work involved him in the analysis of potential hydrocarbon basins in 38 countries, and the initiation and implementation of exploration projects in Africa, Europe, Australia, New Zealand and Indonesia. Silenzi took part in major oil discoveries in Italy, the North Sea and New Zealand. In November 1995, he was appointed Vice President International at Eurogas Corporation, a Calgary-based oil and gas company. The company was involved in development of the Yaro-Yakinsk Field in western Siberia and, in Tunisia, in the drilling of test wells.[477] Sandro was appointed honorary vice consul by the Italian government and supported a number of community initiatives including establishment of the Italian Language School.

Davide (David) Colonna also had a profession when he arrived in Calgary in January 1963.[478] He came to visit his sister Antonietta Iavasile and her husband Giovanni, and was initially not

[474] David Parker, "Father-son team serves up success," *Calgary Herald*, June 11, 2013.

[475] Spada, *The Italians in Canada*, 349.

[476] *Ibid.*, 349.

[477] Eurogas Corporation, news release "Eurogas Corp. (TSE,VSE:EUG) announces the appointment of Dr. Sandro Silenzi to the position of Vice President International," November 9, 1995, URL https://www.thefreelibrary.com/Eurogas+Corporation+-+Corporate+Update.-a017615208, retrieved January 20, 2018.

[478] David Colonna interview, Peoples of Southern Alberta Oral History Project, October 19 and December 2, 1987, Glenbow Archives RCT-281.

impressed with the weather or Canada. He was 25 years old and his father owned a furniture factory in Termoli, Campobasso, Molise. While his brothers embraced the family business, his passion was fashion. He attended L'Istituto Salesiano San Ambrogio, Milan, where he studied fashion and trained as a tailor. He began work with Emilio Federico Schuberth, whose clientele included Rita Hayworth, Ingrid Bergman, Bette Davis, Brigitte Bardot, Sofia Loren, Gina Lollobrigida and Anna Magnani.

To understand Colonna's disappointment in Calgary's fashion scene, it is important to note that, in 1962, Italian fashion and film were recognized worldwide. They were part of the reputation that Italy was building as a purveyor of luxury goods and the City of Milan was at the centre of this. David found Calgary parochial; however, he fell in love and decided to stay. He attended English-language classes at the Calgary Italian Club and obtained work with the Hudson's Bay Company as a tailor and, after six months, moved on to O'Connor's Men's Wear. In 1964, David Abel, founder of David L. Abel Clothiers, invited him to join the firm and Colonna bought a 25 percent interest. In 1978, David purchased the company renaming it David Colonna Clothiers. At this time, Calgary was positioning itself as a centre of Canadian business but this required a certain life style and image. Colonna was the right person in the right place at the right time: he understood European high style as well as Calgary's corporate vibe. He stocked high fashion men's suits including Italian and North American brands and started a "suit club" to encourage employees of companies such as Shell, Aquitaine, BMO and the Bank of Commerce to shop at his store. In 2014, he opened a new store in the Bantrell Building.

Journalist David Parker described David's success as follows: "He played and coached soccer for the local Juventus team and was a member of the team that won the Stanley Matthews World Cup in Long Beach, Calif. He served as vice-president of the Italian Club, and it is his contacts and business smarts that have allowed him to become a developer, ranch owner and collector of some very fine automobiles – plus two Vespas that he keeps at his home in Italy."[479] In an oral history interview, Colonna asserted his belief that Canada was "the land of opportunity" and that it had given him a comfortable life. He observed that Canada was a less stratified society and there were fewer barriers to advancement. He strongly believed that his children would have a better future in Canada and was joined in the business by sons Marco and Anthony. Though he was a Canadian citizen, he considered his heritage Italian. While his family in Italy appears to have been well-established not only his sister and her husband but also brothers Italo and Benito immigrated to Calgary.

---

[479] David Parker "Keeping Calgarians in Style," *Calgary Herald*, May 9, 2014. URL: https://www.pressreader.com/canada/calgary-herald/20140509/282093454757457

While most immigrants were delighted with the opportunities that leaving Italy offered, some left their homeland reluctantly. Giuseppe Fanella was forced to leave Italy because of a job loss. He was born in Foggia, Puglia in southern Italy, the son of an Italian federal police officer and a seamstress. Giuseppe attended school to the age of 16 and then was apprenticed to a carpenter. In 1955, he completed compulsory military service and began work in a furniture shop. He considered immigrating but his family opposed this and he felt guilt at the thought of "abandoning them."[480] But the decision would ultimately be taken out of his hands: he lost his job and had wife Maria Di Filippi, whom he had married in 1961, and two children to support. He allowed his sister and her husband, who had immigrated in 1965 and were established in Calgary, to sponsor them. Giuseppe, Maria, daughter Antonella and son Nick arrived in Calgary in February 1968. The arrival in winter inspired immediate regret about leaving their homeland. With Giuseppe and Maria, the feeling of isolation and depression did not go away and would mark the remainder of their lives in Canada. His brother-in-law found him work with Italian-owned Paragon Construction, the majority of whose employees were immigrants. In 1971, Giuseppe was able to join the United Brotherhood of Carpenters and Joiners who negotiated solid contracts, and ensured that their members received good pay. In a 1987 interview, he observed that Italian employers were anxious to rise in status as quickly as possible, so they were more likely to exploit their own ethnic group in order to earn high profits and establish themselves in the construction industry.[481]

Giuseppe appears not to have integrated with the Italian community or the community at large. His opinion of the Italian community is decidedly negative – he viewed jealousy and competition as the norm. There is the suggestion in the interview that he had some negative experiences that he could not talk about. He also believed that Canadians viewed Italians as inferior and that they had not fully accepted their presence in their country. While Giuseppe affirmed that coming to Canada was right because of the opportunities for economic betterment as well as his children's future prospects, his life in Canada appears to have been unhappy. He was proud that Antonella was a University of Calgary graduate and that son Nick was studying at Mount Royal College.

Maria Fanella was born in Foggia, the daughter of a railway engineer and seamstress.[482] She was one of six children and had the opportunity to attend school (the Italian equivalent of grade nine). The declaration of war in 1940 ended her school days; according to Antonella, this was

---

[480] Fanella, *With Heart and Soul*, ix.

[481] Giuseppe Fanella interview, Peoples of Southern Alberta Oral History Project, May 21, 1987, Glenbow Archives RCT-764.

[482] Maria Fanella interview, Peoples of Southern Alberta Oral History Project, May 27, 1987, Glenbow Archives RCT-765.

because the Mussolini regime closed schools so that the premises could be used to train soldiers. The family had extremely bad experiences with Fascism: while the Depression had resulted in many losses, it would be the Fascists who stripped them of other assets. After the war ended, Maria returned to school briefly to write final exams and, at the age of 16, went to work in a tobacco factory. In 1958, she went to Milan where a sister and brother were residing hoping to find better work. Marriage in 1961 liberated her from this toil and her expectations were that her economic lot would improve. The forced immigration to address Giuseppe's job loss was very hard for her.

In Calgary, Maria was a lonely woman and it was her husband who suggested that she get a job to get out of the house. An acquaintance helped her obtain work as a steam-press operator at the Rosedale Cleaners. Most of the workers were Chinese or other immigrant women. The women worked the 10- to 12-hour nightshift so that they could care for their children during the day while their husbands were at work. This made for a fragmented and stressful home life; the entire family could only be together on weekends and, in addition, because of childhood illnesses, there were many sleepless nights so fatigue was a constant companion. The double income, however, was a boon enabling the couple to buy a house. Maria stopped work after surgery, in 1974, but when her depression returned she became a cook at the University of Calgary's dining centre, and worked there from 1976 to 1979. At this point, Giuseppe insisted that she quit because their financial circumstances were comfortable but again she was not happy at home and, in 1981, went to work at the Caffè dello Sport, established by Frank Lucente, in 1973. Illness finally forced her retirement in 1983.

Maria was a woman of strong beliefs and notes in the oral history interview that Canada gave people independence and personal freedom; in addition, women in Canada were freer and able to work. She also believed that when Italians became too Canadian, this prejudiced family values and also made them more materialistic. She shared her husband's negative opinion of Canadians and believed that they were jealous of immigrants' success and more interested in having a "good time" than hard work and sacrifice. Stereotyping was, thus, not confined to Anglo-Canadians alone. What is surprising is her belief that the North American image of the Italian wife as docile and obedient was wrong and that, in fact, Italian marriages were more equal than North American ones. She also affirmed that, while Italian men were "traditional," most changed their attitudes in Canada. This would appear to be the perspective of a woman content in her marriage but this view was certainly not shared by other Italian women, who came to realize, in a more liberal society, how restricted their lives were. While the immigrant experience for Giuseppe and Maria Fanella was not a happy one, it must be acknowledged. Immigration would bring material improvement to many but it did not always bring happiness.

Antonietta (Toni) Colonna is an example of a self-confident Italian woman who faced down challenges in her immigration journey. She was born in Termoli, Campobasso in 1940, the daughter of Giuseppe, a furniture-maker and shopkeeper, and Angelina, a seamstress. The family considered itself middle class and she completed the *terza media* (the first three years of secondary school). In 1958, Giovanni Iavasile returned to Italy to marry her. He was a friend of her brother and had immigrated in 1954 and found a job with the CPR at the Ogden shops. According to Toni, they had a long-distance romance. Since she was not yet 18, consular officials advised her to wait before she joined him in Canada. Thus, she travelled alone and arrived in Halifax in July and then travelled by train to Calgary.

In a 1987 interview, Toni described the sense of adventure that she felt about immigration.[483] She did not experience the doubts or fears expressed by some peers; she did, however, mention that because she had no family or friends, she felt "let down." To combat these negative feelings, Toni went straight to work in a dry cleaning plant. The earnings were small (75 cents an hour) but gave her a sense of achievement, which coupled with being out of the home and inter-acting with others, made her life richer. But her husband, who she described as a very traditional Italian male, did not want her to work and forced her to quit. But she prevailed and, in February 1959, returned to work as a seamstress at the Sears store. Toni was highly-motivated and taught herself to read and speak English fluently. (She noted that she had some knowledge of English before immigrating.) At Sears, she started in draperies, then worked in the tailor shop and, finally, as a commission sales person. This suggests that her competence in English was excellent. Toni confessed that her life was comfortable in Italy and she would have continued to be well off if she had remained. Her job enabled her to socialize with the "English" community but the couple also socialized with other Italians. When asked about exploitation of Italian immigrants, she admitted that it happened but not to her.

Toni was joined in Calgary by three brothers and a sister (two brothers chose to remain in Italy). Her brother David, as has been noted, arrived in 1967 as did her sister Lucia Calvitti, who came with her husband Raffaele and son. A number of Italian families were divided in this way. In many instances, those who remained prospered and this put in doubt the whole reason for immigrating. Toni became a citizen in 1977 but believes that the ceremony did not make her a Canadian and that she did this for herself. The couple had a daughter, Rosaria (Rose), and Toni believes that she was not better off economically or educationally in Canada, though she felt her daughter was a better person for having grown up in Canada.

---

[483] Antonietta Iavasile interview, Peoples of Southern Alberta Oral History Project, June 1, 1987, Glenbow Archives RCT-766.

Gloria Marin was born in Vittorio Veneto, Treviso and grew up on her family's farm.[484] Like so many others, she experienced the negative impacts of war among them the disruption of her schooling, which ended at grade three. She apprenticed as a seamstress but could not obtain work; in a 1987 interview, she observed that most tailoring shops were family-owned and did not hire outsiders. So she went to work in a factory making baked goods. The wage was low and the working day was from 12 to 16 hours. In 1959, marriage to Damiano Marin freed her from this toil. Her husband had immigrated in 1954 and had returned to Italy to marry. He returned to Canada and Gloria joined him a few months later arriving in Halifax in August 1959. They settled in Calgary and she got a job at the coffee shop in the St. Louis Hotel. The couple lived in modest accommodations near the hotel. Gloria worked there for about six months and then got a job as a seamstress with Macleod Brothers Ltd. From the outset, the couple decided that they were going to make money and return. In the 1987 interview, she noted that she returned in 1962 with their two-year-old son, Walter, and her husband in 1964. But the old proverb that you can never go home again applied in this situation as well. Her husband was not only unhappy with the changes in Italy but also found that their savings did not go very far. They returned to Canada the following year and Gloria returned to work at Macleod Brothers Ltd. and worked there from 1965 to 1979. From there, she moved to Jo Anne's fashions where she worked until 1987. The couple adjusted to life in Canada and had no regrets. While they socialized within the community, they did not participate in any club activities.

Anna Ferrara was another strong woman whose immigration experience was positive. She and future husband Vincenzo Mandaione were born in Monteforte Irpino, Avellino, in central Italy. Her father owned a farm and was also a lumber merchant. Anna remembers having to help him with her five siblings. While her brothers were allowed some freedom, she was not and resented this. After the war, her brothers immigrated to Buenos Aires, Argentina but returned to Italy in 1954. Her marriage to Vincenzo, in 1959, freed her from parental supervision but she had to assist his mother in running the family's hardware store, thus, she had no memories of not working. In 1961, the couple headed to Stuttgart, Germany where Vincenzo had obtained work as a carpenter. That year was important because Germany and Italy signed an agreement that established freedom of movement of labour. The Mandaiones were part of a flood of more than 580,000 workers from central and southern Italy who went to Germany. Stuttgart had a large Italian community of "guest workers" and she enjoyed the life there. Although happily settled, at the prompting of her husband's sister, they returned to Italy in 1967, and found the conditions there limiting.

---

[484] Gloria Marin interview, Peoples of Southern Alberta Oral History Project, June 30, 1987, Glenbow Archives RCT-774.

On an exploratory mission, in June 1967, Vincenzo visited cousins in Calgary and, because of his carpentry skills, found work at the Alberta Trailer Company. The company was established by S. D. and R. D. (Ron) Southern, in 1947, to provide trailers to accommodate workers at industrial sites such as the Leduc and Redwater fields. The company was the first in a unique market niche and eventually became ATCO, a worldwide enterprise with about 8,000 employees and a net worth of $19 billion. It is interesting to note how many Alberta companies benefitted from immigrant labour. Vincenzo returned to Italy to arrange for the family's move but, because Anna was expecting their third child, he remained until February 1968 when he returned to Calgary. She and the children joined him in April.

In Germany, Anna had worked in a factory so it was natural for her to seek employment. She joined her husband at Alberta Trailer working the day shift while he worked nights. This continued until her mother-in-law's arrival in 1970 when she took over the child care. The work was heavy for her and, after two years, she developed rheumatic pain and had to quit. On average, every two-or-three years until 1986 she changed jobs. Employers included the Southern Alberta Institute of Technology, MacLeod Brothers men's wear, and a tile business. She then returned to MacLeod Brothers and remained there until 1986 when she retired. Because Anna was interviewed alone, the female perspective on immigration comes through strongly.[485] She expressed no doubts about the decision to immigrate and, while she did hear negative comments about immigrants in the workplace, she indicated that she did not experience discrimination herself. While she and her husband socialized with other Italians, they were not members of any Italian organizations. She expressed the very liberal view that it was not necessary for their children to marry other Italians or even Catholics. This last is surprising since she was a church-goer. She had seen social change in Italy as well including a rise in the rate of divorce. She expressed the opinion that Canada belongs to everyone and that her children's success made every sacrifice worthwhile.

Immigration to Other Urban Centres

The 1991 census provided the following rankings for Alberta cities based on percentage of Italians in the population: Lethbridge, 3.3 percent; Edmonton, 3.1 percent; Calgary, 3.0 percent; Medicine Hat, 2.3 percent; Red Deer, 2.1 percent; Grande Prairie, 1.6 percent; and Fort McMurray, 0.3 percent. Unfortunately, there is little archival material and oral and community histories do not

---

[485] Anna Mandaione interview, Peoples of Southern Alberta Oral History Project, September 11, 1988, Glenbow Archives RCT-855.

exist for Alberta's "second" cities. However, the profiles that I have been able to create demonstrate the same immigration patterns as in Edmonton and Calgary.

Family sponsorship brought a number of immigrants to Lethbridge who would become leaders in the Italian community. Many were from Calabria. In 1948, Lethbridge herbalist Nicholas Alvau sponsored his son Paolo (Paul) Rosario and his wife Virginia Lavorato and children Rose, Maria and Nick. Paul and Virginia were likely the first Italian post-war immigrants to arrive in Lethbridge. He was active in the Italian community and, besides the Italian Canadian Club, helped to found the Associazione Nazionale Combattenti Sezione di Lethbridge (Italian Veterans Society of Lethbridge). Virginia was a member of the Fraternal Order of Eagles, the Catholic Women's League and the Italian Canadian Club.

Virginia sponsored her sister Giuseppina (Lavorata) and husband Francesco Mazzuca; both were born in Piane Crati, Cosenza. Their son John was born in 1933. The family arrived in Lethbridge in 1953. Father and son, for a number of years worked at a range of jobs in Alberta and BC including the railways, in construction and for the gas company. All were seasonal leaving them without income for half the year. This prompted Francesco, who was a trained shoemaker, to set up a shop in Natal and eventually he moved to Lethbridge and continued to run the shop until his retirement. In 1957, John began to work for the Pink and Chiste Electric Company and studied to become a journeyman electrician. In 1972, with friend and co-worker Luciano (Lou) Travaglia, John set up L. & J. Electric. Travaglia had arrived in Lethbridge in 1952. The partnership continued until Lou's death in 1996. John then worked on his own until 2007 when he retired. In 1961, he returned to Italy and married Ermelinda (Linda) Salfi and the couple had two sons and a daughter. John and Linda were leaders in Lethbridge's Italian community helping to found the Romulus & Remus Club, the city's first Italian society. John was president for 30 years. He loved music and played the accordion and the band he set up was popular at weddings and community dances.

Lou Travaglia worked as an electrician but his real love was soccer: he played, refereed and coached. He served on the board of the Lethbridge Soccer Association for 22 years and saw the league grow from several hundred members to 2,000 players. The team he coached won the western Canadian championships in 1976. Lou was also instrumental in the development of indoor soccer so that the game could be played year round. Lou was a member of the Italian Club as well as the Knights of Columbus.

Silvio Mauro was born in Grimaldi, Cosenza, Calabria and was an only child raised by his mother – his father had immigrated to Canada and was a sojourner working in Trail and other communities. Silvio trained as a cabinetmaker and, at the age of 23, married Rosina Vercillo. In 1951, he decided to follow family members to Canada and left his wife and two young sons behind. He travelled with 14 young men from his hometown and arrived in Halifax with $72 in his pockets. Immigration officials took him aside and gave him $50, which his aunt in Trail had sent. Silvio settled in Trail and the family joined him in 1954; shortly after, they moved to Lethbridge where he found employment in construction. He became immersed in the life of the growing Italian community. He was a founding member and served as president of the Italian Club; the local soccer association; and the Italian Veterans Society. The last had 35 members and reflected the fact that the men of the post-war generation who came to Canada had served in the military. A renowned storyteller, Silvio particularly enjoyed talking about his Italian roots and immigration experience to school groups at the Galt Museum.[486] In 2000, Silvio attracted media attention because of a large replica of the Leaning Tower of Pisa that he built for a float for the Italian Club and, then, stored in his back yard. It was featured on the CBC television series *On the Road Again*, hosted by Wayne Rostad.[487] The Lethbridge Herald showcased the event in two articles: "Silvio's On the Road" and "Silvio leans towards Italy after honours from Pisa." The latter referred to the fact that Silvio was honoured by the Mayor of Pisa in summer 2000 when he visited Italy.

Ruggero (Roger) Giordano Algeri Sergo was born in 1921 in Pozzino, Tuscany and began work aged 13 delivering bread and cleaning for a bakery.[488] In 1937, he became an apprentice at the Decleva Luigi Bakery. At the age of 19, in 1941, he joined the Italian Navy. After the war, he worked in a wool factory. In 1951, he decided to come to Canada where he hoped to be able to practice his trade. He travelled from Naples on a boat with 1,400 other immigrants. During the passage, he worked as a baker for an agreed-upon wage of $1 a day. On his arrival in Halifax, his pay did not materialize. Setbacks continued to dog him: he was supposed to work in a bakery in Montreal but lack of English prevented him from doing so, and he had to go to work in a logging camp. To learn English, he also worked in a restaurant. In spring 1952, the promise of work on a sugar beet farm brought him to Lethbridge. He moved on to work in the Western Canadian Collieries in Bellevue. In 1956, he heard of a job at Penny's Bakery in Lethbridge, applied and was hired. It was a wholesale operation in which he did only one job and he did not find it fulfilling. In 1959, he moved to the National Bakery.

In 1961, Roger married Dorina (Doris) Whitcroft, whom he had met in 1952 in Bellevue. Doris' father, John Scodellaro, left Udine and settled in Bellevue in 1909 and worked in the

---

[486] A session featuring Silvio Mauro and junior high students at the Galt Museum was filmed in 1996, Galt Archives AN-19971070002. Silvio donated some of his wine-making equipment to the Galt.

[487] Ron Devitt, "Silvio's On the Road," *Lethbridge Herald*, January 19, 2000; and Sherri Gallant, "Silvio leans towards Italy after honours from Pisa," *Herald*, September 5, 2000.

[488] Roger Sergo's stepdaughter Maxine Whitcroft Strain donated biographical notes and photographs to the Galt Archives.

mines.[489] Doris was born in 1923, completed grade 9 and then attended the Home Service Training School in Calgary.[490] Her first job was with a wealthy Calgary family doing light cleaning and preparing supper. In 1943, she moved to Windsor where she worked as a housekeeper. According to daughter Maxine, she used the name "Doris Scott" to avoid discrimination against Italians during the Second World War. In 1946, she married Herbert Whitcroft and the couple had two children, Richard and Maxine. The marriage did not work out and, in 1951, she returned to Bellevue with her children and worked at the Quality Meat Market and, later, at the post office. As a divorced woman, she would have experienced some stigma in the Italian community, but this did not prevent her from raising her children with the help of her family until she married Roger. The couple's daughter Darlene was born in 1962, the same year that he went to work in the Woolworth Bakery in Lethbridge. Maxine describes her stepfather as "a man who found his talent and passion early in life and didn't give up (taking many other jobs) until he was able to fulfill that dream." Maxine observes:

> Dad went to work at 1 am or 2 am, so the baked goods would be ready and fresh for opening each day. If there were 2 bakers, one would start at 1, the other at 2:00 am. In those days, nothing was "pre-mixed." Everything was made from scratch. Today bakers use "pre-mix" packages. Dad would create his own recipes. Using a scale, he would measure in pounds (lbs) and ounces (ozs). In 1962, he leased the Marquis Bakery premises in the Marquis Hotel. His customers would come for their favorites. They would follow him from bakery to bakery for his famous rye bread.[491]

In 1962, Roger became manager of the Marquis Bakery located in the hotel of the same name and Doris, Maxine and Richard helped him. His fresh buns, vanilla slices, cakes and donuts including Boston Crème ones with custard filling became popular and Roger ran the bakery for seven years. He also catered weddings and other events. His extreme work ethic likely caused burnout and he went to work at the IGA Bakery. He ended his career at the Safeway Bakery at Mayor Magrath South. Richard tells an interesting story: when Roger first arrived in Canada, he sought help from the church (one assumes a Catholic church in Montreal) but did not get it. He next went to the Salvation Army and they gave him a room, a bed, fed him and gave him

---

[489] The entry on John Scodellaro in *Crowsnest and Its People* was submitted by Doris (Scodellaro) Sergo, 830-831.

[490] Information on Dorina (Doris) Scodellaro appears on a Scodellaro Family genealogical site, URL: http://scodellaro.com/page11-Doris.html, retrieved October 26, 2017.

[491] Maxine Whitcroft Strain, family history, Galt Archives.

cigarettes. This memory stayed with him and, when he had his own bakery, he sent day-old pastries to the local Salvation Army.

Red Deer saw the arrival of a number of families from Calabria. Gregorio (Greg) Mancuso was born in Cicala, Catanzaro, one of nine children in a farming family. Contract work for the CPR enabled him to immigrate in 1955.[492] In the same year, he married Immacolata (Emma) whose family had arrived in Canada in the early 1950s. Greg and Emma settled in Red Deer and he started cleaning in the evenings after work. They saved and, in 1958, Greg started his own company, Mancuso Janitorial Service, and he became a pioneer in the carpet and upholstery cleaning industry. Son Paolo described his father as "an 18-hour-a-day guy." In 1992, on his father's retirement, he took over Mancuso Carpet and Upholstery Cleaning Services. After her children were in school, Emma worked for the Michener Centre, the home for physically and developmentally challenged individuals, from 1972 to 1987.

Gregorio sponsored his younger brother Pasquale, who had five years of education and was apprenticed to a bricklayer. Pasquale arrived in Red Deer in 1959 and went to work as a labourer in construction; shortly after, he was joined by wife Tina. He saved and, in 1964, bought an old truck, some wheelbarrows, shovels and a power trowel, and went into the construction business with a friend. They worked out of a garage in the Parkvale neighbourhood of downtown Red Deer. After his friend left the business, he and Tina incorporated Pasquale Mancuso Concrete Services Ltd. in 1968. The company quickly gained a reputation for excellence in small residential projects including sidewalks, driveways and patios. The business soon required its own building. Pasquale next moved into institutional and commercial work and benefitted from the building boom in the 1960s and 1970s.

In a 1985 interview Pasquale observed that, in the past 15 years, his company had done about 75 percent of the concrete work in Red Deer with peak years being 1975 and 1982. Projects included the Bower Place Shopping Centre, Capri Centre expansion, the Black Knight Inn, Red Deer Lodge, civic water treatment plant, City Hall addition, the Provincial building and all four petrochemical plants in the region. Pasquale also talked about the impact of the recession resulting from the drop in the price of oil and revealed optimism about the future: "I feel everything will come back in our economy. We all got hurt by the recession and a lot of companies in the construction industry went bankrupt. In our own Mancuso operations here, we had to cut back our staff from a peak of 35 employees in 1981 to a low of 10. We are now back up to having 20 employees. I am most pleased that we always have been able to pay our bills, although this has

492 Greg Mancuso obituary, *Red Deer Advocate*, November 16, 2006.

meant working long hours for me. We lost on some jobs and made up on others."[493] One of the projects that indicated an improvement in the economy was the new hospital in Ponoka, at the time the company's largest contract. With renewed oil industry activity in central Alberta, new clients continued to emerge and, in 1990, the rebranded PMCL Partnership expanded into construction of foundations for oil and gas facilities. Sons Domenico and Rino grew the company to the next level ensuring continuity. Pasquale also noted the trend to "do-it-yourself" in home renovations and established Northland Construction Supplies, in 1978.

Medicine Hat received a number of post-war Italian immigrants. Nello Angelo De Valter was born in Galliera Veneta, Padua, and immigrated in 1949. He found work at Alberta Clay Products.[494] An earlier generation of De Valters, likely cousins, arrived in the first decades of the twentieth century and worked in the potteries. Nello returned to Italy in 1957 and married Dina Beghetto, a local girl, and they returned to Medicine Hat. He obtained work with I-XL Industries, a supplier of brick, stone and other products, and remained there until retirement in 1985. What is unusual about this family is that it appears that none of his siblings joined him in Canada.

Giuseppe Votta was born in Calvello, Potenza and married Serafina Giase in September 1947.[495] In 1951, he immigrated to Canada and settled in Medicine Hat; he was joined by Serafina and their first child in 1952. Giuseppe worked for Medalta Pottery, Hycroft China and the McAvity Foundry and retired from the last in 1975. In 1955, T. McAvity & Sons (Western) Ltd. was established in Medicine Hat to cover the western market. Giuseppe and Serafina had eight children: four sons and four daughters.

The marriage of Aldo Rossetto and Amalia Dalla Longa in 1951 was followed by immigration to Medicine Hat from San Vito di Valdobbiadene, Treviso. His parents, Silvio and Fiorina, operated a shoe shop and the trade was in his blood. In 1961, he started Aldo's Shoe Repair on Third Street in the downtown. The couple had three children, two sons and a daughter. Son Mario studied business and, in 1985, went to work with his father eventually taking over the shop. He was one of the individuals featured in a 2018 exhibit titled "Hands at Work in Medicine Hat" at the Yuill Family Gallery at Medalta.[496]

[493] George Yackulic, "Mancuso found perfect foundation for concrete business in city," *Red Deer Advocate*, August 1, 1985.

[494] Nello Angelo De Valter obituary, *Medicine Hat News*, May 4, 1996.

[495] Giuseppe Votta obituary, *Medicine Hat News*, April 26, 1996.

[496] Medalta website, "Hands at Work in Medicine Hat," URL: https://medalta.org/hands-work-medicine-hat/, retrieved January 19, 2019. Photographer James K. Farrell created 39 black and white photographs documenting the work of 17 "makers" in the city.

The Dal Molin family straddles two eras of immigration history. Both generations got their start in the clay industry and then found secure work with the City of Medicine Hat. Luigi and Fortunata Dal Molin were the first generation to immigrate and two of their three sons were born in the city: Lino in 1922 and Italo in 1928. The couple returned to Italy in 1933; perhaps they were badly affected by the Depression or simply missed their home. Third son Aldo was born in 1935 in Italy. Lino married Teresa Castaldo in 1952 and, in 1954, their son Louis was born. In 1956, the young family immigrated to Medicine Hat and he found work with Alberta Clay Products.[497] Lino's next job was with the City where he worked in the Cemetery Department until his retirement in 1982. Aldo Dal Molin was reunited with his older brothers in 1957 and worked at Medicine Hat Brick and Tile for 42 years. He was renowned for his gardening skills and even succeeded in growing grapes. He entered his produce in the annual Medicine Hat Exhibition and won many prizes.

The resource towns of Exshaw and Jasper saw the arrival of a number of immigrants including Osvaldo Borsa and Guido Moro. Borsa left Pian dei Zocchi, San Nazario, Veneto in 1955 at the age of 21, attracted by Government of Canada advertisements for skilled labour. He travelled with friend Tony Moro who had settled in Surrey, BC and returned to Italy for a visit. The two were met in Calgary by Tony and Maxine Lazzarotto, who were related to Moro. Osvaldo relied on friends to help him find work and observes: "Several job openings came available with C.P. Rail and Loders Lime. The best way to settle the job issue between Tony and I was to flip a quarter. Tony got the job working for C.P. Rail and I started working for the lime plant. For the first while I stayed at the bunkhouse in Kananaskis and ate in the cookhouse. Over the 45 years of employment with the lime plant, I've worked in the positions of labourer, welder and millwright."[498]

Osvaldo saved and sponsored his childhood sweetheart Silvana Moro, who came over in 1958 to marry him. She found work as a cook in the company bunkhouse until their son Maurizio's birth in 1962. Her father Giacchino Moro joined them in 1965 and also went to work at Loders Lime. After the children went to school, Silvana worked at the school in maintenance for 12 years. In 1970, the couple returned to Italy and though Silvana does not explain why this move was taken, it was likely homesickness coupled with work frustrations. They returned after two years and Osvaldo got his job back and they moved to a company house in Kananaskis Village. Their sons Maurice and John went to work for Baymag Inc.

A third member of the Moro family, Guido, had worked on the family farm near Rivalta, Turin, done his military service and took on a number of labouring jobs including work in

---

[497] Lino Luigi Dal Molin obituary, *Medicine Hat News*, May 16, 2009.
[498] Osvaldo and Silvana Borsa, "Borsa: Osvaldo and Silvana – 1955," in *Exshaw*, 451.

Switzerland before deciding to immigrate. He arrived in Exshaw in 1957 and went to work in the lime plant; wife Ida and son Giacomo joined him the following year. Ida had washed clothes to make money and, in the family history, notes that they were desperate to improve their economic condition. She described the journey to Canada as follows:

> The boat trip was in February, and was very rough and very scary. It took 11 days. I was seasick for five days which made it difficult, as I had Giacomo to look after. We landed in New York, where there was a metre of snow and travelled by train to Toronto with a police escort to make sure we did not get off the train in the States. They even followed us to the bathroom. That train from New York did not have any heat and it was -18 C. My boy got a terrible cold. I took my coat off to cover him because we did not have a blanket. The next train had heat. We took it from Toronto to Calgary and then Canmore. We did not have much luggage; just a trunk and a suitcase. Now we have too much.[499]

Ida recounts that she taught herself English with the help of some other Italian women, including Maxine Lazzarotto, and that watching television helped. She also read her son's books when he went to school. She writes of her settlement experience: "I had to learn a different way of life. It was rough starting; especially not knowing the language. It was worth it because I was married to a man that I loved. I started baking bread and pasta, etc., and every spring I would buy fifty chicks for eggs and meat. Between Guido and I, we started a vegetable garden. I tried to help Guido pay the rent and the trip to Canada."[500] When her children went to school, she worked cleaning the school, initially part-time and then full-time, for a total of 23 years. She notes of her husband's work: "When he started at the plant, he was bagging the lime but it burned his skin, so he worked on the crusher breaking rock with a hammer for six or seven years. They had to crush the bigger rock because the crusher would not take it. After that, they got a newer plant and it was easier."[501] The couple wanted better lives for their children and she proudly reported that son Giacomo had his own business in Calgary as a heavy-duty mechanic; Johnny worked as a painter for the Calgary school board; and Dennis was a chef with his own candy stores – The Fudgery and The Candy Bears' Lair in Banff and Jasper, respectively.

Italian immigrants, a number from Calabria, ended up working in Jasper for the CNR. Domenico Borelli arrived in Jasper in August 1953 and started working for CN at midnight the

---

[499] Ida Moro, "Moro: Ida and Guido – 1957," in *Exshaw*, 466.
[500] *Ibid.*, 466.
[501] *Ibid.*, 467.

same day.[502] He moved from work as a labourer to machinist's helper and then machinist. He was joined by wife Elvira and three-year-old daughter Francesca (Frances) in 1954. When diesels replaced steam engines in 1957, he was laid off. For a time, he worked at the Athabasca Hotel as a bartender and then for Parks Canada. In 1962, he was re-employed by CN and worked for the company until his retirement in 1984. Frances and Maria attended the University of Alberta and obtained B Ed degrees and taught in Edmonton. Both married Jasper boys: Frances wed Angelo Timoteo, and Maria, Tony De Rosa.

John De Rosa at the age of 23 left his wife and three children and went to work in the mines in Russia. He did not like working underground or the politics and returned to Italy. In 1953, he travelled to Halifax and joined one of the Welch gangs in Kamloops. He worked for two years "in the bush" and eventually walked from Geikie to Jasper and got a job in the CN shop. The family history notes: "Every day, after he finished his job at the CN, he helped people with building projects, dug wells, and did any odd job that came his way, constantly stashing away every dollar he could make. In 1955, he reached his goal, and the whole De Rosa family became a part of Jasper life. The children attended school and were talking English like veterans in a month or so."[503] John worked for CN until retirement in 1990. Son Vincenzo married Rena Timoteo of Jasper and the couple operated a restaurant in St. Paul. Tony with wife Maria Borelli moved to Edmonton where he worked for CN and she taught. Frances married Joe Caputo, who worked for Parks Canada in Jasper and the couple also owned L and R Fashions. Maria married Leo Giampo and the couple lived in Edmonton where he worked as an electrician.

Quinto Odorizzi, aged 27, arrived in Edmonton in 1955 from northern Italy but missed the mountains and travelled to Jasper where he found work as a section man for CN near Miette. The year after, he was transferred to the shops in Jasper. Around 1958, he travelled to Italy for a holiday and met Rita Leonardi and they were married. He worked for CN as a labourer, coach cleaner, auxiliary cook and foreman until retirement in 1985. Once their three daughters were in school, Rita worked at the Parkview store and as a hostess, first at Smitty's restaurant and, then, at the Marmot Motor Lodge. Quinto served on the Jasper School Board for four three-year terms; on the Family Community Social Services Board; and was also a member of the Lions Club. The couple were keen gardeners and also acted as informal guides to Jasper National Park.[504]

Giovanni (John) Forabosco was sponsored by his sister Angelina and husband Lino Fadi and arrived in August 1956. In the family history in *Jasper Reflections*, he writes:

---

[502] *Ibid.* "Borelli, Domenico," 62-63.
[503] *Ibid.*, "DeRosa, John and Rosa," 120-121.
[504] *Ibid.*, "Odorizzi, Quinto and Rita," 317-318.

A couple of days later I started to work for "Welch" (a railroad gang organization) building a stone wall between the tracks and the main street. This job lasted a couple of months and I then got a job in the Roundhouse for the CNR. Some of the foremen were Bill Corrins, Albert Lusk (may they rest in peace) and Bob Key (a tough cookie). This job lasted until the fall of 1958.... I worked night shifts in the Roundhouse and sometimes on slow nights we used to hop in the cab of the steam engine and go to sleep, driving the foreman crazy. As everything comes to an end, so did the steam engines and in came diesels. Now there were massive layoffs in the Roundhouse and I was one of them. Wasting no time, the following day I had a job with Parks Canada.[505]

In 1958 when he joined Parks Canada, he was designated a truck driver and joined a crew patching roads between Jasper and the Park's East Gate. His future wife, Josie, emigrated with her family from Holland to Hardisty, Alberta, and in 1959 came to work at the Seton Hospital. She noted in the family history: "We also used to call Jasper 'Little Europe' because there were so many people of different nationalities but most of them Italian."[506] They met at a dance at the Spero's Hall and were married in February 1960. John lost his job with Parks Canada and worked at the Mountain Motors Garage for a time. His next employment was with Cy Whitfield, the Imperial Oil Bulk Agent, delivering heating fuel to Jasper clients. John did this for eight years and, on Whitfield's retirement in 1967, he purchased the business. In 1968, the business required that they relocate to Whitecourt. In 1973, the couple returned to Jasper and purchased the Roche Bonhomme Bungalows; in 1978, they purchased the Jasper House Bungalows. The family history proudly notes: "In 1988, the last two children graduated from high school. John Jr. went to the University of Calgary and graduated with a four year degree in Fine Arts. Sandi is in Education at the University of Alberta and will graduate in 1995. Marina has a degree in Sociology and Psychology, and later went into Education and is now teaching in Kamloops. Anita is in the University of Alberta Nursing Program and seems to enjoy it. She will be finished July 1994."

Aldo Leonardi, the youngest of 13 children, was sponsored by his sister Rita Odorizzi and arrived in Jasper in 1963; he was 18.[507] Aldo loved Jasper, which reminded him of his northern Italian home near Trentro where he had skied and climbed mountains. His initial work was as a cook for the crew erecting the communications tower on Pyramid Mountain. The catering company next sent him to Vancouver Island to cook at a zinc mining camp that was accessed via

[505] Jasper Community History Committee, *Jasper Reflections* (Jasper, AB: Jasper Community History, 1996), "Forabosco, John and Josie," 145-148.
[506] *Ibid.*, "Forabosco, John & Josie," 145-148.
[507] *Ibid.*, "Leonardi, Aldo and Shirley,"240-241.

a small aircraft. He hated the remoteness and returned to Jasper and was hired by CN as a coach cleaner. Aldo spent the next 30 years working for CN as a car repairman, auxiliary cook and crane operator. In 1970, he married Shirley Urness, who was working during the summer months at the Astoria restaurant to make money to attend university. Like many Italians, Aldo acquired a number of trades and helped community members with home repairs and renovations. Shirley taught at the Jasper Elementary School.

Giovanni Pooli arrived in Canada in 1954 and joined his brother Roberto and other family members in Toronto. Hearing of work opportunities in the West, they headed to Edmonton where Giovanni briefly worked at St. Joseph's Hospital as a cook. They then headed to Kitimat, BC, where they worked in the aluminum mines. They did not care for the work and moved to Jasper where they worked for CN. The family history notes:

> Roberto and I rebuilt a chicken shed and sent for Roberto's wife Teresa and their three year old son to come out from Trento, Italy. So the chicken shed was our home together. The stations along the line from Jasper were Mosley, Rainbow, Grantbrook, Jackman and Red Pass and we worked along as linemen. When I was in Red Pass in 1961, I returned briefly to Trento to marry Pia, Theresa's sister. Pia came to Canada in May 1961 to our small house in Red Pass. Though we knew very little English, we found we were in a good community. There was a store, the RCMP station and the school. We came to Jasper along the Yellowhead Trail to see the doctor and to shop from time to time. In winter, the snow lay deep and covered the house, we often had to shovel our way out for water from the creek, and run down the path to the outhouse. The bears looked in at the window and sometimes tried to get in via the back door! It was November 1970 before we packed up and came to live in Jasper at 824 Geikie Street.[508]

Giovanni worked for CN as a section foreman until retirement in May 1985. Daughter Elda attended Grant MacEwan College in Edmonton and, then, the University of Alberta and worked in Edmonton as a nutrition consultant. Son Roberto studied civil engineering at NAIT and worked in Edmonton.

Emilio Cesco, another Northern Italian from near Venice, arrived in Canada in 1956 with a group including two brothers and two cousins and took the train to Jasper to start work for CN on a Welch gang. In an interview in 1999, he recalled arriving at night and seeing the mountains.[509]

---

[508] *Ibid.*, "Pooli, Giovanni and Pia," 338-339.
[509] "Emilio Cesco," Jasper Information Centre Oral History Project, March 19, 1999, Jasper-Yellowhead Museum & Archives AN 001.06.05.

He noted that the rock work on the buildings resembled that on buildings in his home town. He spent his first winter at the Tangle Camp which housed about 150 men. Working hours were from 8 am to 5 pm daily and weekends were spent in town. They made 82 cents an hour, which he felt was "good money." In the spring, he was moved to the camp at Mile 45, then to Mile 31 (Ranger Creek) and then to the Miette Hot Springs Road. Emilio welcomed the hard work and saved money in order to marry a hometown girl – Lina Pradetto – who had gone to England to work. He sponsored her and they married in Edmonton in 1960 and had two children. The couple returned to Italy in 1964 but all did not go as they had hoped and they returned to Jasper. At this point, he got a job as a labourer with the Canadian Parks Service. He assisted Joe Calabretta, a master mason, on the rockwork for the Pyramid Mountain tower, the viewpoint at Tangle Creek and other projects. The next year he went to work in the carpentry shop and was involved in a range of repair work on the old Parks Administration Building and other structures. He became the Trades Foreman in 1985 and retired in 1992.

In the early 1950s, Bruno Mannella, Amerino Gatti, Domenico Borrelli and Ugo Albo from southern Italy decided to go to Canada. They found work in Jasper and decided to send for their families. Bruno sponsored his sister, Concetta (Connie) and she, in turn, sponsored her 18-year-old sweetheart, Gino Tassone, whose family lived in Serra San Bruno, Vibo, Calabria. He arrived in winter, 1957, wearing lightweight clothing but was undeterred by the cold and the couple married a few weeks later. Gino started work at the Jasper Park Lodge as a painter. In 1958, his mother came for a visit and decided to stay. Other family members joined them: first, sister Maria, who was married to a distant cousin, Francesco (Frank) Tassone; next, Maretta, who was married to Bruno Zaffino; and, finally, brother Franco and wife Stella and their three children. Pauline (LaMothe) Tassone writes in the family history: "It can be said that the Tassones and Zaffinos, while they arrived having had little education and knowing next to no English were very resourceful: working as nightclerk at the Athabasca Hotel, providing janitorial services to parks Canada and to the schools, working for CN when the opportunity arose, and buying and managing property as funds became available. While English may have been lacking at first, they found ways of making themselves understood."[510]

A final brother, Cosmo, and wife Rafaela were the last to arrive in 1961. He changed the spelling of the family surname to Tassoni. Cosmo, for the next 30 years, worked in various positions for the Parks Service including caring for the local fire hall, maintaining equipment and driving an ambulance. Evelyn Saurette in an article in the *Jasper Booster* noted: "It was an absolute devotion to his family that drove the gentle Italian to continue to work several jobs for more than

---

[510] Pauline Tassone, "The Jasper Tassones," unpublished family history, 2014, Jasper-Yellowhead Museum.

30 years. With five successful children and five grandchildren who continue to live in Jasper, he says he has been repaid many times over."[511] Rafaela also worked initially as the building manager at the Perrier Apartments where they first lived. This enabled the couple to purchase their first home. She also ran a successful bed and breakfast. The couple were renowned for their garden. Eventually, a number of members of this extended family moved to Edmonton and Penticton, BC.

Joe Calabretta's immigration story took him to Argentina in 1949 where he joined his brother and sister.[512] He was apprenticed to a bricklayer and worked all day and attended school at night for the next seven years. Unrest dominated the political life of the country: Juan Peron was in power; the military ruled; and violence was common. Joe decided that he wanted to leave and let his friend Michaela Garcea know; Garcea had left Argentina and gone to Jasper, sponsored by his daughter, Rosina Bossio. It was Rosina, who arranged a match with her friend Francesca Mantini who worked at the Seton Hospital. Joe travelled to Jasper in 1959 and his first job involved cementing the rebar in the foundation of the lower terminal of the Whistler Tramway. He next worked at Pyramid Mountain where the CN telecommunications tower was being built. He earned $3 an hour plus overtime, which he considered good money. According to the family history, he was a great believer in overtime! Joe next got work with the Government of Canada as a stonemason. In an oral history interview, he noted that his first work was with the team renovating the old Administration Building. Joe also helped in the maintenance of the old mineral springs' pool at Miette and remembers a midnight call when the creek was flooding. He helped fill sandbags and take them to Miette to prevent water from getting into the powerplant. He observed that the sulphur in the water "could chew everything."

Joe's trade was valued in Jasper because of the many structures that reflected the Craftsman style of the early part of the twentieth century that featured large, uncut rocks and logs. His first stonework project was the viewpoint at Tangle Hill; Emilio Cesco also worked on this project and they stayed in a small heated shack nearby. The rocks were all local and were selected by Joe (he wanted to ensure that they would fit together) and taken to the site by dump truck and loader. In 1964, Joe built the boundary markers at the Sunwapta Pass between Banff and Jasper. The work crew had to construct a shack for protection from not only the weather but also bears; it was heated by a coal oil stove and propane heater. Rocks were obtained from the Medicine Lake area and from the CN Rock Mine at Henry House. Other projects included rockwork monuments at the cold sulphur springs, goat viewpoint, the Columbia Ice Fields (later demolished) and four pedestals

[511] Ron Rowson, "Key ingredient in gardening still good old TLC," in *Jasper Booster*, Wednesday, April 24, 1991.
[512] Joe Calabretta interview, Jasper Information Centre Oral History Project, March 10, 1999, Jasper-Yellowhead Museum AN 001.06.02.

with plaques in the area. Joe also built the rock foundation for the Miette Lake warden's cabin and was particularly proud of the stairway that he constructed at Mount Edith Cavell. He also completed the east and west park boundary markers and the gun tower at Marmot Basin used, in his words, "to shoot the avalanches." Shots were fired to precipitate the fall of loose snow thereby diminishing avalanche danger. Eventually, he had three apprentices working with him. Joe also did private contract work including builting a rock fireplace/barbeque at the Tekarra Lodge. Joe left behind an incredible stonework legacy.

Tony Bruni-Bossio left Grimaldi, Calabria in 1960, aged 16. He worked initially in construction in Edmonton, likely for New West Construction, before joining one of the Welch gangs in the BC interior. In 1963, he met his wife Rosina in Jasper and started work with Parks Canada. Shortly after, he got a job with CN and worked for the company for 30 years. He learned masonry and did this throughout his working life. On retirement, it became his full-time job and he was responsible for much fine rockwork in Jasper including fireplaces in homes and hotels as well as brick frontages on buildings including the Chamber of Commerce and Jasper Information Centre. He also created stone bases for a number of signs such as the Patricia Lake Bungalows, Pyramid Resort, Jasper House Bungalows, Tekarra Lodge, Alpine Village, Mt. Robson Motel, Sawridge Hotel, Mountain Park Lodges and the Catholic Church.[513]

Some Observations

The federal government's desire to generate economic growth through industrial development brought many Italian young men to Canada. They found skilled and unskilled labouring positions in cities and towns as well as the resource hinterlands of Alberta. They buckled down and, together with their wives, many of whom also worked, set out to improve the lot of their children. The postwar wave of immigration is unique not only in the sheer numbers that came to Canada and Alberta but also the speed in which the movement from working class to middle class occurred. A typical immigrant household by the 1970s and 1980s comprised a father who worked in some type of labouring or trades job, a mother who worked as a seamstress or in retail, and children who were teachers, lawyers or accountants. Immigrants who had professions in Italy, while not necessarily able to move straight into similar work, mostly ended up in "white collar" jobs. The businessmen and entrepreneurs came from both the labouring and educated classes and, through hard work and sacrifice, were able to achieve wealth perhaps beyond their wildest dreams when they left Italy.

---

[513] Information provided by son, Vince Bruni-Bossio, July 30, 2007 to the Jasper-Yellowhead Museum for an exhibit on "Masons in Jasper."

Thus, Italian immigrants as a cohort were extremely upwardly mobile. While this movement had occurred in the first decades of the twentieth century, it was not to this extent. In the earlier era, for example, multiple generations stayed in railway and mining work. While some experienced discrimination, oral history evidence reveals that very few allowed this to limit their development whether in the work place or in the community. The frequent refrain is, "it didn't happen to me but I know it happened to others." For most, discrimination was simply an obstacle to overcome in order to prosper. Many parents were delighted when their children's achievements exceeded those of their "Canadian" neighbours.

A group of Italian immigrants pictured in July 1957 in Genoa just before boarding the Cristoforo Colombo ship bound for Canada. Back row (left to right): unknown; unknown; unknown; Giovanni Giacomin; unknown; unknown; Angelo Giacomin; Valentia Da Barp; unknown; unknown; unknown. The Giacomin brothers were bound for Calgary and Angelo sponsored Valentina in 1958 and they were married in Calgary. Photo courtesy of Glenbow, Archives and Special Collections, University of Calgary NA-5590-29.

Aldo Rossetto at his work bench in Aldo's Shoe Repair shop in Medicine Hat, ca 1980. He arrived in the city in the 1950s as part of the post-war wave of immigration. Photo courtesy of Esplanade Archives 0964.0001.

Luisa Marzetti Rossi with son Domenico (born 1937) and daughter Maria (born 1935) in Villa San Leonardo, Ortona, Chieti, ca 1940. Domenico joined his Father at the age of 16 and immediately went to work. He completed high school through night school at age 26 and then attended the University of Alberta to become an engineer. Photo courtesy of Domenico Rossi.

CHAPTER VIII

Child Immigrants and the First Generation

THE POST-WAR WAVE OF IMMIGRATION comprised mostly young married men who subsequently sponsored their wives and children. There was thus a cohort of "child immigrants" who received some or all of their education in Canada. The fact that they did not speak the language, and felt different with respect to the way they dressed, the values of their parents and their life style, marked them. With their "born in Canada" siblings they grew up with a sense of "otherness" that manifested itself in a desire to conform but also to excel to prove that they were as good as everyone else. Many became over-achievers in whatever career path they chose. They became doctors, lawyers, teachers, accountants, engineers, civil servants, historians, academics, artists, politicians and some excelled in the business world. Many would make their mark as Canadian society changed in the 1970s and 1980s as a result of passage of multiculturalism legislation that legitimized being ethnic and a "hyphenated" Canadian.

Teen Immigrants

Perhaps the least fortunate were children aged 14 to 17: parental commitment to education or lack thereof affected their opportunities and career prospects. This created the not uncommon situation where within one family older children were unskilled labourers or trades people while younger siblings entered the professions. The fact that this "class" divide did not lead to jealousy is a testament to the stability of the Italian immigrant family and value placed on mutual support. The Vecchio family of Edmonton provides an example. Maria Teresa and younger children Tony, Silvano and Rita arrived in Edmonton in 1955. Tony, who was born in 1939, went to school briefly but left because he felt out of place in the classroom. He followed in his older brother Sam's footsteps and became a fitter in the welding industry. Silvano and Rita were able to complete their education and he became a medical doctor and she, a teacher. This was also true of the Mantello family of Lethbridge. Oldest son Joe became a welder while younger brother Silvio attended university and became a teacher.

Likely the most disadvantaged group was girls in their mid-teens since parental expectations were different for them. While they could enter the workforce, it was expected that they would marry and further education was a luxury that the family could not afford (or so some parents thought). Maria (Minardi) Mosca was born in 1948 in Aprigliano, Cosenza, and came to Canada with her parents in 1962. She was one of five children born to farm labourers Guglielmo Minardi and Carmela Spadafora. Her schooling in Italy ended in grade five. The family initially settled in Natal, BC, and a year later moved to Calgary where Guglielmo could find better work. Maria had to go to school because she was younger than the school leaving age of 16 but she was put into grade one and hated it. She quit school and the family did not try to dissuade her. With virtually no education and little English, she had no option but to do some type of menial work. Her first job was at Arrow Dry Cleaners where she earned 75 cents an hour. In a 1987 interview, she observed that her employers were demanding but overall fair. She stayed there for five years and quit only when she was refused a raise. This suggests that she had a sense of what was right and also what she was worth. Not everyone would have had the courage to do this. Her decision paid off and she was invited back and given a raise. She continued to work there until the business went bankrupt. Her next job was also at a drycleaners, at the Glenmore Shopping Centre. She then moved on to Cleanitizing Dry Cleaners. Until her marriage, part or all of her income went to her parents to contribute to the family's upkeep.

Maria's story is also typical with respect to the control that her parents exerted over her life. She was not allowed to date so the only way she could meet a suitable future husband was through church-going or through family or friends. Some families, even in Canada, arranged marriages. Maria was always accompanied by a chaperone, either a parent or an older brother. In 1966, at the age of 18, she married a fellow Calabrese, Carmine Mosca. The oral history interviewers noted that Maria was reluctant to be interviewed and that a pre-interview had to be done to re-assure her. This is not surprising: many immigrants from rural backgrounds and with little education were ashamed of their early circumstances. It is touching that Maria expressed very strongly that immigration was the right thing for her family and that she wished that her parents had forced her to stay in school. What is unsaid is her realization that schooling would have opened up more career options for her. Maria proudly mentioned that her oldest daughter was studying at university; thus, she and her husband were able to do for their children what her parents could not do for them. She expressed pride in their beautiful home and the material comforts the family enjoyed. Maria also observed that the older a woman was at the time of immigration, the more difficult it was for her to adjust. Her mother never adjusted to leaving Italy. Maria also noted the importance of working outside the home to aid women in the adjustment process.

There is no better example of "the passion for education" than Domenico Rossi who has written a memoir titled *The Quest for an Education*. His father, Antonio Rossi, was a farmer, who with wife Luisa Marzetti, tended a small vineyard near Villa San Leonardo, Ortona, Chieti. Antonio fought with the Italian army and was taken prisoner and interned; he did not return home until 1946. Poverty forced him to immigrate in 1951 and he was sponsored by an uncle, Donato Rossi, who worked in the mines in the Crowsnest Pass. Antonio found work in the Bellevue Mine but, due to a work shortage, moved to Fernie, in 1952, and worked in the mines at Michel. When Antonio left Italy, 14-year-old Domenico, the second-oldest child, was left to look after the land. His dream of finishing his education crumbled – the school in Villa San Leonardo went only to grade five, so he would have had to take a bus to Ortona to continue, and the family had no money for the fare. In 1953, he joined his father in Fernie where he received about three months of education from nuns in the local Catholic school. Domenico then went to work because money was needed to bring over the rest of the family. His older sister Maria arrived in 1954 and Luisa and the remaining children, Ada, Theorino (Terry) and Giselda, in 1955.

While Domenico continued to work, he did not forget his dream of continuing his education. He had a good job at the Galloway Lumber Company but there were no means to further his education. In 1956, he moved to Calgary thinking that there would be greater opportunities in a large urban centre and found work at Dominion Bridge. His father insisted that he continue to contribute to household expenses even though he had moved out. It would not be until September 1960 that Domenico would be able to begin night school classes. This was on top of full-time work. He convinced the principal, Mr. Churchill, that he had the equivalent of grade 8 (this was a lie) and the educator took a chance on him. Churchill challenged Domenico to complete Chemistry 30 and Social Studies 30 and, if he received passing grades, he would allow him to go on with Physics 30 and Math 30. Over the next three years, Domenico completed most of the required subjects but English 30 continued to trouble him. He sat the exam three times and finally passed. He studied Math 31 via correspondence and, because he needed a language, went to Edmonton to sit the exam for Italian. (At that point Edmonton had an Italian program while Calgary did not.) Domenico finished high school in January 1964, aged 26, and decided to go to university to study engineering. After completing two years at the University of Alberta, Calgary Campus, he had to move to Edmonton to finish. He obtained a Bachelor of Engineering degree in June 1968 at the age of 31.

Domenico went to work as a substation design engineer for Calgary Power in May 1968 (the company later became TransAlta). He rose through the ranks and his final position was as manager of risk management and insurance. He retired in 1993 and continued to volunteer in the Italian community. He served as president at the Calgary Italian School from 1988 to 2006 and was involved with the Abruzzese Club. He joined the board of the National Congress of Italian Canadians and, in 1988 Calgary hosted the national biennial conference. In 1994, he became the national president, the only person to hold this position who was not from either Toronto or Montreal. In 2006, the Government of Italy honoured him with the Cavaliere dell'Ordine della Stella della Solidarità Italiana.

Frank Cairo arrived in Edmonton from Celico, Cosenza, Calabria in 1955, at the age of 16, joining his father Giuseppe, who had immigrated in 1952. While other young men his age were put off by having to learn English the only means of which was entering a conventional classroom, he did not allow this to defeat him. Having studied hair dressing, he obtained a job in a salon and, three years later, at the age of 19, started his own. The salon became the "go-to" place for young Italian women but his clientele was not limited to community members. At that time, women working in offices and banks and even housewives who could afford it went in for a weekly "do." Not only was Frank an excellent stylist renowned for his skill in cutting hair, he was also an entrepreneur and, eventually, expanded the business to 11 salons (10 in Edmonton and one in Jasper). He was assisted in administration by wife Shauna Thompson. He competed internationally and won; he also created Cairo Équipe, a team of specialists who travelled to beauty shows in North America and provided on-the-spot training.

In 1975, Frank decided to focus on education and sold his salons and purchased the Edmonton and Calgary Marvel Beauty Schools, which offered training in hairstyling. He proved to be an inspired educator and was instrumental in the creation of the Alberta Association of Career Colleges and had the first school in Alberta to be accredited by the National Accrediting Commission of Career Arts and Sciences. He blended classroom instruction with practicum experience, and also provided instruction in subjects required to run a successful business. Frank expanded into the teaching of aesthetics and, in 1987, into fashion design. He also redeveloped the school infrastructure so that the buildings looked like high-end salons and spas. The old "beauty school" name was changed to Marvel College and he set up branches in Red Deer, Saskatoon, Kelowna and Winnipeg. In 2000, the business became the MC College Group, which was taken over after Frank's retirement by sons Joe and Dino. Frank has been an active volunteer in the Italian community and, in 2013, was awarded a Queen Elizabeth II Diamond Jubilee Medal.

Entering the Professions

By far the largest number of young Italians of this generation became teachers. In 1965, Rita Vecchio (later Cavaliere) with Tony Caria and Tony Falcone, who came from Italy as young men, were the first teachers of Italian descent hired by the Edmonton Catholic School Board. Others, who either came as young children or were born in Canada included Dolores Antonello, Adeline (Piazza) Cairo, Joe Feula, Joe Petrone, E. R. (Rudy) Cavaliere, Reny Clericuzio, Pasqualino Gatto, Giancarlo (Charles) Grelli, Carmela Marino, Josephine (Clericuzio) Parrotta, Nick Parrotta, Silvio Pino, Liliana (Varsallona) Potestio, Carmelo Rago, Flora (Ricioppo) Rizzuto, Mario Rizzuto, Gigliola (Mazzotta) Russo, Joe Russo, Vincenzo Russo, George Santarossa, Frank Sdao, Savino Solinas, Dominic Spatafora, Sandra Talarico, Theresa (Sdao) Wasylenko and Maria Teresa (Vecchio) Romano.[514] Many siblings and/or cousins went into education and some teachers married teachers. Most worked in the Catholic system and some also taught at the Dante Alighieri School. Antonella Ciancibello was a teacher and principal at the School and has also taught Italian for the Faculty of Extension at the University of Alberta.

Rudy Cavaliere, a math and science specialist, was one of the first teachers in Edmonton to embrace computers in education.[515] St. Mark's School purchased an Atari computer and Rudy re-wrote the program so that student records could be entered. From 1983 to 1985, he was the first Computer Literacy Facilitator with the Edmonton Catholic School District. This involved visits to elementary schools to introduce personal computers. The District next purchased 10 Apple II computers, which he took to schools to do training. With Eugene Kozak, the district's Computer Consultant, he also did in-service for teachers. As computers became more user-friendly, his work became easier. This knowledge and experience became useful for the *Il Congresso* newspaper, which he co-founded, and Rudy used Aldus Pagemaker, beginning in 1985, to do page layout on a Mac computer. He co-founded the National Congress of Italian Canadians, Edmonton District; the Junior Appennini Dancers; and a range of other organizations. He served on the building committee of the Santa Maria Goretti Community Centre and as president, as well as doing a range of work for the parish. Rudy was also the "go to" guy when any club needed a program or brochure designed. He received the Queen Elizabeth II Silver Jubilee Medal for his volunteer activities.

Calgary also had a number of young Italians entering the teaching profession including Serafino Scarpino, Nick Borelli, Aldo Barbuto, Bruno Arena, Joseph and Tony Audia, Milvia Marzetti and Kathy (Iafolla) Harradance. Scarpino arrived in Calgary with his mother and siblings in 1962 at the age of 14. He completed secondary education and then enrolled at the University of Calgary in the Faculty of Education. He had wanted to be a teacher, specifically, a math teacher, from the age of eight and also loved languages. (He started to study French in Italy.) In 1972, he obtained a B Ed degree from the University of Calgary in French and Psychology and, in 1981, an M Ed with specialties in curriculum and administration from Gonzaga University

514 Thanks are owed to Rudy Cavaliere for his help in identifying teachers.
515 Telephone interview with Rudy Cavaliere conducted by the author, January 19, 2018.

in Spokane, Washington. He began his teaching career at two Calgary elementary/junior high schools: St. Margaret and St. Alphonsus. Serafino taught at the former in the morning and the latter in the afternoon. He accepted a permanent post at St. Margaret's the following year and taught there for eight years. In 1973-1974, he was involved in setting up the Italian Language School and drafted the curriculum. In 1981, with Alberto Romano and others, Serafino worked on the curriculum for the high school teaching of Italian in the Calgary Catholic system and, later, at the elementary and junior high levels. Serafino also supported Italian studies at the University of Calgary.

Having retired from teaching in 2003 (his last job was heading the modern languages department at St. Francis High School and serving as vice principal), he ran for the position of Trustee with the Calgary Separate School Board. He was successful and served four terms including as chair. He was the board's representative on the Alberta School Board Association and chaired two task forces on governance and infrastructure. He also served as vice president of the Alberta Catholic Schools Trustee Association for four years. When he stood for re-election as a trustee in 2013, he noted: "Alberta has one of the best education systems in the world, we have been rated in the top 10 systems in the world for a good number of years, however, there are always pressing issues that must be addressed. Our biggest challenge at the moment is addressing our fast growth and infrastructure needs. Alberta's economy continues to be strong; therefore, people from other countries and provinces continue to arrive in our city in good numbers. We must ensure that we are well prepared to meet this challenge."[516] From personal experience, he knew the special needs of child immigrants in particular those from war-torn countries. Serafino was an active volunteer and was involved with the Calgary Italian Sportsmen's Dinner, serving as president of the organization for 20 years. He also served on the Alberta Cultural Heritage Council and the board of the National Congress of Italian Canadians (he was vice president Western Region). He was awarded an Alberta Achievement Award for volunteerism.

Silvio Mantello's immigration journey ended in Sparwood, BC, in 1957, when he was 10. His father was working in the mines when he, his mother and sister arrived. Silvio received his education in BC and, in 1965, went to the newly-established University of Lethbridge and obtained a BA degree with a history major and, subsequently, a B Ed. He began teaching for the Lethbridge School District in 1971 and remained there until retirement in 2006. Silvio's focus remained on elementary education with specialties in social studies, French and special education. His passion for history led him to volunteer at the Galt Museum. He was fascinated by his

516 Lorraine Hjalte, "Serafino Scarpino – Candidate for Calgary Catholic School District in Wards 1, 2 and Cochrane," *Calgary Herald*, October 15, 2013.

family's immigration experience, and has written biographical and creative non-fiction accounts. The last chapter of a semi-autobiographical novel about his last year in Grimaldi received second prize in a 2017 writing contest established by the Alberta Retired Teachers Association. It was published in their magazine.

Barbara (Mazzuca) Brown was born in Lethbridge where her parents, John and Linda, were prominent members of the post-war Italian community. She obtained a B Ed from the University of Lethbridge (1991) with a major in mathematics and minor in physical sciences and, then, an M Ed from the University of Alberta (2000) specializing in secondary education. Barbara taught for the Edmonton Catholic School Board for 10 years. Her husband was transferred to Calgary and she taught at the junior and senior high level and also served as the first educational technology supervisor for the Calgary Catholic School District. Her doctorate at the University of Calgary, completed in 2013, focused on leadership, technology and educational change. She is director of professional graduate programs in education and director of research and innovation for the Galileo Educational Network in the Werklund School of Education, University of Calgary.

Other child immigrants and members of the first generation became lawyers and accountants. Among the former were Joseph O. Segatto, who was called to the Alberta Bar, in 1978. He has spent most of his career with the Alberta Department of Justice and the Office of the Solicitor General in Edmonton. Anthony (Tony) Cairo qualified for the Alberta Bar and, sadly, died in 2005, at the age of 58. Salvatore (Sam) Amelio focused on business law and was appointed Queen's Counsel. Terry Antonello, who was called to the Alberta Bar in 1983, specialized in Aboriginal, banking and commercial lending, corporate, real estate and Italian law. He provided legal advice to the Italian consulate and was recognized with a knighthood.

Rosanna Saccomani was admitted to the Alberta bar in 1984 and specialized in corporate-commercial litigation, fatal accident law, medical malpractice, general insurance law, employment, and family and criminal law. In May 7, 2014, she was appointed a judge of the Edmonton Region Provincial Court. She is the recipient of a number of awards including the Queen Elizabeth II Diamond Jubilee Medal, the Alberta Civil Trial Lawyers Association President's Award and the Kevin Carr Neuman Theological Award. She co-founded the Kids Kottage Foundation, a crisis nursery for the prevention of child abuse and neglect, and has served on the boards of various charitable organizations.

A number of young Italians in Calgary entered the legal profession including Domenic Venturo, Joe Amantea, Andrea Riccio, Alec Silenzi and Sam Durante. Silenzi continued his father Sandro's involvement in the petroleum industry but not as a geologist. He obtained a BA from the University of Calgary in 1990 and an LL B degree from the University of Alberta in 1994. He is a domestic and international business law specialist and has worked in the oil and gas sectors (both within legal practices and directly for energy companies) throughout his career. His work has involved him in a range of international jurisdictions.

Prominent accountants in Edmonton have included Agostino (Augie) Annichiarico, Tony Scozzafava and Peter Bruno. Augie received a B Com degree from the University of Alberta (1968) and was admitted to membership in the Institute of Chartered Accountants of Alberta in 1970. He has served with a number of national accounting firms and, in 1977 was a founding partner at Yaremchuk & Annicchiarico LLP. He has volunteered extensively both within the Italian community and the community at large. In 1982, he helped to raise over $400,000 for Italian earthquake relief. This was donated to the Red Cross and he assisted them to generate tax receipts. He subsequently served on the Board.

Tony Scozzafava received a B Com degree with distinction from the University of Alberta and received a CA designation. He worked at Enbridge and KPMG and then joined EPCOR where he was part of the team that, in 2009, spun-off the Capital Power Corporation. Tony served as Vice President of Taxation and Treasury as well as CFO for Capital Power Income LP, a publicly-traded income fund sponsored by the company. Tony rejoined EPCOR in 2018 and serves as Senior Vice President and CFO. He is a member of the board of Wellspring, a non-profit that offers non-medical services to cancer victims and their families.

Peter Bruno obtained a Diploma in Business Administration with a major in accounting from NAIT in 1984 and also completed courses at the Institute of Management Studies. He obtained work with H & R Block Canada and steadily rose through the ranks serving as Chief Operating Officer from 2013-2017. In July 2017, he became president and is responsible for overseeing growing revenues and market share. He has been Treasurer of the National Congress of Italian-Canadians for many years and instrumental in the success of the Italian Pavilion at Heritage Days.

Brothers Angelo and Luciano Scarpino graduated in chemical engineering from the University of Calgary and found work in the oil patch. Angelo has served in management at Dome Petroleum and International CH2M Hill, a global engineering company. Son David, also a chemical engineer, works for Nexen. Luciano has worked at Pan Canadian and Cenovus Energy where his responsibilities included management of operations in Saskatchewan. He was to retire in 2017 but Cenovus asked him to stay on to assist in selling assets to pay down debts. In September 2017, Cenovus released information of the sale of its Pelican Lake assets; and, in October, of Palliser crude oil and natural gas assets in southeastern Alberta to Torxen Energy and Schlumberger for $1.3 billion. The third sale was of Cenovus's Weyburn, Saskatchewan carbon-dioxide enhanced oil-recovery operation for cash proceeds of $940 million in 2017.

Several individuals have reflected and written about Alberta's history. John G. Fainella was born in Antrodoco, Rieti and settled in Calgary where he obtained his first degree. In 1975, he published a booklet titled *Cultural background and Italian settlement in Calgary* and, in 1984, his essay "The Development of Italian Organizations in Calgary," was published in *Alberta History*.[517] He moved to Montreal to pursue a sociology degree based on studies of the Molisani in Italy and Canada. He has authored a number of fiction and non-fiction works.

Antonella Fanella, a University of Calgary graduate, described her fascination with Italian immigration history in the Preface to her book *With Heart and Soul: Calgary's Italian Community*: "For me, it means wanting to understand and appreciate our heritage, our community and our sense of tradition. That desire was first manifested in a university class on ethnic groups in Alberta. Annoyed that the Italians were left out of the mosaic, I chose to rectify the situation by persuading the professor to include the Italians in a research project on the history of ethnic groups in Southern Alberta."[518] Her Masters' thesis was the basis of her book, which was published in 1999. Antonella has worked in the Glenbow Archives and has undertaken a range of writing projects including a history of the Calgary YWCA.

The author, Adriana (Albi) Davies, completed BA and MA degrees at the University of Alberta and, then, a PhD at the University of London, England, in 1971. In 1980, she was appointed Science Editor of Mel Hurtig's *The Canadian Encyclopedia*, which was published in 1985. Volunteer work for the Italians Settle in Edmonton historical project, in 1983, ignited her interest in Italian settlement history and, in 2002, she created the *Celebrating Alberta's Italian Community* website as part of the Alberta Online Encyclopedia, which she established and edited as Executive Director of the Heritage Community Foundation. It was the first comprehensive multimedia website to deal with an ethnocultural community and included clips from oral histories. She explored the Prohibition history of Alberta and BC in an exhibit and accompanying book titled *The Rise and Fall of Emilio Picariello*. She has published historical and biographical works and was recognized by investiture in the Order of Canada and an Italian knighthood.

A number of immigrant children became authors and some combined this with academic work. Caterina Edwards was born in Earls Barton, England to a Welsh father and Italian mother. The family immigrated to Calgary in the mid-1950s. In 1968, Caterina enrolled at the University of Alberta to undertake a BA degree. In 1973, she completed an MA in creative writing and has taught at Grant MacEwan Community College (now MacEwan University), the University of Alberta and Athabasca University. She served as writer-in-residence at MacEwan and the University of Alberta. Caterina has written short stories, novellas, novels and a play that draw on her

[517] Fainella, "The Development of Italian Organizations in Calgary," in *Alberta History*, vol. 32, Winter 1984, 20-26
[518] Fanella, *With Heart and Soul*, x.

experiences of being an Italian-Canadian. Publication of her first novel, *The Lion's Mouth*, in 1982, made her the first Italian-Canadian woman writer in western Canada. *Finding Rosa*, published in 2009, was awarded the Wilfred Eggleston Award for Nonfiction (Writers Guild of Alberta) and, in 2010, the Bressani Prize for Writing about Immigration. The book deals with her mother's decline as a result of the onset of Alzheimer's and Caterina's journey (physical and intellectual) to understand her mother's and her own roots.

Giuseppe (Joe) Pivato was born in Tezze sul Brenta, near Venice, and grew up in Toronto. He moved to Edmonton in 1970 to begin work on an MA degree in comparative literature at the University of Alberta. After completing this, in 1971, he pursued doctoral studies and obtained a Ph D in 1977. He began teaching at Athabasca University, the newly-established distance learning centre in northern Alberta. In 1984, he was a Research Fellow in the Ethnic and Immigration Studies Program at the University of Toronto. In 1985, *Contrasts: Comparative Essays on Italian-Canadian Writing* was published. This subject became core to his academic studies and teaching. In 1986, he was a founder of the Association of Italian-Canadian Writers. In 1998, his book *Italian-Canadian Writing* showcased 53 authors writing in English, French and Italian. Pivato has published a number of works of criticism and is also a published poet.

Giuseppe Albi arrived in Edmonton at the age of five in 1951. He attended the Alberta College of Art in Calgary from 1966-1968 and, then, l'École des beaux-arts in Montreal in 1968-1969. In 1970, he moved to Europe and continued informal art studies and was a practising artist in London and Amsterdam. In 1971, he had an exhibit in the Galerie de Sfinx, Amsterdam and, in 1973, in the KES Mosaics Gallery in Edinburgh. Giuseppe returned to Canada in 1974 and, while continuing to have a studio, worked in exhibit design and event development for Northlands. He next became the Manager of Events Edmonton responsible for the Taste of Edmonton and First Night festivals. His work is abstract and he is an innovator in the use of acrylics. He has exhibited in both public and commercial galleries and highlights include the exhibit "Aspects of Contemporary Art in Alberta" at Glenbow in Calgary (1987); the Alberta Biennial of Contemporary Art at the Edmonton Art Gallery and Nickle Arts Museum in Calgary (2002); and a special exhibit at the Istituto Italiano di Cultura in Vancouver (2008). In 2006, Giuseppe was awarded a commission by the National Congress of Italian Canadians, Edmonton District to create a commemorative sculpture as a gift to the people of Alberta on the Province's centenary. In 2007, the stone neo-classical column on a concrete base overlaid with bronze casts of labourers' tools was set in place at the Legislature grounds in Edmonton. Giuseppe was a co-founder of the Latitude 53 Society of Artists in Edmonton and has served on various boards including the Alberta Foundation for the Arts and Harcourt House Arts Centre as well as the City of Edmonton Design Committee. His works are in both public and private collections.

Running for Political Office

In the 1980s, Alberta's Italian communities focused on electing community members to political office at the three levels of government. Candidates included immigrants who had come as young men or children of immigrants. Tony Falcone ran as a Progressive Conservative against Ray Martin in provincial elections in 1982 and was narrowly defeated (Martin obtained 4,855 votes and Falcone 4,778). The same year, Al Iafolla ran for the Liberals federally in the riding of Edmonton-East and was defeated though he obtained about 6,000 votes. Things got complicated when Falcone and Iafolla ran against each other in provincial elections in 1986 in Edmonton-Calder, a working class neighbourhood with a large Italian population. They split the Italian vote and both lost.

Danny Dalla-Longa broke down barriers against Italian candidates when he was elected to the Alberta Legislature in 1993. His father, Reno Dalla-Longa, was born in San Vito, Treviso in 1927 and immigrated to Medicine Hat. Fiancée Giovanna joined him, in 1952, and they were married; the couple had three children. Danny grew up in The Hat and obtained a B Ed degree from the University of Calgary. He ran as a Liberal in the riding of Calgary-West and his victory was a major upset since the riding was previously held by Premier Peter Lougheed. He served only one term and returned to his career in finance. He has served as CEO, president and chair of Luca Capital Inc., which he co-founded with Al J. Kroontje in 2005. He has also worked for i3 Capital Partners Inc., a Calgary-based merchant bank serving the energy and technology sectors.

Four individuals have served as city aldermen: Joe Mauro in Lethbridge; Roberto Noce and Tony Caterina in Edmonton: and Joe Ceci in Calgary. Mauro, the son of Silvio and Rosina Mauro, attended the University of Lethbridge and obtained a BA degree with a major in Sociology. He served as a long-time city of Lethbridge alderman. Joe was extremely popular with constituents and, in the 2001 election, received the highest number of votes cast for an aldermanic candidate – 15,330 (66.3 percent of the total votes cast). He ran for mayor in 2004 and 2017 and was unsuccessful.

Noce obtained an LL B degree from the University of Alberta in 1991 and joined the Alberta Bar in 1992. He ran for City Council in 1995 and, at the end of the term in 2001, decided to throw his hat in the mayoral ring. Many voters were deterred by his youth and he was defeated by pro-business incumbent Bill Smith, a former Edmonton Eskimo football player and businessman. Roberto ran again in 2004 and some critics including Councillor Stephen Mandel, who went on to defeat him, faulted Noce for his youth. Mandel, a successful developer, saw this as an obstacle in the complex negotiations with the public and private sectors that the mayor was involved in. Roberto returned to the practice of law with a focus on municipal law, real estate development, condominium, and corporate/commercial matters. Noce is an occasional columnist with the

Edmonton Journal and *Calgary Herald* on condominium matters. He was appointed Queen's Counsel in 2007 and is the recipient of a Queen Elizabeth II Diamond Jubilee Medal.

Tony Caterina was born in Montagano, Campobasso, Italy and immigrated with his family arriving in Edmonton in 1962, when he was six years old. He attended the University of Alberta and switched from Education to an Art History program. In 1974, he started several clothing businesses and, subsequently, an industrial pipe insulation company. His interest in politics arose out of his service on the board of the Alberta Avenue Business Association. Tony ran for Edmonton City Council in 2004 in Ward 3 but did not succeed. In the same year, he ran in Edmonton-Centre for a seat in the Legislative Assembly of Alberta and was also unsuccessful. He ran again for Edmonton City Council in 2007 in Ward 6 and was elected. He championed keeping the Edmonton Municipal Airport open which was unpopular since it would have meant closure of the International Airport. He was re-elected in 2010 and 2013. In 2015, he ran provincially for the Progressive Conservative Party in the riding of Beverly-Clareview but was defeated. He retained his seat on City Council.

The individual who, next to Mike Maccagno, has held the highest political office is Joe Ceci. Maccagno ran for the Liberals and was elected to the Alberta Legislature and, in 1968, became Leader of the Opposition. Ceci, who ran on behalf of the NDP, was elected in the constituency of Calgary-Fort, in May 2015. Premier Rachel Notley appointed him President of Treasury Board. Ceci has a Bachelor of Social Work from the University of Western Ontario and a Master of Social Work from the University of Calgary. From 1981 to 1987, he worked as a social worker with the City and also served as the public policy manager of a Calgary charity. For 15 years, he served on Calgary City Council. Joe has a long history in the charitable sector and has served on the boards of the Calgary Folk Festival Society, Habitat for Humanity and the Calgary Bridge Foundation for Youth. He is the recipient of a lifetime achievement award for advocacy from the Family and Community Support Services Association, a Queen's Diamond Jubilee medal and an Alberta Centennial Medal.

Retailers and Entrepreneurs

A number of Italian-Canadian children have taken over family businesses and excelled. Carlo Facchin went to work for his father, Vittorio, at Roma Pasta and when his father sold the business in 1987, he was employed by the new owners, Primo Foods, a division of Nabisco Ltd. Canada. He became convinced that selling was not the right move and, in 1996, he partnered with some farmers from Altona, Manitoba, and bought the plant back. They renamed the company Prairie

Harvest Canada Ltd. and, because of the high cost of building a new plant in Manitoba, chose to stay in Edmonton. At the time there were five dry-pasta plants in Canada and Prairie Harvest was the smallest. To improve their chances of success, the partners established a market niche – organic pasta made using the best Durum semolina flour. In a 2000 interview, Carlo mentioned that the six new types of organic pasta they had introduced comprised only about a quarter of their production but that he expected it to increase.[519] The company chose not to sell in eastern Canada because of the competition with existing brands such as Primo and Catelli. Noting the emergence of the "gluten-free" market, Prairie Harvest moved into this creating not only pasta but also a line of sauces. The San Zenone brand includes the company's organic corn and rice pasta lines. In 2016, the company won the Canadian Grand Prix Award in the "shelf stable prepared foods and entrees category" for their new line of organic coconut blend pasta.[520]

Teresa Spinelli inherited her father Frank's entrepreneurial skills. She was born in Edmonton in 1961 and graduated with a degree in psychology from the University of Alberta.[521] She grew up playing among the grocery aisles and learned the business from the ground up. In 1983, on completing her studies, she began work with her father in the area of administration. She found that she loved the work and abandoned her dream of becoming a social worker. Her younger brother Pietro was intended to take over the family business but his untimely death at the age of 32 in 1996 meant that Teresa became the heir. Her father's death of cancer in 2000 made her president. She has told journalists that she had "big shoes to fill" and that she experienced some "pushback" as to whether she could continue to run the business not only from staff who thought that it was not a woman's role but also from the larger community. Some employees left the company.

She began a series of expansions including two more stores in Edmonton and one in Calgary, and also grew the wholesale empire. She introduced higher wages and better benefits and also a profit-sharing scheme with staff (some had worked in the store for over 30 years). She is quick to admit that, without loyal staff, neither she nor her father could have built the business. The staff numbers have grown from 30 to over 500; the core comprising individuals of Italian descent (mostly in managerial positions) with floor and wholesale staff from a range of ethnicities. Sales have climbed from $8 million in 2000 to over $65 million in 2017.[522] Teresa also expanded

[519] Sean Pratt, "Little Pasta Plant on the Prairies," *The Western Producer*, May 1, 2000.

[520] Prairie Harvest website, *Prairie Harvest News*, May, 2016.

[521] Rina and Teresa Spinelli interview, Celebrating Alberta's Italian Community Oral History Project, 2002, Heritage Community Foundation Fonds, University of Alberta Archives.

[522] See Alex Migdal, "Employees Share in Successes at Italian Centre Shop," in *Edmonton Journal*, January 17, 2017.

the range of merchandise to cater to shoppers with ethnicities beyond Western Europe. In an interview at the second annual Women and Wealth conference in Edmonton in 2017, she noted that women have come a long way in business but they need to go further. She observed that at business gatherings that she attends with her husband Mike Newberry, others think he is the business owner. *Profit* magazine has repeatedly named her one of Canada's Top Women Entrepreneurs. She has continued her father's work in community building including involvement in festivals in Giovanni Caboto Park as well as committees dedicated to improving conditions in the Boyle-McCauley inner-city neighbourhoods that include Edmonton's Chinatown and Little Italy. Teresa is a recipient of the Queen's Diamond Jubilee Medal, Global Woman of Vision Award and University of Alberta Alumni Award. In 2018, she was appointed the Dr. Charles Allard Chair in Business at MacEwan University recognizing business excellence.

Louis and David Bontorin as children played hide-and-seek among the flour sacks in their parents' Calgary Italian Bakery. They started work filling bags with a dozen buns and received 25 cents an hour. While David studied in the Faculty of Science at the University of Calgary intending to become a doctor, he was drawn into the family business in 1988 when Luigi was treated for cancer. Louis and David took over the business. By 2006 when Calgary's economy was booming, the company had difficulty finding workers. David flew to the Philippines to interview potential staff and they brought in 36 workers. The next year, 15 more were hired. At a time when other employers were exploiting foreign workers, the Bontorins welcomed them and provided a furnished apartment at a low rent. They helped them establish bank accounts and sponsored them for citizenship. In the first 45 years of the bakery's existence, Italian recipes were not used: Luigi had tried in the 1960s but there was no interest. In mid-2010, the Bontorins introduced "heritage" products to reflect the emerging public interest in the baking traditions of people of different cultures. While Louis and David's children have worked at the bakery, the brothers, as yet, do not know whether the business will survive to a third generation. What they do know is that they have outsurvived all of their competitors. In 2013, the Bontorins donated $50,000 to the Tom Baker Cancer Centre.

Carmelo Rago trained as a teacher but made his mark in Edmonton as a restaurant entrepreneur. His father, Pasquale Rago, owned a flour mill in Zungoli, Avellino, Italy, before immigrating to Ontario in 1953. The elder Rago did not have his family join him until 1961. Carmelo, who was 11 at the time, finished his studies and went on to Eastern Illinois University in Charleston on a soccer scholarship and completed an education degree. He came to Edmonton to teach and married Stella, daughter of Maurizio and Maria Saccomanno. Carmelo tells the story that he, his uncle and father-in-law went to a pizza restaurant in Castledowns in 1979, and found that the owner was ceasing operations. Carmelo and Maurizio felt this was an omen and decided to purchase it and name it Sorrentino. While Maurizio had successfully operated a restaurant with his brother Frank, Carmelo had no business experience. He observed: "When I got involved I became so obsessed. I spent all my time in the restaurant, which resulted [*sic.*] at the price of my family. Yet I needed that passion, otherwise I would have no chance in making it. It gave me a chance to get involved with people, talk to my guests and learn the business. In the end, my lack of knowledge worked for me because it forced me to talk directly to the guests, suppliers and staff."[523]

Maurizio died tragically in 1991 in a car accident and did not live to see the success of the Sorrentino Restaurant Group expansion into multiple restaurants, cooking classes and catering. This has involved Stella and Carmelo's sons – Maurizio, Carmelo Jr., Pasquale and Antonio – as well as other family members. In the early 1990s, the Ragos started a Garlic Festival that continues to the present day; not only starters and main courses but also deserts include the locally-grown herb. Stella established Sorrentino's Compassion House Foundation in 1998 to build a facility to support northern Alberta women suffering from breast cancer. The house quickly exceeded capacity and, in 2010, a fundraising campaign was launched. Over $5 million was raised and, in 2012, construction began on an extension. The enhanced facility re-opened in September 2013. Events such as the Garlic Festival and an annual fashion show support Compassion House. The Rago family also supports prostate research, the Lois Hole Hospital and NAIT's Culinary Institute.

Paolo Mancuso continued Mancuso Carpet and Upholstery Cleaning Services started by his father Greg in Red Deer. He began helping his father at the age of six but did not see himself following in his father's footsteps. After completing high school, he worked for a number of years in the family business. In 1986, he enrolled at the University of Alberta and completed a B Ed degree with majors in home economics and fine arts. He taught for two years but saw that with his specializations it would be difficult to find permanent work. It was at this time that his father announced that he wanted to reduce his workload, and Paolo stepped in to help. His knowledge of textiles helped him to understand the science behind cleaning and he became fascinated by the business. In 1992, he took over from his father and introduced industry standards that he helped to formulate. Paolo assisted Alberta Advanced Education and Career Development in creating the occupational profile for carpet and upholstery cleaning in Alberta. Paolo was awarded the Better Business Bureau of Central and Northern Alberta's Torch Award for Ethics in 2000.[524]

---

[523] Nerissa McNaugton, "Sorrentino Restaurant Group," company website, URL: https://www.sorrentinos.com/about-us/ , retrieved September 13, 2017.
[524] Harley Richards, "Textile Cleaning from the floor up," *Red Deer Advocate*, November 2, 2004.

Builders and Developers

Child immigrants have also excelled in the construction industry. Tom Mauro of Albi Homes in Calgary was born in Albi, Italy and attended the Southern Alberta Institute of Technology. He graduated in 1978 and immediately set up as a contractor but the timing was not great because the drop in the price of the barrel resulted in a recession.[525] He persevered and, in 1982, with wife Debra, started Albi Homes, a quality home building business. The company prospered and supports the School of Construction at SAIT as well as employing their graduates. In 2015, Brookfield Residential Alberta acquired the company.

Aldo and Tony Laratta took their parents' business, Laratta Homes, to the next level. Aldo received a BA from the University of Calgary and joined the company in 1987; brother Tony, a successful realtor, joined in 1994. On their father's retirement, Aldo became president and Tony vice-president. In a 2009 interview, Aldo observed: "I had been accepted into law school in Eastern Canada, but decided to stay and help with the family business. We built our first really high-end house in McKenzie Lake in 1991. It won numerous SAMs (Sales and Marketing awards from the Canadian Home Builders' Association – Calgary Region) and was a springboard for us into the high end. The customer was so pleased with the quality of workmanship that we probably got to high-end referrals from that."[526]

They have built custom homes in a number of Calgary subdivisions including Elbow Valley, Stonepine, Grandview Park, Priddis, Heritage Point, Church Ranches, Mount Royal, Roxboro, Altadore and Britannia. In 2016, Laratta became one of the preferred builders in the Slopes of Sylvan Lake development near Red Deer.[527] The company's homes are in the $2 to $4 million range and in a 2010 interview, Aldo observed: "People who traditionally buy in the high end are recession proof. They are not employment dependent for their wealth and don't have to worry about interest rates and the economy. It's always been like this – a percentage of people who are very fortunate."[528] To celebrate its thirtieth anniversary in 2009, the company chose to use monies earmarked for a celebration to support organizations doing research on breast cancer and Alzheimer's. They also support the Mustard Seed Ministry working in Calgary's inner city and Habitat for Humanity.

---

[525] Colleen Lavender, "How to Build an Empire, one satisfied homeowner at a time," in *SAIT ALUMNI LINK*, Winter 2010, 10-13.

[526] *Ibid.*

[527] Marty Hope, "Slopes of Sylvan Lake: tranquil setting with natural beauty," *Calgary Herald*, June 24, 2016.

[528] Kathy McCormick, "High-end homes 'recession-proof': Calgarians with the big bucks are buying million-dollar houses," *Calgary Herald*, December 11, 2010.

Nick Matera, in 1983, established M.A.P. Water & Sewer Services Ltd. in Edmonton and later added two other divisions, M.A.P. Earthworks Ltd. and Williamson Equipment. The companies have over 500 employees. Mario Pagnotta worked for Forest Construction for 20 years before turning to concrete work. In 1992, he set up Edmonton-based Pagnotta Industries focused on formwork and concrete towers. They are part of the building boom resulting from city infrastructure projects and revitalization of Edmonton's downtown.

George Cantalini obtained a business degree in 1984 from Sir Wilfred Laurier University. He started work with Toronto development company Tridel in investor relations; the company was founded in 1927 by Italian stonemason, Jack Del Zotto, who started to build homes. Today the company is among the largest builders of condominiums in the Toronto area. Cantalini rose through the ranks and was sent to Edmonton in 1991 to head up the western division, Beaverbrook Developments. With the economic downturn of 1997, Tridel wanted to leave Edmonton and Cantalini, wife Teresa and some local Italian-Canadian investors purchased the company's land holdings.[529] Beginning with development of 100 lots, by peak year 2014, the number had increased to 1,000. The company also expanded beyond Edmonton to Spruce Grove. More recently, the company has begun to do infill housing. In 2017, Beaverbrook began work on the West Block on Stony Plain Road and 142 Street, a major development including offices, retail, and residential and seniors housing.

Adrian Bussoli took the New Hatchwear Uniform Company, purchased in 1971 by Pete and Ida Fornaro and continued by their son Victor, to the next level. Adrian was born in Fossacesia, Chieti, in 1952, and arrived in Calgary with parents Francesco and Luisa the following year. He completed a BA with a major in political science at the University of Alberta in 1974. He noted in a 1988 interview that his parents stressed the importance of education throughout his growing up; his father worked for the City of Calgary and the Catholic School Board until his retirement. Adrian's first employment was with Canada Manpower as a supervisor of industrial training programs. He then became Director of Student Finance in charge of student loans for southern Alberta. In 1981, he decided to move into the private sector and joined New Hatchwear as the sales and marketing manager. In 1988, he became the co-owner and took over the company when Victor Fornaro retired. He created Alberta Garment Manufacturing specializing in flame resistant, safety clothing and other workwear.

While other garment manufacturers in Alberta suffered from international competition, Bussoli with the assistance of partners Mohamed Pakir and son Michael Bussoli, beginning in

[529] Anon., "Beaverbrook Developments," *The Canadian Business Journal*, November 2017, vol 10, issue 11.

2012, orchestrated major changes that would result in growth and new markets.[530] He approached Western Economic Diversification for support in creating the Alberta Apparel Innovation Centre and Olds College was brought onboard as the educational partner. The partners operated the Fashion Institute in Calgary at Bow Valley College. In 2014, WED approved $2.9 million to support the purchase of new equipment for the Apparel Centre, which is located in Alberta Garment's plant. The chosen research focus for the centre was innovation in cold climate clothing, which makes sense in Alberta where much industrial activity occurs outdoors. The focus is on fabric research, testing, product development and training for students in the apparel industry.

Domenico (Dom) and Rino Mancuso began work in their parents' construction business in Red Deer and became shareholders in their teens. The company was started in 1968 and undertook small residential concrete projects and grew to be a leading construction company in the region including undertaking oil industry activity. The company was rebranded in 1990 as PMCL. Under the brothers' leadership, the company took on ever-larger projects not only in Alberta but also in BC and Saskatchewan. The Northland Construction Supply stores, established by their parents to serve the do-it-yourself market, were expanded by the brothers to Edmonton (1989), Calgary (1992), Fort McMurray (1997) and Lethbridge (2012). Dom has served as the president of the Red Deer Chamber of Commerce and on the executive of the Alberta Chamber of Commerce. The family set up two $1,000-scholarships at the Red Deer College: the Pasquale Mancuso Family Scholarship for Leadership Excellence in Carpentry and the Pasquale Mancuso Family Athletic Excellence Award.

David and Randy Dal Molin were born in Medicine Hat and are graduates in computing science from the University of Calgary; David, in 1984 and, Randy, in 1990. David has been president of Venture Software Corp. since 1992 and, since 2009, senior director of application development at ComplyWorks Ltd., Calgary. Randy has worked as a software engineering manager for Dynalco in Fort Lauderdale, Florida, and as a project manager for Hoerbiger, an international leader in the fields of compression drive technologies and hydraulics. Their sister, Linda, and her husband Colin Kryski set up Potti Corp, a Calgary-based personal hygiene and waste containment company in 2001 He serves as president and she as VP Sales.

---

[530] See David Parker, "Alberta Garment Tests Clothing for Extreme Weather Conditions," *Calgary Herald*, January 15, 2016.

Some Observations

While many of the teen and younger child immigrants experienced some difficulties in both their educational and work lives, their achievements exceeded their parents' wildest dreams. Few took on or remained in labouring jobs. Most used their education to enter the professions and the middle class. Many have left their mark not only on their chosen career paths but also in contributing to Italian community organizations. Those in "life style" occupations such as restaurants and shops have been purveyors of the idea of what it is to be Italian as something that is life enhancing. Academics and artists have explored the immigration experience not only as it has shaped them but also the larger community. The post-war wave of immigration resulted in a "golden age" for Alberta's Italian community.

Alessandra Albi with son Raffaele, daughter-in-law Estera and grand-daughters Adriana (left) and Rosa in Grimaldi, Cosenza, Calabria, ca 1945. Raffaelle arrived in Edmonton in 1949 and was joined by his wife and children in 1951. Photo courtesy of Albi Family.

Members of the Vecchio family from Grimaldi, Cosenza, Calabria. Front row: children Antonio, Rita and Silvano; back row: Aunt Giuseppina and Uncle Raffaele Vecchio, Maria Teresa (mother), and older children Vittoria and Fiore. Photo courtesy of Rita and Rudy Cavaliere.

Italian ladies' society in Blairmore, Alberta, July 1, 1929. The men's fraternal societies promoted creation of the women's lodges and the Fernie Loggia Speranza d'Italia was likely the first. Front row (l-r): S. De Marin, C. Rinaldi, A. De Cecco, A. Catellano, I. Toppano, M. Montalbetti, M. Salvador, I Fontana, F. Rizzo and G. Alampi; second row (l-r): L. Scquarella, R. Milo, D. Orlando, C. De Cecco, M. Venera, L. De Cecco, R. Scarrella, A. Benedetto; D. Zolli and M. Zolli; third row (l-r): A. Curcio, G. Celli, C. D'Appolonia, B. Benedetto, I. Macchi, B. Aschacer, D. De Cecco, I. Bovio and A. Rossie; fourth row (l-r): F. Oliva, C. Nastasi, M. Comisso, E. Nastasi, M. Pelle, A. Iorio, M. Serra and M. Stella. Photographer: Thomas Gushul. Photo courtesy of Glenbow, Archives and Special Collections, University of Calgary NA-3903-88.

CHAPTER IX

Organizations and Institutions

WHILE FAMILIAL TIES FOLLOWED BY COMMUNITY and regional bonds were the bedrock of Italian communities, in order for immigrants to get ahead, formal organizations were required. The first society established was work-related, the *società di mutuo soccorso*, the fraternal or mutual aid society. Organizations of a cultural, sport, recreational, educational or religious nature developed later. The immigration boom from the 1950s to the 1980s was accompanied by a parallel boom in organizational development. Government multicultural policies and funding stimulated growth of organizations and facilities. Educational programs focused on the Italian language, and culture, both at the K-12 and the post-secondary levels, also developed. Membership in a mutual aid society brought tangible and intangible benefits such as sick and death benefits, on the one hand, and a sense of "brotherhood" and being a part of a collective, on the other. With respect to cultural organizations, membership initially was an affirmation that being of Italian origin was something to take pride in. Later, another dimension came into play: the sense of an Italian-Canadian identity, distinct from Italian birth and citizenship, that was to be cultivated and affirmed in the community at large. Community leaders emerged from the volunteer pool and many left their mark on one or more organizations as either founders or service volunteers.

Società di mutuo soccorso

While craft guilds had existed in Italy since at least the Middle Ages, Italian independence resulted in a new type of organization. In 1862, the Associazione Operaia di Mutuo Soccorso Giuseppe Garibaldi di Macerata (Macerata Giuseppe Garibaldi Workers Association for Mutual Support) was established.[531] Its objects were: "to promote mutual support to overcome the hardships of life, facilitate the obtaining of work, the improvement of arts and crafts, civil progress and morality

---

[531] See Archivio di Stato di Macerata, Archivio Societa Operaia di Mutuo Soccorso "G. Garibaldi" – Macerata (1886 – 1937, Inventario), URL: http://www.icar.beniculturali.it/Inventari/ASMC/Societa_operaia_MC.pdf, retrieved December 8, 2017.

of associates in order to accomplish their duties, among the most prominent being the rights of citizenship."[532] The intent was to stimulate solidarity among workers in order to provide them with supports in a time of rapid industrialization following on unification. The choice of Garibaldi as patron reflected his libertarian values and a historic battle that took place in the city of Macerata in 1849. According to historian Donald Avery, mutual aid societies were popular with Italian, Finnish and Ukrainian immigrants and, in 1885, there were about 4,896 in Italy with over 791,296 members.[533] As well as being vehicles for self-help, these organizations predisposed Italian immigrants to membership in unions.

The Galileo Galilei Society, established in Milwaukee in 1883, was among the oldest such organizations in North America.[534] In 1908, the Società Di Mutuo Soccorso Giuseppe Garibaldi was established; it was the eighth Italian organization in the city and focused on companionship and social activities. Members wore dark uniforms with red hats and carried ceremonial swords as did the Masons, Oddfellows and the Catholic Knights of Columbus. The last was named in honour of the "discoverer" of North America and was founded in New Haven, Connecticut in 1882 by Father Michael J. McGivney.

In Western Canada, the earliest Italian mutual aid societies were established in BC to support mine workers. These included: Giordano Bruno Lodge (1899), founded by Angelo Maura in Rossland, a gold and copper mining area; Felice Cavalotti Lodge (1900) in the coal mining community of Extension on Vancouver Island; Emanuele Filiberto Duca D'Aosta Society (1903) in Michel; and the Società di Mutuo Soccorso Cristofero Colombo (1905) in Trail. In the first decade of the twentieth century, mining activity was booming in the East Kootenays and the most prominent community was Fernie. As early as May 1905, it had the Circolo Operaio Italiano XX Settembre (Labour Circle September XX), which was incorporated on September 9, 1913 as the Società Felice Cavalotti, Loggia No. 146 under the Federazione Colombiana della Società Italo-Americane (Colombian Federation of the Italo-American Society).[535] The Fernie society is enormously important because it would eventually become the grand lodge embracing all Alberta mutual aid societies.

---

[532] *Ibid.* The translation is by the author; the original states: "lo scopo sempre costante di 'reciproco fratellevole appoggio dei soci nelle ristrettezze della vita, la facilitazione al lavoro, il miglioramento delle arti e mestieri, il progresso civile e morale di ciascun socio e l'efficace adempimento dei doveri, non meno che il più largo uso dei diritti del cittadino....'"

[533] Donald Avery, "*Dangerous Foreigners,*" 46.

[534] The Galileo Galilei Society, 1884-1954, records are held by the Milwaukee County Historical Society, Mss-3265.

[535] Three letters from Cosimo Crisafio of the Circola Operaio Italiano XX Settembre Fernie to Signor V. Maniago (August 21 August 29, 1911 and September 11, 1911) are found in the Crowsnest Museum files (2016.017.0022, 2016.017.0021 and 2016.017.0020). The Fernie Lodge files are missing.

The societies were named for historical figures or heroes of the emerging Italian nation: Bruno, a philosopher and freethinker, developed a model of the universe; Cavalotti, a politician and poet, fought with Garibaldi; and the Duca d'Aosta was a member of the Italian Royal House of Savoia. Fernie's Circolo Operaia XX Settembre refers to the capture of Rome on September 20, 1870, the last battle in the process of Italian unification. Others were named after individuals who espoused left-wing views such as Cesare Battista and Leonida Bissolati. The spellings of names of such societies frequently do not conform to Italian spelling; however, since they are legal names, they cannot be corrected.

An Italian Department of External Affairs 2003 publication observed that: "The years that preceded the First World War saw a decrease in the pace of development of local organizations and the birth of unitary organizations. In this sense, there are two important moments: the involvement of Italians in the union movement and the birth, in 1905, of the Ordine dei Figli d'Italia (Order Sons of Italy) in America, in the tri-state area (Connecticut, Eastern New Jersey and New York)."[536] These unitary societies replaced the earlier generation of local lodges and fraternal societies. According to historian Jason Kaufman, at the root of this movement were ambitious individuals who adopted American business and profit models. In the next decade, the Ordine dei Figli d'Italia succeeded in replacing virtually all earlier entities.[537]

Historian Raymond Culos states that a mutual aid society, the Sons of Italy, was established in Vancouver in January 1905. There were 59 founding members under the direction of Agostino Ferrera, the city's first consular agent.[538] There is an interesting parallelism at work: in New York on June 22, 1905, physician Vincenzo Sellaro established the Supreme Lodge of the Ordine Figli d'Italia in America (later the Order of the Sons of Italy in America). Based on Culos' dating, the Vancouver society preceded the American one. The fact that similar societies were established in Vancouver and New York at roughly the same time is not impossible since consular agents in the US and Canada communicated with each other. From the beginning, Canada was viewed as part of the catchment area of the US organization. There are other resemblances between the Vancouver and New York societies: the motto of both is "Liberty, Equality and Fraternity." Culos summarized the goals, which were based on those formulated by Sellaro, as follows:

---

[536] Ministero degli Affari Esteri, *Gli Italiani nelli Stati Uniti d'America* (Italians in the United States of America), QCS Ob. 1, 200-2006, la Direzione Generale per gli Italiani all'Estero e le Politiche Migratorie (DGIEPM), 2003, 25-26. Translation by the author.

[537] See Jason Kaufman, *For the Common Good?: American Civic Life and the Golden Age of Fraternity* (Oxford, UK: Oxford University Press, 2002).

[538] Raymond Culos, *Vancouver's Society of Italians* (Madeira Park, BC: Harbour Publishing, 1998), vol 1, 18-19.

... to reunite in one single family all Italians scattered through the Americas and Canada; to promote moral, intellectual and material betterment among them; to be a school of mutual benevolence and humanitarian foresight; to participate with all its forces in protecting each member; to keep alive the culture of Italy; to spread the conviction that participation in American and Canadian political life is a factor of social betterment; to provide for the spread of the Italian language; to help in welfare activities on behalf of Italians; and to champion all those causes that infuse the conviction that Italians are valuable workers.[539]

The Federazione Colombiana with its roots in mining communities in the US, however, was more significant with respect to fraternal society development in southeastern BC and Alberta.[540] Founded in Chicago, Illinois on October 12, 1893 and incorporated on October 31, 1898, the secretariat was based in Clinton, Vermillion County, Indiana. Delegates from BC and Alberta lodges attended conferences in Clinton and Pueblo, Colorado. The former was a coal mining centre and a destination for Italian immigrants. Many also worked in the steel mills in Pueblo and the Cristofero Colombo Lodge had the distinction of having gifted a bust of the explorer to the city in 1905. It is believed that it was the first community to celebrate Columbus Day, which became the pre-eminent Italian celebration in the US.[541]

Alberta's earliest mutual aid society was established in Lille in the Crowsnest Pass in March 1906 and was initially known as the Società Operaia di Muttuo Soccorso (Workers Mutual Aid Society). It was a branch of the Federazione Colombiana. According to Ferucio De Cecco in *Crowsnest and Its People*, 72 Italian miners were the founding members.[542] Minute and rule (*rituale*) books, banking records and correspondence are located in the Crowsnest Museum and Archives. These provide insight into how the society operated and the labour conditions of the time. In 1906, the society had $425 in assets based on membership fees. The account book devotes a page to each member and the dues book lists members by name and payments made for dues and death benefits. The minute books are formal, with motions made and seconded, and claims for sick leave addressed, supported by medical certificates. Charter members included Joe and

---

[539] Joseph Scafetta, Jr., "A Biography of Vincezo Sellaro, M.D. (1868-1932), URL: https://www.osia.org/documents/Sellaro-Full-Bio.pdf, retrieved January 1, 2018.

[540] According to the Sons of Italy of Canada website, there are 15 lodges in Canada as follows: Brantford, Hamilton (2), Niagara Falls, Sault Ste. Marie, Thorold (2), Toronto, Welland (2), Winnipeg (2) and Kelowna. This contrasts with the over 3,000 in the US. . See URL: http://ordersonsofitalycanada.com/history/, retrieved December 15, 2017.

[541] The bust by sculptor Pietro Piati in Pueblo, Colorado, URL: http://vanderkrogt.net/statues/object.php?webpage=CO&record=usco02, December 11, 2017.

[542] Ferucio De Cecco, "Italian Benevolent Society 1906" in *Crowsnest and Its People*, 322-323.

Enrico Cocciolone, Joe Montalbetti, Domenico Gramacci, Francesco Alampi, Joe Nastasi, Frank D'Ercoli, Joe Troinani and the Cantalini brothers.

The Lille records cover the period 1906 to 1911 and there is significant correspondence with the American parent organization and branches. On April 1, 1910, Domenico Gatto of the Cristoforo Colombo Loggia No. 2 Federazione Colombiana, Lead City, South Dakota, a gold mining centre, wrote to P. Toppano at the Lille lodge thanking him for his intention to come to the upcoming conference.[543] A poignant letter dated April 3, 1911 from Frank Favano, Secretary, Società di Mutuo Soccorso Emanuele Filiberto Duca d'Aosta, Loggia no. 106, Michel, to V. Maniago includes a remittance in the amount of $20 to cover death payments for two of their members killed in a mining accident.[544] On June 26, 1911, Pietro Savio, Secretary General of the Federazione Colombiana, wrote to Signor V. Maniago, Secretary of the Loggia # 123 Lille, Alberta, noting that the membership fees for their 37 members were in arrears.[545] Another letter from H. Chiariglione of Pueblo, dated August 8, 1911, promoted the upcoming conference in that city and noted that the Lille delegate would only have to pay a percentage of the railway fare.[546] A third letter encouraged them to name a delegate. The Federazione Colombiana also published a journal – *L'unione*. Other correspondence deals with American suppliers in New York for minute and dues books, regalia and Columbus souvenirs.

The financials for the first quarter of 1911 show a healthy bank balance of $862.85. On the debit side, there are anticipated costs of $60 for attendance at the upcoming "Congress" and $100 for the amputation of the right leg of "brother" Francesco Nicolai. There are also a number of expulsions likely for non-payment of dues.[547] The language of correspondence is Italian with formal address being used including the terminology of brotherhood. These documents do not bear out the generalization that all miners were ill-educated or illiterate. The benefit system appears to have been well-run – there are copies of doctors' certificates as well as "proof of healing." On October 4, 1911, A. Vendrasco wrote to D. (Donato) Bertoia, Secretary, Lille, Loggia, including his certificate of healing; he notes that he hopes to return to work.[548]

---

[543] Letter from Domenico Gatto, to P. Toppano dated April 1, 1910, Crowsnest Archives 2016.017.0044.

[544] Letter from Frank Favano, to V. Maniago dated April 3, 1911, Crowsnest Archives 2016.017.0045.

[545] Letter from Pietro Savio, Secretary General of the Federazione Colombiana, to Signor V. Maniago, Secretary of the Loggia # 123 Lille, Alberta, dated June 26, 1911 Crowsnest Archives 2016.017.0026.

[546] Letter from H. Chiariglione, to the Loggia # 123 Lille, Alberta, dated August 8, 1911 Crowsnest Archives 2016.017.0024.

[547] Balance sheets for first trimester of 1911, Crowsnest Archives 2016.017.0050 and 2016.017.0051.

[548] Letter from A. Vendrasco, to D. Bertoia dated October 4, 1911, Crowsnest Archives 2016.017.0052.

A letter dated April 20, 1911 from Cosmo Crisafio, secretary of finance of the Circolo Operaio Italiano in Fernie to L. Vendrasco, the secretary of finance at the Lille Loggia, shows that there was collaboration among the loggias. He asks for funding support for a needy member and writes to his "Dear Friend and Brother" noting that: "Nazareno di Stefano is a member in good order of our Society. He has had the misfortune of losing his young wife in the flower of youth leaving him with two small children aged 2 and the other just born. He has been unemployed for a long time and has incurred many expenses. I appeal to the good heart of each of our brothers to see whether it is possible to give him a hand."[549] In another letter, dated April 15, Crisafio sends V. Maniago in Lille a cheque for $10 to assist members after the Bellevue Mine disaster of Friday, December 9, 1910.[550]

The Crowsnest Museum also holds a collection of artifacts including the sashes worn by members and table officers, and the reversible ribbons worn for ceremonial occasions. The ribbon has an enamel bar pin and badge with a star; on one side, it features the colours of the Italian flag (green, white and red) and the other side is black for use at funerals and memorial occasions. The Union Jack and Italian flags appear on the flag-coloured side of the ribbon. The men wore the regalia proudly in formal portraits and at community events including parades and funerals.

In 1912, the mine and coke ovens at Lille were closed because of a lack of orders and the local lodge was shut down. The men moved on to mining jobs in Coleman, Bellevue, Hillcrest and Blairmore. In the same year, the Loggia Operaia No. 3 Coleman was established with Giuseppe Troinani as president, Donato Bertoia, secretary, and Domenico Gramacci, treasurer. An attempt was made to start a lodge at Hillcrest but this failed and Coleman became the lodge for all miners in The Pass. In its first year of operations, it made use of the old stationery simply crossing out "Lille" and replacing it with a handwritten "Coleman." This is the case with the letter from Bertoia to Domenico Prazzara dated August 8, 1912, in which he responds to the latter's complaint about his request for benefits being turned down. Bertoia observed that, while the decision was made "con tutte le regole" (according to the regulations), he suggests a meeting to discuss the matter because he does not want to upset a "brother."[551] Doing things according to the book is evident in a letter from Dr. N. W. Connolly that gives a would-be member – Achile Salustri – a clean bill-of-health. It notes that Salustri is 34 years old and married, and provides a comprehensive

[549] Letter from Cosmo Crisafio, to L. Vendrasco dated April 20, 1911, Crowsnest Archives 2016.017.0039.
[550] Letter from C. Crisafio, to L. Maniago dated April 15, 1910, Crowsnest Archives 2016.017.0038.
[551] D. Bertoia to Domenico Prazzara, letter dated August 8, 1912, Crowsnest Archives 2016.017.0059.

medical history noting: "No chronic cough or lung disease in family in so far as applicant knows." (This would have been a pre-existing condition that would not be covered.)[552]

The affairs of the Coleman Lodge were run on an extremely business-like basis and the membership at its peak climbed to about 130 (over the years, it ranged from 90 to 130). The records, spanning the period 1912 to 1996, the year the society was dissolved, are a treasure trove.[553] There is no collection like it in Alberta or southeastern BC and it demonstrates the continuity of mining in the Crowsnest Pass and the Italian involvement. After the introduction of health care and other benefits and strong union negotiations, the original purpose of the society became redundant and it morphed into a social organization continuing to serve the community until the children of the pioneers who founded it were too old to continue to run it, and it was dissolved.

In 1912, the Lodge purchased two adjacent buildings at a prominent corner in Coleman on Main Street (now 7601 - 17 Avenue) for a home for the society. The larger, two-storey building, built around 1904, had housed a general store. In 1935, the exterior clapboard walls were covered with stucco with Art Deco features. Two small balconies on the front and west sides allowed for people attending events in the second-floor dance hall to view the street. The Italian Hall served not only as a gathering place but also as a source of income: the ground floor housed the Italian Co-operative Store initially and later Charlie Milo's Pool Hall and Beauty Salon. Apartments were located in the back of the building. A painted sunburst detail centred on the mold of clasping hands decorates the upper gabled parapet on the front façade of the second-storey. According to Alice Feregotto, whose husband Dave was a member of the executive in the final years, the hands indicated the benevolent nature of the society.[554]

The year 1921, saw major changes in the Italian miners' societies in BC and Alberta: the principal lodges organized themselves as the Ordine Indipendente Fior d'Italia (Independent Order Flower of Italy) with the grand lodge located in Fernie. The impetus for this was that the Federazione Colombiana lodges had joined the American Sons of Italy. During the First World War, the latter provided the families of members in active service with welfare cheques, which though small built loyalty. By 1918, there were a total of 960 lodges with 125,000 members located in 24 states. Among them, were members from two Canadian provinces: the Sault Ste. Marie Lodge in Ontario was established in 1915, and the Calgary Lodge, in 1918.

---

[552] N. W. Connolly, M.D. to Societa Operaia di Mutuo Soccorso, Loggia No. 123, Coleman, Alberta, letter dated October 20, 1912, Crowsnest Archives 2016.017.0056.

[553] Dave and Alice Feregotto and others members ensured the preservation of these records by donating them to the Crowsnest Museum. On September 15, 1995, the society sold their Block 11, lots 9 and 10, to John Spina and Wayne Clark.

[554] Community Design Strategies Inc., *Heritage Inventory Project Phase 1 - Municipality of Crowsnest Pass Coleman and Area*, September 2013, "The Italian Hall," 67-68.

While some historians note that the western Canadian miners' fraternal societies joined the American Figli d'Italia, there is no documentary evidence of this; this does not mean that it did not happen. Raymond Culos claims that, in 1918, a branch of the Sons of Italy was established in Fernie. Since the Fernie fraternal society records have not survived, it is impossible to determine the truth of this statement. Whether the relationship between the Fernie Lodge and the American parent society went sour and this resulted in the creation of the Fior d'Italia cannot be verified; however, a 1983 interview with Henry Butti suggests that this might have been the case:

> They [the Americans] had lodges you know…. wherever there were Italian settlements. And they had it here in Canada as well. But, their headquarters was in New York and you know how they are down in the States; us Canadians, well heck, we live in the snow and igloos. So, we couldn't get too much satisfaction from them so some of the people, especially in the West, they formed their own and they called it Fior d'Italia. In all these mining camps, there was an Italian society. Their headquarters was at Fernie, BC, and we had our insurance with them.[555]

Butti had first-hand knowledge – he and father Pietro belonged to the Nordegg Lodge and he was elected deputy to the Grand Lodge in Fernie.

The Statutes of the Ordine Indipendente Fior d'Italia (Independent Order Flower of Italy) were passed at a meeting in Fernie on November 1, 1921; the signatories were Francesco Santoni, Constantino Picco, Natale Valpiola, A. P. Bonamico, Pietro Fantana, Giuseppe Troiani, Virgilio Collina, Pietro Giovanetti, Ferruccio Trevisan, Giuseppe Maio, Leopoldo Cappello, Anselmo Pradolini, Nicola Sarra, Carlo Zarini, Angelo Nusco, Enrico Colombo, Stefano Basso, Niccolo Gardin, Pietro Baldassi and Dr. Antonio Milan.[556] The substitution of "Figli" with "Fior" suggests that the Fernie Lodge had become a member of the Ordine Indipendente Figli d'Italia when the Federazione Colombiana ceased to exist, and therefore chose the same initials. They would have had a stock of ribbons and sashes, and could thus recycle them. The phrase "Flower of Italy" is symbolic and evocative: youth are universally viewed as the "flower" of a nation. The first article states that the Order is constituted in Canada and, by implication, is not part of an American umbrella organization. By and large, the articles are based on the American counterpart with emphasis on the values of the homeland (including preservation of the Italian language) and

---

[555] Enrico Butti interview, Italians Settle in Edmonton Oral History Project, 1983, PAA.
[556] Statutes of the Independent Order Fior D'Italia, 1921, Crowsnest Archives 2016.017.0003.

brotherhood.[557] Procedural matters such as election of officers, discipline, etc. are set out in 60 pages; and six pages are devoted to mutual benefit purposes.

The benevolent purposes are enshrined in a financial provision: "A fund intended for mutual help is instituted by the Great Lodge, among the members of the Independent Order Fior d'Italia. Such a fund has been termed 'Unique Fund'."[558] Membership of individual lodges in the Unique Fund was made obligatory and the claim process was centralized in Fernie. The death benefit was set at $175 and the illness subsidy at $7.50 per week, although an individual must have been ill for six months before being able to access it. In the case of an incurable illness confirmed by a doctor where the individual must return to Italy or to go to a "health resort" in the US, travelling expenses would be paid. Other provisions included: $200 for the loss of one arm; $150 for the loss of one leg; $100 for the loss of one eye and also for inability to work as a result of partial paralysis. Total blindness and loss of an arm, or leg, resulted in a subsidy of $600. Anyone who received this subsidy was not entitled to any more even if death occurred.

The definition of illness did not include "intemperance, immorality, or for diseases already in existence before the admission of the member to the Order." No subsidy is paid for wounds, either self-inflicted or caused by fighting. A more liberal attitude is taken with respect to suicide where it is specified that heirs can receive the indemnity if the member had contributed to the Unique Fund for two years. The document reveals a social policy attitude that would later become entrenched in government health care and worker compensation programs. In 1934, the tiered annual fees were as follows: aged 16 to 30: $8; aged 30 to 40, $10; aged 40 to 50, $12; and contribution to the Fondo Unico, $100. Butti described the functioning of the Lodge as follows:

> We used to have a meeting once a month and if you had any grievances to bring up, even on your work, you know, we would help out. Because, you've got to remember that you used to hear so much about the Italian worker, but, in them days, if you couldn't speak for yourself, you got pretty well exploited too by some of these guys that knew more than you. And this was the only way that some of them who couldn't speak English, they wanted a letter sent some place, well, they'd come to the society and there was always somebody there that could help them out.[559]

---

[557] *Ibid.*

[558] *Ibid.*, 53-60.

[559] Enrico Butti interview, 1983.

The minute books reveal the continuity of the organization including changes in the executive, for example, in 1920 the new officers were D'Appolonia, Alampi, Toppano and Dececco. The financial statements show the fiscal health of the organization: those for March 1918 show a bank balance of $2,977.11 with outgoings totaling $333.50, the majority being sick benefit payments.[560] The December financial statements saw higher payouts totaling $679.46.[561] In the period 1918 to 1936, there were fewer claims than in the 1910 to 1920 period. An explanation might be fewer accidents; another, was declining production particularly in the 1930s. According to the 1924 Ledger, the *Tassa di Amessione* (membership fee) was $1.25 for young, fit men; older men paid more in the tiered fee system. There were 104 members listed.

On a lighter side, financial records provide insight into the social life of the community. For example, monies were approved for A. Toppano to find a band for the New Year's party at the hall. All hall rentals were approved via motions. This included community events such as a "ball" (likely a wedding ball) for "G. Salvador's sister." The event took place "the Monday after Easter 1931" and the rental cost was $10. The 1930 Minute Book has a motion to approve the use of the hall on the fourth Sunday of the month for a meeting of the Soc. Stella d'Italia (Star of Italy Society), the Loggia's companion women's society. In March 1931, a motion approved the purchase of $950 for tables and other objects to be supplied by G. Venera. The society raised funds through a raffle in 1931 and a copy of the book is in the records.

The relations between the Coleman Lodge and the Grand Lodge in Fernie did not always progress smoothly: a motion at the meeting of February 21, 1931 approved a delegation comprising Giovanni Dandrea, Sebastiano Dappolonia and Angelo Toppano going to Fernie to talk things out. The BC and Alberta members of the Order met annually and these events were commemorated by formal photographs. Financial statements in the Coleman papers set out the 1923 and 1924 expenditures of the Grand Lodge and these included travel expenses paid out for individual members to attend the annual conference.[562] The records also include some material relating to member loggias, for example, the 1910-1917 Minute Book for Michel. This suggests that the Grand Lodge in Fernie may have gathered some foundational documents and somehow they ended up in the Crowsnest Pass. Another explanation is that the secretary of the Michel Loggia may have moved to Coleman for work and brought the book with him. The 1921 statutes and other organizational material appeared in a number of editions of the Rule Book. The lodges either printed their own or used the Fernie rule book.

---

[560] Financial Statements, December 1918, Crowsnest Archives 2016.017.0001.
[561] *Ibid.*
[562] Fernie Grand Lodge, 1923 financial records, Crowsnest Archives 2016.017.0006.

By the early 1950s many mines had closed and the March 1, 1953 Coleman Lodge records show a bumper crop of claims. This was a direct result of the aging membership. The difficulty of policing claims also came up. The minutes of January 18, 1953 dealt with problems with regard to the status of Doro Peressini and E. Folino. A registered letter was sent to each requiring that they attend the next meeting. They did not turn up and, in the minutes for the meeting of February 7, a motion was passed to go and visit them. Whether this was done is not recorded; however, at the March 1 meeting, they are still waiting for Peressini to attend a meeting. On March 29, 1953, a motion was passed to suspend his health benefits for failing to attend meetings to substantiate his claim. It is noteworthy that the minutes are less literate in the 1950s than they were in the early years. This suggests that the new workers coming in as part of the post-war immigration boom were less well-educated.

The Records for the Leonida Bissolati Lodge No. 5, Coalhurst (1916-1926) have not survived. The Galt Archives has a 10-year commemorative photograph of the membership.[563] The society ceased to exist shortly after. The Loggia Operaia No. 6, Lethbridge was established in 1918 but the only proof of its existence is, again, a photograph in the Galt Archives. According to oral history evidence, the societies ended as a result of a dispute between the pro- and anti-Fascist forces in the community in the mid-1920s. The Glenbow Archives has documents relating to the Cesare Battisti Lodge in Nordegg, established in 1918, including minute books, membership and dues books, and the rule book.[564] These belonged to members of the Marasco family.

The early 1920s saw the formation of companion women's societies within the Order Flower of Italy. This was not only a reflection of the increasing number of women in mining communities but also the fact that women's orders existed among mainstream fraternal societies. For example, the Ray of Hope Rebekah Lodge, No. 67, Bellevue, was established in 1919 and was the companion of the Oddfellows.[565] The first women's lodge was the Speranza d'Italia (Hope of Italy) Loggia No. 101 in Fernie. The charter is dated October 20, 1923 and the signatories were Concetta Borelli, Virginia Giacomazzi, Maria Schianni, Rosaria Maio and Caterina Rossi (all of their husbands were miners). The officers of the men's lodge were also signatories. The women were in their late twenties and early thirties, and represented a generation who had learned English and wanted to assert themselves in the new Canadian world order. They were no doubt aware of women's suffrage gains – Alberta women obtained the vote in 1916.

---

[563] Photograph titled "Ricordo Loggia Leonida Bissolati #5 Ordine Indipendente Fior d'Italia Order of the Flowers of Italy, Coalhurst, Galt Archives 19841076024.

[564] Ordine Indipendente Fior d'Italia, Cesare Battisti Loggia No 9 Papers, 1918-1980, Glenbow AN M7715.

[565] See "Ray of Hope Rebekah Lodge, No. 67, Bellevue," entry in *Crowsnest and Its People*, 322.

Other women's orders followed: Loggia Rose d'Italia No. 102, Lethbridge; Loggia Adelaide Cairoli No. 103, Calgary; Loggia Stella d'Italia No. 105, Coleman; Loggia Eleonora Duse No. 106, Drumheller; and Loggia Principessa Maria Jose No. 9, Revelstoke. The names were either based on Roman Catholic symbolism or paid tribute to Italian heroines: the rose represented the Blessed Virgin Mary (Rose of Sharon); Cairoli was an important supporter of Italian independence and her son Benedetto Cairoli became premier of Italy in 1878; Duse was an important Italian actress; and Maria Jose was the last Queen of Italy.

A few records of the Loggia Rose d'Italia No. 102, Lethbridge have survived and provide insight into the functioning of women's lodges.[566] A typescript document in Italian on letterhead with the date "193_" (the last digit is not filled in) sets out the organization's fee structure.[567] It is a tiered system like the men's order and sick and death benefits were paid. The fee schedule is as follows: ages 16 to 25, $1; ages 25 to 30, $2; ages 30 to 35, $3.50; ages 35 to 40, $6; ages 40 to 45, $8; and ages 45 to 50, $10. There are several more tiers than in the men's order and there is a cutoff age of 50. Article 12 clarifies this: "According to our Constitution this loggia does not give a subsidy to any sister for illnesses associated with the change of life or resulting from the change of life [menopause]."[568] No sick benefits were provided for the first four days of illness or accident, and a medical certificate was required to be presented every 30 days. The death benefit differs from that of the men. Article 19 specifies: "In the case of the death of a sister, all of the active sisters will be taxed at the rate of 25 cents to be given to the widower or orphans of the deceased sister, if the sister is celibate [the actual term used is "celebre," which means famous and is therefore a misspelling], the said tax will go to the father or mother, and if these are deceased, then a small memorial will be created."

The financial records from 1925 to 1936 are hand-written on a series of sheets rather than appearing in a ledger; for example, the 1925 records are simply a listing of deposits made by the secretary of finance Giulia Baceda. Giulia Briosi came to Lethbridge at the age of 17 with her family and her father Davide went to work in the mines. Her first job was washing dishes in the Arlington Hotel and, in 1922, she married Joe Baceda. She was a founding member of the Rose d'Italia. The society appears to have continued as a women's club until April 1970 when it was

---

[566] Loggia Rose d'Italia No. 102, Lethbridge, Galt Archives 19931049006 to 19910530024.
[567] The Galt record indicates that the Loggia Rose No. 102 was founded around 1925 but the constitution document appears on letterhead with the date "193_" so a later date is possible. Galt Archives LETH-1915.
[568] The translation is the author's.

dissolved. The last secretary, Elda Jorgensen, donated the papers to the Galt Archives. Elda was born in Udine in 1920 and raised in Coalhurst where her father worked in the mines. The family then moved to Lethbridge where she completed high school and later married Clarence Jorgensen. She worked at Sears for over 25 years rising to the position of credit manager.[569]

A series of balance sheets dating from 1955 to 1960 in the Coleman papers provide evidence of a network of fraternal societies in southern BC and Alberta under the Grand Lodge at Fernie. The following societies are listed: Loggia Operaia No. 3, Coleman; Loggia Duca Degli Abruzzi No. 4, Revelstoke; Loggia Operaia No. 6, Lethbridge; Loggia F. Cavallotti No. 7, Fernie; Loggia Italian Club No. 8, Calgary; Loggia C. Battisti No. 9, Calgary; Loggia C. Colombo No. 11, Kamloops; Loggia C. Colombo No 14, Cranbrook; Loggia V. Emanuele III No. 15, Michel; Loggia E. Caruso No. 16, Drumheller; Madre [Mother] Loggia, Fernie; Loggia Speranza d'Italia No. 101, Fernie; Loggia Rose d'Italia No. 102, Lethbridge; Loggia Adelaide Cairoli No. 103, Calgary; Loggia Stella d'Italia No. 105, Coleman; Loggia Eleanora Duse No. 106, Drumheller; and Loggia Princ. Maria Jose No. 9, Revelstoke. The balance sheets include sources of funding as follows: contributions to the *Fondo Unico* (Unique Fund); contributions to death benefits; *Cap. tax* (head tax/membership fee); and *diverse* (other). These documents are important because they reveal the range of Italian fraternal societies most hitherto unknown because no records have survived.

The Società Duca d'Abruzzi, established in Venice shortly after the colony was set up in 1914, served the needs of the agricultural colonists. An article in the *Edmonton Bulletin* of January 5, 1917, provides some insight into its functioning:

> The Duca d'Abruzzi Society of Venice, a few miles south of here, invited all their compatriots of the Colony to a Christmas celebration at the residence of A. Piemonte. There was a huge Christmas tree and a fine feast, dainties from sunny Italy, presents for the signoras and nuts, candies, cakes and oranges for the bambinos. The Society, whose main object is the colonizing of Italians in the forming districts of Venice and the neighbourhood, extends free guidance to desirable homesteads to newcomers and helps them otherwise. It is extending its scope by furnishing its members with free medical aid and pecuniary assistance in case of sickness. The presidents are F. A. Billas [O. J. Biollo] and A. Piemonte and the directors are Messrs. A. Guerra, L. Rizzoli, E. Manca, T. Piemonte and P. Bonifacio.[570]

---

[569] Elda Jorgensen obituary, *Lethbridge Herald*, June 30, 2000.
[570] Cited in *Hylo-Venice: Harvest of Memories*, 179.

Tony Bonifacio in *Venice Alberta* 1914 mentions that another society was formed in 1926 in the nature of a co-operative enterprise. Efisio Manca was the chairman and president, and the members included Pio Bonifacio, Joe Michetti, Augusto Marini, Attilio and Frank Macor, Ascenzio and Vincent Varze. The group pooled their cash and also borrowed to purchase a tractor, brush breaker, grain crusher, stationary one cylinder motor and a circular saw. The group remained together until the equipment became obsolete.

Calgary's Italian Societies

Historian John G. Fainella noted: "In Calgary, the Giovanni Caboto Loggia No. 8 was born in 1918 as a branch of the fraternal insurance association Ordine dei Figli d'Italia (Order of the Sons of Italy) which was founded in New York in 1905.... The Calgary lodge was organized under the direction of a Mr. Santone from Fernie, B.C."[571] According to Ovindolo Onofri, the Calgary Loggia lost its Dominion Charter in 1920 because it was not satisfying its members.[572] With the establishment of the Ordine Indipendente Fior d'Italia, in 1921 in Fernie, the Calgary Lodge became part of this entity, as did the women's lodge, the Loggia Adelaide Cairoli No. 103. Nick Gallelli, who arrived in Calgary in 1899, was one of the founding members and worked as a teamster in construction.

Initial meetings were held in members' homes until an old garage was acquired in the early 1920s at the Edmonton Trail NE and Third Avenue. The Loggia organized dinners and annual picnics and also supported an Italian band. Visual evidence of this can be found in the Glenbow Archives – a 1921 photo shows the Italian Band relaxing at Shouldice Park. The conductor was Lawrence Faletti, who also established the H. W. McNeill Co.'s Colliery Band and the Elk's Band in 1923 in Canmore. He died in 1926 and was succeeded by oboist John J. Pompilio, who led the orchestra from 1928 to 1932. Band members included J. M. De Paoli, G. Terzi, R. Laudadio, E. DiPaolo, Charles Garossino, Conrad Lagger, H. Manzara, G. and F. Corradetti, S. Ciuffa, E. and L. Marocco; and M. Grassi. Pompilio, who gave music lessons, also set up the Calgary Italian Boy's Band, which performed in the Stampede Parade in 1930, but it lasted only a brief time.

Two new organizations challenged the Calgary Loggia's supremacy: the Associazione Italo-Canadese (Italo-Canadian Association), also an affiliate of the Ordine Indipendente Fior d'Italia, was established in 1933 and the Piemontese Society in the mid-1930s. The Loggia responded by renovating the existing building but larger forces came into play. On June 10, 1940, Italy declared war on Great Britain and, by extension, Canada; this resulted in enemy alien designation and

---

[571] Fainella "The Development of Italian Organizations in Calgary," 22.
[572] *Ibid.,* 22.

internment, which halted all Italian organizational activities. The Lodge sold its premises and went dormant during the war while the two other societies shut down. In an oral history interview, Flavia Santucci noted that the building was sold to the Polish Club.

The end of the war saw a resuscitation of the Calgary Loggia but it was soon challenged by a new society with largely social aims. On May 1, 1952, the Italo-Canadian Society of Calgary was established with the following objectives: acquire lands; erect or otherwise provide a building for social and community purposes; provide a meeting place for the consideration and discussion of questions affecting the interests of the community; and provide a centre and suitable meeting place for various activities of the community. There were a total of 65 members and E. Sciore was the founding president. The Society initially met in members' homes and social gatherings were held in Luca Carloni's Isle of Capri Restaurant. The Club continued to provide sickness and death benefits. The monthly dues were set at $1. The fraternal practices, however, did not last long since the various levels of government introduced social assistance programs.

In 1955, the Loggia and the Italo-Canadian Society merged forming the Calgary Italian Club. Augostino di Paulo was the founding president and served for a year; he was succeeded by V. Barbaro, who served from 1957 to 1960. [573] On May 1, 1959, the Club purchased a barn at 416 - 1st Avenue NE for $17,000. According to Giulia Gallelli, the Club had difficulty making payments on the loan but eventually was able to pay it off. The barn's ground and second floors were renovated to provide meeting and banqueting space; later, the basement was also developed. As a result of massive volunteer efforts, revenues were increased and the Society was able to purchase adjoining properties.

The club became the centre of community activities and evolved to meet community needs. The large number of young men who arrived from Italy wanted to play soccer and the Juventus Soccer Club was formed in 1956. [574] This initiative was led by Alberto Romano, Lino Massolin, Angelo Ciono, Terry Ius and Mario Finot. In 1958, the club joined the Second Division and a soccer rivalry began with Edmonton. In 1962, Juventus incorporated and officially registered as a sports club. In the following years, it expanded involvement into Calgary's sporting community and, in 2000 it started a foundation and presented scholarships to Calgary soccer players who excelled in the sport and in academic subjects. David Colonna participated as both a player and coach for

---

[573] Early Calgary Italian Club presidents were as follows: 1953-54, E. Sciore; 1955, A. Di Paolo; 1956, V. Barbaro; 1957-60, A. Di Paolo; 1961-62, V. Barbaro; 1963, F. Verdis; 1964, E. Martina; 1965, F. Verdis; 1966, L. De Paoli; 1967, A. Sanguin; 1968, G. Sperman; 1969-73, J. De Paoli; 1974-75, S. Scarpino; 1976, J. De Paoli; 1977-79, S. Scarpino; 1980, V. Fornaro; 1981-82, C. Duri; 1983, V. Finot; 1984-86, A. Bussoli; 1987, R. Blasetti; 1988-92, J. De Paoli; 1993-97, L. Blasetti; 1998, G. Violini; 1999, V. Finot; and 2000, A. Riccio.
[574] Anon. "A Tribute to the Longevity of Juventus," in *Il Congresso*, year 19, no 5, May 5, 2002.

12 years. Juventus produced some fine soccer players and, over the years, won tournaments for both male and female players. It also established the Pocaterra Tournament, named in honour of pioneer rancher George Pocaterra; this brought together teams from across Western Canada. In 2002, the Club celebrated its 45th anniversary at the Calgary Italian Club and the event drew over 200 individuals. Besides the adult soccer club, junior boys and girls teams were established.

In keeping with its benevolent roots, in 1960, the Italian Club established the Columbus Savings and Credit Union to assist recent immigrants needing loans. This effort was led by Luca Carloni and Alberto Romano, who as a real estate agent was aware of difficulties in borrowing. Carloni's son-in-law Tony Valerio served as the Credit Union's secretary from 1963 until, in his words, "it went belly up" 20 years later when it was no longer needed. In 1975, the Columbus Savings and Credit Union assets surpassed $1 million.

Calgary's Italian community was very conscious of the importance of business develop-ment and to raise awareness of Italian businesses and raise funds, the Italian Club established the Sportsmen's Dinner in 1963; 97 people attended. Carloni, again, played a leadership role in this initiative. The event got bigger and bigger and monies raised supported not only the Club's activities but also activities in the community at large.

A major governance change occurred in 1974: the Italian Club severed its ties with the Fior d'Italia and became part of a national umbrella organization, the National Congress of Italian Canadians, established in the same year. The Ottawa-based NCIC grew out of the Federation of Italian Canadian Associations. The Calgary Italian Club move was strategic: the Fior d'Italia was rooted in the past while the NCIC represented a new generation of politically-savvy community leadership interested in political lobbying as well as preservation of Italian culture, language and traditions. A Calgary District Branch of the NCIC was established but, unlike its Edmonton counterpart, it did not initiate programming and the Italian Club remained the major provider of activities. A major achievement was the establishment of the Calgary Italian Saturday School with a seed grant from the federal government and funding support from the Italian government. To assist in the communication of community activities, the Italians for Community Action organization was established and produced a program on community events for the Capital Cable Television Co. Ltd. (later Shaw Cable).

The highs were inevitably accompanied by lows: on October 11, 1976 fire destroyed the club's premises just as a half-million dollar renovation was to begin. Members accelerated fund-raising and the club was rebuilt. While new facilities could be erected, a far more serious problem began to emerge based on regional divisions in the Italian community. Differences manifested themselves through conflict and negativity and culminated in the establishment of new organi-zations that challenged the programming supremacy of the Italian Club. To add insult to injury, some of these new entities were the result of Club initiatives. The angst that resulted is very evident in oral history interviews conducted in 1985 and 1988. Many of the people interviewed in the 1985 project, which was a Calgary Italian Club initiative, were elderly pioneers, and they lamented the fact that the Club's membership had dropped dramatically. All pointed to disputes between Northern and Southern Italians. In addition, the organization was experiencing financial difficulties and was confronted by the possibility of foreclosure on its debts.

In 1985, Domenico Ambrogiano, who arrived in Canada in 1948 as a contract labourer, noted with respect to the declining membership, that the Italian community was closer when people were poorer and needed each other.[575] He also saw an emerging trend of the younger generation not respecting elders and, by extension, the organizations they supported. In a 1988 interview, Tony Valerio agreed that the club was failing to attract young members but also noted that club meetings were very male-oriented and that more had to be done to attract women. Pier Siccardi, also interviewed in 1988, went so far as to reject the notion that Calgary had an Italian "community," which implied shared interests and values, preferring the more neutral term "population." He noted that the Italian Club's membership was only 200 and that there were few social activities. He also observed that Calgary was the only city with a significant Italian population that had never elected anyone to public office and expressed disappointment at the failure of the Italians for Community Action, the organization producing the Italian television program in which he was involved. The program had shut down because community members were critical of its format; it failed to attract young people as participants; and also had difficulty attracting guests.[576] Historian Antonella Fanella sums up the conflict as follows:

> The board of directors, which was dominated by northern Italians was regularly accused of misappropriating funds. Heated arguments and bitter confrontations over mismanagement of the club ended with resignations and the turning in of memberships. Often as one member resigned, his relatives followed suit. Past presidents were harshly criticized and even ostracized in the community. The creation of regional clubs, such as the Fogolar Furlan (northern Italians from Friuli-Venezia Giulia) and the Abruzzesi Association, simply made the problem worse, as there was not enough money for these groups to have separate buildings.[577]

[575] Mr. and Mrs. Giovanni Ambrogiano interview, Calgary Italian Club Historical Project, May 23, 1985, Glenbow Archives RCT-869-1 & 2.

[576] Unlike Edmonton, which had a number of radio programs, two newspapers and a television program, Calgary was not able to achieve this. A newspaper, *Il Panorama*, was established in 1968 but existed only for a couple of years. G. Carozzi was editor and was assisted by C. Graighero, V. Pana and G. Puco.

[577] Fanella, 58.

The issues at the club were, however, larger than regional differences: they were symptomatic of a phenomenon typical in established immigrant communities. After 35 years of immigration growth, a large number of members of the Italian community were well-established and economic betterment signaled an exodus from inner-city areas. In addition, they no longer needed the benefits that the club provided. David Colonna is representative of this shift. On his arrival in 1963, he attended language classes at the club and met many people. The club provided necessary moral and psychological support and he remained involved for about 12 years when business pressures drew him away.[578] Vincent Davoli, who was brought to Calgary as a one-year-old child in 1956, noted that his parents were extremely involved in the club but, when they moved from Bridgeland, their contact lessened. Davoli was a director of the Club from 1982 to 1984 and served on the sport and building committees. In 1984, he chose to distance himself from the Club and the Italian community.[579]

Rather than accepting defeat, the club's core membership redoubled fundraising efforts organizing casinos, bingos and also initiating a series of Ferrari raffles, the proceeds of which were used towards mortgage payments. According to Adrian Bussoli, the majority of the board initially opposed the raffle thinking it a risky endeavour. Younger board members prevailed and the Club continued to hold the raffle every two years. In the early years, the raffle generated over $500,000, which was shared between the Calgary Italian Club and other charitable groups. The club succeeded in paying down its mortgage on May 10, 1986. The larger problem of its aging membership still existed and great efforts had to be made to encourage younger members to join. In 1987, the club collaborated with the Calgary Italian School, and created the Italian-Canadian Folk Dancers of Calgary, later the Calgary Italian Folk Dancers.

The process of renewal was by and large successful and a key factor was that the club looked outward, beyond the Italian community, and became part of philanthropic efforts involving the community at large. The intent was to show the strength and civic-mindedness of the Italian community. This applied not only to club initiatives but also organizations that had spun off from the club such as the Calgary Italian Sportsmen's Association. The club also partnered strategically to do good works; for example, co-hosting, with the Calgary Firefighters Burn Treatment Society,

---

[578] David Colonna interview, Peoples of Southern Alberta Oral History Project, October 19 and December 2, 1987, Glenbow Archives RCT-281.

[579] Vincent Davoli interview, Peoples of Southern Alberta Oral History Project, March 24, 1988, Glenbow Archives RCT-836. The statistics are cited by Tom Babin in a November 26, 2011 *Calgary Herald* article titled "Modestino Carbone: 'I didn't leave Italy for more of the same."

the annual Ladies Night Out in support of the Foothills Burn Treatment Society. A more recent initiative is the "Food for Friends" program that involves the feeding of local homeless people on three occasions through the year. The Club has also been involved in a range of disaster relief activities in partnership with the National Congress of Italian Canadians. These included the Friuli earthquake on May 6, 1976, and the earthquake at Eboli, south of Naples, on November 23, 1980. The Club raised $50,000 for the former and more than $1 milllion for the latter (including some provincial funding). During the Calgary Winter Olympics, in 1988, the club hosted teams and officials from Italy and took on the role of "Casa Italia."

The Italian Sportsmen's Association, in 2017, held its 55th dinner and has branded itself as "Calgary's premier sportsmen's dinner where we celebrate everything Italian – food, wine, culture, camaraderie and good times." [580] Scholarships worth $5,000 each are provided to three high school students of Italian descent who excel in athletics and academics. Key speakers are sports personalities whether players, coaches or management. The past and current directors comprise a who's who of leaders of Calgary's Italian community. Serafino Scarpino served as president for 20 years; Domenic Venturo, QC, became president in 2017. The organization has raised more than $1.5 million and beneficiaries have included the Calgary International Film Festival, Alberta Children's Hospital and The Bill Powers Media Scholarship.

In 2006, the Italian Sportswomen's Association was established and founders noted: "The focus of our organization is to provide scholarships to young women of Italian heritage who have demonstrated excellence in athletics, academics, leadership, fine arts and volunteering. The scholarship recipients are then honored at a premier dinner event that allows us to shine the spotlight on the successful recipients and on our Italian culture. We are proud to provide financial assistance to some exceptional young women to assist them in pursuing post-secondary educational goals."[581] The board in 2017 comprised Teresina Bontorin, Leah Conforti, Gabrielle Enns, Andrea Loria, Dora Osterling, Ashley and Chelsea Paolini, and Carmelina Riccio. Bontorin, a lawyer, is also the Honorary Consul of Italy in Calgary.

---

[580] Calgary Italian Sportsmen's Dinner Association website, URL: http://www.italiansportsmen.com/, retrieved December 13, 2017.
[581] Italian Sportswomen's Association website, URL: http://www.calgaryitaliansportswomen.ca/home.html, retrieved December 13, 2017.

Edmonton Italian Organizations

The first Italian organization in Edmonton – the Società Vittorio Emanuele Terzo (Vittorio Emanuele Third Society) – was established in 1913 by Lorenzo Cantera. It was likely a miners' fraternal society since Edmonton had many Italians working in local coal mines. O. J. Biollo became the next president. Together with the newly-established Venice Society it supported the Venice and Hylo colonies in northern Alberta. Both are mentioned in newspaper accounts of the colonization and oral histories. They do not appear to have survived and were succeeded by the Edmonton Fascio in 1924. In 1932, the Cristoforo Colombo Club, also referred to as the Italo-Canadese Society, was established by 32 community members with Henry Butti as president and Louis Biamonte as treasurer. In a 1983 interview, Butti noted: "We used to gather about once a month and have some discussions and we started a bingo among ourselves to try and raise some money, and we were going to buy some books.… and we were going to start a little library and the war broke out and that finished everything."[582] Butti mentioned that, at the end of the war, they tried to re-establish the society and even called a meeting: "The first thing they wanted to know is, well, what's in it for me if I join the society? … You see, some of the misconceptions of some of these new immigrants that came right after the war, they thought that, well, we're all millionaires here." At that point, he gave up.

Because of the large number of young male immigrants, the first post-war organization estab-lished was the Cristoforo Colombo Soccer Club, founded in 1955. This was planned at a meeting at the Sacred Heart Church Hall. The first board comprised Terry Peron, president; Giovanni Guerrato, vice president; Ugo Bagatin, treasurer; A. Durante, secretary; and directors, Giuseppe Bendin, E. Bonetto, C. Borin, R. Bossio, Giovanni Segato and Henry Butti. Butti became the team's unofficial photographer as well as donating money to buy the first uniforms; it is likely that he also suggested the name to commemorate the earlier society. Mario Molinari became involved in the team's management and Fidenzio Pasqua, a young immigrant from Grimaldi, Cosenza, became a leading player.

Through some well-connected Italian builders, the team had been given land by the City of Edmonton for development of a soccer field and club house but couldn't raise the funds so they continued to play at Clarke Stadium. The club won the City of Edmonton championship and defeated Calgary's Millican United to win the President's Cup, emblematic of Alberta soccer supremacy. Pasqua scored four times to lead the team to a 5-1 victory. In 1957, after a fight at

---

[582] Henry Butti oral history interview, August/September 1983, Italians Settle in Edmonton Oral History Project, PAA PR0915.

a game and disciplinary action, the club suspended operations. In 1958, the newly-established Santa Maria Goretti Parish created Azione Cattolica (Catholic Youth Organization) and started the Juventus Soccer Team. Mario Zecchini was the manager and Pasqua served as coach for a time as did Mario Paulon. Players included Franco and Luigi Binassi, Mario Mazzotta, Joe and Tony Caria, Emilio Gatto, Mario Rizzuto, Silvano Vecchio, Francesco Sicolo and Tony Campoli.

Frank Spinelli, in 1960, created the Ital Canadian Soccer Club; many team members had played with the Cristoforo Colombo Club. In 1964, they won the Bay Cup and, in 1966, defeated the Calgary Callies to capture their first Alberta Cup. Coaches included Mike Trafficante, who ended up coaching nationally, and Mimmo Longo. Players included Mario Paulon, who was the goalie; Dirk Gaudmans, a Dutchman who played with the Italians; Silverio Mazzotta; Giuseppe (Joe) Petrone; and Sergio Berti. Petrone, a social studies teacher, became the top scorer in the history of Alberta soccer. He continued to be involved in every soccer venture in Edmonton including professional team FC Edmonton of the North American Soccer League.

Media organizations were the next to be established. This was an area that had not prospered in Calgary and is perhaps emblematic of a difference between the Italian communities of Alberta's largest cities. In 1959, Mariano Covassi founded Edmonton's first Italian-language radio program, "Piccola Italia," on CKUA. In 1962, it was taken over by Sab Roncucci of the Dante Alighieri Society and renamed "Panorama Italiano." In 1974, Adriano Zenari and three University of Alberta students ran the program for about three months and then ceased operations. A range of other radio programs succeeded it. Fathers Giovanni Bonelli and Rino Ziliotto of Santa Maria Goretti Parish began a program on the French-language station CHFA. The priests played Italian music, provided news from the homeland and offered community messages. Frank Spinelli, Joe Bocchinfuso and Lorenzo Bagnariol began the secular "Programma Italiano," also on CHFA, which ran for 25 years. The year 1974 saw another Italian-language radio program, "Italianissimo," started by Tony DeRose and broadcast from Wetaskiwin on radio station 1441 AM. In 1980, Leo Sorgiovanni started "Ciao Italia" on CKER radio, Edmonton's multicultural station. It ran every Sunday from 9 am to 12:30 pm from 1980 to 1988. In 1988, Sorgiovanni began "Buongiorno all'Italiana" and it lasted until 1994. The "Mezz'ora con Voi" (Half an Hour with You), produced by Father Luciano Cortopassi of Santa Maria Goretti Parish, began around the same time and focused on church activities.

In 1975, the "Panorama Italiano" Italian-language television program began on the new Capital Cable Television Co., incorporated in Edmonton in 1966. It assumed the name of the earlier radio program and was supported by Ernie Poscente, the cable company's first Programming Manager, who was the son of Italian immigrants. In 1983, the company became Shaw Cable Systems Ltd. (and later still Shaw Communications). Fathers Augusto Feccia and Raniero Alessandrini of Santa Maria Goretti Parish initiated the program. Milena Alzetta was the videographer, editor and sometimes interviewer for over 30 years. Carlo Amodio and Frank Cappellano took over in 2010 and continued until 2014 when the program was shut down because Shaw Cable demanded better quality programming. This was not possible because of a lack of volunteers and interest from the younger generation.

While the Calgary Italian Club experienced a splintering off of new societies, the situation in Edmonton was the reverse: individual societies preceded collective organizations. The first such entity was the Associazione Nazionale Alpini (ANA), established in 1960 as a fraternal society of former members of the Italian Alpini Regiment. Tony Zenari was a founder. Besides a range of social activities, the group still undertakes annual Remembrance Day activities. The group also established the Alpini Choir.

In 1961, the Dante Alighieri Society was established and affiliated with the main society in Rome founded in 1889 to help promote Italian culture and language abroad. The Edmonton society is one of 425 branches worldwide. The founding executive were Sab Roncucci, president; Olga De Girolamo, vice president; Felice Toniate, vice president; Ruggero Battistuzzi, secretary; Vittorio Cocco, corresponding secretary; and Gianni Segatti, treasurer; and directors, Mira Butti, Antonio Falcone, Peter Caffaro and Enrico Musacchio.[583] The society has organized a range of cultural and educational activities over the years including the Italian-language school, public lectures, concerts, a radio program and a range of activities promoting citizenship and human rights. In 1973-1974, it undertook an oral history project, the first in Alberta's Italian community, with funding support from Alberta Culture. As a centenary legacy for Canada in 1967, the society donated a bust of Dante and some Italian books to the Edmonton Public Library.

In 1978, the Italian Pioneers Club was formed to organize social and recreational activities for members and their families. Activities included visiting and helping sick members; helping families of deceased members; and organizing social gatherings such as an annual dinner-dance for members and their families and friends. Vincenzo Funaro was one of the founders. As the pioneers died, the club ceased to exist.

Provincial legislation and cultural policies began to impact on the Italian community in the late 1970s and resulted in a proliferation of societies. The Province of Alberta was a leader in embracing multiculturalism and, under Horst Schmid, Minister of Culture, Youth and Recreation, proclaimed the *Alberta Heritage Day Act*, in 1974. This established the first Monday in August as a cultural heritage holiday. The provincial government set up the Cultural Heritage Council and

[583] Presidents have included Sabatino Roncucci, Tony Falcone, Tony Caria, Nando Zenari, Ubaldo Aloisio, Joe Pivato, Giovanni Bragaglia, Giancarlo Grelli, Enrico Musacchio, Reny Clericuzio and Michele Bruni-Bossio.

the Cultural Heritage Foundation with the mandate to operate a grants program for qualifying groups. This new policy had an enormous impact on Edmonton's Italian community. Three Italian centres were built supported by the Community Facilities Enhancement Program, which funded the building and renovation of structures throughout Alberta including cultural, educational, sports and recreational facilities as well as community and church halls.

The Edmonton Heritage Festival (now SERVUS Heritage Festival) was established in 1977. Under the leadership of Sab Roncucci, representing the Dante Alighieri Society, the Italian community took part. The year 1978 saw the number of participating groups increase to 30. Mayfair Park (renamed Hawrelak Park in 1982) became the Festival's permanent home. A group was required to take on this programmatic role and, in 1979, the National Congress of Italian-Canadians, Edmonton District (NCIC) was established. The NCIC was incorporated under the *Societies Act* of Alberta and its foundation is a registered charity. Besides running the Italian pavilion at the Heritage Festival, the Congress undertakes a range of community building work including liaison with other ethnocultural communities and with the various levels of government. The founders included Carlo Amodio, Rudy Cavaliere, Tony Mazucca and Sab Roncucci. From the outset, presidents including Amodio, Cavaliere, Mazucca, Fausta Marazzo, Adriana (Albi) Davies and Sam Amelio emphasized that multiculturalism was more than food and dance. Activities included donation of the waterfall in the Shaw Conference Centre on the occasion of the City of Edmonton's 75th birthday (the centre opened in 1983); raising funds for earthquake relief in Italy and to benefit the people of Eritrea; construction of Piazza Italia Seniors Residence; talent shows and concerts; and the donation of a monument to the Province of Alberta on the occasion of its centenary in 2005. The Heritage Festival in August, one of Canada's largest ethnocultural festivals, spans the entire August long weekend. Running the Italian Pavilion is a major volunteer commitment and has been headed for many years by Carlo Amodio and Peter Bruno. Revenues generated allow NCIC to provide grants to Italian community organizations, individuals with projects benefitting the Italian community, Italian-language students, Italian courses at the University of Alberta as well as the opera program of the Department of Music.

Initial efforts to bring the existing Edmonton societies under the NCIC "umbrella" were unsuccessful; however, a few societies support NCIC initiatives. In 2002, NCIC provided financial support to the Heritage Community Foundation to create the *Celebrating Alberta's Italian Community* website, which is part of the *Alberta Online Encyclopedia*.[584] In 2013, the NCIC partnered with the Celebrating Italian Families of Edmonton Society (CIFES) to develop celebratory activities to

---

[584] Adriana A. Davies, Executive Director of the Heritage Community Foundation and Editor-in-Chief of the *Alberta Online Encyclopedia* created the *Celebrating Alberta's Italian Community* website in 2002 and authored thematic pieces.

commemorate the bicentenary of the birth of composer Giuseppe Verdi – the Edmonton Verdi Festival. The six-month festival was the largest festival outside of Italy and provided a showcase for musical talent. Partners from outside the Italian community included the Edmonton Opera and Chorus, the Edmonton Youth Orchestra, Citie Ballet and the Suzuki School.

The NCIC also created *Il Congresso*, an Italian newspaper with a provincial mandate, established by Carlo Amodio, Rudy Cavaliere and Alessandro Urso. The first issue was published in April 1984. Within the first year of operations, the paper became independent and the founders set up CURA Enterprises Ltd. The paper focused on Italian community news and articles were in English and Italian. News from Italy was relegated to a minor position and, in any case, another newspaper, *Il Mondo*, established by Vittorio Coco, covered this terrain drawing on content from Italian wire services (it was eventually replaced by *Il Nuovo Mondo* edited by Josephine Sicoli). *Il Congresso* nurtured columnists including Sab Roncucci, Frank Albi of Portland, Oregon, Adriana Davies and Vice Consul of Italy Giovanni Bincoletto, who wrote under the pseudonym "Il Gatto Pardo." The paper operated for 25 years until 2010 and is an important archival resource on Alberta's Italian communities.[585]

The Junior Appennini Dancers (later the Italian Appennini Dancers) was established, in 1979, by the founding members of the NCIC, Edmonton District to promote folk dancing and music. The group was named after the Appennini Mountain Range, the "spine" unifying all regions of Italy. The dancers became a feature of the Italian Pavilion stage at Heritage Days and have also peformed at festivals in Calgary, Jasper, Banff, Lake Louise, Saskatchewan and various regions of Italy. The dancers also present at seniors and extended care facilities. Directors and choreographers have included Sab Roncucci (1979-1985), Rosanna Verdicchio (1986-1998), Frank Cappelano (2000-2005), and, more recently, Frances Pagnotta, Sonia Pileggi and Ann Bodson.

Just as in Calgary, tensions between Northern and Southern Italians peaked in Edmonton in the late 1970s. The catalyst was the building of the Santa Maria Goretti Community Centre, which, according to some community members, was dominated by Calabrese. In 1979, this resulted in the creation of the Italian Cultural Society, first known as the Tri-Veneti Nel Mondo Cultural Society. The signatories to the application for society status were Assunta and Mario Cancian, Amalia Pozzobon, Giovanni Facchin, Alberto Del Moro and Giovanni Capra. Leadership was provided by Gino Antonello and Benito Zenari, who served as the founding

[585] Selected articles can be found on a database on the *Celebrating Alberta's Italian Community* website, URL: http://wayback.archive-it.org/2217/20101215215930/http://www.albertasource.ca/abitalian/illcongresso/ilcongresso_lifeways.php, retrieved December 17, 2017.

president. Other Board members included Frank Fraccaro, Mario Cancian, Vince Di Luigi, Lorenzo Giacobbo and Donato Calista.

The founders wanted a facility and, since the City of Edmonton had set aside land off the St. Albert Trail for multicultural communities to establish purpose-built centres (it was named the Peter Lougheed Multicultural Village in 1985), they looked to locate there. Land was obtained and fundraising begun but planning was brought to a halt when two Edmonton Italian societies complained to the city that the building of a centre based solely on an Italian region would be divisive for the Italian community. The City put the land approval on hold and members of the Italian Cultural Society had to make their case again. In order to move ahead, the founders brought together about 20 existing Italian societies and invited them to participate in the building project promising them a home in the Centre. The Italian Cultural Society would, however, remain in charge. This had been a bone of contention because, as a parish facility, the Santa Maria Goretti Centre was unable to offer a home to independent, non-religious organizations. The Italian Cultural Society made a presentation to the City of Edmonton Appeal Board and was successful in obtaining land.

More than $60,000 was raised and Victor Losa, former Italian honorary consul, gave a leadership gift of $30,000. The largest banqueting hall was named in his honour. Both the provincial and federal governments provided grants. Members involved in the construction industry, including new President Lorenzo Giacobbo, built the centre located at 14230 - 133 Avenue. Facilities include bocce court, offices, meeting rooms, a cafe/bar and card room. Societies with members of largely Northern Italian origin housed there include the Associazione Nazionale Alpini (founded in 1960); Società Bocciofila (1980); Fogolar Furlan (1981); Trevisani nel Mondo (1985); Associazione Nazionale Marinai d'Italia (National Association of Italian Sailors, 1992); Regione Molise – Associazione dei Sanniti (1991); Associazione Nazionale Combattenti e Reduci d'Italia (National Association of Fighters and Veterans of Italy, 1991); Vicentini nel Mondo (Citizens of the city of Vicenza in the World, 1992); and Associazione Lazio (1993). The Dante Alighieri Society made the Centre the location of its Italian language school and library for many years and still retains ties to the Centre.

The year 1981 saw Alfonso (Al) Iafolla, who had recently arrived from Calgary, initiate a petition for the re-naming of Patricia Park in Little Italy as Giovanni Caboto Park. The 10,000-name petition was brought to City Council and the re-naming was approved. The park's naming was intended to honour the sea captain, likely from Genoa, who sailed for King Henry VII of England, under the pseudonym John Cabot, to find new lands in the western hemisphere. The Giovanni Caboto Cultural Society of Alberta was established in 1981, and the first initiative was creation of a one-day festival held in the park on the last Sunday of June. Frank Spinelli of the Italian Centre Shop, supported these initiatives and daughter Teresa Spinelli has served as president of the society. These efforts helped to reinforce the "Little Italy" brand for the area. For the Caboto Festival in June, the block immediately adjacent to the Park was closed off creating a large piazza and merchants located carts and tables there, and sold various types of Italian food from sausages to ice cream. Activities included a cycle race (reminiscent of the Tour of Italy), pasta eating contest, climbing a greased pole as well as cultural displays and entertainment. The organizers ran out of steam in the early 2000s and the festival was not held for several years. Local businesses decided to revive it and, in 2011, it was rebranded "Viva Italia: Viva Edmonton," and became part of the East Meets West Festival that honours "Multicultural McCauley," Edmonton's inner city neighbourhood.

In 1982, the NCIC built the Piazza Italia Seniors Residence in Little Italy to allow seniors to remain near Santa Maria Goretti Parish and Italian shops when they could no longer live in their own homes. Funding for the six-storey, independent-living facility located at 9521 - 108A Avenue was provided by Canada Mortgage and Housing Corporation. Piazza Italia's governing board for many years included founding members Carlo Amodio, Rudy Cavaliere and Tony Mazzuca. Services to residents included medical support and a range of recreational activities. A professional manager was hired to run the facility. (Franco Mauro served in this capacity for many years.) Board chairs have included Adriana Davies and Sam Amelio. While, initially, the Centre was dedicated to Italian seniors who occupied about two-thirds of the suites, the changing demographics of McCauley saw the majority of Italians moving away from the inner city. When this occurred, residency requirements were expanded to include people of all ethnocultural backgrounds. Vista Housing for Seniors is the management agency responsible for running the provincially-owned facility. Sam Amelio has served as the NCIC representative on the board of Vista Housing for many years.

In 1983, the Italian Cultural Society established the Edmonton Juventus Sports Club with the objectives of offering recreational and competitive soccer, and road and track cycling for youth and adults. The club organized teams in a city-wide league leading to provincial and national championships for players aged 12 to 18. Early coaches included Ferdinando Zenari, Robert Moscie, Robert Pozzobon, Terry Antonello, Vito Loconte, Franco Bruni, Mike Fiorillo and John Contessa. The club affiliated with the Alberta Soccer Association and the Alberta Cycling Association. The club continues strong and its two branches – Edmonton Juventus Cycling and Edmonton Juventus Soccer – partnered, in 1995, with the Argyll Velodrome Association to take over that facility, built for the 1978 Commonwealth Games. Olympic Gold Medalist Lori-Ann Muenzer is a member of the Juventus Cycling Club.

Club Calabria was established in 1983 to promote the culture and traditions of the region. Founders included Enrico Potestio (president) and Bruno Romano (vice president). The group undertook social activities to raise funds for scholarships and held a Miss Calabria contest. In 1987, the club started an annual wine-making competition under the leadership of Tony Falcone and Ottavio Rosanova. Funds raised were used to provide scholarships for students of Italian descent. The organization operated for about 10 years.

The Teatro Libero (Free Theatre) was established in 1983 to promote the works of well-known Italian playwrights, and facilitate performances of Italian touring troupes. The group staged works by Luigi Pirandello, Dario Fo and Eduardo de Filippo. In July, 1984 Teatro Libro performed two comedies by Fo: *Non tutti i ladri vengono per nuocere* and *La Marcolfa*. They reprised these productions in February, 1985 in the Yates Theatre in Lethbridge and in the Italian Romulus and Remus Centre. Pasqualino Gatto, who taught English and Drama at Victoria Composite High School, was instrumental in setting up Teatro Libero and also directed a number of productions including De Filippo's *Natale in Casa Cupiello*. Carlo and Lina Amodio played the husband and wife and three performances were held at the Edmonton Public Library Theatre in Churchill Square. Another active volunteer, Maria Teresa Vecchio, a teacher and specialist in drama, also served as president. The society ceased to exist when volunteers were no longer available to carry on the work.

In 1985, the Patronato INAS (Italian Institute of Social Assistance) was created to help Italian immigrants residing in Alberta apply for social and health assistance provided by the Italian government. The young immigrants of the 1950s were now close to retirement and needed this type of help. The office initiates the administrative work to enable applicants who believe they are entitled, within the parameter of the bilateral accord between Italy and Canada, to certain social benefits (such as pensions). It is linked with the head office in Toronto and with offices in Montreal, Hamilton, Guelph and Mississauga.

The Ital-Canadian Seniors Association was established in 1986 at the urging of Father Augusto Feccia of Santa Maria Goretti Parish. Arnaldo Zanon was the founding president. The goal was to provide senior citizens with a drop-in centre and range of services. The Centre is located adjacent to the church at 9111-110 Avenue. In 2009, the Association set up the Alberta Italian Museum under the leadership of President Maria Mauro with the assistance of Adriana Davies. A mezzanine was built above the bocce courts to house exhibits. Luigi Zorzetto, a construction project supervisor, volunteered his services for planning and construction, and engineer Frank Cavaliere volunteered as structural consultant. Over 30 percent of the work was accomplished by volunteers. A grant from the Alberta Lottery Fund paid for 50 percent of the construction costs with the remainder contributed by the Association (its catering operations are revenue generating) and other donors. Work was completed in October 2009. Artifacts for displays were donated by members of the community and the Centre became the permanent home of travelling exhibits developed by Adriana Davies in partnership with the Galt Museum in Lethbridge: "Alberta's Italian Community" and "People of the Coal Mines: The Italian Community."

Societies continued to be developed even after immigration from Italy had effectively ceased. The Associazione Abruzzese of Edmonton was established in 1990 to promote the region's culture and traditions. It founded the Coro Folcloristico Abruzzese (Abruzzese Choir). Antonio Ranieri has served as president and Rosanna Verdicchio has been the choir director. The Celebrating Italian Families of Edmonton Society (CIFES) was created in 1996 to celebrate Italian families through the support of youth projects and seniors' events. The organization collaborates with the Santa Maria Goretti Parish, the three Italian Centres and other Italian associations. A primary activity is the 20 Regions of Italy Extravaganza Weekend; this raises funds for charitable purposes. Antonella Ciancibello-Normey was the founding president and still leads the organization.

The Lethbridge Italian Club

The post-war wave of immigration created a need for an organization to bring Italians together and, according to John Mazzuca, efforts were made as early as 1954 but nothing solidified. Efforts continued but no-one wanted to assume the role of president with its attendant responsibilities. Finally, in 1960, the Romulus & Remus Italian Canadian Club was established. On December 18, 1964, the group hosted a dinner at the Lethbridge Exhibition Pavilion to commemorate 100 years of Italian settlement in Canada. Attendees included Governor General Georges Vanier, Dan Innuzzi, centennial chairman for Canada, and the Italian consul-general.[586] Guests were greeted by Club president Frank Conti.

In 1972, a board was struck with Giulio Di Rocco, as president; Luigi Valerio, vice president; Nick Palazzo, treasurer; Luciano Travaglia, recording secretary; and directors Mike Vercillo, Mike Viani, Pietro Fiorino, Aldo Vercillo, Fernando Rose, Aldo Meli and John Mazzuca.[587] In 1972, John Mazzuca took on the vice presidency. The board began to plan for a building and, in 1975,

[586] Anon., "Italians to Mark Their Centennial," *Lethbridge Herald*, December 18, 1964.
[587] For the Lethbridge Italian Club history I have drawn on an unpublished document shared with me by John Mazzuca in 2018.

when Mazucca became president, it became a priority. Provincial funding was secured and board and committee members committed personal funds amounting to $8,700 to purchase a lot from the city. The Club set up debentures to support the building fund and, in the end, called them shares, not knowing that it was illegal to do so. People of Italian ancestry were targeted and asked to contribute $100 to the building fund; eventually, $60,000 was raised.

On May 24, 1977, the Italian Canadian Cultural Centre was completed at 1511 Street and Edward Boulevard N at a cost of $75,000. An issue arose when some of the "shareholders" wanted their money back. In order to do this, a bank loan was explored but because of the high interest rate proposed (22 percent), this option was rejected. In the end, Valerio Matteorri agreed to loan the money at 15 percent interest. The names of 300 donors are commemorated on an engraved plaque in the foyer of the building. The membership at the time was about 400. Nadia Zacchigna became the volunteer manager and the club began to generate money from rentals and was able to pay down the debt. The Ladies Auxiliary was formed in 1977 and the youth group soon after. Italian-language instruction was begun and activities for children included Christmas programming around La Befana, the witch who brings gifts to good boys and girls and coal to bad ones. Other events included seniors and family suppers, a summer picnic and camp out, a fall grape harvest supper and dance and a New Year's Ball.

A dance group, the Gioventu Italiana (Italian Youth), was started around 1979 and Sab Roncucci was brought down from Edmonton to coach and choreograph works. The group had 40 youth aged four to 20 and performed traditional folk dances. The dancers performed at Expo '86 in Vancouver and in Italian communities.[588] The Club established the Romulus & Remus Italian Canadian Scholarship at Lethbridge College and the University of Lethbridge. The 25th anniversary celebration, in April 2002, was attended by 460 individuals including guests Pierluigi Trombetta, Italian Consul from Edmonton; representatives from the civic, provincial and federal governments; Carlo Amodio, from the National Congress in Edmonton; and Cecilia Cupido from the Calgary National Congress. John Mazzuca, who served as president for the entire period of the Club's existence, was recognized as was wife Linda Mazzuca, who had volunteered the entire time. As the founders aged and died, membership declined and, to address this issue, restriction of membership to Italian-Canadians was abolished. The Italian Centre became a community organization and is still going strong.

---

[588] John Mazzuca, "Italiani di Lethbridge à Expo 86," *Il Congresso*, November 1986.

Religious Organizations

In the early years of Italian settlement, individuals who were strong Roman Catholics worshipped at established churches in their communities. Italian-speaking priests occasionally said Mass. With the establishment of the Diocese of Calgary, in 1912, St. Mary's became the Cathedral and Italians who settled in Riverside (later renamed Bridgeland), worshipped there. In 1916, Bishop McNally established St. Angela's Chapel, and some Italians switched their allegiance to this church. In 1929, Our Lady of Perpetual Help was built in Bridgeland and became the church of choice for many in the Italian community. In Edmonton, Italians initially worshipped at Francophone churches such as Église Catholique St. Joachim, built in 1898-1899 in the Oliver neighbourhood. The Église Cœur Immaculé de Marie (Immaculate Heart of Mary Church) was built next at 96 Street and 108 Avenue. In 1913, Sacred Heart Church opened across the street and served the growing Anglophone community. Italians began to worship at Sacred Heart in the McCauley neighbourhood. Mass in Italian was said occasionally by Oblates in the basement of the church. In the post-war period, Mass was also said in the Chapel at the General Hospital by Father Luigi, a member of the Salesian order of missionary priests.

While Edmonton, Calgary and the Crowsnest region had significant Italian populations, it would be the Venice agricultural colony that built the first church, Il Redentore (Holy Redeemer), in 1924. An article in the Edmonton *Journal* of December 6, 1924 noted that the cornerstone for the "Redentore" (Redeemer) church was laid on November 30th and that a blessing was performed by the Rev. Charles (Carlo) Fabris, the delegate from His Grace Archbishop O'Leary. It continues:

> The church which will be completed in a few weeks is situated near Venice station and is being built according to the plans of the architect, Edward Underwood of Edmonton. It will be of artistic design.
>
> It is hoped to see in the very near future a large influx of population in the colony and already Father Fabris, who was called direct from Rome by His Grace the Archbishop is working incessantly towards this end and the united efforts are sure to bring the desired results.[589]

Undoubtedly, Archbishop Henry Joseph O'Leary was influenced by Consular Agent Felice de Angelis.[590] Father Fabris bought the windows, doors and hardware for the church; Pio Bonifacio, Salvatore Giacobbo, Joe Michetti, Frank and Attilio Macor, and Leonardo Guerra volunteered

---

[589] Cited in *Hylo-Venice: Harvest of Memories*, 191.
[590] *Ibid.*, 12.

labour; and some lumber was provided by the De Angelis/Marini sawmill. The importance of the priest to the community is noted by Tony Bonifacio, who observes of Father Fabris: "He had many ambitious dreams, and one was the pine trees that were planted around the church in 1927. When planted by the parishioners in 1927 they were about three to four feet tall."[591] According to Tony, the trees were planted to resemble the Colonnade of the Vatican in Rome. He also noted: "During this time, my mother walked from farm to farm, collecting donations of money to purchase a statue of The Holy Redeemer to set up in the church. The statue was bought and shipped from Italy and was in the original church until it was demolished. Also, there was a cast iron bell in the steeple of the old church. The whereabouts of the bell and statue are unknown today."[592] Father Fabbris also wanted a convent school and went scouting for possible students in communities with large Italian populations.[593] He did not succeed and left the community in 1927. He was the first and only Italian-speaking priest.

Three individuals were instrumental in getting an Italian church built in Edmonton: Angelo Biasutto, a cook at the St. Mary's Home for Boys; Henry Butti, owner of an electrical business; and Pat Giannone, owner of the Cromdale Hotel. They were aware of the reputation of the Scalibrini Fathers (Missionaries of St. Charles), an order that served Italian immigrant communities in North America, and believed they might be the best option to run a parish.[594] Archbishop Anthony Jordan gave his approval and, in December 1957, fathers Giovanni Bonelli and Rino Ziliotto arrived from Chicago. Biasutto and Butti, who were involved with the Cristoforo Colombo Soccer Club, knew that land had been offered for a soccer pitch and that the club did not have the money to build. They suggested that the land, on 110 Avenue and 90 Street, be offered as a church site. A committee began planning and obtaining pledges to cover construction costs. Two saint's names were presented to the Archbishop – St. Cecilia and Santa Maria Goretti – and he decided that the latter would be closer to Edmonton's Italian community since she was a "saint of our days." The sod turning took place on September 8, 1958 with Mayor William Hawrelak in attendance and the wooden truss and stucco building was dedicated on December 21. Shortly after, a small rectory and church hall extension were completed. In 1966, a new rectory was built. By 1973, all building costs had been paid.

---

[591] Tony Bonifacio, *Venice Alberta 1914.*

[592] Anthony P. (Tony) Bonifacio, "Bonifacio, Pio and Lucia Bonifacio, Anthony and Rina (nee Macor)," *Hylo-Venice: Harvest of Memories*, 277.

[593] *Hylo-Venice: Harvest of Memories*, 13.

[594] At the time of the order's centenary in 1987, there were 750 Scalabrinian fathers working in 20 countries with immigrants of various nationalities.

The priests understood the need to create vehicles for social interaction that would make the church the centre of community life. They established the Donne del Santo Rosario (Ladies of the Holy Rosary) and Azione Cattolica (Catholic Action). The former society was established, in 1958, to help promote Christian values and to support Santa Maria Goretti Parish financially, through a variety of fundraising activities, and spiritually with a variety of auxiliary tasks. Leaders in the early days were Mary Giannone, Myra Butti, Iolanda Segatti, Rosa Biasutto, Rina Vanoni and daughter Julie Ciochetti, Lucy Sartor and Florence Biamonte. Catholic Action allowed young people to meet without parental supervision and was the means by which many couples fell in love and married. The hall became the location for meetings of societies as well as weddings, anniversaries, and parties to celebrate baptisms, Holy Communions and Confirmations.

A new surge of activity happened with the arrival of Father Augusto Feccia from Chicago in 1979. Born in Chiavenna Rochetta, Piacenza, after taking holy orders, he was sent to serve as associate pastor at the Italian parish in Chicago, which he did until 1965. From 1965 to 1970, he served as pastor of the Italian American Federation and became interested in the documentation of Italian-American history. From 1970 to 1979, he was the founder and director of the Italian Cultural Centre in Illinois and worked with volunteers to convert an old building into a centre dedicated to religion, art, culture and music. He wanted this for Edmonton and, in 1981, set up a volunteer committee to investigate the possibilities. The executive comprised Pat Giannone, chair; Peter Caffaro, first vice-chair; Frank Cairo, second vice-chair; Agostino Annichiarico, treasurer; and Carlo Amodio, secretary. Peter Batoni, Rudy Cavaliere, D. Gulli, S. Pompei, Mario Scrivano and Luigi Zorzetto were members-at-large. Cairo subsequently became chair and other members were added including Carmen Naccarato, Angelo Biasutto, Tony Cairo, Ugo Fioretti, Silvio Pino, Carmen Rago, Tony Spadafore, Dick Tomat and Livio Cabrelli.

An aggressive fundraising campaign culminated in 1987 with an application for funding to the Government of Alberta's Recreational Cultural Funding Program. The following objectives were set out: establishment of a community facility with significant cultural, artistic, social and recreational components; revitalization of one of Edmonton's oldest and historically Italian neighbourhoods; and promotion of Italian cultural heritage amongst second and third generation Italian-Canadians. Eight bids were received for construction of the Santa Maria Goretti Centre ranging from $1.6 to $1.9 million. More than $350,000 was raised through bingos, casinos and donations, and $800,000 was lent by the Archdiocese of Edmonton. The centre was built at a cost of about $2 million. A new rectory was built at the same time. The gala opening in July 1986 included a day-time procession to the Centre led by Father Feccia followed by representatives from the various Italian societies with their banners. A sold-out gala dinner was attended by community members, Vice Consul of Italy Giovanni Bincoletto and civic, provincial and federal officials. A non-profit society was established to run the Centre.[595] Sunday *pranzo*, after the 11 am Mass, became a tradition, and the two main halls and meeting rooms became popular venues for community celebrations as well as theatrical productions, concerts, talent shows, art exhibits, fashion shows and conferences. Additional renovations occurred in 2004.

Edmonton was well on its way to becoming a "mini" Chicago. The 25th anniversary of the parish, in 1983, provided an opportunity to undertake a legacy project. Father Feccia was proud of the parish's service to the community including the solemnization of 1,000 marriages, the baptizing of over 4,000 children and confirmation of over 2,400 children. He established the Italians Settle in Edmonton Historical Society, in 1982, with Frank Sdao, a teacher at St. Joseph's High School, as president. Sdao outlined the objectives as follows: "Write the story of the Italian community of Edmonton and region; create materials based on the track established by Canadian multiculturalism; keep the community informed of the contributions, experiences and aspirations of Italian-Canadians; render materials created accessible to the City and Provincial Archives; collect materials that will assist in the teaching of history in the City and Province of Alberta; and Prepare publications of interest to the general public."[596] Feccia also recruited Adriana Davies as volunteer lead researcher; at the time she was the Science and Technology Editor of the *Canadian Encyclopedia,* Mel Hurtig's visionary gift to the people of Canada for Alberta's 75th anniversary.

David Goa, Curator of Folk and Religious Life at the Provincial Museum of Alberta, and Jim Parker, University of Alberta Archivist, were recruited to train volunteers. Rudy Vecoli, founder of the Immigration History Research Center at the University of Minnesota, was brought in as a resource person. He had served as president of the American Italian Historical Association from 1966 to 1970. Project deliverables included oral histories, a photographic exhibit and commemorative booklet (written by Davies and translated into Italian by Tony Falcone). Other volunteers included Rita Arnieri, Anna Maria Bruni, Tony Caria, Rita Cavaliere, Elizabeth Crump-Dumesnil, Philip Fiorillo, Carmela Marino, Mario Rizzuto, Severina Rossi, Joe Russo, Teresa Sdao, Josephine Sibilani and Alessandro Urso. Father Feccia's work in Edmonton ended in 1990 when he was appointed director of Villa Scalabrini in California. In 2016, the Board of the Santa Maria Goretti Community Centre named one of their halls in his honour.

---

[595] Presidents have included: Frank Cairo, Carlo Amodio, Agostino Annichiarico, Rudy Cavaliere, Salvatore Amelio, Tony Mazzuca, Frank Cairo, Joe Bocchinfuso, Fausto Franceschi, Tiz Benvenuto, Rita Raimuno, Ben Raimundo and Luigi Zorzetto and Mario Palazzo.

[596] Frank, Sdao, "Insediamento Italiano in Edmonton Un Progetto Di Ricerca Storica," (Italian Settlement in Edmonton: A Historical Research Project), *Il Congresso,* year 1, no 3, June 1984. Translation was done by the author.

In 2002, the Scalibrini Order left Santa Maria Goretti Parish and the parish became part of the Archdiocese of Edmonton. Its priests were aging and their founding mission was no longer relevant since there had been no significant immigration from Italy for many years. As members of Edmonton's Italian community left the inner-city, many did not return to Mass at the church though some continued to attend functions at the Centre. Another difficulty was that Italian priests could not be found to come to Edmonton, although this has been addressed by bringing in priests, such as Father George Puramadathil, who speak Italian. The shrinking congregation remains an issue.

In Calgary, Italian-speaking priests continued to say Mass in local parishes until the early 1960s. Among them was Father Gene Violini, a member of a prominent Calgary Italian family, who said Mass at St. Mary's Cathedral.[597] It would be the arrival of Monsignor Angelo Sacchi, in 1963, that stirred discussion about a dedicated Italian church. Bishop Francis Carroll approved the purchase of St. Andrew's, an old Presbyterian church in Inglewood, and it became La Parrocchia di Sant'Andrea (St. Andrew's Parish). Antonella Fanella notes that the timing was right: "In comparison to the pre-war migrants, who were sporadic in church attendance, the post-war immigrants became closely attached to St. Andrew's. While they claim to have felt comfortable in the 'English' church, the immigrants needed their own church. Only an Italian parish could accommodate their special cultural traditions such as compareggio (godparenthood), le feste dei santi (festivals of patron saints), first communion, weddings, or a special mass for a deceased relative in Italy."[598]

The community restored Sant'Andrea and it opened on September 14, 1965. By the early 1980s, congregation growth required an expansion, or another church. According to Fanella, this was opposed by the community at large but Bishop Paul O'Byrne supported it and, in June 1985, Our Lady of Grace Italian and English Church was opened.[599] Father Riccardo Bezzegato, a Scalabrinian who was assigned to the parish, observed in a 1988 interview that his focus, besides pastoral work, was to pay down the mortgage.[600] He felt that social activities could be developed later and, in any case, the Italian Club addressed this need and he did not see the church competing with them. Bezzegato was well aware of the turmoil in Edmonton when Santa Maria Goretti

[597] Kathy Roe presents Father Gene's life, in *Memories of Fr. Violini* (Calgary, AB: Kathy Roe, 2014). He was the son of immigrant parents and served in Calgary parishes as well as Mission churches including St. Joseph's at Cowley, Alberta. She describes miracles attributed to him.

[598] Fanella, 56.

[599] Norman Knowles, *Winds of Change – A History of the Roman Catholic Diocese of Calgary since 1968* (Calgary, AB: Roman Catholic Diocese of Calgary and St. Mary's University, ca 2004).

[600] Father Riccardo Bezzegato interview, Peoples of Southern Alberta Oral History Project, January 27, 1988, Glenbow Archives RCT-818.

Parish built a large cultural centre initiating a north/south controversy, and did not want to see this replicated in Calgary. He bemoaned the fact that the many families lived far away and did not attend.

Educational Organizations and Programs

Edmonton's Italian community played a key role in introducing Italian language instruction in Alberta. The work was accomplished by some dynamic individuals including Sab Roncucci who was a natural educator. He arrived in Edmonton from Milan with his family in 1958 and had a good command of English since he had served as a translator for the Allies at the end of the war. He set up his own tailoring business and also taught at the Northern Alberta Institute of Technology. The Edmonton branch of the Società Dante Alighieri established the Scuola di Lingua e Cultura Italiana (Italian Language and Culture School) in 1962. It was housed at the Santa Maria Goretti Church Hall.[601] There were 36 students enrolled in the Saturday morning classes. Tony Falcone served as the first director and teacher. Myra Butti, member of a pioneer family, served as secretary; Enrico Musacchio, newly-arrived professor of Italian at the University of Alberta, was instructional counsel; and Peter Caffaro, became legal counsel. In the second year, the school moved to two classrooms in Sacred Heart School, also in the inner city. Other teachers were added, including Tony Caria, and they were paid an honorarium of $2.50 per lesson.[602]

The school next moved to the Italian Cultural Centre where its library is still located. Principals have included Antonella Ciancibello, Reny Clericuzzio and Aristide Melchionna. Ciancibello and Chiaricuzzo attended the University of Alberta and Melchionna, who came to Edmonton as an adult, was educated in Italy and at the University of Alberta. Today, the Dante School offers instruction to children and adults not only within the Italian community but also the community at large. Enrolment continued to increase and, by 1996, there were 172 students. Roncucci was a founder of the Northern Alberta Heritage Languages Association (1978) and the Dante School program served as a model for other ethnocultural groups for the retention of heritage languages.

In 1970, the Dante Society contacted Minister of Education Robert Clark and the Edmonton Catholic School Board with respect to the introduction of Italian into the school curriculum.

[601] The Dante Alighieri School website was developed by Adriana Davies at the Heritage Community Foundation in 2008. See URL: http://www.ladanteedmonton.org/en/school/history.html, retrieved December 21, 2017.
[602] Teachers have included Lina Amodio, Loretta Moscardelli, Francesca Cardilem, Patrizia Farrar, Hilario Saccarello, Mirella Cristello, Melania Stavale, Angela Mack, Eleonora Mannarino, Natascia Mazzotta, Loretta Moscardelli-Bacon, Catrina Mandalit and Francesca Cardile.

The request was accepted by Alberta Education and Tony Falcone and Tony Caria combined material obtained from the Government of Ontario with Dante School instructional materials to create the first curriculum. In 1971, Italian language instruction at the grade 7 level was introduced at Sacred Heart School. The year 1973 saw Caria introducing Italian 10 at Archbishop O'Leary. In the same year, the junior high Italian program was moved from Sacred Heart School to Cardinal Léger School in the west end. This move reflected a shift of the Italian population from the inner-city to the inner-ring of suburbs. Italian programs continued to be introduced to Edmonton Catholic schools including St. Joseph's High School (1974, Tony Petrone), Archbishop MacDonald and St. Francis Xavier high schools and St. Cecilia Junior High. Caria was succeeded at Sacred Heart by Carmelo Rago, in 1975.

In 1976, Manuel Da Costa, who at the time was working for the Secretary of State, provided a $7,500 grant to create a workbook. This was accomplished by Caria, who served as course administrator, and Falcone, as language teacher. In 1982, a proposal was sent to the Edmonton Catholic School Board to move the program from "a system-based option to a provincially recognized core language option." Falcone and Caria created the curriculum, which was piloted in 1983. Edmonton Catholic then sold the curriculum to Calgary Catholic for introduction to the school system there. Alberta Education created a committee with representation from the province's Italian teachers and a provincial program was established in 1994. By 1996, 379 students received Italian language instruction in Edmonton Catholic schools. In 1999, Italian was introduced at St. Philip Elementary School. The program of studies was developed by Ida Renzi, Valeria Palladino and Silvia Franzese. Adult evening classes had been introduced in 1972, by the Department of Continuing Education of the Edmonton Public School Board. The average annual enrolment was 40 but, as interest declined, courses were terminated and this need was filled by the University of Alberta Faculty of Extension.

In Calgary, Italian language instruction came later: with the support of the Calgary Italian Club, in 1973, Giovanni Germano, Consul General of Italy, met with community leaders to address this gap.[603] Supporters included Alberto Romano, Serafino Scarpino, Jimmy Barbaro, Joe Commissotti, Norma Massolin, Cosma Ius, Rodolfo Pacione, Gary Cioni, Eda De Santis, Honorary Vice Consul Sandro Silenzi and Valeria Sestieri Lee, who had recently arrived in Calgary and was a graduate of the University of Rome. To establish need, a list of potential students was compiled by Romano and Scarpino and it totaled 120. The first curriculum was developed by Serafino Scarpino. The Italian Consul General in Vancouver provided funding support of $1,000

[603] See Calgary Italian School website, "History," URL: https://italianschoolcalgary.com/?page_id=4, retrieved January 23, 2019.

and this enabled classes at the Calgary Italian School to begin in January 1974 at St. Alphonsus and St. Michael schools with an enrolment of 200. In 1976, classes moved to St. Mary's and, in 1978, to the Calgary Italian Club where they have remained. Instruction at grades 10, 20 and 30 was introduced at St. Francis, Bishop Grandin and Father Lacombe high schools in the early 1980s. Scarpino moved to St. Francis High School to instruct and, because of high enrolments, a second teacher, Maria Amoru, was hired (Scarpino had taught her).

The classes attracted not only Italian students but also those of other ethnocultural backgrounds. In 1981, a joint curriculum was developed in a partnership between the Dante School in Edmonton and the Calgary Italian School. To encourage the study of Italian, in 1985, the Calgary Italian School introduced a $500 scholarship, awarded to the student receiving the highest grade in Italian 30. The year 1988 saw the establishment of a scholarship to attend a course at the Università per gli Stranieri in Perugia. In 1998, as part of a mandated provincial curriculum review, the Calgary Italian School developed a new curriculum and, in 2004, six new classrooms were added to the school. The year 2006 saw Italian as a Second Language (ISL) instruction introduced at two Catholic elementary schools in the city.

The length of volunteer commitment was staggering not only on the part of teachers but also the board. Alberto Romano served as president for 14 years retiring in 1988. Domenico Rossi succeeded him and served for 18 years and was, in turn, followed by Caterina Greco-Mangone in 2006. She studied law and romance languages at the University of Alberta and had worked as a multicultural consultant and, later, human rights officer for the Government of Alberta.

University Italian Programs

University level instruction in the Italian language and culture in Alberta universities was introduced by professors who received their education in Italy. They were succeeded by American and Canadian-trained individuals. In 1962, Enrico Musacchio became a professor in the Department of Romance Languages, Faculty of Arts, at the University of Alberta. He received a doctorate in philosophy from the Università degli Studi, Rome. Having Italian studies at the university was an important milestone for Alberta's Italian community and the majority of the students in Musacchio's first class were drawn from the community. The program grew beyond language courses to include Italian literature and culture, and Italian grew from a minor to a major in the undergraduate degree program. On his retirement in 1996, Musacchio became a professor emeritus of modern languages and comparative studies at the University.

In 1980, Massimo Verdicchio, joined the Romance Languages Department and succeeded Musacchio as program head. Verdicchio was born in Naples and immigrated to Canada with his family at the age of 16 in 1961; the family first lived in Ottawa and then made their home in Vancouver. Verdicchio received a Ph D from Yale University in 1978 and specialized in Dante and Petrarch, and theory of the novel and anti-novel. On retirement, he became an emeritus professor. William Anselmi served as first associate professor and, then, as professor of Italian and Italian-Canadian literature and culture. He received a Masters' degree from Carleton University in 1983 and a Ph D in Comparative Literature in 1992 from the Université de Montréal.[604] He is a specialist in Italian poetry of the neo-avant-garde and experimentalism as well as Italian-Canadian literature and culture.

In 2006, Patrizia Bettella became the Italian Language Program Coordinator and held this position until 2014. She studied at the Università Cattolica di Milano and obtained a Ph D from Johns Hopkins University in Washington, DC. Her research interests include women literary figures of the Middle Ages and Baroque in Italy. She has also written about the cinematic treatment of women and children during the Fascist period in Italy. She has served as Vice-President of the Canadian Society for Italian Studies and as review editor for *Quaderni d'italianistica.*

An additional dimension was added to Italian studies when Helenà Fracchia ahd Maurizio Gualtieri joined the Classics Department (later History Department). Fracchia studied at the University of California at Berkeley and obtained a Ph D in Classical Archaeology. Gualtieri, a specialist in pre-Roman and Roman Italy, obtained a degree in Letters and Philosophy from the University of Naples (1965) and a Ph D from the University of Pennsylvania (1977). In the early 1980s, the husband-and-wife team established the University of Alberta School in Cortona and, in the following years, undertook archaeological work at Rocca Gloriosa and Oppido Lucano. Fracchia became the Scientific Director of the University of Alberta's Archaeological Field School at Ossaia. In a 1984 article in *Il Congresso*, Gualtieri described the first digs as follows:

> As in the previous two years, during the months of June and July 1984, the University of Alberta held a summer course in archaeology in Italy, to provide experience in the technology of the archaeological dig to teachers and students. At a time when the study of the past and archaeology, in particular, are experiencing a "boom" period in North America, a course of this type is the best vehicle to provide enthusiasts with technological knowledge and skills. At the same time, it allows students from various parts of Canada an opportunity to experience directly the culture and life of Italy.[605]

---

[604] Wikipedia, "William Anselmi," https://en.wikipedia.org/wiki/William_Anselmi, retrieved December 22, 2017.
[605] Maurizio Gualtieri, "L'Universita dell'Alberta in Italia," *Il Congresso*, year 1, no 2, May 1984.

The "boom" was a reference to the Indiana Jones series of films, beginning with *Raiders of the Lost Ark* released in 1981, which stimulated interest in classical archaeology. The summer courses were funded by the Social Sciences and Humanities Research Council of Canada. In 2015, the University introduced a non-credit course led by Fracchia. The prospectus noted:

> For the first time this fall, the Faculty of Arts is offering a "Mosaic Course" in Cortona, Italy to alumni and the general public for nine days of learning and adventure, led by academics who live, work and research in the region — including History & Classics professor Helena Fracchia, archeologist and director of the UAlberta School in Cortona. Participants will enjoy academic discussions on ancient and modern Italy, visits to museums, traditional Italian cooking (including an olive oil and truffle lesson), language instruction, wine tasting and guided archeological tours.[606]

This is not an academic offering but, rather, a "life style" course and, as part of its promotion, the University states: "Did you know that Italian is the fourth most studied language in the world? Italy is the 8th largest economy in the world, and is home to 50 UNESCO World Heritage Sites. Studies in Italian could lead you to many careers including those in import/export, art restoration, music, teaching, high fashion, and film."[607] This brand is very different from that at the initiation of Italian studies in the early 1960s.

It was Fracchia's and Gualtieri's dream to bring a major archaeological exhibit to the Provincial Museum of Alberta in Edmonton. This came to fruition (without their involvement because of pressures of academic work) in October, 2002 when the exhibit "Ancient Rome" opened at the Provincial Museum of Alberta (now the Royal Alberta Museum), as a result of efforts by Director Bruce McGillivray. It received funding support from the Italian consulate and was curated by Joel Christianson.

Italian studies at the University of Calgary were pioneered by Valeria Sisterio Lee. She was born in Rome and attended its namesake university receiving a degree in the Humanities with an Art History major in 1959. She found it difficult to obtain a job and held a series of short-term appointments including as museum curator and even as a secretary in a government public health institution. Valeria applied for jobs teaching Italian at various American universities and, in 1962, accepted a position at the University of Illinois at Urbana. She married Egmont Lee in

[606] See Donna McKinnon, "Italy for the Intellectually Curious Traveler, *WOA/Work of Arts*, July 16, 2015.
[607] University of Alberta description of the Italian program, URL: https://www.ualberta.ca/modern-languages-and-cultural-studies/undergraduate-program-information/areas/italian, retrieved December 22, 2017.

1963 and completed a Ph D at the University of Illinois in 1967. In 1968, Egmont obtained a job in the History department at the University of Calgary. Valeria initially worked as a tutor in the History Department and, then, taught in the Department of French, Italian and Spanish as a part-time instructor. When an Italian program did not immediately develop, she left the University and taught at the Italian School. She returned to the University in 1977 when the program was expanded. Egmont, whose specialty was the Italian Renaissance, added to the University's offerings. For a number of years, he was the director of the Canadian Academic Centre in Italy and was asked to join the Roman Gruppo dei Romanisti. In 1976, he established the Calgary Institute for the Humanities at the University. Both Valeria and Egmont promoted international exchanges to enrich the experience of their students. In a 1987 interview, she noted that it was not just students of Italian ancestry who took Italian courses at the University; students came from all ethnic backgrounds.

More recently, Italian Studies became part of the University of Calgary's School of Language, Linguistics, Literature and Culture and its focus, according to the program description, is "the multidisciplinary examination of Italian language, literature, culture, art and history." Available as a major and minor for undergraduate degrees in Arts and Education, it is also marketed as part of the University's focus on multicultural diversity. An annual event, supported by the Italian Consulate General in Vancouver and the Italian Cultural Institute in Toronto, is the "Settimana della Lingua Italiana" (Week of Italian Language) that brings in international personalities including writers and scholars. In the late 1990s, a Masters program was added and Serafino Scarpino and others helped to bring this about.

The Italian Studies Program is linked with Perugia's Università per Stranieri and for-credit courses can be taken there. Exchanges can also be done with universities in Bologna and Verona. "Life-style" non-credit course are also offered in Perugia. Emilia Spoldi, who obtained a degree in Italian Language and Literature from the University of Milan, has been the Director of the University of Calgary Study Abroad Program since 2007. She is a member of the Italian Language Education Consortium and the Canadian Society for Italian Studies. Francesca Cadel, who has a doctorate in Italian Studies from the University of Sorbonne-Paris IV (1999) and a Ph D in Comparative Literature from the City University of New York (2002), is also part of the current faculty. The program receives funding support from various sources including the Italian consulate in Vancouver and Calgary Italian societies such as the Fogolar Furlan.

For members of Alberta's Italian community who fought for university studies in Italian, the programs at the universities of Alberta and Calgary have been a source of both pride and frustration. Some hoped that they would espouse Italian-Canadian history. This did not happen since universities are driven by their own agendas. Former University of Athabasca professor and author

Joseph J. Pivato takes them to task for their lack of support for Italian-Canadian authors. Pivato observes: "Italian studies programs in North America, Australia and elsewhere are in a colonial position with regard to Italy. They are materially dependent on the publications from there and ideologically dependent on the conservative ideals of nostalgia for the country of origin. In this colonial space there is no room for criticism of this very position, nor for theoretical questioning of European assumptions."[608]

Some Observations

The history of the development of Italian societies in Alberta reveals that the first societies, the mutual aid societies, financially supported recent immigrants who were in a disadvantaged position in the work place. They also had a social dimension since they were fraternal in nature. Focused largely on the mining community, they ceased to be relevant with closure of many mines in the 1950s and also the introduction of workers compensation and health benefits. While more purely "social" organizations were established, they were dealt a death blow by enemy alien designation and internment in the Second World War.

The massive wave of immigration, beginning in the 1950s, gave birth to a range of cultural, social, religious and educational societies. These were an affirmation that Italians had come to stay and become a part of Canadian democracy. These societies had a foot in the past (all affirmed the importance of Italian language and culture) and the future: many adopted multicultural statements as part of their program plans. They all benefitted from multicultural policies that frequently had financial support for programming and facilities.

With the passage of time, children, grandchildren and great grandchildren became Canadian, in simple terms, they became assimilated, and this challenged the modus operandi of existing societies. Aging board members and volunteers clung to the traditions of the past and could not understand the lack of interest in their work on the part of the younger generation. In addition, many organizations experienced conflict based on the division between North and South that immigrants had brought to Canada from Italy. This can clearly be seen in the conflict at the Calgary Italian Club, which saw splintering into a range of other societies. In Edmonton, since there was no comparable society, regionally-based clubs formed first and were followed by the establishment of the National-Congress of Italian Canadians, Edmonton District, which attempted to set itself up as an umbrella organization. This was only moderately successful and, by the

---

[608] Joseph J. Pivato, "Italianista vs. Italian-Canadian Writing," URL: *http://engl.athabascau.ca/faculty/jpivato/italianistica. php*, retrieved December 23, 2017.

early 1990s, there were over 40 Italian societies in Edmonton. The difference in the character of the two cities is also manifested in their societies. Calgary's emphasis on business is evidenced not only in the important role that business people have played in the leadership of the Calgary Italian Club but also initiatives such as the extremely successful Sportsmen's Dinner. Edmonton's societies remained staunchly cultural, social, religious and educational in nature and, because of Edmonton's position as provincial capital, the leadership of the National Congress, Edmonton District, was extremely engaged in debates around multiculturalism.

What is evident, as members of the Italian community prospered, societies focused on cultural identity ceased to have relevance. This problem is not confined to the Italian community. It has affected and continues to affect ethnocultural and mainstream organizations alike. Organizations incapable of change simply cease to exist. Educational organizations offer some useful examples. While the teaching of the Italian language began through Saturday morning language schools operated by registered societies, it was taken over by Alberta Education and school boards when a demand was demonstrated. At the university level, instruction of "romance" and other languages has become part of a larger construct – languages, culture and society – and, at the adult level, a part of "life-style" activities rooted in language and culture.

The Loggia Giovanni Caboto No. 8, Calgary's first Italian society, had its headquarters in an old garage on 4th Street and 2nd Avenue NE in 1925. Photo courtesy of Glenbow, Archives and Special Collections, University of Calgary NA-5124-3.

Santa Maria Goretti Church, built in Edmonton in 1958, saw many weddings as a result of the immigration boom in the late 1950s and 1960s. Photo courtesy of Provincial Archives of Alberta A10969.

Celestina Andrenacci mixing eggs and flour to make tagliatelle pasta in the first International Food Fair sponsored by the Calgary Canadian Citizenship Council, January 1955. Italians were one of the 13 ethnocultural communities that participated in the event. The event was a foretaste of ethnocultural festivals such as Edmonton's Heritage Days which showcased food and dance. The Albertan January 29, 1955. Glenbow Archives NA-5600-7110a.

CHAPTER X

Cultural Identity and Belonging

THE 1950s THROUGH THE 1970s was a period of hard work and material betterment for Italian immigrants in Alberta. At the leadership level, it was one of engagement with the various levels of government. Policy changes in the areas of immigration and culture would have a profound impact on the process of integration and assimilation. In 1961, the Report of the Royal Commission on Bilingualism and Biculturalism, besides furthering the English/French "founding nations" theory, suggested that support be provided to other cultural groups. It would take another 10 years for this to take effect: in October 1971, Prime Minister Trudeau in the Canadian Multiculturalism Policy recognized Canada's diversity defined in terms of language, customs, religion, and other areas of difference. In the debate in the House of Commons, Trudeau noted: "It was the view of the royal commission, shared by the government and, I am sure, by all Canadians, that there cannot be one cultural policy for Canadians of British and French origin, another for the original peoples and yet a third for all others. For although there are two official languages, there is no official culture, nor does any ethnic group take precedence over any other. No citizen or group of citizens is other than Canadian, and all should be treated fairly."[609]

At the provincial level, in 1971, Premier Harry E. Strom introduced a "New Cultural Policy for the Province of Alberta." The year 1973 saw establishment of the Cultural Heritage Council and a secretariat to implement multicultural policies and co-ordinate programs. In June of that year, Minister of Culture, Youth and Recreation, Horst Schmid, a German immigrant, unveiled the new policy directions in a keynote paper titled "Keystone of our Cultural Tomorrow" at a conference at the University of Alberta. Schmid became the first Minister of Culture and Multi-culturalism. In 1974, the *Alberta Heritage Day Act* proclaimed the first Monday in August as a provincial holiday to celebrate cultural heritage. In 1977, Schmid sponsored the first Ethnocultural Language Teachers' Seminar through the new Cultural Heritage Branch. In 1978, the Alberta Ethnic Language Teachers' Association was incorporated with northern and southern Alberta branches. Edmonton Mayor Lawrence Decore was the first elected civic official to champion

[609] Pierre Elliott Trudeau, House of Commons Debates, October 8, 1971, 8545-8548.

multiculturalism and it was entrenched in a policy paper titled "A Cultural Policy for Edmonton." This was a recommendation of the Mayor's Task Force on Culture, established in 1984. In 1985, Alberta Culture and the Cultural Heritage Division of the Secretary of State for Multiculturalism sponsored a conference on heritage language schools; this was held in Red Deer on November 15-16.[610]

These liberalizing measures culminated, in 1982, with the recognition of multiculturalism in section 27 of the Canadian Charter of Rights and Freedoms and, in 1988, with the *Canadian Multiculturalism Act*, the first in the world. The last was enacted under PM Brian Mulroney. The *Constitution Act*, 1982, Part I, defines the fundamental freedoms shared by all Canadians as "(a) freedom of conscience and religion; (b) freedom of thought, belief, opinion and expression, including freedom of the press and other media communication; (c) freedom of peaceful assembly; and (d) freedom of association." The impact of these changes on the building of ethnic pride and a sense of belonging in Alberta's ethnic communities cannot be understated. At the most basic level, the policies and legislation affirmed that, while of different ethnicity, immigrants were part of the fabric of Canada. They were no longer "strangers at the gates" waiting for permission to enter but never truly belonging. Thus, new and established immigrant communities were validated and brought into the public life of the country and the functioning of Canadian democracy.

In the past fifty years, the relationships of Italian-Canadians to all levels of government in Canada and Italy changed. In the process, opportunities arose for debate around the issue of citizenship and what it is to be a Canadian, Italian or both. The cultural arena and identity were thus politicized and funding became the carrot.

Provincial Relations

Alberta's pioneer role in defining and implementating multiculturalism allowed Italian community members to play a leadership role. The Cultural Heritage Council included Edmonton's Sab Roncucci, Carlo Amodio, Nando Zenari, Al Iafolla and Tony Falcone; Calgary's Alberto Romano, Giovanni de Maria, Serafino Scarpino, Ralph Grossi and Sara Lacentra; and Maria Siegle and Nick DeSimone of Lethbridge. Council members helped to create a new relationship between the Government of Alberta and ethnocultural communities. In a 1985 article in *Il Congresso*, Amodio wrote:

---

[610] There were a series of meetings in the mid-1980s; see Adriana Albi Davies, "Heritage Languages Conference," *Il Congresso*, year 3, no. 11, November 1986.

In February 1974, the Council approved a recommendation that requested the ministry to provide financial support to those groups offering heritage language classes. The government approved this recommendation and established a $15 subsidy for each student in an ethnic language school. This directive had a direct correlation with the establishment, in 1975, by the departments of Instruction and Human Rights of Immigrant Centres in Calgary and Edmonton. In the following years, the Council took a strong position against any activity that could be offensive or derogatory towards ethnic communities. An example was the strong reaction when the CBC aired a program on the Mafia which appeared to denigrate the Italian community in Canada. Through radio station CKUA and its relation to ACCESS (Alberta Education Communication Corporation) the Council obtained excellent results in the creation of radio programs and various activities of interest to the community.[611]

The establishment of ethnic radio and television programs in Edmonton (efforts to do this in Calgary failed) can be attributed to these recommendations. While the Edmonton Italian language school, run by the Dante Alighieri Society, was of an earlier generation, it benefitted from the new subsidy. The funding support arrived just in time for the newly-established Calgary Italian language school. Thus, public policy changes served to empower community leaders and impacted on the day-to-day-life of the community.

Creation of the Cultural Heritage Division of Alberta Culture established another vehicle for funding, the Alberta Cultural Heritage Foundation. Amodio wrote: "By way of this foundation, which is funded through the provincial lottery program, funding support can be obtained for special programs including: dance, newspapers, theatre and other activities. Grant requests must be presented by the end of May of each year."

Sab Roncucci worked closely with the province in launching a number of initiatives. With respect to the Heritage Days Festival, there were many naysayers who felt that the proposed event would conflict with the traditional summer exhibition (at the time called Klondike Days) and would therefore not succeed. In the July 1986 issue of *Il Congresso*, Sab wrote: "[T]he first Heritage Day was celebrated in August 1974 at Fort Edmonton. The participation of ethnocultural groups and the public was modest, but encouraging. I had the honour of being the co-chairman of the 1975 Heritage Days event. Ten groups participated and there were 11,000 visitors at the

[611] Carlo Amodio, "Cosa È L'Alberta Cultural Heritage Council?" (What is the Alberta Cultural Heritage Council), *Il Congresso*, year 2, no. 12, December 1985, 15.

mini-festival."[612] The 1976 festival was moved to Hawrelak Park in the River Valley and since then has gone from strength to strength including expansion to three days (the entire August holiday weekend) and draws crowds in excess of 400,000 to Hawrelak Park. The Italian pavilion was there from the beginning.

Gene Zwozdesky, teacher, Ukrainian dancer and choreographer, became the executive director of the Alberta Cultural Heritage Foundation and was responsible for the development of over 70 ethnocultural profiles for use in Alberta schools; this was done in consultation with community leaders and teachers since they were created as curriculum resources.[613] The *Alberta People Kit* was published in 1984 by the Government of Alberta. Roncucci and others provided information.

The final piece in legitimizing and empowering ethnocultural communities occurred through the Community Facilities Enhancement Program, which directed Alberta Lottery Fund monies to communities for new buildings and renovations to existing buildings. This was the final set of policy changes that leveled the playing field between mainstream organizations and those created by immigrants. The program was accessed to support the building of a number of Italian centres and enhancement of existing ones, in particular, in Edmonton. Some critics would say that it created the problem of an "edifice complex" – individuals wanted to see their names on plaques acknowledging the contribution of the provincial government and local MLAs. But this was no different than in mainstream organizations.

The Italian community was introduced to the art of lobbying and every community activity had obligatory civic, provincial and federal representatives in attendance. Their staff also assisted in the grants process. This was a simpler time when lobbying was viewed as a legitimate way of doing business with government. Politicians also actively cultivated the Italian vote. Edmonton Mayor William Hawrelak began this in the 1950s and had close relationships with prominent Italian builders, including Giannone and Battoni, and, in some instances, business relationships. That is why land adjacent to Clarke Stadium was promised to the Cristoforo Colombo Soccer Club and was ultimately used for construction of Santa Maria Goretti Church. Adelaide Carloni observed that her husband Luca helped "to bring in the Italian vote" in Calgary as did Angelina Rebaudengo. Whether this was truly the case cannot be proved; Carloni did, however, host

---

[612] Sab Roncucci, "Heritage Festival: Un Monumento alla Libertà Culturale e al Volontarismo" (Heritage Festival: A Monument to Cultural Liberty and Voluntarism), *Il Congresso*, year 3, no. 7, July 1986.

[613] The Alberta People Kit profiles can be found on the Heritage Community Foundation's website *Albertans: Who Do They Think They Are*, 2000, part of the *Alberta Online Encyclopedia*, URL: http://wayback.archive-it. org/2217/20101208160622/http://www.abheritage.ca/albertans/index.html, retrieved February 1, 2018. The Cultural Heritage Foundation was disbanded in the early 1990s and the granting function was taken over by civil servants and eventually ceased altogether.

politicians at his popular Isle of Capri restaurant as did Gene Cioni at La Villa. In Edmonton, Tita's Restaurant, operated by Rudy Tosta and Sal Acampore, and Sceppa's, operated by Ralph and Bonnie Maio, saw their share of lobbying lunches.

The first co-ordinated lobbying effort related to an important aspect of the Italian heritage – wine-making in the home. This activity, while innocent in Italy, was illegal in Alberta where liquor production and sales were strictly controlled by the province. This was a legacy of Prohibition, which had not worked. A November 1964 raid by the RCMP on Italian households in Calgary's Italian community, between the hours of midnight and 3 am, caused a great deal of trauma. For those who had lived through the war-time years of enemy alien designation, the intrusion of the police into their personal lives reawakened old fears. Wine-making equipment and wine were seized and destroyed. The fine imposed for illegal distilling was $100. To add insult to injury, those affected realized that there were informants within the community. Again, this brought up memories of the Second World War. Adelina Carloni noted in an interview that everybody made a little wine but you had to beware of "spies" and that sometimes even the "best of friends could report you."[614] Elia Martina, a former secretary and president of the Calgary Italian Club, in a 1985 interview, noted that 17 families in Bridgeland were raided.[615] The Club began a protest that focused on changing the *Liquor Control Act* to allow for home wine-making. Luca Carloni, Alberto Romano, Elia Martina, Tony Sanguin and others joined Edmonton counterparts including Frank Spinelli, Lorenzo Bagna-riol and Tony Falcone in lobbying efforts that resulted in legislative change in 1967. The revision to the Act permitted families to produce 25 gallons of wine for every person over the legal drinking age.

This was a relatively easy win; electing individuals of Italian descent to political office proved more difficult. While in the previous 80 years some Italian immigrants had served on municipal councils and run in provincial elections and succeeded, among them Social Credit MLAs Angelo Montemurro (Mayerthorpe) and Antonio Aloisio (Athabasca), and Liberal MLA Mike Maccagno, there was an almost feverish quality in contemporary efforts. The reasons were twofold: on the one hand, the various levels of government were actively courting the "ethnic" vote; on the other, there was a realization that to assert their presence and be counted, community members needed to be among the political ruling class. Individuals who threw their hats in the political ring included Calgary's Darryl Raymaker (his mother was of Italian ancestry) and Edmonton's Tony Falcone and Al Iafolla.[616]

---

[614] Adelina (Adelaide) Carloni, oral history, June 10, 1985, Glenbow Archives RCT-869-5.

[615] Elia Martina oral history, June 19, 1985, Glenbow Archives RCT-869-16.

[616] Raymaker joined the Liberal Party as a young man, in 1963. His political coming of age is described in *Trudeau's Tango: Alberta Meets Pierre Elliott Trudeau, 1968-1972* (Edmonton: University of Alberta Press, 2017).

Il Congresso newspaper became an important vehicle for supporting political campaigns. In a 1986 interview with Frank Spinelli, grocer extraordinaire and community leader, Amodio asked what was his personal motto and Spinelli responded: "The motto that has always guided me is that it is important to give in order to receive." Amodio concluded the interview with the following, tongue-in-cheek observation: "Notwithstanding the fact that we did not have time to talk about politics and political affiliations, it is well known that Spinelli is a fervent Liberal and that his motto has also infiltrated into this field [that is, politics]. This demonstrates the fact that not only Liberal leaders but also those of other parties must make their way to 95 Street and 109 Avenue [Italian Centre Shop] when it is necessary."[617] Amodio's statement should not be viewed as implying that Spinelli expected personal political favours; he did not, he simply wanted what was best for the Italian community. In order for this to happen, Italian-Canadians had to be at the political table.

David King, the PC incumbent in the Edmonton-Highlands riding placed an ad in the April 1986 issue of the paper with the following text: "David King is a proven friend of the Italian people. He has worked hard for the Italian community. He participates in many community activities, listens to Italians, and values their thoughts and ideas. David King asks for your support on May 8, to give Italians another effective voice in the provincial government." The accompanying photo was taken in front of the Italian Centre Shop and includes Spinelli. King had been an MLA since 1971 and had served as Legislative Secretary to Premier Peter Lougheed, Minister of Education and Minister of Technology. He was well-known for his advocacy in the creation of multicultural educational resources. King was defeated in the 1986 election by NDP candidate Pam Barrett, who also had an ad in the paper accompanied by a photograph of herself beside Spinelli in his store. The original text passage is in Italian, and the translation is as follows:

> Pam Barrett and the New Democrats defy the Conservatives for the continuing increase in unemployment, reduction of funds to education, the politics that continues to ruin small business owners and the reduction in funding for health and child assistance.
>
> Pam Barrett knows that this type of politics corrodes our communities, an important resource for the future of Alberta as well as our petroleum industry and our wheat industry.
>
> It's time for a change! It's time to have a new voice in the Legislative Assembly of Alberta![618]

---

[617] Carlo Amodio, "I Volti della Communità: Franco Spinelli" (The Faces of the Community: Franco Spinelli). *Il Congresso*, year 3, no. 2, February 1986, 10.
[618] Pam Barrett campaign ad, *Il Congresso*, year 3, no. 4, April 1986, 7.

Barrett defeated King and went on to become the NDP party leader. It is intriguing that these party battles took place in ridings in which Italians could provide the swing vote.

The April issue had as its lead article, "Calder: Italiano" (Italian Calder), a reference to the fact that well-known community members Tony Falcone, a Conservative, and Al Iafolla, a Liberal, were running against each other in the provincial elections. Author Lina Amodio notes:

> … leaving aside the political divergence, it is with great satisfaction that we Italians unite in support of our two candidates: we are now challenged by excellent choices. We can take pride in the fact that our community has reached a level of maturity in which we accept our responsibilities in the public life of our country and can demonstrate to the community at large that we can provide our perspective in shaping our country. Today, we can make ourselves appreciated not only because of our songs and spaghetti but also because of our intellectual stature.[619]

Playing in the political arena meant that the community had finally made it to the "big leagues." The election saw the unseating of a number of Conservatives including King, Julian Koziak, Gerry Amerongen, Mary LeMessurier and Milton Pahl. Lina comments on the Calder riding as follows:

> Our sympathies go with T. Falcone and A. Iafolla, whose efforts were appreciated by their fellow countrymen. We are well aware of campaign pressures that resulted in squabbling and insults since they are the order of the day; it saddens us that such incidents, which could have been avoided, also happened with our candidates.
>
> Our community has reached a level of maturity that enables it to participate civilly in the political life of Alberta, but it is important that improvements occur to ensure that incidents do not occur that blot the quality of our candidates. We hope that in the future such incidents will be a thing of the past and will not mar the success of our candidates and the reputation of our community.[620]

The candidates in Calder split the Italian vote and lost. Success at the provincial level would finally occur with the election of Danny Dalla-Longa (Liberal, 1993) and Joe Ceci (NDP, 2015) in Calgary. An individual of Italian descent has yet to be elected in Alberta at the federal level. The most success has been experienced at the civic level.

---

[619] Lina Amodio, "Calder: Italiano" (Italian Calder), *Il Congresso*, year 3, no. 4, April 1986, 1.
[620] *Ibid.*, "Elezioni '86" (Elections '86), *Il Congresso*, year 3, no. 5, May 1986, 1.

The Falcone/Iafolla incident is a demonstration that sometimes Italian community leaders are their own worst enemies. Alessandro Urso, a co-founder of *Il Congresso*, in a critical editorial titled "Clubs, Quanti Clubs" (Clubs, How Many Clubs), in 1986 took a stab at what he considered the "individualism," and, by extension, "egotism," in the community. He pointed out that there were 35 Italian societies in Edmonton; if the Italian population totaled 20,000, each club would have a membership base of 571 people. Urso ascribed this excess to ambitious individuals who wanted to head an organization, as he notes, "Viva la presidentomania!" He noted:

> The Italian community is in a formative state and other ethnic groups have and are continuing to contribute solidly to the formation of the Canadian mosaic because they are well coordinated and united. Let us look at the Ukrainians, the Germans, the Dutch, the French, the English and primarily the Chinese. This last group has understood that now is the time to contribute. The month of Chinese culture (last November was designated Chinese Awareness Month), commercial exchanges, twinning with other cities in China, participation in the political process and many other activities are evidence of a concrete and active presence in the political process and many other activities testify … to an active presence of this group in this country.[621]

The subtext in Urso's message is that, if factionalism in Italian communities persisted, they would be unable to access the "glittering prizes" offered by governments.

The sense of urgency to stand up and be counted was felt by community leaders who were regularly invited to participate in government round tables and discussions. In 1992, the City of Edmonton commissioned cultural profiles of its ethnocultural groups; Sab Roncucci and Adriana Davies created the Italian one. While Urso noted the need for unity for Edmonton's Italian community, this did not happen, either at the local or provincial level. While the National Congress of Italian Canadians in Edmonton and Calgary convened periodic meetings and talked about collaboration, this did not occur in other than informal ways when the need arose.

Relations with Italy

In 1982, the Government of Italy appointed Giovanni Bincoletto as Vice Consul in Alberta and he arrived in Edmonton with his family. This ended the era of honorary consuls and signalled an interest on the part of the Government of Italy in strengthening trade ties. Of particular importance was sale of technology to Alberta's petroleum industry. Bincoletto had served in Paris in

---

[621] Alessandro Urso, "Clubs, Quanti Clubs" (Clubs, How Many Clubs), *Il Congresso*, year 3, no. 12, December 1986, 3.

1970, and, in 1976, chose an appointment at the Ottawa Embassy. Besides doing trade attache work, he became involved in the life of the Italian community and, whenever possible, made available funding support for educational and cultural activities. He wrote for *Il Congresso*, under the pseudonym "Gatto Pardo" (The Leopard), a fact that was known only to the management team until after his retirement in 1990. By this point, he and wife Laura were so entrenched in the life of the community that they decided to stay in Edmonton.

Community leaders basked in the attention of the Italian government and welcomed visits from the Italian ambassador in Ottawa, dignitaries, musicians and artists. The most significant event was the Second Rome Conference on Immigration, which took place from November 28 to December 3, 1988. The conference theme was "Gli Italiani all'Estero" (Italians Abroad). Bincoletto appointed the presidents of the Edmonton and Calgary National Congresses, Adriana Davies and Domenico Rossi, as the official Alberta delegates. They became part of the Canadian delegation, which met jointly with the American delegation in New York (June 1988) and alone in Toronto (November 1988) to formulate positions on various conference themes including culture, language retention, political rights, pensions, etc. Discussions were heated and were complicated by Italian party political differences as well as regional differences, which also impacted on the opinions of American and Canadian delegates. As well, there were among the representatives more recent immigrants who had kept their Italian citizenship and truly considered themselves "Italians abroad." They wanted to retain full rights of Italian citizenship while making a living abroad.

The Pre-Conference meetings in New York were launched by Giulio Andreotti, Minister of Foreign Affairs and Minister of Labour Rino Formica. Similar pre-conferences occurred in Buenos Aires, Strasbourg and Melbourne. Andreotti emphasized the interest that Italian Parliamentarians had in the opinions and needs of Italians abroad. He also discussed the waves of immigration to the Mediterranean from former colonies as an issue facing the government. The New York pre-conference was attended by 450 delegates of which perhaps 40 to 50 were Canadian. The Canadian contingent eventually compromised on all themes except the most potentially divisive: the establishment of local consular committees, the proposed COEMIT (Comitati Emigrazione Italiani). The reason that the National Congress opposed them was that they believed that Italian-Canadian societies needed to determine their own priorities, separate from those of the Government in Italy. The "culture" paper was developed by Davies, who also presented in Rome. On the theme of cultural retention, she concluded:

> Cannot the Italian government aid Italian communities abroad, which desire to retain a strong link with the culture and traditions of their homeland, by providing a mechanism for free cultural exchange, making use of all of the benefits of modern technology. This, besides scholarships

to facilitate study in either country, materials for Italian language schools could be provided free or at a cost through Italian consulates; cultural institutes could facilitate visits by artist and performers; copyright arrangements could be made to permit use of Italian video materials. The list of concrete examples of cultural co-operation is endless.[622]

The total number of conference attendees was 2,239 (1,189 were delegates, 600 invited guests, 50 observers and 400 journalists). Travel and accommodation expenses were paid. Countries represented ranged from Algeria to Venezuela. Most of Italy's parliamentarians attended at least some of the sessions.

Was the Rome conference an exercise in self-interest on the part of the Italian government? This was certainly the view of many delegates. They speculated that allowing Italians abroad to reclaim Italian citizenship might give Italy an advantage within the European Economic Community and also pointed out that monies sent back to Italy by immigrants were a significant part of the country's finances. After much deliberation, the delegates made three key recommendations: the establishment of a general council of Italians living abroad to be given constitutional powers and, later, the right to vote for representatives to the Italian Parliament; acceptance of dual citizenship; and establishment of local Comitati dell'Emigrazione Italiana (Committees of Italian Immigration).[623] These last would be established by the Italian government through an election process in continents with significant Italian populations. The possibility of elections was an issue that worried Canadian delegates because a foreign power would be acting at a political level within Canada; this harkened back to the days of the Fascio when Mussolini attempted to control Italians living abroad.

The dual citizenship policy was implemented immediately. In Edmonton, Vice Consul Bincoletto, in the January 1989 issue of *Il Congresso* made a formal request that Italian-Canadians desiring to reclaim their Italian citizenship should register with the consulate. Giuseppe Imbalzano, who succeeded him in 1990 and had been involved in the organization of the Rome Conference, implemented the policy. Imbalzano also implemented the Comitati degli italiani all'estero (Committees of Italians Abroad) or COMITES, even before the passage of legislation, which did not occur until 2003. This was opposed by the President (Adriana Davies) and the Board of the NCIC, Edmonton District, in keeping with directives from its national counterpart. The result was friction in the community and Imbalzano initially selected members for his committee personally.

---

[622] Adriana Albi Davies, "A Canadian Viewpoint: Reflections on Multiculturalism," *Il Congresso*, year 5, no. 8, August 1988.
[623] *Anon.*, "Affermazioni di Principio E Strade Per L'Emigrazione" (Affirmation of Principle and Roads to Immigration), *Il Congresso*, year 6, no. 1, January 1989; translated by Adriana Davies.

Over the next decade, members of the executive included Domenico Marazzo, Luciana de Santis, Maria Mauro, Leo Sorgiovanni and Giuseppe Sabiti from Edmonton and Domenico Rossi and Luigi Mangone from Calgary. The COMITES was charged with adjudicating grant requests for educational and cultural programs (this had previously been done by consular staff).

The passage of legislation by the Italian Parliament on October 23, 2003 empowered the Minister of External Affairs and the Minister of Italians Abroad, a new position, to facilitate voting in Italian elections in any consular jurisdiction with over 3,000 Italians who retained or had regained Italian citizenship.[624] The policy also resulted in the implementation of procedures to vote for candidates living abroad who would have seats in the Italian Parliament. Committees were established in various European countries; Ireland; the United Kingdom; North, Central and South America; Africa; and Australia. The first elections occurred in 2003. According to Domenico Rossi, in about 2012, there was dissent in the Alberta COMITES and he and others resigned.

With respect to the issue of greater aid to help Italian-Canadians preserve their culture and traditions, Italy's worsening economy resulted in the closing of many Italian consular offices throughout the world. Edmonton lost its consulate in June 2008. This was viewed as short-sighted by most community members. The last incumbent was Arnaldo Minuti, a young career diplomat, who took up his appointment in September 2004. Alberta is now part of the Vancouver consulate's region and there is an honorary consul in Calgary (Teresina Bontorin) and a consular office in Edmonton for passport, pension and other matters. The Italian government has continued to bestow the cavaliere (knighthood) on Italian-Canadians whose achievements have brought honour to Canada and Italy. A complete list is not available but many community leaders in Edmonton and Calgary have been recognized.

Federal Relations

The Italian community's relationship with the federal government was, by-and-large, built through the evolution of multiculturalism policies. Sab Roncucci was one of the most ardent supporters of multiculturalism in Alberta. His column in *Il Congresso*, titled "La rubrica dell'opinioni" (A Guide to Opinion), dealt with various aspects of policy implementation as well as human rights issues. At the basis of his assertions was the fact that in an officially bicultural and bilingual country, there was a "third group" of "others" whose numbers were increasing and who felt marginalized. He wrote in a 1986 article:

---

[624] *Anon.*, "I Comites – Comitati degli Italiani residenti all'estero," Calabresi.net: The Portal of the Calabresi in the World, URL: http://www.calabresi.net/i-comites-comitati-degli-italiani-residenti-allestero/, retrieved February 14, 2018.

If we examine the demographic development of the population of Canada, we see that Canadians of non-English and non-French origin were 18.4 % in 1781; 15.9 % in 1911; 19.9 % in 1931. Later, in 1971, the figure had reached 16.7 %. It is therefore logical that the cultural politics of the country needed to change drastically in order to reflect the presence of a great number of citizens representing more than 70 diverse cultures. A new state politics and social philosophy were required that went beyond mere tolerance, be it sincere or paternalistic.[625]

As well, Roncucci anticipated the negative side of politicizing ethnicity. As early as August 1970, in a presentation at a conference at the University of Alberta on the theme of "Multiculturalism for Canada," he noted that cultural identity was becoming an "artificial" construct "promoted and kept alive by vested interests such as: ethnic businesses, ethnic churches, phony ethnic leaders, and petty ethnic politicians." He continues: "In other words, by overplaying the possible loss of the group's tradition and culture, they generate a psychosis of fear and tension inside the group (between the most progressive and the most conservative, between the young and the old), as well as tension and prejudices between the group and the rest of Canadian society."[626] His observations are as pertinent today as they were then. Cultural "politics" came to dominate the relationship between ethnocultural groups and the federal government (as well as other governmental levels). In addition, different ethnic groups jockeyed for position and groups were played off against each other.

The implementation of multiculturalism policies empowered several ethnocultural groups to address painful periods in their history in Canada. Beginning in the 1970s, Japanese-Canadians spoke out about internment in the Second World War, and the National Association of Japanese Canadians (NAJC) began to campaign for reparations. The terrible experiences of Canadian soldiers in Japanese prisoner of war camps, uppermost in the minds of many Canadians, prevented anything from happening at that time. In the mid-1980s, however, PM Mulroney demonstrated a willingness to discuss redress. The NAJC hired accountants to calculate Japanese-Canadian losses and these exceeded $443 million in 1986 dollars. In September 1988, the Government of Canada apologized to Japanese-Canadians for their internment, which began after the attack on Pearl Harbour of December 7, 1941. About 22,000 were interned of whom 14,000 were born in

---

[625] Sab Roncucci, "Un Po di Storia del Multiculturalism" (A Bit of the History of Multiculturalism), *Il Congresso*, year 3, no. 8, August 1986.

[626] *Ibid.*, "Comments on Multiculturalism for Canada," a paper presented at the "Multiculturalism for Canada" conference, University of Alberta, August 28-29, 1970; reprinted in *Il Congresso*, year 3, no. 8, August 1986.

Canada. They were removed from their homes and relocated to camps in the interior of BC and to farms across the country including southern Alberta around Taber. They lost homes, possessions and businesses. The government awarded over $300 million in compensation.[627]

Ukrainian-Canadians, since 1985, sought acknowledgement and redress for the internment of about 6,000 Austro-Hungarians, many of whom were in fact ethnic Ukrainians, during the First World War. The campaign was led by the Ukrainian Canadian Civil Liberties Association. In November 2005, Bill C-331 was passed acknowledging the internment of persons of Ukrainian origin and obliging the Government of Canada to negotiate an agreement determining educational and commemorative measures to be undertaken. In May 2008 the government established a $10 million fund (held in trust by the Ukrainian Canadian Foundation of Taras Shevchenko) and a vehicle for disbursing interest monies to qualifying projects. The Canadian First World War Internment Recognition Fund (CFWWIRF) was implemented in September 2009. The government avoided the issue of compensation of individuals.

Redress efforts for Italian-Canadians interned during the Second World War were led by the National Congress under President Annamarie Castrilli, a Toronto lawyer. At the time, she was a member of the board of governors of the University of Toronto. (She later served as chair.) The nucleus of community leaders involved in this lobbying effort had also taken part in the Government of Italy's Immigration conference and had established a relationship of trust. In discussions at NCIC meetings and also in correspondence, there was an overwhelming consensus that Italian internment had been wrong and that internees were innocent. Research was undertaken to determine the number of individuals arrested and interned; incidences of confiscation of property; loss of jobs; and other impacts. A brief was prepared and reviewed by the executives of regional congresses across the country.[628] The NCIC succeeded in obtaining a verbal apology from Mulroney at a luncheon in Concord, a Toronto suburb, on November 4, 1990 attended by 500 members and guests.[629] This event was the highlight of the NCIC biennial meeting. Some members of the Italian community wanted more than an apology; they wanted compensation. For them, the issue continues to be a sore point.

After the apology, nothing happened since it was an unofficial gesture that had taken place outside of the workings of Parliament. In 2005, PM Paul Martin included $25 million in the

---

[627] A similar redress bill was approved in Washington six weeks earlier.

[628] As President of the Edmonton District Congress, I provided feedback on several drafts.

[629] Adriana Albi Davies, "P.M. Apologizes to Italian-Canadians," *Il Congresso*, year 7, no. 11, November 1990, 1.

budget to address claims for communities seeking redress. He side-stepped the issue of compensation to families by placing funds within a new program – the Acknowledgement, Commemoration and Education (ACE) Program. PM Stephen Harper, in 2006, replaced this with the Community Historical Recognition Program (CHRP), established to formally distribute monies to community initiatives. In 2009, Liberal MP Massimo Pacetti from the Quebec riding of Saint-Léonard-Saint-Michel brought forward a private member's bill, Bill C-302. Pacetti specified that he wanted a formal apology in Parliament by the PM, $2.5 million to produce educational materials related to Italian-Canadian history for use in the school system, and a commemorative stamp. The bill was passed in the House of Commons on April 28, 2010 though opposed by Conservative MPs. Since it did not get a Senate review, it did not become law. In fact, at a meeting at the Biennial Conference of the National Congress in Montreal in April 2011, Pacetti recommended that lobbying continue and that a different Italian-Canadian MP put forward a new private member's bill to finish the work. This did not occur.

Mulroney's apology did have a positive outcome: it spurred academics, mostly of Italian descent, to undertake research to discover whether Fascism had gained a foothold in Canada and, by implication, the guilt or innocence of internees. By and large, the focus was on Ontario and Quebec since the majority of internees came from these provinces. This led to a new generation of scholarship culminating in the book *Enemies Within: Italian and Other Internees in Canada and Abroad* edited by Franca Iacovetta, Roberto Perin and Angelo Principe, which was published in 2000. In their summative essay, Iacovetta and Robert Ventresca noted:

> The history of Italian Canadians in the Second World War was far more complicated, sordid, and turbulent than the community version permits. The streamlined story of internment fails to convey the intensely dramatic developments of those heady years, such as Fascism's popular appeal among immigrants, its totalitarian nature, and the hypocrisy and ironies revealed in the behaviour both of Canadians in general (including state authorities) and of Italian-Canadians in particular (especially towards each other)....[630]

This view did not sit well with community members who believed that everyone arrested was innocent.

In 2010, the Columbus Centre in Toronto initiated a research project intended to "acknowledge and commemorate the experience of Italian Canadians during World War II." Funding

---

[630] Franca Iacovetta and Robert Ventresca, "Redress, Collective Memory, and the Politics of History," in *Enemies Within*, 398-399.

support was obtained from the Community Historical Recognition Program, Citizenship and Immigration Canada. An Advisory Committee was struck including academic and popular historians from across the country; staff and contractors were hired to undertake research including oral histories with descendants.[631] There were four project deliverables: an educational website (*Italian Canadians as Enemy Aliens: Memories of World War II*); a permanent exhibit at the Columbus Centre and a travelling version; the anthologies *Beyond Barbed Wire: Essays on the Internment of Italian Canadians* and its companion volume *Behind Barbed Wire: Creative Works on the Internment of Italian Canadians*; and a monument by artist Harley Valentine located at the Columbus Centre. The statue includes three images: a grandfather, pregnant mother and a child representing the generations. Archival material gathered is held at the Centre.[632] It was determined that about 31,000 Italian-Canadians were designated as enemy aliens and about 600 were interned. A list of internees with biographical information is available on the website.

Memorials

As a result of the emphasis on cultural identity of the past decades, in 2002, the National Congress of Italian Canadians, Edmonton District decided to partner with the Heritage Community Foundation in developing a website to showcase Alberta's Italian history.[633] The Foundation, under Executive Director Adriana Davies, had made the worldwide web the vehicle for connecting Albertans and Canadians with their heritage through discovery and learning. At a time when the web was becoming the vehicle of choice for information sharing, this made sense. The new website was titled "Celebrating Alberta's Italian Community" and through text, images, documents, oral histories and video elements told the community's stories. It did this in a Canadian and international context as well as through regional profiles, thematic articles and short biographies of pioneers. Funding support was provided by the Edmonton District Congress, the City of Edmonton and the Heritage Community Foundation. The website was the first of its kind and received substantial visitation; in addition, emails were received from descendants who wanted

---

[631] The Advisory Committee members were as follows: Vittorina (Vikki) Cecchetto, Adriana A. Davies, Nicholas DeMaria Harney, Steven High, Francesca L'Orfano, Sam Migliore, James H. Morrison, CM, Christine Sansalone, John Potestio, Carl Thorpe and Ernesto Virgulti.

[632] An educational publication was also created in this period. See Pamela Hickman and Jean Smith Cavalluzzo, *Italian Canadian Internment in the Second World War: Righting Canada's Wrongs* (Toronto, ON: James Lorimer, 2012).

[633] Adriana A. Davies, *Celebrating Alberta's Italian Community* website, *Alberta Online Encyclopedia*, Heritage Community Foundation, URL: http://wayback.archive-it.org/2217/20101215215929/http://www.albertasource.ca/abitalian/index.html, retrieved February 6, 2018.

to track their ancestors. It became the prototype for other websites developed by the Foundation in partnership with ethnocultural groups. These formed part of the Alberta Online Encyclopedia (www.albertasource.ca), which on June 30, 2009, the Foundation gifted to the University of Alberta in perpetuity for the benefit of all Albertans.

Alberta's centenary in 2005 spurred two commemorative exhibits. The Galt Museum undertook a Year of the Coal Miner Project that linked communities from Drumheller to the Elk Valley in BC. Besides a physical exhibit at the Galt projects included a small travelling exhibit titled "People of the Coal Mines: The Italian Community" and a website, *When Coal Was King*, part of the *Alberta Online Encyclopedia*. Adriana Davies developed the exhibit and the website. Funding support was provided by the Canada's Cultural Capitals Program as well as several partners. The project lead was the Galt's Executive Director Ron Ulrich. Italian Vice Consul Arnaldo Minuti provided funding support for a second exhibit, titled "Alberta's Italian community," designed to commemorate Alberta's centenary. The exhibit was developed by Davies and built by the Galt. Besides being displayed in Edmonton, it travelled to Calgary in spring 2007 where Domenico Rossi arranged for its placement at City Hall for two weeks. In 2007, the Italian Consulate provided the Ital-Canadian Seniors Association with a small grant to bring both exhibits to Edmonton where they were permanently installed in the new Alberta Italian Museum located in the Seniors Centre.

Finally, the NCIC wanted to create a commemorative project for the provincial centenary that would be a gift from Alberta's Italian community to the people of Alberta. Since other groups had monuments on the grounds of the Legislative Assembly in Edmonton, the board decided to pursue this option. A commemorative sculpture was determined to be the best project and Tony Lupino, then Director of the Art Gallery of Alberta, was put in charge of the selection process. Artists were asked to submit concepts and Giuseppe Albi was selected as the sculptor. A fundraising campaign was launched in the community and a grant was obtained from the Government of Alberta's Community Initiatives Program. In 2007, Albi's sculpture comprising a marble column with bronze casts of tools and musical instruments at the base was unveiled. The bronze artifacts were intended to be tangible tokens of what Italian pioneers brought to the province. The official opening on October 27, 2007 was attended by Domenico Campione, president of the NCIC, Toronto; Italian Ambassador Gabriele Sardo; Italian Consul in Edmonton, Arnaldo Minuti; Mayor Stephen Mandel; MP Laurie Hawn; MLA Hugh MacDonald; Tony De Somma and Domenico Rossi representing Calgary's Italian community; John Mazzuca representing the community in Lethbridge; and City of Edmonton Alderman Tony Caterina. [634]

---

[634] Alessandro Urso, ""Inaugurato il monumento degli Italiani in Alberta" (Inauguration of the Monument of Italians in Alberta), *Il Congresso*, year 24, no. 10, October 2007, 1-2.

Identifying Ourselves

Identity is a central aspect of the intangible heritage of a people manifesting itself in a range of ways from memories to things done in our daily lives that are customary. It is also present in works of art. There are two important literary portraits of Italians relating to Alberta's history that are archetypal in nature: Caterina Edward's inhabitants of an Italian boarding house in *Terra Straniera* (Strange Land) and Peter Oliva's miners in *Drowning in Darkness*. The first was written in 1986 and the latter, in 1993. The mood of both is somber. Lina Amodio in her review of the former notes: ·

> In her new play the author presents with sensitivity the joys and sufferings that are typical of all immigrants who confront life in a new country. A group of "paesani" who live in the same boarding house, at the end of the 1950s, experiences the same melancholy that is common to all immigrants. Canada appears cold and sterile in comparison to the country left behind.
>
> It is not only the climate that appears cold, but the society in general; in this new world no-one understands, no-one sings, no-one cries. Every protagonist attempts to resolve these issues in different ways, but when the tragedy erupts the inhabitants of the house know that they cannot count on that cold world for help, that their strength is in their unity, and their need for each other.[635]

This was the first play about an Italian theme put on at the Edmonton Fringe Festival. In the play and novel, women are hard-working and submissive and the new world has not altered their circumstances. While some oral histories bear out these themes, it is only a minority that experienced these extreme feelings of alienation. The majority of immigrants rose to the challenges and forged very successful lives as is evidenced in accounts in the previous chapters. There is thus a "disconnect" between the fictional accounts and the reality of the immigration experience. That is not to say that the fictional accounts are false, simply that real life was more complex and richer. Allowing immigrants to speak in their own voices as recorded in family and community histories as well as the rare memoir is necessary for a full understanding of the immigrant experience.

Those who built successful lives in Canada moved very quickly from a sense of being "outsiders" to being more-or-less integrated into Canadian society. They were able to separate the past from the present and retained only those aspects of their culture and traditions necessary to a sense of wholeness. In the 1970s and 1980s many participated in multicultural events in which they

---

[635] Lina Amodio, "Terra Straniera," *Il Congresso*, year 3, no. 8, August 1986.

demonstrated aspects of their ethnicity – food and dance – but it was in their private lives that they struggled with what to keep and what to dispose of "in becoming Canadian."

While the phase of struggle was very real for the Italian community, which experienced discrimination, in the end, the passage of time resulted in assimilation. While treated as a "visible" minority throughout the three eras of immigration spanning the end of the nineteenth century to the 1980s, Italians were, in fact, Europeans and part of Western culture and tradition. It was racism and selective immigration policies that placed them outside the bounds. Once this was more-or-less done away with, they could be assimilated. This simply required the passage of time.

In 1985, Frank Trovato, a University of Alberta sociology professor, examined demographic trends in Canadian society. With respect to the Italian community, he noted that a look at census data from 1961, 1971 and 1981, revealed that Italians were more educated and also that their socioeconomic position had significantly improved. He further observed:

> Increasing education and professionalization have very positive implications of course, but there are latent consequences worth recognizing as well. As children of Italian parents become highly educated, and attain professional certification, they will be more likely to relocate away from their ethnic communities in search of work and opportunities in other parts of the country. To the extent that ethnic members relocate, the viability of an ethnic community is weakened in direct proportion to the number of people leaving it. Moreover, the process of upward mobility is often associated with the loss of tradition.[636]

Thus, the very success of Italian immigrants in professionalizing and becoming Canadian has eroded the sense of a distinct Italian community. This was mentioned by interviewees in the Calgary Italian Club oral histories in the mid-1980s. The seniors lamented that the next generation had become "Canadian" and that they were no longer interested in what the Club had to offer. This occurred in Edmonton and Lethbridge as well. In Calgary, revitalization of the Club occurred because of the larger numbers in the community and also because the Italian language school and other activities had an appeal for the community at large. In Lethbridge, the board decided to open up the membership to others to ensure survival. Edmonton's Italian societies are facing these issues today with aging boards and facilities requiring ongoing maintenance. The child immigrants of the 1950s and 1960s, who are currently running Italian organizations, are struggling to involve young people. *Il Congresso* newspaper ceased publication after 25 years in

---

[636] Frank Trovato, "Implications for the Italian Community in Canada," *Il Congresso*, year 2, no. 12, December 1985, 3-4.

December 2009; in its last years, the number of wire service articles from Italy came to dominate coverage of the Italian community. As the management team comprising Carlo Amodio, Rudy Cavaliere and Alessandro Urso and their contributors aged, it became more-and-more difficult to cover community events and publish a monthly paper. In addition, with Italian content being readily available on television initially through Tele-Latino and, later, RAI (the Italian broadcasting company), what was printed in *Il Congresso* was less timely.

The question arises as to whether it is important that Italian community organizations and activities survive? The brutal answer is that this will only happen if they can find a new function within the Italian community, which is now part of mainstream Canadian society. Italian-Canadians are no longer in a position requiring redress; the community has nothing to prove to anyone. It is the new generations of immigrants that are repeating the cycle of arriving on the shores of a strange land with different languages, cultures and traditions, and needing to bridge the divide. Many are truly visible minorities with cultures and traditions that are not part of Graeco-Roman civilization.

In 1986, Sab Roncucci stated at a multiculturalism conference in Edmonton: "I consider myself: First: A human being; Second: A Canadian Citizen; Third: A person of Italian origin." Most if not all individuals of Italian ethnicity today would likely say the same. But it took the struggles around multiculturalism and the politicizing of cultural identity to empower and enable Italian-Canadians to embrace all aspects of citizenship including rights, freedoms and responsibilities.

25ᵐᵒ Anno di servizio alla Comunità

Il Congresso

December 15 Dicembre 2009   Anno 26 Numero 9

E' stato un piacere!!!

di Carlo Amodio

Forse voi non lo sapete ma ogni anno o due, su iniziativa di Rudy Cavaliere, abbiamo creato libri che mettono assieme tutti i giornali che abbiamo pubblicato negli ultimi 25 anni. Per cui nel decidere come salutare i nostri cari lettori ho deciso di sfogliare questi 16 libri. Mentre sfogliavo queste pagine storiche il tutto diventava un viaggio nel passato, un interessantissimo viaggio di 25 anni di avvenimenti documentati con dedicazione, pazienza e passione. Posso dirvi che in questo periodo di tempo hanno scritto costantemente per questo giornalino oltre 140 persone. Ed essi sono (in ordine di apparenza, più o meno!):

Alessandro Urso, Carlo e Lina Amodio, Giovanni Bincoletto, Sabatino Roncucci, Gianna Ponzo, Maurizio Gualtieri, Nino Cappelletto, Bruno Romano, Agostino Annicchiarico, Padre Augusto Feccia, Antonella Ciancibello, Tony Falcone, Alex Munzel, Giovan-

vanni Marchisio, Nando Zenari, Tino Sannio, Silvio Pino, Silvia Rossi, Anna Calabrese, John Oliverio, Salvatore Amelio, Donna Marie Artuso, Paolo Giuntella, Del Iannucci-Calgary, Michele Iacchetta-USA, Frank Lunginotti-Calgary, David Kilgour, M.P., Maria Assunta Tamman, Peter Caffaro, Peter

continua a pagina 10

ni Bragaglia, A Nigritto, MariaSofia Boag, Fausta Marazzo, Paola Tessaro, Dick Tomat, Vincenzo Funaro, Ma - ria Grazia Ferrara, Tony Zenari. Dr. William Green.

Rudy Cavaliere, Carlo Amodio e Alessandro Urso.

Il Congresso arriva al suo capolinea

di Alessandro Urso

Con questo numero Il Congresso passa negli annali della storia della Collettività italiana di Edmonton. Di esso presto rimarrà solo la memoria del ricordo. Il ricordo di 25 intensi anni di attività comunitarie, il ricordo di persone conosciute, di avvenimenti trattati, di amicizie

all'allora Console Onorario Giovanni Bincoletto, e ricevette l'immediata benedizione dal Parroco della Chiesa Santa Maria Goretti, Padre Augusto Feccia (il mecenatismo di Padre Feccia fu in seguito continuato da Padre Giovanni Bonelli).

Con questi due assi nella manica ed un po' alla

The management team of Il Congresso: Rudy Cavaliere, Carlo Amodio and Alessandro Urso, at Heritage Days in 2009. The article, in the last issue, December 2009, notes, "É stato un piacere" ("It was a pleasure!"). The paper documented Alberta's Italian community and connected Italian-Canadians with issues in Italy for 25 years. Image courtesy of Il Congresso.

Commemorative sculpture by artist Giuseppe Albi commissioned by the National Congress of Italian Canadians, Edmonton District, to celebrate Alberta's centenary in 2005. It was erected on the grounds of the Alberta Legislature in Edmonton in 2007. At the base of the classical column are casts of tools and musical instruments used by Italian immigrants. Photo courtesy of Adriana A. Davies.

Select Bibliography

Books

Alexander, Rob. *The History of Canmore*. Banff, AB: Summerthought Publishing, 2010.

Alexander, Rob, and Dene Cooper, eds. *Exshaw: Heart of the Valley*. Exshaw, AB: Exshaw Historical Society, 2005.

Amantea, Gisele. *The King v. Picariello and Lassandro*. Toronto, ON: Frank Iacobucci Centre for Italian Canadian Studies at the University of Toronto and Dunlop Art Gallery, Regina Public Library, 2007.

Amodio, Carlo. *Downloading my memories: From Naples to Edmonton*. Edmonton, AB: nd, self-published.

Appleby, Edna (Hill). *Canmore: The Story of An Era*. Calgary, AB: D.W. Friesen & Sons Ltd., 1975.

Avery, Donald. *"Dangerous Foreigners": European Immigrant Workers and Labour Radicalism in Canada 1896-1932*. Toronto, ON: McClelland and Stewart, 1979.

------------. *Reluctant Host: Canada's Response to Immigrant Workers, 1896 to 1994*. Toronto, ON: McClelland & Stewart Inc., 1995.

Bachusky, Johnnie. *"Ghost Town Stories of Alberta: Abandoned Dreams in the Shadows of the Canadian Rockies*. Victoria, BC: Heritage House Publishing, 2009.

Bagnell, Kenneth. *Canadese: A Portrait of the Italian Canadians*. Toronto, ON: Macmillan, 1989.

Barrhead and District Historical Society. *The Trails Northwest: A History of the District of Barrhead, Alberta*. Barrhead, AB: Barrhead and District Historical Society, 1967.

Bercuson, David J., *Alberta's Coal Industry, 1919*. Edmonton, AB: Alberta Records Publication Board, Historical Society of Alberta, 1978.

Blue, John. *Alberta Past and Present: Historical and Biographical*. Chicago, ILL: Pioneer Historical Publishing Co., 1924.

Canton, Licia, Domenic Cusmano, Michael Mirolla and Jim Zucchero, eds. *Beyond Barbed Wire: Essays on the Internment of Italian Canadians*. Toronto, ON: Guernica Press, 2012.

Carbone, Stanislao. *The Streets were not Paved with Gold: A Social History of Italians in Winnipeg*. Winnipeg, MB: Manitoba Italian Heritage Committee, 1993.

———. *Italians in Winnipeg: An Illustrated History*. Winnipeg, MB: University of Manitoba Press, 1998.

Coalhurst Historical Society. *Our Treasured Heritage: A History of Coalhurst and District*. Lethbridge, AB: Coalhurst Historical Society, 1984.

Cioni, Mary. *Spaghetti Western: How My Father Brought Italian Food to the West*. Calgary, AB: Fifth House, 2006.

Coalhurst History Society. *Our Treasured Heritage: A History of Coalhurst and District*. Lethbridge, AB: Coalhurst History Society, 1984.

Commission of Conservation Canada, *Report of The Eighth Annual Meeting Held at Ottawa January 16-17, 1917*. Montreal, PQ: The Federated Press, 1917.

Community Design Strategies Inc. *Heritage Inventory Project – Phase 2: Municipality of Crowsnest Pass Blairmore and Frank*. Calgary, AB: CDS Inc., 2014.

Costa, Elio, and Gabriele Pietro Scardellato. *Lawrence Grassi: From Piedmont to the Rocky Mountains*. Toronto, ON: University of Toronto Press, 2015.

Cresciani, Gianfranco. *Fascism, Anti-fascism and Italians in Australia 1922-1945*. Canberra, ACT: Australian National University Press, 1980.

Crowsnest Historical Society. *Crowsnest and Its People*. Coleman, AB: Crowsnest Historical Society, 1979.

———. *Crownest and Its People Millenium Edition*. Lethbridge, AB: Crowsnest Historical Society, 2000.

Culos, Raymond. *Vancouver's Society of Italians*. Madeira Park, BC: Harbour Pub., 1998-2002, 2 vols.

———. *Injustice Served: The Story of British Columbia's Italian Enemy Italians during World War II*. Montreal, PQ: Cusmano Books, 2012.

Davies, Adriana. *Italians Settle in Edmonton*. Edmonton, AB: Tree Frog Press, 1983.

Davies, Adriana A. *The Rise and Fall of Emilio Picariello*. Fernie, BC: Oolichan Press, 2015.

Delia Craigmyle Historical Society. *The Delia Craigmyle Saga*. Lethbridge, AB: Southern Printing Company Limited, 1970.

Den Otter, A. A. *A Social History of the Coal Branch*. Edmonton, AB: University of Alberta Press, 1967.

Diamond City Historical Society. *The History of Diamond City and Commerce*. Diamond City, AB: Diamond City Historical Society, [1996].

Drumheller History Association. *The Hills of Home: Drumheller Valley*. Drumheller, AB: Drumheller Valley History Association 1973.

East Longview Historical Society. *Tales and Trails: A History of Longview and Surrounding Area.* Longview, AB: Tales and Trails History Book Society, 1974.

Epp, Marlene, and Franca Iacovetta. *Sisters or Strangers? Immigrant, Ethnic, and Radicalized Women in Canadian History.* Toronto, ON/Buffalo, NY/London, UK: University of Toronto Press, end ed. 2016.

Fanella, Antonella. *With Heart and Soul: Calgary's Italian Community.* Calgary, AB: University of Calgary Press, 1999.

Friesen, Gerald. *The Canadian Prairies: A History.* Toronto, ON/Buffalo, NY/London, UK: University of Toronto Press, 1987.

Gadd, Ben. *Bankhead: The Twenty Year Town.* Calgary, AB: The Coal Association of Canada and Canadian Parks Service, 1989.

Government of Canada. *The Royal Commission Appointed to Inquire Into the Immigration of Italian Labourers to Montreal and the Alleged Fraudulent Practices of Employment Agencies.* Ottawa, ON: King's Printer, 1905.

Hamblin, Jennifer and David Finch. *The Diva & the Rancher: The Story of Norma Piper and George Pocaterra.* Surrey, BC: Rocky Mountain Books, 2006.

Hanson, Eric J. *Dynamic Decade: The Evolution and Effects of the Oil Industry in Alberta.* Don Mills, ON: T. H. Best Printing Company, Ltd., 1958.

Harney, Robert F. *Italians in North America.* Toronto, ON: Multicultural History Society of Ontario, ca. 1980.

———. *From the Shores of Hardship: Italians in Canada: Essays by Robert F. Harney*, edited by Nicholas Harney. Welland, ON: Soleil Publishing Inc., 1993.

——— and J. Vincenza Scarpaci, eds. *Little Italies in North America.* Toronto, ON: Multicultural History Society of Ontario, 1981.

Hlady, Ernest. *The Valley of the Dinosaurs: Its Families and Coal Mines.* East Coulee, AB: East Coulee Community Association, 1988.

Hickman, Pamela and Jean Smith Cavalluzzo. *Italian Canadian Internment in the Second World War: Righting Canada's Wrongs.* Toronto, ON: James Lorimer, 2012.

Histoire de Legal History Association. *Vision, Courage, Heritage: Legal 1894-1994, Vimy – Waugh – Fedorah."* 2 vols. Altona, MB: Histoire de Legal History Association, 1995.

Hylo-Venice History Book Committee. *Hylo-Venice Harvest of Memories.* Hylo, AB: Hylo-Venice History Book Committee, 2000.

Iacovetta, Franca, Roberto Perin and Angelo Principe, eds. *Enemies Within: Italian and Other Internees in Canada and Abroad.* Toronto, ON: University of Toronto Press, 2000.

Jansen, Clifford J. *Fact-Book on Italians in Canada*. North York, ON: Institute for Social Research, York University, 1987.

Jasper Community History Committee. *Jasper Reflections*. Jasper, AB: Jasper Community History, 1996.

Johnston, Alex, Keith G. Gladwyn and L. Gregory Ellis. *Lethbridge: Its Coal Industry*. Lethbridge, AB: The Lethbridge Historical Society, Occasional Paper No. 20, 1989.

Lysachok, Jeanette (Grigg), ed. *Three Trails Home: A History of Mayerthorpe and Districts, Alberta, Canada*. Skokie, IL: Inter-Collegiate Press, 1980.

Mayerthorpe and District History Book Society. *Three Trails Home: A History of Mayerthorpe and Districts, Alberta, Canada*. Mayerthorpe, AB: The Inter-Collegiate Press 1980.

McMullen Belliveau, Anne. *Small Moments in Time: The Story of Alberta's Big West Country Upper North Saskatchewan River Corridor, Shunda Basin, Brazeau Collieries and Nordegg*. Calgary, AB: Detselig Enterprises Ltd., 1999.

Michaud, Marie-Christine. *From Steel Tracks to Gold-Paved Streets: Italian Immigrants and the Railroads in the North Central States*. New York, NY: Center for Migration Studies, 2005.

Millarville, Kew, Priddis and Bragg Creek Historical Society. *Our Foothills*. Calgary, AB: Millarville, Kew, Priddis and Bragg Creek Historical Society, 1975.

Oliva, Peter. *Drowning in Darkness*. Dunvegan, ON: Cormorant Books, 1993.

Oltmann, Ruth. *Baroness of the Canadian Rockies*. Exshaw, AB: Ribbon Creek Publishing, 1983.

Palmer, Howard. *Land of the Second Chance: A History of Ethnic Groups in Southern Alberta*. Lethbridge, AB: The Lethbridge Herald, 1972.

Palmer, Howard, and Tamara Palmer, eds. *Peoples of Alberta: Portraits of Cultural Diversity*. Saskatoon, SK: Western Producer Prairie Books, 1985.

Peck, Gunther. *Reinventing Free Labour: Padrones and Immigrant Workers in the North American West, 1880 to 1930*. Cambridge, UK: Cambridge University Press, 2000.

Perin, Roberto, and Franc Sturino, eds. *Arrangiarsi: The Italian Immigration Experience in Canada*. Montreal, PQ: Guernica Editions, third edition, 2006.

Peterson, M. *287 Garry Street: Garrick (Wellington) Hotel)*. A report prepared for the City of Winnipeg Historical Buildings & Resources Committee, April 2016.

Pivato, Joseph, ed. *Contrasts: Comparative Essays on Italian Canadian Writing*. Montreal, PQ: Guernica, 1985.

Poplar Ridge Historical Committee. *The District's Diary: 95 Years of History of the Crossroads, Poplar Ridge, Norma and Durham Districts*. Red Deer, AB: Poplar Ridge Historical Committee, 1981.

Potestio, John, ed. *The Memoirs of Giovanni Veltri*. Toronto, ON: The Multicultural History Society, 1987.

————. *In Search of a Better Life: Emigration to Thunder Bay from a Small Town in Calabria*. Thunder Bay, ON: Thunder Bay Historical Society, 2000.

Pozzetta, E. George, and Bruno Ramirez, eds. *The Italian Diaspora: Migration Across the Globe*. Toronto, ON: The Multicultural History Society of Ontario, 1992.

Principe, Angelo. *The Darkest Side of the Fascist years: The Italian-Canadian Press; 1920-1942*. Toronto, ON: Guernica Press, 1999.

Ramirez, Bruno. *On the Move: French-Canadian and Italian Migrants in the North Atlantic Economy, 1860-1914*. Toronto: Oxford University Press Canada, 1998, ca. 1991.

Readymade Historical Society. *Readymade and District*. Lethbridge, AB: Readymade Historical Society, 1977.

Riva, Walter J. *Survival in Paradise: A Century of Coal Mining in the Bow Valley*. Canmore, AB: Canmore Museum and Geoscience Centre, 2008.

Rosoli, Gianfausto, ed. *Un secolo di emigrazione italiana 1876-1976*. Roma, IT: Centro studi emigrazione, 1978.

Ross, Toni. *Oh The Coal Branch: A Chronicle of the Alberta Coal Branch*. Calgary, AB: D. Friesen and Sons Ltd., 1974.

Scardellato, Gabriele Pietro, and Manuela Scarci, eds. *A Monument for Italian-Canadian Immigrants: Regional Migration from Italy to Canada*. Toronto, ON: Department of Italian Studies, University of Toronto, and Italian-Canadian Immigrant Commemorative Association, 1999.

Spada, A. V. *Canada Ethnica VI: The Italians in Canada*. Ottawa, ON/Montreal, PQ: Riviera Printers and Publishers Inc., 1969.

Sturino, Franc. *Forging the Chain: A Case Study of Italian Immigration to North America*. Toronto, ON: Multicultural History Society of Ontario, 1990.

Sunnyside Area Historical Society. *Sunnyside Area: A History of the Royal View/Eight Mile Lake and Crystal Lake School* Districts. Lethbridge, AB: Sunnyside Area Historical Society, 1988.

Taber History Committee. *From Tank 27 to Taber Valley: A History of Taber, Its District and People*. Taber, AB: Taber History Committee, 1977.

Vangelisti, P. Guglielmo. *Gli Italiani in Canada*. Montreal, PQ: Chiesa italiana di N. S. della difesa, 1958.

Whitehead, Margaret, ed. *They Call Me Father: Memoirs of Father Nicolas Coccola*. Vancouver, BC: University of British Columbia Press, 1988.

Whyte, Jon. *Tommy and Lawrence: The Ways and the Trails of Lake O'Hara*. Banff, AB: Lake O'Hara Trails Club, 1983.

Wood, Patricia K. *Nationalism from the Margins: Italians in Alberta and British Columbia*. Montreal, PQ & Kingston, ON, London, UK, Ithaca, NY: McGill-Queen's University Press, 2002.

Woodsworth, J. S. *Strangers Within Our Gates, Coming Canadians*. Toronto, ON: Frederick Clarke Stephenson, Missionary Society of the Methodist Church, Canada, 1909.

Zucchi, John E. *The Italian Immigrants of the St. John's Ward, 1875-1915: Patterns of Settlement and Neighbourhood Formation*. Toronto: Multicultural History Society of Ontario, 1981.

———. *Italians in Toronto: Development of a National Identity, 1875-1935*. Montreal, PQ/ Kingston, ON: McGill Queen's University Press, 1988.

Articles

Alberta Agriculture and Forestry. "Briosi, Andrew Arthur – 1982 Hall of Fame Inductee." In *Alberta Agriculture Hall of Fame* website, URL: http://www1.agric.gov.ab.ca/$Department/deptdocs.nsf/all/info1982?opendocument, retrieved October 18, 2017.

Alberta Sports Hall of Fame. "Bruno Comis." Alberta Sports Hall of Fame & Museum website, URL: http://ashfm.ca/hall-of-fame-honoured-members/browse/speed-skating/comis-bruno, retrieved January 11, 2018.

Alessio, Francesco. "Il piu grande esodo della storia moderna." Associazione Internet degli Emigrati Italiani (Internet Association of Italian Immigrants), URL: http://www.emigrati.it/Emigrazione/Esodo.asp, retrieved July 26, 2017.

Allison, Garry. "Building St. Basil's was a community effort." In *Lethbridge Herald*, October 1, 2000.

Anon. "I Comites –Comitati degli Italiani residenti all'estero." Calabresi.net: The Portal of the Calabresi in the World, URL: http://www.calabresi.net/i-comites-comitati-degli-italiani-residenti-allestero/, retrieved February 14, 2018.

Anon. "James Anselmo Points to Guideposts for Success." In *Construction World*, May 1958, 40-41, 82.

Avery, Donald. "European Immigrant Workers and Labour Protest in Peace and War, 1896-1919." In *The History of Immigration and Racism in Canada: Essential Readings,* Barrington Walker, ed. Toronto: Canadian Scholars' Press Inc., 2008.

Basilici, Paolo. "Il Pittore Roberto Basilici." Edizione aggiornata a marzo 2016, URL: http://www.basilici.info/personaggi/roberto.pdf, retrieved August 17, 2017.

Cataneo, Claudia. "John Forzani on the right time to sell." In *Financial Post*, May 16, 2011.

Cole, Catherine C. "Accommodating an Increasingly Diverse Work Force." In *Piece by Piece: The GWG Story* website, Royal Alberta Museum/Virtual Museum of Canada, URL: https://www.royalalbertamuseum.ca/exhibits/online/GWG/en/labourforce/middleeast.html, retrieved January 21, 2018.

Davies, Adriana A. "The Black-Shirted Fascisti Are Coming to Alberta." In *Beyond Barbed Wire: Essays on the Internment of Italian Canadians*. Licia Canton, Domenic Cusmano, Michael Mirolla and Jim Zucchero, eds. Toronto, ON: Guernica Press, 2012, 251-271.

———. "There Were No Safety Nets: 1900 to 1920." Edmonton: Edmonton Heritage Council, City as Museum, Cultural Mapping Project, 2016, URL: http://citymuseumedmonton. ca/2016/08/30/edmontons-italian-community-1900-to-1920/, retrieved January 22, 2017.

———. "There Were No Safety Nets: 1921 to 1945." Edmonton: Edmonton Heritage Council, City as Museum, Cultural Mapping Project, 2016, URL: http://citymuseumedmonton. ca/2016/09/06/edmontons-italian-community-1921-to-1945/, retrieved January 22, 2017.

———. "There Were No Safety Nets: 1949 to the Present." Edmonton: Edmonton Heritage Council, City as Museum, Cultural Mapping Project, 2016, URL: http://citymuseumedmonton.ca/2016/09/13/edmontons-italian-community-1949-to-the-present/, retrieved January 22, 2017.

Den Otter, A. A. "Social Life of a Mining Community: the Coal Branch." In *Alberta Historical Review 17*, Historical Society of Alberta, 1969, 17-4, Autum, 1-11.

Di Cintio, Marcello. "Give Us This Day Our Daily Bread." *Swerve* (Calgary Herald), May 31, 2012.

Fanella, Antonella. "The Rebaudengo Family." In *Beyond Barbed Wire: Essays on the Internment of Italian Canadians*. Licia Canton, Domenic Cusmano, Michael Mirolla and Jim Zucchero, eds. Toronto, ON: Guernica Press, 2012, 274-280.

Fainella, John G. "The Development of Italian Organizations in Calgary." In *Alberta History*, vol. 32, Winter 1984, 20-26.

Fenton, Allan. "New West Construction – From horse to computers." In *Engineering and Contract Record*, December 1967, 60-63

Finch, David. "Romancing the Dudes." In *Research Links: A Forum for Natural, Cultural and Social Studies*, vol 5, no 3, Winter 1997, 5.

Gallant, Collin. "Hat's favourite burger man passes." In *Medicine Hat News*, April 15, 2014.

Grossutti, Javier. "Immigration from Friuli Venezia Giulia to Canada." University of Trieste, undated, URL: http://www.ammer-fvg.org/_data/contenuti/allegati/eng/en_grossutti_canada. pdf, retrieved February 14, 2018.

Harney, Robert F. "Montreal's King of Italian Labour: A Case Study of Padronism." In *Labour/ Travail*, vol. 4 /vol. 4e (1979), 57-84.

———. "Boarding and Belonging: Thoughts on the Sojourner Institutions." In *Urban History Review*, Immigrants in the City, Numero 2-78, October, 1978, 1-37.

Konotopetz, Gyle. "Life's El Grande for Calgary's Nacho King." In *Business Edge News Magazine*, January 15, 2003.

Krawchuk, Peter. "Interned Without Cause." *Socialist History Project* website, URL: http://www.socialisthistory.ca/Docs/CPC/WW2/IWC05.htm, retrieved February 13, 2018.

Milani, Ernestro R. "Appunti per una storia dei lombardi in Canada" (Notes for a History of the Lombards in Canada). *Lombards in the World* portal, URL: http://portale.lombardinelmondo.org/nazioni/nordamerica/Articoli/storiaemi/canada, retrieved April 26, 2017.

Norrie, Kenneth H. "The National Policy and the Rate of Prairie Settlement." In *The Prairie West: Historical Readings*, R. Douglas Francis and Howard Palmer, eds. Edmonton, AB: The University of Alberta Press, 1992, 243-263.

Peck, Gunther. "Mobilizing Community: Migrant Workers and the Politics of Labour Mobility in the North American West." In *Labor Histories: Class, Politics, and the Working Class Experience 1900-1910*, edited by Eric Arnesen, Julie Greene and Bruce Laurie. Urbana and Chicago, IL: University of Illinois Press, 1998 175-200.

Palmer, Howard. "Strangers and Stereotypes: The Rise of Nativism, 1880-1920." In *Prairie West: Historical Readings*, R. Douglas Francis and Howard Palmer, eds. Edmonton, AB: University of Alberta Press, 1992, 308-334.

Pratt, Sean. "Little Pasta Plant on the Prairies." In *The Western Producer*, May 1, 2000.

Ramirez, Bruno. "Brief Encounters: Italian Immigrant Workers and the CPR 1900-30." In *Labour/Travail*, vol. 17, Spring 1986, 9-28.

———. "CORDASCO, ANTONIO." *Dictionary of Canadian Biography*, vol 15, University of Toronto/Université Laval, 2003–, URL: http://www.biographi.ca/en/bio/cordasco_antonio_15E.html, retrieved March 2, 2017.

Seward, Karen Davidson. "Gebo/Gibeau: Cousins reunited in the Crowsnest Pass." In *Heritage News: Discover Crowsnest Heritage*, Issue 5, September 15, 2010, unpaginated.

Svatek, Genevieve. "Banff loses a legend: Louis Trono remembered for his stories, humour, talent, love and music." In *The Banff Crag & Canyon*, May 25, 2004.

Wait, N. A. "Grassi of Canmore." *The Canadian Golden West*, 1969, 24-25.

Wood, David. "Picturing Conservation in Canada: The Commission of 1909-1921." In Studies in Documents, *Archivaria: The Journal of the Association of Canadian Archivists* 37 (Spring 1994), 64-74.

Wood, Patricia K. "Borders and Identities among Italian Immigrants, 1880-1938." In *Parallel Destinies: Canadian-American Relations West of the Rockies*. Kenneth S. Coates, John M. Findlay, eds. Seattle, London, Montreal and Kingston: Center for the Study of the Pacific Northwest with the University of Washington Press and McGill-Queen's University Press, 2002, 104-122.

Archival Resources

Angelo Toppano Fonds, Provincial Archives of Alberta paa-6932, PR0649

Basilici Family Fonds, Glenbow Archives NA-3917

Berlando/Berlanda Family Fonds, Galt Archives AN 19821019001

Biollo Family Fonds, Provincial Archives of Alberta PR1370, PR1976.0204

Cantalini Fonds, Esplanade Archives MED-753

Gus Dotto Fonds, Provincial Archives of Alberta PAA paa-7626

Emilio PicarielloFonds, Glenbow Archives M-6242, PA-2945, PA-3169, NA-5067, NA-5309

Emilio Picariello Fonds, Provincial Archives of Alberta GR2002.0056/1675

Felice de Angelis Fonds, Provincial Archives of Alberta PR1995.0022

Gallelli and Sons Ltd. Fonds, Glenbow Archives M-9113, M-9222, PA-3675

George and Norma Piper Pocaterra Fonds, Glenbow Archives M-6340-1 to 181, M-4405, M-6340-198 to 206

Ginger (Pavan) Erickson Fonds, Galt Archives 2012 1067

Giovanni Mamini Fonds, Glenbow Archives M-807

Gus Dotto Fonds, Provincial Archives of Alberta PR1400

Italian Society Ledgers, Crowsnest Archives 1906-1917, 95.08.04 A-L (12 books), 1936-1962: 95.08.02 a-k; 95.08.01a-k (23 books), 1918-1936 95.08.03 a-k (10 books, missing k)

Italian Women's Society (Rose d'Italia No. 102) Fonds, Galt Archives 19931049006.

J. McKinley Cameron (Picariello/Lassandro Trial) Fonds, Glenbow Archives M 6840, NA 4691

Lawrence Grassi Fonds, Whyte Museum of the Canadian Rockies Archives M45/240.

Marquis Bakery Company (Roger Sergo) Fonds, Galt Archives AN 2017.1084

Ordine Indipendente Fior d'Italia (Cesare Battisti Loggia no. 9) Fonds, Glenbow Archives M-7715

Palmetto Bakery Fonds, Glenbow Archives glen-2729

Purity Dairy (Fabbi Family) Fonds, Galt Archives 2009.1033007

Roy Berlando Fonds, Provincial Archives of Alberta PR 1882

Theses and Unpublished Manuscripts

Tony Bonifacio, "Venice Alberta, 1914: The Pioneers and Others that Lived There." Unpublished manuscript, ca. 1990s. Bonifacio Family.

Gallelli, Delores. "The Story of Nick and Julia Gallelli and Family: Founders of the Gallelli Company: A Pioneer Calgary Firm." Unpublished manuscript, 2009. Gallelli and Sons Ltd. Fonds, Glenbow Archives M-9113, M-9222, PA-3675.

Lake, David W. "The Historical Geography of the Coal Branch." MA thesis, University of Alberta, 1967.

McBride, Michelle. "From Internment to Indifference: An Examination of RCMP Response to Fascism and Nazism in Canada from 1934 to 1941." MA thesis, Memorial University, 1997.

Pocaterra, George, and Norma Piper Pocaterra. "Son of the Mountains." Unpublished manuscript, 1970, Glenbow Archives.

Pucci, Antonio. "*The Italian Community in Fort William's East End in the Early Twentieth Century.*" Master's thesis, Lakehead University, 1977.

Villeneuve, Loretta. "Luigi Biamonte Family History." Unpublished manuscript, undated. Biamonte/Villeneuve Family.

Newspapers

Banff Crag & Canyon

Blairmore Enterprise

Calgary Albertan

Calgary Herald

Drumheller Mail

Edmonton Bulletin

Edmonton Journal

Edson-Jasper Signal

Il Congresso

Edson-Jasper Signal

Lethbridge Herald

Lethbridge Daily Herald

Medicine Hat News

National Post

Red Deer Advocate

Rocky Mountain Outlook

Oral Histories

Dante Alighieri Society Oral History Project, 1973, Provincial Archives of Alberta
Interviewers: Sabatino Roncucci and Gian-Carlo (Charles) Grelli
Interviewees: Louis Biamonte AN 74.106/1, Mrs. Gisella Biollo and Mike Biollo AN 74.106/2, Father Giovanni Bonelli AN 74.106/3, Camillo Bridarolli AN 74.106/4, Henry and Myra (Mira) Butti AN 74.106/5, John Camarta AN 74.106/6, Domenico Chiarello AN 74.106/7, Joe Fabbri AN 74.106/8, Mario Grassi AN 74.106/9, Victor Losa AN 74.106/10, Mrs. Mamie Meardi [nee Marini] AN 74.106/11, Tony Nimis AN 74.106/12, Giorgio Pocaterra AN 74.106/13, Mrs. Norma Pocaterra AN 74.106/14, Mr. and Mrs. John Segatti AN 74.106/15, Romano Tedesco and Irma Giacobbo AN 74.106/16

Italians Settle in Edmonton Oral History Project, 1983, Provincial Archives of Alberta
Interviewers: Anna Bruni, Tony Caria, Rita Cavaliere, Adriana Davies, Tony Falcone and Carmela Marino
Interviewees: Raffaele Albi, Mr. and Mrs. Enrico Butti, Mr. and Mrs. Domenico Chiarello (Nella Anselmo), Gus and Assunta Dotto (Emilia Raffin), Attilio and Stella Gatto, Gus Lavorato, Giovanni Paron, Louie Protti, Mr. and Mrs. Sartor, Sam Scrivano, Silvio Tona and Paolo Veltri (AN PR0915)

Calgary Italian Club Oral History Project, 1985, Glenbow Archives
Interviewers: Rosanne Audia and Kathy Savoia
Interviewees: Mr. and Mrs. Ambrogiano RCT-869-1 & 2, Renato Antenucci RCT-869-3, Anthony Audia RCT-869-4, Adelina Carloni RCT-869-5, Severno Coppola RCT-869-6, Gino DePaoli RCT-869-7, Joseph DePaoli RCT-869-8, Angelo DePaolo RCT-869-8A, Camila Dileandro RCT-869-8A, Mrs. Dipaolo RCT-869-9, Mr. and Mrs. Pasquale Fornaro RCT-869-10, Mr. R. Fornasero RCT-869-11, Julia Gallelli RCT-869-12, Donato Giammarino RCT-869-13, Mr. and Mrs. P. Giammarino RCT-869-14, Mario Grassi RCT-869-15, Elia Martina RCT-869-16, Gabriel Medori RCT-869-17, Mr. and Mrs. R. Pacione RCT-869-18, Mr. and Mrs. Libero Pittana RCT-869-19, Angelina Rebaudengo RCT-869-20, Mario Rebaudengo RCT-869-21, Alberto Romano RCT-869-22, Flavia Santucci RCT-869-23, Mrs. Savoia RCT-869-24, Adelmo Stante RCT-869-25 and Gerardo Zaghetto RCT-869-26.

People of Southern Alberta Oral History Project, 1987, Glenbow Archives
Interviewers: Marianne Fedori and Tonya (Antonella) Fanella
Interviewees: Riccardo Bezzegato RCT-818, Raymond Blassetti RCT-835, Adrian Bussoli RCT-850, David Colonna RCT-821, Zuppe D'Amico RCT-857, Vincent Davoli RCT-836, Giuseppe Fanella RCT-764, Maria Fanella RCT-765, Violeta Gallardo RCT-822, Vincenzo Girimonte RCT-767, Toni Iavasile RCT-766, Valeria Lee RCT-773, Frank Lucente RCT-787, Anna Mandaione RCT-855, Gloria Mrin RCT-774, Maria Mosca RCT-768, Angelina Rebaudengo RCT856, Alberto Romano RCT-788, Italo Sartorio RCT-837, Per Siccardi RCT-817, Tony Valerio and Nina Valerio RCT-854 andCharles Violini and Lina Violini RCT-858.

Jasper Information Centre Oral History Project, March, 1999, Jasper-Yellowhead Museum & Archives
Interviewer: Vicki Wallace Jasper, AB,
Interviewees: Emilio Cesco AN 001.06.05, Joe Calabretta AN 001.02

Heritage Community Foundation Celebrating Alberta's Italian Community Oral History Project,
2002, Provincial Archives of Alberta
Interviewers: Adriana Davies and David Ridley
Interviewees: Carlo and Lina Amodio, Mary Biollo Doyle, Tony Falcone, Sabattino Roncucci,
Rina and Teresa Spinelli, Allessandro and Lina Urso and Fiore M. Vecchio

Ital-Canadian Seniors Centre Memory Lane Oral History Project, 2007, Ital-Canadian Seniors Centre
Interviewers: Adriana Davies and youth volunteers: Stellina Gatto, Andrea Melchionna, Brandon
Panice and Michael Vecchio
Interviewees: Peter Caffaro, Julie Ciocchetti, Maria d'Andrea, Adriana Albi Davies, Luciana De
Santis, Wanda Dominelli, Aurora and Antonio Frattin, Nicola Loconte, Oronzo Loparco, Giuseppe
Mauro, Maria Mauro, Carmela Marino, Vitalia Marino, Aristide Melchionna, Salvatore Noce,
Gina Principe, Frank and Maria Saccomanno, Teresa Spinelli, Silvano Vecchio and Luigi Zorzetto.

Oil Sands Oral History Project, Canadian Petroleum Society, August 23, 2012, Glenbow Archives
M-9491
Interviewer: Gordon Jaremko
Interviewee: Neil Camarta

Websites

Canadian Museum of Immigration at Pier 21. *Italian Immigration, National Statistics.* Pier 21,
    URL: https://www.pier21.ca/culture-trunks/hungary/statistics, retrieved January 10, 2018.
Columbus Centre/Villa Charities, *Italian Canadians as Enemy Aliens: Memories of World War II*,
    URL: http://www.italiancanadianww2.ca/collection/details/icea2011_0009_0001, retrieved
    October 12, 2017.
Davies, Adriana A. *Celebrating Alberta's Italian Community,* 2002, Heritage Community Foundation:
    Alberta Online Encyclopedia, URL: http://wayback.archive-it.org/2217/20101215220218/
    http://www.albertasource.ca/abitalian/background/edmonton.html, retrieved January 21,
    2017.
———. *When Coal Was King,* 2005, Heritage Community Foundation: *Alberta Online Encyclo-
    pedia,* URL: http://wayback.archive-it.org/2217/20101208160414/http://www.coalking.
    ca/industry/coal_types.html, retrieved March 23, 2017

Library and Archives Canada. *Moving Here, Staying Here. The Canadian Immigrant Experience*, URL: https://www.collectionscanada.gc.ca/immigrants/index-e.html, retrieved February 11, 2018

Royal Alberta Museum, *Piece by Piece: The GWG Story*, URL: *https://www.royalalbertamuseum.ca/exhibits/online/gwg/en/images/3-1-4.html*, retrieved October 10, 2017.

About the Author

ADRIANA (ALBI) DAVIES was born in Grimaldi, Cosenza, Italy and grew up in Canada. She received B.A. and M.A. degrees from the University of Alberta, and a Ph.D. from the University of London, England. Her thesis topic was "The Art for Art's Sake and Decadent Movements in Nineteenth Century English and French Literature."

For more than 40 years, she has worked as a researcher, writer, editor, lecturer, executive director and curator in England and Canada. Professional accomplishments include: Science and Technology Editor, *The Canadian Encyclopedia*; Executive Director, Alberta Museums Association; and creator and Editor-in-Chief of the *Alberta Online Encyclopedia* – www.albertasource.ca. In 2009, the 84 multimedia websites were gifted to the University of Alberta.

Dr. Davies has a range of publications including authoring about one-third of the entries for the *Collins' Encyclopaedia of Antiques* (London: Collins. 1973; New York: Random House, 1974); *Dictionary of British Portraiture*, Volume 1 (London: Batsford, 1979) and *Dictionary of British Portraiture*, Volume 4 (London: Batsford, 1981).

Her most recent publications are the critical biography *From Realism to Abstraction: The Art of J. B. Taylor* (Calgary: University of Calgary Press, 2014); *The Rise and Fall of Emilio Picariello* (Fernie: Oolichan Books, 2015); and *The Frontier of Patriotism: Alberta and the First World War* (Calgary: University of Calgary Press, 2016), an anthology that she co-edited with Jeff Keshen, former Dean of Arts, Mount Royal University, Calgary. Her newest publication, "From Sojourners to Citizens: Alberta's Italian History" will be published by Guernica Editions in Spring 2021. It documents the settlement history and contributions of Italian immigrants who worked on the railways, in the coal mines of Alberta and BC, homesteaded and also set up a range of small and large businesses. She gives Italian immigrants their rightful place in the narrative of province and nation building.

She has contributed entries to the *Dictionary of Canadian Biography* for psychiatrist Charles Arthur Baragar, horticulturist George Harcourt, and city planner and administrator Christopher James Yorath.

For over 30 years she has worked in the museum sector in Alberta (including as Executive Director of the Alberta Museums Association) and is well-known for advocacy on behalf of the sector. She served on the Government of Canada's Cultural Sector Initiative and co-chaired the Research Steering Committee, Capacity Joint Table, responsible for designing the first-ever National Survey of Non-Profit and Voluntary Organizations as well as the benchmarking study on charities in 40 countries done by Johns Hopkins University for UNESCO. Dr. Davies has served on various cultural advisory committees adjudicating grants and making policy decisions including the Canada-France Cultural Accord.

She has undertaken a range of curatorial work including obtaining loans from French and British museum collections for the millennium exhibit *Anno Domini: Jesus through the Centuries* at the Royal Alberta Museum. She curated two travelling exhibits: "People of the Coal Mines: The Italian Community" for the Galt Museum covering communities from the Elk Valley to Drumheller; and, "Alberta's Italian Community" with funding support from the Italian Consul General in Edmonton. In 2012, she curated the exhibit "J. B. Taylor and the Idea of Mountains" for the Whyte Museum of the Canadian Rockies and, in 2015, a travelling exhibit titled "The Rise and Fall of Emilio Picariello" for the Fernie Museum.

On July 1st, 2010, she was invested in the Order of Canada for her role in creating the *Alberta Online Encyclopedia* and for her contribution to the promotion and preservation of Canada's cultural heritage. In 2012, she was awarded the Queen's Diamond Jubilee Medal. As a Member of the Order of Canada she officiates at Canadian citizenship ceremonies. Other awards include: the Alberta Museums Association Life Time Achievement Award, Province of Alberta Centennial Medal, Global Woman of Vision Award and the YWCA Woman of Distinction Award in the Arts. In 2015, the Association canadienne-francaise de l'Alberta awarded her the Prix Roger Motut for helping to preserve the Francophone Culture and Language of Alberta and the Italian government awarded her a knighthood (Cavaliere d'Italia) for preserving the Italian language, culture and traditions as well as her scholarship. In September 2020, the Edmonton Heritage Council awarded her its inaugural Heritage Writers' Reserve Award.